FIFTH EDITION

JUSTICE CRIME AND ETHICS

MICHAEL C. **BRASWELL**   EAST TENNESSEE STATE UNIVERSITY

BELINDA R. **McCARTHY**   UNIVERSITY OF CENTRAL FLORIDA

BERNARD J. **McCARTHY**   UNIVERSITY OF CENTRAL FLORIDA

 LexisNexis®

 **anderson publishing**
A member of the LexisNexis Group

Justice, Crime, and Ethics, Fifth Edition

Copyright © 1991, 1996, 1998, 2002, 2005
Matthew Bender & Company, Inc., a member of the LexisNexis Group

Phone 877-374-2919
Web Site www.lexisnexis.com/anderson/criminaljustice

LexisNexis and the Knowledge Burst logo are trademarks of Reed Elsevier Properties, Inc.
Anderson Publishing is a registered trademark of Anderson Publishing, a member of the LexisNexis Group

Braswell, Michael C.
    Justice, crime, and ethics / Michael C. Braswell, Belinda R. McCarthy.--5th ed.
        p. cm.
    Includes bibliographical references and index.
    ISBN 1-58360-562-2 (softbound)
        1. Criminal justice, Administration of--Moral and ethical aspects. I. Braswell, Michael.
    II. McCarthy, Belinda Rodgers. III. McCarthy, Bernard J., 1949-
    HV7419.J87 2005
    174'.9364--dc22   2004030547

Cover design by Tin Box Studio, Inc./Cincinnati, Ohio
Photo © Koichiro Shimauchi/Photonica

EDITOR   Ellen S. Boyne
ACQUISITIONS EDITOR   Michael C. Braswell

Dedication

To our parents:
Martha and Calvin Braswell
Barbara and William "Buck" Rodgers
Bernard and Claire McCarthy

A Note about the Fifth Edition

The fifth edition of *Justice, Crime, and Ethics* continues to evolve toward addressing moral issues and concerns of our justice process in personal, social, and criminal justice contexts. A philosophical foundation is provided for exploring and applying ethical principles to a wide range of criminal and social justice issues. New chapters have been added on police ethics, lawyers as legal advocates and moral agents, punishment philosophies and their ethical dilemmas, restorative justice, the death penalty, and the ethical ramifications of the war on terrorism, and additional chapters have been revised.

To stimulate discussion and reflection, case studies, problem-solving exercises, discussion questions, and lists of key concepts are included in the text. In addition, a separate Student Study Guide accompanies the text. Please note that all persons and situations described in case studies and exercises are fictional and have been constructed to illustrate ethical dilemmas characteristic of the criminal justice field.

Finally, we want to give credit to faculty who have filled out comment forms or talked to us at conferences, offering their suggestions on ways to improve the text. Many of the changes found in each of the editions reflect their recommendations. We want to acknowledge and thank our editor, Ellen Boyne, for her substantial efforts in making this a better book.

MB
BM
BM

Table of Contents

Section I: Introduction

> **Vision brings a new appreciation of what there is. It makes a person see things differently rather than see different things.**
>
> —Herbert Guenther

Our personal and social values shape and color the way we perceive the world in which we live. While we are concerned with achieving personal goals and ambitions, we also come to realize at a rather early age that the needs and desires of others are also forces to be reckoned with. The question for us then becomes one of reconciling the pursuit of our individual dreams within the context of the larger community. Maintaining our individual integrity, our personal sense of right and wrong, and, at the same time, conforming to what is best for the majority of persons in our society can often become a perplexing challenge. Yet we are all connected to each other in one way or another, such as with parents and children, and inmates and correctional staff. We are even connected to our physical environment as evidenced in the quality of air we breathe and water we drink. As potential criminal justice practitioners, our professional choices and policies will emanate from our personal beliefs and values—from our personal philosophies. How much do we care about trying to honestly and effectively address the pressing justice issues of the day? Are we truly mindful of the ways we are connected to our problems? Do we have a long-term as well as short-term sense of what the costs of our proposed solutions will be?

Cultivating a greater understanding of our own philosophical perspectives can provide us with a foundation for making more informed decisions about the diverse social issues we face and the way our system of justice responds to such issues.

All Knowledge is interconnected - all LIFE is interconnected.

1

Ethics, Crime, and Justice:
An Introductory Note to Students

Michael C. Braswell

As you approach the study of ethics, crime, and justice, it is important that you view your study as a search, journey, or exploration. This search in many ways will yield more questions than answers. It is a creative endeavor in which a number of your beliefs and assumptions will be challenged. Questions such as "Can moral or ethical behavior be illegal and legal actions be immoral?" and "Can we have a more equitable criminal justice system without addressing social problems like poverty and discrimination?" will test the limits of your personal values and beliefs (Braswell & LaFollette, 1988). This study will also encompass a variety of disciplines that contribute to criminal justice, including law, economics, psychology, sociology, philosophy, and theology. For the purposes of our exploration we will use the terms "ethical" and "moral" interchangeably.

KEY CONCEPTS:

ethics

morals

wholesight

What is ethics? In a general sense, ethics is the study of right and wrong, good and evil. Who decides what is right and wrong? What one person may believe is right, another person may feel is wrong. Our beliefs and values regarding right and wrong and good and evil are shaped by our parents and friends, by the communities we are a part of, and by our own perceptions. Codes of conduct are also influenced by the law and our religious beliefs. Professional organizations involving such areas as law, medicine, and criminal justice also offer professional codes of ethics as a benchmark for persons who fulfill those professional roles. This study involves all aspects of who we are—our minds, hearts, relationships with each other, and the intentions and motives for our actions regarding both our inner and outer environment. We are inclined to believe that ethical persons act in good or right ways, while unethical people commit evil acts and other forms of wrongdoing. Then again, it is not only a matter of a person acting "unethically"; also at issue are persons who could chose to do good but instead do nothing, allowing others to do evil. So it is not simply a matter of my committing an evil or wrongful act, it is also a matter of my being an indirect accomplice to evil by silently standing by, letting evil occur when I could stand for what is right. As a result, unethical acts can occur by the commission of wrongdoing or by omission—by allowing wrongdoing to occur. Thomas Merton (as quoted in Woods, 1966), in examining a fundamental problem of omission, wrote "moral paralysis...leaves us immobile, inert, passive, tongue-tied, ready and even willing to succumb."

The study of justice and ethics, of the good and evil we do to each other, also involves a sense of community. We often hear that problems of crime and violence are the result of a breakdown in family and community values. What does our community consist of? Our community includes our family, neighbors, even the land we grow food on to eat and the air we breathe. Is it important that we act in ethical ways regarding our physical environment as well as with regard to people we come in contact with? Within our community of interdependent parts exist three contexts, or perspectives, that can help us approach a better understanding of justice, crime, and ethics.

THREE CONTEXTS FOR UNDERSTANDING JUSTICE, CRIME, AND ETHICS

A way of understanding the idea of justice in human experience is to think of it as a process that moves within three contexts or concentric circles (see Figure 1.1). The first context or innermost circle is the "personal," which represents our individual sense of justice. This context examines right and wrong, good and evil—life experienced and lived, for better or worse, from the inside out. "My" life experiences come to form a set of perceptions, some easily changed and others being very resistant to change, that form my personal sense of justice—my way of looking out into the world as a safe or dangerous place, with hope or despair.

The second circle represents the social context of justice. This circle includes all that is the world without—the physical environment I live in, be it rural, urban, or suburban, and the people with whom I interact through choice or necessity. I may live in a relatively just or unjust community. I may live as an oppressed member of my community or I may act as the oppressor. During our lifetimes, perhaps on one occasion or another, and in one way or another, we will taste the experience of both.

Persons do not commit crimes in isolation. Crimes also require circumstances and victims. Crimes are related to social circumstances and conditions as well as being subject to the law and criminal justice system. Why did the abused wife kill her husband? In the broader social context, we might look at the abuse she suffered before making her husband a victim of a homicide. What was her relationship to her parents and other family members? What about her neighbors? Did she have access to adequate social and support services? Could something have been done to prevent her own victimization and subsequent crime?

The social context of ethics suggests that we cannot be concerned with criminals only after they have committed crimes but must also better understand the conditions and environments that encourage people to become criminals, whether such offenders physically rape their victims or economically violate them through such means as stock market fraud. We also need to remember that offenders who are incarcerated in prisons typically return to the communities from whence they came whether they become rehabilitated or more criminalized.

The social context is not concerned just with how we judge others as being good or evil, but also how we judge ourselves in relationship to others. Frederick Buechner (1973) writes, "We are judged by the face that looks back at us from the bathroom mirror. We are judged by the faces of the people we love and by the faces and lives of our children and by our dreams. Each day finds us at the junction of many roads, and we are judged as much by the roads we have not taken as by the roads we have."

Figure 1.1
Three Contexts for Understanding Justice, Crime, and Ethics

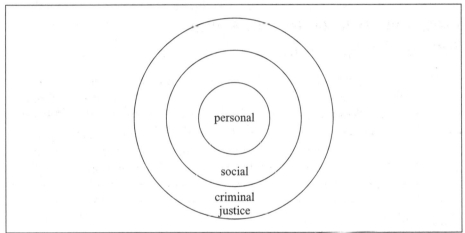

The third context we can use in our efforts to better understand justice, crime, and ethics is perhaps the most specific one; it centers around the *criminal justice process*. Too often, the criminal justice process is the only context or perspective we consider. It is important that we include both the personal and social contexts of ethics when exploring the criminal justice process. Due process, police corruption, and punishment are examples of important issues that require us to consider personal beliefs, social factors, and criminal justice consequences simultaneously. For example, I explore any new law being proposed regarding the punishment of offenders in terms of my personal beliefs. How does this proposed law square with my own value system? How do I feel about it? The proposed law also should be examined on the basis of how it will affect the social community. Is it just and fair to all parts and groups within the community? Will it contribute to the community's sense of safety and security, or is it perhaps more of a public relations or election-year gimmick?

Can the criminal justice process and system effectively implement the law? Are there adequate resources to finance and manage the changes that will occur in the system as the result of the proposed law?

The criminal justice context also sets legal limits for what we can do to each other. Those of us who inflict harm on others may experience legal consequences ranging from fines to imprisonment to having to forfeit our lives. Sometimes what is legal is also what is right or good, but that is not the primary function of criminal justice. We need to remember that our justice system, due to existing laws and community attitudes, may also support tyrants or various forms of injustice and corruption on occasion, leading to suffering and oppression in our communities. Our personal and communal sense of morality (what is right and wrong) may often stand outside the limits of the law. In fact, some politicians often seem to confuse what is moral with what is legal. For example, although gambling may be illegal, a given community may consider it desirable and ignore the law, even demonstrating a sense of collective pride in such activities. In addition, during one period of our history, it was considered illegal for women or minorities to vote or to help persons who were enslaved escape to freedom. In such cases, what was legal was immoral and what was moral was illegal. Some of us did what was right and good at great peril and personal cost during such times even though we broke the law. Others of us remained responsible, law-abiding citizens and, by omitting to do the good we could have done, allowed others to experience unimaginable suffering and injustice.

It is important to note that each of the circles are more like membranes than concrete lines of demarcation. Like ocean tides, they bend and flow with each other, remaining distinct but always connected and interacting. Finally, the area beyond the third context represents the "unknown." From our personal beliefs and values to our social relations and interaction within and outside the rule of law—all are subject to the effects of the unknown. We may call it coincidence, luck, fate, destiny, or the will of God. Whatever we call it, the outcome of our individual lives as well as the fate of our larger community includes an air of mystery, of the unexpected—sometimes welcomed and other times feared. What we can count on is that if we act as ethical persons of integrity we will increase the odds that we will work and live in responsible and caring communities where the chance for justice will be greater for all who live there.

In addition to examining our study of ethics from a personal, social, and criminal justice context, it is also useful to identify several specific goals as we begin to explore issues regarding justice, crime, and ethics.

FIVE GOALS FOR EXPLORING ETHICS

The initial goal for exploring ethics is to *become more aware and open to moral and ethical issues.*

As we try to become more aware of ethical issues, we will discover a number of contradictions in our moral beliefs and values. We will find that there is often a difference between appearances and reality, that things are often not what they seem. What we are taught as children may be challenged by our adult experiences. As a result, some choices seem clearly to be right or wrong, while other events seem more ambiguous and less certain.

A part of our becoming more open includes our learning to be more aware of the full range and nature of moral and ethical issues—from telling a small lie to committing perjury, from cheating on one's income taxes to engaging in major bank fraud. This broad range of moral issues reminds us that where justice is concerned, personal values, social consequences, and criminal justice outcomes are often intertwined.

As we become more open to moral and ethical issues, it is important that we approach our second goal, which is to *begin developing critical thinking and analytical skills.*

As young children, we were often creative, as evidenced by our active imaginations. As we grew older, we learned to stand in line, follow instructions, and be seen more than heard when it came to the process of learning. In a word, we learned to become obedient. Over time, we began to lose confidence in our point of view as being anything of value. In such a context, as students, we are inclined to become more interested in asking *how* rather than *why*, in becoming more like technicians rather than philosophers. However, Albert Einstein (as quoted in Castle, 1988), in discussing science and creativity, suggested that "[t]o raise new questions, new possibilities, to regard old problems from a new angle, requires creative imagination and marks real advances in science." In other words, if we do not first ask the right questions, our solutions, no matter how well-intended and efficient, simply add to our difficulties. Asking why, then, is an important aspect of developing critical thinking and analytical skills.

Asking meaningful questions requires clarity in our thinking and a sense of mindfulness as we explore moral and ethical issues. Critical thinking and analytical skills help us to distinguish concepts such as justice and liberty from principles such as "the ends do not justify the means." For example, we might discuss capital punishment both as a concept and in principle. However, our critical thinking and analytical skills will allow us to go even further as we search for the truth regarding capital punishment. What are the short-term and long-term costs of such a sanction? How does it affect our criminal justice system and our society in general? What will future generations think about our decisions, laws, and policies regarding capital punishment? While we may never be able to arrive at a perfect position on capital punishment, critical thinking and analytical skills can aid us in exploring more openly and with more integrity the various issues surrounding it. These skills encourage openness and perseverance rather than blind acceptance and obedience based upon ignorance.

There will always be disagreement on such issues as capital punishment. As with any moral issue, there is a cost for the attitudes we hold and the choices we make; there is inevitably an upside and a downside, a pro and a con. As we explore such issues, critical thinking and analytical skills can help us see more clearly what the costs will be.

Becoming more open to moral and ethical issues and developing critical thinking and analytical skills will help us to more fully realize our third goal: *becoming more personally responsible.* Before we can become more responsible, we must increase our ability to respond. The first two goals aid us in this endeavor. As we persevere in an open exploration and search for the truth regarding moral and ethical issues, we will feel more empowered and have more hope for the future.

A fourth goal of our ethics education is that we *understand how criminal justice is engaged in a process of coercion.* Giving tickets to drivers who exceed the speed limit and sentencing offenders to prison are examples of this process. In exploring the morality of coercion, we come to realize that, in large part, criminal justice is about forcing people to do things they do not want to do. Having the authority to be coercive, combined with the discretionary nature of such authority, creates the potential for corruption and abuse. Can you think of any examples where the coercive role of police, courts, or corrections could be corrupted? On a more personal level, how might parental or peer influences exercise coercion in an unethical way (Sherman, 1981)?

The fifth goal of our exploration concerns what Parker Palmer (1983) refers to as *developing wholesight.* It is important that we become more open to moral and ethical issues, that we develop critical thinking and analytical skills, that we increase our sense of personal responsibility, and that we understand the morality of coercion. Yet all of these abilities and skills need to be tempered by our intuitive nature. We need to explore these issues not only with our minds but also with our hearts. Our mind or intellect can often become more preoccupied with immediate problems and how to solve them. The heart asks why and looks not only to the immediate dilemma but also to the deeper level of difficulty, and it asks what the costs might be in the long run. Wholesight creates a vision in which our minds and hearts, our thinking and feeling, work together for the common good as we explore the ethical and moral issues that we as individuals and as members of a community face.

Figure 1.2
Five Goals for Exploring Ethics

1. Greater awareness of moral/ethical issues
2. Develop critical thinking/analytical skills
3. Become personally responsible
4. Understanding coercion in criminal justice
5. Develop wholesight

The following sections of this book will introduce you to some of the philosophical theories that can provide a framework for you to study and analyze ethical and moral issues in crime and justice. The police, courts, and corrections, which comprise the criminal justice system, will be explored in the light of ethical concerns. Criminal justice research and crime control policy will also be examined. Finally, a justice ethic for the future is offered for your consideration. What kind of future do you want to be a part of? What price are you willing to pay?

REFERENCES

Braswell, M. & H. LaFolette (1988). "Seeking Justice: The Advantages and Disadvantages of Being Educated." *American Journal of Criminal Justice*, (Spring):135-147.

Buechner, F. (1973) *Wishful Thinking*. New York: Harper & Row, p. 48

Castle, T. (ed.) (1988). *The New Book of Christian Quotations*. New York: Crossroads, p. 52

Palmer, P. (1983). *To Know As We Are Known*. San Francisco: Harper & Row.

Sherman, L.W. (1981). *The Study of Ethics in Criminology and Criminal Justice*. Chicago: Joint Commission on Criminology and Criminal Justice Education and Standards, p. 181.

Woods, R. (ed.) (1966). *The World Treasury of Religious Quotations*. New York: Garland, p. 647.

DISCUSSION QUESTIONS

1. Define and discuss the term "ethics" from your own perspective.

2. Explain what "ethics" is using the three contexts presented in this chapter for understanding justice, crime, and ethics.

3. Explain the five goals of exploring ethics and the impact that each has on the other.

CHAPTER 2

Utilitarian and Deontological Approaches to Criminal Justice Ethics

Jeffrey Gold

Over the past 10 to 15 years, interest in professional ethics has grown steadily. Business ethics, medical ethics, and environmental ethics are all flourishing as components in most college and university curricula. Despite this fact, until recently, "higher education programs in criminology and criminal justice have largely neglected the systematic study of ethics" (Sherman, 1981:7). This is unfortunate because the ethical issues that arise in the area of criminal justice are significant and complex. And, even though many of the ethical issues that arise in criminal justice are common to other professions, there are other issues that are specifically tailored to criminology and criminal justice. The most significant example, as mentioned in Chapter 1, involves the use of force and physical coercion. Sherman points out: "Force is the essence of criminal justice . . . The decisions of whether to use force, how much to use, and under what conditions are confronted by police officers, juries, judges, prison officials, probation and parole officers and others. All of them face the paradox . . . of using harm to prevent harm" (Sherman, 1981:30). Because the use of force is central to criminal justice, this distinguishes criminal justice from other professions.

KEY CONCEPTS:

categorical imperative

consequentialism

deontology

hypothetical imperative

John Stuart Mill

Immanuel Kant

normative ethics

universalizability

utilitarian calculus

utilitarianism

In addition to the issue concerning the use of force, there are other factors that seem to distinguish the moral decisions of criminal justice agents from other professionals. Sherman (1981) discusses two of them:

First, criminal justice decisions are made on behalf of society as a whole, a collective moral judgement made in trust by a single person. That would entail a far greater responsibility than what other vocations are assigned. Second, the decisions criminal justice agents make are not just incidentally, but are primarily, moral decisions. An engineer designs a building that may or may not kill people, but the decision is primarily a physical one and only incidentally a moral one. When a police officer decides to arrest someone . . . when a judge decides to let that person out on a suspended sentence, the decisions are primarily moral ones (p.14).

As we can see, the moral issues that arise in the field of criminal justice are both distinctive and significant.

It is sometimes helpful, when trying to solve certain specific ethical issues, to begin with more general, theoretical questions. When we get a handle on the more theoretical issue, we can apply that to a specific moral problem. So, with respect to criminal justice, we might begin by raising more general questions about the nature of justice. Theories of justice address broad social issues including human rights, equality, and the distribution of wealth. We might even go up one more level of generality: justice is itself a branch of an even wider sphere, that of ethics. It seems important that we view issues in criminal justice from the larger framework of ethics and morality. It would be a mistake to assume that issues in criminal justice could emerge outside of the larger social and ethical context of our culture. Therefore, this essay will explore the field of ethics with the hope that such a study will provide us with a set of concepts that will shed some light on specific moral issues in the field of criminal justice. That shall be done by presenting a study of two of the major philosophical theories in the field of normative ethics.

NORMATIVE ETHICS

Normative ethics is the study of right and wrong. A normative ethical theorist tries to discover whether there are any basic, fundamental principles of right and wrong. If such principles are discovered, they are held to be the ground or foundation of all of our ethical judgments. For example, we ordinarily say lying, cheating, stealing, raping, and killing are wrong. The ethical theorist asks: Do these very different activities of lying, stealing and killing all have something in common that makes them all wrong? If so, what is that common characteristic?

One of the most important figures in the history of Western philosophy, Socrates, was famous for seeking the universal in ethical matters.[1] In other words, when Socrates asked "What is Justice?" or "What is Virtue?", he was not asking for a list of actions that are just or a list of examples of virtue; rather, he was seeking the universal characteristic that all just or virtuous actions have in common.[2] Just as all squares, no matter how large they are or what color they are, have something in common (four equal sides and four right angles), the ethical theorist wants to know if all morally right actions (whether they are cases of honesty, charity, or benevolence) also have something in common. If such a common characteristic is found, it is held to be the ground or foundation or fundamental principle of ethics. We shall now turn to our study of two standard ethical theories in an effort to locate such a foundation for ethics.

UTILITARIANISM

The most famous version of utilitarianism was developed in Great Britain in the eighteenth and nineteenth centuries by Jeremy Bentham (1970) and John Stuart Mill (1979). Utilitarianism is classified as a consequentialist ethical theory. In other words, the utilitarian holds that we judge the morality of an action in terms of the consequences or results of that action. Mill (1979) states: "All action is for the sake of some end, and rules of action, it seems natural to suppose, must take their whole character and color from the end to which they are subservient" (p. 2). The insight that motivates consequentialism is this: a moral action produces something good; an immoral action produces a bad or harmful result. Put in the simplest possible way, cheating, stealing, and murder are all wrong because they produce bad or harmful consequences, and charity and benevolence are good because they produce something beneficial. To summarize, the consequentialist holds that the morality of an action is determined by the consequences of that action—actions that are moral produce good consequences, actions that are immoral produce bad consequences.

At this point, two questions come up: (1) What do we mean by good consequences (and bad consequences)? (2) Consequences for whom? Actions have consequences for many different people. Which people should we consider when contemplating the consequences of our actions? By giving concrete answers to these two questions, the utilitarian carves out a unique and specific version or type of consequentialist moral theory.

In order to explain utilitarianism, we shall begin with the first question. How does the utilitarian define or characterize good and bad consequences? The most famous version of utilitarianism (the one advocated by Bentham and Mill) is called hedonistic utilitarianism. According to Mill, the fundamental good that all humans seek is happiness. Aristotle agrees with that point, even though he is not a utilitarian. In his discussion of the highest good, Aristotle (350 BCE) says: "As far as its name is concerned, most people would agree: for both the common run of people and cultivated men call it happiness." Mill (1979) holds that "there is in reality nothing desired except happiness" (p. 37). Mill's view is that all people desire happiness and everything else they desire is either a part of happiness or a means to happiness. Thus, the basic and fundamental good, according to hedonistic utilitarianism (hereafter called utilitarianism), is happiness.

According to both Bentham and Mill, happiness is identified by pleasure. Mill (1979) claims: "By happiness is intended pleasure and the absence of pain; by unhappiness, pain and the privation of pleasure" (p. 7). In his discussion of pleasure, Mill includes not only the pleasures of food, drink, and sex, but also intellectual and aesthetic pleasures. In fact, Mill considers the "higher order" pleasures, that is, the intellectual, emotional, and aesthetic pleasures that nonhuman animals are not capable of experiencing, to be of a higher quality than the "lower order" pleasures that many species of animals experience. The pleasures of poetry and opera are, in Mill's view, qualitatively superior to the pleasures of drinking and playing pinball.

Consequentialism holds that the morality of an action is determined by the consequences produced by the action. For the utilitarian, the morally right action produces happiness (pleasure and the absence of pain) and the morally wrong action produces unhappiness (pain and suffering). Mill (1979) states: "The creed which accepts as the foundation of morals 'utility' or 'the greatest happiness principle' holds that actions are right in proportion as they tend to promote happiness; wrong as they tend to produce the reverse of happiness" (p. 7). Bentham (1970) states, "By the principle of utility is meant that principle which approves or disapproves of every action whatsoever, according to the tendency which it appears to have to augment or diminish the happiness of the party whose interest is in question: or, what is the same thing in other words, to promote or to oppose the happiness" (p. 2). Before we examine the theory with any more sophistication, we can already feel the intuitive appeal of the theory. Why do we think that murder, rape, cheating, and lying are immoral? Because those actions cause pain to the victims and the families of the victims. Why do we think that charity and benevolence are righteous actions? Because they produce pleasure or happiness.

Let us now move to the second question. Because utilitarianism holds that we ought to produce happiness or pleasure, whose happiness or pleasure ought we to consider? After all, the thief gets a certain amount of pleasure from a successful burglary. The utilitarian answer to this is that we ought to consider all parties affected by the action, and calculate the pain and pleasure of everyone who is influenced. After due consideration, the action that is morally correct is the one that produces the greatest good (amount of happiness) for the greatest number of people. If all the alternatives involve more pain than pleasure, the morally right action is the one that produces the least amount of pain.

For example, the thief wants money to accord himself a certain lifestyle. Stealing will bring him jewelry or other valuable items that he can trade for money that will make him feel good. However, such actions would also have another consequence: those persons who were stolen from would become victims with the accompanying feelings of sorrow, anger or, perhaps, even fear. As a result, their pain outweighs his pleasure. "The greatest good for the greatest number" creates the context for community. The proportionality of pain and pleasure must be judged in this context.

In calculating the amount of pleasure and pain produced by any action, many factors are relevant. Bentham (1970:29-32) creates a hedonistic calculus in which he lists those factors. I shall briefly describe some of the major elements in Bentham's calculus. First, we must consider the *intensity* or strength of the pleasure or pain. A minor inconvenience is much less important than a major trauma. We must also consider the *duration* of the pleasure or pain. For example, in the case of a rape, psychological scars may last a lifetime. Additionally, we must consider the *long-term consequences* of an action. Certain actions may produce short-term pleasures but in the long run may prove to be more harmful than good (for example, alcohol and drugs). Finally, we must consider the *probability* or likelihood that our actions will produce the consequences we intend. For example, the prisons are full of thieves who in a personal (and not merely community) context did not make a good utilitarian choice. For instance, a certain offender commits an armed robbery to acquire money to spend on a lavish lifestyle that would make her feel good. Instead, because the offender did not consider the probability of being caught, she spends 15 years experiencing the pain of imprisonment.

Let me briefly summarize. The ethical theorist is interested in discovering the basic, fundamental principle of morality, a foundation upon which all moral judgments rest. The utilitarian claims to have found such a principle and identifies it as the greatest happiness principle. According to utilitarianism, an action ought to be done if and only if that action maximizes the total amount of pleasure (or minimizes the total amount of pain) of all parties affected by the action.

The entire criminal justice system can be justified on utilitarian grounds. Why do we need a police force? To serve and protect. That is to say, it is in the long-term interests of a society (produces the greatest amount of happiness for the greatest number of people) to pay police officers to protect the community from burglars, murderers, rapists, and drunk drivers. The utilitarian would argue that what we call criminal activities tend to produce much more pain than pleasure. Therefore, a criminal justice system is instituted in order to lower the amount of crime, thereby lowering the amount of pain produced by crime.

Despite that fact that utilitarianism can be used to justify the criminal justice system, there are certain times when we say a police officer is justified in arresting (or ticketing) a citizen even though that arrest does not lead to the greatest good for the greatest number. For example, suppose a man is in a rush to pick up his daughter at school. He is driving on the freeway on a bright, sunny day and there is virtually no traffic. Suppose he exceeds the speed limit by 15 miles per hour (the speed limit is 55 mph and he is driving at 70 mph). The police officer stops him and gives him a ticket for $75. One might argue that, in this case, the painful consequences of giving a ticket outweigh the pleasurable consequences. First of all, the driver is caused pain by having to pay the ticket. Secondly, by getting the ticket, the driver is late to pick up his daughter, which causes the daughter anxiety. The delay also causes inconvenience for the principal at school. What are the pleasurable consequences for giving the ticket? Who is made happier? Had the officer just given the driver a warning, the driver, the principal, and the child would all be happier. No one would be less happy. So, on utilitarian grounds, the officer should not issue a ticket in the set of circumstances just described.

The previous example leads some people to say that the officer has a *duty* to issue the ticket regardless of the consequences. This leads us to our next moral theory, namely, deontological ethics.

DEONTOLOGICAL ETHICS

The word *deontology* comes from two Greek roots: *deos*, meaning duty, and *logos*, meaning study. Deontology is therefore the study of duty. Deontologists have argued that human beings sometimes have duties to perform certain actions regardless of the consequences. Police officers have a duty to issue traffic tickets even when doing so does not produce the greatest good for the greatest number. Teachers have the obligation or duty to fail students who do failing work even if failing that student produces more misery than happiness.

The most famous deontologist is Immanuel Kant, an eighteenth-century German philosopher. Kant believed that all consequentialist theories missed something crucial to ethics by neglecting the concept of duty. But that is not all. Kant also believed that by focusing solely on consequences, utilitarian-type theories missed something even more basic to morality, namely, a good will or the intention to do what is right. He begins his treatise on ethics as follows: "It is impossible to conceive anything at all in the world, or even out of it, which can be taken as good without qualification, except a *good will*" (Kant, 1964:61). In other words, the key to morality is human will or intention, not consequences.

Consider the following example: Suppose John is driving down the road and sees someone on the side of the road having difficulty with a flat tire. John notices that the car is a brand-new Cadillac and the driver of the car (an elderly woman) is wearing a mink coat. John thinks to himself, "If I help this woman, she will give me a large reward." So, John stops his car and helps the woman fix her flat tire. In the second case, Mary drives down the road and sees someone on the side of the road having difficulty with a flat tire. Mary says to herself, "That woman seems to be in trouble. I think I should help her." And she does help her. Kant would argue that there is a moral difference between case one and case two, despite the fact that the consequences in the two cases are identical. In both cases, John and Mary (on a utilitarian view) did the right thing by helping the woman, thereby producing the greatest good for the greatest number. However, Kant would argue that even though John and Mary both did the right thing (Kant would say they both acted in accordance with duty), there is still a moral difference. Mary did the act because it was her duty, whereas John was motivated by self-interest. Kant would not say that John was immoral. After all, he didn't do anything wrong. In fact, he did the right thing. But, because he didn't do it for the right reason, his action has no moral worth. He did the right thing for self-ish reasons (which is still better than doing the wrong thing, that is to say performing an action inconsistent with duty). Kant (1964:65-67) draws a distinction between actions that are merely in accordance with duty and actions that are taken for the sake of duty. And, he holds that only actions that are done for the sake of duty have moral worth.

Having established the importance of a good will (doing an act for the right reason), Kant moves to the question: What is our duty? In other words, just as the utilitarians have a fundamental principle of morality (act so as to produce the greatest good for the greatest number), Kant argues for a different fundamental principle of morality.

The Categorical Imperative

Kant calls the fundamental principle of morality the *categorical imperative*. An imperative is a command. It tells us what we ought to do or what we should do. The categorical imperative contrasts with what Kant calls hypothetical imperatives. A *hypothetical imperative* is a command that begins with "if," for example, *if* you want to get a good grade, you ought to study, or *if* you want to make a lot of money, you should work hard, or *if* you want to stay out of jail, you should not break the law. The categorical imperative is unhypothetical, no ifs whatsoever. Just do it! You ought to behave morally, period; not: *if* you want people to like you, you should behave morally; not: *if* you want to go to heaven, you should behave morally. It is just "you ought to behave morally." In other words, the categorical imperative commands absolutely and unconditionally.

What is the categorical imperative? Kant gives several formulations of it. We will focus on two formulations. The first formulation emphasizes a basic concept in ethics called "universalizability." The basic idea of universalizability is that for my action to be morally justifiable, I must be able to will that *anyone* in relevantly similar circumstances act in the same way. For example, I would like to cheat on my income tax, but could I will that *everyone* cheats on income taxes, thereby leaving the government insufficient funds to carry out programs I support? I would like to tell a lie to extricate myself from an uncomfortable situation, but could I will that someone else lie to me in order to get him or herself out of a difficult situation? Kant's formulation of the categorical imperative is as follows: "Act only on that maxim [a maxim is a principle of action] through which you can at the same time will that it should become a universal law" (1964:88).

Kant's insight is that morality involves fairness or equality—that is, a willingness to treat everyone in the same way. I am acting immorally when I make myself an exception ("I wouldn't want others behaving this way, but it is fine for me to behave this way"). Put in that way, we see a similarity to the Golden Rule, which states, "Do unto others only as you would have them do unto you."[3] Kant's idea is that you should do only what you are willing to permit anyone else to do. The idea is that there is something inconsistent or irrational about saying that it is fine for me to lie to you, cheat you, steal from you, but it is not justified for you to do those things to me.

The next formulation of the categorical imperative focuses on the fact that human beings have intrinsic value (that is, value in and of themselves). Because human beings have intrinsic value, they ought always to be treated with reverence and never to be treated as mere things. When I treat someone as a thing, an object, a tool, or an instrument, I am treating that person as a means to my own ends. For example, if I marry someone to get her money, I am using her as a means to my own ends. I am not treating her with dignity, respect, or reverence, but as a mere thing. It is the classic case of using someone. When I was about 10 years old, a friend and I wanted to go to a movie. My mother could drive one way, but my friend's mother was busy and couldn't drive that day. So we decided to call a neighbor (Richard). I still remember the conversation. I said, "Hi, Richard. Would you like to go to a movie with me and Kenny?" Richard responded affirmatively, saying he would enjoy that very much. I then said, "Could your mother drive one way?" Well, Richard exploded. Richard immediately recognized that we were not inviting him because we especially wanted him to come, but rather we were using him to get a ride from his mother. Unfortunately, Richard was right. That was precisely why we called him.

Kant (1964) speaks of a human being as "something whose existence has in itself an absolute value" (p. 95). He goes on to say that "man, and in general every rational being, exists as an end in himself, not merely as a means for arbitrary use by this or that will" (p. 95). On the basis of this, he offers the following formulation of the categorical imperative: "Act in such a way that you always treat humanity, whether in your own person or in the person of any other, never simply as a means, but always at the same time as an end" (p. 96).

Kant believed that these two seemingly different formulations of the categorical imperative really come to the same thing. Perhaps the reasoning goes as follows: What maxims or principles of action would I be willing to universalize? Only those that treated others as ends in themselves and not as things. Why? Because I want to be treated with reverence, respect, and dignity. Because I want to be treated as a being with intrinsic value, I can only universalize maxims that treat other people as having intrinsic value.

COMPARING UTILITARIANISM AND DEONTOLOGY

Before concluding this essay, let us contrast deontological ethics with utilitarianism on a specific issue related to criminal justice. The issue is: What are the legitimate restraints a society should impose on police officers in the apprehension of suspected criminals? To limit this rather broad topic somewhat, let us focus on the use of techniques of deceit including entrapment, telephone bugging, and undercover operations. In this example, I will not try to predict the answer that a utilitarian or a deontologist will give. Instead, I will simply contrast the approach or the strategy they will use in thinking about the issue.

Let's begin with utilitarianism. Utilitarianism is a consequentialist moral theory. We decide the legitimacy of deceptive tactics on the basis of the consequences of using those tactics. In particular, we must weigh the positive results against the negative results in deciding what to do. On the positive side are entrapment, bugging operations, and undercover operations work. As a result of the use of such tactics, we are able to apprehend some criminals that might otherwise go free. And, as a result of apprehending those criminals, we may deter future crime in two ways: (1) we keep known criminals behind bars where they are unable to commit further crimes; and (2) we show, by example, what happens when someone breaks the law and thereby deter other citizens from risking incarceration.

On the negative side, we have certain individuals' right to privacy being violated by the use of deceptive tactics. The utilitarian will now weigh the positive benefits of apprehending criminals, and thereby protecting society, against the negative consequence of violating certain citizens' rights to privacy.

Kant would approach the issue from a very different reference point. As a deontologist, he would not approach this issue from the perspective of "What consequences are likely to occur?" Rather than focusing on the results or ends of the behavior, he or she would look at the behavior itself to see if it conforms to the categorical imperative. Concentrating on the universalizability formulation of the categorical imperative, a Kantian might ask: "Would I consent to having my telephone bugged if there were reason to suspect that I was guilty of a crime?"

Or, if we were to attend to the second formulation of the categorical imperative, a Kantian might ask: "Does the use of manipulative techniques in law enforcement constitute treating suspected criminals as mere means to our ends (by manipulating them, we are using them), or does it constitute treating them as ends in themselves (mature, responsible citizens who must answer to their behavior)?"

These are difficult questions to answer. But the point of the example is not to show how a utilitarian or deontologist would solve an ethical issue in criminal justice, but rather to illustrate how they would approach or think about such an issue.

JUSTICE AND DUTY

Both Kant's categorical imperative and Mill's principle of greatest happiness capture some of our moral intuitions. Treating people as ends and producing the greatest amount of happiness both seem to be credible guides to the moral life. Nonetheless, both theories seem to have trouble with a certain range of cases. Utilitarianism appears to have difficulty with certain cases of injustice, and Kant's deontology seems to have no way to handle cases of conflicting duties. In this final section, I will look at the weak points in both theories and propose an integrated Kantian-utilitarian ethic to handle the alleged weaknesses of both theories.[4]

According to utilitarianism, an action is moral when it produces the greatest amount of happiness for the greatest number of people. A problem arises, however, when the greatest happiness is achieved at the expense of a few. For example, if a large group were to enslave a very small group, the large group would gain certain comforts and luxuries (and the pleasure that accompanies those comforts) as a result of the servitude of the few. If we were to follow the utilitarian calculus strictly, the suffering of a few (even intense suffering) would be outweighed by the pleasure of a large enough majority. A thousand people's modest pleasure would outweigh the suffering of 10 others. Hence, utilitarianism would seem to endorse slavery when it produces the greatest total amount of happiness for the greatest number of people. This is obviously a problem for utilitarianism. Slavery and oppression are wrong regardless of the amount of pleasure accumulated by the oppressing class. In fact, when one person's pleasure results from the suffering of another, the pleasure seems all the more abhorrent.

The preceding case points to a weakness in utilitarianism, namely, the weakness in dealing with certain cases of injustice. Sometimes it is simply unjust to treat people in a certain way regardless of the pleasurable consequences for others. A gang rape is wrong even if 50 people enjoy it and only one suffers. It is wrong because it is unjust. To use Kant's formulation, it is always wrong to treat anyone as a mere means to one's own ends. When we enslave, rape, and oppress, we are always treating the victim as a means to our own ends.

There are several cases related to criminal justice in which this issue comes up. However, when it comes up in these cases, it is not as simple as the slavery and gang-rape cases. It is complex, subtle, and controversial. The cases I am considering involve the excessive use of force. Suppose, for example, that we want to keep order in our communities or in our prisons. Would we be justified in using excessive force on one offender as an example to the rest? If we were to beat a few citizens or prisoners severely for certain crimes, those public beatings might deter future crimes, thereby increasing the general happiness. But do we have the right to treat one offender with excessive violence in order to teach others a lesson? A case like this is apt to produce a lively debate, and the debate would involve utilitarian and Kantian sentiments. The utilitarian might point out that although public canings are brutal, Singapore (which uses such punishments) is virtually crime-free. The Kantian would say that the beating of some citizens to protect others is too high a price. It is simply unjust to mistreat one citizen in order to benefit others. The ambivalent feelings we have in this case show how deeply we have internalized the voices of both Kant and Mill.

We see from the above cases (especially the slavery case) that utilitarianism has trouble dealing with situations involving the maximization of pleasure for the majority at the expense of the minority. We also see that Kant (with his emphasis on treating people as ends in themselves) can easily handle those cases. Kant's moral theory, however, has problems of its own. In particular, although Kant talks extensively of duty, he seems to have no way to deal with cases of conflicting duties. Suppose, for example, you borrow a gun from a friend for target practice, and promise to return the weapon. After you borrow the weapon, your friend becomes emotionally upset and vows to shoot someone. He then demands that you return the gun that you promised to return. He says he needs the gun back to commit a murder. On the one hand, you have a duty to keep your promises and return what you owe. On the other hand, you have a duty to try to prevent a murder. Kant gives us no guidance here. Treating people as ends and not means is a nice formula, but how does it apply in this case? If you do not return the gun, aren't you treating your friend as a means? If you do return the gun, aren't you treating the potential murder victim as a means? Kant provides no obvious solution. It is precisely at this point that a utilitarian calculus might help. The utilitarian would estimate the harm done by returning the gun against the harm done by keeping the gun. Presumably, much more harm would be caused by returning the weapon.

It appears, therefore, that Kant's theory is strong where Mill's is weak, and vice versa. Kant's emphasis on justice provides a moral reason to reject slavery even when it maximizes pleasure. The utilitarian calculus gives us a method of determining what to do in cases of conflicting duties.

Perhaps we can combine the insights of both utilitarianism and deontology and formulate a "Utilitarian Kantian Principle." Cornman and Lehrer (1974) propose the following integrated principle:

> An action ought to be done in a situation if and only if (1) doing the action, (a) treats as mere means as few people as possible in the situation, and (b) treats as ends as many people as is consistent with (a), *and* (2) doing the action in the situation brings about as much overall happiness as is consistent with (1) (p. 506).

This integrated Kantian utilitarian principle avoids the problem of the many enslaving the few because such an act would violate point 1. It also avoids the problem of conflicting duties because point 2 provides a way of deciding what to do when I am faced with a conflict of duties.

Deontology and utilitarianism are two of the most significant, influential ethical theories in Western thought. Much of the moral reasoning we daily engage in is guided by utilitarian and/or deontological reflection. This is true both generally and specifically in cases involving criminal justice. The criminal justice system itself is usually justified on either utilitarian grounds (it is in the best interest of most citizens to punish criminals) or Kantian grounds (it is our duty to punish wrongdoing). The hope is that this essay will provide some tools that we can use in trying to understand and solve some of the tough ethical decisions facing our criminal justice system.

NOTES

1. In the *Metaphysics* (987b1), Aristotle states: "Now Socrates was engaged in the study of ethical matters, but not at all in the study of nature as a whole, yet in ethical matters he sought the universal and was the first to fix his thought on definitions."

2. See Plato, *Laches* 191c, *Euthyphro* 5c-d, *Meno* 72a.

3. See Matthew 7:12; Luke 6:31.

4. I first discovered the idea of integrating Kant and Mill in James Cornman and Keith Lehrer, *Philosophical Problems and Arguments: An Introduction*, 2d ed. (New York: Macmillan, 1974), pp. 504-508.

REFERENCES

Aristotle (350 BCE). *Nicomachean Ethics*, 1095a 15-20.

Bentham, J. (1970). *The Principles of Morals and Legislation*. Darien, CT: Hafner.

Cornman, J. & K. Lehrer (1974). *Philosophical Problems and Arguments: An Introduction*, 2nd ed. New York: Macmillan

Kant, I. (1964). *Groundwork of the Metaphysics of Morals* (translated by H.J Paton). New York: Harper & Row.

Mill, J.S. (1979). *Utilitarianism*. Indianapolis: Hackett.

Sherman, L.W. (1981). *The Study of Ethics in Criminology and Criminal Justice*. Chicago: Joint Commission on Criminology and Criminal Justice Education and Standards.

DISCUSSION QUESTIONS

1. Compare and contrast utilitarianism and deontology. Which of the two do you feel explains human behavior most effectively? Why?

2. Explain and discuss Kant's categorical imperative. How appropriate are his views in today's criminal justice field?

3. Think of a difficult ethical decision that someone working in the criminal justice field might be facing. Using one of the theories discussed in this chapter, illustrate how it might be used to improve upon that situation, including the person's understanding of his or her dilemma.

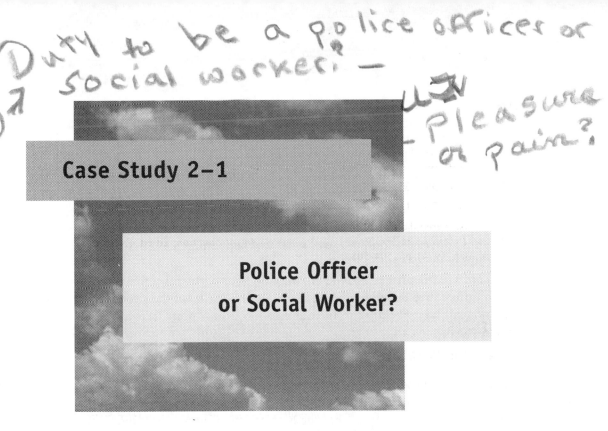

Duty to be a police officer or social worker? — Pleasure or pain?

Case Study 2–1

Police Officer or Social Worker?

Jack and Ann Smith are a married couple with three children ranging in age from five months to six years. Jack is unemployed and is 60 percent disabled from a wound he received in Vietnam. Ann has to provide primary care for the children and also has a part-time job at a nearby grocery store. Jack and Ann live in a housing project where the rent is based on the government welfare checks they receive.

It is near the end of the month and the food stamps have almost been depleted. Jack spent what little money they had left on beer for himself and his friends. Over the years, Jack has continued to feel bitter about his disability and apparently tries to drown his problems with alcohol.

Jack and Ann had an argument earlier in the day over the amount of money Jack spends on beer and wine. Ann was also becoming increasingly upset over Jack frequenting bars and not trying to help with household responsibilities and chores. Ann even accused Jack of feeling sorry for himself and of being a failure in general. Jack responded by slapping Ann several times and leaving the house in a fit of temper.

While Jack was gone, the two eldest children began fighting with each other, which resulted in the youngest child crying. Although Ann had carefully cleaned the apartment the day before, the children had again made a mess of the house. Her patience wearing thin, Ann rocked the youngest child in a rocking chair in an effort to stop his crying. After substantial threats from their mother, the two oldest children started playing in the kitchen and

From Larry S. Miller and Michael Braswell, *Human Relations and Police Work,* 4th ed. (Prospect Heights, IL: Waveland Press), 1997. Reprinted with permission.

eventually broke several dishes that were on the table. That was the last straw! Ann began whipping [beating] the oldest child for breaking the dishes. Full of anger and frustration, she whipped the child so hard that he fainted and was apparently unconscious.

Jack came back to the apartment a short time later, intoxicated and still upset over the argument in which he and Ann had engaged earlier. He found the younger children crying, the oldest child badly beaten, and Ann sitting in a kitchen chair sobbing. In a fit of rage, Jack began beating Ann.

The next-door neighbor, aware of what was happening, called the police and explained the situation.

You are a patrol officer assigned to the call. Your partner is a female officer with little police experience. Not knowing for sure what the situation is, you do not call for a backup car. In your opinion, at this point, it is a routine family disturbance call.

As you stand outside the Smiths' apartment door, you hear children sobbing. No one answers the door or speaks to you when you knock. You think to yourself, "These people need a social worker, not a police officer." Your partner looks at you, uncertain and waiting for instructions. You take a deep breath and try to decide what the best course of action will be.

Based on what you have read, answer the following questions:

> Examine this case from utilitarian and deontological perspectives. How would each approach differ from the other in resolving the crisis? How would they be similar? Which approach do you feel would be best?

CHAPTER 3

Peacemaking, Justice, and Ethics

Michael C. Braswell & Jeffrey Gold

The evolution of legal and social justice in America often has found itself pulled between the retribution and punishment agendas of such ancient traditions as the law of Moses, the Koran, and the rehabilitation and redemption traditions of New Testament Christianity. The tension between these traditions of retribution and rehabilitation, and punishment and reform, has been substantial.

Peacemaking as a justice and criminology perspective has been heralded in some quarters as a contemporary, "new age" phenomenon. The New Age movement itself appears to be essentially a middle-class movement that focuses on such issues as metaphysical inquiry, mind control, emotional healing, and

KEY CONCEPTS:

caring

connectedness

mindfulness

peacemaking

financial well-being. While peacemaking concerns may be compatible with some of these issues, they seem more grounded in age-old traditions such as Christianity, Judaism, Islamism, Buddhism, and Hinduism. In particular, these ancient traditions emphasize the value and usefulness of suffering and service, which is often deemphasized or nonexistent in New Age movements (Bartollas & Braswell, 1993).

Peacemaking, as evolved from ancient spiritual and wisdom traditions, has included the possibility of mercy and compassion within the framework of justice. To put such thinking in a more personal perspective, we might consider our own experiences—times when we have been the victim and other occasions when we have been the offender. Perhaps we have never committed a crime and, hopefully, most of us have never been harmed by an offender. Yet, in our own way we have been both victim and offender. We have been betrayed by those we trusted, whether the heartbreak of a romance gone sour or the cruel gossip of a broken confidence. How did we feel when we were betrayed? What did we want from the one who hurt us? Typically, we wanted to strike back; we wanted revenge, retribution, our pound of flesh. What about the occasions when we have been the offender, when we have committed the betrayal? When our best friend found out that we were the source of the criticism or cruel gossip, what did we want? As the one who offended, what did we hope for? Did we hope for mercy and forgiveness, perhaps another chance? Can we have it both ways? Can we be for revenge and violence when we are the victim and for mercy and peace when we are the offender? Can we expect to have it both ways?

What we will try to do in this chapter is explore three themes of peacemaking: (1) connectedness, (2) care, and (3) mindfulness. It is our hope that through this exploration we will be able to better understand the possibilities of peacemaking for us as criminal justice professionals as well as on a personal level.

CONNECTEDNESS

The first and perhaps most important theme is demonstrated in the dedication to the book *Inner Corrections: Finding Peace and Peace Making,* which says, "to the keeper and the kept, the offender and the victim, the parent and the child, the teacher and the student, and the incarcerator and the liberator that is within each of us" (Lozoff & Braswell, 1989). This simple statement suggests what Eastern philosophers such as Lao-tzu and Western philosophers such as Plato advocated ages ago—that human beings are not simply isolated individuals, but each one of us is integrally "connected" and bonded to other human beings and the environment. This environment includes not only the outer physical environment but our inner psychological and spiritual environment as well. Chief Seattle of the Duwamish tribe, in a letter to the president of the United States, wrote the following in 1852:

> Every part of this earth is sacred to my people. Every shining pine needle, every sandy shore, every mist in the dark woods, every meadow, every humming insect . . . . We know the sap which courses through the trees as we know the blood that courses through our veins. We are part of the earth and it is part of us. The perfumed flowers are our sisters. The bear, the deer, the great eagle, these are our brothers. The rocky crests, the juices in the meadow, the body heat of the pony, and man, all belong to the same family . . . This we know: the earth does not belong to man, man belongs to the earth. All things are connected like the blood that unites us all. Man did not weave the web of life, he is merely a strand in it. Whatever he does to the web, he does to himself.[1]

In that letter, Chief Seattle emphasizes our connection to the natural world. One can find a similar position in several different Eastern philosophies. Bo Lozoff (1987:11), articulating the position found in Yoga, states: "In Truth, we (everybody and everything in the Universe) are all connected; most of us just can't see the glue."

The idea that we just can't see the glue (that is, we can't see the connection linking ourselves to others) is the Hindu concept that we misperceive ourselves as isolated and disconnected from one another and the world. As we become more aware of how we are connected to all that we are a part of, we are encouraged to take more personal responsibility to do the best we can. Wendell Berry, a noted conservationist, writes, "A man who is willing to undertake the discipline and the difficulty of mending his own ways is worth more to the conservation movement than a hundred who are insisting merely that the government and industries mend *their* ways" (in Safransky, 1990:51). Thomas Merton suggests that "instead of hating the people you think are war makers, hate the appetites and the disorder in your own soul, which are the causes of war." (in Safransky, 1990:115). Insofar as we see ourselves as apart from nature rather than a part of nature, we end up with pollution, acid rain, destruction of forests, and the depletion of the ozone layer. As Berry and Merton indicate, an important aspect of connectedness is looking within, taking personal responsibility, and acting in a more responsible way.

In this regard, it is interesting to contrast two metaphors concerning the earth. The older metaphor of "mother earth" contrasts dramatically with the contemporary metaphor of the earth as a collection of "natural resources." A mother is someone to whom we feel connected and bound. To perceive the earth as one's mother is to see oneself as coming out of the earth. The connection could not be any more intimate. To perceive the earth as an assortment of natural resources is another matter entirely. To conceive of the earth as merely a provider of goods for our own purposes is, to borrow Kant's expression, to see the earth as merely a means of our own ends. The danger in that attitude is now obvious. Insofar as we do not consider the earth to be sacred or precious (as Chief Seattle did), but instead see it as a commodity with no intrinsic worth, we find ourselves in a world with places like Prince William Sound, Three Mile Island, Love Canal, and Chernobyl. To put such thinking in a Judeo-Christian context, does "dominion over the earth" refer to our being responsible stewards of the earth and its resources, or does it allow us to attempt to dominate the earth, exploiting its resources for profit and convenience with little or no regard for breaking environmental laws or for our children's future?

Once we accept the assumption that we are connected to everyone and everything around us, it becomes clear that our actions do not take place in a vacuum but within a complex web of interconnected people and things. Whatever I do has an impact upon those around me. My actions have consequences. This is the Hindu and Buddhist concept of *karma*. The law of karma is the law of cause and effect. All actions have effects or consequences. The law of karma is neither good or bad. It simply is what it is.

When we integrate the notion of karma (lawful consequences) with the notion of connectedness, it becomes clear that, since we are connected to everyone around us, our actions affect those who are connected to us even when we cannot see the connections. Insofar as we have an impact on someone we are connected with, we have an impact upon ourselves. In other words, our actions ultimately come back to us. What goes around comes around. What we do to others, in one way or another, we also do to ourselves. It is the biblical idea that we reap what we sow. It is Chief Seattle's idea that "Man did not weave the web of life, he is merely a strand in it. Whatever he does to the web, he does to himself. Plant seeds of violence and reap violent fruits. Plant seeds of compassion and reap compassionate fruits." Bo Lozoff (1987:9) states: "Every thought, word, and deed is a seed we plant in the world. All our lives, we harvest the fruits of those seeds. If we plant desire, greed, fear, anger and doubt, then that's what will fill our lives. Plant love, courage, understanding, good humor, and that's what we get back. This isn't negotiable; it's a law of energy, just like gravity."

When we speak of karma, we are not talking about retribution, revenge, or punishment. Rather, we are speaking of the consequences of actions. We do not say of someone who jumps from a third-story window that his broken leg is a punishment for jumping. It is simply a consequence. Rather than thinking of karma as retribution, it is better to think of it as the principle, "You've made your bed, now you must lie in it." We must inhabit the world we create. If we pollute the world, we must live in a polluted world. If we act violently or choose to ignore violence and injustice, we must live in a violent and unjust world.

According to proponents of the idea of karma (the idea that each one of us reaps what he or she sows), no one can ever get away with one's actions. Perhaps we won't get caught by the police, but the action still has an impact on our own life. For a philosopher like Plato, the consequences are consequences for our own psyche. In Plato's *Gorgias,* Socrates compares physical health with psychological health.[2] To understand this comparison, consider the following example. I live a sedentary life, eat a diet of junk food and soda pop, smoke cigarettes, and drink alcohol excessively. This life of no exercise, poor nutrition, cigarettes, and alcohol will eventually catch up with me. After I become adjusted and acclimated to it, I may believe that I feel just fine. But from the fact that I believe that I feel fine, it does not follow that I am in an optimal state of physical health. The reason that I believe that I feel fine is precisely because I no longer even know what it is like to feel healthy. It is like a severely nearsighted boy who has never worn glasses. He will not know that his sight is not optimal; he will think the world is supposed to look the way he sees it. He will not know that there is a better way to see. Similarly, I, as the person who lives a sedentary life and eats exclusively at fast food restaurants, may not know that there is a better way to feel. But the fact that I do not know it does not stop the junk food and cigarettes from continuing to affect my physical condition. One simply cannot avoid the consequences of an unhealthy diet and lifestyle.

This is also a useful analogy for understanding suffering and violence within families. There is often a sense of disconnectedness, inconsistency, and neglect regarding relationships in unhealthy and abusive families. Over a period of years, trust becomes nonexistent, and feelings of anger and unhappiness begin to appear normal to such families. They forget how it felt to be happy and at peace (if they ever experienced such feelings). When children grow up full of pain and inconsistencies, they, along with their families, often reap a harvest of drug abuse, spousal battering, and other forms of criminality—even suicide or homicide. They did not realize things had gotten so bad. In a sense, the connections, both hidden and obvious, that animate the consequences of our actions are like a dance (and there are no spectators in the dance of life). "The flailing arms of the abusive parent and the contortions of the victim-child are locked in a dance of pain and sorrow no less significant than the dance of joy experienced by the loving elderly couple" (Braswell, 1996:87).

In *Gorgias,* Plato argues that the same is true with injustice and psychological health. One can never escape the consequences of injustice. One may escape detection by the police, one may never be brought to trial, one may never go to prison—but injustice continues to affect one's psyche, whether we know it or not. We must inhabit the unjust world that we have created. According to Plato, injustice brings strife, disharmony, and conflict. There will be strife and conflict in an unjust city. Similarly, there will be strife and conflict in an unjust individual (a lack of psychic health and wholeness). Just as the physically unhealthy man may not know he is unhealthy and the nearsighted child may not know his eyesight is poor, the unjust man may not know that he is in a state of psychic disharmony and imbalance. That is because he has become adjusted and acclimated to an unjust and violent life. He simply doesn't know what it is like to feel balanced, harmonious, and whole. Of course, consequences of poor physical or psychic health may also offer a person opportunity to learn and grow from his or her experience. For example, what does it mean when a person who ridicules and feels prejudice toward disabled persons finds himself or herself the parent of a disabled child? Some persons might suggest that such a consequence is a form of punishment. Perhaps on a deeper level, the consequence is also an opportunity—another chance for the disconnected person to see and experience the connection that his or her disabled child is lovable and an important part of the web of life. The same can be said of the harsh, uncaring critic of the drug addict, who comes to find that his own daughter or son suffers from such an affliction.

To summarize, according to what we are calling theories of connectedness, people are not isolated, disconnected beings. Rather, we are earthly beings and social beings; that is, we are creatures integrally connected to the earth and to other people on the earth. What we do has direct consequence on those to whom we are connected, whether or not we see the connection. Our actions directly affect the world in which we live. We must live in the world created by our own actions. If we act violently, cruelly, and unjustly, we will live in a world filled with violence, cruelty, and injustice. If we act compassionately and benevolently, we will live in a world that is more compassionate and benevolent.

This metaphysical view naturally leads to an ethics of nonviolence. The Sanskrit word *ahimsa,* meaning nonviolence, is a fundamental concept in Hinduism and Buddhism. Mahatma Gandhi, who advocated an ethic of nonviolence, is a contemporary representative of that idea. A Christian representative is Martin Luther King Jr. Both believed in changing the world and rectifying the injustices they saw, but both insisted on using nonviolent strategies. Martin Luther King Jr., accepting the Nobel Peace Prize, said, "The nonviolent resisters can summarize their message in the following simple terms: We will not obey unjust laws or submit to unjust practices. We will do this peacefully, openly, cheerfully, because our aim is to persuade. We adopt the means of nonviolence because our end is a community at peace with itself" (Cohen, 1971:40). The idea is that violence breeds violence. You don't fight fire with fire, rather you put out fire with water. You don't end violence by violently resisting it. Perhaps that is what Jesus meant by "resist not evil" (Matthew 5:39). You don't end violence by creating more of it. If we must inhabit the world we create and we want to live in a world that is just and peaceful, we ought to act in just and peaceful ways. Richard Quinney (1993) writes, "Instead of a war on crime ("on criminals") we need to be waging peace on the economy, in the society, and within ourselves." In other words, we need to wage peace, not war.

An example of the relevance of this to criminal justice can be found in our contemporary prisons. Contemporary prisons are typically violent institutions that tend to perpetuate rather than diminish violence. According to the theories presented in this section, we must begin to treat criminals in less violent and more compassionate ways. We must stop thinking in terms of revenge, retribution, and recrimination, and begin to think in terms of reconciliation, compassion, and forgiveness. In recent years, there have been innovations and increasing numbers of alternative programs on mediation, conflict resolution, restitution, and community action. They are a part of an emerging criminology of peacemaking, a criminology that seeks to end suffering and reduce crime (Quinney, 1993). This approach to corrections is not a weak, "bleeding heart" approach. Sometimes love may have to be firm love. Still, if we choose to acknowledge our connectedness and desire to be peacemakers, we will insist on treating persons as a part of our humanity, whether they deserve such treatment or not.

The following Zen story presents this philosophy in its most radical form:

> One evening as Shichiri Kojun was reciting sutras a thief with a sharp sword entered, demanding either his money or his life. Shichiri told him: "Do not disturb me. You can find the money in that drawer." Then he resumed his recitation. A little while afterwards he stopped and called: "Don't take it all. I need some to pay taxes with tomorrow." The intruder gathered up most of the money and started to leave. "Thank a person when you receive a gift," Shichiri added. The man thanked him and made off. A few days afterwards the fellow was caught and confessed, among others, the offence against Shichiri. When Shichiri was called as a witness he said: "This man is no thief, at least as far as I am concerned. I gave him the money and he thanked me for it." After he had finished his prison term, the man went to Shichiri and became his disciple (Reps, 1919:41).

Along the same lines, Jesus teaches that if anyone sues you for your coat, let him also have your cloak (Matthew 5:40). He goes on to say: "Love your enemies, bless them that curse you, do good to them that hate you, and pray for them who despitefully use you, and persecute you" (Matthew 5:44). The radical message of these philosophies is that we should cease to repay violence with violence, whether that repayment be called "retribution" or "just deserts." Instead, we must learn to, as Paul puts it, "overcome evil with good" (Romans 12:21). Jesus also reminds us that whatever we do to the "least of those" in our society, we do to him. In terms of criminal justice, that would involve a complete reform of what we now call "corrections."

Figure 3.1
Peacemaking Practice

Life is short
Make a difference
Perseverance more than ability is key
Keep trying

Even when you are the victim of injustice
Even when you yourself are unjust
Keep trying

Be kind to those around you
Be kind to yourself as well
And when you are not
Keep trying

And be encouraging
Especially when there is no reason to be

Seek completion not perfection
Seek truth not power
Sooner or later the truth will set you free
But not before it beats the hell out of you
Keep trying

Answers long forgotten, the question remains:
when will the peace that passes understanding come?
Not at the end of conflict but in its midst

Peace is a longshot
Justice even more so
Sometimes longshots come in
Believe that they will

From peace within to peace without
From being just to justice for all

Source: Braswell, 2004:6.

CARING

In the previous chapter, we presented reasons in support of the utilitarian version of the fundamental rule of morality, namely, that we ought to produce the greatest good for the greatest number. We advanced Kant's arguments for what he considers to be the basic moral principle, that we ought to treat others as ends in themselves and not as mere means. We have just explored how theories of connectedness defend the moral absolute of nonviolence. Though each of the three theories differ from one another, all share a similarity of approach. All attempt to prove, by means of argument, justification, and reason, a specific moral rule or principle. According to Nel Noddings (1986), proving, justifying, and arguing for rules and principles is a masculine approach to ethics. In *Caring: A Feminine Approach to Ethics and Moral Education,* she outlines an alternative. Noddings claims:

> Ethics, the philosophical study of morality, has concentrated for the most part on moral reasoning . . . Even though careful philosophers have recognized the difference between "pure" or logical reason and "practical" or moral reason, ethical argumentation has frequently proceeded as if it were governed by the logical necessity characteristic of geometry. It has concentrated on the establishment of principles and that which can be logically derived from them. One might say that ethics has been discussed largely in the language of the father: in principles and propositions, in terms such as justification, fairness, justice. The mother's voice has been silent. Human caring and the memory of caring and being cared for, which I shall argue form the foundation of ethical response, have not received attention except as outcomes of ethical behavior. One is tempted to say that ethics has so far been guided by Logos, the masculine spirit, whereas the more natural and perhaps stronger approach would be through Eros, the feminine spirit (p. 1).

According to Noddings (1986:2), the masculine approach (the approach of the father) is a detached perspective that focuses on law and principle, whereas the feminine approach (the approach of the mother) is rooted in receptivity, relatedness, and responsiveness. Noddings advocates the feminine perspective. She goes on to point out that "this does not imply that all women will accept it [the feminine perspective] or that men will reject it; indeed, there is no reason why men should not embrace it" (Noddings, 1986:2).

The masculine perspective is an approach to ethics, an approach through justification and argument. The feminine perspective, on the other hand, "shall locate the very wellspring of ethical behavior in human affective response" (Noddings, 1986:3). Noddings's point is that ethical caring is ultimately grounded in natural caring—for example, the natural caring a mother has for her child. Noddings's emphasis on natural caring leads her to the conclusion "that in truth, the moral viewpoint is prior to any notion of justification" (Noddings, 1986:95). In other words, rather than viewing reason and justification as the process by which one comes to the moral perspective, Noddings indicates that the moral perspective is a natural perspective, as natural as a mother caring for her infant.

An ancient Chinese philosophy, Taoism, advocates a position that is similar to the one we find in Noddings. The two major Taoist philosophers, Lao-tzu and Chuang-tzu, suggest that not only is natural caring prior to reason, justification, and principle, it is superior to those activities. In fact, the Taoists claim that principles of ethics actually interfere with caring. Just as Nel Noddings is responding to a particular masculine tradition in Western ethics, the Taoists are responding to a particular tradition in Chinese ethics, namely, Confucianism. The Confucianists were very rule- and principle-oriented—rules for filial piety, rules for those who govern, rules for those who are governed. The Taoists responded by claiming that those rules, because of their artificiality, destroyed true, natural caring and replaced it with forced or legislated "caring."

From the Taoist perspective, the danger of advocating ethical rules and principles is that they will replace something far superior to those principles, namely, natural caring. Chuang-tzu (1964) says: "Because [the doctrine of] right and wrong appeared, the Way was injured" (p. 37).

Lao-tzu (1963) makes a similar claim. Lao-tzu doesn't make the strong claim that the doctrine of right and wrong destroyed the Way (the Tao). However, he does claim that only in unnatural states does the doctrine of right and wrong arise. In the *Tao Te Ching*, Lao-tzu says:

> Therefore, when Tao [the natural Way] is lost, only then does the doctrine of virtue arise.
>
> When virtue is lost, only then does the doctrine of humanity arise.
>
> When humanity is lost, only then does the doctrine of righteousness arise.
>
> When righteousness is lost, only then does the doctrine of propriety arise.
>
> Now, propriety is a superficial expression of loyalty and faithfulness, and the beginning of disorder (p. 167).

Notice how Lao-tzu concludes by discussing the superficiality of notions of propriety and how such notions are the beginning of disorder. In another section of the *Tao Te Ching*, Lao-tzu summarizes the preceding by saying, "When the great Tao [Natural Way] declined, the doctrine of humanity and righteousness arose" (p. 131). Lao-tzu is saying that artificial doctrines of virtue, humanity, and righteousness, doctrines that tell us how we ought to behave, arise only in unhealthy situations. Something is already terribly wrong when we tell a mother she ought to feed her child or that she has a duty to feed her child. Feeding one's child is a natural, caring response. Lao-tzu says: "When the six family relationships are not in harmony, there will be the advocacy of filial piety and deep love to children" (p. 131).

Given that we live in and are inculcated into a patriarchal society, a society of rules, principles, and laws, do the Taoists have any suggestions as to how to break free from patriarchal modes of thought, how to return to a more natural and caring way of living in the world? As you might expect, the answer to this is yes. The Taoist position can be put in the following way: Moral reasoning is the product of a mind that discriminates and draws distinctions (between right and wrong, good and bad, just and unjust). According to Taoism, these categories and distinctions are artificial and conventional, not natural. To put oneself into a more natural state, which according to the Taoist view on human nature would be a more caring state, one must undo, erase, or transcend all the conventional, artificial dualisms that have been inculcated into us. We perceive the world the way we have been taught to perceive the world. So, we must begin to unlearn the categories that have been programmed into us.

In a more contemporary vein, Myers and Chiang (1993) also compared the prevailing legalistic, masculine approach to law enforcement—which focuses on analysis, rationalization, and punishment—with the feminine perspective of nurturing, care, and treatment.

Martin (1993) examined the usefulness of incorporating transpersonal psychology into the justice and corrections process. This discipline integrates Western scientific and Eastern and Western spiritual traditions, which could open a fresh way to develop policy and treatment strategies that are more positive and growth-oriented.

An ancient story involving the teacher, Ryokan, and his delinquent nephew offers another interesting, if unorthodox, approach in utilizing the ethic of care:

> Once his brother asked Ryokan to visit his house and speak to his delinquent son. Ryokan came but did not say a word of admonition to the boy. He stayed overnight and prepared to leave the next morning. As the wayward nephew was lacing up Ryokan's sandals, he felt a drop of warm water. Glancing up, he saw Ryokan looking down at him, his eyes full of tears. Ryokan then returned home, and the nephew changed for the better (in Safransky, 1990:115-116).

It goes without saying that caring is not the exclusive property of Taoism or Yoga. Mother Teresa, a recipient of the Nobel Peace Prize, encompasses this ethic of caring from a Christian perspective. She started her work as a one-woman mission in Calcutta, India, ministering to and caring for the dying. Generally speaking, in some ways we might consider the dying poor even more undesirable than incarcerated offenders. Yet Mother Teresa's Missionaries of Charity grew from a one-woman operation to a group of active missions found all over the world. When asked how she could emotionally handle constantly being around so many dying persons, she responded that when she looked into the eyes of the dying she saw "Christ in a distressing disguise."[3]

MINDFULNESS

Mother Teresa is perhaps the embodiment of the ethic of care. Internalizing such an approach requires that one develop a compassionate vision through mindfulness. The following example from one of her public addresses demonstrates such a vision in action:

> A gentleman came to our house and he told me, "There is a Hindu family with about eight children who have not eaten for a long time." So I took some rice quickly and went to their family and I could see real hunger on the small faces of these children and yet the mother had the courage to divide the rice into two and she went out. When she came back, I asked her, "Where did you go? What did you do?" And she said: "They are hungry also." "Who are they?" "The Muslim family next door with as many children." She knew that they were hungry. What struck me most was that she knew and because she knew she gave until it hurt. I did not bring more rice that night because I wanted them to enjoy the joy of giving, of sharing. You should have seen the faces of those little ones. They just understood what their mother did. Their faces were brightened with smiles. When I came in they looked hungry, they looked so miserable. But the act of their mother taught them what true love was (de Bertodano, 1993:53).

Mindfulness allows us to experience a more transcendent sense of awareness. It allows us to be fully present, aware of what is immediate, yet also at the same time to become more aware of the larger picture both in terms of needs and possibilities. Mindfulness allowed the Hindu mother not only to receive the rice from Mother Teresa with gratitude, but also allowed her to see how she was connected to the hungry Muslim family and how to have the courage to care enough to share her meager resources, thus teaching her own children one of life's greatest lessons.

Mindfulness can encourage us to move from the passion of single-minded self-interest to a growing sense of compassion that includes others and their needs. We often wring our hands about those who are victims of physical abuse and the homeless. Yet how often do we volunteer to help? (Braswell, 1990). Mindfulness can help us, like the Hindu mother, to act on our concerns. As Wang Yang Ming states, "To know and not to do is in fact, not to know" (Lozoff & Braswell, 1989:63). Developing wholesight can help us to become more mindful in turning our knowing into doing. As mentioned in Chapter 1, Parker Palmer (1983) suggests that wholesight includes both the heart and the head in one's decisionmaking.

A strategy or process that can help us become more mindful is meditation. Meditation is a practice through which the meditator quiets or stills the contents of the mind: the thoughts, the emotions, the desires, the inner chatter. Successful meditation culminates in the cessation of mental activity, a profound inner stillness. (See Figure 3.1.)

Recall that Taoism teaches us to return to a more natural state, a state in which we are not controlled by the artificial modes of thought that have been inculcated into us by our society. The practice of meditation can teach us to control and still those modes of thought. By freeing ourselves from conventional ways of thinking, we return to a more natural state, a more connected and caring state. Some persons are concerned that emptying the mind meditatively could lead to some form of mind control. The truth of the matter is that meditation is more likely to lead to a greater sense of self-control, because most of us stay preoccupied with thoughts of things to do or things left undone. Busy, noisy minds often result in confused and unclear thoughts. We are less likely to be misled or do something we regret if our minds are quiet, strong, and clear.

Figure 3.2
A Guide for a Simple Meditation

1. Find a quiet, special *place* in which to meditate.
2. Find a *time* to practice meditation when the area is quiet and there are no distractions, preferably twice daily. Many persons practice meditation at the beginning of the day and at the end of the day.
3. Try to meditate for a designated period of time during each meditation experience, usually at least 10 minutes, and preferably 20 minutes.
4. Sit in a straight-backed chair, keeping the spine as straight as possible.
5. For the designated period of time, practice the following sequence:
   A) Sit silently for a few moments and become *aware* of how you are breathing;
   B) Gently and gradually begin to breathe more *smoothly;*
   C) Now begin to breathe a little more *deeply,* gradually increasing the depth of your breathing;
   D) Finally, begin to *slow* down the rate of your breathing;
   E) No matter what distractions or thoughts may occur, simply acknowledge them and let them pass, then return to breathing *smoothly, deeply,* and *slowly* for the designated period of time.

The relevance of this approach in ethics to criminal justice can be seen in the work of Bo Lozoff, director of the Prison Ashram Project. Lozoff works with prisoners, teaching them techniques of meditation. Lozoff (1987:xvii) is "helping prisoners to use their cells as ashrams [places of spiritual growth], and do their time as 'prison monks' rather than convicts." In his book *We're All Doing Time,* Lozoff has a chapter on meditation in which he describes and teaches a number of meditation techniques. Much of his work in prisons involves teaching these techniques to convicts.

Lozoff (1987:29) describes meditation as "sitting perfectly still—silence of body, silence of speech and silence of mind. The Buddha called this 'The Noble Silence.' It's just a matter of STOPPING." To connect this with Taoism, we might say that by achieving a state of inner silence in which we stop all the conventional modes of thinking and reasoning that have been inculcated into us, we return to a more natural state, a more caring state. And from this caring and compassionate state, we can become more mindful of how our inner and outer experiences are connected to those around us, even to our physical environment. This awareness can become a kind of awakening, encouraging us to make more informed and ethical decisions about the way we live our lives.

CONCLUSION

If we choose to develop a greater capacity for peacemaking through connectedness, care, and mindfulness, it should follow that as persons and criminal justice professionals we will act more morally and ethically. In addition, we are more likely to teach offenders such values from the inside out, because we will be living that way ourselves. For peacemaking to work, we have to take it personally first. We have to be grounded in the reality of where we are in terms of criminal justice problems, but at the same time peacemaking encourages us to have a vision of what we can become. Peacemaking offers us a vision of hope grounded in the reality of which we are a part. John Gibbs (1993:2) suggests that "the best strategy for individual peacemakers is to adopt one which emphasizes personal transformation, has a spiritual base, and avoids ideology." Mother Teresa writes, "There can be no peace in the world, including peace in the streets and peace in the home, without peace in our mind. What happens within us, happens outside us. The inner and outer are one" (de Bertodano, 1993:7).

If we choose to try to become peacemakers, it does not necessarily follow that our lives will be less difficult. As Frederick Buechner (1973:39) suggests in discussing the teachings of Jesus, "peace seems to have meant not the absence of struggle but the presence of love." Bo Lozoff (1994), who along with his wife, Sita, have dedicated their lives to teaching offenders peacemaking, writes in response to an inmate's letter:

> Life is funny that way. We tend to expect a nice, easy, smooth life as a result of prayer and meditation. But more often than not, our spiritual practice seems to create *more* problems instead of fewer. And then we often freak out and miss the point entirely.
>
> Pain, separation, misfortune are a part of human life . . . . Did the martyrs of every religion avoid being tortured for their beliefs? Divine beings, saints and sages have come into this world to show us how to *respond* to pain, separation, misfortune, and death—not how to escape them. By their example, they have shown us the humility, patience, forgiveness, courage, compassion, and ultimate freedom which are our own divine nature (p. 5).

Peacemaking acknowledges that while we do not control what life brings us, we do have a choice in how to respond to whatever life brings us. Through connectedness, care, and mindfulness, we can begin to change ourselves first, then others by our example, and finally our system of justice—from the inside out.

Figure 3.3
Thoughts on Peacemaking

I have decided to stick with love. Hate is too great a burden to bear.

—Martin Luther King Jr.

Love cures people—both the ones who give it and the ones who receive it.

—Karl Menninger

The love we give away is the only love we keep.

—Elbert Hubbard

In all conflict with evil, the method to be used is love and not force. When we use evil methods to defeat evil, it is evil that wins.

—Sri Rodhakrishnan

The inner ear of each man's soul hears the voice of life, (find your work, and do it!). Only by obedience to this command can he find peace.

—Frank Crane

If you do your work with complete faithfulness . . . you are making as genuine a contribution to the substance of the universal good as is the most brilliant worker whom the world contains.

—Phillips Brooks

The vocation of every man and woman is to serve other people.

—Leo Tolstoy

In real love you want the other person's good. In romantic love you want the other person.

—Margaret Anderson

Once we learn to touch this peace, we will be healed and transformed. It is not a matter of fact; it is a matter of practice.

—Thich Nhat Hanh

He who knows when enough is enough will always have enough.

—Lao-tzu

We must be the change we wish to see in the world.

—Mahatma Gandhi

NOTES

1. The entire letter can be found in Joseph Campbell, *The Power of Myth* (New York: Doubleday, 1988), pp. 32-35.

2. Plato, *Republic*, 351d-352a.

3. This quotation is from the documentary film, *Mother Teresa*, directed by Richard Attenborough.

REFERENCES

Bartollas, C. & M. Braswell (1993). "Correctional Treatment, Peacemaking, and the New Age Movement." *Journal of Crime & Justice*, 16:43-59.

Braswell, M. (1990a). "Peacemaking: A Missing Link in Criminology." *The Criminologist*, 15:1, 3-5.

Braswell, M. (1990b). *Journey Homeward.* Chicago: Franciscan Herald Press.

Braswell, M. (2004). "Peacemaking Boogie." *Justitia*, 3(1):6.

Buechner, F. (1973). *Wishful Thinking.* New York: Harper & Row.

Chuang-tzu (1964). *Basic Writings.* New York: Columbia University Press.

Cohen, C. (1971). *Civil Disobedience.* New York: Columbia University Press.

de Bertodano, T. (ed.) (1993). *Daily Readings with Mother Teresa.* London: Fount.

Gibbs, J. (1993). "Spirituality, Ideology, and Personal Transformation: Some Considerations for Peacemaking." Unpublished paper.

Lao-tzu (1963). *The Way of Lao-tzu (Tao Te Ching).* Indianapolis: Bobbs-Merrill.

Lozoff, B. (1987). *We're All Doing Time.* Durham, NC: Human Kindness Foundation.

Lozoff, B. (1994). "Letters." *Human Kindness Foundation Newsletter*, 5.

Lozoff, B. & M. Braswell (1989). *Inner Corrections: Finding Peace and Peace Making.* Cincinnati: Anderson.

Martin, R. (1993). "Transpersonal Psychology and Criminological Theory: Rethinking the Paradigm." *Journal of Crime & Justice*, 16:43-59.

Myers, L. & C. Chiang (1993). "Law Enforcement Officer and Peace Officer: Reconciliation Using the Feminine Approach." *Journal of Crime & Justice*, 16:31-43.

Noddings, N. (1986). *Caring: A Feminine Approach to Ethics and Moral Education.* Berkeley, CA: University of California Press.

Palmer, P. (1983). *To Know As We Are Known.* San Francisco: Harper & Row.

Quinney, R. (1993). "A Life of Crime: Criminology and Public Policy and Peacemaking." *Journal of Crime and Justice*, 16:3-11.

Reps, P. (ed.) (1919). *Zen Flesh, Zen Bones: A Collection of Zen and Pre-Zen Writings*. Garden City, NY: Doubleday.

Safransky, S. (ed.) (1990). *Sunbeams: A Book of Quotations*. Berkeley, CA: North Atlantic Books.

DISCUSSION QUESTIONS

1. List and discuss the three themes of peacemaking, and explain the impact they have on traditional police or corrections values.

2. In your opinion, can peacemaking, justice, and ethics ever become fully realized? Why or why not?

3. Choose one theme of peacemaking and explain why you think it would have the greater impact on justice and ethics.

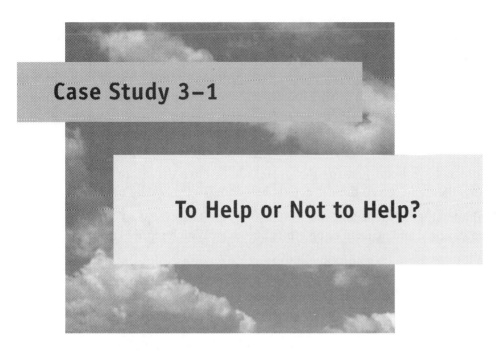

Case Study 3–1

To Help or Not to Help?

To help or not to help? At 8:15 P.M., a criminal justice professor had just arrived on a flight from Albuquerque, where he had lectured the previous day at the International Academy in Roswell.

After picking up his luggage, the professor exited the airport gate and stood in line with the other passengers who were waiting for the next shuttle bus. A few minutes later, a young couple who appeared to be married arrived and elbowed their way in line, ahead of the professor and others. The professor politely called the matter to their attention, asking them to observe the social principle of "first come, first served." The couple ignored the professor's remark. When the professor repeated his request that they move to the end of the line, the husband became hostile, accusing the professor of being rude. Rather than escalate the conflict, the professor said nothing more. He and the other passengers were tired and the hour was late. When the shuttle finally arrived, everyone got on board and remained silent.

Upon reaching his car, the professor packed his luggage in the trunk and drove toward the parking lot exit. As he approached the exit, he noticed two persons flagging the passing cars for assistance to no avail. Taking a closer look at the two stranded individuals, the professor was surprised to find that they were the same two persons who had broken into line and the man was the one who had insulted the professor 25 minutes earlier. Although he was tempted to continue driving, he stopped and after rolling down his window asked the couple what kind of assistance they needed. When they realized who he was, the man and woman were clearly both surprised and

From a conversation with Professor Sam Souryal, Sam Houston State University

41

embarrassed. They were unable to look the professor in the eye as they explained their predicament. In response, the professor procured a jumper cable from the trunk of his car. Within five minutes he had brought their dead battery back to life. During that time, not a word was spoken. As the couple prepared to drive off, they finally looked at the professor and thanked him. The wife added, "We are sorry."

Questions

1. Would it have been just for the professor to have driven on by the stranded couple, given their previous behavior? Why or why not?

2. Evaluate this incident and the professor's response from utilitarian, deontological and peacemaking ethical models. Which model fits best?

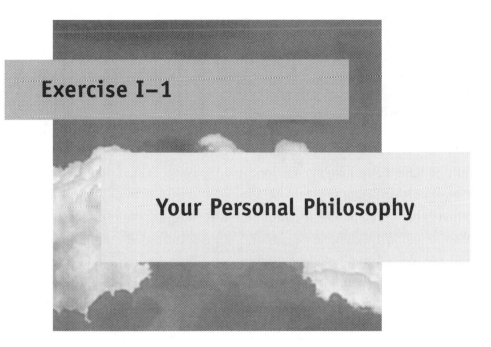

Exercise I–1

Your Personal Philosophy

What is your personal/professional philosophy? The most important aspect of our personal and professional growth involves the values and beliefs that we hold dear. Now that you have covered the first three chapters, with which theories and ideas do you agree or disagree? What are your personal values and what beliefs are they based upon? How do you plan to put these values and beliefs into practice in the work environment of your chosen profession?

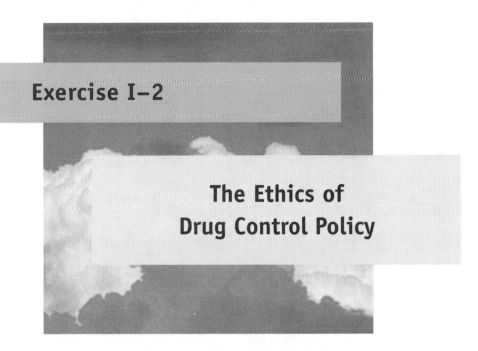

Exercise I-2

The Ethics of
Drug Control Policy

The United States is currently confronting a drug crisis. While drug use in the general population seems to be declining, drug use and sales among criminals is continuing to increase. Some citizens are calling for stiffer penalties for illegal drug use, while others are calling for decriminalization, a greater emphasis on treatment, and even legalization of certain drugs. Suppose you were a staff assistant to a congressperson whose committee was investigating the ethics of drug control policy.

What issues would be relevant to this assessment?

How could a morally correct approach to drug/crime policy be developed?

Whose rights would have to be protected?

What societal benefits and deficits would you consider?

How could this policy be developed in a way that promoted caring and concern for all in society?

Section II: Ethical Issues in Policing

> **Man becomes great exactly in the degree in which he works for the welfare of his fellow man.**
>
> —Mahatma Gandhi

Police work has been called a "morally dangerous" endeavor, and with good reason. Not only are the temptations faced by the average patrol officer much greater than those confronted in other occupations, but the nature of the work itself requires activities that can easily cross over the line from acceptable to unethical conduct.

Police corruption is a broad area of concern. For some observers, it includes everything from the simple acceptance of a free meal from a small business owner, to the receipt of kickbacks from attorneys and tow truck drivers, to police-organized theft.

Many of the problems of police corruption are linked to the tremendous amount of discretion possessed by the patrol officer. Most of us would agree that it is sometimes acceptable to use this discretion to avoid giving a ticket or making an arrest. When good judgment determines that no action is necessary or there are other means of addressing the problem, discretion is clearly being put to good use. But, when these discretions are influenced by offers of money, drugs, or sexual favors, the use of discretion becomes tainted and the actions corrupt.

Situations confronting police officers offer temptations of their own. The money found on a drunk, the cash and drugs found at the scene of a crime—these can tempt officers who are on their honor to report what they find. In the area of narcotics control, such temptations are always present.

There are still other dilemmas confronting the police officer who does not give in to the temptations of corruption. In many ways, crime control efforts foster an "ends justifies the means" mentality. To the extent that due process guarantees are seen as somehow interfering with crime control efforts, attempts to work around these "technicalities" come to be viewed as justified. This is especially true in regard to the control of vice and narcotics activities, where proactive and deceptive methods, such as "sting" operations and undercover work, are routine.

In many ways, police officers must walk a fine line. Overzealousness and the use of unnecessary force is undesirable, but so is a reluctance to intervene or back up another officer when the situation requires it. When officers use patrol time to avoid their responsibilities rather than to execute them, the professional image of the entire department suffers.

To avoid corruption, police departments must attempt to recruit and hire honorable men and women. These persons must be educated and trained to deal with whatever problems they confront. There is also a need for the police organization to take steps to keep standards high. These efforts include the development of explicit policy covering the variety of potentially corrupting situations and the implementation of active internal affairs units. Perhaps more important, however, is the creation of an organizational climate that fosters candid and open public examination of police practices, and a responsiveness to line officers and the dilemmas they confront.

CHAPTER 4

Learning Police Ethics

Lawrence Sherman

There are two ways to learn police ethics. One way is to learn on the job, to make your moral decisions in haste under the time pressures of police work. This is by far the most common method of learning police ethics, the way virtually all of the half million police officers in the United States decide what ethical principles they will follow in their work. These decisions are strongly influenced by peer group pressures, by personal self-interest, by passions and emotions in the heat of difficult situations.

There is another way. It may even be a better way. You can learn police ethics in a setting removed from the heat of battle, from the opinions of co-workers, and from the pressures of supervisors. You can think things through with a more objective perspective on the issues. You should be able to make up your mind about many difficult choices before you actually have to make them. And you can take the time to weigh all sides of an issue carefully, rather than making a snap judgment.

KEY CONCEPTS:
apologia
contingencies
ethics
metamorphosis
moral career
moral experience
morals
occupational career

The purpose of this article is to provide a basis for this other, less common way of learning police ethics, by making the alternative—the usual way of learning police ethics—as clear as possible. This portrait of the on-the-job method is not attractive, but it would be no more attractive if we were to paint the same picture for doctors, lawyers, judges, or college professors. The generalizations we make are not true of all police officers, but they do reflect a common pattern, just as similar patterns are found in all occupations.

Lawrence Sherman, "Learning Police Ethics," (as appeared in *Criminal Justice Ethics*, Volume 1, Number 1 [Winter/Spring 1982] pp. 10-19). Reprinted by permission of the Institute for Criminal Justice Ethics, 899 Tenth Avenue, New York, NY 10019-1029.

LEARNING NEW JOBS

Every occupation has a learning process (usually called "socialization") to which its new members are subjected. The socialization process functions to make most "rookies" in the occupation adopt the prevailing rules, values, and attitudes of their senior colleagues in the occupation. Very often, some of the existing informal rules and attitudes are at odds with the formal rules and attitudes society as a whole expects members of the occupation to follow. This puts rookies in a moral dilemma: Should the rookies follow the formal rules of society or the informal rules of their senior colleagues?

These dilemmas vary in their seriousness from one occupation and one organization to the next. Young college professors may find that older professors expect them to devote most of their time to research and writing, while the general public (and their students) expects them to devote most of their time to teaching. With some luck, and a lot of work, they can do both.

Police officers usually face much tougher dilemmas. Like waiters, longshoremen, and retail clerks, they may be taught very early how to steal—at the scene of a burglary, from the body of a dead person, or in other opportunities police confront. They may be taught how to commit perjury in court to insure that their arrests lead to conviction, or how to lie in disciplinary investigations to protect their colleagues. They may be taught how to shake people down, or how to beat people up. Or they may be fortunate enough to go to work in an agency, or with a group of older officers, in which none of these violations of official rules is ever suggested to them.

Whether or not rookie police officers decide to act in ways the wider society might view as unethical, they are all subjected to a similar process of being taught certain standards of behavior. Their reactions to that learning as the years pass by can be described as their *moral careers:* the changes in the morality and ethics of their behavior. But the moral career is closely connected to the *occupational career:* the stages of growth and development in becoming a police officer.

This article examines the process of learning a new job as the context for learning police ethics. It then describes the content of the ethical and moral values in many police department "cultures" that are conveyed to new police officers, as well as the rising conflict within police agencies over what those values should be. Finally, it describes the moral career of police officers, including many of the major ethical choices officers make.

BECOMING A POLICE OFFICER

There are four major stages in the career of anyone joining a new occupation:[1]

- the *choice* of occupation
- the *introduction* to the occupation

- the first *encounter* with doing the occupation's work

- the *metamorphosis* into a full-fledged member of the occupation

Police officers go through these stages, just as doctors and bankers do. But the transformation of the police officer's identity and self-image may be more radical than in many other fields. The process can be overwhelming, changing even the strongest of personalities.

Choice

There are three aspects of the choice to become a police officer. One is the *kind of person* who makes that choice. Another is the *reason* the choice is made, the motivations for doing police work. The third is the *methods* people must use as police officers. None of these aspects of choice appears to predispose police officers to be more or less likely to perform their work ethically.

Many people toy with the ideal of doing police work, and in the past decade the applicants for policing have become increasingly diverse. Once a predominately white male occupation, policing has accepted many more minority group members and attracted many more women. More college-educated people have sought out police work, but this may just reflect the higher rate of college graduates in the total population.

What has not changed, apparently, is the socioeconomic background of people who become police. The limited evidence suggests police work attracts the sons and daughters of successful tradespeople, foremen, and civil servants—especially police. For many of them, the good salary (relative to the educational requirements), job security, and prestige of police work represent a good step up in the world, an improvement on their parents' position in life.

The motivation to become a police officer flows naturally from the social position of the people who choose policing. People do not seem to choose policing out of an irrational lust for power or because they have an "authoritarian personality"; The best study on this question showed that New York City police recruits even had a *lower* level of authoritarian attitudes than the general public (although their attitudes become more authoritarian as they become adapted to police work, rising to the general public's level of authoritarian attitudes).[3] Police applicants tend to see police work as an adventure, as a chance to do work out of doors without being cooped up in an office, as a chance to do work that is important for the good of society, and not as a chance to be the "toughest guy on the block." Nothing in the motivation to apply for a police position seems to predispose police officers towards unethical behavior.

Nor do the methods of selecting police officers seem to affect their long-term moral careers. There was a time when getting on the force was a matter of bribery or political favors for local politicians, or at least a matter of knowing the right people involved in grading the entrance examinations and sitting on the selection committees. But in the 1980s the selection process appears to be highly bureaucratic, wherein impersonal multiple-choice tests scored by computers play the most important role in the process.

To be sure, there are still subjective background investigations, personal interviews, and other methods that allow biases to intrude upon the selection process. But these biases, if anything, work in the direction of selecting people who have backgrounds of unquestioned integrity. Combined with the high failure rate among all applicants—sometimes less than one in twenty is hired, which makes some police departments more selective in quantitative terms than the Harvard Law School—the selection process probably makes successful applicants feel that they have been welcomed into an elite group of highly qualified people of very high integrity.

Introduction

But this sense of high ideals about police work may not last for long. The introduction to policing provided by most police academies begins to convey folklore that shows the impossibility of doing things "by the book" and the frequent necessity of "bending the rules."

Police recruit training has changed substantially over the past thirty years. Once highly militaristic, it has recently taken on more the atmosphere of the college classroom. The endurance test-stress environment approach, in which trainees may be punished for yawning or looking out the window, may still be found in some cities, but it seems to be dying out. Dull lectures on the technical aspects of police work (such as how to fill out arrest reports) and the rules and regulations of the department are now often supplemented by guest lectures on theories of crime and the cultures of various ethnic groups.

But the central method of *moral* instruction does not appear to have changed. The "war story" still remains the most effective device for communicating the history and values of the department. When the instructor tells a "war story," or an anecdote about police work, the class discipline is relaxed somewhat, the interest and attention of the class increase, and an atmosphere of camaraderie between the class and the instructor is established. The content of the war story makes a deep impression on the trainees.

The war stories not only introduce police work as it is experienced by police officers—rather than as an abstract ideal—they also introduce the ethics of police work as something different from what the public, or at least the law and the press, might expect. Van Maanen recounts one excerpt from a police academy criminal law lecture that, while not a "story," indicates the way in which the hidden values of police work are conveyed:

> I suppose you guys have heard of Lucky Baldwin? If not, you sure will when you hit the street. Baldwin happens to be the biggest burglar still operating in this town. Every guy in this department from patrolman to chief would love to get him and make it stick.

> We've busted him about ten times so far, but he's got an asshole
> lawyer and money so he always beats the rap. . . . If I ever get a
> chance to pinch the SOB, I'll do it my way with my thirty-eight
> and spare the city the cost of a trial.[3]

Whether the instructor would actually shoot the burglary suspect is open to
question, although he could do so legally in most states if the suspect attempted
to flee from being arrested. More important is the fact that the rookies spend
many hours outside the classroom debating and analyzing the implications of
the war stories. These discussions do help them decide how they would act in
similar circumstances. But the decisions they reach in these informal bull sessions are probably more attributable to peer pressure and the desire to "fit in"
to the culture of the department than to careful reflection on moral principle.

Encounter

After they leave the academy, the rookies are usually handed over to Field
Training Officers (FTOs). In the classic version of the first day on patrol with
the rookie, the FTO says, "Forget everything they taught you in the academy,
kid; I'll show you how police work is really done." And show they do. The rookie
becomes an observer of the FTO as he or she actually does police work. Suddenly the war stories come alive, and all the questions about how to handle tough
situations get answered very quickly and clearly, as one police veteran recalls:

> On this job, your first partner is everything. He tells you how to
> survive on the job . . . how to walk, how to stand, and how to speak
> and how to think and what to say and see.[4]

The encounter with the FTO is only part of the rookie's "reality shock" about
police work. Perhaps even more important are the rookie's encounters with the
public. By putting on the uniform, the rookie becomes part of a visible minority group. The self-consciousness about the new appearance is heightened by
the nasty taunts and comments the uniform attracts from teenagers and others.[5]
The uniform and gun, as symbols of power, attract challenges to that power simply because they are there.[6] Other people seek out the uniform to manipulate
the rookie to use the power on behalf of their personal interests. Caught frequently in the cross fire of equally unreasonable citizen demands, the rookie
naturally reacts by blaming the public. The spontaneous reaction is reinforced
by one of the central values of the police culture: the public as enemy.[7]
This is not different from the way many doctors view their patients, particularly patients with a penchant for malpractice suits. Nor is it different from
the view many professors have of their students as unreasonable and thick-
headed, particularly those who argue about grades. Like police officers, doctors and professors wield power that affects other people's lives, and that
power is always subject to counterattack. Once again, Van Maanen captures
the experience of the rookie:

> [My FTO] was always telling me to be forceful, to not back down and to never try to explain the law or what we are doing to a civilian. I really didn't know what he was talking about until I tried to tell some kid why we have laws about speeding. Well, the more I tried to tell him about traffic safety, the angrier he got. I was lucky just to get his John Hancock on the citation. When I came back to the patrol car, [the FTO] explains to me just where I'd gone wrong. You really can't talk to those people out there; they just won't listen to reason.[8]

It is the public that transforms the rookie's self-conception, teaching him or her the pains of exercising power. The FTO then helps to interpret the encounters with the public in the light of the values of the police culture, perhaps leading the rookie even further away from the values of family or friends about how police should act.

The FTO often gives "tests" as he or she teaches. In many departments, the tests are as minor as seeing if the rookie will wait patiently outside while the FTO visits a friend. In other departments, the test may include getting the rookie involved in drinking or having sex on duty, a seriously brutal slugfest against an arrestee, or taking bribes for nonenforcement. The seriousness of the violations may vary, but the central purpose of the test does not: seeing if the rookie can keep his or her mouth shut and not report the violations to the supervisors. A rookie who is found to be untrustworthy can be, literally, hounded and harassed from the department.

Finally, in the encounter stage, the rookie gets the major reality shock in the entire process of becoming a police officer. The rookie discovers that police work is more social work than crime fighting, more arbitration of minor disputes than investigations of major crimes, more patching of holes in the social fabric than weaving of webs to catch the big-time crooks. The rookie's usual response is to define most of the assignments received as "garbage calls," not *real* police work. Not quite sure whom to blame for the fact that he or she was hired to do police work but was assigned everything else, the rookie blames the police executive, the mayor and city council, and even previous U.S. presidents (for raising public expectations). But most of all the rookie blames the public, especially the poor, for being so stupid as to have all these problems, or so smart as to take advantage of welfare and other social programs.

Metamorphosis

The result of those encounters is usually a complete change, a total adaptation of the new role and self-conception as a "cop." And with that transformation comes a stark awareness of the interdependence cops share with all other cops. For all the independence police have in making decisions about how to deal with citizens, they are totally and utterly dependent on other police to save their lives, to respond to a call of an officer in trouble or in need of assistance, and to lie on their behalf to supervisors to cover up minor infractions of the many rules the department has. This total change in perspective usually means that police accept several new assumptions about the nature of the world:

- loyalty to colleagues is essential for survival

- the public, or most of it, is the enemy

- police administrators are also the enemy.

- any discrepancy between these views and the views of family and friends is due simply to the ignorance of those who have not actually done police work themselves.

These are their new assumptions about the *facts* of life in police work, the realities which limit their options for many things, including the kinds of moral principles they can afford to have and still "survive," to keep the job, pay the mortgage, raise the kids, and vest the pension. This conception of the facts opens new police officers to learning and accepting what may be a new set of values and ethical principles. By the time the metamorphosis has been accomplished, in fact, most of these new values have been learned.

CONTENT OF POLICE VALUES TEACHING

Through the war stories of the academy instructor, the actions and stories of the FTO, the bull sessions with other rookies and veterans, and the new officer's encounters with the public, a fairly consistent set of values emerges. Whether the officer accepts these values is another question. Most students of police work seem to agree that these are the values (or some of them) that are taught:

1. Discretion A: *Decisions about whether to enforce the law, in any but the most serious cases, should be guided by both what the law says and who the suspect is.* Attitude, demeanor, cooperativeness, and even race, age, and social class are all important considerations in deciding how to treat people generally, and whether or not to arrest suspects in particular.

2. Discretion B: *Disrespect for police authority is a serious offense that should always be punished with an arrest or the use of force.* The "offense" known as "contempt of cop" or P.O.P.O. (pissing off a police officer) cannot be ignored. Even when the party has committed no violation of the law, a police officer should find a safe way to impose punishment, including an arrest on fake charges.

3. Force: *Police officers should never hesitate to use physical or deadly force against people who "deserve it," or where it can be an effective way of solving a crime.* Only the potential punishments by superior officers, civil litigation, citizen complaints, and so forth should limit the use of force when the situation calls for it. When you can get away with it, use all the force that society should use on people like that—force and punishment which bleeding-heart judges are too soft to impose.

4. Due Process: *Due process is only a means of protecting criminals at the expense of the law-abiding and should be ignored whenever it is safe to do so.* Illegal searches and wiretaps, interrogation without advising suspects of their Miranda rights, and if need be (as in the much-admired movie, *Dirty Harry*), even physical pain to coerce a confession are all acceptable methods for accomplishing the goal the public wants the police to accomplish: fighting crime. The rules against doing those things merely handcuff the police, making it more difficult for them to do their job.

5. Truth: *Lying and deception are an essential part of the police job, and even perjury should be used if it is necessary to protect yourself or get a conviction on a "bad guy."* Violations of due process cannot be admitted to prosecutors or in court, so perjury (in the serious five percent of cases that ever go to trial) is necessary and therefore proper. Lying to drug pushers about wanting to buy drugs, to prostitutes about wanting to buy sex, or to congressmen about wanting to buy influence is the only way, and therefore a proper way, to investigate these crimes without victims. Deceiving muggers into thinking you are an easy mark and deceiving burglars into thinking you are a fence are proper because there are not many other ways of catching predatory criminals in the act.

6. Time: *You cannot go fast enough to chase a car thief or traffic violator nor slow enough to get to a "garbage" call; and when there are no calls for service, your time is your own.* Hot pursuits are necessary because anyone who tries to escape from the police is challenging police authority, no matter how trivial the initial offense. But calls to nonserious or social-work problems, like domestic disputes or kids making noise, are unimportant, so you can stop to get coffee on the way or even stop at the cleaner's if you like. And when there are no calls, you can sleep, visit friends, study, or do anything else you can get away with, especially on the midnight shift, when you can get away with a lot.

7. Rewards: *Police do very dangerous work for low wages, so it is proper to take any extra rewards the public wants to give them, like*

free meals, Christmas gifts, or even regular monthly payments (in some cities) for special treatment. The general rule is: take any reward that doesn't change what you would do anyway, such as eating a meal, but don't take money that would affect your job, like not giving traffic tickets. In many cities, however, especially in the recent past, the rule has been to take even those awards that do affect your decisions, as long as they are related only to minor offenses—traffic, gambling, prostitution, but not murder.

8. Loyalty: *The paramount duty is to protect your fellow officers at all costs, as they would protect you, even though you may have to risk your own career or your own life to do it.* If your colleagues make a mistake, take a bribe, seriously hurt somebody illegally, or get into other kinds of trouble, you should do everything you can to protect them in the ensuing investigation. If your colleagues are routinely breaking the rules, you should never tell supervisors, reporters, or outside investigators about it. If you don't like it, quit—or get transferred to the police academy. But never, ever, blow the whistle.

THE RISING VALUE CONFLICTS

None of these values is as strongly or widely held as in the past. Several factors may account for the breakdown in traditional police values that has paralleled the breakdown of traditional values in the wider society. One is the increasing diversity of the kinds of people who join police departments: more women, minorities, and college graduates. Another is the rising power of the police unions which defend individual officers who get into trouble— sometimes even those who challenge the traditional values. A third factor is the rise of investigative journalism and the romantic aura given to "bucking the system" by such movies as *Serpico.* Watergate and other recent exposés of corruption in high places—especially the attitude of being "above the law"—have probably made all public officials more conscious of the ethics of their behavior. Last but not least, police administrators have increasingly taken a very stern disciplinary posture towards some of these traditional police values and gone to extraordinary lengths to counteract them.

Consider the paramount value of loyalty. Police reformer August Vollmer described it in 1931 as the "blue curtain of secrecy" that descends whenever a police officer does something wrong, making it impossible to investigate misconduct. Yet in the past decade, police officers in Cincinnati, Indianapolis, New York, and elsewhere have given reporters and grand juries evidence about widespread police misconduct. In New York, police officers have even given evidence against their colleagues for homicide, leading to the first conviction there (that anyone can recall) of a police officer for murder in the line of duty. The code of silence may be far from breaking down, but it certainly has a few cracks in it.

The ethics of rewards have certainly changed in many departments over the past decade. In the wake of corruption scandals, some police executives have taken advantage of the breakdown in loyalty to assign spies, or "field associates," to corruption-prone units to detect bribe-taking. These officers are often recruited for this work at the police academy, where they are identified only to one or two contacts and are generally treated like any other police officer. These spies are universally hated by other officers, but they are very hard to identify. The result of this approach, along with other anti-corruption strategies, has been an apparent decline in organized corruption.[9]

The ethics of force are also changing. In the wake of well-publicized federal prosecutions of police beatings, community outrage over police shootings, and an explosion in civil litigation that has threatened to bankrupt some cities, the behavior and possibly the attitude of the police in their use of force have generally become more restrained. In Los Angeles, Kansas City, Atlanta, New York, Chicago, and elsewhere, the number of killings of citizens by police has declined sharply.[10] Some officers now claim that they risk their lives by hesitating to use force out of fear of being punished for using it. Even if excessive use of force has not been entirely eliminated, the days of unrestrained shooting or use of the "third degree" are clearly gone in many cities.

The increasing external pressures to conform to legal and societal values, rather than to traditional police values, have generated increasing conflict among police officers themselves. The divide-and-conquer effect may be seen in police officers' unwillingness to bear the risks of covering up for their colleagues now that risks are much greater than they have been. Racial conflicts among police officers often center on these values. At that national level, for example, the National Organization of Black Law Enforcement Executives (NOBLE) has been battling with the International Association of Chiefs of Police (IACP) since at least 1979 over the question of how restrictive police department firearms policies should be.

These conflicts should not be over-emphasized, however. The learning of police ethics still takes place in the context of very strong communication of traditional police values. The rising conflicts are still only a minor force. But they are at least one more contingency affecting the moral choices police officers face as they progress through their careers, deciding which values to adopt and which ethical standards to live by.

THE POLICE OFFICER'S MORAL CAREER

There are four major aspects of moral careers in general that are directly relevant to police officers.[11] One is the *contingencies* the officer confronts. Another is the *moral experiences* undergone in confronting these contingencies. A third is the *apologia,* the explanation officers develop for changing the ethical principles they live by. The fourth and most visible aspect of the moral careers of police officers is the *stages* of moral change they go through.

Contingencies

The contingencies shaping police moral careers include all the social pressures officers face to behave one way rather than another. Police departments vary, for example, in the frequency and seriousness of the rule-breaking that goes on. They also vary in the openness of such rule-breaking, and in the degree of teaching of the *skills* of such rule-breaking. It is no small art, for example, to coax a bribe offer out of a traffic violator without directly asking for it. Even in a department in which such bribes are regularly accepted, a new officer may be unlikely to adopt the practice if an older officer does not teach him or her how. In a department in which older officers explicitly teach the techniques, the same officer might be more likely to adopt the practice. The difference in the officer's career is thus shaped by the difference in the contingencies he or she confronts.

The list of all possible contingencies is obviously endless, but these are some of the more commonly reported ones:

- the values the FTO teaches
- the values the first sergeant teaches
- the kind of citizens confronted in the first patrol assignment
- the level of danger on patrol
- whether officers work in a one-officer or two-officer car (after the training period)
- whether officers are assigned to undercover or vice work
- whether there are conflicts among police officers over ethical issues in the department
- the ethical "messages" sent out by the police executive
- the power of the police union to protect officers from being punished
- the general climate of civic integrity (or lack of it)
- the level of public pressure to control police behavior

Contingencies alone, of course, do not shape our behavior. If we were entirely the products of our environment, with no freedom of moral choice, there would be little point in writing (or reading) books on ethics. What contingencies like these do is push us in one direction or another, much like the waves in the ocean. Whether we choose to swim against the tide or flow with the waves is up to us.

Moral Experiences

The moral experience is a major turning point in a moral career. It can be an agonizing decision about which principles to follow or it can be a shock of recognition as you finally understand the moral principles implicit in how other people are behaving. Like the person asleep on a raft drifting out to sea, the police officer who has a moral experience suddenly discovers where he or she is and what the choices are.

Some officers have had moral experiences when they found out the system they worked for was corrupt: when the judge dismissed the charges against the son of a powerful business executive, or when a sergeant ordered the officer not to make arrests at an illegal after-hours bar. One leading police executive apparently went through a moral experience when he was first assigned to the vice squad and saw all the money that his colleagues were taking from gamblers. Shocked and disgusted, he sought and obtained a transfer to a less corrupt unit within a few weeks.

Other officers have had moral experiences in reaction to particular incidents. One Houston police rookie was out of the academy for only several weeks when he witnessed a group of his senior colleagues beat up a Mexican-American, Joe Campos Torres, after he resisted arrest in a bar. Torres drowned after jumping or being pushed from a great height into a bayou, and no one knew how he had died when his body was found floating nearby. The officer discussed the incident with his father, also a Houston police officer, and the father marched the young man right into the Internal Affairs Division to give a statement. His testimony became the basis of a federal prosecution of the other officers.

Other officers may have a moral experience when they see their ethics presented in public, outside of the police culture. New York City police captain Max Schmittberger, for example, who had been a bagman collecting graft for his superiors in New York's Tenderloin district, was greatly moved by the testimony of prostitutes he heard at the hearings of the Lexow Committee investigating police corruption in 1893. He told muckraking reporter Lincoln Steffens that the parade of witnesses opened his eyes to the reality of the corruption, so he decided to get on the witness stand himself to reveal even more details of the corruption.

No matter what contingencies occur to prompt a moral experience, the police officer faces relatively few choices about how to react. One option is to drift with the tide, letting things go on as they have been. Another option is to seek an escape route, such as a transfer, that removes the moral dilemma that may prompt the moral experience. A third option is to leave police work altogether, although the financial resources of police officers are not usually great enough to allow the luxury of resigning on principle. The fourth and most difficult option is to fight back somehow, either by blowing the whistle to the public or initiating a behind-the-scenes counterattack.

Not all moral experiences are prompted by criminal acts or even by violations of rules and regulations. Racist jokes or language, ethnic favoritism by commanders, or other issues can also prompt moral experiences. With some officers, though, nothing may ever prompt a moral experience; they may drift out to sea, or back to shore, sound asleep and unaware of what is happening to them.

Apologia

For those officers with enough moral consciousness to suffer a moral experience, a failure to "do the right thing" could be quite painful to live with. "Even a bent policeman has a conscience," as a British police official who resigned on principle (inadequate police corruption investigations in London) once observed.[12] In order to resolve the conflict between what they think they should have done and what they actually did, officers often invent or adopt an acceptable explanation for their conduct. The explanation negates the principle they may have wished they actually had followed, or somehow makes their behavior consistent with that principle.

Perhaps the most famous apologia is the concept of "clean graft": bribes paid to avoid enforcement of laws against crimes that don't hurt people. Gambling and prostitution bribes were traditionally labeled as "clean graft," while bribes from narcotics pushers were labeled "dirty graft." (As narcotics traffic grew more lucrative, however, narcotics bribes were more often labeled "clean.")

The apologia for beating a handicapped prisoner in a moment of anger may draw on the police value system of maintaining respect for authority and meting out punishment because the courts will not. The apologia for stopping black suspects more often than white suspects may be the assumption that blacks are more likely to be guilty. No matter what a police officer does, he or she is apt to find *situationally justified* reasons for doing it. The reasons are things only the officer can understand, because only the officer knows the full story, all the facts of the *situation*. The claim of situational expertise, of course, conveniently avoids any attempt to apply a general moral principle to conduct. The avoidance is just as effective in the officer's own mind as it would be if the apologia were discussed with the officer's spouse, clergyman, or parents.

Perhaps the most important effect of the apologia is that it allows the officer to live with a certain moral standard of behavior, to become comfortable with it. This creates the potential for further apologias about further changes in moral standards. The process can clearly become habit-forming, and it does. The progression from one apologia to the next makes up the stages of moral change.

Stages

The stages of moral change are points on a moral continuum, the different levels of moral improvement or of the "slippery slope" of moral degeneration. Such descriptions sound trite and old-fashioned, but they are commonly used by officers who get into serious trouble—such as being convicted for burglary—to account for their behavior.

The officers caught in the Denver police burglary ring in 1961, for example, appear to have progressed through many stages in their moral careers before forming an organized burglary ring:

1. First they suffered moral experiences that showed them that the laws were not impartially enforced and that judges were corrupt.

2. Then they learned that other police officers were dishonest, including those who engaged in "shopping," i.e., stealing goods at the scene of a nighttime commercial burglary, with the goods stolen by the police thus indistinguishable from the goods stolen by others.

3. They joined in the shopping themselves and constructed an apologia for it ("the insurance pays for it all anyway").

4. The apologia provided a rationale for a planned burglary in which they were burglars ("the insurance pays for it anyway").

5. The final stage was to commit planned burglaries on a regular basis.

These stages are logically available to all police officers. Many, perhaps most, officers progress to Stage 3 and go no further, just as most professors steal paper clips and photocopying from their universities, but not books or furniture. Why some people move into the further stages and others do not is a problem for sociology of deviance, not ethics. The fact is that some officers do move into the more serious stages of unethical conduct after most officers have established the custom in the less serious, but still unethical, stages.

Each aspect of police ethics, from force to time to due process, has different sets of stages. Taken together, the officer's movement across all the stages on all the ethical issues makes up his or her moral career in police work. The process is not just one way; officers can move back closer to legal principles as well as away from them. But the process is probably quite connected across different issues. Your moral stage on stealing may parallel your moral stage on force.

LEARNING ETHICS DIFFERENTLY

This article has treated morality as if it were black and white, i.e., as if it consisted of clear-cut principles to be obeyed or disobeyed. Many issues in police ethics are in fact clear-cut, and hold little room for serious philosophical analysis. One would have a hard time making a rational defense of police officers stealing, for example.

But what may be wrong with the way police ethics is now taught and learned is just that assumption: that all police ethical issues are as clear-cut as stealing. They are not. The issues of force, time, discretion, loyalty, and others are all very complex, with many shades of gray. To deny this complexity, as the formal approaches of police academies and police rule books often do, may simply encourage unethical behavior. A list of "dos" and "don'ts" that officers must follow because they are ordered to is a virtual challenge to their ingenuity: catch me if you can. And in the face of a police culture that has already established values quite contrary to many of the official rules, the black-and-white approach to ethics may be naive.

As indicated above, an alternative approach may be preferred. This would consider both clear-cut and complex ethical issues in the same fashion: examining police problems in the light of basic moral principles and from the moral point of view. While there may be weaknesses in this alternative approach, it may well be the sounder road to ethical sensitivity in the context of individual responsibility.

NOTES

1. See John Van Maanen, "On Becoming a Policeman," in *Policing: A View from the Street,* eds. Peter Manning and John Van Maanen (Santa Monica, CA: Goodyear, 1978).

2. See John McNamara, "Uncertainties in Police Work: The Relevance of Recruits' Backgrounds and Training," in *The Police: Six Sociological Studies,* ed. David J. Bordua (New York: Wiley, 1967).

3. Van Maanen, "On Becoming a Policeman," p. 298.

4. Ibid., p. 301.

5. See William Westley, *Violence and the Police* (Cambridge, MA: M.I.T. Press, 1970), pp. 159-60.

6. See William Ker Muir, Jr., *Police: Streetcorner Politicians* (Chicago: University of Chicago Press, 1977).

7. See Westley, *Violence,* pp. 48-108.

8. Van Maanen, "On Becoming a Policeman," p. 302.

9. See Lawrence Sherman, "Reducing Police Gun Use" (Paper presented at the International Conference on the Management and Control of Police Organizations, Breukelen, the Netherlands, 1980).

10. Ibid.

11. Cf. Erving Goffman, "The Moral Career of the Mental Patient," in *Asylum: Essays on the Social Situation of Mental Patients and Other Inmates* (Garden City, NY: Anchor Books, 1961), pp. 127-69.

12. See Sherman, "Reducing Police Gun Use."

DISCUSSION QUESTIONS

1. Why is it difficult for police officers to make moral judgments that are not in line with those of their peers? Do you think you would "buck the system"? Why or why not?

2. Why do you feel there are value conflicts between citizens and police? If you were a police chief, how would you resolve the conflicts between citizens and your department?

3. What type of instruction would be of the greatest value to new recruits in the police academy regarding professional ethics?

4. Can you demonstrate professional ethics without having personal ethics? Why or why not?

Case Study 4-1

Liberty and Justice for All

You are a police officer in a large metropolitan city. For the past eight months you worked in a middle- and upper-class suburban patrol zone. Most of the people with whom you came in contact were respectable members of the community. You had good rapport with most of the community and they were generally quite cooperative with the police. Now you are being transferred to another patrol zone which is in a lower-class area near the inner city.

The first week you are in the new zone, you are assigned to work with Mike, a veteran officer who has been working this zone for almost four years. Mike drives you around, pointing out informants, drunks, thieves, and places where they hang out. You immediately notice that Mike has a somewhat harsh, even punitive attitude regarding the people with whom he comes in contact on his beat.

"You have to treat these people tough, intimidation is the only way to communicate with them," Mike explains.

After one week in your new zone, you become aware of a great difference in police work with different types of people. You rarely made arrests in your old zone. Most problems there could be worked out by talking rationally with the people with whom you came in contact. In this zone, however, you have made more arrests and have had to use more force with people. It becomes apparent to you that there are even more drunks and criminals living in the new zone than you had ever expected. People living in the slums seem to be more apathetic as well.

From Larry S. Miller and Michael Braswell, *Human Relations and Police Work,* 4th ed. (Prospect Heights, IL: Waveland Press), 1997. Reprinted with permission.

Mike has told you that if you need information on criminal activity, just pick somebody up and threaten to arrest them if they do not tell you what you need to know. This method worked, as your new partner seemed to demonstrate frequently. Mike would "plant" drugs or a gun on somebody, then threaten to arrest them if they did not give him information or become an informant for him. Mike has occasionally beat confessions out of suspects, then threatened to "get them" if they did not plead guilty to offenses.

You become aware of more violent crimes in you new zone. There are more murders, assaults, and rapes here than would happen in the middle- and upper-class neighborhoods. Mike defines rape "victims" as those persons who did not get paid for their services. "Not even worth writing a report on," Mike tells you. Murder investigations are routinely handled by the investigators in this zone. The detectives seldom perform a comprehensive investigation on any offense here. In the middle- and upper-class zone, all offenses were investigated thoroughly and the victims were given excellent attention by investigating officers.

You find that more police officers are assaulted in the lower-class zone than in your old zone. The people living in the lower-class zone do not appear to respect the police. It seems they only respect force.

"Don't ever turn your back on these people. And if you have to put one of these thugs down, be sure there ain't no damned video camera around," Mike advises you. Mike also advises you to have your gun ready at all times.

"Shotgun's the best, they're really scared of 'em," says Mike. You also notice that more officers in this zone use deadly force than officers in other zones of the city. The police shot five people here last year.

"And probably a few more they didn't count," Mike chuckles.

After working in the new zone for two months and seeing what kind of people live in this area, you find yourself agreeing more and more with Mike's attitudes and methods. You and Mike receive a radio call to back up another unit a couple of blocks away. As you pull up beside the other cruiser, you see two police officers beating up a young man in the alley.

"C'mon Mike, you want a piece of this?" shouts one of the officers. Mike takes out his slapjack and moves in with the other two officers beating the youth.

"What did he do?" you ask.

"He made the mistake of calling us names," responds one of the officers. "We're going to let this one be an example."

The young man could not be over seventeen years old and appears to be badly hurt. You know the officers will leave him in the alley when they are finished beating him. Of course, there will be no arrest.

You begin to think about how you have changed. Mike always says, "Fight fire with fire." Right now you are wondering who the criminals are. What should you do?

Questions:

1. Explain the metamorphosis of the officer taken out of his middle-class environment. Why would there be increased conflict between citizens and police in the lower-class neighborhood? Could this increased conflict explain the behavior of the other veteran officers in this precinct?

2. From a deontological perspective, what must this new officer do to preserve his moral integrity?

3. How might an *apologia* be used to defend the actions of the veteran officers? Would utilitarianism allow for the battering of a minor in this case?

CHAPTER 5

The Ethics of Deceptive Interrogation

Jerome H. Skolnick & Richard A. Leo

INTRODUCTION

As David Rothman and Aryeh Neier have recently reported, "third degree" police practices—torture and severe beatings—remain commonplace in India, the world's largest democracy.[1] Police brutality during interrogation flourishes because it is widely accepted by the middle classes.[2] Although this may seem uncivilized to most Americans, it was not so long ago that American police routinely used physical violence to extract admissions from criminal suspects.[3] Since the 1960s, and especially since *Miranda* [*v. Arizona*], police brutality during interrogation has virtually disappeared in America. Although one occasionally reads about or hears reports of physical violence during custodial questioning,[4] police observers and critics agree that the use of physical coercion during interrogation is now exceptional.

KEY CONCEPTS:

fabricated evidence

Fourteenth Amendment

interrogation

interview

Miranda v. Arizona

role playing

slippery slope argument

Wickersham Report

This transformation occurred partly in response to the influential Wickersham report,[5] which disclosed widespread police brutality in the United States during the 1920s; partly in response to a thoughtful and well-intentioned police professionalism, as exemplified by Fred Inbau and his associates; and partly in response to changes in the law which forbade police to "coerce" confessions but allowed them to elicit

Jerome H. Skolnick and Richard Leo, "The Ethics of Deceptive Interrogation," (as appeared in *Criminal Justice Ethics*, Volume II, Number 1 [Winter/Spring 1992] pp. 3-12). Reprinted by permission of the Institute for Criminal Justice Ethics, 899 Tenth Avenue, New York, NY 10019-1029.

admissions by deceiving suspects who have waived their right to remain silent. Thus, over the last fifty to sixty years, the methods, strategies, and consciousness of American police interrogators have been transformed: psychological persuasion and manipulation have replaced physical coercion as the most salient and defining features of contemporary police interrogation. Contemporary police interrogation is routinely deceptive.[6] As it is taught and practiced today, interrogation is shot through with deception. Police are instructed to, are authorized to—and do—trick, lie, and cajole to elicit so-called "voluntary" confessions.

Police deception, however, is more subtle, complex, and morally puzzling than physical coercion. Although we share a common moral sense in the West that police torture of criminal suspects is so offensive as to be impermissible—a sentiment recently reaffirmed by the violent images of the Rodney King beating—the propriety of deception by police is not nearly so clear. The law reflects this ambiguity by being inconsistent, even confusing. Police are permitted to pose as drug dealers, but not to use deceptive tactics to gain entry without a search warrant, nor are they permitted to falsify an affidavit to obtain a search warrant.

The acceptability of deception seems to vary inversely with the level of the criminal process. Cops are permitted to, and do, lie routinely during investigation of crime, especially when, working as "undercovers," they pretend to have a different identity.[7] Sometimes they may, and sometimes may not, lie when conducting custodial interrogations. Investigative and interrogatory lying are each justified on utilitarian crime control grounds. But police are never supposed to lie as witnesses in the courtroom, although they may lie for utilitarian reasons similar to those permitting deception at earlier stages.[8] In this article, we focus on the interrogatory stage of police investigation, considering (1) how and why the rather muddled legal theory authorizing deceptive interrogation developed; (2) what deceptive interrogation practices police, in fact, engage in; and—a far more difficult question—(3) whether police should ever employ trickery and deception during interrogation in a democratic society valuing fairness in its judicial processes.

THE JURISPRUDENCE OF POLICE INTERROGATION

The law of confessions is regulated by the Fifth, Sixth, and Fourteenth Amendments. Historically, the courts have been concerned almost exclusively with the use of *coercion* during interrogation. Although a coerced confession has been inadmissible in federal cases since the late nineteenth century, the Supreme Court did not proscribe physically coercive practices in state cases until 1936.[9] In *Brown v. Mississippi*, three black defendants were repeatedly whipped and pummeled until they confessed. This was the first in a series of state cases in which the Court held that confessions could not be "coerced," but had to be "voluntary" to be admitted into evidence.[10]

Whether a confession meets that elusive standard is to be judged by "the totality of the circumstances." Under that loose and subjective guideline, an admission is held up against "all the facts" to decide whether it was the product of a "free and rational will" or whether the suspect's will was "overborne" by police pressure. Over the years, however, certain police practices have been designated as presumptively coercive. These include physical force, threats of harm or punishment, lengthy or incommunicado interrogation, denial of food and/or sleep, and promises of leniency.[11] In 1940, the Supreme Court ruled—in a case in which a suspect was first threatened with mob violence, then continuously questioned by at least four officers for five consecutive days—that psychological pressure could also be coercive.[12]

One reason for excluding admissions obtained through coercion is their possible falsity. But, beginning with *Lisenba v. California*[13] in 1941, and followed by *Ashcraft v. Tennessee*[14] three years later, the Supreme Court introduced the criterion of *fairness* into the law. Whether in the context of searches or interrogations, evidence gathered by police methods that "shock the conscience" of the community or violate a fundamental standard of fairness are to be excluded, regardless of reliability.[15] This rationale is sometimes twinned with a third purpose: deterring offensive or unlawful police conduct.

In its watershed *Miranda* decision, the Supreme Court in 1966, prescribed specific limitations on custodial interrogation by police.[16] The five-to-four majority deplored a catalog of manipulative and potentially coercive psychological tactics employed by police to elicit confessions from unrepresented defendants. In essence, the court could not reconcile ideas such as "fairness" and "voluntariness" with the increasingly sophisticated and psychologically overbearing methods of interrogation. In response, it fashioned the now familiar prophylactic rules to safeguard a criminal defendant's Fifth Amendment right against testimonial compulsion. As part of its holding, *Miranda* requires that (1) police advise a suspect of her right to remain silent and her right to an attorney, and (2) the suspect "voluntarily, knowingly and intelligently" have waived these rights before custodial interrogation can legally commence. An interrogation is presumed to be coercive unless a waiver is obtained. Once obtained, however, the "due process-voluntariness" standard governs the admissibility of any confession evidence. In practice, once a waiver is obtained, most of the deceptive tactics deplored by the majority become available to the police.

In retrospect, *Miranda* seems to be an awkward compromise between those who argue that a waiver cannot be made "intelligently" without the advice of an attorney, who would usually advise her client to remain silent, and those who would have preferred to retain an unmodified voluntariness standard because police questioning is "a particularly trustworthy instrument for screening out the innocent and fastening on the guilty," and because the government's obligation is "not to counsel the accused but to question him."[17]

In sum, then, three sometimes competing principles underlie the law of confessions: first, the truth-finding rationale, which serves the goal of *reli-*

ability (convicting an innocent person is worse than letting a guilty one go free); second, the substantive due process or *fairness* rationale, which promotes the goal of the system's integrity; and third, the related *deterrence* principle, which proscribes offensive or lawless police conduct.

The case law of criminal procedure has rarely, however, and often only indirectly, addressed the troubling issue of trickery and deceit during interrogation. We believe this is the key issue in discussing interrogation since, we have found, interrogation usually implies deceiving and cajoling the suspect.

Police deception that intrudes upon substantive constitutional rights is disallowed. For example, the Supreme Court has ruled that an officer cannot trick a suspect into waiving his *Miranda* rights. But apart from these constraints, the use of trickery and deception during interrogation is regulated solely by the due process clause of the Fourteenth Amendment, and is proscribed, on a case-by-case basis, only when it violates a fundamental conception of fairness or is the product of egregious police misconduct. The courts have offered police few substantive guidelines regarding the techniques of deception during interrogation. Nor have the courts successfully addressed the relation between fairness and the lying of police, or the impact of police lying on the broader purposes of the criminal justice system, such as convicting and punishing the guilty. As we shall see, the relations among lying, conceptions of fairness, and the goals of the criminal justice system raise intriguing problems.

A TYPOLOGY OF INTERROGATORY DECEPTION

Because police questioning remains shrouded in secrecy, we know little about what actually happens during interrogation. Police rarely record or transcribe interrogation sessions.[18] Moreover, only two observational studies of police interrogation have been reported, and both are more than two decades old.[19] Most articles infer from police training manuals what must transpire during custodial questioning. Our analysis is based on Richard Leo's dissertation research. It consists of a reading of the leading police training manuals from 1942 to the present; from attending local and national interrogation training seminars and courses; from listening to tape-recorded interrogations; from studying interrogation transcripts; and from ongoing interviews with police officials.

A. "Interview" versus "Interrogate"

The Court in *Miranda* ruled that warnings must be given to a suspect who is in custody, or whose freedom has otherwise been significantly deprived. However, police will question suspects in a "noncustodial" setting—which is defined more by the suspect's state of mind than by the location of the questioning—so as to circumvent the necessity of rendering warnings. This is the most fundamental, and perhaps the most overlooked, deceptive stratagem police employ. By telling the suspect that he is free to leave at any time, and by having him acknowledge that he is voluntarily answering their questions, police will transform what would otherwise be considered an interrogation into a non-custodial interview. Thus, somewhat paradoxically, courts have ruled that police questioning outside of the station may be custodial,[20] just as police questioning inside the station may be non-custodial.[21] The line between the two is the "objective" restriction on the suspect's freedom. Recasting the interrogation as an interview is the cleanest deceptive police tactic since it virtually removes police questioning from the realm of judicial control.

B. *Miranda* Warnings

When questioning qualifies as "custodial," however, police must recite the familiar warnings. The Court declared in *Miranda* that police cannot trick or deceive a suspect into waiving *Miranda* rights.[22] The California Supreme Court has additionally ruled that police cannot "soften up" a suspect prior to administering the warnings.[23] However, police routinely deliver the *Miranda* warnings in a flat, perfunctory tone of voice to communicate that the warnings are merely a bureaucratic ritual. Although it might be inevitable that police would deliver *Miranda* warnings unenthusiastically, investigators whom we have interviewed say that they *consciously* recite the warnings in a manner intended to heighten the likelihood of eliciting a waiver. It is thus not surprising that police are so generally successful in obtaining waivers.[24]

C. Misrepresenting the Nature or Seriousness of the Offense

Once the suspect waives, police may misrepresent the nature or seriousness of the offense. They may, for example, tell a suspect that the murder victim is still alive, hoping that this will compel the suspect to talk. Or police may exaggerate the seriousness of the offense—overstating, for example, the amount of money embezzled—so that the suspect feels compelled to confess to a smaller role in the offense. Or the police may suggest that they are only interested in obtaining admissions to one crime, when in fact they are really investigating another crime. For example, in a recent case, *Colorado v. Spring*, federal agents interrogated a suspect on firearms charges and parlayed his confession into an additional, seemingly unrelated and unimportant, admission of first-degree murder.[25] Despite their pretense to the contrary, the federal agents were actually investigating the murder, not the firearms charge. This tactic was upheld by the Supreme Court.

D. Role Playing: Manipulative Appeals to Conscience

Effective interrogation often requires that the questioner feign different personality traits or act out a variety of roles.[26] The interrogator routinely projects sympathy, understanding, and compassion in order to play the role of the suspect's friend. The interrogator may also try to play the role of a brother or father figure, or even to act as a therapeutic or religious counselor to encourage the confession. The best-known role interrogators may act out is, of course, the good cop/bad cop routine, often played out by a single officer. While acting out these roles, the investigator importunes—sometimes relentlessly—the suspect to confess for the good of her case, her family, society, or conscience. These tactics generate an illusion of intimacy between the suspect and the officer while downplaying the adversarial aspects of interrogation.

The courts have routinely upheld the legitimacy of such techniques—which are among the police's most effective in inducing admissions—except when such role-playing or manipulative appeals to conscience can be construed as "coercive," as when, for example, an officer implies that God will punish the suspect for not confessing.[27]

E. Misrepresenting the Moral Seriousness of the Offense

Misrepresentation of the moral seriousness of an offense is at the heart of interrogation methods propounded by Inbau, Reid, and Buckley's influential police training manual.[28] Interrogating officials offer suspects excuses or moral justifications for their misconduct by providing the suspect with an external attribution of blame that will allow him to save face while confessing. Police may, for example, attempt to convince an alleged rapist that he was only trying to show the victim love or that she was really "asking for it"; or they may persuade an alleged embezzler that blame for her actions is attributable to low pay or poor working conditions. In *People v. Adams*, for example, the officer elicited the initial admission by convincing the suspect that it was the gun, not the suspect, that had done the actual shooting.[29] Widely upheld by the courts, this tactic is advertised by police training manuals and firms as one of their most effective.

F. The Use of Promises

The systematic persuasion—the wheedling, cajoling, coaxing, and importuning—employed to induce conversation and elicit admissions often involves, if only implicitly or indirectly, the use of promises. Although promises of leniency have been presumed to be coercive since 1897, courts continue to permit vague and indefinite promises.[30] The admissibility of a promise thus seems to turn on its specificity. For example, in *Miller v. Fenton*, the suspect was repeatedly told that he had mental problems and thus needed psychological treatment rather than punishment. Although this approach implicitly suggested a promise of leniency, the court upheld the validity of the resulting confession.[31]

Courts have also permitted officers to tell a suspect that his conscience will be relieved only if he confesses, or that they will inform the court of the suspect's cooperation, or that "a showing of remorse" will be a mitigating factor, or that they will help the suspect out in every way they can if he confesses.[32] Such promises are deceptive insofar as they create expectations that will not be met. Since interrogating officials are single-mindedly interested in obtaining admissions and confessions, they rarely feel obliged to uphold any of their promises.

G. Misrepresentations of Identity

A police agent may try to conceal his identity, pretending to be someone else, while interrogating a suspect. In *Leyra v. Denno*, the suspect was provided with a physician for painful sinus attacks he began to experience after several days of unsuccessful interrogation.[33] But the physician was really a police psychiatrist, who repeatedly assured the defendant that he had done no wrong and would be let off easily. The suspect subsequently confessed, but the Supreme Court ruled here that the confession was inadmissible. It would be equally impermissible for a police official or agent to pretend to be a suspect's lawyer or priest. However, in a very recent case, *Illinois v. Perkins*, a prison inmate, Perkins, admitted a murder to an undercover police officer who, posing as a returned escapee, had been placed in his cellblock.[34] The Rehnquist Court upheld the admissibility of the confession. Since Perkins was in jail for an offense unrelated to the murder to which he confessed, the Rehnquist Court said, Perkins was not, for *Miranda* purposes, "in custody." Nor, for the same reason, were his Sixth Amendment *Massiah* rights violated.[35] Thus, the profession or social group with which an undercover officer or agent identifies during the actual questioning may—as a result of professional disclosure rules or cultural norms—be more significant to the resulting legal judgment than the deceptive act itself.[36]

H. Fabricated Evidence

Police may confront the suspect with false evidence of his guilt. This may involve one or more of five gambits. One is to falsely inform the suspect that an accomplice has identified him. Another is to falsely state that existing physical evidence—such as fingerprints, bloodstains, or hair samples—confirm his guilt. Yet another is to assert that an eyewitness or the actual victim has identified and implicated him. Perhaps the most dramatic physical evidence ploy is to stage a line-up, in which a coached witness falsely identifies the suspect. Finally, one of the most common physical evidence ploys is to have the suspect take a lie-detector test and regardless of the results—which are scientif-ically unreliable and invalid in any event—inform the suspect that the poly-graph confirms his guilt.[37] In the leading case on the use of police trickery, *Frazier v. Cupp*, the Supreme Court upheld the validity of falsely telling a sus-pect that his crime partner had confessed.[38]

THE CONSEQUENCES OF DECEPTION

Although lying is, as a general matter, considered immoral, virtually no one is prepared to forbid it categorically. The traditional case put to the abso-lutist is that of the murderer chasing a fleeing innocent victim, whose whereabouts are known by a third party. Should the third party sacrifice the innocent victim to the murderer for the cause of truth? Few of us would say that she should. We thus assume a utilitarian standard regarding decep-tion. So, too, with respect to police interrogation.

Interrogatory deception is an exceedingly difficult issue, about which we share little collective feeling. How are we to balance our respect for truth and fairness with our powerful concern for public safety and the imposition of just deserts? We are always guided by underlying intuitions about the kind of community we want to foster and in which we want to live. Which is worse in the long run—the excesses of criminals or the excesses of authorities?

Few of us would countenance torture by police in the interests of those same values. One reason is that violence may produce false confessions. As Justice Jackson observed in his dissent in *Ashcraft*: ". . . [N]o officer of the law will resort to cruelty if truth is what he is seeking."[39] But that is only partly cor-rect. Cruelty can also yield incontrovertible physical evidence. We reject tor-ture for another reason—we find it uncivilized, conscience-shocking, unfair, so most of us are repelled by it. That leads to a third reason for opposing tor-ture. If effective law enforcement requires public trust and cooperation, as the recent movement toward community-oriented policing suggests, police who torture can scarcely be expected to engender such confidence.

What about police deception? Does it lead to false confessions? Is it unfair? Does it undermine public confidence in the police? A recent and fas-cinating capital case in the Florida Court of Appeal, *Florida v. Cayward*, the facts of which are undisputed, is relevant to the above questions.[40] The defen-dant, a nineteen-year-old male, was suspected of sexually assaulting and smothering his five-year-old niece. Although he was suspected of the crime, the police felt they had too little evidence to charge him. So they interviewed him, eventually advised him of his rights, and obtained a written waiver.

Cayward maintained his innocence for about two hours. Then the police showed him two false reports, which they had fabricated with the knowledge of the state's attorney. Purportedly scientific, one report used Florida Department of Criminal Law Enforcement stationery; another used the stationery of Life Codes, Inc., a testing organization. The false reports established that his semen was found on the victim's underwear. Soon after, Cayward confessed.

Should this deception be considered as akin to lying to a murderer about the whereabouts of the victim? Or should police trickery, and especially the falsification of documents, be considered differently? We unsystematically put this hypothetical question to friends in Berkeley and asked about it in a discussion with scholars-in-residence at the Rockefeller Study Center in Bellagio, Italy. The answers, we discovered, revealed no common moral intuition. For some, the answer was clear—in either direction. "Of course the police should lie to catch the murdering rapist of a child," said one. "I don't want to live in a society where police are allowed to lie and to falsify evidence," said another. Most were ambivalent, and all were eager to know how the Florida court resolved the dilemma.

Citing *Frazier v. Cupp* and other cases, the court recognized "that police deception does not render a confession involuntary *per se*." Yet the court, deeply troubled by the police deception, distinguished between "verbal assertions and manufactured evidence." A "bright line" was drawn between the two on the following assumption: "It may well be that a suspect is more impressed and thereby more easily induced to confess when presented with tangible, official-looking reports as opposed to merely being told that some tests have implicated him."[41]

Although we do not know the accuracy of the conjecture, it assumes that false police assertions such as "Your fingerprints were found on the cash register" are rarely believed by suspects unless backed up by a false fingerprint report. But in these deception cases, we do not usually encounter prudent suspects who are skeptical of the police. Such suspects rarely, if ever, waive their constitutional rights to silence or to an attorney. As in *Cayward*, and many deception cases, the suspect, young or old, white or black, has naively waived his right to remain silent and to an attorney.

Would such a suspect disbelieve, for example, the following scenario? After two hours of questioning, the telephone rings. The detective answers, nods, looks serious, turns to the suspect and says: "We have just been informed by an independent laboratory that traces of your semen were found, by DNA tests, on the panties of the victim. What do you say to that?"

A verbal lie can be more or less convincing, depending upon the authority of the speaker, the manner of speaking, its contextual verisimilitude, and the gullibility of the listener. False documentation adds to verisimilitude, but a well-staged, carefully presented verbal lie can also convince. The decision in *Cayward*, however well-written and considered, is nevertheless bedeviled by the classic problem of determining whether Cayward's confession was "voluntary."

No *contested* confession, however, is ever voluntary in the sense of purging one's soul of guilt, as one would to a religious figure. "The principal value of confession may lie elsewhere, in its implicit reaffirmation of the moral order," writes Gerald M. Caplan. "The offender by his confession acknowledges that he is to blame, not the community."[42] That observation focuses on the offender. Sometimes that is true, sometimes it is not. Those who contest their confessions claim that they were unfairly pressured, and point to the tactics of the police. The claim is that the police violated the moral order by the use of unfair, shady, and thus wrongful tactics to elicit the confession. Had the police, for example, beaten a true confession out of Cayward, it would indeed seem perverse to regard his confession as a reaffirmation of the moral order.

If Cayward had been beaten, and had confessed, we would also be concerned that his confession was false. Assuming that all we know are the facts stated in the opinion, which say nothing of corroborating evidence or why Cayward was suspected, should we assume that his confession was necessarily true? However infrequent they may be, false confessions do occur. Moreover, they do not result only from physical abuse, threats of harm, or promises of leniency, as Fred Inbau and his associates have long maintained;[43] nor are they simply the result of police pressures that a fictionalized reasonable person would find "overbearing," as Joseph Grano's "mental freedom" test implies.[44] They may arise out of the manipulative tactics of influence and persuasion commonly taught in police seminars and practiced by police and used on Cayward.

Psychologists and others have recently begun to classify and analyze the logic and process of these false confessions,[45] which are among the leading causes of wrongful conviction.[46] Perhaps most interesting is the "coerced-internalized" false confession, which is elicited when the psychological pressures of interrogation cause an innocent person to temporarily internalize the message(s) of his or her interrogators and falsely believe himself to be guilty.[47] Although Cayward was probably factually guilty, he might have been innocent. Someone who is not altogether mature and mentally stable, as would almost certainly be true of a nineteen-year-old accused of smothering and raping his five-year-old niece, might also have a precarious and vague memory. When faced with fabricated, but supposedly incontrovertible, physical evidence of his guilt, he might falsely confess to a crime of which he has no recollection, as happened in the famous case of Peter Reilly,[48] and, more recently, in the Florida case of Tom Sawyer,[49] both of which were "coerced-internalized" false confessions.[50]

If Cayward was, in fact, guilty, as his confession suggests, the court was nevertheless willing to exclude it. Presumably, he will remain unpunished unless additional evidence can be produced. Characterizing the falsified evidence as an offense to "our traditional notions of due process of law," the Florida court was evidently alarmed by the *unfairness* of a system which allows police to "knowingly fabricate tangible documentation or physical evidence against an individual."[51] In addition to its "spontaneous distaste" for the conduct of the police, the court added a longer-range utilitarian consideration. Documents manufactured for such purposes, the court fears, may, because of their "potential of indefinite life and the facial appearance of authenticity,"[52] contaminate the entire criminal justice system. "A report falsified for interrogation purposes might well be retained and filed in police paperwork. Such reports have the potential of finding their way into the courtroom."[53] The court also worried that if false reports were allowed in evidence, police might be tempted to falsify all sorts of official documents "including warrants, orders and judgements," thereby undermining public respect for the authority and integrity of the judicial system.

Yet the slippery slope argument applies to lying as well as to falsification of documents. When police are permitted to lie in the interrogation context, why should they refrain from lying to judges when applying for warrants, from violating internal police organization rules against lying, or from lying in the courtroom? For example, an *Oakland Tribune* columnist, Alix Christie, recently received a letter from a science professor at the University of California at Berkeley who had served on an Alameda County (Oakland) murder jury. He was dismayed that a defendant, whom he believed to be guilty, had been acquitted because most of the jurors did not believe the police, even about how long it takes to drive from west to east Oakland. "The problem," writes Christie, "predates Rodney King. It's one familiar to prosecutors fishing for jurors who don't fit the profile of people who distrust cops." She locates the problem in "the ugly fact that there are two Americas." In the first America, the one she was raised in, the police are the "good guys." In the other, police are viewed skeptically.

Police misconduct—and lying is ordinarily considered a form of misconduct—undermines public confidence and social cooperation, especially in the second America. People living in these areas often have had negative experiences with police, ranging from an aloof and legalistic policing "style" to corruption, and even to the sort of overt brutality that was captured on the videotape of the Rodney King beating in Los Angeles. Community-oriented policing is being implemented in a number of American police departments to improve trust and citizen cooperation by changing the attitudes of both police and public.

Police deception may thus engender a paradoxical outcome. Although affirmed in the interest of crime control values by its advocates like Fred Inbau—who, along with his co-author John Reid, has exerted a major influence on generations of police interrogators—it may generate quite unanticipated consequences. Rarely do advocates of greater latitude for police to interrogate consider the effects of systematic lying on law enforcement's reputation for veracity. Police lying might not have mattered so much to police work in other times and places in American history. But today, when urban juries are increasingly composed of jurors disposed to be distrustful of police, deception by police during interrogation offers yet another reason for disbelieving law enforcement witnesses when they take the stand, thus reducing police effectiveness as controllers of crime.

Conservatives who lean toward crime control values do not countenance lying as a general matter. They approve of police deception as a necessity, measuring the cost of police deceit against the benefits of trick-ery for victims of crime and the safety of the general public. Police and pros-ecutors affirm deceitful interrogative practices not because they think these are admirable, but because they believe such tactics are necessary.[54]

The Florida police officers who fabricated evidence did so for the best of reasons. The victim was a five-year-old girl, and the crime was abhorrent and hard to prove. Nevertheless, the Florida court excluded the confession on due process grounds, arguing that police must be discouraged from fab-ricating false official documents. Many persons, but especially those who, like Fred Inbau, affirm the propriety of lying in the interrogatory context, tend to undervalue the significance of the long-term harms caused by such autho-rized deception: namely, that it tends to encourage further deceit, undermining the general norm against lying. And if it is true that the fabrication of doc-uments "greatly lessens," as the Florida court says, "the respect the public has for the criminal justice system and for those sworn to uphold and enforce the law,"[55] doesn't that concern also apply to interrogatory lying?

There is an additional reason for opposing deceitful interrogation prac-tices. It does happen that innocent people are convicted of crimes. Not as often, probably, as guilty people are set free, but it does happen. Should false evidence be presented, a suspect may confess in the belief that he will receive a lesser sentence. In a study in 1986, of wrongful conviction in felony cases, C. Ronald Huff and his colleagues conservatively estimated that nearly 6,000 false convictions occur every year in the United States.[56] Hugo Bedau and Michael Radelet, who subsequently studied 350 known miscar-riages of justice in recent American history, identified false confessions as one of the leading sources of erroneous conviction of innocent individuals.[57]

There are no easy answers to these dilemmas, no easy lines to suggest when the need to keep police moral and honest brushes up against the imperatives of controlling crime. Phillip E. Johnson, who has proposed a thoughtful statutory replacement for the *Miranda* doctrine,[58] would not allow police to "intentionally misrepresent the amount of evidence against the suspect, or the nature and seriousness of the charges,"[59] as well as other, clearly more coercive tactics. But he would allow feigned sympathy or compassion, an appeal to conscience or values, and a statement to the sus-pect such as "A voluntary admission of guilt and sincere repentance may be given favorable consideration at the time of sentence."[60] Johnson states no formal principle for these distinctions, but does draw an intuitively sensi-ble contrast between, on the one hand, outright *misrepresentations*, which might generalize to other venues and situations; and, on the other, *appeals* to self-interest or conscience, which seem to draw upon commonly held and morally acceptable values. If, however, as we have argued, rules for police conduct, and the values imparted through these rules, produce indirect, as well as direct, consequences for police practices and the culture of policing, Johnson's distinctions are persuasive. This resolution, we suggest, is quite different from the direction recently taken by the Rehnquist Court.

We have earlier argued that when courts allow police to deceive suspects for the good end of capturing criminals—even as, for example, in "sting" operations—they may be tempted to be untruthful when offering testimony. However we think we ought to resolve the problem of the ethics of deceptive interrogation, we need always to consider the unanticipated consequences of permitting police to engage in what would commonly be considered immoral conduct—such as falsifying evidence. The Supreme Court has moved in recent years to soften the control of police conduct in interrogation. In *Moran v. Burbine*, for example, the Court let stand a murder conviction even though the police had denied a lawyer—who had been requested by a third party, but without the suspect's knowledge, prior to his questioning—to the suspect during interrogation. The dissenters decried the "incommunicado questioning" and denounced the majority for having embraced "deception of the shabbiest kind."[61]

More recently, the notoriety of the Rodney King beating overshadowed the significance of the Rehnquist Court's most significant self-incrimination decision, *Arizona v. Fulminante*.[62] Here, a confession was obtained when a prison inmate, an ex-cop who was also an FBI informer, offered to protect Fulminante from prison violence, but only if he confessed to the murder of his daughter. In a sharply contested five-to-four opinion, the Court reversed the well-established doctrine that a coerced confession could never constitute "harmless error." Whether the ruling will be as important in *encouraging* police coercion of confessions as the King videotape will be in discouraging future street brutality remains to be seen. But in concert with other recent U.S. Supreme Court decisions that have cut back on the rights of defendants, the *Fulminante* decision may also send a message that police coercion is sometimes acceptable, and that a confession elicited by police deception will almost always be considered "voluntary."

NOTES

For helpful advice, criticism, and counsel, we would like to thank the following individuals: Albert Alschuler, Jack Greenberg, James Hahn, Sanford Kadish, Norman LaPera, Paul Mishkin, Robert Post, Peter Sarna, Jonathan Sither, Amy Toro, Jeremy Waldron, and, especially, Phillip Johnson.

1. Rothman & Neier, *India's Awful Prisons*, N.Y. Rev. Books, May 16, 1991, at 53-56.

2. Id. at 54.

3. *See* E. HOPKINS, OUR LAWLESS POLICE: A STUDY OF UNLAWFUL ENFORCEMENT (1931), and E. LAVINE, THE THIRD DEGREE: A DETAILED AND APPALLING EXPOSE OF POLICE BRUTALITY (1930).

4. "Confession at Gunpoint?" 20/20, ABC NEWS, March 29, 1991.

5. NATIONAL COMMISSION ON LAW OBSERVANCE AND ENFORCEMENT, LAWLESSNESS IN LAW ENFORCEMENT (1931).

6. Richard Leo, From Coercion to Deception: An Empirical Analysis of the Changing Nature of Modern Police Interrogation in America (paper presented at the Annual Meeting of the American Society of Criminology, Nov. 19-23, 1991).

7. *See* G. MARX, UNDERCOVER: POLICE SURVEILLANCE IN AMERICA (1988).

8. *See* Skolnick, *Deception by Police*, CRIMINAL JUSTICE ETHICS, Summer/Fall 1982, at 40- 54.

9. Brown v. Mississippi, 297 U.S. 278 (1936).

10. Caplan, *Questioning Miranda*, 39 VANDERBILT LAW REVIEW 1417 (1985).

11. The Supreme Court's very recent ruling that coerced confessions may be "harmless error" will undermine this general rule. Arizona v. Fulminante, U.S. LEXIS 1854 (1991).

12. Chambers v. Florida, 309 U.S. 227 (1940).

13. 314 U.S. 219 (1941).

14. 322 U.S. 143 (1944).

15. *See* Rochin v. California, 342 U.S. 165 (1952), Spano v. New York, 360 U.S. 315 (1959), and Rogers v. Richmond, 365 U.S. 534 (1961).

16. Miranda v. Arizona, 384 U.S. 436 (1961).

17. Caplan, *supra* note 10, at 1422-23.

18. The state of Alaska requires, as a matter of state constitutional due process, that all custodial interrogations be electronically recorded. *See* Stephan v. State, 711 P.2d 1156 (1985).

19. Wald, et al., *Interrogations in New Haven: The Impact of Miranda*, 76 YALE L. J. 1519-1648 (1967), and N. MILNER, COURT AND LOCAL LAW ENFORCEMENT: THE IMPACT OF MIRANDA (1971).

20. Orozco v. Texas, 394 U.S. 324 (1969).

21. *See* Beckwith v. United States, 425 U.S. 341 (1976), Oregon v. Mathiason, 429 U.S. 492 (1977), and California v. Beheler, 463 U.S. 1121 (1983).

22. However, police may deceive an attorney who attempts to invoke a suspect's constitutional rights, as to whether the suspect will be interrogated, and the police do not have to inform the suspect that a third party has hired an attorney on his behalf. *People v. Moran*, 475 U.S. 412 (1986).

23. People v. Honeycutt, 570 P.2d 1050 (1977).

24. *See* O. STEPHENS, JR., THE SUPREME COURT AND CONFESSIONS OF GUILT 165- 200 (1973) for a useful summary of studies assessing the impact of *Miranda* in New Haven, Los Angeles, Washington, D.C., Pittsburgh, Denver, and rural Wisconsin. These studies indicate that police obtain waivers from criminal suspects in most cases. Additionally, the Captain of the Criminal Investigation Division of the Oakland Police Department told one of the authors that detectives obtain waivers from criminal suspects in 85-90% of all cases involving interrogations.

25. Colorado v. Spring, 107 S.Ct.851 (1987).

26. Consider the following passage from R. Royal and S. Schutt, THE GENTLE ART OF INTERVIEWING AND INTERROGATION (1976): "To be truly proficient at interviewing or interrogation, one must possess the ability to portray a great variety of personality traits. The need to adjust character to harmonize with, or dominate, the many moods and traits of the subject is necessary. The interviewer/interrogator requires greater histrionic skill than the average actor. . . . The interviewer must be able to pretend anger, fear, joy, and numerous other emotions without affecting his judgment or revealing any personal emotion about the subject" (p.65).

27. People v. Adams, 143 Cal.App.3d 970 (1983).

28. F. INBAU, J. REID, & J. BUCKLEY, CRIMINAL INTERROGATION AND CONFESSIONS (1986).

29. People v. Adams, *supra* note 27.

30. Bram v. United States, 168 U.S. 532 (1897).

31. Miller v. Fenton, 796 F.2d 598 (1986).

32. Kaci & Rush, *At What Price Will We Obtain Confessions?* 71 JUDICATURE, 256-57 (1988).

33. Leyra v. Denno, 347 U.S. 556 (1954).

34. Illinois v. Perkins, 110 S.CT. 2394 (1990).

35. In Massiah v. United States, 377 U.S. 201 (1964), the U.S. Supreme Court held that post-indictment questioning of a defendant outside the presence of his lawyer violates the Sixth Amendment.

36. *See* Cohen, *Miranda and Police Deception in Interrogation: A Comment on Illinois v. Perkins*, CRIMINAL LAW BULLETIN 534-46 (1990).

37. *See* Skolnick, *Scientific Theory and Scientific Evidence: Analysis of Lie Detection*, 70 YALE LAW JOURNAL 694-728 (1961); and D. LYKKEN, A TREMOR IN THE BLOOD: USES AND ABUSES OF THE LIE DETECTOR (1981).

38. Frazier v. Cupp, 394 U.S. 731 (1969).

39. Ashcraft v. Tennessee, *supra* note 14, at 160.

40. Florida v. Cayward, 552 So.2d 971 (1989).

41. *Id.* at 977.

42. Caplan, *Miranda Revisited*, 93 YALE L.J. 1375 (1984).

43. F. INBAU, LIE-DETECTION AND CRIMINAL INTERROGATION (1942).

44. Grano, *Voluntariness, Free Will, and the Law of Confessions*, 65 VA. L. Rev. 859-945 (1979).

45. *See* Kassin & Wrightsman, *Confession Evidence*, in THE PSYCHOLOGY OF EVIDENCE AND TRIAL PROCEDURE (S. Kassin & L.Wrightsman eds. 1985). G. GUDJONSSON & N. CLARK, SUGGESTIBILITY IN POLICE INTERROGATION: A SOCIAL PSYCHOLOGICAL MODEL (1985); Ofshe, *Coerced Confessions: The Logic of Seemingly Irrational Action*, 6 CULTIC STUD. J. 6-15 (1989); Gudjonsson, *The Psychology of False Confessions*, 57 MEDICO-LEGAL J. 93-110 (1989); R. Ofshe & R. Leo, The Social Psychology of Coerced-Internalized False Confessions (paper presented at the Annual Meetings of the American Sociological Association, August 23-27, 1991).

46. Bedau & Radelet, *Miscarriages of Justice in Potentially Capital Cases*, 40 STAN. L. Rev. 21-179 (1987).

47. Kassin & Wrightsman, *supra* note 45.

48. *See* J. BARTEL, A DEATH IN CANAAN, (1976); and D. CONNERY, GUILTY UNTIL PROVEN INNOCENT (1977).

49. State of Florida v. Tom Franklin Sawyer, 561 So.2d 278 (1990). *See also* Weiss, *Untrue Confessions*, MOTHER JONES, Sept., 1989, at 22-24 and 55-57.

50. Ofshe & Leo, *supra* note 45.

51. Florida v. Cayward, *supra* note 40, at 978.

52. *Id.*

53. *Id.*

54. Inbau, *Police Interrogation—A Practical Necessity*, 52 J. CRIM. L., CRIMINOLOGY, & POL. SCI. 421 (1961).

55. Florida v. Cayward, *supra* note 40, at 983.

56. Huff, Rattner & Sagarin, *Guilty Until Proven Innocent: Wrongful Conviction and Public Policy*, 32 CRIME & DELINQ. 518-44 (1986). *See also* Rattner, *Convicted But Innocent: Wrongful Conviction and the Criminal Justice System*, 12 L. & HUM. BEHAV. 283-93 (1988).

57. Bedau & Radelet, *supra* note 46.

58. P. JOHNSON, CRIMINAL PROCEDURE 540-50 (1988).

59. *Id.*, at 542.

60. *Id.*

61. Moran v. Burbine, 475 U.S. 412 (1986).

62. Arizona v. Fulminante, *supra* note 11.

DISCUSSION QUESTIONS

1. Differentiate between the various typologies of interrogatory deception. Which type do you think would be more problematic for an officer to engage in morally? Legally?

2. How does police deception differ from torture? Does police deception, especially in the interrogation phase, lead to false confessions? Explain.

3. What are the consequences of police deception?

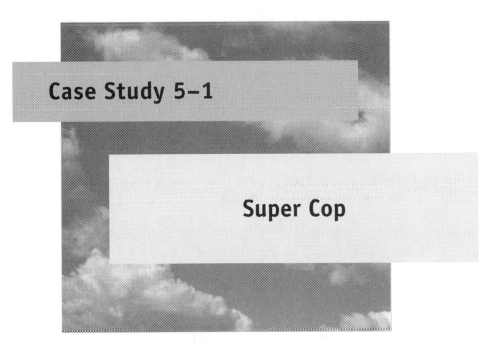

Case Study 5–1

Super Cop

Bill Hammonds's name appears once again on the "Best Detective of the Month" roster.

It is the sixth time in a row that Hammonds has received the honor. Hammonds was promoted from patrol to investigations just nine months ago.

"How does he do it?" you ask yourself aloud.

"Hammonds is doing a damn good job, isn't he?" Pete Rowe comments as he steps up to the bulletin board.

"That's not the word for it. Look at the difference in all of our case loads and conviction rates and then look at Hammonds'. His conviction rate is almost 80 percent while the average is around 20 percent," you point out.

"Well, I've heard that he's got a whole army of snitches working for him," Pete says as he walks away from the bulletin board.

"Snitches" is a slang word for informants. Without good informants, an investigator can do very little with an investigation. But it takes time for an investigator to develop good informants.

Hammonds did not seem to have any trouble developing informants during his first weeks as an investigator. It took you almost two months to develop a couple of snitches, and Hammonds seemed to have an "army" of snitches working for him during the first several weeks of his detective assignment.

From Larry S. Miller and Michael Braswell, *Human Relations and Police Work,* 4th ed. (Prospect Heights, IL: Waveland Press), 1997. Reprinted with permission.

"How does he do it?" you ask yourself again.

That afternoon your captain calls you into his office. "Mike, how's that investigation coming on the country club burglary?" the captain asks.

"It's a pretty tight case, Captain. I've got a couple of leads and I'm waiting for a response from the crime lab," you explain.

"I've been getting some pressure up the ranks to get this thing resolved. You've been working on the case for about two weeks. I'm going to put both you and Hammonds on the case and see if we can't get this thing solved," the captain says.

Walking out of the captain's office, you feel as though you have been slapped in the face. It seems obvious that the captain feels you are not as competent as Hammonds would be in solving the case. It is an insult, but one you will have to live with.

The next day, Hammonds walks up to you, sporting a grin.

"Mike, I hear you're having trouble with a burglary at the country club?" Bill asks, somewhat snidely.

"Very funny, Hammonds. C'mon, let's contact some of your snitches and see if they know anything," you retort as you grab your overcoat.

Hammonds will not allow you to talk with any of his informants. Hammonds always insists that you stay in the car while he gets out to talk. You are not very concerned because several other detectives are "protective" of their sources and do not like others around while talking with them. After a while, you begin to wonder what kind of informants Hammonds has working for him. Almost all of Hammonds's snitches seem to be either drug users or pushers.

"Now all we have to do is sit back and wait for a phone call," Hammonds says as he begins to drive back to the station.

"Did any of your snitches know anything?" you ask.

"No, not yet. But one will turn up something real soon," Hammonds says as he begins to drive back to the station.

That afternoon, Hammonds comes into the detective office with a warrant in his hand. "This is it, Mike. I've got a warrant for Jake Lennan, the one that broke into the country club." Hammonds says as he waves the warrant in your face.

"Ok, Hammonds, now tell me how you did it," you say, looking over the warrant.

"It was easy, Mike. My snitches came through with the information. Besides, I think there is a real good chance that Mr. Jake Lennan will want to talk and confess to the break-in as well as return the stolen property," Hammonds comments.

You look at Hammonds in disbelief. Hammonds, noticing the expression on your face, continues to explain.

"Look, if this Jake guy doesn't talk and confess I'd sure hate to be in his shoes when my snitches get hold of him."

Hammonds' last statement puts a thought in your mind. Apparently Hammonds is using his informants to do the investigative work for him. Hammonds' informants may even be using force on suspects like Jake Lennan to confess and return stolen property. It seems Pete was right about Hammonds having an army of snitches. You begin to wonder what Hammonds is giving his informants in return for their services.

"What're you paying your snitches for doing your work for you?" you ask with increasing skepticism.

"Nothing much. I may let them slide on a few things they may be involved with," Hammonds responds as he turns and walks away.

It is becoming more apparent to you that Hammonds may be solving cases by using his informants to do the investigation work, as well as engaging in other inappropriate activities. Hammonds' use of drug addicts and pushers as informants led you to other possible conclusions. He could be ignoring violations of narcotics laws by his informants in return for information and services. You decide to confront Hammonds with your suspicions.

"Well, why not?" I'm solving more cases than anyone else here. Why not let snitches slide on some things in return for good convictions? I haven't put one thug in jail that didn't deserve to go. It's throwing back the little fish for the big ones," Hammonds argues.

Hammonds continues to explain to you how he has been using his informants to "catch" the crooks and make them confess to their crimes.

As you think about what Hammonds said, you wonder if that is the way an investigation should be handled. His argument seems to have some merit and does produce results. It does not seem right to you that a police officer should ignore the illegal activities of one group and arrest others. You decide to ask your captain.

"Look, Mike, in our business it's give and take. We have to look at our priorities. We have to look at the worst offenses and let the others slide. We can use that to our advantage the way Hammonds is doing. We've all done it as investigators—maybe not to the extent that Hammonds has, but if all of us would take that advantage, we would solve more cases," your captain explains.

The captain's statement still does not satisfy you. You still believe Hammonds' methods are unethical, even if "that's the way it is" in detective work.

You wonder what you will have to do to become "Detective of the Month."

Questions:

1. Justify the actions of Hammonds from a utilitarian perspective.

2. What types of problems may be generated by Hammonds's actions?

3. Do you agree with the Captain and Hammonds?

CHAPTER 6

Ethical Dilemmas in Police Work

Joycelyn Pollock & Ronald Becker

There is a growing body of literature on the importance of teaching ethics in criminal justice curricula (Kleinig, 1990; Pollock, 1994; Schmalleger & McKenrick, 1991; Silvester, 1990). Police ethics has received the most attention in the literature. One issue dealt with is where such teaching should be conducted. The focus of such debate is usually an argument over the benefits of the college classroom versus the police academy, but there is increasing recognition that both locales are important. Another discussion concerns whether teaching ethics is properly placed in an academy recruit class or as part of in-service training. Again, it is probably true that there is a need for a focused, guided discussion of ethical issues at both periods of a career in policing.

Police ethics is particularly relevant, according to Kleinig (1990:4), because of the number of issues relevant to police, the discretionary nature of policing, the authority of police, the fact that they are not habitually moral, the crisis situations, the temptations, and the peer pressure. The goals of police training typically include all aspects of how to perform tasks related to the job. More recently, other information has been introduced, such as communication skills, multicultural understanding, and dealing with child abuse and the "battered woman syndrome." However, the role of the police in a free society and the due process and ethical issues involved in investigation and enforcement often are not included in the training schedule.

In this chapter, ethics training for police officers will be the topic of discussion. Usually the content of such courses is developed as a combination of philosophy and discussion of ethical dilemmas that practitioners might face in the field. Swift, Houston, and Anderson (1993), for instance, suggest that utilitarianism is the appropriate philosophical system because most offi-

> **KEY CONCEPTS:**
>
> **discretion**
>
> **duty**
>
> **gratuities**
>
> **loyalty**
>
> **police ethics**
>
> **utilitarianism**

cers (they also included correctional officers in their study) can identify with the concepts of utilitarianism and use them intuitively. Other authors also suggest exploring a philosophical foundation as well as practitioner issues as being an important part of the content for such a course (Kleinig, 1990; Schmalleger, 1990; Souryal, 1992).

The content of ethical dilemmas for police officers can be gleaned from newspapers, books in the field, and articles. Delattre's (1989) book, for instance, can be used as a source for a number of ethical dilemmas, as can Cohen and Feldberg (1991). Pollock (1994) provides dilemmas for police personnel as well as for corrections and other criminal justice professions. Pollock (1993) discusses a number of sources for police ethics, and these can be used to develop other dilemmas.

Perusing the literature, one can identify the following issues (although these by no means form an exhaustive list): gratuities, corruption, bribery, "shopping," whistleblowing and loyalty, undercover tactics, the use of deception, discretion, sleeping on duty, sex on duty and other misfeasance, deadly force, and brutality. Barker and Carter (1994) develop a typology of officer deviance including use of force, misconduct (violation of rules or laws), and corruption (gratuities and/or any misuse of position for expected reward). One might assume that these issues are the most problematic ethical issues in police work because they are what is primarily addressed in the literature. However, it may not necessarily be true that these issues are perceived by officers themselves as the most problematic. For example, although undercover tactics (i.e., deception) have received a great deal of attention in the literature, many officers are never faced with such issues because they are in patrol and not in criminal investigation. The issues of deadly force and brutality are certainly important, but they may not be day-to-day concerns for most officers who are rarely faced with such encounters. In addition, while most of the ethical issues mentioned thus far involve officer deviance, there are some ethical issues that do not involve misconduct. In fact, there may be situations in which neither decision that could be made by the officer is clearly wrong. Few attempts have been made to determine what ethical concerns are identified by the officers themselves. If such an attempt has been made in academy classrooms, the findings have not found their way into the literature.

One of the few instances in which officers were asked their views on ethical issues was a study done by Barker (1978). In this study he asked 50 officers in a small police department how many of their number participated in specific examples of unethical activity other than corruption. The categories were: "excessive force," "police perjury," "sex on duty," "drinking on duty," and "sleeping on duty." Barker also had them rank the perceived seriousness of such acts. Findings indicated that officers believed that sleeping on duty and engaging in sex while on duty were the most frequent forms of misconduct, and they were also rated as relatively less serious than other forms of unethical behavior. The police officers ranked the activities in the following way from most serious to least serious: drinking on duty, police perjury, sleeping on duty, sex on duty, brutality. Another measure of seriousness is in the officers' willingness to report another officer for the activity. In answer to this question, the officers responded in the following way: 56 percent would always report drinking on duty; 28 percent would always report perjury; 19 percent would always report sex on duty; 14 percent would always report sleeping on duty; and 12 percent would always report brutality.

One might expect that the perceived extent and seriousness of various types of wrongdoing may vary from city to city. In an informal survey using the same choices as Barker's, one of the authors found that officers in a large city reported that their fellow officers engaged in significantly more drinking and less sex and brutality. It could also be that the changes are related to the time period in which the surveys were conducted because Barker's study took place in the late 1970s before officers were sensitized to the problem of police brutality.

Barker's study still does not fully explore what officers themselves perceive to be problematic issues because it uses a restricted list of activities. This chapter will discuss an approach to teaching ethics to an audience of police officers that allows class participants to submit their own ethical dilemmas and to analyze these using a philosophical framework. The approach is premised on the assumption that officers will submit dilemmas that have relevance to them. Personalizing course content and providing practitioners with a basic understanding of ethical analysis will hopefully help them to recognize ethical issues and resolve them.

Each of the authors has had the opportunity to teach ethics to police officers. As a pedagogical tool, one instructor utilized ethical dilemmas turned in by class participants as the basis for half the course content. The procedure operates as follows. First, the instructor defined the term *ethical dilemma* as: (1) a situation in which the officer did not know what the right course of action was, (2) a situation in which the course of action the officer considered right was difficult to do, or (3) a situation in which the wrong course of action was very tempting. Then, the officers in each class were asked to write down a difficult ethical dilemma they had faced. This assignment took place after several hours of introductory material on ethics, morals, and value systems, but before any issue-based material was presented, so officers were not yet focused on one or another specific type of dilemma (i.e., gratuities or brutality).

It is unclear whether officers reported ethical dilemmas according to frequency or seriousness or perhaps some other criteria. As mentioned previously, issues that pose the most serious ethical concerns, (e.g., use of deadly force and brutality) may be those that are least commonly faced. Officers may have identified an example of the most serious incident, the most recent incident, or the incident most frequently presented to them. This exercise does present a useful way of obtaining relevant, realistic classroom material upon which to base a discussion of ethics.

Another exercise that was used in every class was to have the officers write their own code of ethics, with the restriction of limiting their code of ethics to one line. In other words, they were instructed to write down what they considered the most important elements of a code for police officers or what makes a good police officer. These short one-sentence codes were collected and then read to the class, which analyzed the values expressed in each and identified the most frequently cited values. In all classes, police officers identified five common elements: (1) *legality* (enforcing and upholding the law); (2) *service* (protecting and serving the public); (3) *honesty and integrity*; (4) *loyalty*; and finally, (5) some version of the *Golden Rule* or respect for other persons. These five elements were mentioned in every class, though the relative rankings or emphasis given to each varied somewhat.

These concepts parallel closely the Code of Ethics promulgated by the International Association of Chiefs of Police. Specifically, legality is represented by the phrase, "I will be exemplary in obeying the law and the regulations of my department," and service as, "my fundamental duty is to serve the community. . . ." Honesty and integrity is reflected in "Honest in thought and deed both in my personal and official life. . . ." The Golden Rule or some version of respect for other persons is exemplified in the lines in the Code that relate to never acting officiously or permitting personal feelings, prejudices, or friendships, among other things, to influence decisions. Loyalty, in fact, is the only issue identified by officers with no direct parallel to the Code. Because it is a subject of concern for both officers and writers in the field of ethics, it is interesting that the Code has taken the opposite approach in a recent revision by specifically exhorting the duty to comply with investigations of wrongdoing in the phrase, "I will cooperate with all legally authorized agencies and their representatives in the pursuit of justice."

The five elements that officers viewed as important to a code of ethics were tied to the dilemmas they identified. *Legality* can be discussed in terms of discretion—what to do in particularly difficult situations in which no good solution presents itself and the law is not very helpful. *Service* is relevant to duty issues. These issues cover those instances in which it would be inconvenient or perceived as a waste of time to do a task that duty calls for. *Honesty* is related to whistleblowing and *loyalty* issues as well as temptations of taking money from a scene or accepting a bribe. Finally, the *Golden Rule* is related to all those incidents in which it is difficult to keep one's temper or treat people respectfully due to anger, the exigencies of the moment, or some other reason. These five elements comprise four categories of dilemmas.

The four categories are: (1) *discretion (legality)*, (2) *duty (service)*, (3) *honesty*, and (4) *loyalty*. The two most frequent categories of dilemmas reflected in the officers' submissions were loyalty versus whistleblowing and the use of discretion in difficult situations. In the remainder of this chapter, these dilemmas and the procedure used to analyze them will be discussed.

DISCRETION

Discretion can be defined as the power to make a choice. Obviously all ethical dilemmas involve making choices (e.g., whether to take a bribe). The situations categorized in this area, however, are within the purview of what is known as police discretion (e.g., whether to arrest, whether to ticket, what to do when faced with any altercation). Some of these dilemmas have not been readily identified as ethical issues in the literature. In these situations, officers either felt uncomfortable about what the law or regulations required them to do, or they were sincerely confused as to what the appropriate course of action was.

Some incidents occur when the officer is faced with a choice of whether to enforce a law, or when the officer feels uncomfortable about enforcing it. Typically the law involved is relatively minor—a traffic citation, enforcing city warrants, or some other misdemeanor. The reason the officer hesitates or feels that the decision presents an ethical dilemma is because of situational elements (e.g., the age or poverty of the offender, or the perception that the person deserves a break). The following examples are representative. All are verbatim transcriptions of officers' submissions:

> Officer received a call regarding business holding a shoplifter. A 75-year-old female was being held for shoplifting needed medications. However, store insisted on filing charges on her.

> Kmart calls for a wagon call. You get there and find a 70-year-old lady arrested for trying to steal hearing aid batteries. She was on a fixed income and unable to purchase items. She even looks like your mother.

> While on patrol one day, I was dispatched to a disturbance at a gas station. Upon arrival I spotted a kid I saw in the neighborhood a lot. I knew this kid lived with his grandmother and that they were barely making ends meet. I had ran into problems before with the kid begging for money and washing people's windows at gas stations without being asked to. The gas station attendant wanted the child arrested for trespassing because he stated the child harasses the customers.

In these situations the offender is usually either poor and/or elderly. The stores often insist on prosecution, leaving the officer in a struggle between compassion and enforcing the law. In the next set of dilemmas or situations, there is no demanding complainant, but the officer feels strict legality may not serve the ends of justice, or at least feels torn about enforcing the law:

> Officer A was faced with arresting a person on a parole violation. Officer, while talking to family members, learned that parole violator had just started a new job, which was verified by employer. What should Officer A do? (Parole violation was for first DWI.)

> I arrested a lady with a baby for numerous traffic warrants. Do you take the baby to juvenile and her to jail, make arrangements for someone else to care for the baby, or just let her go and tell her to take care of the warrants on her own? She has no money and gave us no trouble.

> Riding with a partner we stopped a person in traffic for multiple violations, no insurance, no driver's license, no ID at all, and who would face going to jail for traffic violations on Christmas Eve. Would you discourage your partner from taking him to jail?

The most numerous type of incidents involve women and/or families with children stopped for some sort of traffic violation. Some officers were very clear as to what criteria they used to guide their discretion, while others were more unsure about the ethical role of the police in traffic enforcement.

Another category of discretion dilemmas involved situations in which no law or policy may be involved, but the officer was still perplexed regarding how to resolve the situation. These situations were often family disputes in which a significant problem existed prior to interaction with a police officer. Here, the officer's dilemma arises from a sincere desire to do the right thing but not being sure what the right thing is. Referral sources in the community, while plentiful, are often unavailable or overused. The large number of these submitted dilemmas indicate that the officers perceive significant ethical issues in this area of policing. For most officers, it was not necessarily a question of doing something wrong, but rather of finding the best solution to a difficult problem.

> What do you do when called to a scene to transport and find some type of housing for an elderly parent whom the family no longer wants because of mental impairment, knowing that the family has used, in the past, the parent's resources as their mainstay?

> Officer A received call in regard to trespassing. Officer spoke with complainant at residence who wanted a female removed from his house. Female had a small child and was complainant's ex-girlfriend who had no family and no place to go.

This last dilemma is the single most frequent type of instance in this category. Typically boyfriends wanted girlfriends removed, girlfriends wanted boyfriends removed, parents wanted children removed, and husbands wanted wives removed, or vice versa. Police officers expressed the frustration inherent in having to deal with what are essentially difficult interpersonal problems, such as the examples below:

> You and your partner are dispatched to a disturbance at a low-income apartment complex. It involves a drunk husband and drunk wife calling the police for no reason. No crime has been committed. After being dispatched to the same apartment unit three or four times in one night, how should an officer resolve the situation? Arrest one or both for public intoxication inside their own residence? Unplug the phone? Continue to return every time they call?

> Officer A goes to a disturbance at a residence. It is his third time there. The problem is the same each time. Father gets drunk, he then tells his son, wife, and kids to leave his home. The son refuses to take his family and leave. The real problem is the father being drunk and stupid, yet the father has a legal right to tell his son's family to leave. What should you do?

Some dilemmas arise because of a personal or professional relationship between the officer and the subject. Typically this involved stopping a speeding car and finding the driver to be another officer or responding to an altercation involving another officer or family member.

> You are on patrol, riding one man, at approx. 10 P.M. You and one other vehicle are stopped at a red light. The light changes and you and the other vehicle start driving. Suddenly you observe the other vehicle weaving from lane to lane. You turn on your lights and siren and after about an eight-block drive the vehicle finally pulls over. You exit your vehicle and find that not only is the driver very intoxicated, but he is also your first cousin. What should you do?

> Working a side job at a nightclub you notice a disturbance on the far side of the club. As you handle the problem, you discover that the instigator of the problem is an off-duty officer, who is extremely intoxicated, and refuses to follow your instructions. Also, the other party involved, who is not an officer, is claiming that the officer assaulted him, although the other party does not know he is an officer.

> Officer A is on patrol. Suddenly he spots a vehicle traveling at a high rate of speed. Officer A stops the vehicle and finds out that the person is a law enforcement officer from a different agency. Officer A observes that he is highly intoxicated. What should he do?

By presenting these as dilemmas, officers indicate that they perceive that special treatment given to other officers is questionable even if they typically defend preferential treatment.

Discussions brought out from dilemmas concerning the use of discretion can be organized around the determination of which criteria may be considered ethical and which have less ethical support in guiding discretion. Because full enforcement is not always considered an option, officers use discretion in their decisionmaking. It is important for them to at least recognize the ethical issues involved in employing that discretion.

DUTY

Duty may involve situations in which there is a real question concerning what the duty of a police officer is in a certain situation. Duty may also involve those situations in which the officer knows that the job requires a particular action, but feels that action is either inconvenient or a waste of time. In the first situation, some of the examples of discretion given above may also apply to duty. For instance, in the case of a family altercation when a police officer responds and finds no crime has been committed, what is his or her duty? Is there or is there not a duty to try to resolve a volatile situation before it erupts into a crime? Some police officers believe they have a duty to help the poor and homeless find shelter, other officers see their job as being free from such responsibilities. This is the type of discussion that inevitably brings out differences of opinion among police officers and is linked to how they view their role in the community. It is also, of course, an ethical issue.

The other type of duty dilemma is more straightforward. Here, the officer knows there is a duty to perform a certain act. A frequent situation was the temptation (and evidently widespread practice) of either driving by an accident scene or avoiding it because it occurs near the end of a shift. There were also dilemmas involving repetitive 911 calls and the temptation to avoid them or respond to them halfheartedly. The following are examples:

> It is 10 minutes to off-duty time. You view an accident. Do you work the accident, even though you want to go home, or do you avoid the accident by sneaking around it?

> It is 10:30 P.M. and you are a late shift unit heading into the station when you notice a large traffic jam. As you near the scene you observe that it is an accident involving two cars and a fixed object. Do you stop and respond, or take the back way to the station?

> You get a disturbance call from the dispatcher at a certain location. You can see the location from inside a building you are in; and see that there is no disturbance at that location. Is it necessary to leave the building to respond to the call?

Another duty dilemma issue arose concerning the risk of contracting AIDS. Finally, there were miscellaneous duty issues, all under the general idea of using regular work hours to conduct personal business.

> You are involved in a situation where someone is injured and is in need of CPR. You know the injured person is a drug addict and a criminal. Do you perform CPR or not?

> To get in service after clearing a call or staying out of service to handle some personal business or affairs.

> An officer works a plainclothes assignment in a division where each squad is small and has its own supervisor. The officer's supervisor is off this day and the likelihood of being noticed leaving early is almost nonexistent. So why not cut out an hour and a half early when it won't be noticed? Your work will not be undone.

Discussion of duty issues in the classroom shows participants that not all police officers view duty in the same way. To move beyond a simple exchange of opinion, it is necessary to apply an ethical framework analysis that helps each officer understand that while his or her position may be justifiable to some extent and legal, it may have less ethical support than other positions.

HONESTY

Under the general heading of honesty, officers submitted dilemmas involving self-protection or enrichment, honesty versus the need to effect an arrest, and bribery. Many participants related dilemmas in which officers are confronted with temptations of money or other goods, typically "found" or at burglary scenes.

> Officer received a call to a robbery and on the way to the call he discovered a brown bag full of money. This officer was alone and no one saw him pick up the bag. The question is what to do with the bag, turn it in or keep it?

> Officer A and B are on the scene of a homicide involving a supposed drug dealer who is lying on the ground dead. No one is present except the officers, who then find $20,000 cash in suspect's pockets. Officer B insists that they should keep and split the money with each other.

> An officer is patrolling through an abandoned apartment complex when he observes a stack of lumber in the back of the complex to be used for remodeling. The officer is working on a project at home and could use a few pieces of the lumber. Nobody else is around. What should he do?

One interesting discussion device is to start with a dilemma using $20 "found" by a police officer and ask what the proper procedure is; then continue the discussion with larger amounts of money. While many officers would feel that it is a minor breach (if any at all) to keep the $20, at some point the amount of "found" money that is kept by the individual becomes perceived as unethical. The issue then becomes "is it the amount or the action" that should determine the ethical nature of the response.

Another type of dilemma involves officers trying to cover up their own wrongdoing by lying or not coming forward when they commit minor acts of wrongdoing. Given the number of dilemmas reported concerning small "fender-benders" with police cars, it may be surmised that the police parking lot is an insurer's nightmare.

> Officer had accident where there was no witnesses. Since it was an auto-fixed object, officer was at fault but he didn't want disciplinary action. The officer was deciding whether or not to suggest another car cut him off to explain how the accident occurred.

In another type of situation, officers must either tell the truth and lose (or risk losing) an arrest, or misrepresent facts to save the arrest. While this is a popular topic in the literature, it was not a frequent dilemma submitted by officers.

> You stop somebody and check his pockets and find some dope. You had no probable cause to search him, but you did anyhow because

> you thought he might be holding. Do you find a reason to arrest
> him and then put in the report that you found the dope after the
> arrest so it won't get thrown out in court?

> Officer A sees a known crack dealer on a corner and searches him.
> He finds drugs, makes arrest, and then lies about or makes up prob-
> able cause for the search in his report and in his courtroom testi-
> mony. Nobody knows but the officer and the suspect. The suspect
> did have the drug, and he is a dealer in that neighborhood.

Bribery is a form of dishonesty that can be discussed under this category of dilemma. It can be defined as some reward for doing something illegal or for not doing something that is required. There were very few submissions from officers dealing with the issue of bribery. It may be that officers do not view it as a dilemma because they seldom receive opportunities, do not want to admit that it occurs, or may not consider it a dilemma because the occupational sub-culture is such that bribe-taking is clearly a serious violation and therefore there is no question as to the response to take when faced with such an opportunity.

> I was offered money for taking care of a ticket. Also offered money
> for giving information about a driver's license or license plate.

LOYALTY

In situations or dilemmas involving loyalty versus whistleblowing, officers must decide what to do when faced with the wrongdoing of other police officers. The literature accurately reflects the saliency of this issue for police officers, given the frequency of this type of submission. Officers' dilemmas ran the gamut from seeing relatively minor wrongdoing (e.g., overtime misuses) to very serious violations (e.g., physical abuse of a suspect or the commission of another crime).

> On a winter afternoon Officers A and B are riding patrol in a rough
> area of town. Officer A spots a possible burglar and stops. After
> a brief chase the suspect is arrested. Officer B uses a little more
> force than necessary. Officer A does not agree, what does he do?

> You are on patrol. Your partner uses more force than you think
> needed when arresting a suspect, and you are asked by the partner
> to lie about how much force was used if asked.

> Whether or not to tell a supervisor of another officer that you see
> verbally or physically abuse a citizen when it's not called for on
> a regular basis.

In fact, the only time abuse of force was mentioned at all was in this category of whether to report a fellow officer who used what was considered to be too much force. The third dilemma above illustrates, however, that the use of appropriate force may be in the eye of the beholder. Is the officer identifying the partner's action as problematic because of its nature, because it is too frequent, or because it is uncalled for? When is it called for? Another set of issues involves observing or believing another officer has committed a crime.

> You are on patrol as you roll up on a possible narcotics transaction involving a known dope dealer. You make the block to set up on the buyer who is in a vehicle. By the time you make the block the buyer is rolling. You go to chase down the buyer and it takes you several blocks to catch up to him. In your mind he is trying to lose you. You manage to catch up to him about a mile away. It turns out the driver is an off-duty sheriff's deputy. What do you do?

> An officer is dispatched as a backup unit where an alarm is going off at a large jewelry store. He insists on doing the report listing items that were taken. A couple of days later you see him wearing items or showing off items he claims to have got a good deal on. These are items you saw in the store burglarized. What should you do?

Finally, there are dilemmas involving actions that may technically be crimes and often pose risks to other officers but are not viewed to be as serious as buying drugs or stealing from the scene of a burglary. Several of these dilemmas again involve minor traffic accidents. Because officers get disciplined for driving errors, it is always a temptation to avoid responsibility.

> You are standing in a parking lot when you notice Officer A backing his car out of his parking space, he hits the car behind him, then drives off. A few seconds later the owner of the car comes out and asks you if you saw what happened. What should you do?

> One day while leaving the parking lot, my partner was driving and accidentally damaged a new patrol car which was parked next to us. We both got out of our patrol vehicle and observed the minor damage to the new vehicle. We both looked around but did not notice anyone else near. My partner told me he would report it to the sergeant at the end of the shift. However, the next day at roll call, the roll call sergeant asked if anyone knew how the new patrol car received the damage.

> Officer A sleeps on duty and doesn't run his calls. What should I (his partner) do?

> Officer A was an alcoholic and consumed alcohol very heavily on a day-to-day basis. Even while on duty, A was highly intoxicated. Joe Blow, a concerned citizen, who owned a liquor store in the beat, knew of A's situation and decided to call Officer B and advised him to talk to A about the problem before it gets out of hand. What should B do?

Because covering up for another officer is more risky now with the possibility of individual civil liability, it may be that fewer officers are willing to draw the "blue curtain." However, it is important to distinguish between reporting on a fellow officer because he or she did something wrong and telling the truth is the right thing to do, and coming forward or telling the truth in an official investigation in order to avoid being disciplined.

GRATUITIES

The subject of gratuities does not emerge as an issue during the exercise involving the Code of Ethics; however, it is a subject that is hard to ignore in any law enforcement ethics class. It is represented in the policing literature and identified by laypersons as a perennial problem among police (e.g., the infamous donut shop). Officers themselves often feel that there is nothing wrong with gratuities. One distinction that can be made in these dilemmas is between situations involving true gratuities (i.e., something given to all police as a policy) and gifts (i.e., something given to an individual in return for a specific action).

> Officer A is new to his beat. Where he worked before, he would stop by a local convenience store and get something to drink and pay for it. He has learned from past experiences that people always expect something in return. In this new beat he stops by the store. The clerk refuses to accept payment. Officer A explains that he would prefer to pay. The clerk, now upset, accuses officer of trying to be better than the others, and will tell his supervisor who also stops by. What does he do?

> Officer A stopped in a store in his beat and was offered anything he wanted in the store within reason: food, cigarettes, Skoal. And the worker offered him lottery tickets, which he may or may not have taken. After several days of going to the store, the worker tells the officer he sometimes has problems and could he give the worker his beeper number to call him if he has problems. The question is should the officer give his beeper number and feel obligated to call this person because he has gotten free articles?

> A guy's car had broken down on the freeway. As an officer on duty, I stopped. I took him home since he only lived a short distance away in my beat. It was early in the morning, and the man was very appreciative. He wanted to buy me breakfast to show his appreciation so he offered me five dollars.

> Officer A is called to a burglar alarm at a Vietnamese business. Officer checks the building and finds that the Vietnamese family lives inside. Officer then checks the inside of the business and finds no sign of forced entry. Officer reassures the Vietnamese family that everything is alright. Vietnamese family then offers officer an envelope filled with unknown amount of cash. What should he do?

Discussion involving the ethics of gratuities can be hampered by defensiveness on the part of police participants, especially if the discussion takes place after lunch and many officers in the classroom have taken advantage of half-price or free meals in nearby restaurants. It is helpful to explore regional differences and clearly discuss definitions (i.e., the difference between gratuities and gifts) and the reason why gratuities to public servants is a problematic issue.

NOW THAT WE HAVE DEFINED THE ISSUES, WHAT DO WE DO WITH THEM?

Descriptions of dilemmas submitted by officers indicate that they may view many relatively mundane issues as problematic. Decisions regarding whether to enforce a warrant or ticket, what to do in a domestic disturbance, and whether to leave early from an assignment are not perceived the same as police brutality or use of deception. Yet, it seems clear that if an ethics course for officers is to be relevant, it should cover these issues as well. The approach one should take in analyzing these dilemmas is up to the individual instructor. What follows is one way to utilize these dilemmas in a classroom.

As discussed previously, any class of police ethics must have a philosophical basis in order to move it beyond a mere "bull" session of opinions. While one may decide to simplify matters and only present one ethical framework, such as utilitarianism, and then use it to analyze ethical dilemmas, another approach may be to compare several ethical frameworks, such as utilitarianism, ethical formalism, and religion.

After dilemmas are submitted, it is useful to group them together in some order so that similar dilemmas are discussed together. This exercise is similar to what was done above. One benefit of this approach is that officers realize they have similar concerns. The anonymity of the method ensures that officers have the opportunity to honestly address and describe the dilemmas they feel are most prevalent and important.

The first form of analysis is to determine at what level there is disagreement. One might ask the following questions: What does the law require? What does departmental policy require? What do personal ethics require? Interestingly, there is often heated discussion regarding legal definitions and policy mandates. This is why some ethics classes become training courses in such things as domestic violence laws and victim rights legislation. There may be agreement on whether there is an applicable law but disagreement on departmental policy. There may be agreement on law and policy but not on an ethical analysis. If there is an applicable law or policy and there is still an ethical concern whether to follow such law or policy, the issue of civil disobedience and duty becomes relevant. Can an officer be considered ethical if he or she follows a personal code of ethics that is contrary to a departmental directive? What if the departmental directive has no support from any ethical system? These are sensitive and important issues.

If there is no applicable law or departmental policy, then the discussion can quickly be directed to an ethical analysis of possible solutions. The instructor can direct discussion in at least two ways. First, participants can be assigned to groups and provided an ethical framework. Then group members can determine a solution that is justified by the ethical framework (i.e., utilitarianism, ethical formalism, ethics of care, etc.). Obviously, there has to be a basic understanding of these frameworks and it may be necessary to provide the groups with a quick review of previously presented material. Another approach is to ask the class what is the best solution to the dilemma and then analyze that solution using the ethical framework. For example, one of the previous dilemmas states:

> Officer received a call regarding a business holding a shoplifter. A 75-year-old female was being held for shoplifting needed medications. However, the store insisted on filing charges on her.

The first set of questions reveals the following. Is there an applicable law? Yes, and the woman obviously broke it. Is there an applicable departmental policy? Obviously, the departmental policy would be to enforce the law, especially if there is a complainant wanting to press charges. Does this resolve the dilemma? For some officers it does. Some officers believe that their duty is to enforce the law, not mediate it. Therefore, in this situation, they merely respond to the event by enforcing the law. Other officers, however, would respond by saying there is still an ethical issue. It is these officers who identify this situation as a dilemma. Their solution may be to try to convince the store owner to drop charges, perhaps even going so far as to pay for the items themselves. Is this their duty? There is obviously no professional duty that dictates such action, but some believe that personal ethics require a more complete response to the situation than merely acting as an agent of the law. The ethical frameworks are now applied to the possible solutions. Utilitarianism would be concerned with the relative costs and benefits of arrest versus some type of intervention. Ethical formalism would be concerned with duties. Ethics of care would focus on need (see Pollock, 1994, for a more complete discussion of some of these applications).

Another dilemma presented previously was the following:

> Officer A was an alcoholic and consumed alcohol very heavily on a day to day basis. Even while on duty A was highly intoxicated. Joe Blow, a concerned citizen, who owned a liquor store in the beat, knew of A's situation and decided to call Officer B and advised him to talk to A about the problem before it gets out of hand. What should B do?

Again, the first question is: Is there an applicable law? Public intoxication laws may be applicable. There certainly is an applicable departmental policy and a violation. What is the ethical issue? Personal loyalty versus whistleblowing. The appropriate solution for any individual officer may be discussed in terms of his or her own value system. Some officers place a higher value on loyalty than any other value, including integrity. Most balance loyalty against the severity of the wrongdoing. Alcohol use is considered less serious than illegal drug use. More officers would take action against an officer using illegal drugs than one abusing alcohol, despite the fact that the resultant effects on the officer may be similar. A discussion concerning this dilemma often involves the perceived unfairness of an administrative response. For example, while other types of professionals may be censured for alcohol problems, police officers often lose their jobs and their career. This can be tied in to an application of utilitarianism. What are the relative costs and benefits associated with turning the officer in, talking to the officer or doing nothing? An application of ethical formalism would be concerned with the duty of the officer with knowledge of the problem. (See Cohen and Feldberg, 1991, for a more complete discussion of similar issues.)

Such discussion will hopefully show that some decisions have little or no ethical rationale. In addition, some rationales for actions can only be described as egoist or primarily self-serving. Officers are seldom forced to present ethical rationales for their decisions. Some do not like the experience. Yet others have indicated that all police officers could benefit from such an experience and it "reminds them of why they entered the law enforcement profession in the first place."

CONCLUSION

This chapter presented the premise that the best ethics course for police officers is one that is relevant to them. One way to achieve that is to utilize their own dilemmas in guiding the discussion of ethics. Most of these problems fall into particular types of categories. The frequency of examples concerning more mundane issues indicates that the literature on police ethics may have missed some important, albeit less "juicy," issues of police ethics. Such dilemmas as what to do with an elderly shoplifter, whether to enforce an outstanding warrant for a poor mother, or whether to report a minor fender-bender during a shift may not be the stuff of "Dirty Harry" movies, but they are experienced by many police officers nonetheless. The method of analysis presented can be utilized for various types of ethical dilemmas, and the benefit of such analysis is that it gives police officers the tools to identify and resolve their own ethical dilemmas.

REFERENCES

Barker, T. (1994a). "Peer Group Support for Police Occupational Deviance." In T. Barker and D. Carter (eds.), *Police Deviance,* 3rd ed. Cincinnati: Anderson, pp. 45-57.

Barker, T. (1994b). "A Typology of Police Deviance." In T. Barker and D. Carter (eds.), *Police Deviance,* 3rd ed. Cincinnati: Anderson, pp. 3-12.

Barker, T. (1978). "An Empirical Study of Police Deviance Other Than Corruption." *Journal of Police Science and Administration*, 6(3):264-272.

Barker, T. & D. Carter (1994). *Police Deviance,* 3rd ed. Cincinnati: Anderson.

Canons of Police Ethics (1992). International Association of Chiefs of Police, Arlington, VA.

Carter, D. (1994). "Theoretical Dimensions in the Abuse of Authority by Police Officers." In T. Barker and D. Carter (eds.), *Police Deviance,* 3rd ed. Cincinnati: Anderson, pp. 269-290.

Carter, D. & D. Stephens (1994). "Police Ethics, Integrity, and Off-Duty Behavior: Policy Issues of Officer Conduct." In T. Barker & D. Carter (eds.), *Police Deviance,* 3rd ed. Cincinnati: Anderson, pp. 29-44.

Cohen, H. (1985). "A Dilemma for Discretion." In W. Heffernan & T. Stroup (eds.), *Police Ethics: Hard Choices in Law Enforcement*. New York: John Jay Press, pp. 69-82.

Cohen, H. & M. Feldberg (1991). *Power and Restraint: The Moral Dimension of Police Work.* New York: Praeger Press.

Delaney, H.R. (1990). "Toward a Police Professional Ethic." In F. Schmalleger (ed.), *Ethics in Criminal Justice: A Justice Professional Reader*. Bristol, IN: Wyndham Hall Press, pp. 78-94.

Delattre, E.J. (1989). *Character and Cops: Ethics in Policing.* Lanham, MD: AEI Press.

Doyle, J. (1985). "Police Discretion, Legality, and Morality." In W. Heffernan and T. Stroup (eds.), *Police Ethics: Hard Choices in Law Enforcement*. New York: John Jay Press, pp. 47-69.

Heffernan, W. (1985). "The Police and the Rules of Office." In W. Heffernan & T. Stroup (eds.), *Police Ethics: Hard Choices in Law Enforcement*. New York: John Jay Press, pp. 3-25.

Heffernan, W. & T. Stroup (eds.) (1985). *Police Ethics: Hard Choices in Law Enforcement.* New York: John Jay Press.

Kleinig, J. (1990). "Teaching and Learning Police Ethics: Competing and Complementary Approaches." *Journal of Criminal Justice*, 18:1-18.

Metz, H. (1990). "An Ethical Model for Law Enforcement Administrators." In F. Schmalleger (ed.), *Ethics in Criminal Justice: A Justice Professional Reader*. Bristol, IN: Wyndham Hall Press, pp. 95-102.

Pollock, J. (1993). "Ethics and the Criminal Justice Curriculum," *Journal of Criminal Justice Education*, 4(2):377-391.

Pollock, J. (1994). *Ethics in Crime and Justice: Dilemmas and Decisions,* 2nd ed. Belmont, CA: Wadsworth.

Schmalleger, F. (ed.) (1990). *Ethics in Criminal Justice: A Justice Professional Reader*. Bristol, IN: Wyndham Hall Press.

Schmalleger, F. & R. McKenrick (1991). *Criminal Justice Ethics: An Annotated Bibliography*. Westport, CT: Greenwood Press.

Sherman, L. (1982). "Learning Police Ethics." *Criminal Justice Ethics*, 1(1):10-19.

Silvester, D. (1990). "Ethics and Privatization in Criminal Justice: Does Education Have a Role to Play?" *Journal of Criminal Justice*, 18:65-70.

Souryal, S. (2003). *Ethics in Criminal Justice: In Search of the Truth*, 3rd ed. Cincinnati: Anderson.

Souryal, S. & D. Potts (1993). "What Am I Supposed to Fall Back On? Cultural Literacy in Criminal Justice Ethics." *Journal of Criminal Justice Education*, 4:15-41.

Swift, A., J. Houston & R. Anderson (1993). "Cops, Hacks and the Greater Good." Presented at the Academy of Criminal Justice Sciences, Kansas City, MO, March 1993.

Wren, T. (1985). "Whistle-Blowing and Loyalty to One's Friends." In W. Heffernan & T. Stroup (eds.), *Police Ethics: Hard Choices in Law Enforcement*. New York: John Jay Press, pp. 26-46.

DISCUSSION QUESTIONS

1. If you were a police officer, what would you consider to be the five most important elements that should be included in a police code of ethics? List and describe each category.

2. Of all the categories listed in the text—discretion, duty, honesty, and loyalty—which do you think is the most important? Explain your answer. Which do you think is the least important? Explain your answer.

3. What are the dangers of accepting even minor gratuities such as free cups of coffee, discounts, or free tickets to sporting or entertainment events? Can the acceptance of gratuities contribute to more serious problems in policing?

4. To what extent should a police department strive to minimize discretion? How can a department minimize or structure police discretion? Do officers welcome limits on their discretion? Why or why not?

CHAPTER 7

Police Ethics, Legal Proselytism, and the Social Order: Paving the Path to Misconduct

Victor E. Kappeler & Gary W. Potter

Crime, deviance, and unethical conduct can be found within almost every occupation and profession. Just open a newspaper, turn on the television, or listen to the radio and you will be exposed to abundant accounts of misdeeds by political leaders, members of the clergy, people in business, and even college professors. Police are not unique in this sense and it is safe to conclude that virtually every American law enforcement agency has witnessed some form of unethical conduct, corruption, or scandal (Bracey, 1989; Kappeler & Alpert, 1998; Sherman, 1974). It is equally important to recognize that many police officers are honest, hardworking citizens, as are many doctors, stockbrokers, or college professors. Many police officers would never consider taking money in exchange for not enforcing the law or intentionally misusing their legal authority to use force. These same police officers, however, might not think twice about accepting a free cup of coffee, using deception during a criminal investigation, or even falsifying a police report to help ensure that a "dangerous" criminal is taken off the street.

If unethical conduct can be found in every profession, why should be we uniquely concerned with police ethics? The answer to this question is complex. Policing is an occupation that shares many of the characteristics of other occupations (Sherman, 1982), but it also has many unique features. Like the clergy, police officers are charged with responding to citizens in times of need and tragedy. Citizens often come in contact with the police during some

KEY CONCEPTS:

appeals to higher loyalties

collective responsibility

condemnation of the condemners

denial of injury

denial of responsibility

denial of the victim

police use of force

techniques of neutralization

of the most difficult times in their lives. A parent who has lost a child in a car accident, a women seeking help to escape a violent relationship, or an abused child may all find themselves coming into contact with the police. In less dramatic cases, citizens may seek out the police for direction, counseling, or a referral to a social service agency. Citizens are likely to call the police for assistance regardless of whether the matter requires a traditional law enforcement response. In this sense, police, like the clergy, hold positions of public trust and are expected not to take advantage of people in their time of need. Moreover, like teachers, police officers are viewed by some (especially children) as role models. In fact, police go to great lengths to promote themselves as role models, frequently participating in school programs and often sponsoring events for children. Police officers who engage in unethical conduct are surely poor role models and set negative examples for young people. Police are perhaps the most visible living symbol of our government. They represent, both symbolically and literally, our systems of government and justice. The decisions made by police officers affect our perceptions of government and justice.

Society's concern with police ethics and the high standards we expect of police officers cannot be solely explained based on the shared characteristics policing has with other occupations. We must consider the unique occupational features of policing to fully understand the importance of police ethics. The police are vested with both powers and responsibilities that few other occupations are accorded. Unlike governmental bureaucrats, the clergy, or teachers, the police have been given the power to detain and arrest persons, to search and seize property, and to use force (up to and including deadly force) in carrying out legal mandates. These aspects of policing alone may require that police be held to a higher standard of behavior than other citizens in exchange for the enormous powers vested in them. In addition, police have the power to open the gates to the justice system and force people down a path they would not choose for themselves. A police intervention, therefore, can forcefully change the course of a life and interfere with our right to self-determination. These powers vest law enforcement officials with a significant amount of authority that distinguishes them from employees in other occupations.

Police in American society are charged with a complex mission and are accorded extraordinary powers. Society has done this with the expectation that they will fulfill their responsibilities in a fair, impartial, and ethical manner (Kappeler, Sluder & Alpert, 1998). This also means the police may be seen by the public in paradoxical roles. The police are a governmental body whose ultimate mission is to protect the rights and liberties of citizens. This responsibility is paradoxical in two senses. First, unethical police officers represent one of the greatest threats to these same rights and liberties. In other words, police who violate the public trust by engaging in unethical behavior are one of the greatest threats to the protections extended to citizens in a free and democratic society. Unethical conduct by police officers involves a threat to the right to be free from unjust and unwarranted government restrictions and intrusions. Second, many of the coercive authorities we grant the police to accomplish their mission consist of the very behaviors from which we desire protection. Police officers are allowed to use violence to prevent violence, they can take away our freedom to protect freedom, and they can seize property to prosecute property crimes. "Having the authority to be coercive, and the discretionary nature of such authority, creates the potential for corruption and abuse" (Braswell, 2001). In all, policing is fraught with contradiction and ethical dilemmas even before an officer pins on a badge or makes a decision.

THE PATH TO UNETHICAL CONDUCT

The path to many forms of unethical conduct does not begin with actions; rather, it begins with a way of thinking. We may not even be aware that the way we think influences our choices and actions. In a broad sense, the way we view the world, our role, and relationship to it, and how we situate behavior all contribute to the choices we make and the actions we take. Many of the decisions we make are really shaped long before we act upon them by our perception of the world around us. Do we see the world as being composed of good and evil people? Do we see ourselves as a corrective force? Is the world a dangerous and disorderly place? Are we responsible for bringing about safety and order? Do we see the world as full of predators who prey on the weak and powerless? Is our role that of the protector? The answers to these questions, of course, depends on our socialization by parents, friends, and peers; the information we are exposed to by the media, schools, and churches; and our life experiences. To some extent, the way we see the world and our relationship to it influences our decisions—even our choice of occupation. People who become police officers are no exception to these observations.

How the police think about themselves, their occupation, and the world around them sets the stage for unethical conduct. Far too many police officers see the world as a black-and-white morality play. The police often reduce their image of the world to simple snapshots. People are cast into roles as good and evil actors, predators and protectors, the forces of disorder and the ensurers of order. People become defined by their behavior in the moment, not by their history, who they are, or where they have been. In this worldview, behaviors are decontexualized and people are dehumanized as becoming the objects of action with all the shades of gray of social life stripped away.

Police work is also imagined in simplistic terms. The police view of the world is jaded by the perception of policing as the most critical of social functions. In this black-and-white world, police begin to believe and project for the public the image that they are the "thin blue line" that stands between anarchy and order. In this drama, police are constantly faced with danger while they attempt to ferret out evil and bring order to a chaotic world. This view of policing is reinforced by slogans and metaphors like "brave cops on mean streets," "police on the front lines of the war on crime," and "better to be tried by twelve than carried by six." The war for social order is seen by the police as so important that it requires sweeping authority and unlimited discretion to invoke the power of law and, if necessary, the use of deadly force—after all, we *are* at war. A free cup of coffee, a discounted meal, a deception in court, protecting the criminal activities of a useful informant, or turning a blind eye to an intentional push or shove of some "bad guy" all seem trivial matters when you are on the front lines of a war. Likewise, using dirty or unethical means to achieve "good" ends seems a relatively minor concern. Isn't everything fair in love and war?

The vast majority of people who choose policing as a profession view themselves as moral and ethical individuals. People become police officers for an array of personal—and even noble—reasons. As Sherman (1982:51) points out, "Police applicants tend to see police work as an adventure, as a chance to do work out of doors without being cooped up in an office, as a chance to do work that is important for the good of society, and not to be the 'toughest guy on the block.'" This observation is accurate; in fact, young people become police officers for a variety of reasons, ranging from a desire to help and protect people and make a difference in their community, to a response to their personal victimization, to a desire for job security and exciting work, or just to get the "bad guys" off the streets. This does not mean, however, that these desires do not flow from a common way of seeing the world or a simplistic view of police work. Although expressed in a variety of forms, the reasons people become police officers usually flow from a black-and-white construction of the world. After all, from where do we get the notion that policing is an adventurous and exciting profession as opposed to dull and boring work? To the ex-offender seeking job skills, the patient needing surgery, or the person experiencing a life crisis, is policing really more important work than teaching, medicine, or tending souls? Is there really an endless supply of really "evil" people to take off the streets and a shortage of "moral" citizens, or do most of us fall somewhere in between? It is not that the people who go into policing are predisposed to unethical behavior, it is that they are predisposed to missing all of the gray aspects of social life.

As good and moral people, police and those desirous of becoming police officers are compelled to believe in the goodness of maintaining order, the nobility of the occupation, and the fundamental fairness of the law and existing social order. To maintain their self-perception, the police are compelled to view disorder, lawbreaking, and lack of respect for police authority as enemies of a civilized society. "They are thus committed ("because it is right") to maintain their collective face as protectorates of the right and respectable against the wrong and the not-so-respectable . . . . Thus, the moral mandate felt by the police to be their just right as the societal level is translated and transformed into occupational and personal terms" (Van Maanen, 1978:227). For many people, policing is not just what they do; it becomes who they are. Law, authority, order, and the profession become extensions of their moral selves. Challenges to any of these are seen as a personal assault on their morality, integrity, and sense of self.

If law, authority, and order are seen as fostering inequity or injustice, the police self-perception would be tainted and the "goodness" of the profession would be questioned by the public and the police themselves. Police could see themselves no longer as partners in justice and protectors of the good but rather as partners in repression—a role most police neither sought nor would be willing to recognize. A black-and-white view of the goodness of order and law can, in fact, blind police to unethical conduct. Enforcing "slave codes" becomes a means of maintaining order, not a way of supporting a criminal system of agricultural production. Carrying out the legal edicts of an immoral regime, such as that of the Nazis, is viewed as supporting social transformation of a society under the rule of law, not as participation in a holocaust. Arresting labor union agitators and civil rights organizers is seen as an action enhancing the "rule of law" as a mechanism of social change, not as the use of brutal force to maintain exploitation and discrimination. Police who begin to question the goodness of the profession, the equity of law, or the criticality of maintaining the existing social order often flee the occupation for other careers, leaving behind those who have the strongest belief in this black-and-white world of morality. Most certainly, unethical or even corrupt police officers do not get up in the morning, look into the mirror, and say to themselves, "I'm really going to be bad or unethical today." The police construction of the world, the occupation role, and the law itself provide more than ample legitimization for departing from ethical expectations.

LEGALLY PERMISSIBLE BUT UNETHICAL CONDUCT

Almost every criminal justice student has heard a professor remark that law, morality, and ethics are very different things. The law is neither a system of ethics nor a moral orientation; it is a set of formal statements of authority that may or may not be in keeping with ethical principles or moral beliefs. The law may represent little more than the brutal use of state force to maintain injustice. Jim Crow and segregation laws in the South, laws allowing for the detention of immigrants, and laws suppressing the right of political protest and free speech are often little more than bald attempts by the state to maintain power. The law may represent little more than the canonization of economic power, allowing corporate criminals to kill and maim with impunity while only criminalizing the actions of the poor. The law may be ambiguous, badly written, and poorly constructed. The law may be little more than a fraud, such as the Racketeer Influenced Corrupt Organizations (RICO) Act passed by the Nixon administration ostensibly to control organized crime. RICO was used not once by that administration against the mob, but was used repeatedly to attack groups opposing the administration's policies in Vietnam. The law may be inherently discriminatory, such as present laws heavily penalizing the use of crack cocaine by the poor but providing far lesser penalties for the use of cocaine hydrochloride by the rich. The importance of this distinction, however, often vanishes when students leave the academic community and enter the world of policing. The transformation from student to police officer involves extensive indoctrination. This process begins with formal training police receive in the academy.

While many police academies provide new recruits with four or five hours of ethics training, this exposure pales compared to the legal training given. During hundreds of hours of legal training, recruits are exposed to a very rigid way of looking at human behavior and what constitutes right and wrong. Recruits are asked to memorize and parrot back to their trainers the elements of literally hundreds of criminal statutes. Rarely are discussions of the ambiguity of the law, the gray areas of human behavior, or the distinctions between ethics and law ever held in these settings. The law is presented as an unquestionable system of rights and wrongs. In the world of police training, the law is not something to be challenged, it is to be mastered as the foundation for action. During this experience, recruits slowly internalize a simple value system—what is legal is good and what is illegal is bad. People, behavior, and the police role are once again cast into simplistic distinctions between right and wrong.

The formality, precision, and seemingly unambiguous nature of the law is seductive to young scholars and recruits struggling to find their moral place in the world. Recruits learn formal statements of authority that support their black-and-white picture of the world. People become defined by their legal behavior and the difference between good and bad is often as simple as the elements of a crime. Recruits also learn that they have a special place in this system of legal authority and that their actions will be judged not by the ethical nature of the choices they make but rather by the extent to which their actions fall within legal bounds. What is good, what is right, and what is ethical become intertwined with what is legally permissible.

The special legal privileges accorded the police provide unprecedented opportunities to engage in legally legitimated conduct that can be ethically questionable. Police, for example, are granted the authority to use force to accomplish their legal objectives. They are legally justified to use force under certain circumstances. The justification and legal authority to use deadly force may, however, mask an unethical use of force. Police have been known to contrive situations that would allow them to use deadly force when lesser means, or no force at all, could be used to accomplish the same legal objective. Sensational cases such as the Federal Bureau of Investigation's storming of the Branch Davidian's home in Waco and the sniper execution of two unarmed members of the Weaver family at Ruby Ridge come to mind. In both cases, constitutional rights were set aside by members occupying the highest levels of federal government. The legal construction of police use of force neither requires police officers to seek out alternatives to the use of force, nor does it recognize the officer's motives for using force as a factor in determining whether a use of force is legally reasonable. Likewise, the government sets aside its own legal rules when it becomes politically inconvenient. In this sense, an unethical use of force can be perfectly legal and considered a "just" or even "righteous" use of force.

The use of the "law" in narcotics investigations provides a similar example. The activities of one drug dealer may be deemed sufficiently reprehensible to allow police to pursue him or her with vigor, often protecting other drug dealers who provide information or facilitate arrests in the process. In this case, the police make a legal decision to grant a crime-committing license to some in order to "get" others. Police frequently construct informant relationships with fences in order to get information on specific thefts, or on the flow of money through the criminal underworld. Here, again, some people are permitted to violate the law to enhance enforcement of the law.

Not long after graduating from the police academy, officers learn that the law is not just a statement of authority that restricts behaviors, but that it can be used to make progress in the war against crime. The law is often written and can be interpreted in ways that give the police sufficient latitude to engage in unethical conduct in their pursuit of their crime control objective. Richard Ericson (1981:91) has noted in this respect that "substantive laws are written broadly enough, and with sufficient ambiguity, that they can be applied across a range of circumstances. Causing a disturbance, a breach of the peace, obstructing police, and many others serve as a pretext for making the arrest." Because of the ambiguity in criminal law and the police situational interpretation of these legal mandates, the law itself contributes to unethical conduct. Ericson's discussion of the legal discretion available to police illustrates how the police can use the law as a tool that facilitates achievement of enforcement objectives rather than as a guide to how those objectives are to be achieved. The structure of the law itself allows for an ends-over-means justification of police misconduct.

In short, manipulation and the situational application of the law to achieve enforcement objectives are often seen as acceptable (or even masterful) police work rather than unethical conduct. For example, identical legal infractions—such as two traffic violations—can result in different outcomes depending not on the violation but on the motives of the police. First, police can merely release the citizen with no more than a verbal warning—there is no legal mandate that the police enforce all minor infractions of the law. Second, the police employ the force of law by issuing a citation or summons for the violation. Third, if police feel that the citizen fits the "mold" or "profile" of one in need of state control, the citizen may be arrested. Fourth, the police may arrest the citizen for the sole purpose of searching the vehicle for criminal evidence. Because the law does not recognize the motives of the officer, and considers only the initial violation, the officer has acted in a legally permissible fashion. Racism, sexism, retribution, or a desire to skirt the Fourth Amendment are all washed away with the "good arrest." Examples of unethical but legally permissible police behavior abound. They can range from stacking or jacking-up charges against citizens for purposes of coercion to contriving situations that allow officers to use deadly force (Kappeler, Sluder & Alpert, 1998).

SOCIALLY SITUATING UNETHICAL BEHAVIOR

Living and working in the world of policing provides officers with the ability to rationalize, excuse, and justify unethical behavior while maintaining a moral self-image. The police occupation provides its members with a handy conceptual tool box that allows officers to engage in unethical behavior without suffering the cognitive dissonance and social stigma normally associated with wrongdoing. Police are, in essence, prepared to act unethically because of their worldview, the way police work is legally and perceptually framed, and the manner in which their actions are socially situated.

Although the police may view themselves as moral agents in a dangerous world full of evil people, they must first frame the use of force as a viable response to citizens and as an effective means of crime control before it can become a course of action. Whether this perceptual frame is expressed or experienced intuitively or learned as legal doctrine, it prepares police to use force. A perceptual frame begins to take shape and become a reality when an "event" unfolds, falls within the pre-established frame, and is incorporated into an actor's collective experience. Our perceptual frames are reinforced and strengthened as events meet our expectations. Events become factors that help interpret future events and courses of action. As Harold Garfinkel (1967:113) instructs, "It consists of the possibility that the person defines retrospectively the decisions that have been made . . . in order to give their decisions some order, . . . "officialness," or justification.

Sykes and Matza's (1957) theory on the techniques of neutralization used by juveniles to explain their delinquency is particularly instructive for understanding how police officers draw upon preconstructed frames of reference to excuse, justify, and rationalize a variety of unethical behaviors. Sykes and Matza theorized that delinquents use techniques of neutralization that allow them to maintain a positive self-image even though they have engaged in wrongdoing. These techniques included: denial of responsibility, denial of injury, denial of the victim, condemnation of condemners, and appeals to higher loyalties.

Denial of responsibility prepares police for unethical conduct and provides a justification following the commission of an unethical act. Denial of responsibility is the belief that the potential or real injury caused by conduct is "due to forces outside the individual and beyond his control . . . ." (Sykes & Matza, 1957:667). Police rationalize their conduct by viewing themselves as little more than "billiard balls on a pool table" rebounding from external influences. Police see themselves as being buffeted back and forth between administrative policies and political decisions made at headquarters by administrators who no longer understand the "reality of the streets," by citizen calls and complaints identifying specific criminal actions to be investigated and acted upon, and by a pervasive panorama of criminality that they see and feel all around them. They are following orders, serving the public, or making their own choices about who is worse among an endless sea of the bad and law-breaking. Political pressures may have them arresting drunk drivers one week, prostitutes the next, and crack dealers the next. They are simply responding to pressures beyond their control and to the actions of a seemingly endless number of miscreants who could have chosen not to be criminal. From this frame of reference, police officers view their actions as predetermined by criminals, events, and situations that they cannot influence or control.

The training police receive in the use-of-force continuum is a good example of how police officers are socialized into viewing themselves as passive actors who are merely responding to the provocative behaviors of citizens. In this training, police are instructed that their use of force is always a response to a citizen's behavior—whether verbal or physical. Police are instructed that when a citizen takes an aggressive action, the officer is to respond to that action with a higher level of force than that of the citizen. No allowance is made for the ambiguity of the situation or the law, for the ability of the citizen to understand or respond, or for the simple human emotions that the citizen may feel. At each stage of action, the police officer moves up the continuum until the citizen's action is halted. This construction of police use of force assumes that police are merely responding to citizens' behaviors and that police action, verbalization, and demeanor have no contribution to the citizen's behavior. Accordingly, police officers are not responsible for their contribution to the situation or their forced response. Defiant citizens are viewed from this frame as provocateurs in need of police control. When police use violence or an unethical application of law, they are merely responding to the provocation of citizens, situations, and events over which they have little or no control and for which they are not responsible regardless of their own contributions to the situation or their departure from ethical principles.

Denial of responsibility provides police with an after-the-fact justification for their abuse of authority. Police who engage in brutal assaults on citizens often allege that they were forced into it because there was no alternative course of action or that it was expedient—the citizen or situation "forced their hand." Waco and Ruby Ridge are two classic examples of the police being "forced" into violence when simply waiting might have resulted in different outcomes. These force choices, however, are constructed by the manner in which police work and the use of force have been constructed. "Never back down," "no duty to retreat," and "no legal obligation to seek out alternatives to the use of force" construct for the police their thinking. By offering these excuses, police can violate ethics while maintaining an ethical self-image. Police can make the legal choice to enforce the requirements of a minor municipal ordinance, such as those governing parades and demonstrations, vigorously and violently while ignoring the overarching reasons for that demonstration. Police in Birmingham, Alabama, can turn dogs and fire hoses on peaceful demonstrators whose only crime is not having a permit while ignoring segregation and racism. Police in Chicago can riot against antiwar demonstrators who have no permit to be in a park after dark while ignoring the immorality of a war. Police can enforce loitering laws against prostitutes while never questioning the social and economic arrangements of a sexist and patriarchal society that makes prostitution a viable alternative for many women. "By learning to view himself as more acted upon than acting," an officer "prepares the way for deviance from the dominant normative system without the necessity of a frontal assault on the norms themselves" (Sykes & Matza, 1957:667). Police are able to sidestep their ethical violations by shifting responsibility to victims and invoking their legal authority and training as the basis for self-evaluation.

Denial of injury is a technique of neutralization that provides police with a host of justifications for their unethical acts. Because many police breaches of ethics do not involve the direct physical injury of a citizen or seem of little consequence to police, they are free to pursue them. From this frame, "wrongfulness may turn on the question of whether or not anyone has clearly been hurt by his deviance, and this matter is open to a variety of interpretations" (Sykes & Matza, 1957:667). Denial of injury occurs when police steal evidence from suspects, when they violate civil rights to make arrests or get convictions, and when they abuse their authority to establish or maintain their personal sense of order. Planting evidence on a suspected drug dealer, committing perjury to justify an illegal search, and harassing prostitutes are all seen to have no deleterious impacts either to the individual or to the rule of law. Changing reports and rehearsing testimony to iron out contradictions and in the end change the facts are all acceptable procedures in prosecuting a war on crime. The police can employ this technique to maintain that the suspect should not have had contraband in the first place, the citizen was a criminal deserving of something less that the full protection of civil rights, or the juvenile had to be "moved along" to prevent crime and ensure order.

For police, the theft of property from a suspect can be socially situated as "confiscation." The padding of overtime records can be viewed as "just compensation" for someone on the front lines of the war on crime. Perjury is just "embellishing" the facts or recalling previously forgotten information to convict someone who is "guilty anyway" and needs to be taken off the street.

Denial of the victim is not the assertion that victims do not exist but rather a characterization of victims and victimization in an attempt to justify unethical behavior. Sykes and Matza explain that "the moral indignation of self and others may be neutralized by an insistence that the injury is not wrong in light of the circumstances. The injury, it may be claimed, is really not an injury; rather, it is a form of retaliation or punishment" (Sykes & Matza, 1957:668). This technique of neutralization provides police with viable targets for victimization by characterizing certain individuals and situations so that police misconduct is seemingly justified given the imputed character of the target and the interpretation of the circumstances. Socially situating people into good and evil, dangerous and friendly, deserving and not so deserving, allows those people to become acceptable victims. For example, consider a situation in which a traffic violator decides to run from the police. The offender and situation can be viewed in several different ways. The officer can perceive the situation as consisting of a relatively minor violation of the law—someone has committed a traffic offense and has overreacted by selecting a very poor course of action. Alternatively, the officer may define the citizen as a dangerous fleeing felon who has taken a drastic and hazardous course of action. Depending on perception and definition, the citizen may be seen as deserving a little more of the full force of law. In these situations, police are prone to exact a pound of flesh. In other words, police reason away their use of force as the justifiable punishment of people deserving of such treatment. In essence, the officer "moves himself into the position of an avenger and the victim is transformed into a wrongdoer . . . To deny the existence of the victim, then by transforming him into a person deserving injury. . ." is to recognize "appropriate and inappropriate targets" for victimization (Sykes & Matza, 1957:668). Denial of the victim also invokes a kind of legitimated prejudice for police. The poor, young, minority-group drug dealer is seen as being less worthy than the drunk-driving middle-class executive. No consideration is made for the family of the drug dealer. No consideration of who will pay the rent, who will buy the food, or who will provide for the children is necessitated by the law. However, the impact of an arrest on the social status of the middle-class drunk driver often allows for a greater and more humane exercise of discretion. It is all legal; it is all justified in the black-and-white world of order maintenance. This pattern repeats itself often in policing. The middle-class housewife victimized by a confidence game is more deserving of protection than the prostitute raped by her john. The middle-class juvenile is more likely to "get help" and straighten out his or her life than the impoverished teen who must be arrested and detained to protect society.

Police often invoke what Sykes and Matza (1957:668) have characterized as the technique of *condemning the condemners*. This technique involves a reaction to the detection of unethical conduct and a response to those who either allege or sanction it. By employing this technique, the police officer "shifts the focus of attention from his own deviant acts to the motives and behaviors of those who disapprove of his violation. His condemners, he may claim are hypocrites, deviants in disguise, or impelled by personal spite" (Sykes & Matza, 1957:668). Police condemn the edicts of external examiners when they conflict with their frames of reference by imputing motive on those justice personnel who attempt to curtail police autonomy, authority, and wrongdoing. The exclusionary rule is used by lawyers who are just out to "make a buck." Those who developed this rule did so just to provide a "loop hole" for criminals and make it more difficult for the police to make progress in the crime war. Criminal charges brought by the police against citizens are reduced in plea bargaining arrangements because judges and prosecutors are "soft on crime." The goodness of the legal code remains, but the actors and the legal process have become corrupted. A second form this technique takes is a condemnation of those people who bring charges of misconduct against the police. Citizens who bring complaints against the police are merely "hostile" toward law enforcement, "resentful" for being ticketed or arrested, or are merely "money-grubbing" individuals out to make a "quick buck" by filing a lawsuit against the police. Certainly, evil people would have no problem with making these unfounded claims. A third use of this technique is to condemn those persons who pass judgment on police conduct. When police officers are convicted of crimes or held liable in civil proceedings, the condemners of police are often characterized as unable to understand the "realities" of police work or the "dangerousness" of criminals. To the police, these people are merely "armchair quarterbacks" who use 20/20 hindsight to pass judgment on actions they do not understand.

As with the other techniques of neutralization, condemning the condemners serves to prepare the police for exploits by predetermining that the legal rules of police conduct, those who may allege misconduct, and those who may be called upon to sanction misconduct are themselves unjust, corrupt, deviant, or ignorant. Through condemnation, police sever the link between their potential courses of action and the negative stigma of unethical conduct. Police reject the exclusionary rule before its application, thus freeing themselves to collect evidence in an illegal manner; they reject allegations of police wrongdoing by citizens by attributing them to resentment and hostility; and they reject challenges to their authority and autonomy by condemning those who pass judgment on them. Police can therefore deviate with a steadfast belief that they are righteous in their actions, even if such actions involve "bending," "sidestepping," or "twisting" ethics.

Police *appeal to higher loyalties* is perhaps the most powerful technique of neutralization used by police. More than any other, this technique allows police to break the bonds of ethical behavior. In Sykes and Matza's (1957:669) words, "internal and external social controls may be neutralized by sacrificing the demands of the larger society for the demands of the smaller social group. . . ." Applied to police, this means that officers may be forced to choose between the sanctions that are associated with violating or adhering to one or another set of values. For example, a police officer who sees her partner brutalize a citizen may be called upon to give testimony. The officer is forced to make a decision between committing perjury (so as not to implicate her partner) or adhering to the police code of secrecy that prohibits "giving up" another cop. The officer can testify that she either saw nothing or that the partner did not engage in brutality, in so doing escaping the sanction of peers but running the risk of being charged with perjury. One might suspect that this is a wrenching decision. The officer must protect her partner but do so in a manner that preserves a law-abiding and conformist self-image. Quite the contrary, though, this decision is often relatively easy. Protecting a fellow officer is expected and even considered noble rather than criminal. The officer who commits perjury to protect a fellow officer has demonstrated loyalty and solidarity to the group by placing himself or herself in harm's way. After all, who is deserving of protection, the police officer on the frontlines of the crime war or the criminal? As Sykes and Matza (1957:669) note, "the most important point is that deviation from certain norms may occur not because the norms are rejected but because other norms, held to be more pressing or involving a higher loyalty, are accorded precedence."

COLLECTIVE RESPONSIBILITY FOR UNETHICAL POLICE CONDUCT

It is not just the police whose black-and-white view of the world makes this ethical quagmire inevitable. The entertainment media contribute with their fictional views of good and evil. There is little ambiguity in police dramas on television. The police are always seen as good, effective, and successful. They must overcome the legal protections provided to citizens, and they must circumvent bureaucratic and administrative controls. The inherent "badness" of the suspect is not mitigated by social concerns or economic circumstances. Television criminals rarely have low IQs that make it impossible for them to understand the law. Television criminals rarely act out of fear, anger, or desperation; instead, they plan and connive to achieve their ends. The news media is not much better. The view of police under siege, the view of police being outgunned and overwhelmed, the view of police as holding back a tide of criminality—all are standard news magazine fare. Politicians also contribute to this worldview. All politicians are anti-crime, pro-police, law-and-order activists. The poor, who bear the brunt of the criminal laws passed by politicians, neither vote in sufficient numbers nor make sufficiently attractive political contributions to gain any consideration in the criminalization process.

Crime becomes a societal passion play, but a very disturbing one when viewed closely. As we watch this black-and-white world portrayed on television and in the newspapers, nagging questions emerge—questions that are all but ignored by the legal orientation of policing. For example, is it really a war on crime we are fighting or is it a war on troublesome and unsettling people? How many mentally ill individuals denied care by this society have become criminal problems? How do we explain the fact that 15 percent of all illegal drug users in this society are black, while 45 percent of all those arrested for drugs and portrayed on the television news as drug dealers are black? Is it law that we are enforcing or is a system of legalized apartheid? And how do we judge the police who enforce those laws in either an ethical or unethical manner? Do we judge them on the basis of narrow legal definitions that protect injustice and promote unethical conduct or on the basis of the social consequences of their actions?

REFERENCES

Bracey, D.H. (1989). "Police Corruption." In Bailey, W.G. (ed.), *The Encyclopedia of Police Science*. New York: Garland.

Braswell, M. (2005), Chapter 1, this volume.

Garfinkel, H. (1967). *Studies in Ethnomethodology*. Englewood Cliffs, NJ: Prentice Hall.

Kappeler, V.E., R.D. Sluder & G.P. Alpert (1998). *Forces of Deviance: Understanding the Dark Side of the Force*, 2nd ed. Prospect Heights, IL: Waveland.

Sherman, L.W. (1974). *Police Corruption: A Sociological Perspective*. Garden City, NY: Anchor.

Sherman L.W. (1982). "Learning Police Ethics." *Criminal Justice Ethics*, 1(1):10-19.

Sykes, G. M., & D. Matza (1957). "Techniques of Neutralization." *American Sociological Review*, 22:664-670.

Van Maanen, J. (1978). "The Asshole." In Manning, P.K. & J. Van Maanen (eds.), *Policing: A View from the Street*. Santa Monica, CA: Goodyear.

DISCUSSION QUESTIONS

1. In preparing for criminal trial, police are frequently interviewed and rehearsed by prosecutors. Words, phrases, and recollections that might lead to troublesome cross-examination are excised, and other terminologies more favorable to the prosecution are substituted. Potential police witnesses are warned about inconsistencies and incongruities in their testimony and reports. In the end, the actual content of the officer's sworn testimony may be substantially changed from his or her original recollection. Is this legal? Is this ethical? When does the rehearsal and preparation of a witness so substantially change the way an incident is portrayed that it becomes perjury?

2. It is common practice in narcotics units to cultivate informants, usually drug dealers or drug users. Information provided to the police by these informants may result in the arrest of other dealers or users. Virtual immunity is often granted to those who cooperate with the police. Where are the ethical lines to be drawn in this arrangement?

3. "Street justice" is a term frequently employed by the police to justify the use of physical force against suspects. "Street justice" is seen as a symbol, a warning, a caution to others that both enhances social control and in some instances protects the police from potential acts of violence. Fre-

quently, these beatings are "legal" in the sense that a narrow legal justification may exist for the incident. Is being legal a sufficient justification? Are such beatings ethical?

4. Should police in slave-holding states have enforced slave codes that required them to track down and return runaway slaves? Should police in Nazi Germany have enforced laws displacing and confiscating the property of jews? Should police enforce laws they know to be unjust and immoral just because they are the law?

5. Do all police officers, regardless of their worldview, have an ethical obligation to report the corruption, brutality, and misconduct of other police officers? If a police officer does not report such illegal conduct, is there any real difference between that officer and other criminals?

Case Study 7–1

Honor Thy Father and Mother

As you park your cruiser next to the curb on Meadowview Street you dance at your watch . . . just about the time you should be going on that coffee break you planned two hours ago. However, two traffic accidents and a drunk'en bar patron later, you still haven't managed to get the caffeine "boost" you've come to rely on for the night shift

You can clearly see a portly woman who looks to be m her fifties standing anxiously in her driveway awaiting your arrival. She must be Mrs. Simms, who called 911. Leaving your cruiser, you introduce yourself.

"Ma'am, I'm Officer Smith. What seems to be the problem?" The woman who is obviously quite anxious, replies in a loud whisper as she looks over her right shoulder at the house next to hers.

"Officer, I'm really scared for my neighbors, the McGillicutys. Ned is in his eighties and his wife, Mildred, is in her late seventies. I heard her scream several times tonight after dinner. My husband told me it was none of our business and maybe he's right . . . but I just can't live with myself if I stand by any longer and let it continue." Mrs. Simms begins to cry softly.

Patiently, you respond, "Let what continue, Mrs. Simms?"

"The beatings," she replies in a choked voice.

After another five minutes of conversation with Mrs. Simms, you have a pretty good picture of what is going on. The McGillicutys had moved in with their divorced son, in his mid-forties, apparently at his request. Mr. McGillicuty had not fully recovered from a stroke six months ago and was,

From Larry S. Miller and Michael Braswell, *Human Relations and Police Work,* 4th ed. (Prospect Heights, IL: Waveland Press), 1997. Reprinted with permission.

for the most part, bedridden. The son Bob had begun to drink heavily. For the last two months, according to Mrs. Simms, he had been progressively abusing his parents, particularly his mother.

You radio in the information to headquarters and are advised that the dispatcher is contacting the state department of social services. A few minutes later, the dispatcher advises that an APS worker is en route to meet you at the McGillicutys' residence, APS, or Adult Protective Services, is a unit similar to Child Protective Services but with a focus on the needs of the elderly and elderly abuse.

You park your cruiser in front of the McGillicutys' house and wait for the arrival of the social worker. While waiting, you notice someone peering out the window of the McGillicutys' house. About twenty minutes later, a car with the familiar state emblem on the door pulls in behind your cruiser.

"Hi, I'm Ann Sheridan with APS."

"Ben Smith. You on call tonight?" you ask, while shaking Ann's hand.

"Yeah, my turn. The dispatcher said you might have an abused elderly woman here?"

You explain what the neighbor had told you as both you and Ann walk to the front entrance to the McGillicutys' house. After you have knocked repeatedly, the front door finally opens, revealing a frightened, elderly woman. There is a large red welt under her left eye, and she is gingerly holding her right wrist.

"Mrs. McGillicuty, I'm Officer Ben Smith and this is Social Services Counselor Ann Sheridan. We understand that you might be in need of assistance."

"Oh, no. Officer," Mrs. McGillicuty replies quickly, "I fell down the basement stairs, but I will be all right. I do appreciate your concern . . ."

You hear her words, but her look tells you much more. You have seen that look too many times. It was the same blank, hidden stare of fear and pain you had seen on the faces of many battered children and women. Before you have a chance to say anything else, a belligerent voice bellows, "Who the hell is at the door?"

From the kitchen emerges a middle-aged man who appears to be over six feet tall and weighing about 230 pounds. He has a partially empty beer bottle in his hand and walks with some degree of unsteadiness. You and Ann take advantage of the moment's confusion and step inside the front door to get a better look inside. The interior of the house is unkempt. Old newspapers are spread around the floor and empty beer bottles indicate that serious problems exist in the McGillicuty family. The son. Bob, addresses you and Ann. "We didn't call for the police. Everything is fine here. I bet it was that nosey neighbor, Mrs. Simms. Hey, you want a cold beer, officer? How about you, honey?"

As the son rambles on, you notice Mrs. McGillicuty hanging on her son's every word. When he finishes his beer and his "everything is fine" speech, his mother quickly backs up everything he had said.

"How is Mr. McGillicuty doing?" You interject.

"He's fine," the son quickly replies.

"Mind if we take a look?" Ann asks.

"Sure, go ahead," Bob replied, "I think I'll get me another beer. Sure you two don't want one?"

"No thanks," you and Ann simultaneously reply as you follow Mrs. McGillicuty to the father's room.

When you enter the bedroom, the stench is almost unbearable, although it doesn't seem to affect Mrs. McGillicuty. Mr. McGillicuty's eyes are closed. He looks like he is in a coma. From the light of the bedside lamp, you can see that he and his bed need changing. You are thinking to yourself, "At least the old fellow doesn't know what's happening," when upon closer inspection you notice a single tear running down his left cheek. Ann takes out a small camera from her purse and tries to inconspicuously take a few photos.

Mrs. McGillicuty tugs on your sleeve and implores you not to report what you have seen.

"Officer Smith, please don't get the wrong impression. Bob isn't a bad boy. He's our only son and we love him. With his delicate emotional balance, any more problems could push him over the edge. He doesn't mean to be rude on occasion, but it's just his nature. I just wish I could be a better mother. If anything ever happened to him, I just don't know what we'd do . . .," she says, her voice trailing off in a muffled sob.

You and Ann return to the living room and find Bob sitting in a recliner, smoking a cigarette and holding a fresh beer. "Bob, how'd your mother get that bruise on her face and hurt her wrist?" Ann asks.

"What did she tell you?" Bob responds.

"She said she fell down the stairs. Doesn't look like the kind of bruises one would get from falling down stairs though, does it?" Ann replies.

"Of course she fell. Hell, she's old. She bruises easily. You fell, didn't you, mommy?" Bob asks in a sarcastic manner.

Mrs. McGillicuty nods her head nervously.

You look at Ann and can see the frustration in her face. You know that had these two people been children, you could take immediate legal action. Unfortunately, child protection laws and spousal abuse laws do not pertain to elderly abuse.

"Ben, I might be able to get a court order on Mr. McGillicuty and have him committed to the state as an incompetent. I might even be able to get home health services out here for him. But I'm concerned more for Mrs. McGillicuty. Unless she wants to press charges on abuse, we can't do anything," Ann whispers to you.

Ann says her goodbyes and leaves to file her report. You stay behind to have a final word with Bob and Mrs. McGillicuty. You make it clear that you will be checking on them from time to time. Walking to your cruiser, you feel a knot in your stomach. "Those people don't deserve a son like that." Muttering to yourself, you start your cruiser; it's time for that coffee.

Questions

1. What are the laws in your state pertaining to protection of the elderly and elder abuse? Do Ben and Ann have a moral as well as legal obligation in this case?

2. What about the feelings and wishes of the elderly parents? Are they still responsible for their adult son even if he neglects and abuses them?

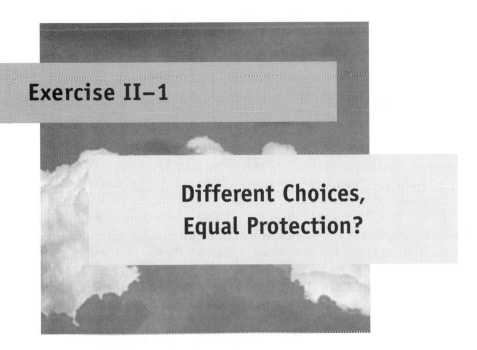

Exercise II–1

Different Choices, Equal Protection?

"You folks need to settle your differences and get along," Sergeant Waddell mumbles as he leaves the apartment with you trailing behind him. The sergeant, a 30-year veteran, switches on the ignition of the cruiser and continues, half-talking to you and half-talking to himself.

"I don't know what the world's coming to! Two men living together like that. It just ain't natural. It's tough enough dealing with the Saturday night husband-and-wife drunks without having to try and calm down the likes of them. They like to call themselves gay, but from the looks of that smaller one, it don't look like he was having too gay of a time! Looked like the bigger feller whipped up on him. Besides, with him being thin like that, I wouldn't be surprised if he didn't have AIDS. I'll tell you one thing. I was glad to get out of there. Who knows what kind of germs was in their apartment?" Lighting a cigarette, he turns to you. "I bet they didn't teach you how to deal with those kind of people in college."

You pause before you respond, not wanting to offend the sergeant, who is also your training officer. "We were taught that it would be difficult and challenging when dealing with the homosexual community, because of AIDS and our own biases and prejudices, as well as a lot of myths that are going around."

"Myths, my ass," Sergeant Waddell interrupts. "That AIDS disease will kill you stone-cold dead. I don't trust the government. You can't tell me you can't catch that stuff from mosquitos either. Who knows how you can catch it? All I know is I want to wash my hands."

From Larry S. Miller and Michael Braswell, *Human Relations and Police Work,* 4th ed. (Prospect Heights, IL: Waveland Press), 1997. Reprinted with permission.

"Well, I would agree that there are a lot of questions," you reply. "But our professors always reminded us that every citizen was entitled to equal opportunity under the law, regardless of their sexual preferences. I was taught that I was to treat them professionally, just as in any domestic disturbance. It seems to me that we should have done something besides just telling them to quiet down and get along with each other. I mean, we should have arrested the big guy just like we would have done if it was a spousal abuse case."

Turning into McDonalds, the sergeant turns once more to you, "Simpson, you're a good kid and I believe you will make a fine officer. But you need to remember that the classroom is one thing and the real world is another. I don't hate those kind of people, but they made their own bed and now they'll have to lie in it. I don't know what else we could have done. They weren't married and, even if they were, I don't believe it's legal in this state. We couldn't take the little guy to a spousal abuse shelter, they'd laugh their asses off at us. And I don't think that domestic violence law covers people like that anyway. Why don't you go order us a couple of black coffees to go while I wash my hands?"

Waiting for the coffee, you reflect on Waddell's words. He is a respected veteran police officer and you understand his uneasiness. You felt it, too. You also remember the look of fear and helplessness on the face of the battered guy, Eddie, who called the police. One part of you wanted to go back and check on him and do something, even if it meant arresting the other guy for domestic violence. Another part of you wanted to stay on Sergeant Waddell's good side. After all, he is your training officer. What are you going to do?

Questions:

1. What police ethics might this new recruit be torn between? Explain.

2. How might a department with stricter objectives or codes of conduct have influenced the behavior of the officers? Explain.

3. Address this case from the three ethical models of utilitarianism, deontology, and peacemaking. Which perspective do you feel would be most helpful in this instance? Why?

4. Research the local laws of your area and report back to the class. Are homosexual relationships covered by the local laws in your area? How might this information affect the officers' behavior?

Section III: Ethics and the Courts

A man can only do what he can do. But if he does that each day he can sleep at night and do it again the next day.

—Albert Schweitzer

It has been argued that while our criminal justice system is not perfect, it does yield a kind of "rough justice." No one is guilty of exactly the crime for which they are convicted, and no one receives exactly the penalty they deserve, but the majority of people do receive a disposition that approximates justice.

This view is probably accurate, but it is also somewhat troubling. While it is an eminently pragmatic approach, one may question the extent to which justice can be "approximated." One can also question the process by which this approximation is achieved. When defense attorneys and prosecutors struggle against each other in the adversary process, is truth the likely outcome or just a lucky possibility? Is the process any more agreeable when there is little real argument, just a negotiation over charge and sentence recommendation?

This is hardly the process one would design to find the right punishment to fit the crime or the criminal. But in whose hands should such decisions be placed? The legislature can attempt to ensure greater consistency through determinate sentencing, but such efforts often result in higher penalties than judicial discretion would yield. And in this period of prison overcrowding, what is the correct use of incarceration? One is forced to juxtapose a moral obligation to minimize prison costs that serve to shortchange state health, education, and welfare programs, with an equally important obligation to protect the community from crime.

The decisions that defense attorneys, prosecutors, judges, and legislators must make are difficult ones, requiring a balancing of sound ethical judgments with the pragmatic realities of their positions. To assist their students in dealing with these problems, law schools provide instruction in professional ethics. This is normally achieved by requiring students to complete a course that addresses the practicing attorney's obligations to the client, to the bar, and to the court. Questions have been raised, however, about the utility of requiring a single isolated ethics course, as opposed to integrating a concern with ethics into the general curriculum. While the former provides more intense and focused study, the latter encourages the incorporation of ethical concerns into every aspect of law. This incorporation may be a more effective means of instilling high standards, because many ethical dilemmas seem to be a direct result of the conflicting obligations inherent in the practice of law.

CHAPTER 8

Whatever Happened to Atticus Finch? Lawyers as Legal Advocates and Moral Agents

Joycelyn M. Pollock

Atticus Finch, the role created by Harper Lee in the book and movie, *To Kill a Mockingbird,* was the epitome of the "gentleman" lawyer: courteous, honest, brave, and intelligent. He was a consummate professional, but more than that, an admirable man. In the plot, he was a comfortable, respected attorney in a small Southern town who agreed to defend a black man accused of raping a white woman. In a time of lynchings, this decision exposed him and his family to ostracism and danger, yet at all times he maintained a professional courtesy, even toward those whose actions were condemning an innocent man to die. In contrast to this ideal of an attorney, there is the stereotype of the "ambulance chaser" lawyer who, like a parasite, exploits and profits from other's misfortune. The criminal defense attorney is often perceived as unscrupulous and uncaring, stopping at nothing to "get his client off." So where is Atticus? Of course, it helped that he defended an innocent client; real-world attorneys are not always so lucky.

KEY CONCEPTS:

active role

client-centered/
friend role

ethics of care

ethics of rights

guru/godfather role

hired-gun role

legal advocate

moral agent

moral dialogues

passive role

One of the reasons for the public's disdain for lawyers is found in the role they play *vis à vis* their clients—are attorneys amoral "hired guns" or are they professionals who balance their clients' interests against respect for the law and some objective standard of justice? This concept of the lawyer as a "legal advocate" (with no individual contribution of morality) versus "moral agent" (whereby the lawyer imposes a personal view of morality into his or her activities for the client) has been discussed and debated vigorously in the literature.

THE LAWYER-CLIENT RELATIONSHIP

Cohen (1991) presented the argument that only an attorney acting as a moral agent had the capacity to be moral. A legal advocate, one who pursued his or her clients' wishes even if they were immoral, could not possibly be considered good because he or she might be doing bad acts. He suggested some principles (see Figure 8.1) that attorneys had to follow in order to be considered moral.

Figure 8.1
Principles for Attorneys as Moral Agents

---

1. Treat others as ends in themselves and not as mere means to winning cases.

2. Treat clients and other professional relations who are relatively similar in a similar fashion.

3. Do not deliberately engage in behavior apt to deceive the court as to the truth.

4. Be willing, if necessary, to make reasonable personal sacrifices—of time, money, popularity, and so on—for what you justifiably believe to be a morally good cause.

5. Do not give money to, or accept money from, clients for wrongful purposes or in wrongful amounts.

6. Avoid harming others in the process of representing your client.

7. Be loyal to your client and do not betray his confidence.

8. Make your own moral decisions to the best of your ability and act consistently upon them

---

Source: Cohen, 1991:136.

Cohen's position that attorneys should be moral agents and decide independently what is right and wrong has been attacked vociferously. For instance, Memory and Rose (2002) argue that a lawyer can be effective and morally good by subscribing to the American Bar Associations' Model Rules of Professional Conduct. They argue, basically, that a lawyer who follows the Model Rules can be a zealous advocate for his or her client, but still never do wrong because the Model Rules prohibit illegal and unethical behaviors, such as lying. They especially do not agree with Cohen's idea that lawyers should apply their own definitions of morality in any case where they are being paid to pursue the client's interest. Morality is "subjective," they argue, and therefore it would only result in a loss of trust in attorneys and damage the client relationship if attorneys were to pursue their own definitions of justice, rather than the clients' definitions.

Cohen (2002), in a rebuttal, continues to argue his case, proposing that the legal advocate becomes used to imposing injury on others and that they do so without feelings of guilt. He argues that the Model Rules do not prohibit all acts that could be defined as unethical and immoral. For instance, they do not prohibit a situation whereby an attorney would maintain silence in an instance that results in third parties being financially harmed. Although Cohen wrote his article before the Enron, WorldCom, and Adelphia debacles, these examples certainly seem to be cases in point because attorneys were involved when corporate officers misled shareholders about the financial holdings of the companies (Rhode & Paton, 2002). As Powell (2003:316) pointed out:

> . . . how could it be . . . that with over a thousand lawyers at Arthur Andersen, over 300 lawyers at Enron, and, minimally, another dozen or so lawyers at Vinson and Elkins, the only person willing to blow the whistle was a senior vice president with a business degree?

Actually, both sides seem to agree that the most egregious acts of attorneys who pursue their client's interests, regardless of truth, justice, or who gets hurt, would be unacceptable for either the moral agent (because these actions offend some larger definition of morality) or the legal advocate (because they violate the Model Rules). However, there are still a number of issues and situations that fall between the two sides. For instance, if a defense attorney had a weak case and the only available tactic was to challenge the credibility of the prosecution's witness, should the attorney expose the witness (who is telling the truth and the defense attorney knows it) with evidence of past misdeeds, current failings of character, and, in general, attack his or her character? What if such treatment ruined the witness's reputation, health, or relationship with a loved one? The legal advocate would have no problem with such behavior; he or she must pursue the client's interest in creating reasonable doubt for the jury. What about the moral agent? If the moral agent refused to attack an honest prosecution witness, what good would he or she be to the guilty defendant who has no other means of obtaining an acquittal? What does a defense attorney owe to his or her client?

Wishman (1981) describes a case in which he challenged a rape victim's account of an alleged brutal rape and sodomy. He was able to convince the jury that she was lying and, months later, was confronted with her anger.

> . . . as all criminal lawyers know, to be effective in court I had to act forcefully, even brutally, at times. I had been trained in law school to regard the "cross" as an art form. In the course of my career I had frequently discredited witnesses. My defense of myself had always been that there was nothing personal in what I was doing. This woman was obviously unwilling to dismiss my behavior as merely an aspect of my professional responsibility; instead of an effective counsel, she saw me simply as a "motherfucker" (Wishman, 1981:6-7).

The literature in jurisprudence is filled with articles seeking to clarify or instruct in the attorney-client relationship. Condlin (2003:220-221, notes omitted) explains the ethical dilemma of attorneys who find themselves forced to decide how to act when pursuing the client's interests:

> Lawyers can find themselves in situations, therefore, in which they have social and moral obligations to behave in one way, and legal and professional obligations to behave in another. When norms collide in this fashion, when what a client asks is legal but also unfair or destructive of societal interests generally, lawyers face a difficult question. Should they be moral or legal, social or self-interested, communitarian or individualistic, or as some put it, persons or lawyers?

Granfield and Koenig (2003:513) observe that law school ethics classes do not help lawyers answer such questions: ". . . the codes do not tell lawyers how to reconcile conflict between their personal sense of ethics and the rules. . . ." In their survey of 40 Harvard graduates they found that many experienced deep personal conflict in representing clients whose tactics or positions with which they disagreed. However, they tended to resolve such conflict by adapting a "role-based morality." In effect, their definition of good became a judgment of their technical competence—they exchanged being good persons with being good lawyers. Those who could not make that adaptation left the field.

Condlin (2003) describes the role of lawyers as falling into one of the following categories: the hired gun role (most similar to our legal-advocate description above), the guru/godfather role (in which the lawyer tells the client what should be done), and what some call the client-centered/friend role (in which, it is assumed, the client can be persuaded not to engage in unethical or immoral practices). Condlin (2003) is critical of those who propose the last category, arguing that, in the end, if the client insists upon immoral actions, the attorney either tells the client "no" (guru/godfather) or does the client's bidding (legal advocate).

While some writers (e.g., Simon, 1993, 1998) argue that the attorney,—even the criminal defense attorney—should balance client interest against social justice, others argue that zealous advocacy is not only desirable, but also honorable (Freedman, 2002). Many advocates for the "client first and foremost" position use a famous quote from Lord Brougham that describes the client-attorney role: ". . . by the sacred duty which he owes his client, knows, in the discharge of that office but one person in the world—that client and no other . . ." (cited in Markovits, 2003:213).

Smith (2003) points out that the whole argument against zealous advocacy presumes that allowing perjury, browbeating victims, and other "aggressive tactics" are rampant. The more typical situation, Smith argues, is that criminal defendants get barely more than a "warm body sitting next to them" and, in fact: "Actually a warm body might be benign compared to some of the dangerous, dim-witted defenders that roam the criminal courts" (2003:91). He presents the case that the more typical attorney barely meets the definition of competent and comes nowhere near zealous in his or her defense of clients' interests.

It should also be noted that not all subscribe to the idea that the lawyer is always seeking the client's best interest. Scheingold (1984:155), for example, argues:

> the practice of defense law is all too often a "confidence game" in which the lawyers are "double agents" who give the appearance of assiduous defense of their clients but whose real loyalty is to the criminal courts.

In this view, lawyers on both sides of the bar have more in common with each other than with the client (or victim), so they really are advocates in name only. Defense attorneys and prosecutors share some vision of what is fair, and the system operates to enforce this vision, regardless of impositions from the outside or drama displayed for the client's benefit (for a discussion of this model and others, see Pollock, 2004).

GUIDANCE FOR LAWYERS: MODEL RULES OF PROFESSIONAL CONDUCT

All attorneys are guided by the American Bar Association (ABA) and the bar association of their own state. The American Bar Association has created and continues to update the Model Rules of Professional Conduct. The most recent revisions were proposed in 2000 and passed in 2002. The Rules cover the client-lawyer relationship, maintaining the integrity of the profession, courtroom behavior, conflicts of interest, use of the media, and relationships with opposing attorneys, among other areas. A standing committee on ethical responsibility, which provides formal and informal written opinions, enforces the Rules. Each state bar association enforces its own rules by sanctions that range from a private censure to disbarment.

Although we have been discussing zealous defense and the extent to which lawyers should ignore their personal ethics to do their client's bidding, it should be noted that the most common complaint lodged with state bar associations is incompetence or negligence. Most clients who are unhappy with their attorney are unhappy because of real or perceived neglect, that is, the attorney doesn't return their calls, the attorney missed a legal deadline, or so on. Very few complaints result in serious sanctions taken against attorneys (Pollock, 2004).

So what do the Rules dictate regarding the relationship between an attorney and client? First, the Rules demand that the lawyer "shall abide by a client's decisions concerning the objectives of representation. . . .[and] shall consult with the client as to the means by which they are to be pursued" (ABA, 2002:Rule 1.2). Barker and Cosentino (2003) point out that the revisions to this rule attempted to clarify the authority of the client and attorney in the relationship. The old rule distinguished between the objectives of the case (with greater authority given to the client) and the means or strategies used (with greater authority given to the attorney). The new rule encourages the client's participation in all decisionmaking, but the use of the term "consult" may be interpreted to mean that the client does not have absolute authority over decisions regarding means or strategies. Mather (2003) argues that the Model Rules are still "vague, contradictory, and ambiguous" in regard to the appropriate power differential in the attorney-client relationships.

This issue becomes extremely relevant in criminal defense cases when clients insist upon courses of action that attorneys feel are self-destructive or not helpful to the defense. Barker and Cosentino (2003) discuss, for instance, cases in which the defendant does not want attorneys to pursue insanity pleas or does wish to present defenses that clearly have no basis in fact. They also note that the revision takes away any disciplinary sanctions for attorneys who decide to go against client's wishes unless the action also violates other laws. This may, they argue, encourage attorneys to act their conscience when a client desires to do something morally repugnant. They conclude, however, that the revised rule continues to leave much ambiguity in who has control over decisionmaking—the client or the attorney.

Mather (2003) finds that an attorney's inclination to let the client take the lead in making decisions about objectives and tactics depends on the type of client. Studies indicated that public defenders were much more likely to believe in an attorney-led relationship, partially because of a belief that the client was too "unsophisticated" or ignorant to make good decisions. Corporate attorneys, on the other hand, were more "client-centered" and more likely to do the client's bidding, regardless of what they personally thought. This was because corporate executives could simply take their business elsewhere and the attorney would lose money. According to Mather (2003:1081):

> The client-sensitive or agent role in representation could become the role of the lackey in situations of unequal power between client and lawyer. As a result, the broader public interest, including the requirements of law, may suffer.

Rule 1.2 also cautions that the lawyer "shall not counsel a client to engage, or assist a client, in conduct that the lawyer knows is criminal or fraudulent . . ." Thus, a lawyer cannot knowingly participate in ongoing criminal or fraudulent activity. One assumes that when a corporate attorney is involved in activities that later are exposed as fraudulent, it is because there is more "wiggle" room in interpreting corporate acts—and more incentive for attorneys to decide that the actions aren't "strictly illegal," even though they may later be defined to be.

The attorney-client privilege refers to the client's right to not have the attorney be called to offer testimony about information obtained during the course of representing the client. The Model Rules have enlarged this privilege to prohibit any form of divulging information that is injurious to the client's interests, except for a few exceptions. Rule 1.6 states that lawyers "may not reveal information relating to the representation of a client unless the client gives informed consent" (ABA 2002: Rule 1.6).

The exceptions to this rule include an exception to prevent "reasonably certain death or substantial bodily harm" or to "prevent . . . a crime or fraud that is reasonably certain to result in substantial injury to the financial interests or property of another and in furtherance of which the client has used or is using the lawyer's services." Seemingly, the last exception is simply a restatement of Rule 1.2, which prohibits the lawyer from participating in an ongoing crime or fraud, but does not allow an attorney to come forward if he or she simply knows of the fraud but his or her services are not being used in furtherance of the activity.

This Rule has been substantially revised from earlier versions. For instance, in the 1983 version of the Rules, the exception was only the prevention of a crime that involved death or substantial bodily harm. In this earlier rule, financial injury, less than substantial physical injury, or the wrongful conviction of another could not justify disclosure (Vogelstein, 2003).

Martyn (2003) discusses both utilitarian and deontological rationales for the attorney-client privilege. Arguably, for instance, the rule is necessary in order for clients to be open with attorneys and share information that they must have in order to conduct an effective defense in criminal law and to further the client's interests in civil law. The deontological rationale is that it is the duty of the attorney to pursue the client's interests above all others. Martyn (2003) gives an example of an attorney who was consulted by a man seeking to sue an apartment manager for wrongful termination. During the course of that conversation, the man told the attorney that he was going to burn down the apartment building. The attorney informed the police, and they caught the man in the act after he had already spread an accelerant. The moral agent attorney could have done nothing else, but some questioned this attorney's actions because he could not have been "reasonably certain" that the man was going to commit arson and he wasn't involved in furthering the crime.

One much discussed case involved two lawyers who knew the location of the bodies of two teenagers who had been killed and buried by their client. Instead of divulging this information, they kept their client's confidence and used the location to bargain for a reduced sentence (for a discussion, see Pollock, 2004). Certainly a legal advocate would have kept quiet, but what would a moral agent have done? A very similar case occurred more recently in Texas when an attorney was compelled by the Texas courts to produce a map drawn by a client that showed the location of a child she had murdered. The court decided that the abandonment of the privilege was necessary because although the client had said that the child was dead, in another interview, she said that the child was still alive, so the location was necessary to prevent a future crime (if the child had still been alive). Because the attorney had to be compelled to produce the map through legal means, can we assume that she knew the child was already dead? A moral agent would have never kept such information to herself, but what about a legal advocate?

Blakleyn (2003) discusses a different sort of confidentiality issue. He asks whether attorneys, as officers of the court, owe a general duty to the public in cases that are sealed, but in which, arguably, the public interest dictates divulging information from the case to a wider audience. His examples included sealed settlements between clergy members who were sued for sexually molesting children. The sealed settlements prohibited any of the parties from breaking the confidentiality clause of the contract, but in some cases, especially when the same clergymen engaged in similar behavior, it is clear that the public's interest would have been served by knowing.

The Michael Jackson case involving a young child is also a good example of how sealed settlements may not be in the public interest. Several years before the charges imposed in December 2003, a family leveled similar allegations but settled the case out of court for an undisclosed sum of money. The family and child refused to cooperate with prosecutors in that case. Now, allegedly, another child has been sexually molested. Do the attorneys in the prior case bear some responsibility, given the fact that they did not divulge information to prosecutors that might have helped prevent future crimes? Would a moral agent attorney have found some way not only to protect the public but also to get a settlement for his or her client? What responsibility does a judge have in this situation? After all, a judge must agree to the confidentiality clause in any settlement agreement.

Vogelstein (2003) presents a description of psychologist Carol Gilligan's "ethics of care" in juxtaposition to the "ethics of rights" approach of the legal system and the ethical principles for lawyers. While the "ethics of care" centers on morality as tied to relationship and the understanding of connectedness, the "ethics of rights" is rule-based and emphasizes legality. Vogelstein applies this reasoning to the specific issue of when attorneys should divulge confidential information to third parties. She argues that the rule contributes to the negative stereotype of attorneys:

> By orchestrating a legal system where "zealous advocacy" for one individual trumps virtually any concern for and responsibility to the collective body, the confidentiality rule contributes significantly to the marred perception of the legal profession currently shared by the American populous (Vogelstein, 2003:159).

Vogelstein (2003) points out that the current Rule has protected more third parties than the earlier versions of the rule, but that it still ignores other types of harm—specifically, commission of a crime or fraud that results in substantial harm but is not furthered by the lawyer's services, wrongful incarceration or execution of another, and substantial emotional injury.

She further points out that to ensure that lawyers do protect the interests of third parties, the rule to disclose should not be a permission to do so, but, rather, should be mandatory. She argues that lawyers have an inclination to protect their clients—for pecuniary reasons if for no other. Therefore, the ABA should use forceful persuasion via the rules to make sure attorneys act as moral agents following an "ethics of care" toward third parties and the public at large.

Rule 2.1 seems to offer support for the proposition that the lawyer is a moral agent by proposing that the lawyer "shall exercise independent professional judgment and render candid advice." Further, the rule goes on to state that "a lawyer may refer not only to law but to other considerations such as moral, economic, social and political factors . . ." (ABA, 2002: Rule 2.1). Dinnerstein and colleagues (2004) explain that attorneys rarely engage in "moral dialogues" with their clients, but they explain how one might go about such a discussion. They also observe that attorneys may approach giving moral advice in an oblique way or couch their argument in practical rather than moral terms. The authors discuss elements of whether to engage in moral arguments, including such things as the seriousness of the issue (see Figure 8.2).

Figure 8.2
Moral Dialogues with Clients: Suggestions for Lawyers

1. The moral stakes of the issue—the more serious the issue, the more reason there is to engage in a discussion about a course of action.
2. The debatability of an issue—if it is in a gray area, there may be more reason to allow client latitude in decision making.
3. The client's capacity to make a moral decision—some clients may not have the intellectual capacity to reasonably make decisions.
4. The presence of shared values—when the attorney is very different from the client there may be more room for disagreement.
5. The nature of a legal relationship—a simple exercise in contract writing may not create the same need for moral discussions as a criminal defense or custody battle.
6. The lawyer's objectivity or self-interest—the attorney needs to be sure that his or her moral advice isn't influenced by self interest.

Source: Dinnerstein et al., 2004.

Rule 3.1 mandates that lawyers "shall not bring or defend a proceeding, or assert or controvert an issue therein, unless there is a basis in law and fact . . ." (ABA, 2002: Rule 3.1). However, in the Rule, there is a special exception or allowance for criminal defense attorneys, who are allowed to defend their clients in a way to "require that every element of the case be established." Therefore, even if the attorney knows the client is guilty, the ethical responsibility of the attorney is to defend the case in a way that challenges every assertion by the prosecution.

This Rule defines why defense attorneys must ethically question prosecution witnesses, even if they know they are telling the truth. They must challenge technicalities and question physical evidence. Their role is to test the evidentiary weight of the prosecution's case and to offer up any evidence that might create reasonable doubt. If they do not, then, arguably, they have failed to live up to their role. This Rule, along with much commentary in the literature, sets the criminal defense attorney apart from the corporate attorney. The distinction, however, does not solve the moral quandaries of some defense attorneys when they "do what they are supposed to do," such as imply that a rape victim is lying.

The most obvious dilemma for attorneys representing guilty defendants is the situation in which the defendant wants to commit perjury or have someone commit perjury to help the case. The Rules state that a lawyer shall not knowingly "make a false statement of fact or law to a tribunal" or "offer evidence that the lawyer knows to be false" (ABA, 2002: Rule 3.3). Although this seems to resolve the matter, criminal cases merit special rules. Rule 3.3 goes on to say that "A lawyer may refuse to offer evidence, other than the testimony of a defendant in a criminal matter, that the lawyer reasonably believes is false."

In the comments section to this Rule, it becomes clear that an attorney must "know" the testimony is false before he or she can ethically refuse to offer it in trial. If the attorney merely "reasonably believes" the testimony is false, then it must be offered. Thus, if a defendant tells an attorney that he was home alone when the crime was committed, but then when the case isn't going well and the client offers a girlfriend who wants to testify that the client was with her the day of the crime, what should the attorney do? The attorney believes that the client was telling the truth the first time, but does she or he *know* the truth? Do the rules require the attorney to use the testimony of the girlfriend? What if the defendant originally confessed to the crime, but then wanted to take the stand and testify that he didn't do it. The attorney tells him that he can't assist in perjury, so the client claims he was lying in his confession. Does the attorney *know* which is the truth? How would an attorney truly know what is the truth or not versus a reasonable belief anyway?

Pellicotti (1990) describes what an attorney does after his or her client commits perjury. The "passive" role is to ignore the perjured testimony during summation or any arguments. The "active" role would be to disclose the perjury to the court. However, as stated before, the rules state the attorney must *know*, not simply reasonably *believe*, that the client has committed perjury. The culture of the defense bar includes the idea that all defendants lie: "I was surprised, at first, that a client would lie to his own lawyer, but after a while I got used to it" (Wishman, 1981:37). Thus the rationale of many defense attorneys is that they don't *know* anything. They ask not whether the person did the crime, but rather, what do they need to know to defend the case.

The proscriptions regarding the attorney's direct use of deception are stringent. In a much publicized case in Colorado in 2002, an assistant district attorney was helping police negotiate with a murderer to surrender. While talking to a police negotiator over the telephone, the murderer had already confessed to brutally killing three women and raping and terrorizing a fourth. He insisted that he would not surrender until he spoke with a public defender. The assistant district attorney pretended to be a public defender and assured him that he would not be harmed if he turned himself in. He did not solicit additional inculpatory information, nor offer legal advice. However, he was brought up on disciplinary charges for violating the Colorado Bar Association's Rule 8.4, which prohibited attorneys from engaging in conduct that involved "dishonesty, fraud, deceit or misrepresentation." Upon appeal, the Colorado Supreme Court affirmed the suspension (Cross, 2003; See *In re Paulter*, 47 P.3d 1175 [Col. 2002]). Was this attorney acting as a moral agent? Should he have been disciplined?

Those who defended the action of this lawyer argued that he was trying to save lives because the murderer might not have surrendered and would have murdered again. It was important to his supporters that he did not acquire any inculpatory evidence; the sole motivation for his deception seemed to be public safety. Those who agreed with the finding that he deserved discipline pointed out that he had other options open to him; that is, he could have gotten get a real public defender to talk him into surrendering. According to this argument, whenever there are alternative options to violating a rule, one should take them.

Finally, Rule 3.4 covers actions taken by the attorney in pursuing his or her client's interests. An attorney cannot "unlawfully obstruct . . . access to evidence or unlawfully alter, destroy or conceal a document or other material having potential evidentiary value," nor can an attorney "falsify evidence" or counsel another to do so. Further, an attorney cannot assert "personal knowledge of facts in issue" or "state a personal opinion as to the justness of a cause, the credibility of a witness, . . . or the guilt or innocence of an accused." Does this mean that the attorney cannot, in closing arguments, profess to the jury that the defendant is innocent if he or she knows him to be guilty? But then again, how would the lawyer *know* for sure? This rule illustrates that, although an attorney must ethically conduct a zealous advocacy, there is a line to be drawn as to what is the difference between ethical zeal and over-the-line aggressive lawyering. The line is difficult to see, to be sure, and there is vigorous debate as to where it is. Some argue that zealous defense is the only ethical approach, while some, as stated above, argue that the lawyer should moderate the client's interests with larger issues of social justice.

Etienee (2003) points out that the federal courts impose a sanction against clients whose lawyers take the aggressive lawyering approach. In this study, it was found that the federal sentencing guidelines allow judges to impose longer sentences on those defendants who show no remorse. Increasingly, judges appear to use longer sentences to punish clients whose lawyers employ "zealous defense" strategies:

> Zealous advocacy is recast as a question of strategy to be balanced against other strategic considerations rather than as a require-ment of ethical and professional representation (Etiennee, 2003).

It seems, therefore, that what one attorney would see as ethical advocacy, another sees as inappropriate "strategy" that deserves sanctions. Ironically, though, when that other person is also a judge, it is the client who is often punished, not the attorney.

THE PROSECUTOR

Most of the discussion thus far has involved defense attorneys or cor-porate attorneys, but the same issues apply to prosecutors. While defense attorneys are supposed to be advocates for the defendant, prosecutors are sup-posed to be advocates for justice. Even so, many have committed actions that violate the ethical rules in their zeal to win. They become, in effect, legal advocates, but instead of pursuing justice, they are merely pursuing con-victions. Wishman (1981:52-53) writes: "Some prosecutors lied out of per-sonal ambition, some out of a zeal to protect society, but most lied because they had gotten caught up in the competition to win."

Gershman (1991) describes cases in which prosecutors engaged in false promises, fraud, and threats during plea bargaining. Other studies have found that prosecutors ignore, suppress, and even conceal exculpatory evi-dence, as well as misrepresent evidence to the jury (Hessick, 2002). For instance, cases are cited in which prosecutors have misrepresented animal blood as human blood in arguments to the jury, hid the fact that the victim had a gun to undercut the defendant's self-defense plea, and concealed evi-dence that showed that the chief witness (not the defendant) was the killer, (Armstrong & Possley, 2002; Columbia Law School, 2000).

Gershman (2003) also writes of prosecutors who willfully misuse foren-sic evidence in a number of ways, including suppressing test results that do not match the theory of the case, using the testimony of forensic experts who are incompetent or biased, rejecting expert reports that are exculpatory, and overstating the findings of forensic experts in summary argument. Obviously, prosecutors who engage in such behavior are not moral agents; nor are they legal advocates—they are violating the law. Unfortunately, sanctions for such behavior are rare (Keith, 2003).

There is a growing perception that prosecutorial misconduct has gotten out of hand, and there has even been a legislative proposal to create an agency that would investigate allegations of such misconduct (Hessick, 2002). Because that task is already supposed to be done by the Department of Justice, the creation of a special agency is unlikely to happen, but it does indicate that some believe that legal advocate prosecutors have forgotten that their client is the public at large—and the public's interests are not served by securing convictions at all costs.

CONCLUSION: RECONCILING THE LEGAL ADVOCATE AND MORAL AGENT VIEWS

There are literally volumes of literature on the ethics of attorneys and, especially, whether they should be pure legal advocates of their client or whether they should abide by and enforce some external moral principles. The dilemma has no easy answer. This may be why the Model Rules have not provided one. Should murderers have attorneys who use "aggressive lawyering" to obtain a dismissal? Should corporations have attorneys that help them thwart judgments that are just and moral? Should attorneys engage in practices that they would not do for themselves but are insisted upon by their clients? In the end, attorneys and their clients must decide for themselves what they feel is the right thing to do. A strong personal ethical or moral code can help everyone make those decisions for themselves.

REFERENCES

American Bar Association (2002). Model Rules of Professional Conduct. Retrieved from the American Bar Association's web site: http://www.abanet.org/cpr/mrpc

Barker, J. and M. Cosentino (2003). "Who's In Charge Here? The Ethics 2000 Approach to Resolving Lawyer-Client Conflicts." *Georgetown Journal of Legal Ethics*, 16:505-520.

Blakleyn, A. (2003). "To Squeal or Not to Squeal: Ethical Obligations of Officers of the Court in Possession of Information of Public Interest." *Cumberland Law Review*, 34:65-93.

Cohen, E. (1991). "Pure Legal Advocates and Moral Agents: Two Concepts of a Lawyer in an Adversary System." In M. Braswell, B. McCarthy & B. McCarthy (eds.), *Justice, Crime and Ethics*, 4th ed., pp. 125-161. Cincinnati: Anderson.

Cohen, E. (2002). "Pure Legal Advocates and Moral Agents Revisited: A Reply to Memory and Rose." *Criminal Justice Ethics*, 21(1):39-55.

Condlin, R. (2003). "What's Love Got to do With it? It's Not Like They're Your Friends for Christ's Sake: The Complicated Relationship Between Lawyer and Client." *University of Nebraska Law Review*, 82:211-311.

Cross, R. (2003). "Ethical Deception by Prosecutors." *Fordham University Law Journal*, 31:215-234.

Dinnerstein, R., S. Ellman, I. Gunning & A. Shalleck (2004). "Connection, Capacity and Morality in Lawyer-Client Relationships." *Clinical Law Review*, 10:755-805.

Etienne, M. (2003). "Remorse, Responsibility, and Regulating Advocacy: Making Defendants Pay for the Sins of Their Lawyers." *New York University Law Review*, 78:2103-2174.

Freedman, M. (2002). "How Lawyers Act in the Interests of Justice." *Fordham Law Review*, 1717-1727.

Gershman, B. (2003). "The Use and Misuse of Forensic Evidence." *Oklahoma City University Law Review*, 28:17-41.

Gershman, B. (2005). Chapter 9, this volume.

Granfield, R. & T. Koenig (2003). "It's Hard to be a Human Being and a Lawyer: Young Attorneys and the Confrontation with Ethical Ambiguity in Legal Practice." *West Virginia Law Review*, 105:495-524.

Hessick, C. (2002). "Prosecutorial Subornation of Perjury: Is the Fair Justice Agency The Solution We have Been Looking For?" *South Dakota Law Review*, 47:255-280.

Keith, R. (2003). "Illinois Court Cites 'Alarming Frequency' of Prosecutorial Misconduct." Salon.com. Available at: http://www.salon.com/news/wire/2003/10/17/prosecutorial _misconduct/print.html

Markovits, D. (2003). "Legal Ethics from the Lawyer's Point of View." *Yale Journal of Law and the Humanities*, 15:209-245.

Martyn, S. (2003). "In Defense of Client-Lawyer Confidentiality." *University of Nebraska Law Review*, 81:1320-1350.

Mather, L. (2003). "Ethics Symposium: What do Clients Want? What do Lawyers Do?" *Emory Law Journal*, 52:1065-1088.

Medwed, D. (2004) "The Zeal Deal: Prosecutorial Resistance to Post-Conviction Claims of Innocence." *Boston University Law Review*, 84:125-183.

Memory, J. & C. Rose (2002). "The Attorney as Moral Agent: A Critique of Cohen." *Criminal Justice Ethics*, 21(1):28-39.

Pellicotti, J. (1990). "Ethics and the Criminal Defense: A Client's Desire to Testify Untruthfully." In F. Schmalleger (ed.), *Ethics and Criminal Justice*, pp. 67-78. Bristol, IN: Wyndam Hall Press.

Pollock, J. (2004). *Ethics in Crime and Justice: Dilemmas and Decisions*. Belmont, CA: Wadsworth.

Powell, B. (2003). "Integrity in the Practice of Law: the Limits of Integrity or Why Cabinets Have Locks." *Fordham Law Review*, 72:311-332.

Rhode, D. & P. Paton (2002). "Lawyers, Ethics and Enron." *Stanford Journal of Law, Business and Finance*, 8:9-8.

Scheingold, S. (1984). *The Politics of Law and Order*. New York: Longman.

Simon, W. (1998) *The Practice of Justice: A Theory of Lawyer's Ethics*.

Simon, W. (1993). "The Ethics of Criminal Defense." *Michigan Law Review*, 91:1703-1743.

Smith, A. (2003). "Promoting Justice Through Interdisciplinary Teaching, Practice and Scholarship: The Difference in Criminal Defense and the Difference It Makes." *Washington University Journal of Law and Policy*, 11:83-140.

Vogelstein, R. (2003). "Confidentiality vs. Care: Re-evaluating the Duty to Self, Client, and Others." *Georgetown Law Journal*, 92:153-171.

Wishman, S. (1981). *Confessions of a Criminal Lawyer*. New York: Penguin Books.

DISCUSSION QUESTIONS

1. Describe the moral agent and legal advocate roles of attorneys. Give examples of how these two groups might make different decisions in criminal or civil cases.

2. What is the source for the definition of what is right or wrong behavior for attorneys?

3. Explain the difference between the ethical obligations of a defense attorney and the ethical obligations of a prosecutor. Explain how these different roles may affect their responsibilities in a criminal trial.

4. What is attorney–client privilege? What justifications are used for its existence?

5. What is the criteria used to decide whether to engage in a "moral dialogue" with a client?

Case Study 8–1

Child Rapist

You are an Assistant District Attorney in a small circuit court region. The region consists of three counties with an average population of 80,000 people per county. The community you serve is primarily composed of middle-class people with middle-class values. Having come from a large city, you were particularly impressed with the small town atmosphere and easy way of life.

The District Attorney General hired you straight out of law school two years ago. You felt that a job with the D.A.'s office would be an excellent opportunity to gain needed experience and develop a reputation as a good lawyer. Your ambition is to enter the political arena and perhaps run for State Representative in a couple of years. You have stressed a "law and order" image in order to accomplish your career ambitions.

As you prepare to look over the court docket for tomorrow's cases, your secretary advises you that Sheriff's Investigator John Wainwright is waiting to see you. "John, come in. I was going to call you about our burglary case tomorrow. You didn't have to come over here in person today."

"Thanks Bill, but I need to talk with you about another matter. You know, we arrested a young man by the name of Fred Granger a couple of days ago for rape and I wanted to fill you in on some details," the investigator begins.

"Yes, I was at the arraignment, remember?" you jokingly respond. Fred Granger is a 22-year-old white male who works in a nearby factory. He has a high school education and no prior felony arrests or convictions, but does have a previous conviction for DUI two years ago and one for possession of

From Michael Braswell, Tyler Fletcher, and Larry S. Miller, *Human Relations and Corrections,* 4th ed. (Prospect Heights, IL: Waveland Press), 1997. Reprinted with permission.

marijuana three years ago. He has been charged with the rape of a 13-year-old girl under state code 37-1-2702:

> Any adult who carnally knows a child under the age of fourteen by sexual intercourse shall be guilty of the capital offense of rape. The punishment for same shall be not less than ten years nor more than thirty years in the state penitentiary without parole. It shall be no defense that the child consented to the act or that the defendant was ignorant of the age of the child.

The punishment for this offense is no different than for the crime of forcible rape in your state. Fred Granger was arrested on a complaint from the parents of a thirteen year old girl named Debbie. It seems Fred picked Debbie up for a date, went to the lake and had sexual intercourse with her. It was a clear violation of the law and an apparently easy conviction since Fred admitted to arresting officers that he had sex with Debbie.

"So, what information do you have for me, John?" you ask.

"We've obtained statements from everyone involved. This is basically what went down. Fred knew Debbie's sister, Nina, who is twenty years old. Fred and Nina had gone out before on a couple of dates in the past and have had intercourse. It seems Nina and her younger sister, Debbie, have the reputation of being "easy." Anyway, Fred called Nina for a date and Nina wasn't at home. Debbie answered the phone and started flirting with Fred. Fred asked Debbie if she wanted to go with him to the lake and Debbie agreed. Debbie apparently wore a very revealing bathing suit and 'came on' to Fred. They had intercourse and Fred dropped Debbie back home. Debbie's parents inquired about her activities for the day and Debbie told them everything, even about the sex. That's when we got the call. Fred states that he thought Debbie was over eighteen and that Debbie consented to having sex with him. Debbie supports this story. Both of them were drinking beer at the lake," the investigator continued.

"Yes, well, I see. But, it's no defense for Fred to be ignorant of her actual age and no defense for him that Debbie consented. He probably got her drunk anyway. The law is clear on this matter," you advise.

"Yes, I know. But this Debbie has a reputation of being very promiscuous. She is very open about the fact that she consented. She now says she's in love with Fred. Needless to say, her parents aren't very happy about her attitude, but they seem to have very little control over her or her sister. In addition, anyone can look at Debbie and make a mistake about her age." The investigator pulls out and shows you a recent photograph of Debbie.

The photograph surprises you. You had not previously seen the victim but from the photography Debbie looks well over twenty years old.

"Hey, she does look twenty," you respond. "She certainly would have fooled me."

"Yeah. Anyone could have made that mistake," the investigator replies.

Looking over the statements that the investigator brought, you begin to feel uneasy about the case. In the legal sense, Fred is a criminal. He violated the state law. He has no legal defense. The girl is under fourteen which means she cannot testify that she consented. The fact that she has had intercourse before cannot be used as a defense for Fred. It seems to be an open and shut case. Fred is looking at ten to thirty years with no chance of parole. Even if he got the minimum ten years, it is still a stiff punishment for ignorance. You decide to call on the District Attorney General for advice.

"Yes, Bill. I see why you are concerned. It seems to me you have three options here. One, you could *nolle prosequi* the case (a formal entry on the record by the prosecuting attorney that he will not prosecute the case further). Two, you could reduce charges through a plea bargain agreement. Or, three, you could prosecute to the fullest extent of the law. It's basically a choice between legal ethics and personal ethics. Legal ethics would dictate that you prosecute to the fullest. A crime by statutes has been committed and you are sworn to uphold the law. In that sense, it would not be legally ethical for you to *nolle prosequi* or plea bargain when you have such a strong case. And, if you did, it might affect your political career. The news media and the public would not take your letting a 'child rapist' off without comment. On the other hand, your personal ethics dictate that this Fred fellow is not a typical criminal. He's guilty of stupidity maybe. But, apparently when you look at Debbie, you can see why. If you prosecuted the case, the jury might see Debbie the way Fred saw her and acquit him. But that is a big chance to take. Juries are unpredictable and you can't bring up the fact that she 'looks' of age. I don't know Bill. It's your decision. I'll back you on whatever you decide."

Questions:

1. Examine this case in terms of the moral agent and the legal agent. Compare and contrast the two in terms of the decision that the prosecuting attorney must make.

2. Develop a position in regard to what you would do if you were the prosecuting attorney. Explain your reasoning. What do you think would be the most likely outcome of this case?

CHAPTER 9

Why Prosecutors Misbehave

Bennett L. Gershman

KEY CONCEPTS:

courtroom misconduct

forensic misconduct

harmless error doctrine

oral advocacy

prosecutorial misconduct

The duties of the prosecuting attorney were well-stated in the classic opinion of Justice Sutherland 50 years ago.[1] The interest of the prosecutor, he wrote, "is not that he shall win a case, but that justice shall be done. As such, he is in a peculiar and very definite sense the servant of the law, the twofold aim of which is that guilt shall not escape or innocence suffer. He may prosecute with earnestness and vigor—indeed, he should do so. But, while he may strike hard blows, he is not at liberty to strike foul ones."[2]

Despite this admonition, prosecutors continue to strike "foul blows," perpetuating a disease which began long before Justice Sutherland's oft-quoted opinion. Indeed instances of prosecutorial misconduct were reported at least as far back as 1897,[3] and as recently as the latest volume of the *Supreme Court Reporter.*[4] The span between these cases is replete with innumerable instances of improper conduct of the prosecutor, much of which defies belief.

One of the leading examples of outrageous conduct by a prosecutor is *Miller v. Pate,*[5] where the prosecutor concealed from the jury in a murder case the fact that a pair of undershorts with red stains on it, a crucial piece of evidence, were stained not by blood but by paint. Equally startling is *United States v. Perry,*[6] where the prosecutor, in his summation, commented on the fact that the "defendants and their counsel are completely unable to explain away their guilt."[7] Similarly, in *Dubose v. State,*[8] the prosecutor argued to the jury: "Now, not one sentence, not one scintilla of evidence, not one word in any way did this defendant or these attorneys challenge the credibility of the complaining witness."[9] At a time when it should be clear that constitutional and ethical standards prevent prosecutors from behaving this way,[10] we ought to question why prosecutors so frequently engage in such conduct.

Much of the above misconduct occurs in a courtroom. The terms "courtroom" or "forensic misconduct" have never been precisely defined. One commentator describes courtroom misconduct as those "types of misconduct which involve efforts to influence the jury through various sorts of inadmissible evidence."[11] Another commentator suggests that forensic misconduct "may be generally defined as any activity by the prosecutor which tends to divert the jury from making its determination of guilt or innocence by weighing the legally admitted evidence in the manner prescribed by law."[12] For purposes of this analysis, the latter definition applies, as it encompasses a broader array of behavior which can be classed as misconduct. As will be seen, prosecutorial misconduct can occur even without the use of inadmissible evidence.

This article will address two aspects of the problem of courtroom misconduct. First, it will discuss why prosecutors engage in courtroom misconduct, and then why our present system offers little incentive to a prosecutor to change his behavior.

WHY MISCONDUCT OCCURS

Intuition tells us that the reason so much courtroom misconduct by the prosecutor[13] occurs is quite simple: it works. From my ten years of experience as a prosecutor, I would hypothesize that most prosecutors deny that misconduct is helpful in winning a case. Indeed, there is a strong philosophical argument that prosecutorial misconduct corrupts the judicial system, thereby robbing it of its legitimacy. In this regard, one would probably be hard pressed to find a prosecutor who would even mention that he would consider the thought of some form of misconduct.

Nonetheless, all of this talk is merely academic, because, as we know, if only from the thousands of cases in the reports, courtroom misconduct does occur. If the prosecutor did not believe it would be effective to stretch his argument to the ethical limit and then risk going beyond that ethical limit, he would not take the risk.

Intuition aside, however, several studies have shown the importance of oral advocacy in the courtroom, as well as the effect produced by such conduct. For example, the student of trial advocacy often is told of the importance of the opening statement. Prosecutors would undoubtedly agree that the opening statement is indeed crucial. In a University of Kansas study,[14] the importance of the opening statement was confirmed. From this study, the authors concluded that, in the course of any given trial,[15] the jurors were affected most by the first strong presentation which they saw. This finding leads to the conclusion that if a prosecutor were to present a particularly strong opening argument, the jury would favor the prosecution throughout the trial. Alternatively, if the prosecutor were to provide a weak opening statement, followed by a strong opening statement by the defense, then, according to the authors, the jury would favor the defense during the trial. It thus becomes evident that the prosecutor will be best served by making the strongest opening argument possible, and thereby [assisting] the jury in gaining a better insight into what they are about to hear and see. The opportunity for the prosecutor to influence the jury at this point in the trial is considerable, and virtually all prosecutors would probably attempt to use this opportunity to their advantage, even if the circumstances do not call for lengthy or dramatic opening remarks.[16]

An additional aspect of the prosecutor's power over the jury is suggested in a University of North Carolina study.[17] This study found that the more arguments counsel raises with respect to the different substantive arguments offered, the more the jury will believe in that party's case. Moreover, this study found that there is not necessarily a correlation between the amount of objective information in the communication and the persuasiveness of the presentation.

For the trial attorney, then, this study clearly points to the advantage of raising as many issues as possible at trial. For the prosecutor, the two studies taken together would dictate an "action packed" opening statement, containing as many arguments that can be mustered, even those which might be irrelevant or unnecessary to convince the jury of the defendant's guilt. The second study would also dictate the same strategy for the closing argument. Consequently, a prosecutor who, through use of these techniques, attempts to assure that the jury knows his case may, despite violating ethical standards to seek justice,[18] be "rewarded" with a guilty verdict. Thus, one begins to perceive the incentive that leads the prosecutor to misbehave in the courtroom.[19]

Similar incentives can be seen with respect to the complex problem of controlling evidence to which the jury may have access. It is common knowledge that, in the course of any trial, statements frequently are made by the attorneys or witnesses, despite the fact these statements may not be admissible as evidence. Following such a statement, the trial judge may, at the request of opposing counsel, instruct the jury to disregard what they have heard. Most trial lawyers, if they are candid, will agree that it is virtually impossible for jurors realistically to disregard these inadmissible statements. Studies here again demonstrate that our intuition is correct and that this evidence often is considered by jurors in reaching a verdict.

For example, an interesting study conducted at the University of Washington[20] tested the effects of inadmissible evidence on the decisions of jurors. The authors of the test designed a variety of scenarios whereby some jurors heard about an incriminating piece of evidence while other jurors did not. The study found that the effect of the inadmissible evidence was directly correlated to the strength of the prosecutor's case. The authors of the study reported that when the prosecutor presented a weak case, the inadmissible evidence did in fact prejudice the jurors. Furthermore, the judge's admonition to the jurors to disregard certain evidence did not have the same effect as when the evidence had not been mentioned at all. It had a prejudicial impact anyway.

However, the study also indicated that when there was a strong prosecution case, the inadmissible evidence had little, if any, effect.[21] Nonetheless, the most significant conclusion from the study is that inadmissible evidence had its most prejudicial impact when there was little other evidence on which the jury could base a decision. In this situation, "the controversial evidence becomes quite salient in the jurors' minds."[22]

Finally, with respect to inadmissible evidence and stricken testimony, even if one were to reject all of the studies discussed, it is still clear that although "stricken testimony may tend to be rejected in open discussion, it does have an impact, perhaps even an unconscious one, on the individual juror's judgment."[23] As with previously discussed points, this factor—the unconscious effect of stricken testimony or evidence—will generally not be lost on the prosecutor who is in tune with the psychology of the jury.

The applicability of these studies to this analysis, then, is quite clear. Faced with a difficult case in which there may be a problem of proof, a prosecutor might be tempted to sway the jury by adverting to a matter which might be highly prejudicial. In this connection, another study[24] has suggested that the jury will more likely consider inadmissible evidence that favors the defendant rather than inadmissible evidence that favors conviction.[25]

Despite this factor of "defense favoritism," it is again evident that a prosecutor may find it rewarding to misconduct himself in the courtroom. Of course, a prosecutor who adopts the unethical norm and improperly allows jurors to hear inadmissible proof runs the risk of jeopardizing any resulting conviction. In a situation where the prosecutor feels there is a weak case, however, a subsequent reversal is not a particularly effective sanction when a conviction might have been difficult to achieve in the first place. Consequently, an unethical courtroom "trick" can be a very attractive idea to the prosecutor who feels he must win.[26] Additionally, there is always the possibility of another conviction even after an appellate reversal. Indeed, while a large number of cases are dismissed following remand by an appellate court, nearly one half of reversals still result in some type of conviction.[27] Therefore, a prosecutor can still succeed in obtaining a conviction even after his misconduct led to a reversal.

An additional problem in the area of prosecutor-jury interaction is the prosecutor's prestige; since the prosecutor represents the "government," jurors are more likely to believe him.[28] Put simply, prosecutors "are the good guys of the legal system,"[29] and because they have such glamour, they often may be tempted to use this advantage in an unethical manner. This presents a problem for the prosecutor in that the "average citizen may often forgive, yea urge prosecutors on in ethical indiscretions, for the end, convictions of criminals, certainly justifies in the public eye any means necessary."[30] Consequently, unless the prosecutor is a person of high integrity and is able to uphold the highest moral standards, the problem of courtroom misconduct inevitably will be tolerated by the public.

Moreover, when considering the problems facing the prosecutor, one also must consider the tremendous stress under which the prosecutor labors on a daily basis. Besides the stressful conditions faced by the ordinary courtroom litigator,[31] prosecuting attorneys, particularly those in large metropolitan areas, are faced with huge and very demanding caseloads. As a result of case volume and time demands, prosecutors may not be able to take advantage of opportunities to relax and recover from the constant onslaught their emotions face every day in the courtroom."[32]

Under these highly stressful conditions, it is understandable that a prosecutor occasionally may find it difficult to face these everyday pressures and to resist temptations to behave unethically. It is not unreasonable to suggest that the conditions under which the prosecutor works can have a profound effect on his attempt to maintain high moral and ethical standards. Having established this hypothesis, one can see yet another reason why courtroom misconduct may occur.

WHY MISCONDUCT CONTINUES

Having demonstrated that courtroom misconduct may in many instances be highly effective, the question arises as to why such practices continue in our judicial system. A number of reasons may account for this phenomenon. Perhaps the most significant reason for the continued presence of prosecutorial misconduct is the harmless error doctrine. Under this doctrine, an appellate court can affirm a conviction despite the presence of serious misconduct during the trial. As Justice Traynor once stated, the "practical objective of tests of harmless error is to conserve judicial resources by enabling appellate courts to cleanse the judicial process of prejudicial error without becoming mired in harmless error."[33]

Although the definition advanced by Justice Traynor portrays the harmless error doctrine as having a more desirable consequence, this desirability is undermined when the prosecutor is able to misconduct himself without fear of sanction. Additionally, since every case is different, what constitutes harmless error in one case may be reversible error in another. Consequently, harmless error determinations do not offer any significant precedents by which prosecutors can judge the status of their behavior.

By way of illustration, consider two cases in which the prosecutor implicitly told the jury of his personal belief in the defendant's guilt. In one case, the prosecutor stated, "I have never tried a case where the evidence was so clear and convincing."[34] In the other case, the prosecutor told the jury that he did not try cases unless he was sure of them.[35] In the first case the conviction was affirmed, while in the second case the conviction was reversed.

Interestingly, the court in the first case affirmed the conviction despite its belief that the "prosecutor's remarks were totally out of order,"[36] Accordingly, despite making comments which were "totally out of order," the prosecutor did not suffer any penalty.

Contrasting these two cases presents clear evidence of what is perhaps the worst derivative effect of the harmless error rule. The problem is that the stronger the prosecutor's case, the more misconduct he can commit without being reversed. Indeed, in the [*People v.*] *Shields* case, the court stated that "the guilt of the defendant was clearly established not only beyond a reasonable doubt, but well beyond any conceivable doubt."[37] For purposes of our analysis, it is clear that by deciding as they do, courts often provide little discouragement to a prosecutor who believes, and rightly so, that he does not have to be as careful about his conduct when he has a strong case. The relation of this factor to the amount of courtroom misconduct cannot be ignored.

Neither can one ignore the essential absurdity of a harmless error determination. To apply the harmless error rule, appellate judges attempt to evaluate how various evidentiary items or instances of prosecutorial misconduct may have affected the jury's verdict. Although it may be relatively simple in some cases to determine whether improper conduct during a trial was harmless, there are many instances when such an analysis cannot properly be made but nevertheless is made. For example, consider the situation when an appellate court is divided on whether or not a given error was harmless. In *United States v. Antonelli Fireworks Co.,*[38] two judges (including Judge Learned Hand) believed that the prosecutor's error was harmless. Yet, Judge Frank, the third judge sitting in the case, completely disagreed, writing a scathing dissent nearly three times the length of the majority opinion. One wonders how harmless error can be fairly applied when there is such a significant difference of opinion among highly respected members of a court as to the extent of harmfulness of trial errors. Perhaps even more interesting is the Supreme Court's reversal of the Court of Appeals for the Second Circuit's unanimous finding of harmless error in *United States v. Berger.*[39] As noted, *Berger* now represents the classic statement of the scope of the prosecutor's duties. Yet, in his majority opinion for the Second Circuit, Judge Learned Hand found the prosecutor's misconduct harmless.

The implications of these contradictory decisions are significant, for they demonstrate the utter failure of appellate courts to provide incentives for the prosecutor to control his behavior. If misconduct can be excused even when reasonable judges differ as to the extent of harm caused by such misbehavior, then very little guidance is given to a prosecutor to assist him in determining the propriety of his actions. Clearly, without such guidance, the potential for misconduct significantly increases.

The *Shields* case presents yet another factor which suggests why the prosecutor has only a limited incentive to avoid misconduct. In *Shields,* the court refused to review certain "potentially inflammatory statements" made by the prosecutor because of the failure of the defense to object.[40] Although this approach has not been uniformly applied by all courts, the implications of this technique to reject a defendant's claim are considerable. Most important, it encourages prosecutors to make remarks that they know are objectionable in the hope that defense counsel will not object. This situation recalls the previous discussion, which dealt with the effect of inadmissible evidence on jurors. Defense counsel here is in a difficult predicament. If he does not object, he ordinarily waives any appealable issue in the event of conviction. If he does object, he highlights to the jury the fact that the prosecutor has just done something which some jurors may feel is so damaging to the defendant that the defense does not want it brought out.

The dilemma of the defense attorney in this situation is confirmed by a Duke University study.[41] In that study, jurors learned of various pieces of evidence which were ruled inadmissible. The study found that when the judge admonished the jury to disregard the evidence, the bias created by that evidence was not significantly reduced.[42] Consequently, when a prejudicial remark is made by the prosecutor, defense counsel must act carefully to avoid damaging his client's case. In short, the prosecutor has yet another weapon, in this instance an arguably unfair aspect of the appellate process, which requires preservation of an appealable issue.[43]

A final point when analyzing why prosecutorial misconduct persists is the unavailability or inadequacy of penalties visited upon the prosecutor personally in the event of misconduct. Punishment in our legal system comes in varying degrees. An appellate court can punish a prosecutor by simply cautioning him not to act in the same manner again, reversing his case, or, in some cases, identifying by name the prosecutor who misconducted himself.[44] Even these punishments, however, may not be sufficient to dissuade prosecutors from acting improperly. One noteworthy case[45] describes a prosecutor who appeared before the appellate court on a misconduct issue for the third time, each instance in a different case.

Perhaps the ultimate reason for the ineffectiveness of the judicial system in curbing prosecutorial misconduct is that prosecutors are not personally liable for their misconduct. In *Imbler v. Pachtman,*[46] the Supreme Court held that "in initiating a prosecution and in presenting the state's case, the prosecutor is immune from a civil suit for damages under Section 1983."[47] Furthermore, prosecutors have absolute rather than a more limited, qualified, immunity. Thus, during the course of a trial, the prosecutor is absolutely shielded from any civil liability which might arise due to his misconduct, even if that misconduct was performed with malice.

There is clearly a need for some level of immunity to be accorded all government officials. Without such immunity, much of what is normally done by officials in authority might not be performed out of fear that their practices are later deemed harmful or improper. Granting prosecutors a certain level of immunity is reasonable. Allowing prosecutors to be completely shielded from civil liability in the event of misconduct, however, provides no deterrent to courtroom misconduct.

CONCLUSION

This analysis was undertaken to determine why the issue of misconduct seems so prevalent in the criminal trial. For the prosecutor, the temptation to cross over the allowable ethical limit must often be irresistible because of the distinct advantages that such misconduct creates in assisting the prosecutor to win his case by effectively influencing the jury. Most prosecutors must inevitably be subject to this temptation. It takes a constant effort on the part of every prosecutor to maintain the high moral standards which are necessary to avoid such temptations.

Despite the frequent occurrences of courtroom misconduct, appellate courts have not provided significant incentives to the prosecutor to avoid misconduct. It is not until the courts decide to take a stricter, more consistent approach to this problem that inroads will be made in the effort to end it. One solution might be to impose civil liability on the prosecutor who misconducts himself with malice. Although this will not solve the problem, it might be a step in the right direction.

NOTES

1. Berger v. United States, 295 U.S. 78 (1935).

2. Id. at 88.

3. See Dunlop v. United States, 165 U.S. 486 (1897), where the prosecutor, in an obscenity case, argued to the jury "I do not believe that there are twelve men that could be gathered by the venire of this court . . ., except where they were bought and perjured in advance, whose verdict I would not be willing to take. . . ." Id. at 498. Following this remark defense counsel objected, and the court held that statement to be improper.

4. See Caldwell v. Mississippi, 105 S. Ct. 2633 (1985) (improper argument to capital sentencing jury); United States v. Young, 105 S. Ct. 1038 (1985) (improper argument but not plain error).

5. 386 U.S. 1 (1967). In this case, the Supreme Court overturned the defendant's conviction after the Court of Appeals for the Seventh Circuit had upheld it. The Court noted that the prosecutor "deliberately misrepresented the truth" and that such behavior would not be tolerated under the Fourteenth Amendment. Id. at 67. [sic]

6. 643 F.2d 38 (2d Cir. 1981).

7. Id. at 51.

8. 531 S.W.2d 330 (Texas 1975).

9. Id. at 331. The court noted that the argument was clearly a comment on the failure of the defendant to testify at trial.

10. See Griffin v. California, 380 U.S. 609 (1965), where the Supreme Court applied the Fifth Amendment to the states under the Fourteenth Amendment.

11. Alschuler, "Courtroom Misconduct by Prosecutors and Trial Judges," 50 *Texas Law Review* 627, 633 (1972).

12. Note, "The Nature and Function of Forensic Misconduct in the Prosecution of a Criminal Case," 54 *Colorado Law Review* 946, 949 (1954).

13. Of course, there is also a significant amount of defense misconduct which takes place. In this respect, for an interesting article which takes a different approach than this article, see Kamm, "The Case for the Prosecutor," 13 U. Tol. L. Rev. 331 (1982), where the author notes that "courts carefully nurture the defendant's rights while cavalierly ignoring the rights of the people."

14. Pyszczynski, "The Effects of Opening Statement on Mock Jurors' Verdicts in a Simulated Criminal Trial," II J. *Journal of Applied Social Psychology* 301 (1981).

15. All of the cited studies include within the report a caveat about the value of the study when applied to a "real world" case. Nonetheless, they are still worthwhile for the purpose of this analysis.

16. In some jurisdictions, attorneys may often use the voir dire to accomplish the goal of early influence of the jury.

17. Calder, "The Relation of Cognitive and Memorial Processes to Persuasion in a Simulated Jury Trial," 4 *Journal of Applied Social Psychology* 62 (1974).

18. See Model Code of Professional Responsibility EC 7-13 (1980) ("The duty of the prosecutor is to seek justice.").

19. Of course, this may apply to other attorneys as well.

20. Sue, S., R.E. Smith, and C. Caldwell, "The Effects of Inadmissible Evidence on the Decisions of Simulated Jurors—A Moral Dilemma," 3 *Journal of Applied Social Psychology* 345 (1973).

21. Perhaps lending validity to application of the harmless error doctrine, which will be discussed later in this article.

22. Sue, note 20 *supra* at 351.

23. Hastie, *Inside the Jury* 232 (1983).

24. Thompson, "Inadmissible Evidence and Jury Verdicts," 40 *Journal of Personality & Social Psychology* 453 (1981).

25. The author did note that the defendant in the test case was very sympathetic and that the results may have been different with a less sympathetic defendant.

26. Of course, this begs the question: "Is there a prosecutor who would take a case to trial and then feel that he didn't have to win?" It is hoped that, in such a situation, trial would never be an option. Rather, one would hope for an early dismissal of the charges.

27. Roper, "Does Procedural Due Process Make a Difference?" 65 *Judicature* 136 (1981). This article suggests that the rate of nearly 50 percent of acquittals following reversal is proof that due process is a viable means for legitimatizing the judiciary. While this is true, the fact remains that there is still a 50 percent conviction rate after reversal, thereby giving many prosecutors a second chance to convict after their original misconduct.

28. See People v. McCoy, 220 N.W. 2d 456 (Mich. 1974), where the prosecutor, in attempt to bolster his case, told the jury that "the Detroit Police Department, the detectives in the Homicide Bureau, these detectives you see in court today, and myself from the prosecutor's office, we don't bring cases unless we're sure, unless we're positive." Id. at 460. [sic]

29. Emmons, "Morality and Ethics—A Prosecutor's View," *Advanced Criminal Trial Tactics* 393-407 (P.L.I. 1977).

30. Id.

31. For an interesting article on the topic, see Zimmerman, "Stress and the Trial Lawyer," 9 *Litigation* 4, 37-42 (1983).

32. For example, the Zimmerman article suggests time off from work and "celebration" with family and friends to effectively induce relaxation.

33. R. Traynor, *The Riddle of Harmless Error* 81 (1970).

34. People v. Shields, 58 A.D.2d 94, 96 (N.Y.), aff'd. 46 N.Y.2d 764 (1977).

35. People v. McCoy, 220 N.W.2d 456 (Mich. 1974).

36. Shields, 58 A.D.2d at 97.

37. Id. at 99.

38. 155 F.2d 631 (2d Cir. 1946).

39. 73 F.2d 278 (1934), rev'd, 295 U.S. 78 (1935).

40. Shields, 58 A.D.2d at 97.

41. Wolf & Montgomery, "Effects of Inadmissible Evidence and Level of Judicial Admonishment to Disregard on the Judgments of Mock Jurors," 7 *Journal of Applied Social Psychology* 205 (1977).

42. Additionally of note is the fact that if the judge rules the evidence [inadmissible] and did not admonish the jury, then the biasing effect of the evidence was eliminated. The authors of the study concluded that by being told not to consider certain evidence, the jurors felt a loss of freedom and that to retain their freedom, they considered it anyway. The psychological term for this effect is called reactance.

43. Of course, this does not mean that appeals should always be allowed, even in the absence of an appealable issue. Rather, one should confine the availability of these appeals to the narrow circumstances discussed.

44. See United States v. Burse, 531 F.2d 1151 (2d Cir. 1976), where the court named the prosecutor in the body of its opinion.

45. United States v. Drummond, 481 F.2d 62 (2d Cir. 1973).

46. 424 U.S. 409 (1976).

47. Id. at 431, 42 U.S.C. 1983 authorizes civil actions against state officials who violate civil rights "under color of state law."

DISCUSSION QUESTIONS

1. If you were a prosecutor, do you feel it would be ethical to engage purposely in courtroom misconduct to win a case? Why or why not?

2. If you were a juror and were asked to disregard stricken testimony, do you feel you could still be objective in the case? Explain.

3. Explain both the advantages and disadvantages of the harmless error doctrine as related to prosecutors.

4. Do you feel it is more acceptable for prosecutors to demonstrate misconduct in felony trials than in misdemeanor trials? Discuss your position.

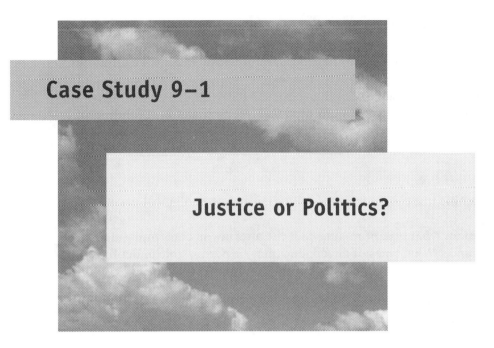

Case Study 9–1

Justice or Politics?

You have been district attorney for 12 years and a prosecuting attorney for almost 25 years. You know you are good with people—all kinds of people. That is why you keep getting elected and why you are the favorite to win the state assembly. As district attorney for Middleview County, you have backed up your tough talk about making "the time fit the crime" for violent offenders. You have "talked the talk and walked the walk." In fact, you have a perfect record concerning first-degree murder cases. You have won them all and in every case the offender has received the death penalty.

Sipping a cup of coffee, you stretch back in your leather chair and consider the case before you. Elroy Dudley, or "the Dude" as he is known in Middleview County, is one "bad" piece of work. Forty-five years old, Elroy has a long history of physically assaulting men and women. You have sent Elroy to state prison on two previous charges, where he has served a total of 10 years. After he finished his last sentence, it was just six weeks before Elroy was involved in a bar room brawl where a man was killed. Apparently, "the Dude" tried to pick up someone else's escort. Shortly thereafter, six to eight men were involved in a free for all. Several people were stabbed, and several shots were fired. The deceased, one Red "Big Red" Smith, was stabbed once in the heart. The people in your county were very afraid of Elroy and had been afraid of Big Red as well. Young and old, male and female, all seemed to feel relief. They also voiced their opinion regarding the wish that "the Dude" had met a similar fate.

Finishing the last of your coffee and drumming your fingers on the open folder, you consider your options. A lot is riding on this case. If you handle it right, you could walk into that state seat blindfolded. There is no direct evidence connecting Elroy to Big Red's death, but he was a central figure in the brawl. Elroy was also a threat to the community. You are certain you could get several of the other "lowlifes" to implicate Elroy with a little coaxing. You aren't certain that Elroy killed Big Red, but there is no doubt he was capable of it. And his personal history of violence speaks for itself. If you could put "the Dude" on death row, you would be doing yourself and everybody else in Middleview County a favor—everyone but Elroy and anyone who cares for him.

Questions:

1. Examine this case in terms of utilitarian and deontological perspectives.

2. Explain what type of misconduct the attorney is contemplating in this instance. What types of misconduct may be permissible under these circumstances?

3. What position would you take in this case? What do you think would be the most probable outcome of this case?

CHAPTER 10

Criminal Sentencing: Ethical Issues and the Problems of Reform

Lawrence F. Travis III

Sentencing is the decision of what to do with the person convicted of a criminal offense. Traditionally, we have responded to criminality by imposing a punishment on the criminal. Von Hirsch (1976:34) defined criminal punishment as "the infliction by the state of consequences normally considered unpleasant, on a person in response to his having been convicted of a crime." Graeme Newman (1983:6) simply states, "Punishment must, above all else, be painful." For our purposes then, criminal punishment is the purposeful infliction of pain on a person as a result of a criminal conviction.

There is an element of reflex in punishment. When we are harmed by someone or something, we tend to strike back in reaction. Mackie (1982) traced the origins of criminal punishments to such reflex responses. Criminal punishment is, at least partly, a return of harm for harm, or wrong for wrong. Yet there is an old saying that two wrongs don't make a right. Others, like Garland (1990), argue that punishment, whatever its origins, is also a product of social structure and cultural values. Who we punish, when we punish, and how we punish are determined by the role of punishment in society. Further, punishment itself affects social values in a number of important ways. These include defining what is improper behavior, building a sense of togetherness among the law-abiding, and supporting our beliefs about the nature of humankind and society.

KEY CONCEPTS:

desert

deterrence

disparity

false negative

false positive

incapacitation

paradox of retribution

prediction

punishment

treatment

truth in sentencing

utilitarianism

If ethics is the study of morality and what is right or wrong, it is likely that no aspect of the criminal justice process is more amenable to ethical examination than sentencing. By committing a crime, the offender has wronged society. By punishing, society arguably "wrongs" the offender. The purpose of this paper is to examine the question, how can punishment be justified? Following that, we will briefly explore ethical issues that remain even if punishment itself is accepted.

While we do not normally apply the saying about two wrongs to the question of criminal punishment, it seems apropos. How can we justify the purposeful infliction of pain, even on those convicted of crimes? What factors make punishment right and whether we should punish are interrelated questions. The answers to these questions depend upon how we define the purpose of punishment.

THE PURPOSE OF CRIMINAL PUNISHMENT

Should we punish? This question is so basic that it is often unasked and unanswered. Yet, when, whom, and how we punish are contingent on why we punish. We tend to believe that criminals should be punished. The wrong they do by committing crimes demands a punitive response. We often disagree, however, on why crime requires punishment. Traditionally, four reasons for punishment have been advanced: deterrence, incapacitation, treatment, and desert.

Deterrence

Deterrence supports punishment as an example of what awaits lawbreakers. This example is expected to convince would-be offenders to avoid criminal behavior. Deterrence is based on a conception of human beings as rational and guided by a pleasure principle. In theory, humans do things that please them and avoid things that hurt them. They weigh the likely consequences of their behavior and choose activities accordingly (Paternoster, 1987).

In order for a punishment to deter, two conditions must be met. First, the penalty must be severe enough so that the pain of the punishment exceeds the benefit of the crime. For example, a $50 fine for theft of $100 would not deter because the crime results in a "net gain" of $50. Second, the penalty must be imposed. If the criminal is unlikely to be caught and/or punished, the threat of the penalty is not likely to be "real." The lower the chance of punishment, the greater the chance of crime.

Deterrence works on two levels. General deterrence applies when the offender is punished so that others will be afraid to commit crimes. Thus the purpose of the punishment is to deter the general public from crime. Specific deterrence occurs when the penalty is designed to convince the particular offender not to commit another crime in the future.

As a justification for punishment, deterrence emphasizes the needs of the collective over those of the individual. The purpose of punishment is to control future crime. A deterrence rationale would allow the imposition of a severe penalty for a minor offense if that penalty would prevent a large enough number of future offenses. For example, a $10,000 fine for a $10 theft could be justified under deterrence if it would prevent at least 1,000 such thefts. Research to date does not indicate that we are very effective at deterrence (Paternoster, 1987; Sherman et al., 1997).

Incapacitation

Like deterrence, incapacitation is a justification for criminal punishment based on the promise of reducing future crime. In contrast to deterrence, however, incapacitation supports penalties that prevent offenders from having the chance to commit new crimes. While deterrence seeks to convince offenders that crime will not pay, incapacitation seeks to limit the offender's ability to commit a new crime.

One reason to incarcerate a convicted offender is that, at least while in prison, that person is not able to harm society by committing more crimes. The primary problem with incapacitation as a justification for punishment is our inability to accurately predict who is likely to commit future crimes (Visher, 1987). Research to date seems to indicate that incapacitative penalties entail a significant increase in prison population (Greenwood, 1982; Van-Dine, Conrad & Dinitz, 1979). To be sure that dangerous offenders are "locked up," we must also incarcerate relatively large numbers of nondangerous offenders (Sherman et al., 1997).

Treatment

Another justification for punishment is to allow for the treatment or rehabilitation of criminal offenders. This philosophy assumes that crime is caused by a variety of reasons, such as poverty, discrimination, or individual pathology. Punishments are designed to change the offender's need or desire to commit crime. Like deterrence and incapacitation, the ultimate goal of treatment is a reduction in future crime. Unlike those other two rationales, treatment emphasizes the individual offender (Cullen & Gilbert, 1982).

Studies of the effects of treatment suggest that most programs currently available are not very effective (Bailey, 1966; Martinson, 1974; Sherman et al., 1997). Efforts to treat criminal offenders continue, and many programs show promise of effectiveness with some types of offenders (Gendreau, 1995; Gendreau & Ross, 1987; Van Voorhis, 1987). As with the prediction problems of incapacitation, treatment attempts are limited by our ability to design and implement effective programs matched to suitable types of offenders (Latessa, Cullen & Gendreau, 2002).

Desert

A final rationale for criminal punishment is desert, which is sometimes called "retribution." This justification for punishment is the only one of the four that is "backward looking." Unlike deterrence, incapacitation or treatment, a desert rationale does not seek to reduce future crime. Rather, desert is based on the idea that the offender deserves to be punished as a result of committing a crime.

As a justification for punishment, desert places limits on both who may be punished and the degree to which someone may be punished. Desert requires that penalties only be imposed on those who have committed a crime. Further, a desert rationale requires that the punishment be commensurate (proportional to) with the severity of the crime committed. In these ways, desert may be considered to emphasize the interests of the individual offender over those of the collective, or society.

UTILITARIANISM VERSUS EQUITY

These four rationales and their varying emphases on the individual or collective interests in punishment highlight the ethical dilemma identified by Packer (1966). The core issue involves the role of social utility in punishment. Utility means benefit, or the "good" expected as a result of punishment. Those who support punishment on the basis of the good it will produce emphasize a utilitarian rationale. In contrast, those who support punishment regardless of effects, based on a notion that crime deserves punishment emphasize equity, or fairness.

In brief, we can say that deterrence, incapacitation, and treatment are utilitarian purposes of punishment. Desert is nonutilitarian. Only the desert principle supports the imposition of punishment regardless of effects. The other rationales depend upon some good resulting from the penalty.

If someone is convicted of a crime, should they be punished? If no one else will know that crime went unpunished and the offender will not commit another crime in the future, there is no reason to punish under a deterrence rationale. No one will be deterred by the penalty. Similarly, given that the offender will not commit a new crime, there is no need to incapacitate or treat the offender. Thus, utilitarian purposes cannot support the imposition of a penalty in this case.

Yet, most of us will be uncomfortable with allowing a criminal to escape punishment. At base, most people support a desert rationale for punishment. Someone who has broken the law has "earned" or deserves a punishment. Because those who don't commit a crime are not rewarded for law-abiding behavior, those who violate the law should be punished. This seems only fair, or equitable.

Mackie (1982) referred to this as the "paradox of retribution." By this he meant that it is not possible to explain or develop a desert rationale within a reasonable system of moral thought, yet it is also not possible to eliminate desert from our moral thinking. Retribution does not make sense. Desert suggests that wrongful acts should be punished but offers no reason for punishment. Mackie resolves the paradox by saying that punishment is essentially a reflex based on emotions. We react to things and people who hurt us by hurting them in return.

Given this emotional need to harm those who harm us, we will punish criminals without regard for possible beneficial effects of punishment. As punishment became institutionalized in society, jurists and philosophers developed more rational justifications for punishment based on utilitarian notions (Garland, 1990). These notions may explain particular punishments and the selection of specific offenders for punishment, but they do not explain why we punish. It is likely that we punish because punishment seems "right." Just as good deeds should be rewarded, bad ones should be punished. People should receive rewards and punishments for their good and bad behavior. This conception of reward and punishment as earned is the core of the concept of equity.

If Mackie's assessment is correct, it means that we will punish criminals routinely without regard to the effects of punishment. Nonetheless, we would like the two wrongs of crime and punishment to make some sort of right—to produce some good. We are not satisfied with a system of penalties that merely reacts to behavior. We want to influence the future. Thus, most criminal sentences involve a mix of equity and utilitarian justifications.

It is these utilitarian purposes of punishment that raise the ethical dilemma of sentencing as a balance between the needs of the collective and those of the individual. During the 1970s, retribution or desert experienced a renaissance (Cullen & Gilbert, 1982). This renaissance defined retribution as a limiting factor in punishment (Fogel, 1975; Frankel, 1972; Twentieth Century Fund, 1976; Von Hirsch, 1976).

The resurgence of desert was directed at fairness in criminal punishments. Proponents of desert-based sentencing were concerned with what they perceived as unfair disparities in criminal punishments. Under the laws of most states, it was possible for offenders convicted of the same offense to receive widely different penalties. One person convicted of burglary might be placed in prison while another might receive probation. Reliance on a desert rationale would narrow this range of penalties, ensuring that similar offenders convicted of similar crimes would experience similar penalties.

Desert would lead to more equitable punishment. Supporters of desert felt that it was unjust to punish similar people differently, as each had "earned" the same penalty. It was also wrong to impose a very harsh penalty on someone in order to deter others or to prevent a possible future offense by the person. Desert required that the offender be guilty of the offense for which punishment was imposed, and that the offense, not the offender, was the subject of punishment.

At the level of fairness to the individual offender, general deterrence and collective incapacitation (Visher, 1987), by which everyone convicted of the same offense receives the same sentence in hopes of reducing general levels of future crime, are less troublesome than individual predictions. If everyone convicted of an offense receives a similar punishment, whether for incapacitative or general deterrent purposes, individual fairness in terms of equivalent penalties is achieved. If these penalties are excessive in comparison to the seriousness of the crime (all burglars receive a term of life imprisonment, for example) while the sentences are equal, they are not equitable. The harm of the punishment exceeds the harm of the crime.

Equity, in terms of retribution is both an explanation of punishment and a limit on punishment. We will punish criminals because they have earned a penalty. We can only punish guilty criminals, and only in proportion to the seriousness of their crime. Von Hirsch and Hanrahan (1979) proposed a "modified just deserts" sentencing rationale that includes these two dimensions of equity. They argued that desert justifies the imposition of a penalty, and sets the outer limits of the punishment. Within these limits, however, utilitarian considerations could be used to allow different penalties to be imposed on offenders convicted of the same offense. Thus, burglary may deserve imprisonment of between one and three years. The sentencing judge would be able to impose a three-year term for incapacitation or treatment or deterrence, but would not be allowed to impose more than the upper limit. So too, the judge could impose a one-year term for the burglary, but not less than one year, because burglary deserves at least that level of punishment.

THE PRACTICE OF PUNISHMENT

Punishment is firmly established in our culture and our history. It seems safe to say that we will continue to punish criminals in the future, just as we have punished them in the past. The core dilemma in punishment is trying to achieve a balance between considerations of equity that are at the base of punishment, and desires for utility that can be realized through punishment. Over time, and across different types of offenders and offenses, this balance shifts. At any time, the practice of punishment reflects the current balance between concern for the interests of the individual as expressed in terms of equity and concerns for the needs of society expressed in terms of utility. The ethical question remains constant, however. That question is: Under what circumstances is the state justified in applying punishment to individuals? And how much punishment is justified?

Is there ever a time when it would be all right to impose the death penalty on someone convicted of theft? Should prison crowding (and the expense of prisons) justify reducing the prison term of a violent offender? As these questions illustrate, sentencing involves the fundamental issue of individual interests versus societal needs. The ethical problem exists in our attempts to determine the "right" balance of the two.

CONTEMPORARY ETHICAL CONCERNS IN SENTENCING

Leaving aside the question of whether we should punish, there are several important ethical considerations in contemporary sentencing. That is, assuming our current system of criminal punishment achieves an acceptable balance between concern for individual interests and social needs, this system contains some ethical dilemmas. Among the most important considerations are those dealing with honesty in the sentencing of criminals, the role of prediction in the allocation of criminal penalties, and the problem of discriminatory punishment.

Honesty about Punishment

Persons sentenced to prison in state courts in 1994 were expected to serve less than 40 percent of the prison term imposed by the judge (Langan & Brown, 1997:4). Of those receiving their first release from state prison on a violent offense conviction in 1994, the average offender had served less than one-half of the original prison term. The sentences announced in court are often quite different from the penalties served by convicted offenders. Growing pressure for criminal justice officials to be more honest about sentencing practices led to federal legislation including incentives to promote "truth in sentencing." A goal of the truth in sentencing movement was to ensure that violent offenders serve at least 85 percent of the prison terms they receive in court.

Several practices led to mistruths in sentencing. Most states award or allow inmates to earn "good time." Good time is a reduction in the length of sentence given for good behavior in the institution. It is common for such reductions to be in the one-third to one-half range, so that a sentence of nine years, if all good time is applied, becomes a term of four and one-half to six years. Discretionary release on parole also affects time served. An inmate sentenced to 10 years might be paroled after serving only three. Even most of those who receive life sentences are expected to be released at some point (Beck & Greenfeld, 1995:2).

Critics of this "dishonesty" in sentencing contend that current practices are wrong. Early release of offenders undermines the deterrent effect of the law and fails to provide adequate protection to the public (incapacitation). In addition to these negative effects on potential utilitarian benefits of punishment, critics also make that point that it is wrong to mislead the public. When citizens learn that offenders are not being punished as they had expected, critics contend, the citizens lose respect for the law and question the integrity of the criminal justice system. There is some evidence to suggest that public awareness that prison sentences are shorter in practice than what is announced in court leads jurors to support capital punishment for some offenders. Assuming that a prison term—even a term of life imprisonment—will result in an early release, jurors vote for the death penalty because the prison alternative is not punitive enough (Foglia, 2003).

The question of honesty in sentencing is complicated. Assuming truth in sentencing is desirable, how can we achieve such honesty? One solution is to simply keep offenders incarcerated for longer periods of time. The problem, of course, is that in doing so we must increase the harm of the punishment relative to past practice, and we must somehow find ways to pay for the increased prison population. Another solution is to lower court-imposed sentences to terms that are closer to what prisoners typically serve. This solution faces the political problem of appearing to lessen the seriousness with which we view crimes, and the perception that criminal justice agents have become "soft on crime." A third, and perhaps most common solution, is to combine the two by increasing the time served by violent offenders while reducing sentences for nonviolent offenders. Of course, as with any compromise, this third solution has the strengths and weaknesses of the first two. It is not clear that the compromise solves the dilemma of dishonesty in sentencing.

One of the pressing issues in sentencing today is how to achieve truth in sentencing. Whatever strategy is selected, we must be aware of the implications of changes in punishment for the balance between individual interests and social needs. If we opt to compromise, then we must re-examine the distribution of punishments. What crimes ought to receive more punishment than they presently do, and which crimes should receive less? If we change the distribution of punishment, what other effects might this have on fairness in punishment?

Prediction in Punishment

A second contemporary (and continuing) ethical issue in sentencing concerns the role of prediction in the assignment of criminal penalties. Clear and O'Leary (1983:35-38) recognized the central role of prediction in all aspects of criminal justice. Society expects its criminal justice apparatus to protect it from crime, and part of this protection involves the identification of risk and taking steps to minimize the chance of future crimes. The assignment of criminal penalties involves the prediction of future criminality and an assessment of the likely harm of that future crime. Indeed, one reason to increase terms for violent offenders and decrease the punishment of nonviolent offenders is because violent crimes are more damaging and thus justice system agents have a greater interest in preventing violent crimes.

In any attempt to predict "dangerousness" among a population of offenders, two types of error are possible. An offender who does not pose a risk of future crime may be erroneously predicted to be dangerous. This type of error is called a *false positive* because the offender was falsely (erroneously) predicted to be positive for danger. Conversely, an offender who actually poses a danger of future crime may be erroneously predicted to be "safe." This type of error is called a *false negative* because the offender was falsely (erroneously) predicted to be negative for danger.

False positives are subjected to greater levels of punishment than they need or deserve based on their actual dangerousness. Because they are predicted to be dangerous, we will incapacitate them or subject them to more severe sanctions to ensure specific deterrence or treatment. False negatives are punished less than they need or deserve based on their actual dangerousness. Because they are predicted to be safe, we return them to society quickly and allow them to commit additional crimes.

If we accept prediction as an appropriate consideration in sentencing, the use of differential sanctions is ethically justifiable based on the need to protect society. Yet, it remains wrong to subject a nondangerous offender to more severe punishment. Similarly, it is wrong not to punish more severely an offender who is actually dangerous. Both false positives and false negatives are treated unfairly, and both errors place increased burdens on society.

We currently do not have total accuracy in our predictions, so we make both kinds of errors. In practice, false positives occur about seven times for every true positive. Further, we correctly predict only about one-half of the truly dangerous offenders, so that our false negative rate is roughly equal to our true negative rate (Wenk, Robison & Smith, 1972). That is, we make many mistakes.

An alternative solution to this dilemma, of course, is to impose harsher penalties on all offenders, as if they were all dangerous. This would lead to "fair" punishment in that everyone receives a similar penalty, but it is a very expensive policy. In addition, critics argue that such a policy is unethical because it subjects all offenders to more severe punishment when most do not deserve it.

Even if we could achieve complete accuracy in our predictions of future crime, the ethical question remains: Should we punish people for crimes they have not yet committed? If I knew you were going to break the speed limit next week, should I collect a fine from you today? If I do, what should I do next week when I catch you speeding? That is, by sentencing based on a prediction, have we allowed the offender to "pre-pay" for crime, so that when the crime actually occurs, there is no punishment after the crime? Must we wait for someone to actually commit an offense before we punish? Suppose we predict that someone will commit a murder. If we incarcerate them now, they do not have the chance to commit the murder, and so the crime never occurs. Because the crime never occurred, do we have a right to imprison the predicted offender? In the movie *Minority Report* this issue was briefly explored. In the movie, the central question involved the accuracy of predictions. While there were some who were concerned about "pre-punishing" offenders, the justice system was allowed to arrest and punish people who were predicted to commit murders before the crimes actually happened.

Concern about repeat offenders and career criminals raises the issue of prediction. Recent attention to "three strikes and you're out" laws illustrates the point. These laws impose long prison sentences on those convicted of their third felony offense. The logic behind such laws is that three-time losers are dangerous and need to be incapacitated. Many states have passed or are considering such laws. The ethical issues around prediction in sentencing are complicated, and do not disappear even if we manage to achieve completely accurate predictions. We must still decide the balance between individual interests and community needs. Does the community's need for safety outweigh the individual's interest in liberty if we predict that the individual will eventually commit a crime? Under what circumstances might the community's needs be more important? Under what circumstances is the individual's interest in liberty most important?

Discrimination in Sentencing

The purpose of prediction is to discriminate between those offenders who require more punishment and those who can be safely given less punishment. A related ethical concern is how the predictive system achieves this discrimination. It is possible that errors in prediction are not random but that they result in differential punishment for some persons as opposed to others (Zimmerman, Martin & Rogosky, 2001). The data concerning the characteristics of persons receiving severe sanctions indicates that sentencing decisions are disproportionate. Males, minority group members, young adults, and the poor are more likely to receive harsh sentences than females, older adults, whites, and the more affluent (Petersilia, 1983; Visher, 1983). The third ethical issue in contemporary sentencing concerns discrimination in the assignment of criminal penalties.

Klein, Turner, and Petersilia (1988) reported that criminal sentences in California were based more on the seriousness of the offense, prior criminal record of the offender, and justice process variables than on race. The fact remains, however, that the ethically acceptable factors that predict future crime and explain sentence severity—prior record, criminal justice history, and offense seriousness, appear to be related to sex, race, age, and social class. The conclusion that these factors are more determinative of punishment than race or sex does not necessarily mean that sentencing decisions do not discriminate.

The problem of the relationships between race, sex, socioeconomic status, age, and the factors that explain sentences are complex. Race, for example, may be related to unemployment because of societal discrimination. In turn, unemployment may be related to involvement in crime and criminal justice processing decisions (bail, probation and parole supervision, and the like), which in turn are related to future criminality. Punishments based on the likelihood of future criminality as predicted from prior record or criminal justice history will reflect the effects of race, sex, and social class. However, because the sentencing decision relies only on prior criminal record and criminal justice history, the effect of race, sex, and class may be hidden from those making the punishment decision.

A related issue concerns definitions of offense seriousness. The war on drugs provides an excellent example. Under federal sentencing rules, offenses involving crack cocaine were treated more severely than those involving powder cocaine. Racial differences in the use of these drugs (blacks were more likely to use crack cocaine; whites more likely to use powder cocaine) resulted in disproportionate sentencing of cocaine offenders as black offenders more often received prison terms, and received longer terms than white offenders. So too, an emphasis on certain types of drug offenses, such as street sales versus possession, produces racial differences in punishment (Barnes & Kingsnorth, 1996). Later research (Kautt & Spohn, 2002) did not support the idea that an interaction between type of drug (crack) and race (African-American) resulted in harsher punishment of minority group members. One possible reason for these results is that federal sentencing judges, learning about the discriminatory effects of the federal law, had changed their decisions to increase fairness.

The ethical problem here is akin to that faced by automobile insurance underwriters. Punishments based on predictions of future crime treat some individual offenders unfairly, just as blanket assignment of certain groups of drivers to "high-risk" classes for insurance. So too, treatment of different kinds of criminal behavior as more serious is like assigning different insurance rates based on the type of automobile driven, not the skill of the driver. At what point, if ever, does this unfair treatment of individual offenders (or drivers) render the assignment process unethical? Is crack cocaine use more serious than use of powder cocaine? If it is, how concerned should we be over racial differences in preference for types of drugs? When, if ever, is discrimination ethically acceptable?

Beyond discrimination as we normally understand it, there is a long-standing concern with sentencing "disparity." Disparity is the unequal punishment of legally similar offenders. If two people who are first offenders are convicted of burglary, we would expect them to receive the same punishment. In practice, similarly situated offenders often received widely different punishments. The difference in punishments is called disparity.

Over the past quarter century there have been numerous efforts to reduce disparity by making sentencing more equitable (Griffin & Katz, 2002). Sentencing laws in most states and the federal system have been changed to include mandatory minimum sentences, sentencing guidelines, and other reforms designed to reduce disparity by making sure that offenders convicted of the same crime get the same penalties. While these changes have managed to reduce some variation in punishments imposed, they have also demonstrated the "perils of reform."

THE PROBLEMS OF REFORM

Sentencing is a complex process that is difficult to change. Changes in sentencing face problems associated with the number and variety of officials who make sentencing decisions, and with the fact that sentencing decisions are closely linked to other aspects of the criminal justice process. Efforts to reduce disparity in criminal sentencing and thus increase fairness and justice have encountered a number of problems. Three-strikes laws have been applied against relatively petty offenders so that life terms have been imposed on people convicted of stealing less than $300 worth of goods. At the same time, other offenders who have committed more serious crimes are not sentenced under the three-strikes provisions (Greenwood et al., 1998). Changes in criminal penalties and sentencing procedures have strengthened the hand of prosecutors at plea bargaining, and the more severe penalties may have increased the willingness of defendants to go to trial, complicating the work of the courts. Brian Johnson (2003) studied sentencing outcomes under a guidelines system in Pennsylvania and concluded that type of conviction (trial or plea) influences the sentence imposed. Despite a guidelines system designed to reduce disparity, Johnson found that race and other nonlegal factors were still associated with sentences.

Sentencing also takes place in local courts, and there is variation in punishment across different courts. Ulmer and Johnson (2004) found that sentences under the Pennsylvania guidelines system differed significantly across different counties. Kautt (2002) also found that sentences under the federal guidelines varied significantly across the different circuits and district courts. While guidelines can reduce some variation in sentencing, there remains substantial local variation in punishment. One of the most vexing problems in sentencing reform is that punishment involves so many actors (prosecutors, judges, parole authorities, legislators, etc.) and takes place in multiple locations (Griset, 2002).

Changes in sentencing can have serious implications for other aspects of the justice process as well. "Truth in sentencing" can produce prison crowding that might result in early release of offenders. States that changed their sentencing laws to achieve truth in sentencing tended to experience increased rates of incarceration of violent offenders. Determinate sentencing and reducing the amount of credit inmates can earn for good behavior in prison may lead to increased rule violations by prison inmates. Concern about expected sentences can lead prosecutors to pursue probation violation sanctions rather than new convictions (Kingsnorth, MacIntosh & Sutherland, 2002). Still, the most frustrating aspect of sentencing reform is that evidence suggests that all too often attempts to reform sentencing practices result in little to no actual changes in sentencing outcomes (Koons-Witt, 2002).

CONCLUSIONS

An examination of the ethics of criminal sentencing raises many questions, but provides few answers. The answers are judgment calls that depend upon the individual doing the judging. A central determinant of how one may resolve these ethical issues is the resolution of the conflict between utility and equity. If the interests of the individual predominate, one is likely to support a desert (possibly treatment) justification for punishment and oppose most predictive efforts. Similarly, one is likely to opt for truth in sentencing by reducing sentences imposed to more closely match time currently served, and to oppose prediction in sentencing and be very cautious about potential discrimination resulting from laws and practices. On the other hand, if one emphasizes utility, it is likely that they will support prediction, solve the truth-in-sentencing problem by increasing penalties (at least for more serious offenses), and be less concerned about potential discriminatory effects of laws and practices. Despite the problems inherent in reforming sentencing, we have an obligation to seek to improve the quality of justice, no matter what are our personal views.

Differences in perspective are reflected in how one views errors of prediction. If false positive errors are more troubling than false negative errors, there is a greater concern for equity than utility. If false negative errors are the more troublesome event, this evidences a greater concern for public safety. Those who emphasize community protection are usually willing to accept false positive errors, arguing that it is not unjust to punish them more severely than their actual risk would warrant.

Each of us may very well answer the questions about sentencing differently. In essence, these are all ethical questions that are asking about what is right or wrong with sentencing and criminal punishment. The ethics of sentencing can be stated as a question of justice. We need to determine what are just punishments and how sentences can be imposed justly. As Von Hirsch (1976:5) stated it, "While people will disagree about what justice requires, our assumption of the primacy of justice is vital because it alters the terms of the debate. One cannot, on this assumption, defend any scheme for dealing with convicted criminals solely by pointing to its usefulness in controlling crime: one is compelled to inquire whether that scheme is a just one and why."

REFERENCES

Bailey, W. (1966). "Correctional Outcome: An Evaluation of 100 Reports." *Journal of Criminal Law, Criminology & Police Science*, 57:153-160.

Barnes, C. & R. Kingsnorth (1996). "Race, Drug, and Criminal Sentencing: Hidden Effects of the Criminal Law." *Journal of Criminal Justice*, 24(1):39-55.

Beck, A. & L. Greenfeld (1995). *Violent Offenders in State Prison: Sentences and Time Served.* Washington, DC: Bureau of Justice Statistics.

Clear, T. & V. O'Leary (1983). *Controlling the Offender in the Community.* Lexington, MA: Lexington Books.

Cullen, F.T. & K.E. Gilbert (1982). *Reaffirming Rehabilitation.* Cincinnati: Anderson.

Fogel, D. (1975). *We Are the Living Proof . . .: The Justice Model for Corrections.* Cincinnati: Anderson.

Foglia, W. (2003). "They Know Not What They Do: Unguided and Misguided Discretion in Pennsylvania Capital Cases." *Justice Quarterly*, 20(1):187-211.

Frankel, M. (1972). *Criminal Sentences: Law Without Order.* New York: Hill & Wang.

Garland, D. (1990). *Punishment and Modern Society.* Chicago: University of Chicago Press.

Gendreau, P. & R. Ross (1987). "Revivification of Rehabilitation: Evidence from the 1980s." *Justice Quarterly*, 4(3):349-407.

Gendreau, P., T. Little & C. Coggin (1995). *A Meta-Analysis of the Predictors of Adult Offender Redivism: What Works!* St. John, Canada: University of New Brunswick.

Greenwood, P. (1982). *Selective Incapacitation.* Santa Monica, CA: Rand.

Greenwood, P., S. Everingham, E. Chen, A. Abrahamse, N. Merritt & J. Chiesa (1998). *Three Strikes Revisited: An Early Assessment of Implementation and Effects.* Washington, DC: National Institute of Justice.

Griffin, B. & L. Katz (2002). "Sentencing Consistency: Basic Principles Instead of Numerical Grids: The Ohio Plan." *Case Western Reserve Law Review*, 53(1):1-75.

Griset, P. (2002). "New Sentencing Laws Follow Old Patterns: A Florida Case Study." *Journal of Criminal Justice*, 30(4):287-301.

Johnson, B. (2003). "Racial and Ethnic Disparities in Sentencing Departures Across Modes of Conviction." *Criminology*, 41(2):449-490.

Kautt, P. (2002). "Location, Location, Location: Interdistrict and Intercircuit Variation in Sentencing Outcomes for Federal Drug-Trafficking Offenses." *Justice Quarterly*, 19(4):633-671.

Kautt, P. & C. Spohn (2002). "CRACK-ing Down on Black Drug Offenders? Testing for Interactions Among Offenders' Race, Drug Type, and Sentencing Strategy in Federal Drug Sentences." *Justice Quarterly*, 19(1):1-35.

Kingsnorth, R., R. MacIntosh & S. Sutherland (2002). "Criminal Charge of Probation Violation? Prosecutorial Discretion and Implications for Research in Criminal Court Processing." *Criminology*, 40(3):553-578.

Klein, S., S. Turner & J. Petersilia (1988). *Racial Equity in Sentencing.* Santa Monica, CA: Rand.

Koons-Witt, B. (2002). "The Effect of Gender on the Decision to Incarcerate Before and After the Introduction of Sentencing Guidelines." *Criminology*, 40(2):297-328.

Langan, P. & J. Brown (1997). *Felony Sentences in State Courts, 1994.* Washington, DC: Bureau of Justice Statistics.

Latessa, E., F. Cullen & P. Gendreau (2002). "Beyond Correctional Quackery: Professionalism and the Possibility of Effective Treatment." *Federal Probation*, 66:43-49.

Mackie, J. (1982). "Morality and the Retributive Emotions." *Criminal Justice Ethics*, 1(1):3-10.

Martinson, R. (1974). "What Works?" *The Public Interest*, (Spring):22.

Newman, G. (1983). *Just and Painful.* New York: Macmillan.

Packer, H. (1966). *The Limits of the Criminal Sanction.* Stanford: Stanford University Press.

Paternoster, R. (1987). "The Deterrent Effect of the Perceived Certainty and Severity of Punishment: A Review of the Evidence and Issues," *Justice Quarterly,* 4(2):173-217.

Petersilia, J. (1983). *Racial Disparities in the Criminal Justice System.* Santa Monica: Rand.

Sherman, L., D. Gottfredson, D. MacKenzie, J. Eck, P. Reuter & S. Bushway (1997). *Preventing Crime: What Works, What Doesn't, What's Promising.* Washington, DC: National Institute of Justice.

Twentieth Century Fund Task Force on Criminal Sentencing (1976). *Fair and Certain Punishment.* New York: McGraw-Hill.

Ulmer, J. & B. Johnson (2004). "Sentencing in Context: A Multilevel Analysis." *Criminology*, 42(1):137-177.

Van Dine, S., J. Conrad & S. Dinitz (1979). "The Incapacitation of the Chronic Thug." *Journal of Criminal Law & Criminology*, 65:535.

Van Voorhis, P. (1987). "Correctional Effectiveness: The High Cost of Ignoring Success." *Federal Probation*, 51(1):56-62.

Visher, C. (1987). "Incapacitation and Crime Control: Does a 'Lock 'em Up Strategy Reduce Crime?," *Justice Quarterly*, 4(4):513-543.

Visher, C. (1983). "Gender, Police Arrest Decisions and Notions of Chivalry." *Criminology*, 21(1):5-28.

Von Hirsch, A. & K. Hanrahan (1979). *The Question of Parole.* Cambridge, MA: Ballinger.

Von Hirsch, A. (1976). *Doing Justice.* New York: Hill & Wang.

Wenk, E., J. Robison & G. Smith (1972). "Can Violence be Predicted?," *Crime & Delinquency*, 18(3):393-402.

Zimmerman, S., R. Martin & T. Rogosky (2001). "Developing a Risk Assessment Instrument: Lessons About Validity Relearned." *Journal of Criminal Justice*, 29(1):57-66.

DISCUSSION QUESTIONS

1. Explain the concept of equity.

2. For punishment to deter, what conditions must be met?

3. List the ethically acceptable factors that predict future crime and explain sentence severity.

4. Explain what "truth in sentencing" is.

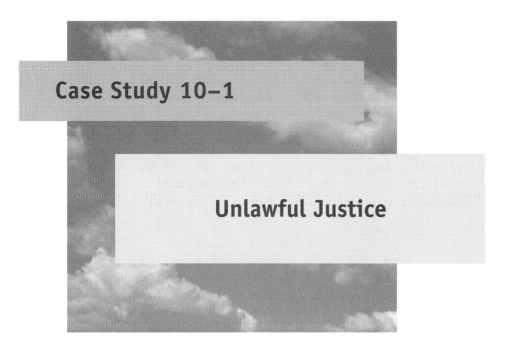

Case Study 10–1

Unlawful Justice

Sam Smith stared at the half-empty cup of coffee on his desk. Reaching down, he picked up the cup and drained its lukewarm contents with a single gulp. He had been District Attorney for 10 years and this was the toughest decision he had ever been faced with. He slowly exhaled as he looked at the file in front of him one more time.

Dexter "Bad Boy" Devlin was a three-time loser who had been incarcerated in three different states for 15 of his last 20 years. Three rapes, four especially aggravated assaults, an armed robbery, and other assorted charges pretty much told the D.A. all he needed to know. Mr. "Bad Boy" was as dangerous a sociopath as they come. There were inmates on death row that weren't as dangerous as this fellow. If anybody deserved to be on death row it was Devlin, and death row was exactly where Sam Smith had put him after a highly publicized trial involving Devlin and two other tattooed freaks who had gange-raped and strangled a teenage female runaway. Now this.

Apparently, Detectives Johnson and Peterson had not bothered to inform Smith or Devlin's defense attorney of some pertinent forensic evidence that had pointed to one Lefty Dirkson as the person who actually strangled the victim. Dirkson was currently serving 15 to 20 years in the state penitentiary for an armed robbery. Johnson and Peterson had a longstanding beef with Devlin from a previous case seven years earlier, in which he had beaten an especially brutal rape case they had worked.

Sam drummed his fingers on his desktop. If he followed the law, the new evidence would get "Bad Boy" off death row, back into the system, and eventually back onto the street to do more harm. Of course, Dirkson was no picnic, but he was in prison, even if for something else. Devlin was a ticking

179

time bomb as far as violence was concerned. It was always just a matter of time and opportunity. If Sam got rid of the evidence, only he and the detectives would know, and both of them would be good for the secret.

The D.A. muttered to no one in particular, "What is justice? Protect the future victims or protect a dangerous scumbag like Devlin?"

Question:

What should the D.A. do in this case? How do the legal aspects of his vocation conflict with his sense of moral virtue? Is there another way to satisfy both the legal requirements and moral and ethical challenges the D.A. faces?

CHAPTER 11

Crime and Punishment: Punishment Philosophies and Ethical Dilemmas

Laurie A. Gould & Alicia H. Sitren

WHAT IS PUNISHMENT?

The punishment of offenders is a central feature of the criminal justice system and highlights the coercive nature of criminal justice. This topic is of great concern to researchers, government officials, correctional employees, and the general public. These stakeholders have varying opinions pertaining to the proper use and justification of punishment. However, before a critical examination can take place, it is necessary to define punishment.

There are many possible definitions for the term punishment. For example, Hudson (2002) notes that we often speak of a punishing work schedule or the punishment of children by their parents, but these examples fail to provide a useful working definition for the punishment of law violators. Von Hirsch (1976) provides one possible definition of punishment: "Punishment means the infliction by the state of consequences normally considered unpleasant, on a person in response to his having been convicted of a crime" (p. 35). In addition, proportionality between the sanction and the offense is an essential ingredient of the punishment process in the United States. Proportionality requires that the severity of the sentence be dependent on the seriousness of the crime (von Hirsch, 1979). For example, a person who commits a petty theft should receive a sanction commensurate with the offense (i.e., a short jail term or probation), rather than the death penalty or a very long prison term.

KEY CONCEPTS:

deterrence

general deterrence

hedonistic calculus

incapacitation

punishment

proportionality

rehabilitation

retribution

specific deterrence

PUNISHMENT AND ETHICS

There are three major frameworks that address the purpose and ethics of punishment—utilitarianism, deontology, and peacemaking. Utilitarianism views the purpose of punishment in terms of the end result. For Bentham, punishment should be utilized to maximize the total pleasure or minimize the total pain of all parties affected by the crime (Gold, 2002). Deontology, which is associated with the work of Immanuel Kant, differs from utilitarianism in that the focus of actions is on the intent and not the consequences (Gold, 2002). For Kant, punishment by a court can never be inflicted simply as a means to promote good for the criminal or society. Instead, punishment must always be inflicted because the offender has committed a crime (Kant, 1996).

Peacemaking as a justice perspective seeks to incorporate three elements into the criminal justice system—connectedness to each other, caring as the primary element in corrections, and mindfulness of the needs of others (Braswell & Gold, 2002; Lanier & Henry, 1998). The peacemaking perspective argues that our correctional system should change its response to crime away from one of violence, through the use of death and prison. Instead it should move, whenever possible, to deescalate violence through the use of meditation, mediation, spiritual growth (Braswell et.al., 2001), dispute resolution, and forms of conciliation (Lanier & Henry, 1998).

WHAT ARE THE PURPOSES OF PUNISHMENT?

The philosophical punishment literature addresses the rationale behind punishment by posing questions of justification. Typical questions raised by philosophical debates include: Why do we punish? How much do we punish? What kinds of punishment should we utilize? Possible answers to these questions include: because offenders deserve to be punished, to protect society from dangerous people, to stop offenders from committing future crimes, and to discourage other people from committing the same criminal act (Hudson, 2002). Specifically, the philosophies of retribution, incapacitation, rehabilitation, and deterrence outline these answers (Clear, 1994; Duff, 1986; Montague, 1995; Murphy, 1995; von Hirsch, 1976).

Typically, one or more of these penal philosophies has dominated throughout the last two centuries. Within the last few decades, the application of punishment has been marked by a move away from rehabilitative efforts and toward more punitive, incapacitative efforts (Feeley & Simon, 1992, 1995; Pratt, 2000). Currently, it seems that punishment "in its very conception is now acknowledged to be an inherently retributive practice" (Bedau, 2003:1). The following discussion will provide an overview of the major justifications for punishment and highlight some important ethical dilemmas and questions currently affecting punishment.

Retribution

One possible reason to punish wrongdoers is for the simple reason that they deserve it—this perspective is known as retribution. Retribution was often dismissed by criminologists as little more than revenge, and it was not afforded the status of penal theory until the 1980s (Hudson, 2002). When we think of retribution, we often think of *lex talionis*—an eye for an eye, a tooth for a tooth, a life for a life (Wesley, 2003). However, contemporary retribution is far different from this view. While revenge is still fundamental in contemporary retribution, the focus now is on proportionality between the criminal act and the punishment. Retribution manifested in contemporary punishment, through the use of determinate sentences.

Up until the 1970s, the primary sentencing rationale to a large extent, had gone unchallenged—the punishment should fit the criminal, not the crime (Juarez, 1976). A typical indeterminate sentence would include a minimum and a maximum term of punishment, with the actual time served being determined by the progress of the offender. Offenders who could demonstrate successful progress toward rehabilitation could be released from supervision by parole authorities (MacKenzie, 2001). Parole was a privilege to be earned only by those offenders who displayed that they were rehabilitated and had ties to the community (Petersilia, 2001).

Great disparity resulted from indeterminate sentences, such that a property offender could end up serving a longer prison sentence than a violent offender. These concerns, coupled with prison riots, prompted the introduction of sentencing reforms by way of determinant sentences (Hudson, 2002). Liberal critics of indeterminate sentences pointed to the gross abuses suffered by inmates, while more conservative opponents of rehabilitation argued that offenders were being treated far too softy. Determinate sentencing schemes were lauded by both liberals and conservatives, but for very different reasons. For the left, determinate sentences offered a way to curb judicial discretion and the disparities that occurred as a result; for the right; it offered a way to "get tough" with offenders (Hudson, 2002).

The resulting sentencing guidelines offered harsh penalties for severe offenders and penalties that were more lenient for lesser offenders. Many states replaced indeterminate sentences with determinate sentences, which clearly identify fixed penalties for crimes. Under this type of sentence, offenders receive a fixed term of punishment, which is determined by guidelines (MacKenzie, 2001; Petersilia, 2001). Once offenders complete their term of punishment, they are automatically released from prison, thus eliminating parole boards (MacKenzie, 2001; Petersilia, 2001). Determinate sentencing does allow the consideration of certain circumstances of the crime to act as either aggravating or mitigating factors, so there is some individualization of justice. In general, the guidelines offer a range of possible sanctions for each type of offense—for example, a crime might carry a penalty of three to five years, with less serious offenders receiving sanctions at the low end of the spectrum.

With regard to actual administration of punishment, retributivists argue that punishment serves as a means of restoring balance between the offender and society. It is argued that the commission of the criminal act has allowed the offender to seize an unfair advantage over law-abiding people—theft of property, excitement, or the release of tension (Hudson, 2002). Punishment, it is argued, is necessary to remove this unfair advantage.

Despite the focus on fairness and proportionality, retribution still has some problems. Because retribution stresses impartiality and fairness above all else, the system becomes depersonalized (Wesley, 2003). Retribution forces the justice system to ignore potentially relevant facts (such as whether the offender was raised in abusive foster homes) in the pursuit of justice. In short, retributive justice leaves little room for the consideration of human needs and focuses on just deserts (Wesley, 2003).

A discussion of retribution would not be complete without introducing the ultimate sanction—death. Capital punishment is often justified primarily in terms of retribution and demands that murderers should suffer in approximately the same way that the victim suffered (Finkelstein, 2002). The retributive argument for the death penalty typically centers on what Byron (2000) calls the "Their Shoes Gambit," that is, if you had a loved one who was murdered, what type of justice would you demand? According to Byron, the gambit goes something like this: People who are opposed to capital punishment imagine themselves in circumstances in which they would be strongly motivated to demand justice. This demand focuses on retribution, or punishing the guilty as much as they deserve . . . [This gambit] heightens the aggrieved person's demand for retribution, in particular on the person's sense that *nothing short of the death of the perpetrator could approach a just retribution for the crime*" (p. 308).

While this argument may be important, Byron (2000) argues that vengeance has no place in public policy and should not serve as a justification for the death penalty in the absence of other salient functions of punishment such as deterrence and rehabilitation. (see also Chapter 12).

Incapacitation

If we hold that neither deterrence nor rehabilitation are effective, then another option is simply to incapacitate offenders in jails and prisons. Supporters might point to the value of maintaining custody and control over offenders, while critics may suggest that incapacitation is little more than warehousing offenders, making it more likely that they will be unable to succeed in any world outside of prison. Many recent attempts have been made by the state to get "hard-core" repeat offenders off the streets. Incapacitation through incarceration or the death penalty is one way to ensure that chronic offenders curtail their criminal activity, but it is certainly not without problems—most notably prediction.

How do we predict chronic offenders? Several studies have attempted to isolate the characteristics of chronic offenders, in an effort to predict the likelihood of chronic offending (see, for example, West & Farrington, 1973). Such studies have been unable to predict with high levels of accuracy whether someone would reoffend. Several ethical dilemmas present themselves when we consider false positives—those individuals who were predicted to offend, but ultimately would not. Because there really is not any way to demonstrate these false positives, it remains a theoretical dilemma.

In an attempt to incapacitate repeat violent offenders, some form of "three strikes and you're out" laws were implemented by 23 states in 1993 (Dickey & Hollenhorst, 1999). For the most part, three-strikes laws had minimal impact in most states. However, California's wide scope of three-strikes law provisions affected many of the state's systems (i.e., political, educational, criminal justice, human services, and budgetary systems) (Meehan, 2000). Cost implementations alone were substantial (Dickey & Hollenhorst, 1999), with increases being seen is almost every area of offender processing. Preconviction jail time, case processing, trials, and prison-building costs have all increased dramatically since the passage of the three-strikes legislation. Because three-strikes laws entail longer prison sentences in addition to reducing good time credits, such laws contribute to prison crowding as well as the long-term costs of incarceration for geriatric inmates.

Additional problems stem from the application of three-strikes laws. In California, for example, prosecutors are able to exercise their wide discretion in the charging decisions of offenders. In some cases, offenders who commit third-strike-eligible offenses are charged with a misdemeanor, instead of a felony. In other cases, relatively minor infractions are charged as felonies, leading to a disproportionately severe punishment (see Figure 11.1). Wide sentencing disparity has resulted so that an offender could receive an eight-month sentence in one county and a 25-to-life sentence in another county for the same crime (Dickey & Hollenhorst, 1999).

Figure 11.1
Severe Punishments

Gary Ewing received a prison term of 25 years to life for stealing golf clubs from a country club in Los Angeles. The prosecutor in the case had the option of charging Ewing with a misdemeanor, but decided to charge him with a felony. Had Ewing been charged with a misdemeanor he likely would have received a short term in jail and possibly a fine.

In a similar case, Leandro Andrade was sentenced to 25 years to life for stealing nine children's videotapes, including "Snow White," "Cinderella," and "Free Willie 2." The estimated value of these tapes was $153.54.

The crime reduction capabilities of three-strikes laws are tenuous at best. Thus far, research findings have not been able to illustrate a link between three-strikes laws and the reduction and/or prevention of crime (Meehan, 2000). Some have noted that increased preventive efforts, such as education and social programs, may be more effective than incapacitative strategies at reducing crime rates in the long run (Dickey & Hollenhorst, 1999).

Rehabilitation

Since the development of the prison, punishment in the modern era has been characterized by a belief that the problem of crime can be solved through the identification and treatment of the root causes of crime (i.e., rehabilitation). Rehabilitation, which has dominated penal strategies for nearly a century and a half (MacKenzie, 2001; von Hirsch, 1976), characterizes the offenders as being sick and in need of treatment. According to this alternative philosophy, the criminal is in need of treatment, reeducation, or reformation (von Hirsch, 1976). In an effort to "treat" the criminal, rehabilitative strategies have relied on a multitude of different medical and education models (von Hirsch, 1976). In the 1970s, Attorney General Ramsey Clark issued a call for rehabilitation programs to address both the addiction problems suffered by inmates as well as the need for vocational training (Clark, 1970).

For some, rehabilitation is often seen as the opposite of punishment. Such a view would be in error in that rehabilitation is in a very real sense a form of crime control—one that attempts to change the offender so that he or she is less likely to reoffend. Thus, a primary goal of rehabilitation is to reduce recidivism (von Hirsch, 1976). Cullen and Gilbert (1982) in their classic work reaffirmed the rehabilitative ideal in the face of the conservative "nothing works" (Martinson, 1974) onslaught, which fueled the get-tough, punishment revival. Cullen and Wright (1996) offer a convincing argument for the measured and responsible use of evolving rehabilitative strategies. They suggest that. with regard to the state's response to offenders, neither liberal "doing for" treatment programs nor conservative "doing to" punishment strategies will offer significant opportunities for offenders to learn and take responsibility for the crimes they committed and, just as importantly, for assisting in shaping the law-abiding citizens they need to become.

A variety of treatment programs have been implemented, such as intensive supervision on the streets, rehabilitative boot camps, well-equipped vocational training programs, the use of probation, behavioral control techniques, and "community-based" programs such as intensive counseling and group therapy. The efficacy of these treatment programs has been monitored by testing the effects of recidivism. Findings from empirical research on these programs have been inconclusive, with some studies indicating a significant reduction in the recidivism of program participants versus nonparticipants and others not finding a significant difference (Alschuler, 2003; Kempinen & Kurlycheck, 2003; Petersilia, 1998; Petersilia & Turner, 1990).

Some rehabilitation programs appear to be effective for some types of offenders. Contemporary movements that complement more traditional rehabilitation and social support models include family therapy, restorative justice, and peacemaking initiatives. For example, McCord, Tremblay, Vitaro, and Desmarais-Gervais (1994) found that a two-year treatment program that focused on family management and social skills resulted in higher school achievement and less antisocial behavior among delinquent boys. Similarly, Gordon, Graves, and Arbuthnot (1995) found that delinquents who received family therapy had a lower rate of adult offenses compared to those delinquents who received only probation service.

Deterrence

Deterrence is a forward-looking punishment philosophy. Because it is recognized that we cannot change the past, forward-looking philosophies, such as deterrence, hold that the best society can do is prevent wrongs from being committed in the future (Wesley, 2003). Deterrence as a penal strategy generally refers to discouraging reoffending, or offending by law-abiding citizens, through the threat and fear of the potential punishment (Hudson, 2002:19).

Deterrence is generally divided into two major categories—general and specific. *General deterrence* seeks to use the offender as an example to the rest of society. Through the use of general deterrence strategies (increasing the fear and certainty of punishment), it is hoped that the general public will be prevented from engaging in criminal acts. Some examples of general deterrence strategies include: increasing police activity in certain areas, the use of special police task forces to target specific crimes such as narcotics, and the death penalty (Siegel, 2003). *Specific deterrence* seeks to influence the future behavior of a particular offender. Specifically, strategies are implemented to prevent the offender from engaging in future criminal acts. For example, the drunk driver who pays a substantial fine and serves some time in jail should, at least, in theory, find the punishment unpleasant enough to refrain from driving drunk in the future (Siegel, 2003).

The philosophy of deterrence was first introduced by Cesare Beccaria and later articulated by Jeremy Bentham. For both classical contemporary deterrence theorists, the criminal is viewed as a rational actor who has free will. Theoretically, an individual's choice can be deterred by the anticipation of punishment if he or she does engage in the criminal act (Hudson, 2002). Essentially, the criminal actor is viewed as a rational actor who weighs the costs and benefits of the criminal act prior to its commission. Bentham termed this calculation the *hedonistic calculus*, and it is based on the idea that people seek pleasure over pain. Thus, if the pain derived from the punishment of the criminal act outweighs the pleasure derived from that act, the rational actor will choose not to engage in crime.

Contemporary deterrence theorists hold that three elements are essential in the deterrence of criminal activity—the likelihood of arrest, the likelihood of conviction, and the severity of punishment (Mendes, 2003). In theory, a government can reduce the crime rate if the likelihood of arrest and conviction are increased and the severity of punishment is increased (Mendes, 2003).

While deterrence theory has several merits, it is not without its problems. For example, there is considerable difficulty in determining what (if anything) will deter individuals from committing crimes. Deterrence assumes that an individual makes a rational decision to commit a crime, and that simply is not the case in all circumstances. In some cases, an individual is unable to weigh the costs and benefits associated with a criminal event. This is particularly true in the case of crimes that occur in the heat of the moment.

There is great debate in the literature regarding the importance of severity and certainty in the ability to deter crime. Some theorists posit that the severity of punishment has little deterrent effect (Decker & Kohfeld, 1990; Eide, 1994; Witte, 1983). Others suggest that the certainty of punishment is more important than the severity of punishment (Becker, 1968; Ehrlich, 1973). Still others believe that certainty and severity are equally important in the deterrence of crime (Antunes & Hunt, 1973; Chambliss, 1966; Gibbs, 1968; Grasmick & Bryjak, 1980; Gray & Martin, 1969; Logan, 1972; Mendes & McDonald, 2001; Tittle, 1969).

Other difficulties arise when we examine the use of different sanctions as a deterrent. For example, it is believed by some that the use of the death penalty serves as a deterrent for would-be murderers (Reitan, 1993). Critics of the deterrence argument point to a brutalization effect of the death penalty, whereby murder rates actually increase following an execution (Cochran & Chamlin, 2000). An examination of brutalization and deterrence by Cochran and Chamlin (2000) revealed only a slight deterrent effect of the death penalty and an increase in the level of nonstranger, argument-based murders. Recent crime statistics reveal that the South has the highest rate of murder, compared to all regions in the United States, with a rate of 6.8 per 100,000 (FBI, 2002). The South also has the highest execution rate in the United States with 80 percent of all executions taking place in southern states (DPIC, 2004). Overall, the majority of research studies have failed to find support for the link between capital punishment and murder, especially when other penalties, such as life without parole, are available (Bailey & Peterson, 1997; Radelet & Borg, 2000).

Unintended Consequences of Punishment

Determinate sentencing strategies and retributive punishments have contributed to the unprecedented increases in the inmate population in the last few decades. Recent statistics indicate that there are approximately 1.3 million adults confined in state and federal prisons (Bonczar, 2004). Furthermore, approximately 5.6 million U.S. adult residents, or one in every 37 U.S. adults, have previously served time in prison (Bonczar, 2004). This boom in incarceration has prompted the concern of system officials about overcrowding and has led many state departments of correction to search for cost-saving alternatives. Full-scale privatization is one solution employed by many states and the federal government as a way to save resources. Unfortunately, privatization leaves many questions unanswered and has some serious ethical implications.

Overcrowding in prisons and jails has severe impacts on the correctional system, most notably in the conditions of confinement. Overcrowding in the correctional system has arguably contributed to the decline of physical, social, and operational conditions inside prison facilities (Tartaro, 2002). Oftentimes, offenders are doubled up in cells meant for one, jam-packed into dormitories, basements, corridors, converted hospital facilities, tents, trailers, and warehouses (Allen, Simonsen & Latessa, 2004).

While the Supreme Court has ruled that "double bunking" does not violate the Eighth Amendment (see, for example, *Bell v. Wolfish*, 441 U.S. 520, 1979; *Rhodes v. Chapman*, 452 U.S. 337, 1981), overcrowding in correctional facilities does cause some problems. For example, overcrowding impedes correctional officers' abilities to classify and separate inmates according to treatment, safety, and security needs (Tartaro, 2002). Additional problems stem from the frequency of medical problems in overcrowded facilities (Allen et al., 2004). State prison inmates suffer from a variety of diseases, including tuberculosis, sexually transmitted diseases, hepatitis, and HIV/AIDS (see Figure 11.2). Because mass screening programs are currently not in place in most correctional facilities, the data regarding inmates with STDs is incomplete. However, anecdotal evidence and results from behavioral studies indicate that inmates likely suffer from STDs at disproportionately high rates (Hammett, Harmon & Maruschak, 1999). Sexually transmitted diseases and other infectious diseases can be exacerbated in overcrowded conditions (Allen et al., 2004).

Figure 11.2
Health Risks in Prison

> • In 2001, approximately 5,754 inmates in U.S. prisons had confirmed cases of AIDS, up from 5,696 in 2000 (Harrison & Karberg, 2003).
>
> • In 2000, an estimated 31 percent of state inmates tested positive for Hepatitis C (Beck & Maruschak, 2004).

Ethical Dilemmas in Punishment

There are a variety of current ethical dilemmas in punishment, including the use of full-scale privatization, the punishment of special populations (such as the mentally ill and juveniles), and the death penalty. Each of these issues raises important questions about the institution of punishment (See Figure 11.3).

Privatization of correctional facilities requires that we ask "who should punish?" While there are a variety of important issues relating to the privatization of prisons, the ethical questions provoke interesting and meaningful debate. Should corrections be a money-making enterprise? Should governments delegate coercive authority to private entities? These represent just some of the ethical questions and concerns about private correctional facilities.

Although privatization can take any number of forms, full-scale privatization of corrections typically refers to those institutions that are privately owned and operated by a corporation (Pratt & Maahs, 1999). Essentially, a private company is contracted by the state to administer correctional services. Those who are vehemently opposed to full-scale privatization believe that "the state is the sole source of legitimate force and that allowing private organizations to wield the coercive power of the state (particularly in the incarceration and punishment of prisoners) undermines the legitimacy of government" (Vardalis & Becker, 2000:136).

The use of the death penalty also poses some ethical problems and requires that we ask "what types of punishments should we utilize?" For some, death, as the ultimate punishment reserved for those persons who are found guilty of committing the most heinous crimes, is just. For others, the death penalty represents an inhumane punishment that violates the Eighth Amendment provision barring the use of cruel and unusual punishments. This reason, coupled with other pressing concerns such as the execution of innocent people, arbitrary application, and the execution of juveniles, has led death penalty opponents to argue that capital punishment presents too many ethical problems and should be stricken from the range of available punishments.

The punishment of special populations, such as the mentally ill and juvenile offenders, presents another range of ethical dilemmas. Mentally ill offenders make up approximately 16 percent of prison and jail inmates (Lunney & Brown, 2002) and pose a variety of unique demands on correctional systems. An ethical issue arises when one is faced with the quality of life for severely mentally ill inmates (Faust, 2003). Such inmates are more likely to be victimized or beaten, and more likely to commit suicide compared to those who are not sick (Faust, 2003). Scholars argue that jails are no place for the mentally ill because they lack adequate resources for treatment services (Faust, 2003; Hodulik, 2001; Pawel; 2001).

Treating juvenile offenders as adults is a key ethical concern (Gaarder & Belknap, 2002; Redding, 1999; Roberts, 2004). According to Gaarder and Belknap (2002), over the past 10 years, there has been a nationwide effort to treat juvenile delinquents as adults, mainly with the get-tough movement. However, many scholars tend to agree that sentencing should be different for juvenile offenders (Gaarder & Belknap, 2002; Roberts, 2004) because the offenders lack the mental development necessary to form intent. Redding (1999) examined the consequences of treating juveniles as adults and found that "criminal prosecution and/or imprisonment retards rather than enhances community protection and diminishes rather than enhances juvenile offenders' accountability and their development of competencies" (p. 97).

Figure 11.3
Ethical Questions

Issue	Ethical Question
Privatization	Who should punish, the state or private correctional firms?
Death penalty	What types of punishments should we utilize, and how severe should they be?
Special populations	Should we punish all offenders the same way?

CONCLUSION

In sum, penal strategies have increasingly moved away from rehabilitation in recent years. While rehabilitation is still espoused by system officials, it is no longer the primary goal of correctional authorities. In place of rehabilitation, correctional policies are increasingly employing retributive and incapacitative strategies. The overall crime rate has witnessed moderate decreases in the past few years (Federal Bureau of Investigation, 2002), possibly due to the implementation of such strategies as well as a variety of other factors. However incapacitative strategies have had the unintended consequence of overcrowding our nation's prison facilities, and thus increasing the number of violent and health-related consequences. Only time will tell if we can implement a penal policy that balances the need for rehabilitation with the need for public safety.

REFERENCES

Allen, H.E., C.E. Simonsen & E.J. Latessa (2004). *Corrections in America,* 10th ed. Upper Saddle River, NJ: Prentice Hall.

Alschuler, A. (2003). "The Changing Purposes of Criminal Punishment: A Retrospective on the Past Century and Thoughts about the Next." *The University of Chicago Law Review,* 70(1):1-22.

Antunes, G. & A.L. Hunt (1973). "The Deterrent Impact of Criminal Sanctions: Some Implications for Criminal Justice Policy." *Journal of Urban Law*, 51(2):145-161.

Bailey, W. & R. Peterson (1997). "Murder, Capital Punishment and Deterrence: A Review of the Literature." In H. Bedau, *The Death Penalty in America: Current Controversies*. New York: Oxford University Press.

Beck, A. & Maruschak. (2004). Hepatitis Testing and Treatment in State Prisons, Special Report. Washington, DC: U.S. Department of Justice, National Institute of Justice, NCJ 199173

Becker, G.S. (1968). "Crime and Punishment: An Economic Approach." *Journal of Political Economy*, 78:169-217.

Bedau, H. (2003). "Punishment." *The Stanford Encyclopedia of Philosophy*, E.N. Zalta (ed.). Available at: http://plato.stanford.edu/archives/sum2003/entries/punishment/

Bonczar, T. (2003). *Prevalence of Imprisonment in the U.S. Population, 1974-2001, Special Report*. Washington, DC: Bureau of Justice Statistics, NCJ 197976.

Braswell, M. & J. Gold (2005). Chapter 3, this volume.

Braswell, M., J. Fuller & B. Lozoff (2001). *Corrections, Peacemaking and Restorative Justice*. Cincinnati. Anderson.

Byron, M. (2000). "Why My Opinion Shouldn't Count: Revenge, Retribution, and the Death Penalty Debate." *Journal of Social Philosophy*, 31(3):307-316.

Chambliss, W. (1966, January). "The Deterrent Influence of Punishment." *Crime & Delinquency*, 12:70-75.

Clark, R. (1970). *Crime in America: Observations on Its Nature, Causes, Prevention, and Control*. New York: Simon & Schuster, p. 220.

Clear, T. (1994). *Harm in American Penology: Offenders, Victims & Their Communities*. Albany: State University of New York Press.

Cochran, J. & M. Chamlin (2000). "Deterrence and Brutalization: The Dual Effects of Executions." *Justice Quarterly,* 17(4):685-706

Cullen, F.T. & K.E. Gilbert (1982). *Reaffirming Rehabilitation*. Cincinnati. Anderson.

Cullen, F.T. & J.P. Wright (1996). "Two Futures for American Corrections." In B. Maguire & P.F. Radosh (eds.), *The Past, Present and Future of American Criminal Justice*. Dix Hills, NY: General Hall.

Death Penalty Information Center. (2004). *Facts about Deterrence and the Death Penalty.* Available at: http://www.deathpenaltyinfo.org/article.php?scid=12&did=167#STUDIES

Decker, S. & C.W. Kohfeld (1990). "Certainty, Severity, and the Probability of Crime: A Logistic Analysis." *Policy Studies Journal*, 19(1):2-21.

Dickey, W.J. & P. Hollenhorst (1999). "Three-Strikes Laws: Five Years Later." *Corrections Management Quarterly*, 3(3):1-18.

Duff, R.A. (1986). *Trials and Punishments.* Cambridge: Cambridge University Press.

Eide, E. (1994). *Economics of Crime: Deterrence and the Rational Offender.* Amsterdam: North Holland.

Ehrlich, I. (1973). "Participation in Illegitimate Activities: A Theoretical and Empirical Investigation. *Journal of Political Economy*, 81(3):521-565.

Faust, T.N. (2003). "Shift the Responsibility of Untreated Mental Illness out of the Criminal Justice System." *Corrections Today*, 65(2):6-8.

Federal Bureau of Investigation (2002). *Uniform Crime Reports.* Available at: http://www.fbi.gov/ucr/cius_02/html/web/index.html

Feeley, M. & J. Simon (1992). "The New Penology: Notes on the Emerging Strategy of Corrections and Its Implications." *Criminology,* 30(4):449-474.

Finkelstein, C. (2002). "Death and Retribution." *Criminal Justice Ethics*, 21(2):12-22.

Gaarder, E., & J. Belknap (2002). "Tenuous Borders: Girls Transferred to Adult Court." *Criminology*, 40(3):481-518.

Gibbs, J.P. (1968). "Crime, Punishment, and Deterrence." *Southwestern Social Science Quarterly*, 48(4):515-530.

Gordon, D.A., K. Graves & J. Arbuthnot (1995). "The Effect of Functional Family Therapy for Delinquents on Adult Criminal Behavior." *Criminal Justice and Behavior*, 22(1):60-73.

Gold, J. (2005). Chapter 2, this volume.

Grasmick, H.G. & G.J. Bryjak (1980). "The Deterrent Effect of Perceived Severity of Punishment." *Social Forces*, 59(2):471-491.

Gray, L.N. & J.D. Martin (1969, September). "Punishment and Deterrence: Another Analysis of Gibbs' Data." *Social Science Quarterly*, 50:389-395.

Hammett, T., P. Harmon & L. Maruschak (1999). "1996-1997 Update: HIV/AIDS, STDs, and TB in Correctional Facilities." *Issues and Practices.* Washington, DC: U.S. Department of Justice, National Institute of Justice, NCJ 176344.

Harrison, P. & J. Karberg (2003). *Prison and Jail Inmates at Midyear, 2002.* Washington, DC: Bureau of Justice Statistics, NCJ 198877.

Hodulik, J. (2001). "The Drug Court Model as a Response to 'Broken Windows': Criminal Justice for the Homeless Mentally Ill." *Journal of Criminal Law and Criminology*, 91(4):1073-1101.

Hudson, B. (2002). *Understanding Justice: An Introduction to Ideas, Perspectives, and Controversies in Modern Penal Theory,* 2nd ed. Philadelphia: Open University Press.

Juarez, G. (1976). "Modifying the Indeterminate Sentence: The Changing Emphasis in Criminal Punishment." *California Law Review,* 64(2):405-418.

Kant, I. (1996). *The Metaphysics of Morals.* Translated and edited by M. Gregor. Cambridge, NY: Cambridge University Press.

Kempinen, C. & M. Kurlychek (2003). "An Outcome Evaluation of Pennsylvania's Boot Camp: Does Rehabilitative Programming Within a Disciplinary Setting Reduce Recidivism?" *Crime & Delinquency,* 49(4):581-602.

Lanier, M. & S. Henry (1998). *Essential Criminology.* Boulder, CO: Westview Press.

Logan, C.H. (1972, September). "General Deterrent Effects of Imprisonment." *Social Forces,* 51:64-73.

Lunney, L. & R. Brown (2002). "Action Speaks Louder than Words: Addressing the Mentally Ill in Jails." *Sheriff,* 54 (6):18-21.

MacKenzie. D. (2001). "Corrections and Sentencing in the 21st Century: Evidence Based Corrections and Sentencing." *Prison Journal,* 81(3):29-312.

McCord, J., R. Tremblay, F. Vitaro & L. Desmarais-Gervais (1994). "Boys' Disruptive Behavior, School Adjustment, and Delinquency: The Montreal Prevention Experiment." *International Journal of Behavioral Development,* 17(4):739-752.

Meehan, K.E. (2000). "California's Three-Strikes Law: The First Six Years." *Corrections Management Quarterly,* 4(4):22-34.

Mendes, S.M. & M.D. McDonald (2001). "Putting Severity of Punishment Back in the Deterrence Package." *Policy Studies Journal,* 29(4):588-610.

Mendes, S. (2004). "Certainty, Severity, and Their Relative Deterrent Effects:Questioning the Implications of the Role of Risk in Criminal Deterrence Policy." *The Policy Studies Journal, Vol. 32, No. 1,* 59-74

Montague, P. (1995). *Punishment as Societal Defense.* Lanham, MD: Rowman & Littlefield.

Murphy, J. (1995). *Punishment and Rehabilitation.* Belmont, CA: Wadsworth.

Pawel, M.A. (2001). "Imprisoning the Mentally Ill: Does It Matter?" *Criminal Justice Ethics,* 20(1):2-4.

Petersilia, J. (1998). "A Decade of Experimenting with Intermediate Sanctions: What Have We Learned?" *Federal Probation,* 62:3-10.

Petersilia, J. (2001). "Prisoner Reentry: Public Safety and Reintegration Challenges." *Prison Journal,* 81(3):360-375.

Petersilia, J. & S. Turner (1990). "Comparing Intensive and Regular Supervision for High-Risk Probationers: Early Results from an Experiment in California." *Crime & Delinquency,* 36(1):87-111.

Petersilia, J. & S. Turner (1993). "Intensive Probation and Parole." In M. Tonry (ed.), *Crime and Justice: A Review of Research*, Vol. 17. Chicago: University of Chicago Press.

Pratt, J. (2000). "The Return of the Wheelbarrow Men: Or, The Arrival of Postmodern Penality?" *British Journal of Criminology,* 40:127-145.

Pratt, T. & J. Maahs (1999). "Are Private Prisons More Cost-Effective Than Public Prisons? A Meta-Analysis of Evaluation Research Studies." *Crime & Delinquency,* 45:358-372.

Radelet, M. & M. Borg (2000). "The Changing Nature of Death Penalty Debates." *Annual Review of Sociology*, 26:43-62.

Redding, R.E. (1999). "Examining Legal Issues: Juvenile Offenders in Criminal Court and Adult Prison." *Corrections Today*, 61(2):92-101.

Reitan, E. (1993). "Why the Deterrence Argument for Capital Punishment Fails." *Criminal Justice Ethics*, 12(1):26-34.

Roberts, J.V. (2004). "Harmonizing the Sentencing of Young and Adult Offenders: A Comparison of the Youth Criminal Justice Act and Part XXIII of the Criminal Code." *Canadian Journal of Criminology and Criminal Justice,* 46(3):301-327.

Siegel, L. (2003). *Criminology,* 8th ed. Belmont, CA: Wadsworth/Thomson Learning.

Tartaro, C. (2002). "The Impact of Density of Jail Violence." *Journal of Criminal Justice*, 3(6):499-510.

Tittle, C. R. (1969). "Crime Rates and Legal Sanctions." *Social Problems*, 16(4):409-423.

von Hirsch, A. (1976). *Doing Justice: The Choice of Punishments*. New York: Hill and Wang.

Wesley, C. (2003). *The Practice of Punishment: Towards a Theory of Restorative Justice*. New York: Taylor & Francis.

West, D. & D. Farrington (1973). *Who Becomes Delinquent?* New York: Crane, Russak & Co.

Witte, A. D. (1983). "Economic Theories." In S.H. Kalish (ed.), *Encyclopedia of Crime and Justice* (Vol. 1). New York: Free Press.

Vardalis, J. & F. Becker (2000). "Legislative Opinions Concerning the Private Operation of State Prisons: The Case of Florida." *Criminal Justice Policy Review*, 11(2):136-149.

DISCUSSION QUESTIONS

1. Compare and contrast punishing for retribution with punishing for deterrence. Discuss the unintended consequences of each.

2. Describe the ideologies for both prevention and treatment. What are their key assumptions about criminality? How does each claim to reduce criminal behavior.

3. What are some of the challenges that special populations face in prison? Examine the ethical implications of incarcerating the mentally ill and juvenile offenders.

4. Compare and contrast contemporary retribution with retribution as revenge. Do you think that revenge has a place in contemporary punishment? Explain your answer.

5. What are the policy implications of retribution, incapacitation, and rehabilitation.

6. Describe the three ethical frameworks for punishment—utilitarianism, deontology, and peacemaking. Which one do you think should serve as the ethical framework for punishment today? Why?

CHAPTER 12

To Die or Not to Die: Morality, Ethics, and the Death Penalty

John T. Whitehead & Michael C. Braswell

The death penalty fascinates: its merits are debated, producers make movies about the death penalty (*Dead Man Walking*, *The Life of David Gale*, *The Green Mile*), and politicians use it as a sign that they are serious about the crime issue. The fascination with the ultimate sanction persists even though most murderers do not receive the death penalty, and of those who are sentenced to be executed, many get off of death row in other ways such as through court appeals.

KEY CONCEPTS:

arbitrariness

death penalty

deterrence

discrimination

incapacitation

In this chapter we will focus on the ethics of the death penalty. First, to put the death penalty in perspective we will present some basic information. Then we will outline how the three ethical theories—deontology, utilitarianism, and peacemaking—approach the issue of the ethics of the death penalty. Finally, we will consider the specific issues concerning the debate on the ethics of the death penalty.

THE DEATH PENALTY IN PERSPECTIVE: FACTS ABOUT THE DEATH PENALTY

The latest information available indicates that states executed 71 individuals in 2002 and that 3,557 persons were on death row at year-end 2002 (December 31, 2002) (Bonczar & Snell, 2003). California led the nation with 614 offenders on death row, followed by Texas (450), Florida (366), and Pennsylvania (241). Death rows were 54 percent white, 44 percent black, and 2 percent all other races. Death row prisoners were overwhelmingly male (98.6%), and more than one-half (52%) had less than a high school diploma or GED (Bonczar & Snell, 2003).

RATIONALE FOR THE DEATH PENALTY

There are two basic questions regarding the death penalty. The first addresses whether we should even have a death penalty. This question is essentially philosophical in nature. Such a question is often argued in terms of religious values and beliefs. For example, one can find both support and opposition for the death penalty among various Christian denominations, often based on scriptural passages from the Old and New Testaments. This aspect will be discussed in more detail later in the chapter. The second question is judicial in nature. Does the criminal justice system process and prosecute capital cases justly and equitably? Are the laws, procedures, and decisions about such cases administered fairly and consistently, or does discrimination occur against any group? Issues such as race, gender, and economic bias are often debated and discussed when attempting to answer this question.

Concerning the philosophical question, some argue that if an individual takes the life of another person, then that individual should have to forfeit his or her own life, while others might contend that two wrongs don't make a right—that the state also commits murder when they execute a convicted murderer. Persons who support this line of thinking would maintain that advanced or evolved societies do not include the death penalty as a punishment option. Individuals who do support the death penalty would counter by suggesting that the ultimate crime requires the ultimate penalty. Proponents of the death penalty might place their argument in a deontological frame of reference: it is society's duty to punish the most serious crime with the most severe penalty.

The late Ernest van den Haag perhaps put it most eloquently: "Can any crime be horrible enough to forfeit the life of the criminal? Can death ever be a deserved punishment. . . . I am confident that the following excerpt may help answer this question." Van den Haag went on to describe a gruesome murder in which two males tortured and sexually abused a female victim, including pouring salt into her wounds before strangling her. Afterward, they broke her neck and arms so that they could fit her body into a trunk, and then dumped her body in a dumpster (for more details, see van den Haag, 2003:235-237).

Van den Haag thinks the answer is simple: a murder as horrendous as this deserves the death penalty—even cries out for the penalty of death. In fact, van den Haag is in favor of the death penalty for all murders that so qualify according to the laws and jury decisions in the death penalty states.

Capital punishment opponents counter that a severe penalty is appropriate for the crime of murder but it does not have to include the taking of a human life. Opponents argue that a severe punishment such as life without parole (LWOP), life with the possibility of parole, or a lengthy prison sentence short of life are serious enough penalties to serve as commensurate punishment for the crime of murder. Additionally, opponents argue that sentences short of capital punishment have the advantage that if any error is made in determining either guilt or sentence, the error can be corrected, to some extent, if the offender is serving a life sentence or a lengthy prison term. If the offender has been executed, however, any mistake that is discovered years after the conviction and sentencing cannot be corrected. So, in a deontological framework, opponents could argue that LWOP, life, or a lengthy prison term can both satisfy the societal duty to demand a severe penalty for a severe offense and also satisfy any societal duty to rectify mistakes to the fullest extent possible (mistakes will be a separate topic below).

Utilitarians go further than simply offering a philosophical justification that capital punishment offers a severe penalty for a severe offense. Utilitarians argue that the death penalty has additional positive consequences that justify or demand its use, such as deterrence and incapacitation. We will discuss each of these issues in turn.

DETERRENCE

One such additional consequence, according to utilitarians, is deterrence. Utilitarians who favor capital punishment argue that capital punishment is a general deterrent: it is so severe a penalty that it deters or frightens individuals who might be contemplating committing a murder out of committing one. Capital punishment proponents usually argue from personal experience or common sense. They argue that most of us can recall experiences where we were tempted to do something wrong, such as shoplift or speed, but saw a police officer or thought of being caught and decided not to steal or speed down the highway. Proponents also offer some empirical evidence. Studies by Ehrlich (1975) and by Cochran and Chamlin claim that capital punishment has a deterrent effect (e.g., Cochran & Chamlin, 2000).

Capital punishment opponents argue that there are several problems with the deterrence argument. First, relying on our own experiences or common sense about deterrence is misleading. Most of us are law-abiding; we are good citizens who have been appropriately socialized. Many of the people who murder may not be so law-abiding and thus may not think about possible penalties. Second, many murders are committed on the spur of the moment or in an unstable emotional state that does not readily allow for a calm assessment of the possible penalty. Many homicides occur in argument situations in which the offender is agitated. Others occur in robbery situations in which both the offender and the victim are under considerable stress. In both situations as well as others, the perpetrators are not thinking rationally about the penalty for murder or other tragic consequences that are likely to result from their actions. Instead, a robber is often quite nervous and might well interpret a normal fear response by a store clerk (for example, a twitch) as a sign that the clerk is going to reach for a gun or alarm button and end up fatally shooting him or her.

Social scientists have conducted some research on the death penalty and on other penalties that shed some light on how much deterrent impact the death penalty has or might have. One of the first studies on the deterrent impact of the death penalty was conducted by Thorsten Sellin. What he did was to compare homicide rates in contiguous states that did have or did not have the death penalty. He chose Ohio, Indiana, and Michigan. These three states are midwestern states that share similar climates and economies. All three have both manufacturing (auto, steel, and related industries) and agriculture (such as soybeans). All three are a mix of both urban, suburban, and rural areas. There are also cultural, political, and social similarities. Comparing homicide rates across these three states over decades, Sellin concluded that there is no discernible impact of the death penalty. States that have the death penalty do not have lower homicide rates than states without the death penalty (Sellin, 1980).

Peterson and Bailey conducted a review of studies on the deterrent impact of capital punishment. After looking at many different types of research studies, they concluded: "In short, the empirical evidence does not support the belief that capital punishment was an effective deterrent for murder in years past. Nor is there any indication that returning to our past execution practices would have any deterrent impact on the current homicide problem" (Peterson & Bailey, 2003:277).

Other studies of deterrence also show negligible impact. For example, in the late 1970s, Scared Straight programs surfaced as a popular way to supposedly prevent delinquency. Scared Straight was the name of a program in New Jersey in which prison inmates gave prison tours to pre-delinquents or delinquents and then literally tried to scare the youths out of committing any further crime. The inmates yelled at the kids and informed them of all the horrible events that could befall them if they wound up in prison, such as physical and sexual assaults, and even being killed in prison and carried out in a body bag. Although the documentary that promoted the program claimed tremendous success, systematic scientific research studies on the effectiveness of Scared Straight–type programs indicate that there is no significant difference between youths who experience such a program and youths who do not (Lundman, 1993).

To be fair, some studies do show some deterrent effects for some punishments. Granted, many of us fear penalties enough to avoid crime. A point to be considered, however, is that opponents to the death penalty are not arguing for no penalties for murder. Rather, they are advocates for either LWOP, life with the possibility of parole, or lengthy prison sentences for murderers. What is at issue is: What is the true effect of the death penalty? This means that proponents for the death penalty need to demonstrate that the ultimate penalty has more impact than a penalty such as LWOP, which to date has not occurred.

Some proponents of the death penalty argue that a serious problem in looking at the deterrent impact of the death penalty is that it is not imposed in such a way that it can be a deterrent. Deterrence theory maintains that for any punishment or sanction to be an effective deterrent, the penalty in question must be severe, certain, and quick. The death penalty is clearly severe, but it is not always certain or quick. Concerning certainty, while most murderers are caught, not all are convicted and not all receive the death penalty. In fact, even those who receive the sentence of the death penalty do not necessarily get executed. Between 1977 and 2002, about 7,000 persons were sentenced to death, but more than one-third (36.7%; 2,535 offenders) received other dispositions. They had their sentences or convictions overturned, received commutations, or died a natural death before they could be executed (Bonczar & Snell, 2003). Quickness is also problematic. The average stay on death row is about 10 years. Death penalty proponents argue that such lack of certainty and lack of speed in imposing the death penalty detract from its effectiveness. They argue that improvements in certainty and quickness could result in findings that deterrence works. A more recent discussion of the research on deterrence, however, disagrees that improvements will result in new findings of effectiveness (Peterson & Bailey, 2003).

One problem with increasing the speed at which death row offenders proceed to execution is that a major reason for the lengthy time on death row is to allow time for appeals. States usually have a mandatory appeal of the case. Then offenders often pursue discretionary appeals in an effort to save their lives. Lieberman and his colleagues have shown that many of the appeals show reversible error. They studied more than 4,500 appeals from 1973 and 1995 and found the overall rate of prejudicial error to be 68 percent. "In other words, courts found serious, reversible error in nearly 7 of every 10 of the thousands of capital sentences that were fully reviewed during the period" (Liebman, Fagan & West, 2000). Death penalty opponents argue that if states were to shorten the time between sentencing and execution, that would cut short the time for appeals. This would reduce the number of errors that are found. So it would become more likely for states to execute individuals who either did not commit the murder or deserved a conviction and sentence for a noncapital offense such as manslaughter that does not involve the death penalty. The question ends up being one of efficiency versus effectiveness, shortening the appeal process versus guarding against error when execution is the penalty to be rendered.

INCAPACITATION

Death penalty proponents are right about one thing: the death penalty is perfect incapacitation. Executing an offender prevents him or her from ever killing again. Therefore, in a way, the death penalty does satisfy the utilitarian goal of incapacitation.

Opponents cannot deny the incapacitative impact of the death penalty but they can argue that other penalties can also achieve very high degrees of incapacitation. LWOP, for example, will ensure that a murderer cannot commit another homicide on the street. He or she may kill a fellow prisoner or a prison guard, but they will not kill another person on the outside. Moreover, the number of killings in prison is quite small. For example, the latest figures show that approximately one prisoner per state is murdered in prison every year, and about 20 prison staff members are killed every five years (Bedau, 1997:177). Any loss of life is tragic, but unfortunately, these statistics are incomplete and dated. These statistics also do not tell us if convicted murderers were in fact the perpetrators of these in-prison crimes.

There is also substantial evidence that if society punished murderers with 10 to 20 years of imprisonment and then released them on parole, the released murderers would have very low recidivism (new crime) rates. Parole statistics consistently show that murderers make good parolees. Paroled murderers have the lowest crime rates of all parolees. One of the best pieces of evidence about the safety of parole for murderers comes from the *Furman* cases. *Furman* was a Supreme Court case that ruled the death penalty, as then practiced, unconstitutional. As a result, death row inmates in affected states were switched to parole-eligible status and were in fact later (after serving years of their sentences) paroled. The so-called *Furman* parolees performed quite well in the community. In one study of 188 murderers who were released on parole and served an average time of 5.3 years on parole, only one committed a new murder. Twenty (10.6% of those released) committed a new felony (Marquart & Sorensen, 1997).

Why do paroled murderers do so well on parole? There are several reasons for the success. One is that parole boards are more careful in deciding whether a murderer gets parole than in deciding, for example, whether a car thief gets parole. If the parole board makes a mistake about a car thief, the damage is just one more stolen car. If they make a mistake about a murderer, there is the possibility that another murder will take place. Parole board members are concerned about avoiding such serious mistakes. A second reason is that even if the parole board releases a murderer, they usually make him or her serve quite a few years (10 or more) in prison before release. Those years allow maturation to occur; the parolee is often not the impulsive and immature person who entered prison. Simple aging also occurs; the released murderer is not as young, energetic, and angry as he or she once was.

As stated previously, the death penalty achieves perfect incapacitation: no executed killer can kill again in society. However, Life Without Parole also prevents killers from killing again on the street. Parole statistics, especially the *Furman* cases, indicate that even parole for murder is not necessarily a costly choice in terms of outcomes. Very few paroled murderers kill again, but a minority (about 10%) do indeed commit a new felony. So if society wants perfect incapacitation, the death penalty delivers perfection in one specific dimension. If society is willing to tolerate some error (e.g., some new crimes but very few murders), then parole is available as an option.

PEACEMAKING PERSPECTIVE

As noted in Chapter 3, the peacemaking perspective focuses on caring, connectedness, and mindfulness. Peacemakers oppose the death penalty because they think that it does not promote caring, connectedness, and mindfulness whereas other penalties do.

A living example of peacemaking and the death penalty is Jarvis Masters. Jarvis is a death row inmate in California. His time on death row has been an opportunity for him to examine his life and turn from crime and violence to Buddhism and promoting peace. By becoming a Buddhist he has come to realize that we are connected so that what each one of us does indeed affect others and oneself as well. In his book *Finding Freedom* (1997), he gives two dramatic examples of connectedness and caring.

One Fourth of July two guards who normally worked another cellblock were assigned to death row. They were anticipating a holiday barbecue that evening, so they were in a hurry to get through the day. Consequently, they practically threw the food at the inmates that day and ignored simple requests for silverware or toilet paper. Their disdain for inmates was causing rage to rise in the prisoners. Masters saw what was happening and felt he should do something to calm the prisoners. He decided that if the inmates stuffed their toilets with towels and flooded the cellblock, the flood would be a way for the inmates to respond to the guards in a controlled way. It would be an expression of prisoner anger, and it would make the guards late for their barbecue that evening because they would have to clean up the cellblock before they could leave work. More importantly, this minor expression of prisoner anger would prevent the inmates' anger from building up to a point at which inmates might attack a guard.

Another incident involved the guards putting a new prisoner into the yard in such a way that they were basically setting him up for an attack. Apparently, the new prisoner was gay and was dressed in some fashion to draw attention to his sexual orientation. At the time, says Masters, there was considerable hatred for homosexuals in San Quentin Prison. Masters saw the guards let this new prisoner onto the yard and, shortly thereafter, saw an inmate coming toward the new prisoner with a shiv (prison weapon). Masters intervened; he simply went up to the new prisoner and asked him for a cigarette. Seeing Masters stopped the inmate from attacking the new prisoner. Afterwards, Masters wondered why he had risked his own life for someone he really didn't know. He asked himself if he was the only Buddhist there.

The example of Jarvis Masters shows that offenders can change in prison and have a positive effect on other prisoners. Although Masters did receive a death sentence, his time on death row allowed him to question his former lifestyle and change to a lifestyle of genuine spirituality. If he had been executed sooner, he would not have had the chance to change. Nor would he have had the chance to do some of the positive things he has done in prison, such as the two examples just noted. Parenthetically, a death penalty proponent might argue that the inmate on death row didn't give his or her victim a chance to mature or experience such personal transformation.

Peacemaking criminologists might also be concerned about the effects of death row on the family members of the death row inmates. One mother of a death row inmate notes that a detective magazine came out with an article depicting her son's "killing spree." She was so distraught that she tried to buy every copy so that her friends and neighbors would not see the story (Letzin, 1999). A few years later, a brother noted his painful experiences when friends would talk about criminals and say that "They ought to hang the bastard" (Lezin, 1999:18).

Sending offenders to death row seems to foster seeing these criminals as outside the human family and permitting the rest of us to depict them as less than human. Unfortunately, those who are parents, spouses, or siblings of the offender have to listen to and live with such depictions. The relative knows the offender as a flawed human, with good and bad traits, but the media and careless citizens may describe a relative on death row as a cold-blooded killer, a monster, an animal, and so on. It is painful to see and hear someone you love depicted in extreme terms.

MISTAKES

Determining who is eligible for the death penalty is far from an error-free process. Juries and judges make mistakes in determining guilt and determining sentences. Mistakes about guilt result in an innocent person being placed on death row and experiencing the stress of anticipating an execution that he or she does not deserve. Mistakes about the penalty—the sentencing phase—mean that a person who perhaps deserves a lengthy prison sentence is instead anticipating death/execution and spends his or her time trying to appeal an incorrect sentence.

A major source of the mistakes in the death penalty decision-making process is the quality of defense representation that many offenders get. Many offenders are poor and cannot attract the best defense attorney available. Moreover, many states are willing or able to spend only a limited amount of money on indigent offender defense representation. Liebman and his associates found that defense lawyers "who didn't even look for—and demonstrably missed—important evidence that the defendant was innocent or did not deserve to die" was one of the most common errors causing a majority of the reversals at the state post-conviction stage (Liebman, Fagan & West, 2000:ii).

In one case in Georgia the state paid for an assigned defense attorney who was actually a talented lawyer. The problem was that he was a skilled divorce attorney who had never worked a death penalty case. To make things worse, the attorney thought that just because he had done the judge a favor before the case, the judge would return the favor in the totally unrelated death penalty case (Letzin, 1999). Some states, such as New York, do provide competitive pay to attorneys assigned to death penalty cases so that they can put forth an adequate defense. However, many other states provide very modest compensation so that it is often difficult if not impossible to attract qualified individuals to work death penalty cases.

Recent studies have shown that in the "death belt" (nine southern states that use the death penalty frequently) more than 10 percent of the attorneys who have represented indigent capital defendants have been disbarred, suspended, or disciplined at rates significantly higher than average, even in those states. In fact, most of the attorneys in the death belt had not handled a capital case before, and the death belt states did not have training programs for these attorneys (Mello & Perkins, 2003:369)

The result is that many death penalty defendants do not get adequate (much less, superior) representation. Less than adequate representation means that some unknown number of death row defendants receive the death penalty improperly. Adequate defense counsel would mean at least a lesser sentence, if not exoneration.

Apart from what O.J. Simpson, Kobe Bryant, or Michael Jackson actually did or did not do concerning their alleged criminal actions, it is clear that these celebrities were able to hire the best defense attorneys they could afford. Many of the persons who wind up on death row quite simply could not afford that level of defense representation. If they could afford such high-quality attorneys, they would probably not end up on death row. The question, then, is whether it is ethical for wealth or the lack of it to have such impact on who is sentenced to capital punishment. One could argue that the prosecution may be at a disadvantage if the person who is tried for first-degree murder is very wealthy, but the prosecuting attorney and state have a substantial advantage if the defendant is poor.

Opponents of the death penalty argue that mistakes stemming from factors such as inaccurate eyewitness testimony and inadequate defense representation occur too frequently and are reason enough to abolish the death penalty. As noted above, the Lieberman (2000) study of appeals found the rate of prejudicial error to be 68 percent. Abolitionists maintain that an error rate this high is simply unacceptable.

The proponent response to the issue of mistakes in the administration of capital punishment is that mistakes happen in all walks of life. Ernest van den Haag still supports the death penalty, arguing that all human institutions are flawed. For example, he has argued that driving to school or work is a very accident-prone activity. Every time we get in our cars and drive somewhere, we are taking our lives in our hands. We trade off the danger of driving for the convenience of driving to work or classes. Even ambulances, notes van den Haag, kill some innocent pedestrians, but they save more innocent people than they kill (van den Haag, 2003:241). In sum, he thinks that the death penalty is justified, despite mistakes, as long as it deters and the mistakes are few.

As noted, the deterrent impact of the death penalty is not as certain as van den Haag contends. Most social scientists conclude that the deterrent impact is either unknown or nonexistent. Moreover, the frequency of mistakes appears to be much more prevalent than few. Former Governor Ryan of Illinois was so concerned about mistakes that he put in place a temporary moratorium on executions. (For a look at the personal impact of mistakes, see Box 12.1.)

Box 12.1
The Personal Impact of Mistakes

> One of the authors of this chapter likes to have his classes consider that because human beings aren't perfect, neither is our system of justice absolutely perfect. Given that reality, is it acceptable to you that there are some mistakes about who gets the death penalty (for instance, one innocent is executed for every 10,000 who are deserving of death)? After the students raise their hands in support of this statement, he says "OK now keep your hands raised if you can live with such a mistake about the death penalty if it is your brother, your son, your spouse, or yourself who is the innocent victim of the mistake?" Without exception, hands drop one by one.
>
> What about you? Are mistakes in determining who goes to death row all right with you? Are they still acceptable if you or a loved one is the one experiencing the mistake? Are you so much in favor of the death penalty that you can still support it even if it means you or a loved one will be wrongfully executed?

DISCRIMINATION AND RACIAL BIAS

As noted at the beginning of this chapter, death row is disproportionately populated by blacks. Although African Americans make up only about 12 percent of the U.S. population, they constitute about 44 percent of the prisoners on death row (Bonczar & Snell, 2003).

The first ethical concern is whether discrimination in fact occurs. The high percentage of African Americans on death row does not in itself prove discrimination. If blacks make up about 44 percent of the murderers in the United States, then they should make up about 44 percent of the persons on death row. More specifically, if blacks commit about 44 percent of the capital murders (the homicides that deserve capital punishment), then they should make up about 44 percent of the prisoners on death row.

A recent review of research on discrimination in the administration of the death penalty led to several conclusions. First, the race of the defendant is not a significant factor in the prosecutor's charging decision. Second, the data "document race-of-victim disparities reflecting more punitive treatment of white-victim cases among similarly aggravated cases, regardless of the race of the defendant" (Baldus & Woodworth, 2003:241). These disparities seem to stem more from the prosecutor's charging decision than from judge or jury decisions. Third, "in several jurisdictions for which data are available, cases involving black defendants and white victims are treated more punitively than cases with all other defendant/victim racial combinations" (Baldus & Woodworth, 2003:241). Fourth, a few studies do show negative impact on black defendants or on defendants who killed white victims; these disparate impacts "arise from disproportionately punitive charging practices in counties with either particularly large numbers of black-defendant cases or particularly large numbers of white-victim cases on their capital case dockets" (Baldus & Woodworth, 2003:242).

The Capital Jury Project has discovered some interesting findings about how jurors make their decisions. Project researchers have found that the number of white males or even the presence of one black juror on a jury can make a significant difference in the decisions made by juries. Specifically, the Capital Jury Project found a "white male dominance" effect in black defendant/white victim cases. That is, the jury voted for the death sentence in only 30 percent of the cases when the jury had fewer than five white male jurors, but the jury voted for death in 71 percent of the cases when there were at least five white male jurors on the jury. The researchers also found a "black male presence" effect: "Having a black male on the jury reduced the probability of a death sentence from 71.9 percent to 37.5 percent in the B/W [black defendant/white victim] cases, and from 66.7 percent to 42.9 percent in the B/B [black defendant/black victim] cases" (Bowers & Foglia, 2003:77).

Discussions regarding the actual extent of discrimination in the death penalty are important and need to continue. It is imperative to eliminate discrimination. It is also important to end any appearance of discrimination. The high percentage of African Americans who receive the death penalty implies to many that there is discrimination. Even if careful investigation shows that discrimination is not occurring, and that prosecutors and juries are perfectly unbiased in their decisions, many individuals interpret the high percentage of blacks on death row as apparent evidence of discrimination. Discrimination or the appearance of discrimination can influence minority members to have negative attitudes toward police, judges, and others in the criminal justice system. Such negative attitudes can affect the administration of justice.

ARBITRARINESS

Closely related to the issue of discrimination is the issue of arbitrary selection of individuals for the death penalty. Although approximately 20,000 murders are committed each year in the United States, fewer than 500 cases result in the death penalty.

Ideally, those 500 cases should be the most deserving of the death penalty. Practically, however, that is simply not the case. As noted above, race appears to play some factor in the selection of cases for the death penalty. For one thing, black defendant/white victim cases are more likely to result in the death penalty than black defendant/black victim cases.

Even apart from any instances of racial impact, other factors such as location, judge, prosecutor, and case notoriety can play a role in determining whether one murderer gets capital punishment while another gets a life sentence or even less.

The deontologist would be quick to argue that arbitrariness should play no role in such a critical decision. The principle of the categorical imperative calls for not making exceptions but treating similarly situated individuals in similar fashion. Given the demonstrated arbitrariness in the death penalty, a deontologist could oppose the death penalty for this reason alone.

Arbitrariness is hard to eliminate. The federal courts now use a guidelines system that is meant to reduce arbitrariness in all criminal sentencing. Problems persist. For one thing, the Federal Sentencing Guidelines allow for reductions based on providing information on other criminals. Therefore, offenders who either have no information to give, or refuse to give information, receive no reductions. One first offender, for example, refused to implicate her own mother and was given a 10-year sentence, while an offender caught with 20,000 kilos of cocaine served only four years in prison because he "cooperated," that is, gave information on other dealers (Schlosser, 2003:61). Another effort to reduce arbitrariness is proportionality review. This means that courts review death penalty cases in the jurisdiction (usually, one state) to attempt to ensure that only the most horrible murders get the death penalty and that all murders less serious than the least serious death penalty case get a sentence less severe than the death penalty. The basic problem is that such a proportionality review is difficult to do (Mandery, 2003). Measuring severity is not as simple as measuring blood pressure, especially in light of the fact that "the fundamental equality of each survivor's loss creates an inevitable emotional momentum to expand the categories for death penalty eligibility" (Turow, 2003:47).

Abolishing the death penalty will not eliminate arbitrariness. Some murderers will get LWOP, some life with the possibility of parole, some shorter prison sentences, and some even probation. However, abolishing the death penalty could end the arbitrariness of some murderers getting executed and others getting much less severe penalties.

CONDITIONS ON DEATH ROW

Because more than 3,500 prisoners are currently on death row, it is important to consider death row conditions. What are death row prisoners experiencing as they wait for execution?

There are two main types of death rows: unreformed and reformed (Johnson, 1998). Unreformed death rows involve a great deal of isolation. Prisoners are kept in solitary cells and are released from their cells only for short periods of exercise or showers. Such prisoners spend a considerable amount of time reading or watching television.

Reformed death rows, on the other hand, allow prisoners to spend much more time out of their cells for work and recreation. Prisoners might work at jobs such as making clothes or entering computer data. Both work and recreation allow for more socializing with other prisoners. One death row resident in Texas spent much of his time painting pictures, including pictures of Jesus and of how he imagined the execution room to look (Frontline: The Execution).

Many think that a reformed death row represents considerable improvement over an unreformed death row because the inmate on a reformed death row is out of his or her cell more often and has more opportunities to work and engage in recreation or socializing with other inmates.

Box 12.2
Donald Cabana: A Former Executioner Speaks Out on Death Row

Former warden Donald Cabana came to have doubts about working in corrections after executing some prisoners that he became quite close to, but he had no doubts about not wanting to supervise any more executions. "Of one thing I was certain, whatever the future might hold, I had privately concluded that I would not supervise another execution" (Cabana, 1996:191).

Several factors had caused Cabana to change. One factor was executing a man that Cabana knew had changed dramatically during his years on Mississippi's death row. "I was absolutely convinced that Connie Ray Evans would never kill again, and that he would present no threat to other inmates if his sentence were commuted to life. . . . Evans had arrived on death row a streetwise drug abuser, bitter and scornfully contemptuous of authority. He had changed, and I personally had watched the change, especially over the past three years." Cabana pleaded for a commutation from the Governor, imploring the Governor that "Isn't that [change] what prisons are supposed to be about?" (Cabana, 1996:179). The Governor, however, refused to commute the sentence to life, and Cabana had to carry out Evans' execution.

If you are preparing for a career in criminal justice and you go to work in a capital punishment state, you too might secure a position like Don Cabana's. He wound up having to supervise executions. You could end up arresting and investigating capital case defendants, prosecuting capital cases, defending capital defendants, guarding death row inmates, or, like Cabana, actually supervising executions. What do you think about actually being involved in executions or death row or capital cases? Would it bother you to be involved in any stage of the process? Now that about 80 percent of the states have capital punishment, a considerable percentage of criminal justice workers may become involved in the process to some extent.

Robert Johnson, a strong opponent of capital punishment, is not so positive about reformed death row environments. Johnson argues that even a reformed death row does not help a prisoner get ready for his or her own death. In fact, Johnson thinks that there will never be a death row environment that truly prepares an inmate for death. Such a death row would be too painful, says Johnson, for both inmates and guards:

> Officials would be unable to ignore the hurt and loss they, as persons, would inflict on their prisoners, whom they would know to be frail human beings. The prisoners, too, no longer dulled to their own feelings, might well suffer greatly. Executions would be traumatic events, the virtual antithesis of their current bureaucratic reality (Johnson, 1998:215).

Aside from Johnson, most inmates and guards as well as most critics would probably endorse the reformed death row over the unreformed one. With more opportunities for work and recreation, the reformed death row seems to be the best that prisons can offer for those condemned to death by the courts.

JURORS IN CAPITAL CASES

Something relatively new in the debate on capital punishment is the examination of juror behavior in capital cases. The Capital Jury Project in particular has brought forth considerable information about how jurors go about making the decision to vote for or against capital punishment. Unfortunately, much of this information is quite disturbing.

First, many jurors make the decision in favor of the death penalty too soon. Specifically, 30 percent of jurors in capital cases make the decision at the guilt stage, prior to the penalty stage. This means that three out of 10 capital jurors decide on the sentence before they have a chance to hear the evidence about sentencing (Bowers, Fleury-Steiner & Antonio, 2003).

Second, many jurors hold inaccurate beliefs about how many years a prisoner would have to serve in prison if he received a prison sentence instead of the death penalty. For example, in both Alabama and California, the mandatory minimum sentence that a prisoner would have to serve would be life without parole. However, jurors thought the mandatory minimum sentences in those two states were 15 years and 17 years, respectively. Therefore, jurors thought prisoners would be out in a decade and a half, whereas the statutes stipulated life without parole. Such erroneous beliefs about alternative prison terms can easily influence jurors to vote for the death penalty in order to prevent perceived heinous murderers from being released from prison.

Third, capital jurors are often confused about mitigating factors, which are a critical part of the decision to impose the death penalty. Many jurors mistakenly think that mitigating factors must be proven beyond a reasonable doubt or that all jurors must agree that a factor is a mitigator (Bowers, Fleury-Steiner & Antonio, 2003).

Finally, as we noted previously, the Capital Jury Project has thrown new light on the issue of the impact of race on the capital punishment decision. If there is no black juror on the jury, compared to the presence of at least one black male juror, a death sentence is twice as likely. In trials with no black juror, the death sentences resulted 71.9 percent of the time versus 37.5 percent of the cases with at least one black male juror (Bowers, Fleury-Steiner & Antonio, 2003). It appears that the presence of at least one black male juror can get the other jurors to consider the evidence more deliberately.

RELIGION AND CAPITAL PUNISHMENT

Many people use religion to justify their views on the death penalty. This is not the place for a thorough theological debate on the death penalty, but because the death penalty debate often includes religious arguments, we think it important to note some of the Judaeo-Christian–based religious arguments surrounding capital punishment.

Sister Helen Prejean is a powerful example of someone who sees the message of Christ and Christianity as condemning the death penalty. While she was a nun working with the poor in New Orleans, a friend asked her to become a spiritual advisor for a death row inmate. That led to being a spiritual advisor for additional inmates and a book and movie entitled *Dead Man Walking* (Prejean, 1994). In the book she outlines her opposition to the death penalty. For example, she once asked a warden the following question:

> Do you really believe that Jesus, who taught us not to return hate for hate and evil for evil and whose dying words were, 'Father, forgive them,' would participate in these executions? Would Jesus pull the switch? (Prejean, 1994:122).

Yet many Christians apparently do not see a contradiction between Sister Prejean's merciful Jesus and a perceived duty to execute. Many Christians point to Paul's Letter to the Romans (13.4) as proof that God endorses the death penalty when used appropriately (see, e.g., the June 2000 Southern Baptist Convention Resolution on Capital Punishment [www. sbc.net/resolutions/]) (supporting "the fair and equitable use of capital punishment by civil magistrates as a legitimate form of punishment for those guilty of murder or treasonous acts that result in death").

Some see the story of Jesus and the woman caught in adultery as another indicator of Jesus' stance against the death penalty. In this incident, the religious leaders brought to Jesus a woman allegedly caught in the act of adultery. The typical penalty was capital punishment, but Jesus told the questioners that "he who is without sin should cast the first stone." Ashamed, they all walked away (John 8:1-11). Many see this as evidence of Jesus' rejection of the death penalty.

One scholar disagrees. H. Wayne House argues that in this incident Jesus is really concerned about the other party, the man who also committed adultery. House argues that under Mosaic Law both parties to adultery should be charged. Furthermore, the witnesses are guilty of a capital crime by charging only the woman. House argues that here Jesus is taking the procedural issues very seriously and thus is not condemning capital punishment but calling for correct process (House, 1997).

In their official statement on the death penalty, U.S. Catholic Bishops urged fellow Christians "to remember the teaching of Jesus who called us to be reconciled with those have injured us (Matthew 5:43-45) and to pray for forgiveness for our sins "as we forgive those who have sinned against us." (Matthew 6:12) (U.S. Catholic Bishops' Statement on Capital Punishment, 1980:7).

While Biblical scholars and theologians can argue about these and other passages, Sister Prejean's comment that it seems incongruous that the Jesus who preaches love and forgiveness (e.g., "Love your neighbor as yourself;" "Forgive seven times seventy") would favor capital punishment seems logical. Furthermore, societal conditions have changed considerably since the time of Jesus. Lengthy prison terms were not the norm (nor viable alternative to capital punishment) 2000 years ago when Jesus walked the earth, but they are quite possible today.

Several Christian churches have issued formal statements against capital punishment based on their interpretation of the teachings of Jesus. For example, both the Roman Catholic Church and the Presbyterian Church have issued formal statements opposing the death penalty (U.S. Catholic Bishops' Statement on Capital Punishment, 1980; Presbyterian Moratorium on Capital Punishment, see http://horeb.pcusa.org/crim_justice/capitalpunishment.htm). On the other hand, as noted above, the Southern Baptist Convention has issued a statement in favor of the death penalty (see http://www.sbc.net/resolutions).

Theologian George Boyd has an interesting opinion about the death penalty. He opposes the death penalty because he thinks that a convicted murderer might think that his or her debt to society can be paid by accepting the death penalty. Boyd does not want any murderer to be able to feel that way: "Murderers should never be allowed the comfort of the illusion that they can 'pay' for their crime" (Boyd, 1988:163).

In conclusion, churches and theologians are not in agreement over the death penalty. Some religious persons such as Sister Helen Prejean are very active in trying to abolish the death penalty. Others, however, such as the Southern Baptist Convention, endorse capital punishment. It is somewhat perplexing that followers of the same religious leader, Jesus Christ, sincerely maintain dramatically different positions on such a fundamental issue as the death penalty. Perhaps this controversy indicates that believers must struggle with such basic issues and try to come up with a workable solution.

ALTERNATIVES TO THE DEATH PENALTY

If states were to abolish the death penalty, the most likely current alternative would be a sentence of life without any possibility of parole (LWOP). In the last five to 10 years, this has been mentioned most frequently as an alternative punishment.

For example, in a 2004 nationwide poll, 50 percent of the respondents favored the death penalty and 46 percent favored LWOP (life without parole), compared to 52 percent favoring the death penalty and 37 percent favoring life without parole in 2000 (Gallup Poll, adapted by Sourcebook of Criminal Justice Statistics Online, http:/www.albany.edu/sourcebook).

Some utilitarians question LWOP in terms of costs. Assuming that it costs approximately $20,000 to keep an offender in prison for one year and assuming about 50 years of incarceration for a typical murderer, LWOP could easily cost the state about $1 million per inmate. That is a considerable expense. It is not uncommon to hear citizens question the expenditure of so much money on someone who has taken a human life! ("Why should I as a taxpayer have to pay to keep a murderer alive?")

Opponents of the death penalty contend that it is in fact more expensive to execute a murderer sentenced to capital punishment. This statement at first seems difficult to believe, but capital cases take extra time and money, states mandate at least one court appeal, defendants usually pursue additional discretionary appeals, and death rows can be expensive if the inmates are not working. When all the costs of capital punishment are added up, it can cost the state from $2.5 to $5 million to execute one individual (Bohm, 2003).

To be fair, if capital punishment were abolished and LWOP were the most serious penalty, it is likely that murderers would pursue many appeals of that sentence as well. It also seems reasonable, though, that trials and other costs of LWOP sentences would never come to equal the time and expense of capital punishment verdicts.

Many murderers would probably accept LWOP sentences instead of capital punishment. Most seem to want to stay alive even if it means endless years in prison. However, it is important to note that not every murderer would agree. One murderer on death row, for example, was very clear in insisting that he was not desirous of spending the rest of his natural life on death row. In his words, he did not want to be "locked in Hell for all of eternity" (Arriens, 1997:82).

The other alternative to the death penalty is a life sentence with the possibility of parole. This option is not very popular at present. Most of the research focuses on either the death penalty or LWOP. A major reason seems to be public sentiment; the pubic wants murderers either executed or locked up permanently.

An argument in favor of the possibility of parole for murderers is the fact that some murderers succeed quite favorable on parole. ABC did a fascinating documentary about 20 years ago that followed the lives of 40 death row inmates in California. A state appeals court overturned the death penalty in California, and the death row prisoners (108 of them at the time) became eligible for parole. Over the years, the parole board paroled 40.

Thirty-four of the individuals succeeded—got jobs, married, raised kids, and even did such things as speaking to high school students to try to encourage them to live positive lives and stay out of crime. Some failed, however; one committed a new murder and one committed a horrible rape.

Although the current climate is not favorable for the option of life with the possibility of parole, evidence that some parole murderers do so well in terms of jobs, relationships, and parenting, raises the issue that perhaps this should be an option for some. (See Box 12.3 for Scott Turow's comments on the death penalty.)

Box 12.3
Scott Turow's Comments on the Death Penalty

> Scott Turow, the author of such best-selling novels as *Presumed Innocent* and *Reversible Errors*, was a prosecutor and recently served on a governor's commission in Illinois looking into the death penalty in that state.
>
> On the one hand, he notes that he himself would be willing to inject the fatal poison if the murderer were a killer such as John Wayne Gacy, who tortured and killed 33 young men. Along these lines, he and the other members of the commission voted to limit capital punishment to five criteria: multiple murders, murder of a police officer or firefighter, a killing in prison, a murder impeding the criminal justice system, or a murder with torture.
>
> On the other hand, Turow is painfully aware that "[n]ow and then, we will execute someone who is innocent . . ." (Turow, 3003:47). Thus when the commission came to a final vote on whether Illinois should have the death penalty or not, Turow reports "I voted no" (Turow, 2003:47).

CONCLUSION

In this chapter we have tried to present some of the ethical questions about the death penalty. This chapter is not meant to provide complete coverage of the topic. For further coverage, see Bohm (2003) or Costanzo (1999).

Utilitarians would consider the consequences of the death penalty such as deterrence, incapacitation, mistakes, and discrimination. Deontologists would consider the duty to punish and whether the death penalty is the deserved penalty for murder or whether other penalties such as life without parole can be a sufficient punishment for the crime of murder. The peacemaking perspective focuses on the core principles of caring, connectedness, and mindfulness as they pertain to the death penalty. As we have noted, many people also bring religious arguments into the debate.

What each person must do is examine the reasons for his or her current position on the death penalty and ask if those reasons seem sufficient. If not, then the individual should investigate further and come to a new position that is in line with the information that is currently available about the death penalty and its administration.

REFERENCES

Baldus, D.C. & G. Woodworth (2003). "Race Discrimination in the Administration of the Death Penalty." *Criminal Law Bulletin*, 39:194-226.

Bedau, H.A. (1997). "Prison Homicides, Recidivist Murder, and Life Imprisonment." In H.A. Bedau (ed.), *The Death Penalty in America*. New York: Oxford University Press, pp. 176-182.

Bohm, R.M. (203). *Deathquest II: An Introduction to the Theory and Practice of Capital Punishment in the United States*. Cincinnati: Anderson.

Bonczar, T.P. & T.L. Snell (2003). *Capital Punishment, 2002*. Washington, DC: U.S. Department of Justice.

Bowers, W.J., B.D. Fleury-Steiner & M.E. Antonio (2003). "The Capital Sentencing Decision: Guided Discretin, Reasoned Moral Judgment, or Legal Fiction." In J.R. Acker, R.M. Bohm & C.S. Lanier, *America's Experiment with Capital Punishment: Reflections on the Past, Present, and Future of the Ultimate Penal Sanction*. Durham, NC: Carolina Academic Press, pp. 413-467.

Bowers, W.J. & W.D. Foglia (2003). "Still Singularly Agonizing: Law's Failure to Purge Arbitrariness from Capital Sentencing." *Criminal Law Bulletin*, 39:51-86.

Boyd, G.N. (1988). "Capital Punishment: Deserved and Wrong." *The Christian Century*, (February 17 1988): 162-165.

Cabana, D.A. (1996). *Death at Midnight: The Confession of an Executioner*. Boston: Northeastern University Press.

Costanzo, M. (1997). *Just Revenge: Costs and Consequences of the Death Penalty*. New York: St. Martin's Press.

Ehrlich, I. (1975). "The Deterrent Effect of Capital Punishment: A Question of Life and Death." *American Economic Review*, 65: 397-417.

Feld, B.C. (2003). "The Politics of Race and Juvenile Justice: The 'Due Process Revolution' and the Conservative Reaction." *Justice Quarterly*, 20:765-900.

Gillespie, L.K. (2003). *Inside the Death Chamber: Exploring Executions*. Boston: Allyn & Bacon.

House, H.W. (1997). "The New Testament and Moral Arguments for Capital Punishment." In H.A. Bedau (ed.), *The Death Penalty in America: Current Controversies*. New York: Oxford University Press, pp. 415-428.

Johnson, R. (1998). *Death Work: A Study of the Modern Execution Process*. Belmont, CA: West/Wadsworth.

Lezin, K. (1999). *Finding Life on Death Row: Profiles of Six Inmates*. Boston: Northeastern University Press.

Liebman, J.S., J. Fagan & V. West (2000). *A Broken System: Error Rates in Capital Cases, 1973-1995*. Available at: http://ccjr.policy.net/proactive/newsroom/release.vtml?id=18200

Lundman, R.J. (1993). *Prevention and Control of Juvenile Delinquency*, 2nd ed. New York: Oxford University Press.

Mandery, E.J. (2003). "The Principles of Proportionality Review," *Criminal Law Bulletin*, 39:157-193.

Masters, J.J. (1997). *Finding Freedom: Writings from Death Row*. Junction City, CA: Padma.

Mello, M. & P.J. Perkins (2003). "Closing the Circle: The Illusion of Lawyers for People Litigating for Their Lives at the *Fin de siecle*." In J.R. Acker, R.M. Bohm & C.S. Lanier, *America's Experiment with Capital Punishment: Reflections on the Past, Present, and Future of the Ultimate Penal Sanction*. Durham, NC: Carolina Academic Press, pp. 347-384.

Peterson, R.D. & W.C. Bailey (2003). "Is Capital Punishment an Effective Deterrent for Murder? An Examination of Social Science Research." In J.R. Acker, R.M. Bohm & C.S. Lanier, *America's Experiment with Capital Punishment: Reflections on the Past, Present, and Future of the Ultimate Penal Sanction*, Durham, NC: Carolina Academic Press, pp. 251-282.

Prejean, H. (1994). *Dead Man Walking: An Eyewitness Account of the Death Penalty in the United States*. New York: Vintage Books.

Schlosser, E. (2003). *Reefer Madness: Sex, Drugs, and Cheap Labor in the American Black Market*. Boston: Houghton Mifflin.

Sellin, T. (1980). *The Penalty of Death*. Beverly Hills, CA: Sage.

Turow, S. (2003, January 6th). "To Kill or Not to Kill: Coming to Terms with Capital Punishment." *The New Yorker*, 40-47.

Van den Haag, E. (2003). "Justice, Deterrence and the Death Penalty." In J.R. Acker, R.M. Bohm & C.S. Lanier, *America's Experiment with Capital Punishment: Reflections on the Past, Present, and Future of the Ultimate Penal Sanction*. Durham, NC: Carolina Academic Press, pp. 223-249.

DISCUSSION QUESTIONS

1. How serious an ethical issue is the problem of mistakes relating to the death penalty? Is the death penalty ethical if there is only one mistake a year? One every five years? Is perfection necessary? Why or why not?

2. Discuss the relative merits and problems of a sentence of life without parole versus the death penalty. Which seems more ethical? What are the problems of each?

3. Would death penalty opponents really be satisfied if life without parole became the most serious penalty? If the death penalty were abolished, would death penalty opponents then try to abolish life without parole, claiming it to be too harsh?

4. Discuss religious arguments for and against the death penalty. What do you think religion suggests we should do about the death penalty?

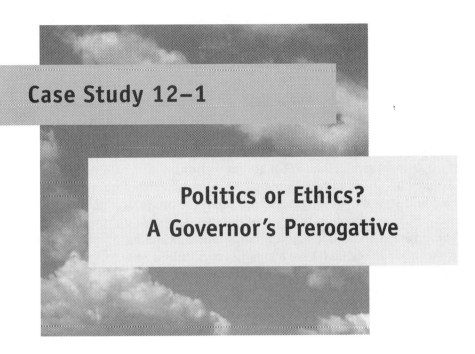

Case Study 12–1

Politics or Ethics?
A Governor's Prerogative

"Joe, get in here. It looks like trouble with that D.A. down in Blackshear County."

The Governor's middle-aged Chief of Staff sat down the leather chair facing the Governor's desk, a fax in his hand.

"It looks pretty bad. Governor. Boscoe's the D.A. down there. It looks like a major political screw-up, not to mention a legal nightmare."

Roy Maden, the Governor of his great state, drummed his fingers impatiently on his desktop. "And of course, Boscoe just happens to be one of the most vocal and high-profile Republicans in our fine state. That will be just dandy with me running for election next year. The Democrats will have a field day."

Joe shifted in his chair as he looked solemnly at his friend of many years.

"No question about Boscoe's political ambition. He has a perfect batting average with capital cases. He's sent 'em all to death row. Fact is, he's sent a little over four times as many to the row as any other D.A. in the state. Most of the folks around here feel like he's setting himself up for a run at Governor after you finish your next term."

"Well, the 'the best laid plans of mice and men' . . ." Boscoe the Bozo wasn't counting that group of law students and their professor taking a closer look at his cases."

Governor Maden rubbed his forehead as he stared out his office window. "Joe, what's the bottom line?"

"According to the legal and forensics experts I've talked to, there's pretty solid buzz that at least a quarter of his cases are bogus and there are questions about a number of others. Missing DNA that's supposed to be on file, withholding evidence from defense attorneys, and, even worse, the names of two detectives keep popping up in the most suspicious cases."

The Governor's eyes widened. "You don't mean . . .?"

"Yes sir, it looks like a criminal conspiracy could be involved."

Roy Maden could feel a headache coming on.

"Give it to me straight, Joe. What are my options?"

Joe stroked his chin and considered the choices at hand before speaking.

"You could stall the investigation until after you are reelected, then go after Boscoe. The downside is that two of the inmates on death row are out of appeals and are scheduled to be executed before the election. I've checked their rap sheets, and they both have a long list of assaults. Some of our folks say that the world would be better off without them."

The Governor looked intently at his trusted friend.

"What do you say, Joe?"

Questions:

1. Discuss the different choices the Governor could make from utilitarian, deontological, and peacemaking perspectives?

2. What would be the most moral and ethical course of action he could take? What would be the probable consequences for the Governor, district attorney, and death row inmates?

Section IV: Ethical Issues in Corrections

> What lies behind us and what lies before
> us are tiny matters compared to what lies
> within us.
>
> —Ralph Waldo Emerson

Can offenders be corrected by encouraging them to behave more ethically? By teaching them how to recognize and analyze moral dilemmas? While few would argue that this practice alone will dissuade many people from crime, it is equally clear that an ability to assess the harmfulness of one's acts and to anticipate consequences may be prerequisites to moral and law-abiding conduct. Given that ability, one can then specify the skills and contexts likely to encourage ethical conduct.

Correctional staffs inside and outside institutional boundaries also need to know how to assess moral dilemmas and how to behave in an ethical fashion. Too often, situational factors work against this objective. Many correctional institutions are plagued by high staff turnover, which means that a high percentage of guards are rookies. These individuals must confront a population of offenders housed in crowded circumstances, inmates whose chief objective is to do their time with as little discomfort as possible. Prison inmates are generally quite interested in paying off guards to improve their living circumstances, to turn a blind eye to various institutional infractions, and/or to bring illicit substances or weapons into the institution. Because these inmates may know as much about running the institution as some of the guards, it is often very easy for correctional officers to become dependent on inmates for assistance in doing their jobs, only to find that inmates expect something in return.

Probation and parole officers face different but related problems. The "burned out" probation or parole officer may be as reluctant to supervise his or her clients as the "burned out" police officer is to answer calls. Or misuse of authority might mean that a probationer or parolee is harassed by his or her supervisor. Discrimination results when the conditions of release are enforced differently against certain offenders.

The ultimate power of the probation or parole officer is the ability to initiate revocation proceedings that can send the offender to prison. The challenge is to use this authority in the same manner as the ethical police officer employs his or her coercive power—with an understanding of humanity but with a willingness to intervene for the greater good.

While probation and parole officers have worked hard to establish themselves as professionals, correctional officers have had greater difficulty in this regard, largely because the positions often require little education and offer very low pay. For many persons, working as a correctional officer is only an interim job.

The Federal Bureau of Prisons offers a notable exception to this pattern. There, the correctional officer's position is viewed as the entry point on a career ladder. This practice, employed in conjunction with the conscientious screening of new employees and the use of a management scheme that serves to discourage corruption, works to make the federal prison system an environment more likely to promote high ethical standards.

CHAPTER 13

Ethical Issues in Probation, Parole, and Community Corrections

John T. Whitehead

INTRODUCTION

It is no accident that more movies and television shows are made about police officers than about probation and parole officers. Because probation and parole are not as dramatic as policing, the ethical issues in probation, parole, and other types of community correctional programs are somewhat more ordinary. Probation and parole officers simply do not have the opportunities to become involved in dramatic matters such as the drug busts and corruption involving some police officers in large cities.

KEY CONCEPTS:

community supervision

parole

probation

whistle-blowing

This does not mean that there are no ethical issues in probation and parole. It just means that the issues are usually less dramatic and more subtle. This chapter will discuss some of the problems that can arise in probation and parole work, including ethical issues concerning intensive supervision, electronic monitoring, and house arrest.

Before delving into the ethical issues in community corrections, it may be helpful to state some assumptions. In this chapter, it is assumed that there are certain values to guide ethical choices, such as truth, honesty, fairness, hard work, and consideration for others. For this discussion, it does not matter whether these values are considered moral absolutes or simply mutually agreed upon conventions. Whatever their sources, the following discussion assumes such values exist and that most individuals subscribe to them. For example, it is assumed that it is ethical for probation and parole employees to put in a full day's work for a full day's pay. Employees who do less are considered to be acting unethically.

THE MISSION OF PROBATION AND PAROLE

The major ethical issue in probation and parole is the definition of the mission of community supervision. This refers to deciding on the purpose or objective of supervision. Traditionally, the mission of probation and parole supervision has been described as some combination of assistance and control, treatment and security, or service and surveillance (Studt, 1973). In other words, officers are supposed to provide services to offenders while also monitoring them so that the community is protected from new crimes.

In the last few years, a number of voices have been calling for corrections to revert back to a very punishment-oriented philosophy. It is not unusual to hear calls for spartan prisons with few or no amenities for prisoners. Critics have voiced their opposition to television (both cable and regular broadcast programming), weightlifting equipment, and athletics as needless frills that prisoners, by virtue of their crimes, simply do not deserve. Extremists call for the reinstatement of chain gangs, while slightly less strident souls simply suggest hard labor for all prisoners to keep them busy and to punish them for their transgressions.

The community corrections corollary to this would be stringent supervision: frequent reporting, curfews, work or community service requirements, fines, supervision fees, and drug testing. These measures would make probation and parole as punitive as possible. The mission would be punishment, pure and simple. The role of the officer would be to make sure that the punishment is being delivered.

Just as prison extremists urge the return of chain gangs, probation-parole extremists urge several harsh changes for community supervision offenders. One is the wearing of insignia to mark one's status as an offender. Offenders would wear shirts or vests or license plates proclaiming their status as an offender (e.g., "drunk driver," "shoplifter," etc.) to the world as they shop at the mall or drive down the street. Society would mark offenders with a "scarlet letter": "D" for drunk driver or "S" for shoplifter, just as puritan New England branded the Hester Prynnes of its day for adultery. (This issue will be considered further in a later section concerning acceptable penal content.)

The new penology (Feeley & Simon, 1992) takes a less strident stance and argues that probation and parole should be efficient monitors of the conditions of supervision. If an offender fails to follow the conditions of supervision, then the officer should be swift to report the failure to the court or the parole board. Sufficiently serious or frequent violations would land the offender in prison. Ironically, failure becomes success in this model. Whereas old-fashioned officers who aimed for the rehabilitation of offenders would consider recidivism (new crimes) a failure of supervision, new penology officers would consider a new crime a success as long as it is noted and used to get the offender back into prison. Here the officer claims that one is doing one's job because signs of continuing criminal tendencies are used to get the offender off the street. The objective is to classify offenders into various categories of risk and to place them into the proper risk-management response. There is no pretense of trying to rehabilitate or cure the offender.

One of the most hopeful philosophies of probation and parole is the restorative justice model. This model of criminal justice is concerned with reparation to the victim and involvement of the victim in the criminal justice process, remorse and accountability for offenders, and peace and justice for the community (Bazemore & Maloney, 1994; Bazemore & Umbreit, 1995). This model argues that neither punishment nor treatment alone is effective in changing offenders or restoring the victim or the community to its pre-crime state. Instead, the model focuses on reparation, restitution, dialogue, and negotiation in order to restore the victim and the community to its pre-crime state. The model involves both a micro dimension (offender reparation and restitution to the victim[s]) and a macro dimension (a community responsibility for crime control and the need for order and safety in the community).

One ethical issue underlying these reconceptualizations of the mission of probation and parole is the question of what society owes the offender. The easy answer is that society owes the offender nothing. The criminal has broken the law, and he or she must pay his or her debt to society. This view is congruent with the current popularity of neoclassical theories of criminal behavior that emphasize free will and accountability (see, for example, Wilson, 1983). Offenders are seen as choosing crime and as responsible for their actions. The only questions are the determination of the debt the offender must pay to society and the control of the offender so new crimes are prevented. Thus, the focus is on retribution, deterrence, and incapacitation. There is little or no emphasis on assistance to the offender.

Positivist theories of crime, on the other hand, contend that crime is not so simple. Biological, psychological, and sociological factors explain criminal behavior (Lilly, Cullen & Ball, 1989). Human behavior reflects all sorts of influences, ranging from genetic makeup to parental upbringing to the availability of educational and job opportunities. Positivist perspectives imply that society has a responsibility to assist the offender because societal factors have contributed to the criminal behavior. Thus, there is a direct link between positivist perspectives and programs to assist offenders in prison and in the community.

The peacemaking perspective outlined in an earlier chapter in this book suggests that all of us have a responsibility to the offender. The principles of caring and connectedness imply that we cannot just ignore offenders—that our common humanity is the basis for remembering that offenders are like us and want and deserve humane treatment and assistance.

The ethical question is this: Can society embrace a neoclassical perspective—assume offenders are totally free and responsible—and simply ignore any consideration of assistance to offenders? Or does society have some obligation to help offenders to some degree?

One answer to this question is that society does have a duty to provide assistance to offenders but that probation and parole should not attempt such a task. Embracing this solution, Rosecrance (1986) argues that other community agencies should provide assistance to offenders and that probation should be limited to investigations and monitoring of court-imposed sentence conditions. Much of the monitoring would be computer-assisted.

Rosecrance argues this drastic solution for several reasons. First, research as well as his own probation experience have convinced him that organizational priorities typically take precedence over concern for the needs of the offender. Both line officers and supervisors are generally more concerned with appearing effective rather than with actually having some impact on clients. As a result, reports of supposedly effective programs must be viewed skeptically. The effectiveness may well reflect organizational manipulations rather than true reformation of offenders. Second, offenders and officers come from different social worlds. As a result, neither party trusts the other, and communication between the two often deteriorates into "patent mendacity" (Rosecrance, 1986:28). Third, if service means counseling or therapy, officers often have no particular expertise in these areas (Rosecrance, 1986). In fact, officers who attempt counseling may harm offender psyches (Dietrich, 1979).

Research on intensive supervision, however, suggests that Rosecrance is wrong. A number of studies on intensive supervision have shown that there is "solid empirical evidence that ordering offenders into treatment and requiring them to participate reduces recidivism [new crimes]" (Petersilia, 1997:187). In one study, recidivism was reduced by 20-30 percent (Petersilia & Turner, 1993).

In light of these studies, it can be argued that the ethical course of action is to provide treatment programs because they both assist the offender and also reduce new crimes. Providing treatment is also consistent with Kant's categorical imperative to treat people as subjects and with peacemaking's precept of caring.

A related consideration that many people forget is the state's obligation to the correctional worker to provide a humane working environment. Even if criminals are seen as deserving only warehouse prisons and some police-like form of probation and parole, some consideration must be given to the employee. What sort of individual would want to work in sparse and spartan prisons? What sort of individual would choose to be a probation or parole officer if the job required only punishment-oriented activities? Because research has indicated that probation officers value a sense of personal accomplishment from involvement with offenders (Whitehead, 1989), any proposal to divorce officers from assistance tasks raises the specter of alienating a substantial number of line officers.

Thus, recent writing on the mission of probation and parole and calls for spartan prisons and punitive probation and parole raise important ethical considerations. Does society have any obligation to provide assistance to offenders? Does the introduction of increased emphasis on controlling offenders result in a work environment that would have negative consequences for officers? These are questions that need attention.

THE EFFECTIVENESS OF COMMUNITY CORRECTIONS

Considerable research has accumulated on the issue of whether probation is effective. A brief review of this research will be presented. Then there will be a consideration of the ethical implications of the effectiveness research.

A 1985 report triggered much of the attention to the question of probation effectiveness. That report, known as the "RAND Report" (Petersilia et al., 1985), found that two counties in California had considerable difficulty with felons placed on probation: 65 percent of the felons studied were rearrested within 40 months and one-third were incarcerated. The report received national attention and caused many to think that probation was a miserable failure. The report was a major factor in the subsequent move to reform probation by developing stricter measures (such as intensive supervision, house arrest, and electronic monitoring programs) for probationers.

There were several problems with the RAND report, however, that did not receive adequate attention. One problem was that the dramatic failure rates noted in the report may have been unique to the two California counties studied. Studies of felony probation in other jurisdictions have shown varying failure rates from quite low to about as high as those found in Los Angeles and Alameda counties (Geerken & Hayes, 1993). Another fact ignored in the report was that most probationers are misdemeanor offenders who typically do quite well on probation.

An ethical question raised by the report is whether workers—officers and managerial personnel alike—are not doing the jobs that they should be doing. If workers and whole agencies are derelict in their responsibilities, ethical irresponsibility on the part of line officers may be the root problem behind the ineffectiveness.

Several factors point to worker malfeasance as contributing to probation ineffectiveness. A unique study on probation undertaken by the General Accounting Office (1976) found that about 60 percent of the court-ordered conditions of sentence were *not* enforced by probation departments. More disturbing was that only 38 percent of the case folders examined had written treatment plans. In other words, in the majority of cases, officers were not even taking the trouble to sit down and write out a set of objectives for the offenders they were supervising. This is equivalent to a college professor not bothering to write a syllabus for a course, having no plan of action for the semester. An in-depth study of parole officers by McCleary found that parole officers "like the rest of us, are interested in doing as little work as possible" (1978:43). McCleary found that parole officers spent much of their time in outside pursuits such as getting a master's degree or running a restaurant. This left less time for their work with parolees.

In short, if community supervision is ineffective, part of the reason may be that officers—and the managers who supervise them—are not doing their jobs. Thus, workers may not be living up to the ethical standard of putting in a full day's work for a full day's pay.

Alternatively, the problem may be that we simply do not really know what to do to help probationers and parolees stay away from crime. Criminology is far from complete agreement on a theory or set of theories about why individuals commit crime or on proven strategies to rehabilitate offenders. Some theories focus on the individual deficits of offenders, others on societal ills, and still others criticize society for defining certain actions as criminal and ignoring other equally harmful actions (Lilly, Cullen & Ball, 1989). Although progress has been made in refining theories about the causes of crime and what are appropriate interventions, criminologists are still exploring both of these issues for better answers. Still another part of the answer involves a clearer definition of the mission of probation and parole so officers have a clear role to perform.

ACCEPTABLE PENAL CONTENT

In the discussion of the mission of probation and parole, it was noted that extremists argue that some offenders should wear shirts or bumper stickers marking them as drunk drivers, shoplifters, or whatever crime the person has been convicted of. In a thought-provoking piece, von Hirsch (1990) notes the ethical concern that any such innovations not insult or demean offenders but satisfy the standard of acceptable penal content:[1]

> Acceptable penal content, then, is the idea that a sanction should be devised so that its intended penal deprivations are those that can be administered in a manner that is clearly consistent with the offender's dignity. If the penal deprivation includes a given imposition, X, then one must ask whether that can be undergone by offenders in a reasonably self-possessed fashion. Unless one is confident that it can, it should not be a part of the sanction (von Hirsch, 1990:167).

Thus, von Hirsch is opposed to shirts or bumper stickers for offenders that make drunk drivers advertise their offense because there "is no way a person can, with dignity, go about in public with a sign admitting himself or herself to be a moral pariah" (1990:168). Similarly, he would be opposed to chain gangs because it is not possible to undergo such a measure with any sense of dignity.

Proponents of identifying labels for offenders would argue that they enhance the punishment value of community corrections. Such marks make probation or parole tougher rather than a lenient "slap on the wrist." Supporters would also argue that there may be deterrent value in the measures. It is embarrassing to wear such markings, and this could serve to deter others from drunk driving or whatever offense results in the added penalty.

Von Hirsch also relates the concept of acceptable penal content to home visits. Traditionally, probation and parole officers have made unannounced home visits to check on offenders and to offer assistance and counseling. Von Hirsch approves of such visits

> only as a mechanism to help enforce another sanction that *does* meet our suggested standard of acceptable penal content.... It is not plausible to assert that, without any other need for it, the punishment for a given type of crime should be that state agents will periodically snoop into one's home (emphasis added) (von Hirsch, 1990:169).

INTENSIVE SUPERVISION ISSUES

For the last decade or more, reformers have advocated intensive supervision as a way to improve regular probation and parole supervision. Giving officers smaller caseloads so that they can provide closer supervision—more frequent contacts—has been supported for both crime control and rehabilitation goals. Intensive supervision raises some ethical concerns.

The major concern about intensive supervision can be labeled a "truth in advertising" issue. Intensive supervision has been promoted as the cure for the failure of traditional probation to decrease the recidivism of felony offenders. The major problem with this claim is that it is simply not true. A major evaluation of several intensive supervision programs concluded that there were no differences between intensive and routine supervision programs (Petersilia, Peterson & Turner, 1992). Many offenders do benefit from the programs, but intensive supervision is not a panacea or cure-all for the ills of ordinary probation. In addition, as noted above, it appears that treatment components rather than control components may be related to offender success (Petersilia, 1997). Second, the programs divert some offenders from prison, but not as many as had been anticipated. Many of the offenders placed into intensive supervision programs would have gone into regular probation if the intensive programs were not available. One study estimated that only one-half of the offenders placed into the program studied would have gone to prison if the program had not been available to judges (Whitehead, Miller & Myers, 1995). Third, ironically, intensive supervision programs can and do operate to *increase* prison populations. The more intensive monitoring involved in these programs (e.g., urinalysis testing) can lead to the detection of illegal drug use or other offenses, which can result in violations. Therefore, offenders on intensive supervision face a higher risk of being detected for behaviors that will send them to prison than do offenders on regular supervision (see Clear & Braga, 1995). Fourth, although intensive supervision can be less expensive than prison, it is more expensive than ordinary supervision.

The ethical issue is whether to continue to promote intensive supervision as a means to reduce recidivism and to reduce prison populations when in fact intensive supervision fails to achieve the dramatic results many had promised. Probably the most honest summary statement about intensive supervision is that it can serve as a probation enhancement. It can make probation tougher than it used to be. This, however, is a much less dramatic claim than was originally made. One wonders if such a reduced claim will be enough to keep intensive supervision popular.

Another concern is that both punitive and risk-control conditions of intensive supervision "are applied across-the-board without much attention to the individual circumstances of the case" (Clear & Hardyman, 1990:54). For example, every intensive supervision offender may be subject to urinalysis checks for drug use even though many have never shown any indication of drug use. This can create a problem of discovering that an offender is adjusting positively on supervision except for recreational marijuana use. The dilemma, then, is how to react to the drug violation. A violation and incarceration would be an ironic twist to the stated intent of many programs to divert offenders from prison. A likely scenario is that "the probation officer is forced to play a type of game—warning the offender and noting the violation but trying to avoid action unless something else happens in the case" (Clear & Hardyman, 1990:54). Such game-playing is hardly new (see McCleary, 1978, for example), but it cannot be avoided in face of the fiscal fact that the "resources simply do not exist to carry out all the threats made in the ISPs [intensive supervision programs] . . ." (Clear & Hardyman, 1990:54).

Another ethical concern is the contention that electronic monitoring is an insidious invasion of the privacy of the home—a principle enshrined in the Fourth Amendment. Corbett and Marx argue that electronic monitoring destroys the privacy of the home:

> Figuratively, prisons have been dismantled, and each individual cell has been reassembled in private homes. Once homes start to serve as modular prisons and bedrooms as cells, what will become of our cherished notion of "home"? If privacy is obliterated *legally* in prison and if EM [electronic monitoring] provides the functional equivalent of prison at home, privacy rights for home confinees and family members are potentially jeopardized (emphasis added) (1991:409).

In short, there are some serious problems surrounding intensive supervision, house arrest, and electronic monitoring. To expect that recent interventions are correctional cure-alls is to invite unnecessary disillusionment.

Officer Concerns in Intensive Supervision Programs

A frequently ignored consideration in the development of intensive programs is what impact such programs will have on the line personnel. Several scenarios are foreseeable. One is popular acceptance by workers. Given the greater role clarity inherent in the recent intensive supervision programs, compared to the role ambiguity and role conflict frequently found in traditional probation, positive worker attitudes are a distinct possibility. Another possible scenario, however, is initial euphoria followed by more negative attitudes. Given the expectations of line officers to monitor offenders 24 hours a day, seven days a week, officers may temporarily experience the special aura of an exciting innovation only to sink into a depression occasioned by unrealistic expectations. Who wants to be on call all hours of the night every day of the week?

Due to the fiscal constraints on state and local government, it is very possible that officers in intensive supervision programs will be called on to perform such Herculean tasks without the resources for backups and relief. Physicians can join group practice arrangements to find some relief from never-ending demands, but the officers in these new programs will not have that luxury. There are too many state and local governments experiencing financial exigency to warrant optimism about the resources that will be allocated to correctional programs.

Another possible reaction of line officers is that officers assigned regular probation caseloads may resent the special status and pay of intensive supervision officers. Regular officers may become envious about the reduced caseloads of intensive officers, especially if officers with regular caseloads suspect that the intensive supervision officers' caseloads show little or no difference in risk levels compared to the regular probationers (Clear & Hardyman, 1990).

Evaluations of intensive supervision in Georgia, Illinois, and New Jersey have reported positive reactions of line personnel (Tonry, 1990). One partial inquiry into the effects of home confinement on a nonrepresentative sample of federal probation officers showed that the officers did not report widespread negative impacts even though overtime was routine (Beck, Klein-Saffran & Wooten, 1990). These findings suggest that negative effects on workers are not a necessary by-product of recent innovations. More research needs to be conducted, however, before firm conclusions are drawn, especially in light of the fact that corrections employment has proven to be conducive to stress and burnout (Whitehead, 1989; Williamson, 1990).

A more specific problem that intermediate punishments may pose for correctional workers is role conflict: "a tension between his control function and his casework function, having to be both a policeman and a social worker" (Morris & Tonry, 1990:183). The enforcement of the conditions of intermediate punishments, such as urinalysis checks for drug use, necessarily places the officer in the role of an enforcer because there "is no way in which effective, regular, but unpredictable urine testing . . . can be made other than as a police-type function" (Morris & Tonry, 1990:185).

One way to resolve this is through team supervision of offenders placed on intermediate punishments. With this approach, one team member emphasizes the enforcement of the conditions of the sanction and the other provides assistance. Another possible resolution is closer cooperation with local police (Morris & Tonry, 1990). Whatever approach is attempted, however, the basic conflict needs to be addressed.

Offender Concerns

Another concern is the reaction of offenders to community supervision pro-grams. Although many assume that offenders would automatically prefer intensive supervision, house arrest, or electronic monitoring to prison, research in Oregon found that one-quarter of the offenders there chose prison over inten-sive supervision (Petersilia, 1990). Byrne interprets this finding to mean that "some offenders would rather *interrupt* their lifestyle (via incarcera-tion) than deal with attempts to *change* it (via compliance with probation con-ditions)" (emphasis added) (1990:23). A more recent study found some offenders opting for prison over community supervision in order to avoid finan-cial conditions such as restitution orders (Jones, 1996). Cynics or conserva-tives may wonder who really cares what offenders think, but probation officers know from experience that the attitude of the offender affects, at the very least, the quality of the supervision experience for officers.

From another perspective, there is concern that class bias may affect deci-sions regarding which offenders are selected for these programs. Some offend-ers may not have a private residence and thus would be ineligible for house arrest. Some offenders may not be able to afford the supervision fees associ-ated with either intensive supervision or house arrest, especially if those fees are high enough to offset the costs of expensive electronic monitoring equip-ment. Consequently, "there may well be a tendency to apply house arrest and electronic monitoring to the more privileged and to deny it to the indigent" (Mor-ris & Tonry, 1990:217-218). In effect, this could lead to a dual system of sanctions: incarceration for the poor and alternatives for the wealthy.

PRIVATIZATION

Another ethical issue is whether states should privatize probation and parole services or continue to keep them public. (This topic is also consid-ered in the chapter on ethical issues and prison.)

Proponents of privatization argue that there are several benefits of turn-ing over various governmental services to private corporations. One alleged benefit is the reduction of operating costs. Proponents claim that private enter-prise can do things more efficiently and less expensively than the government. Government operation is equated with waste and inefficiency. Some of this is attributed to the civil service system, which guarantees job tenure except in extreme circumstances when jobs are abolished. Civil service workers are not under the same pressures as workers in private industry, who must con-sistently show a profit.

Opponents of privatization argue that government agencies *can* be effi-cient and effective. According to this perspective, government offices can adopt efficiency- and effectiveness-enhancing strategies just as do pri-vately run agencies.

Perhaps the main argument against privatization is whether it is appropriate for the government to turn over functions as basic as the correctional supervision of offenders to private businesses. Many question whether the symbolic task of punishing offenders should be handed over to workers who wear uniforms that say "Brand X Corrections" rather than the "State of ____" (American Bar Association, 1986). The most dramatic example of this would be for "Brand X Corrections" to carry out capital punishment. Should the state surrender the symbolism of the state executing an offender? Less dramatically, is it right for the state to contract out prison operations that involve the deprivation of liberty and serious disciplinary measures such as solitary confinement? Set against this context, is it ethical to allow a private company to operate a probation or parole operation that involves the very important decision of whether to allow an offender to remain in the community or be revoked for a violation and sent to prison? Or does the deprivation of liberty involve a basic right that ought not to be relinquished by the government?

Another concern with regard to privatization is whether the profit motive can debase corrections. For example, would private probation or parole agencies be under pressure to keep clients under supervision beyond an appropriate release time so as to keep caseloads and reimbursements high? Would private agencies try to pay their employees fair salaries, or would profit pressures work to minimize salaries and benefits for officers? Would private agencies try to cut services for offenders (e.g., counseling, drug treatment) to a minimum?

In the nineteenth century, the profit motive did operate to cause significant problems in many state prison systems. In one juvenile system, for example, boys were leased out to private contractors for their labor. Hardworking boys would be kept under supervision longer than necessary because the contractor did not want to lose their productivity (Pisciotta, 1982).

A more recent example of the profit motive perhaps having a negative effect occurred in Texas in 1997. Guards in a Texas jail were videotaped apparently shooting offenders with stun guns, kicking offenders in the groin, allowing dogs to bite the offenders, and making offenders crawl on their hands and knees. These guards were Texas jailers supervising Missouri offenders who had been sent to excess jail space in Texas because of overcrowding in Missouri—at a charge of $40 per day per offender to the state of Missouri (MSNBC, August 19, 1997). This situation is sort of an in-between area between public and private enterprise, in which one state offers a service to another state for a profit. Arguably, the profit motive influenced Texas officials to be lax in their training and/or supervision to the extent that this brutality occurred.

One response to such problems is spelling out a private agency's responsibilities to offenders in a carefully devised contract and then monitoring the implementation of the contract. If state inspectors enforce the contract conditions, then problems can be prevented or quickly resolved. If a private agency does not resolve any problems, they are in violation of the contract and the agency can be dropped. Opponents of privatization argue that there is a problem with this argument. If the state wants to end a contract, there may not be another service provider willing and able to step in and take over the contracted service. At the very least, it would take some time for another company to be ready to provide the needed service.

Still another problem with privatization is that private agencies can be overly selective of the clients (offenders) they want to manage. Private agencies in corrections and in areas such as welfare (for example, training public assistance clients to become job-ready) have been criticized for picking the most capable clients (Rosin, 1997). The criticism is that these individuals may have been able to succeed on probation or in getting off of public assistance with little or no help. Statistics showing them to be success stories are thereby misleading. Private agencies have selected the individuals most likely to succeed and ignored the individuals most in need of intervention, leaving the state to deal with the more difficult cases.

In summary, proponents of privatization argue that private agencies can provide needed services such as probation and parole supervision more effectively and efficiently than the government has done in the past. Opponents argue that government agencies can themselves become more effective and efficient, and that there can be serious problems with privatization. They question whether it is right to allow the state to give away the highly symbolic function of depriving citizens of their freedom and supervising the deprivation of liberty.

SUPERVISION OF SEX OFFENDERS

In 1997, a California law took effect mandating that several classes of convicted sexual offenders be given injections of medroxyprogesterone acetate (Depo-Provera) as a condition of parole. Among others, the law targeted anyone who was convicted of molesting a child under age 13 (Turk, 1997). This law and similar measures, such as requiring a woman convicted of child abuse to be implanted with Norplant (a birth control device), raise several ethical issues.

A basic issue is whether it is permissible for the state to deprive an offender of the right to procreate. (The drug acts as a birth control device for women but not for men.) Another issue is whether it is ethical to force the drug on offenders whose molesting problem is not necessarily related to their hormones. For example, the behavior of some sex offenders may be related to an alcohol problem and the drug may actually have no effect. This is important, given the possible side effects of any drug. Even a drug that has no known side effects at present may be found to have harmful side effects at a point later in time.

Still another issue is that such draconian measures may be counterproductive. Kear-Colwell and Pollock (1997), for example, argue that confrontational therapy may be antitherapeutic as opposed to motivational therapy. Although confrontational strategies may impress the public with the appearance that the state is doing something to control sex offenders, such harsh measures may in fact be failing to address the underlying causes of sex offending and, thus, not serving the community.

USE OF VOLUNTEERS

Several ethical issues arise in the use of volunteers in probation and parole. The basic issue is whether it is responsible to use volunteers in the first place. If volunteers are sought merely to save a government agency from hiring needed probation or parole officers, some people (e.g., officers and their unions) would argue that this represents an unethical use of volunteers, and that offenders, officers, and society are being shortchanged. According to this argument, when volunteers are employed, offenders do not receive the professional supervision and assistance they need; officers (actually would-be officers) are denied jobs because volunteers are being used instead of hiring additional officers; and, finally, society does not get the effective supervision it desires.

On the other hand, if volunteers are being used for tasks that officers cannot and should not be doing, then there is a valid use for volunteers. An example of this type of volunteer activity is the establishment of a one-to-one relationship with the offender. Here the volunteer acts as a "big brother/big sister" or friend in relation to the offender. Officers do not have the time to establish such personal relationships with offenders, nor would it be proper for officers to do so, given their authority over offenders. Because such one-to-one relationships are the most frequent volunteer assignments (Shields, Chapman & Wingard, 1983), it appears that many volunteers are being used properly.

The critical issue is whether volunteers are doing what additional officers would be doing or whether they are making unique contributions to the department. A complicating issue is the fiscal fact that many probation and parole departments must proceed with reduced funding. Los Angeles County Probation, for example, lost approximately one-third of its staff due to voter-approved cost-cutting. As a result, caseloads doubled. One part of the department's response to this crisis was to use more than 1,000 volunteers to provide a number of services (Nidorf, 1996). Ideally, a sufficient number of paid officers should be budgeted for every department in the country. Realistically, many government bodies are facing financial limitations and are not funding the number of officer positions that are needed. In such circumstances, volunteers may allow a department to provide services it otherwise could not provide.

CORRUPTION

Like police officers and prison guards, probation and parole officers can become involved in corruption. They can take money from clients improperly or they can sexually harass clients. It appears that such problems have not been as widespread in community corrections as in policing, but such problems do sometimes occur.

In some cases, the problem is easy to resolve. An officer in one agency was pocketing the fine and restitution money he was collecting from offenders. The agency discovered the problem and changed its collection system from having the individual officer collect such monies to having a cashier's office do so. Under the new system, offenders would go to the cashier's office to make payments and get a written receipt, and officers and supervisors would receive a printout each week detailing payments and outstanding balances. The new system removed any possibility of individual officers pilfering payments. Finding a solution to corruption, however, is not always so direct. Managers must be vigilant to detect corruption, yet they must also foster a sense of trust among their employees.

SUMMARY

Although the problems of community corrections may not be as dramatic as those involved in policing, this chapter has shown that ethical problems do arise. One of the principal ethical issues is the question of the purpose or mission of probation, parole, and other types of community corrections. Many are calling for punitive approaches to the supervision of offenders. Others, such as those in the peacemaking school, remind us that religious strands in the American tradition teach us to respect the humanity of offenders even when it appears that such offenders have done horrible deeds and seem to no longer merit humane treatment. This very basic conflict of ideas is prominent in probation and parole—and it affects other issues such as privatization and corruption. As the new century unfolds, it will be important to watch how states and counties decide to answer such questions about the supervision of offenders in the community.

NOTE

1. Much of the material in this section on acceptable penal content and the following section on intensive supervision issues is a revision of an earlier analysis of community corrections written for a chapter in a different book (Whitehead, 1992).

REFERENCES

American Bar Association (1986). *Section of Criminal Justice, Report to the House of Delegates*. Chicago: American Bar Association.

Bazemore, G. & D. Maloncy (1994). "Rehabilitating Community Service: Toward Restorative Service Sanctions in a Balanced Justice System." *Federal Probation*, 58(1):24-35.

Bazemore, G. & M. Umbreit (1995). "Rethinking the Sanctioning Function in Juvenile Court: Retributive or Restorative Responses to Youth Crime." *Crime & Delinquency*, 41:296-316.

Beck, J.L., J. Klein-Saffran & H.B. Wooten (1990). "Home Confinement and the Use of Electronic Monitoring with Federal Parolees." *Federal Probation*, 54(4):22-31.

Byrne, J.M. (1990). "The Future of Intensive Probation Supervision and the New Intermediate Sanctions." *Crime & Delinquency*, 36:6-41.

Clear, T.R. & A.A. Braga (1995). "Community Corrections." In J.Q. Wilson & J. Petersilia (eds.), *Crime* (pp. 421-444). San Francisco: Institute for Contemporary Studies.

Clear, T.R. & P.L. Hardyman (1990). "The New Intensive Supervision Movement." *Crime & Delinquency*, 36:42-60.

Corbett, R. & G.T. Marx (1991). "No Soul in the New Machine: Technofallacies in the Electronic Monitoring Movement." *Justice Quarterly*, 8:399-414.

Dietrich, S.G. (1979). "The Probation Officer as Therapist." *Federal Probation*, 43(2):14-19.

Feeley, M. & J. Simon (1992). "The New Penology: Notes on the Emerging Strategy of Corrections and Its Implications." *Criminology*, 30 449-474.

Geerken, M. & H. Hayes (1993). "Probation and Parole: Public Risks and the Future of Incarceration Alternatives." *Criminology*, 31:549-564.

General Accounting Office (1976). *State and County Probation Systems in Crisis*. Washington, DC: U.S. Government Printing Office.

Jones, M. (1996). "Voluntary Revocations and the "Elect-to-Serve" Option in North Carolina Probation." *Crime & Delinquency*, 42:36-49.

Kear-Colwell, J. & P. Pollock (1997). "Motivation or Confrontation: Which Approach to the Child Sex Offender?" *Criminal Justice and Behavior*, 24:20-33.

Lilly, J.R., F.T. Cullen & R.A. Ball (1989). *Criminological Theory: Context and Consequences*. Newbury Park, CA: Sage.

McCleary, R. (1978). *Dangerous Men: The Sociology of Parole*. Beverly Hills, CA: Sage.

Morris, N. & M. Tonry (1990). *Between Prison and Probation: Intermediate Punishments in a Rational Sentencing System*. New York: Oxford University.

MSNBC, August 1997.

Nidorf, B.J. (1996). "Surviving in a 'Lock Them Up' Era." *Federal Probation*, 60(1):4-10.

Petersilia, J. (1990). "Conditions that Permit Intensive Supervision Programs to Survive." *Crime & Delinquency*, 36:126-145.

Petersilia, J. (1997). "Probation in the United States." In M. Tonry (ed.), *Crime and Justice: A Review of Research* (Vol. 22) (pp. 149-200). Chicago: University of Chicago Press.

Petersilia, J., S. Turner, J. Kahan & J. Peterson (1985). *Granting Felons Probation: Public Risks and Alternatives*. Santa Monica, CA: RAND.

Petersilia, J., J. Peterson & S. Turner (1992). *Intensive Probation and Parole: Research Findings and Policy Implications*. Santa Monica, CA: RAND.

Petersilia, J. & S. Turner (1993). "Intensive Probation and Parole." In M. Tonry (ed.), *Crime and Justice: A Review of Research* (Vol. 17) (pp. 281-336). Chicago: University of Chicago Press.

Pisciotta, A.W. (1982). "Saving the Children: The Promise and Practice of *Parens Patriae*, 1838-98." *Crime & Delinquency*, 28:410-425.

Rosecrance, J. (1986). "Probation Supervision: Mission Impossible." *Federal Probation*, 50(1):25-31.

Rosin, H. (1997). "About Face: The Appearance of Welfare Success." *New Republic*, 217 (August, 4):16-19.

Shields, P.M., C.W. Chapman & D.R. Wingard (1983). "Using Volunteers in Adult Probation." *Federal Probation*, 46(2):57-64.

Studt, E. (1973). *Surveillance and Service in Parole: A Report of the Parole Action Study*. Washington, DC: National Institute of Corrections.

Tonry, M. (1990). "Stated and Latent Functions of ISP." *Crime & Delinquency*, 36:174-191.

Turk, C. (1997). "Kinder Cut: A Limited Defense of Chemical Castration." *New Republic*, 217 (8: August 25, 1997):12-13.

von Hirsch, A. (1990). "The Ethics of Community-Based Sanctions." *Crime & Delinquency*, 36:162-173.

Whitehead, J.T. (1989). *Burnout in Probation and Corrections*. New York: Praeger.

Whitehead, J.T. (1992). "Control and the Use of Technology in Community Supervision." In P.J. Benekos & A.V. Merlo (eds.), *Corrections: Dilemmas and Directions*. Cincinnati: Anderson.

Whitehead, J.T., L.S. Miller & L.B. Myers (1995). 'The Diversionary Effectiveness of Intensive Supervision and Community Corrections Programs." In J.O. Smykla & W.L. Selke (eds.), *Intermediate Sanctions: Sentencing in the 1990s* (pp. 135-151). Cincinnati: Anderson.

Williamson, H.E. (1990). *The Corrections Profession*. Newbury Park, CA: Sage.

Wilson, J.Q. (1983). *Thinking about Crime*, rev. ed. New York: Vintage Books.

DISCUSSION QUESTIONS

1. What do you think is the mission of community corrections? Give reasons for your choice.

2. Discuss the privatization of correctional services. What are some of the arguments for and against privatization?

3. An ethical issue when considering the job of the probation/parole officer is what, if anything, society owes the offender. Can society embrace a neoclassical perspective, assume offenders are totally free and responsible, and simply ignore any consideration of assistance to offenders? Or does society have some obligation to help offenders to some degree? How does the author feel about this issue? What is your opinion? Explain.

4. Considering the author's discussion of whistle-blowing, what would you do if you knew that one officer was going home two hours early every day? What would it take to make you "blow the whistle," or would you feel it was not your responsibility? Explain.

5. How much involvement should victims have in judgments related to their offender(s) (e.g., parole release)? How can their involvement lead to unequal treatment of offenders?

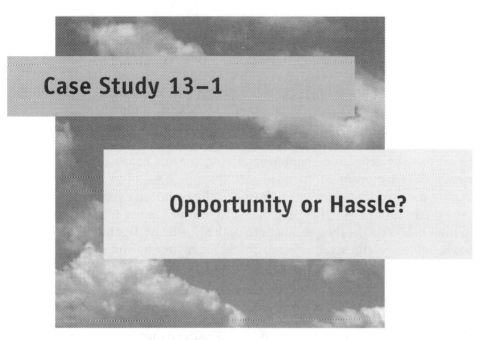

Case Study 13–1

Opportunity or Hassle?

Drinking the last drops of a lukewarm cup of coffee, you stare out the window of your office, which overlooks the agency parking lot. It is beginning to rain. Your name is Gene Hill and, at age 59, you have been a state probation officer (PO) for the past 29 years, longer than anyone else in the office. Although the younger POs often kid you about being over the hill, you enjoy a special bond of affection with them, helping them avoid pitfalls as they learn the "ins and outs" of what it means to be a professional probation officer in the new millennium. Huge case loads and modest pay make it difficult to retain the best ones because they can drive 20 miles and receive a 25 percent raise by doing the same thing in an adjoining state.

As if life wasn't difficult enough, a local judge sent a young priest and Protestant minister to talk to you about some new-fangled victim-offender reconciliation program in which the victim and perpetrator of a crime meet with one another under supervision to try and resolve their differences. The meeting would involve the victim expressing the pain and suffering they endured as a result of the crime and the offender expressing remorse and beginning to pay some form of restitution. The judge indicated that he would be willing to try out the program on an experimental basis if you as the senior PO were willing to work with these two "men of the cloth."

The case that has been proposed for the initial effort involves a feisty 65-year-old retired school teacher, Beth Finely. She is well-known in your town as a hard-core, liberal Democrat, always demonstrating for one cause or another. Apparently, Finely's VCR, television set, and (perhaps most painfully) her framed portrait of all the Democratic Presidents from Franklin D. Roosevelt forward were stolen by George "Little Gus" Simpkins, a 20-

year-old high school dropout who works by day at the local bakery and free-lances at night as a burglar. Simpkins specializes in electronic and entertainment equipment. There has never been any violence associated with Simpkins. He is, however, a nuisance offender. This is his second arrest in five years. He received probation on his two prior offenses, and the local District Attorney is ready to make an example out of "Little Gus" Simpkins. "Little Gus" is married and has a two-year-old son. His wife, who has worked at a local supermarket for five years, is currently recovering from an extended illness. She depends on her husband's income and health benefits to make ends meet and cover her medical care.

Yesterday, the two clergymen had enthusiastically endorsed the program and offered their services as volunteers, citing case after case of success in several similar programs in other jurisdictions in the Northeast. But then, you think, this is not the Northeast; this is the South. No matter how much they pledge their support, in your mind's eye, only one thing is certain: "More work for you!" Moreover, the Assistant District Attorney has called to inform you that the District Attorney wanted the program killed, which would be easy enough for you to accomplish.

Still, there is a part of you that would like to believe that it is possible to make a real difference in helping victims and correcting offenders rather than just processing them through a criminal justice assembly line. Sometimes new programs have been much ado about nothing but, on other occasions, they really have made a difference. The bottom line is that, either way, you will end up having to do a lot of work. In addition, you will make the District Attorney angry. You could give it a try and take the heat, or disappoint the two clergymen and Simpkins and his family. Who knows how Finely really felt? You find yourself wondering, "What is the right thing to do? When will it stop raining?"

Questions:

As the PO in charge, you can give the restorative justice program a chance or end it before it gets started. You already have legal and state-sanctioned procedures to address the case in question. Beyond that, consider what would be the best and most just option for the victim, the community, and the offender. How to satisfy the victim, allay the fears of the community, and correct the offender is a tall order to fill.

CHAPTER 14

Responsibility and Restorative Justice

John Braithwaite & Declan Roche

Restorative justice owes part of its growth in popularity to its broad political appeal, offering something to politicians of varying stripes. In particular, "getting offenders to take responsibility for their actions" has been part of the political appeal of restorative justice. So has "getting families to take responsibility for their kids." While it may seem appropriate to exploit such political appeal, restorative justice must have a more meaningful sense of responsibility than this. Restorative justice cannot sell itself in these terms yet simultaneously distance itself from similar sounding neoconservative ideas of responsibility, without clearly articulating its own conception of responsibility. As O'Malley says, "Discourses of responsibility for crime and crime prevention are . . . not possessions of the political Right, and they do not imply only a punitive response to offending" (O'Malley, 1994:22). Responsibility is a fundamental and contestable part of any scheme of justice, including restorative justice.

KEY CONCEPTS:

active responsibility

causal fault

compassion

conferences/circles

empowerment

passive responsibility

reactive fault

restorative justice

victim-blaming

The purpose of this chapter is to explore the concept of responsibility within a restorative justice framework. As a starting hypothesis, let us see if restorative responsibility might be conceived as that form of responsibility most likely to promote restoration—of victims, offenders, and communities. Given that framework, we will first find a useful distinction between active responsibility and passive responsibility. Then we show how that distinction maps onto distinctions between active and passive deterrence, rehabilitation,

From Gordon Bazemore and Mara Schiff, *Restorative Community Justice* (Cincinnati: Anderson), 2001. Reprinted with permission.

and incapacitation. We then seek to develop the rudiments of a jurisprudence of active responsibility. Finally, we consider some worries about the restorative conception of responsibility we have developed.

ACTIVE AND PASSIVE RESPONSIBILITY

Carol Heimer (1999:18) makes a distinction between being held accountable for the wrong one has done in the past and taking responsibility for the future. Mark Bovens (1998:27) makes a similar distinction between passive responsibility and active responsibility. Twentieth-century Western retributive justice has been mostly concerned with passive responsibility. Restorative justice, we will argue, shifts the balance toward active responsibility.

Bovens says that in the case of passive responsibility "one is called to account after the event and either held responsible or not. It is a question of who *bears* the responsibility for a given state of affairs. The central question is: 'Why *did* you do it?'" (Bovens, 1998:27). Bovens sees passive responsibility as requiring transgression of a norm, a causal connection between conduct and damage, blameworthiness, and sometimes a special relationship of obligation toward the person(s) harmed (Bovens, 1998:28-31). The literature is full of debates about the best way to conceive of passive responsibility (see, for example, Mulgan, 1997; Thomas, 1998). We will not add to those debates here. While we have some doubts about Bovens's conception of passive responsibility, we will not discuss them, as our interest is to move on to the special appeal for restorative justice theory of his concept of active responsibility.

First, however, it must be said that restorative justice cannot do without some concept of passive responsibility. For example, a restorative justice conference is held after the commission of a crime ("after the event," in Boven's terms) and in light of the admission of guilt by the offender (which determines "who bears responsibilty"). Furthermore, a conference, at least in its early stages, will often involve asking the offender why he or she did it. Our argument is not that restorative justice abandons passive responsibility, but that restorative justice uses passive responsibility to create a forum in which active responsibility can be fostered. Restorative justice, then, is about shifting the balance from passive responsibility toward active responsibility.

So what is active responsibility, according to Bovens? He sees active responsibility as a virtue, the virtue of taking responsibility when something needs to be done to deal with a problem or put things right: "[T]he emphasis lies much more on action in the present, on the prevention of unwanted situations and events . . . The central question here is: 'what *is* to be done?'" (Bovens, 1998:27).

To interpolate in a restorative justice frame, active responsibility entails seeking to take responsibility to repair harm, and especially to restore relationships. According to Bovens, active responsibility requires: (1) an adequate perception of threatened violations of a norm, (2) consideration of consequences, (3) autonomy, and (4) taking obligations seriously. Restorative dialogue, in which the problem rather than the person is put in the center of the circle (Melton, 1995), and in which respectful listening is a central value, seems well designed to cultivate Boven's virtue of active responsibility. As Heimer and Staffen (1998:369) put it, "it is the humanity of other people that inspires responsibility." Bovens also sees active responsibility as requiring "conduct based on a verifiable and consistent code"(Bovens, 1998:36). This seems to be an excessively positivist requirement; families can nurture active responsibility through restorative dialogue without codifying their norms.

We argue that restorative justice reconceptualizes responsibility, so that when people claim that restorative justice offers *better* responsibility than traditional court sentencing,[1] they are impliedly making a claim about what is accomplished by active responsibility.

Those who favor retribution are concerned with passive responsibility because their priority is to be just in the way that they hurt wrongdoers. The shift in the balance toward active responsibility occurs because the priority of restorative justice proponents is to be just in the way that they heal.

While it is clear that a backward-looking, deontological theory such as retributivism is clearly concerned more with passive than active responsibility, the influence of passive responsibility also permeates forward-looking, consequentialist theories. Utilitarians along the lines of Jeremy Bentham are equally preoccupied with hurting rather than healing, and with passive rather than active responsibility. We will argue that utilitarians have an inferior theory of deterrence, rehabilitation, incapacitation, and crime prevention to that of restorative justice theorists. At the root of this inferiority is the utilitarian's obsession with passive responsibility to the exclusion of active responsibility.[2] First, we will show how under the restorative alternative, while passive responsibility maps onto passive deterrence, active responsibility maps onto active deterrence—and the latter is more powerful. Then we will do the same for rehabilitation and incapacitation.

Passive and Active Deterrence

Deterrence is not an objective of restorative justice. In fact, to make deterrence of wrongdoing a value would destroy restorative justice for the same reason that making shaming a value would destroy it. As Kay Pranis (1998:45) puts it, "An intention to shame [we add deter] is not respectful. An intention to help a person understand the harm they caused and to support them in taking full responsibility for that harm is respectful."[3] However, this is not to deny that theories of shame and deterrence can help us understand why restorative processes might have more preventive potential than retributive/deterrent processes.

Most deterrence literature in criminology indicates that the severity level of punishment rarely has a significant deterrent effect. While a criminal justice system with no passive deterrence would clearly be one with a lot of crime, the data give utilitarians reason to be discouraged that increasing the quantum of passive deterrence will reduce crime (or that reducing passive deterrence will increase crime). Active deterrence, we will suggest, is a different story.

Ayres and Braithwaite (1992:19-53) have argued that deterrence theory in criminology is primitive compared to deterrence theory in international relations because it is excessively passive. When the United States seeks to deter a form of international behavior, it does not announce in advance that the punishment if states do X will be Y, if they do 2X, it will be 2Y, and so on with a passive deterrence tariff. Instead, its deterrence strategy is active in two important senses. First, the United States uses its power to persuade other states on whom the rogue state is dependent for some reason (for example, trade) to intervene (actively) to persuade the rogue state that it should refrain from the rogue action. What is being mobilized by this kind of active deterrence is a web of complex interdependency (Keohane, 1984). Second, the United States' strategic deterrence is active in the sense of being dynamic rather than passive. The deterrent threat does not just sit there as a passive promise of punishment; deterrence is escalated up and down an enforcement pyramid in response to the level of cooperative response and the concessions made by the rogue state. International relations theory has escaped the shackles of Benthamite thinking about certain response with punishments calibrated to be passively optimal.

Restorative Justice and Deterrence

How could restorative justice theory do better than legal deterrence theory? Let us illustrate with some restorative justice analogies to active webs of complex interdependence. Consider the restorative approach that has been developing in Australian business regulation. First, the regulator meets with the agents in the corporation who seem most passively responsible for the law-breaking, along with some victims (where appropriate). Because the corporate actors most directly responsible have the most to lose from a criminal conviction of the corporation, they will be hard targets, difficult to deter. They are likely to fight passive deterrence by denial of responsibility. For Benthamite corporate crime fighters, that is the end of the story—another contested court case that they do not have the resources to fight, another defeat at the hands of those who control corporate power. However, what we know is that causal and preventive power over corporate crime is, as the philosophers say (Lewis, 1986), overdetermined. So what we do is move up the organization, widening the circle of dialogue, convening another conference to which the boss of the passively responsible agent of the corporation is invited. Often the boss will turn out to be a hard target as well. When that fails, we convene another conference and invite her boss. Fisse and Braithwaite (1993:230-232) have described one restorative justice experience in which the process led right up to the Chief Executive Officer, who was the "toughest nut" of them all. After that, though, the Australian Trade Practices Commission widened the circle to include the Chair of the Board, who was shocked at this recalcitrant unwillingness to restore the victims' losses and reform the corporation's compliance systems. The Chair actually fired the CEO. (Not very restorative! A case of active deterrence leading to passive deterrence.)

In other more extended treatments of the deterrence theory of restorative justice, Braithwaite (1997a, 1999) has argued that corporate crime is not different from common crime in that it is mostly a collective, or at least a socially embedded, phenomenon, in which there are many actors with preventive capabilities. For example, one interpretation for the success of whole-school anti-bullying programs in reducing bullying up to 50 percent (Olweus, 1993) is in these terms. Whenever a fourth grader is bullying another child, many children in the school (particularly from the fifth grade up) are in a position to intervene to prevent the bullying. From a deterrence theory perspective, therefore, whole-school anti-bullying programs work because the deterrence target shifts from the bully (a hard target to deter passively) to active deterrence of responsible peers of the bully.

One reason that empowerment is a central value of restorative justice is that it encourages people to take active responsibility—and active responsibility delivers, among other things, active deterrence. The environmentally conscious citizen of the corporation intervenes to stop the environmental crime even though she has no passive responsibility for causing it. A school friend intervenes to stop bullying even though she bears no passive responsibility for it. An ideal of the design of restorative institutions is to create democratic spaces for the nurturing of the virtue of active responsibility among citizens, young and old.

In the context of violence against women, Braithwaite and Daly (1994) have argued that restorative justice is more likely to be attempted, taken seriously, and to actually work, if it is located within a dynamic enforcement strategy in which the upshot of repeated failure of restorative conferences will be escalation to deterrence and incapacitation. This is not to advocate restorative justice transacted on the basis of threat. Rather it is to say that powerful criminals are more likely to succumb to the entreaties of restorative justice when deterrence is threatening in the background instead of threatened in the foreground (for the theory, see Ayres & Braithwaite, 1992:47-51). The idea is not that deterrence is there as an ever-present passive threat but that everyone knows it is democratically available as an active possibility if dialogue fails or is spurned. Because "everyone knows" this, there is no need to make threats; indeed, to do so is counterproductive. So an offender who chooses not to participate in a conference knows the alternative is an appearance in court, where he or she will be subject to passive responsibility.

THE RESTORATIVE JUSTICE PROCESS AND RESPONSIBILITY

Conferences and circles provide opportunities to nurture active responsibility. If you empower citizens in a punitive society to decide how to put right a wrong, many choose to do so punitively against the wrongdoer. Kathleen Daly suggests that restorative justice does deliver a deal of retribution (Daly, 2000). Moreover, because restorative justice processes of confronting victims and their own families are often grueling even for hardened offenders, and because we know that "the process" in all systems is usually the greater part of punishment (Feeley, 1979), restorative justice also delivers a lot of process-related passive deterrence.

However, the empirical experience of restorative justice is that victims and other citizens are not as punitive as we expected they would be, and not as punitive as they are in the context of adversarial courtroom justice. When courts do intervene to overturn decisions of restorative justice conferences, it is rarely to make them less punitive; instead, it is usually to increase punishment (Maxwell & Morris, 1993). So it seems that while people have the opportunity to pursue punitiveness and passive responsibility, they choose to do so far less than we might expect.

A conference convened by one of the authors of this chapter provides an example. A middle-aged married couple came to the conference to meet the young person who had stolen and damaged beyond repair the car the husband had spent three years and thousands of dollars restoring. In the conference, it was explained to the offender that he had done great damage to the car, probably without realizing it. After the man explained that, his wife shared that her stoic husband had been privately shattered about the loss of the car that he had hoped to display at car shows—and that since the offense, he did not have the heart to start over. She also explained that their daughter was in the advanced stages of a difficult pregnancy and the loss of the car made it difficult to help with tasks such as collecting their grandchildren from school and doing grocery shopping. Yet, despite the harm, the couple declined offers of physical labor from the offender, insisting that the only outcome that would help them was one that helped him (in this case, taking small steps to resume his education). In Boven's terms, the couple was concerned that the young person exercise his active responsibility in respect to this incident in a way that nurtured the virtue of active responsibility in him for the future.

A process that allows victims to meet the offender and his or her family often generates compassion for the offender and a better understanding of his or her actions. Compassion contributes to the pursuit of restoration and active responsibility more than it does to the pursuit of punishment. However, there is not always compassion in conferences and there often is retribution. How can this be an alternative model of justice if citizens often choose to deter or seek revenge? One response is to draw an analogy to democracy. If you set up a democracy, citizens often vote for candidates with anti-democratic values. What is happening there is that we honor the institution (democracy) that conduces to a shift to democratic values rather than honoring the values themselves. To take democracy away from people as soon as they chose to manifest anti-democratic values would be not only perverse but a prescription for historically unsustainable democracy. What we do instead is write constitutions that put limits on anti-democratic action.

Likewise, restorative justice must be constitutionalized so that limits are placed on the pursuit of deterrence. Thus, people can (if they insist) pursue anti-democratic or anti-restorative aims to the extent to which those systems allow.[4] We think these limits should constrain restorative justice conferences against any incarcerative or corporal punishment, any punishment that is degrading or humiliating,[5] and any punishment in excess of that which would be imposed by a court for the same wrongdoing.[6]

Active and Passive Rehabilitation

> "Support without accountability leads to moral weakness. Accountability without support is a form of cruelty."
> —Harriet Jane Olsen, *The Book of Discipline of the United Methodist Church* (1996)

Having outlined in some detail the story of active and passive deterrence, we hope we can briefly state how to apply the same principles to active and passive rehabilitation (for more detail, see Braithwaite, 1998, 1999). There is much evidence that the least effective way of delivering rehabilitation programs is for the state to decide what is best and to require criminals to be passive recipients of that benevolence. In the most empowering restorative justice programs, such as one described by Burford and Pennell (1996), which is designed to deal with family violence, the victims, offenders, and their communities of care are not subjected to rehabilitative prescription but are empowered with knowledge. Experts come into the conference to explain the range of rehabilitative options available. State monopolies of provision of rehabilitative services are replaced by a plurality of service providers from civil society, private enterprise, and the state. More radically, resourcing can be available for professional help for communities of care to craft and operate their own rehabilitative interventions.

The two variables in play here that we know are associated with superior rehabilitative outcomes are: (1) active choice as opposed to passive receipt, and (2) embedding of that choice in networks of social support (Cullen, 1994) rather than choice by isolated individuals. We suspect that the reason for active rehabilitation being superior to passive rehabilitation goes beyond the documented effects of commitment and social support. We also suspect that communities of care empowered with good professional advice will actually make technically superior choices from among a smorgasbord of rehabilitative options, because of the richer contextual knowledge they have of the case (Bazemore, 1999; Bazemore and Dooley, this volume). This is particularly plausible in a world in which, for example, psychotherapy often seems to work but in which there is no consistent evidence showing that one school of psychotherapy works better than another. The hope is that contextually informed community-of-care choices (assisted by professional choice brokers) will be better on average than individual or state choices (Braithwaite, 1998).

Active and Passive Incapacitation

In Braithwaite and Daly's (1994) family violence enforcement pyramid, most of the options for escalation are in fact more incapacitative than deterrent. They include options like "a relative or other supporter of the woman moving into the household," "the man moving to a friend's household," and imprisonment. Once we move beyond a passive conception of incapacitation, which is statically linked to confinement in state prisons, we can see that *capacitation of victims* can be theoretically equivalent to *incapacitation of offenders*. Hence, in a family violence enforcement pyramid, giving a victim the capacity to leave by putting a bank account or funding for alternative accommodation at her disposal (victim capacitation) can be functionally equivalent to removing the offender from the home (offender incapacitation).

Court-ordered incapacitation is notoriously less effective than it would seem. Violent men continue to perpetrate assault and rape in prison. Drug dealers continue to entice vulnerable young people. Judges incapacitate drunk drivers by canceling their licenses only to find that a majority of them continue to drive (Barnes, 1999).

By contrast, the active intervention of communities of care evokes alternative modalities of incapacitation. If the problem is that it is only on Friday and Saturday nights that the offender gets out on the town, Uncle Harry can take responsibility for holding the keys to the car on Friday and Saturday nights and ensuring that the car stays in the garage. Alternatively, the girlfriend can volunteer to call a taxi every time. Or the drinking mates can sign a designated driver agreement at the conference. Or the owner of the pub or club where the offender drinks can agree to train the staff to intervene so that someone else in the bar drives the offender home. We have seen all these forms of active incapacitation negotiated at restorative drunk driving conferences. All of them require cultivation of the virtue of active responsibility. We never see them in drunk driving court cases, which last an average of seven minutes in Canberra, compared with 90 minutes for conferences (Barnes, 1999).

Active Crime Prevention, Active Grace

Braithwaite (1998, 1999) has argued that crime prevention programs mostly fail for four reasons: (1) lack of motivation, (2) lack of resources, (3) insufficiently plural deliberation, and (4) lack of follow through. He argued that making restorative justice conferences a site of crime prevention deliberation in the community can help remedy those four reasons for the failure of crime prevention programs. Motivation, resources, and follow-through on crime prevention have more momentum when coupled to the mainstream processing of criminal cases than when ghettoized into specialized crime prevention units. We will not reiterate the four sets of arguments here, but one way of summarizing them is that they are concerned with the way restorative justice deliberation nurtures the virtue of active responsibility. Active responsibility does not come naturally in response to a plea to attend a Neighborhood Watch meeting. It comes more naturally in reply to a plea from a neighbor who has been a victim of crime to support them in a conference/circle. Similarly, an occupational health and safety poster in the workplace proclaiming "Reporting (accidents) is everyone's responsibility" does not foster a sense of active responsibility in the way that conferences held to discuss specific workplace injuries do.

Serious crime is an opportunity to confront evil with a grace that transforms human lives to paths of love and care. Desmond Tutu would want us to evaluate his Truth and Reconciliation Commission less in terms of how it prevents crimes of violence and more in terms of how its healing lays the foundation of a more humane South Africa. While we can never expect restorative justice institutions to be the most important institutions of community building, they can play their part in the nurturing of active responsibility that is the indispensable ingredient of community development.

If we believe that reintegrative shaming is what is required to deal with the wrongdoing of a Winnie Madikizela-Mandela and a P.W. Botha alike,[7] no one is required to take active responsibility for saying "shame on you" for the killings and the racism under an evil regime. The testimony of the victims and the apologies (when they occur, as they often enough do) are sufficient to accomplish the necessary shaming of the evil of violence. However, there can never be enough citizens active in the reintegration part of reintegrative shaming. If is true that reintegrative shaming prevents crime, and if it is true that it is the reintegration part that is always in short supply, then the particular, if limited, kind of integration into communities of care that is transacted in restorative justice rituals has a special humanitarian significance.

Toward a Jurisprudence of Active Responsibility

So far, we have conceived of active responsibility as the essential element for securing restoration. At the same time, we have argued that without passive responsibility there is risk of injustice. For example, a minimum requirement for punishing an offender for doing wrong would be an inquiry to demonstrate causal responsibility for the wrong.

Now we will complicate this picture by arguing that while passive responsibility remains indispensable to justice in this way, restorative justice propels us to develop a more just notion of criminal liability, on which passive responsibility depends. That is, the emphasis on active responsibility is not only a matter of the jurisprudence of restoration but also of the normative theory of justice.

We turn to Brent Fisse's (1983) theory of reactive fault (further developed in Fisse and Braithwaite, 1993) for key insights here. All criminal justice systems incorporate notions of causal fault and reactive fault. Causal fault is about being causally responsible, while reactive fault is about how responsibly one reacts after the harm is done. The balance between the two varies enormously from system to system. Western criminal justice systems (such as that of the United States) are at the causal end of the continuum; Asian systems (such as that of Japan) tend to be at the reactive end. Yet, even in the West, reactive fault sometimes dominates causal fault, as evidenced in our intuition that with hit-and-run driving, the running is the greater evil than the hitting. Early guilty pleas in court and "remorse" also result in sentence reductions. In *Crime, Shame and Reintegration*, Braithwaite (1989:165) told two stories to illustrate the extremes in the cultural balancing of causal and reactive fault, the first from Haley (1982:272), the second from Wagatsuma and Rosett (1986:486):

> The first is of two American servicemen accused of raping a Japanese woman. On Japanese legal advice, private reconciliation with the victim was secured; a letter from the victim was tabled in the court stating that she had been fully compensated and that she absolved the Americans completely. After hearing the evidence, the judge leaned forward and asked the soldiers if they had anything to say. "We are not guilty, your honor," they replied. Their Japanese lawyer cringed; it had not even occurred to him that they might not adopt the repentant role. They were sentenced to the maximum term of imprisonment, not suspended.

> The second story is of a Japanese woman arriving in the U.S. with a large amount of American currency which she had not accurately declared on the entry form. It was not the sort of case that would normally be prosecuted. The law is intended to catch the importation of cash which is the proceeds of illicit activities, and there was no suggestion of this. Second, there was doubt that the woman had understood the form which required the currency

> declaration. After the woman left the airport, she wrote to the Customs Service acknowledging her violation of the law, raising none of the excuses or explanations available to her, apologizing profusely, and seeking forgiveness. In a case that would not normally merit prosecution, the prosecution went forward *because* she has confessed and apologized; the U.S. Justice Department felt it was obliged to proceed in the face of a bald admission of guilt. (emphasis in original)

These are stories about how the United States justice system creates disincentives for reactive fault, while the Japanese justice system requires it. Fisse (1983) advocates "reactive fault" as the core criterion of criminal fault. In its most radical version, this would mean in a case of assault, the alleged assailant would go into a restorative justice conference not on the basis of an admission of criminal guilt but on the basis of admitting responsibility for the *actus reus* of an assault ("I was the one who punched her").[8] Whether the mental element required for crime was present would be decided reactively, on the basis of the constructiveness and restorativeness of his or her reaction to the problem caused by the act (Braithwaite, 1998). If the reaction were restorative, the risk of criminal liability would be removed; only civil liability would remain. However, if reactive criminal fault were found by a court to be present,[9] that would be insufficient for a conviction; the mental element for the crime would also have to be demonstrated before or during its commission.[10] However, reactive fault would be a more important determinant of penalty than causal fault.

This gives us an answer to the retributivist who says: "Where is the justice with two offenders who commit exactly the same offense: one apologizes and heals a victim who grants him mercy; the other refuses to participate in a circle and is punished severely by a court." The answer is that while the two offenders are equal in causal fault, they are quite unequal in reactive fault. Viewed in terms of passive responsibility, they might be equal; in terms of active responsibility, though, they are not.[11]

The Major Worry about Active Responsibility

In restorative justice conferences, sometimes victims say they are responsible for their own victimization or others blame them for it. This is not a worry when victims blame themselves for leaving open the window through which the burglar entered; indeed, it can be a good thing if it motivates victims to invest in target hardening to protect them from a repeat victimization.[12] Similarly, a victim of a schoolyard fight may reflect on the provocation of the offender that led to the assault. It is a different matter, though, if a girl who is a victim of sexual assault is blamed for wearing a short skirt. What is the difference? It is that this type of victim-blaming is connected to a history of subordination of young women, and the denial of their freedom, which has been much exacerbated by victim-blaming.

Restorative justice implies a grave risk of the occurrence of oppressive victim-blaming. The hope is that when it occurs, participants in the circle will speak up in defense and support of the victim—that there will be reintegrative shaming of victim-blaming. The fact that we cannot guarantee that this will occur is deeply troubling.

Defenders of formal legal processes might further protest that criminal trials do incorporate formal guarantees against victim-blaming. Most of these, however, come into play at the level of proving that sexual assault occurred—guarantees not relevant to normal restorative justice processes that are not concerned with the adjudication of guilt. In any case, it is hard to argue that victim-vilification does not occur in criminal trials.[13] As Hogg and Brown put it, "Police, lawyers and judges have often been derisory in their treatment of complainants who have acted in . . . 'sexually provocative' ways" (1998:65). Indeed, restorative justice advocates argue that the problem with the criminal trial is that it creates incentives for the prosecution to vilify defence witnesses, and vice versa. This is what puts the vulnerable most at risk of stigmatization. The problems that formal legal guarantees against victim-blaming seek to redress are in part problems created by the formal adversarial process.

In terms of the impact of victim-blaming on traditional adversarial justice, we should not confine our examination to trials and sentencing. Ngaire Naffine suggests that in light of the statistics on the extent of unreported rapes, rapes without active resistance (and we would suggest, rapes involving other types of victim-blaming) are "much less likely to find their way into a court of law . . . (and) are more likely to be filtered out of the criminal justice system" (Naffine, 1992:761). Hence, it is clear that victim-blaming is a problem at every level.

What can be said in favor of restorative justice is that while the criminal trial assembles in one room those capable of inflicting maximum damage on the other side, the restorative justice conference assembles in the room those capable of offering maximum support to their own side—be it the victim or the offender side. It is in this structural difference, and in the ethic of care and active responsibility that it engenders, that restorative justice places its hope against victim vilification.

It will be a hope that will continue to be disappointed from time to time, we fear. There are few higher priorities for research and development than to improve the micro-design of conferences/circles. Videos shown to participants before they go into their first conference could not only show how conferences work and how participants can be actively responsible citizens within them, but perhaps they could also warn against victim-blaming and urge a responsibility to speak out against victim-blaming should it occur. Training for convenors should also address this risk. For both court and conference processes, research should be able to test a variety of innovations in order to discover which procedures best protect victims from stigmatization.

Restorative Justice—Beyond Responsibilization

In its traditional criminological forms, utilitarianism tended to objectify and infantilize offenders. In contrast, many writers see newer crime prevention and community policing as involving a new form of subjectification and responsibilization (Crawford, 1997; Garland, 1997; O'Malley, 1992). Garland, for example, identifies a new mode of governing crime, which he characterizes as a "responsibilization strategy": "This involves the central government seeking to act upon crime not in a direct fashion through state agencies (police, courts, prisons, social work, etc.) but instead by acting indirectly, seeking to activate action on the part of non-state agencies and organizations" (Garland, 1996:452). Garland says that this is a response to the predicament that "having taken over control functions and responsibilites which once belonged to the institutions of civil society, the state is now faced with its own inability to deliver the expected levels of control over criminal conduct"(Garland, 1996:449). The recurring message of this approach, as Garland puts it, "is that the state alone is not, and cannot effectively be, responsible for preventing and controlling crime" (Garland, 1996). Clearly, it is possible to read our account of restorative justice in this frame.

There are some distinctions that must be drawn, however. Responsibilization strategies vary in their approaches to achieving responsibility. Foucault's work is the theoretical influence underlying the responsibilization literature. Subjects are "taught to become 'responsible'" (Garland, 1997:191) by "techniques of the self" for cultivating a security-conscious *homo prudens*. This Foucauldian interpretation is contrasted with one in which individuals are assumed to be "'naturally' capable" of responsible action (Garland, 1997:191). Our conception of restorative responsibility is closer to the end of the continuum that assumes a natural capability for responsibility. At least we assume that the simple process of human beings talking through the consequences that have been suffered as a result of wrongdoing is all that is needed to elicit spontaneous proffering of active responsibility. At the same time, though, however natural and unforced the dialogue within it, we must concede that the creation of the institution of a restorative justice conference is itself a regulatory move designed to cultivate this "natural capability" for responsibility.

There are many unattractive features of responsibilization trends from which restorative justice must keep its distance. We see the worst manifestation of responsibilization in laws that hold parents legally liable for the delinquencies of their children. The normative theory of restorative justice should make it clear that only individual actors who are passively responsible (causally responsible) for crime should be held legally or morally responsible for it. Active responsibility of all kinds, including offers of help and support, forgiveness, care, compassion, love, and participation— all the things on which restorative justice most depends for success, should be conceived as gifts rather than moral duties, and certainly not as legal duties. They are supererogatory,[14] to put the claim formally. The legal system rightly recognizes parents as having duties of care to their children. In the context of a restorative justice conference for a criminal offense, though, a decision by parents to refuse to attend (or do anything the conference asks) should not be viewed as a breach of any duty.[15] No one, including the offender, has a duty even to attend.[16]

Restorative justice works because people are prepared to assume an active responsibility (particularly when they have a personal involvement) beyond any allocated passive legal or moral responsibility. Active responsibility often involves an assumed collective responsibility that can provide restoration and crime prevention in ways that courts restricted to allocating passive responsibility (enforced responsibility) cannot. A more structural worry about responsibilization is that it passes gender-related burdens of care down to individuals. This worry is that what is going on is a move by the state to slough off some of its social welfare obligations. A comparable concern arises with using restorative justice to deal with regulatory offenses; it may be part of a state's strategy to walk away from its obligations to regulate in areas such as environment (where it has clear responsibilities) by delegating them to civil society.

Christine Parker's (1999) work is a useful corrective here (see also Braithwaite and Parker, 1999). Parker sees a need for two-way communication. She wants institutions in which the justice of the law filters down into the justice of the people as manifest in restorative justice processes (so that, for example, respect for fundamental human rights constrains informal justice). Obversely, Parker wants a restorative justice that gives the justice of the people an opportunity to percolate up to influence the justice of the law. In terms of active and passive responsibility, we want the active responsibility to have an influence on the passive responsibility. The same theme is apparent in recent writings of Clifford Shearing (1995) and Jurgen Habermas (1996) on how the state can open itself up to "the input of free-floating issues, contributions, information, and arguments circulating in a civil society set apart from the state" (Habermas, 1996:183-184). According to Habermas (1996:442), the theory is clear:

> [T]he public sphere is not conceived simply as the back room of the parliamentary complex, but as the impulse-generating periphery that *surrounds* the political center: in cultivating normative reasons, it affects all parts of the political system without intending to conquer it. Passing through the channels of general elections and various forms of participation, public opinions are converted into a communicative power that authorizes the legislature and legitimates regulatory agencies, while a publicly mobilized critique of judicial decisions imposes more-intense justificatory obligations on a judiciary engaged in further developing the law.

The theory sounds fine, but it all seems rather romantic to imagine the day-to-day work of conferences bubbling up to influence the law. Cumulatively and potentially, though, this is not necessarily romantic. In communities in which conferencing is widespread, justice dilemmas that arise in conferences are discussed in civil society (at dinner parties, for example, including those attended by judges.)[17]

We can already cite specific conferences in New Zealand that have had an impact, albeit small, on the law. In the Clotworthy case, the decision of a conference for community service and victim compensation to fund cosmetic surgery needed as a result of a vicious knife attack was overruled by the Court of Appeal.[18] To the disappointment of restorative justice advocates, the Court of Appeal ordered a custodial sentence. However, the sentence was reduced in response to the wishes of the victim as articulated in the conference. Moreover, the Court did recognize the principle that the demands of restorative justice can affect sentences in very serious cases. Put another way, conferencing is in a position not dissimilar to the routine processing of cases in the lowest courts. Although what happens in the lowest courts might be the bulk of the law in action (and therefore "is" the law), rarely does it have any impact on the law in the books, or formal law. In rare strategic cases, though, the Magistrates "bubble up" the Clotworthy case.

One can imagine how restorative justice processes might achieve this task in a variety of contexts. A conference for schoolgirls caught smoking marijuana could communicate to school principals that passive responsibility such as expulsion is excessive and inappropriate. Conferences can and do also "bubble up" community disapproval of certain investigative techniques by the police, which tend to be suppressed in court. This capacity can be reinforced by making an inquiry of how fairly participants have been treated by the police in this formal part of the restorative justice process. Where there is a concern, the police, as a signatory of the conference agreement, can commit to report back to the participants about the results of an internal or ombudsman investigation of their conduct.

Fisse and Braithwaite (1993:232-237) have documented how a series of conferences exposed the victimization of Australian Aboriginal people in remote communities through fraudulent practices by major insurance companies. One of the decisions of the meetings between offending companies, regulators, victims, and Aboriginal Community Councils was to call a press conference. The abuses exposed were so systemic and shocking that the Prime Minister asked to be briefed by the regulatory agency. Significant change to regulatory law and practice ensued.

While it would be overly optimistic to hope that conferences would often be the transmission vehicle to percolate the justice of the people into the justice of the law, such cases show this is a possibility that can be realized. The Aboriginal insurance cases show that just as restorative justice can serve to responsibilize individuals in a way that relieves the state of burdens, so is it possible for powerless individuals to use restorative justice to responsibilize the state when the state is failing in its regulatory or welfare obligations.

Restorative justice is empowering in that it takes a ball away from the feet of a judge and puts it at the feet of a group of citizens. The type of responsibilizing that then goes on depends on how those citizens decide to exercise their political imagination in the use of that little piece of power. To use a soccer analogy, many will kick their own goals by taking responsibility for awesome burdens of care for which the state should be giving them more help. Others will learn from the example of those Aboriginal Community Councils from far North Queensland and kick the goals of state responsibilization.

CONCLUSION

A neglected part of the restorative justice research agenda has been the development of a restorative conception of responsibility—the kind of responsibility that will maximise restoration of victims, offenders, and communities. We have seen that restorative responsibility will be very different from traditional conceptions of criminal responsibility. It will involve a balance between passive and active responsibility with a substantial shift toward the latter.

We have seen that restorative responsibility has:

1. An important political rationale;

2. A strong philosophical foundation in responsibility for action and responsibility as a virtue;

3. A promising jurisprudential future through development of Fisse's notion of reactive fault; and

4. Practical promise in its links to theories of crime prevention.

At the same time, there remain unsolved worries about responsibilization, such as the risks of blaming victims of sexual assault and foisting unreasonable expectations on single parents who already are expected to do too much with too little support.

ENDNOTES

1. The recent Canadian Supreme Court decision *R. v. Gladue* (1999) provides an example of such a comparison: "Central to the (restorative justice) process is the need for offenders to *take* responsibility for their actions. By comparison, incarceration obviates the need to *accept* responsibility" (emphasis added) (at 72)

2. Some readers might question whether an approach that aims to prevent future events can be characterised as passive responsibility. After all, active responsibility is about the prevention of unwanted events. But it is our contention that one can seek to avoid future

events using passive responsibility or active responsibility. At the heart of the difference between the active and passive forms of these theories is the distinction between people taking responsibility (the active form) and risking being held accountable (the passive form).

3. The normative force of Pranis's assertion arises in our view from the normative claim that respectfulness (Braithwaite, 1989) ranks beside non-domination (Braithwaite and Pettit, 1990; Pettit, 1997) and empowerment (Braithwaite, 1999b) as central restorative values.

4. Some critics might argue that punitiveness on one hand, and active responsibility and restorative justice on the other, are not mutually exclusive: that is, if active responsibility is the taking of responsibility to restore harm, and a punitive outcome is what is required to restore some victims' harm (by satisfying their desire to punish), then punitive outcomes can involve active responsibility. However we would say if a punitive outcome is imposed on an offender without their consent it in no way involves active responsibility. If an offender does seek or actively consent to a punitive outcome, then it may involve active responsibility, but we would nevertheless seek to impose limits on such outcomes.

5. For instance, the International Covenant on Civil and Political Rights prohibits inhuman or degrading treatment or punishment (Article 7).

6. For example, under the legislation governing one conferencing scheme in Australia, the outcome must "not (be) more severe than those that might have been imposed in court proceedings for the offence" (Section 52(6)(a)Young Offenders Act 1997 (NSW)).

7. The allegations against Winnie Madikizela-Mandela included the murder of a child in her pursuit of political objectives on behalf of the African National Congress. P.W. Botha was the South African head of state during a period when his Cabinet is alleged to have authorized murder and other atrocities against those opposed to Apartheid.

8. Functionally, New Zealand law already accomplishes this result by putting cases into family group conferences not on the basis of an admission of criminal guilt, but on the basis of formally "declining to deny" criminal allegations.

9. An example of this would be if a report from a conference said that the offender simply cursed the victim and refused to discuss restitution.

10. Brent Fisse takes the more radical view that if criminal liability is about punishing conduct known to be harmful and if failure to respond responsibly is harmful, then such reactive fault can be sufficient to establish criminal liability.

11. This is not the whole answer, however. The other part of it is that the just deserts theorist is seen as morally wrong to consider equal justice for offenders a higher value than equal justice for victims (Braithwaite, 1999).

12. Having just been a victim of burglary is the single biggest predictor of burglary victimisation (Pease)

13. In Victoria, Australia, a man who raped a woman received a sentence that took into account that the woman's experience as a prostitute meant it was reasonable to assume that she suffered less psychological harm than would have been suffered by other victims of sexual assaults [*Hakopian*, 1991, unreported, Victorian County Court (see Cass 1992 for case summary and comment)].

14. See Mellema, 1991; Heyd, 1982.

15. Of course, this would not be the position with care and protection as opposed to a criminal justice conference, where the legal subject of the conference is whether parents are meeting their legal duty to care for and protect their child.

16. The only duty here rests with the police and prosecutor, who have a duty to take sufficiently serious cases to court when the opportunity for voluntary acts of responsibility in a restorative framework are spurned.

17. Indeed judges will attend conferences during their lifetimes as supporters of victims or of their own children who get into trouble as offenders.

18. *The Queen v. Clotworthy* (CA 114/98, 29 June 1998, NZ Court of Appeal) allowing appeal from sentence of District Court Judge Thorburn, 24 April 1998.

REFERENCES

Ayres, I. & J. Braithwaite (1992). *Responsive Regulation: Transcending the Deregulation Debate*. Oxford, England: Oxford University Press.

Barnes, G. (1999). "Procedural Justice in Two Contexts: Testing the Fairness of Diversionary Conferencing for Intoxicated Drivers." Ph.D. dissertation, University of Maryland.

Bazemore, G. (1999). "After Shaming, Whither Reintegration: Restorative Justice and Relational Rehabilitation." In G. Bazemore & L. Walgrave (eds.), *Restorative Juvenile Justice: Repairing the Harm of Youth Crime*. Monsey, NY: Criminal Justice Press.

Bazemore, G. & M. Dooley (2000). "Restorative Justice and The Offender: The Challenge of Reintegration." In G. Bazemore & M. Schiff (eds.), *Restorative Community Justice*. Cincinnati: Anderson.

Bovens, M. (1998). *The Quest for Responsibility*. Cambridge, England: Cambridge University Press.

Braithwaite, J. (1989). *Crime, Shame and Reintegration*. Cambridge, England: Cambridge University Press.

Braithwaite, J. (1997a). "On Speaking Softly and Carrying Sticks: Neglected Dimensions of Republican Separation of Powers." *University of Toronto Law Journal*, 47:1-57.

Braithwaite, J. (1998). "Linking Crime Prevention to Restorative Justice." In *Conferencing: A New Response to Wrongdoing*. Proceedings of the First North American Conference on Conferencing, August 6-8, Minneapolis.

Braithwaite, J. (1999). "Restorative Justice; Assessing Optimistic and Pessimistic Accounts." In Michael Tonry (ed.), *Crime and Justice: A Review of Research*.

Braithwaite, J. & K. Daly (1994). "Masculinities, Violence and Communitarian Control." In T. Newburn & E. Stanko (eds.), *Just Boys Doing Business*. London and New York: Routledge.

Braithwaite, J. & C. Parker (1999). "Restorative Justice is Republican Justice." In G. Bazemore & L. Walgrave (eds.), *Restoring Juvenile Justice: Repairing the Harm of Youth Crime*. Monsey, NY: Criminal Justice Press.

Braithwaite, J. & P. Pettit (1990). *Not Just Deserts: A Republican Theory of Criminal Justice*. Oxford, England: Oxford University Press.

Burford, G. & J. Pennell (1996). "Family Group Decision Making: New Roles for 'Old' Partners in Resolving Family Violence." *Implementation Report Summary*. St.Johns, Newfoundland: Family Group Decision Making Project.

Cass, D. (1992). "Case and Comment: Hakopian." *Criminal Law Journal*, 16:200-204.

Crawford, A. (1997). *The Local Governance of Crime: Appeals to Community and Partnerships*. Oxford, England: Clarendon Press.

Cullen, F.T. (1994). "Social Support as an Organizing Concept for Criminology: Presidential Address to the Academy of Criminal Justice Sciences." *Justice Quarterly*, 11(4):527-559.

Daly, K. (2000) "Revisiting the Relationship Between Retributive and Restorative Justice." In H. Strang & J. Braithwaite (eds.), *Restorative Justice: Philosophy to Practice*, pp. 33-54. Aldershot, England: Dartmouth.

Eckel, M.D. (1997). "A Buddhist Approach to Repentance." In A. Etzioni & D.E. Carney (eds.), *Repentance: A Comparative Perspective*. New York: Rowman and Littlefield.

Feeley, M. (1979). *The Process is the Punishment*. New York: Russell Sage.

Fisse, B. (1983). "Reconstructing Corporate Criminal Law: Deterrence, Retribution, Fault, and Sanctions." *Southern California Law Review*, 56:1141-1246.

Fisse, B. & J. Braithwaite (1993). *Corporations, Crime and Accountability*. Cambridge, England: Cambridge University Press.

Garland, D. (1996). "The Limits of the Sovereign State: Strategies of Crime Control in Contemporary Society." *The British Journal of Criminology*, 36(4):445-471.

Garland, D. (1997). "'Governmentality' and the Problem of Crime: Foucault, Criminology, Sociology." *Theoretical Criminology*, 1:173-214.

Habermas, J. (1996). *Between Facts and Norms: Contributions to a Discourse Theory of Law and Democracy*. London: Polity Press.

Haley, J.O. (1982). "Sheathing the Sword of Justice in Japan: An Essay on Law Without Sanctions." *Journal of Japanese Studies*, 8(2):265-281.

Heimer, C. (1999). "Legislating Responsibility," unpublished manuscript.

Heimer, C. & L. Staffen (1998). *For the Sake of the Children: The Social Organization of Responsibility in the Hospital and the Home*. Chicago: The University of Chicago Press.

Heyd, D. (1982). *Supererogation: Its Status in Ethical Theory*. Cambridge, England: Cambridge University Press.

Hogg, R. & D. Brown (1998). *Rethinking Law and Order*. Sydney: Pluto Press.

Keohane, R. (1984). *After Hegemony: Cooperation and Discord in World Politics*. Princeton, NJ: Princeton University Press.

Lewis, D. (1986) "Causation" and "Postscript: Redundant Causation." In *Philosophical Papers*, Vol. II. Oxford, England: Oxford University Press.

Makkai, T., and J. Braithwaite (1994a). "Reintegrative Shaming and Regulatory Compliance." *Criminology*, 32(3):361-385.

Maxwell, G.M. & A. Morris (1993). *Family, Victims and Culture: Youth Justice in New Zealand*. Social Policy Agency and Institute of Criminology, Victoria University of Wellington, New Zealand.

Mellema, G. (1991). *Beyond the Call of Duty: Supererogation, Obligation and Offence*. Albany: State University of New York Press.

Melton, A.P. (1995). "Indigenous Justice Systems and Tribal Society." *Judicature*, 79:126-133.

Mulgan, R. (1997). "The Processes of Public Accountability." *Australian Journal of Public Administrion*, 56(1):25.

Naffine, N. (1992). "Windows on the Legal Mind:The Evocation of Rape in Legal Writings." 18 MULR 741.

Olweus, D. (1993). "Annotation: Bullying at School: Basic Facts and Effects of a School Based Intervention Program." *Journal of Child Psychology and Psychiatry*, 35:1171-1190.

O'Malley, P. (1992). "Risk, Power and Crime Prevention." *Economy and Society*, 21:252-275.

O'Malley, P. (1994). "Responsibility and Crime Prevention: A Response to Adam Sutton." *The Australian and New Zealand Journal of Criminology*, 27:21-24.

Parker, C. (1999b). *Just Lawyers*. Oxford, England: Oxford University Press.

Pease, K. (1998). "Repeat Victimization: Taking Stock." Crime Detection and Prevention Series, Paper 90. Police Research Group, London.

Pettit, P. (1997). *Republicanism*. Oxford, England: Clarendon Press.

Pranis, K. (1998). "Conferencing and the Community." In *Conferencing: A New Response to Wrongdoing*. Proceedings of the First North American Conference on Conferencing. August 6-8, Minneapolis.

Shearing, C. (1995). "Reinventing Policing: Policing as Governance." In *Privatisierung staatlicher Kontrolle: Befunde, Konzepte, Tendenzen. Interdisziplinare Studien zu Recht und Staat*, 3:69-88.

Thomas, P. (1998). "The Changing Nature of Accountability." In G. Peters & D. Savoie (eds.), *Taking Stock: Assessing Public Sector Reforms*. Montreal:McGill–Queen's University Press

Wagatsuma, H. & A. Rosett (1986). "The Implications of Apology: Law and Culture in Japan and the United States." *Law and Society Review*, 20:461-498.

DISCUSSION QUESTIONS

1. Why is responsibility an important concept in restorative community justice? How does this model conceive of responsibilty differently than traditional justice models?

2. Distinguish between passive responsibility and active responsibility. How does restorative community justice engage active responsibility? Can you identify occasions when restorative justice might not do this?

3. How could the restorative community justice concept of responsibility change the focus of deterrence, incapacitation, and rehabilitation?

4. What is active deterrence? Compare and contrast active incapacitation and passive incapacitation.

CHAPTER 15

Keeping an Eye on the Keeper: Prison Corruption and its Control

Bernard J. McCarthy

In the introduction to this book, Michael Braswell states, "ethics is the study of right and wrong, good and evil." This chapter focuses on a troublesome and damaging problem in the administration of justice involving conduct that is both wrong and evil in American prison systems. It involves a personal choice by employees to engage in behavior that is clearly wrong and damaging.

Corrupt practices within the criminal justice system undermine and neutralize the administration of justice as well as destroy public confidence in the system. Corruption serves to negate the goals and processes of corrections and breeds disrespect for the process and the aims of justice. The purposes of punishment are also undermined.

The prison system is one of the most visible and symbolic aspects of the coercive nature of criminal justice, yet at the same time it is one that is most closed to the public. As Supreme Court Justice William Kennedy (2003) stated to the American Bar Association, "Even those of us who have specific professional responsibilities for the criminal justice system can be neglectful when it comes to the subject of corrections. The focus of the legal profession, perhaps even the obsessive focus, has been on the process for

KEY CONCEPTS:

corruption

corruption through default

corruption through friendship

corruption through reciprocity

malfeasance

material accommodations

misfeasance

nonfeasance

"pains of imprisonment"

power accommodations

status accommodations

Adapted from Bernard J. McCarthy, "Keeping an Eye on the Keeper: Prison Corruption and Its Control," *The Prison Journal*, 64(2):113-125.

determining guilt or innocence. When someone has been judged guilty and the appellate and collateral review process has ended, the legal profession seems to lose all interest. When the prisoner is taken way, our attention turns to the next case. When the door is locked against the prisoner, we do not think about what is behind it." This chapter takes a glimpse of what goes on behind the door—and exposes the student to a little known area of ethical misconduct.

With the exception of the imposition of death, the deprivation of liberty is the most serious action society takes against an offender. The prison represents society's ultimate penalty. By being sent to prison, offenders are involuntarily removed from the community through a legal process and placed in a confinement facility where their liberties are circumscribed. In the United States, prison systems are a huge and expensive enterprise. The 50 states, the federal government, and the District of Columbia all operate prisons. More than 1.5 million people are confined in prisons, with terms ranging in length of time from one year to life without parole. In addition, based upon the threat the individual poses to society and the crime committed, inmates are confined in conditions that severely restrict their freedom, and they are deprived of goods, services, and liberties from which nonincarcerated citizens are free to choose. More recently, prisons in America have become more punitive in their outlook and operating philosophy, and conditions of confinement have become more severe. A book (*Harsh Justice*) by James Q. Whitman, a Yale law professor, makes the controversial suggestion that the goals of the American prison system have shifted from rehabilitation to purposes that degrade and demean prisoners.

In this chapter, the problem of corruption and its control are examined as one form of ethical misconduct in state correctional systems. Historically, prison corruption has been a persistent and pervasive feature of corrections, periodically erupting in the form of scandals that are usually brought to our attention by the press. No prison system is immune from this problem; in recent years, major prison scandals have been reported in Alabama, California, Delaware, Hawaii, Illinois, New York, Pennsylvania, and Tennessee. Political payoffs, organized crime, large-scale street gangs, and the general avarice of people who have been hired to work in prisons have contributed or played a role in a number of these scandals. Other than media reports and the occasional state investigation, little is known about the problem. Prison systems are not open to the public, and much of what goes on inside is hidden from the public view. In fact, Supreme Court Justice Kennedy, in a speech to the American Bar Association, described the prison as "the hidden world of punishment; [and] we would be startled by what we see" if we were to look.

Periodically the prison becomes exposed to the general public when extreme abuses make their way to the public eye, as in the case of the charges of torture and sexual abuse occurring in the military prison in Abu Grahib.

The Role of Staff in Prison Misconduct

One of the most critical elements in any correctional system is the quality of the staff hired to work in prisons. The critical role played by employees in the correctional enterprise has long been noted by correctional practitioners and prison reformers:

> [It] is obvious, too, that the best security which society can have, that suitable punishments will be inflicted in a suitable manner, must arise from the character of the men to whom the government of the prison is entrusted (Boston Prison Discipline Society, 1827:18).

In 1870, the Reverend James Woodworth, Secretary of the California Prison Commission, stated:

> Until it [prison guard reform] is accomplished, nothing is accomplished. When this work is done, everything will be done, for all the details of a reformed prison discipline are wrapped up in this supreme effort, as oak is in the acorn (Fogel, 1979:69).

Jessica Mitford reported in a critical study of prisons:

> The character and mentality of the keepers may be of more importance in understanding prisons than the character and mentality of the kept (Reid, 1981:211).

Generally, in the area of public service, the integrity of government workers has been viewed as a significant factor in the effective and efficient operation of government. The most visible forms of corruption occur in the front end of the criminal justice system and involve the police. In criminal justice, a voluminous literature exists on police corruption, yet this subject represents one of the least understood areas in corrections. This chapter shifts the focus to prisons and the types of corrupt practices occurring behind the walls (both figuratively and literally). We will examine the forms, functions, and impact of corrupt practices on the correctional process.

Corrupt practices in prison range from simple acts of theft and pilferage to large-scale criminal conspiracies (e.g., drug trafficking, counterfeiting rings, sale of paroles, etc.). These forms of correctional malpractice may be directed at inmates and their families, other employees, the state, and the general community.

The impact of such practices cannot be underestimated. They are destructive and dangerous. In terms of their impact on the criminal justice system, corrupt practices undermine and erode respect for the justice system by both offenders and the general public and lead to the selective nullification of the punishment and the "pains of imprisonment" (i.e., the correctional process for certain offenders). For example, offenders may be able to arrange the purchase of paroles and pardons, arrange for confinement in a less secure setting, or drastically improve their standard of living in custody. Corrupt practices may also lead to a breakdown in the control structure of the organization and to the demoralization of correctional workers. It also dramatically increases the threat to their safety when drugs, cell phones, or weapons are smuggled into prison. The existence of corrupt practices also undermines the impact of correctional programs designed to change offenders. For example, the importation of drugs into a prison may completely undo the efforts of maintaining a drug-free facility.

The pernicious effects of employee misconduct were pointed out by the Massachusetts Public Safety Director Edward A. Flynn when commenting upon the injust treatment suffered by a prison inmate that lead to his death. Flynn said, "if nothing else, inmates must leave our custody with a belief that there is a moral order in the world . . . If they leave our care and control believing that rules and regulations do not mean what they say they mean, that rules and regulations can be applied artibitrarily or capriciously for personal interest then we fail society. We fail them and we will unleash people more dangerous than when they went in" (Belluck, 2004).

As one might expect, the incentives and opportunities for corrupt behavior for employees engaged in low-visibility discretionary actions in prison systems are many. From the offenders' perspective, they have everything to gain to persuade staff to make decisions that benefit them personally (i.e., the so-called pains of imprisonment may be neutralized or their release from custody secured) and very little to lose. Some inmates seek to exploit any weaknesses they may find in the system, including those of the staff. From the employees' perspective, corrupt practices represent a lucrative, albeit illicit, way to supplement one's income (and, in some systems, usually without significant risk). In one investigation nicknamed "Operation Bad Fellas," U.S. Bureau of Prison correctional officers where charged with smuggling heroin, marijuana, steroids, Italian food, vodka, wine, vitamins, clothing, and electronic equipment into a federal correctional facility in New York City. Bribes received by staff ranged from $100 to $1,000 per delivery (Suro, 1997).

In examining staff corruption within a prison system, three basic questions are raised: First, what is corruption, and what forms does it take in a prison setting? Second, what factors appear to be associated with it? Third, what steps should be taken to control the problem?

DEFINING CORRUPTION IN A CORRECTIONAL ENVIRONMENT

In the correctional literature, the concept of corruption has been used frequently, usually referring to a general adulteration of the formal goals of the correctional process (Rothman, 1971; Sykes, 1956, 1958). The literature on corruption, particularly police corruption, provides a much narrower definition, which aids researchers interested in studying the more specific problem (see Kleinig, 1996). For the purposes of this paper, corruption is defined as the intentional violation of organizational norms (i.e., laws, rules, and regulations) by public employees for personal material gain.

This definition was formulated on the basis of a review of the corruption literature—particularly the literature on police corruption—and guides our discussion of the issue. As one might expect, varying definitions and corresponding approaches to the study of corruption exist (Heidenheimer, 1970). In the research on police corruption, most studies appear to use what has been referred to as a public office–centered definition of corruption (Simpson, 1978). The public office–centered definition views corruption as essentially a violation of organizational norms by a public employee for personal gain (Heidenheimer, 1970). Examples of this approach may be found in the writings of Sherman (1974), Meyer (1976), Goldstein (1977), Barker (1977), and Kleinig (1996), and the approach has been adopted in this paper. Corruption occurs when a public servant (prison employee) violates organizational rules and regulations for his or her own personal material gain.

In operationalizing this definition of corruption for research purposes, certain conditions must be satisfied before an act can be defined as corrupt. First, the action must involve individuals who function as employees. Second, the offense must be in violation of the formal rules of the organization. Third, the offense must involve an employee receiving some personal material gain (something of value) for the misuse of one's office. These conditions are used to distinguish corrupt behavior clearly from other forms of staff misconduct, such as excessive use of force. A standard definition of corruption, consistent with the general literature, is critical in building an information base regarding corrupt practices in corrections and for comparative purposes with the larger criminal justice system.

TYPES OF PRISON CORRUPTION

Unlike the literature on police corruption, very little is known regarding the types of corrupt practices experienced by correctional agencies. One way to study this problem is to examine the internal affairs records of a state correctional agency (see McCarthy, 1981).

An internal affairs unit has the responsibility for investigating all allegations of misconduct by staff or inmates. The cases during a specific time period were reviewed first to identify those that fit the above definition of corruption and, second, to identify and analyze the range and types of corrupt practices experienced by this agency. Admittedly, this information source provides a limited view of the problem because it is based on official statistics. However, as researchers in the field of police corruption have suggested, the records of the internal affairs unit represent one of the best available sources of information for examining this topic (Myer, 1976; Sherman, 1979).

A content analysis of the case files identified several types of corrupt conduct: theft, trafficking in contraband, embezzlement, misuse of authority, and a residual or miscellaneous category.

Theft generally involved accounts of items reported as stolen from inmates during frisks and cell searches (drugs, money, jewelry), visitors who were being processed for visiting, and staff members. This form of misconduct was generally committed by low-level staff (e.g., correctional officers) and was opportunistic in nature.

Trafficking in contraband involved staff members conspiring with inmates and civilians to smuggle contraband (drugs, alcohol, money, steroids, food, and weapons) into correctional facilities for money, drugs, or services (usually of a sexual nature). The organization of this activity varied considerably. Some were large-scale conspiracies involving street gangs or organized crime officials on both the inside and the outside. Others were individuals acting on their own. As part of their sentence, inmates are deprived of access to many things that are accorded to free-world citizens. The items smuggled into prisons range from items such as food, makeup, and cigarettes to much more serious items such as drugs, guns, bullets, and explosive devices. In recent years, dozens of staff and inmates across the country have been arrested for smuggling in cell phones to inmates. These phones have been used to continue outside criminal activities (organized crime), intimidate witnesses, and engage in criminal activities such as drug smuggling. According to one recent report in Philadelphia, guards were indicted for smuggling drugs, cigarettes, and cell phones. One guard made up to $10,000 for bringing in cigarettes and a phone before being caught (Butterfield, 2004).

Acts of embezzlement were defined as systematically converting state property for one's own use. This offense was differentiated from theft. Theft tended to occur in single events that were opportunistic in nature. Embezzlement involved employees, sometimes with the help of inmates, systematically stealing money or materials from state accounts (inmate canteens or employee credit unions), state property, and warehouses.

Misuse of authority is a general category involving the intentional misuse of discretion for personal material gain. This form of corruption consisted of three basic offenses directed against inmates: the acceptance of gratuities from inmates for special consideration in obtaining legitimate prison privileges (e.g., payoffs to receive choice cells or job assignments); the acceptance of gratuities for special consideration in obtaining or protecting illicit prison activities (e.g., allowing illegal drug sales or gambling); and the mistreatment or extortion of inmates by staff for personal material gain (e.g., threatening to punish or otherwise harm an inmate if a payment is not forthcoming).

An additional form of misuse of authority is the taking of bribes by correctional administrators to award contracts to private vendors for services needed by the correctional system. As the privatization movement continues to grow in corrections, we can expect more reports of this form of misconduct as some companies vie for an unfair advantage. The use of an open bidding process for contracts helps to minimize this problem.

Another form of misuse of authority that is getting attention in the media is sexual misconduct involving staff and inmates, staff against staff, and staff and offender family members/friends. A National Institute of Corrections (2000) study found roughly one-half of the agencies in the Department of Corrections have been involved in litigation related to sexual misconduct. At least 22 state correctional agencies were facing class action or damage suits as a result of sexual misconduct by staff. One major reason for this upswing in allegations and charges is the use of cross-gender assignments in prisons, that is, male officers assigned to supervise females and female officers assigned to supervise male offenders. Several recent studies have concluded that this is a major problem in corrections (see, for example, Buell et al., 2003).

Staff sexual misconduct with other employees usually involves a supervisory relationship and exploits the imbalance in power. Sexual exploitation of family members and friends of inmates occurs when a staff member either accepts an offer of sexual favors and or takes advantage of the power relationship he or she has over the inmate and his or her family by extorting sexual services.

THE ROLE OF DISCRETION

All forms of corruption involve the misuse of discretion by public employees. The role played by discretion in corrections is significant. Correctional officials are provided with a broad mandate by law to develop and administer correctional agencies. This broad authority extends to devising rules, regulations, and procedures designed to control and otherwise handle offenders under custody. Corruption occurs when officials misuse this discretionary power for personal material gain.

At a general level, three forms of discretionary misconduct can be identified: misfeasance, malfeasance, and nonfeasance. For the purpose of understanding the relationship between corrupt practices and the misuse of authority, the different forms of corruption have been sorted into three categories of discretionary misconduct (see Table 15.1).

Misfeasance refers to the improper performance of some act that an official may lawfully do (*Black's Law Dictionary*, 1968). Offenses in corrections that fall into this category include the acceptance of gratuities for special privileges or preferential treatment (e.g., assignment to honor blocks, access to phone calls), the selective application of formal rewards and punishments to inmates for a fee, the sale of paroles or other forms of releases, and the misuse or misappropriation of state resources for one's own personal gain. All these acts involve an employee misusing the lawful authority vested in his or her office for personal gain.

Corrupt practices falling into the category of misfeasance are directed at improving the living conditions of inmates and, as a result, they reduce the deprivations associated with imprisonment. The misuse of lawful authority appears to be in an area in which line staff have the greatest opportunities to maximize their personal gain (especially in supplementing their income through the commission of illicit acts), because the nature of their work permits them the greatest influence over routine prisoner conditions. These acts are also considered low-visibility ones with little oversight at the lowest levels.

Malfeasance refers to direct misconduct or wrongful conduct by a public official or employee, as opposed to the improper use of legitimate power or authority (*Black's Law Dictionary*, 1968). Corrupt practices that fall in this category involve primarily criminal acts and include theft; embezzlement; trafficking in contraband; extortion; exploitation of inmates or their families for money, goods, and services; protection rackets; assisting escapes (as opposed to arranging paroles or sentence communications); running prostitution rings; and engaging in criminal conspiracies with inmates for such purposes as forgery, drug sales, and counterfeiting.

Acts of malfeasance appear to represent more aggressive and serious acts by staff to supplement their incomes. This type of offense is similar to the grass-eater/meat-eater distinction found in studies of police corruption (Knapp Commission, 1973). Meat-eaters are viewed as aggressively exploiting every possible situation for personal gain. Grass-eaters, on the other hand, take whatever comes their way. For instance, a meat-eater might sell drugs in prison, while a grass-eater might respond to an inmate's request for drugs. This type of behavior is destructive to the correctional environment and in a very real way poses a danger to inmates and staff.

The last category is nonfeasance. *Nonfeasance* refers to the failure to act according to one's responsibilities, or the omission of an act that an official ought to perform (*Black's Law Dictionary*, 1968). McKorkle (1970) has suggested that nonfeasance is more responsible for corrupting correctional officers than malfeasance. Two types of corrupt practices appear to be involved in this type of decision: (1) selectively ignoring inmate violations of institutional rules, such as permitting inmates to engage in sexual activities with visitors or looking the other way when marijuana or other drugs are smuggled into the facility by visitors in return for payment; and (2) the failure to report or stop other employees involved in misconduct. This second practice might typically consist of a low-level employee not informing on a fellow officer or superior because of an implied or direct promise of personal gain, such as promotion, transfer, or time off or reduced duties. In other cases, an administrator may fail to stop staff misconduct for fear of public scandal and possible loss of position.

Table 15.1
Pattern of Corruption by Type of Decision

Corrupt Acts by Discretionary Decisions	Officials Involved
Misfeasance	
Provide preferential treatment and special privileges	Line Staff
Selective application of rewards and punishments	Line Staff
Forms of legitimate release	Administrators
Misappropriation of resources	Administrators
Malfeasance	
Trafficking (cell phones, drugs, alcohol, weapons, and money)	Line Staff
Extortion/exploitation	Line Staff
Protection rackets	Line Staff
Embezzlement/theft	Line Staff & Administrators
Criminal conspiracies	Line Staff
Facilitation of escapes	Line Staff
Nonfeasance	
Failure to enforce regulations	Line Staff
Coverups	Administrators & Line Staff

As Braswell aptly points out in this book's introductory chapter, "our beliefs and values regarding right and wrong are shaped by many forces . . . being unethical is not simply committing an evil or wrong act (commission), it is also a matter of being an indirect accomplice to evil by silently standing by when evil occurs (omission)." In prisons this might occur when misconduct is committed and you know about it and don't do anything about it. For instance, recent revelations of torture in the U.S. prisons in Iraq were brought forward by individuals who were working there and bore witness to the actions of their fellow soldiers. The conduct is wrong and involves both action and witness: commission and omission.

FACTORS ASSOCIATED WITH CORRUPTION

Research has shown certain factors are associated with varying levels of corruption in an agency. In a U.S. Department of Justice study on municipal corruption (1978), two factors were identified as having a major influence on the level and degree of corruption experienced by a particular governmental agency. These factors were: (1) the opportunities for corruption, and (2) the incentives within the workplace to make use of those opportunities (Gardiner & Lyman, 1978). In the following section, these two factors will be examined within the context of a prison environment.

A third driving force identified by other studies of public corruption was the influence of politics (Gardiner, 1970; Sherman, 1978). Sherman suggests that a leading explanation for police corruption was the capture of the department by the political environment. Prison systems come under the executive branch of government, and its leaders are political appointees. As such, corrections is not immune from the power of politics. Correctional programs at the state and local levels are influenced by the political process, particularly in terms of the appointment of administrative staff and the allocation of resources.

THE ROLE OF OPPORTUNITIES

Three external forces influence prison systems and directly affect the incentives and opportunities for corruption. One is the continuing trend to incarcerate criminals. This has led to unprecedented levels of crowding in state and federal prison systems. Second, career criminals are receiving longer sentences as the public sentiment toward punishment continues to harden (e.g., "three strikes and you're out" laws), and these long-term offenders are making up a larger percentage of the inmate population. A third is that citizen attitudes toward the treatment of prisoners have led to a toughening of programs directed at prison inmates (e.g., chain gangs, the introduction of tobacco-free prisons, and the elimination of amenities such as college-level educational programs and recreation). These forces increase the deprivations associated with imprisonment and provide extra incentive to inmates to attempt to mitigate or neutralize the pains of imprisonment.

The opportunities for corruption arise from the tremendous amounts of discretionary authority allocated by the legislature to correctional officials. As Costikyan has noted, "Corruption is always where the discretionary power resides" (1974). In the prison, employees—particularly low-level ones (e.g., correction officers, counselors, and other line workers)—are responsible for monitoring and controlling virtually all inmate behavior. These officials constantly make low-visibility discretionary decisions that reward positive behavior and penalize negative behavior. These decisions directly affect the day-to-day living conditions experienced by inmates in custody.

In a prison environment, staff members, armed with a limited arsenal of formal rewards and punishments, are given the task of controlling a reluctant, resistant, and sometimes hostile inmate population. Special privileges in the form of extra television time, phone calls, job assignments, cell changes, conjugal visits, transfers, and furloughs may be used to reward positive behavior. Punishments, in the form of withdrawal of privileges, transfers, or various forms of deprivation (from restriction of calls to solitary confinement and loss of good time), are used to control inmates.

The way that staff members apply these rewards and punishments has both short-term and long-term consequences for inmates and their experiences in the correctional system. Accordingly, when one considers the conditions of confinement, one recognizes the many incentives and pressures for inmates to attempt to corrupt staff as one means of improving their living conditions or for staff to exploit their power. Individuals sentenced to prison are subjected to various levels of deprivations, commonly referred to as "pains of imprisonment," that affect both the physical and psychological stated of the individuals. Sykes defined these pains of imprisonment as the deprivation of liberty, goods and services, heterosexual relations, autonomy, and security (Sykes, 1958). In dealing with these "pains" associated with confinement, inmates make various adaptations to their immediate environment to help soften its psychological and physical impact. One of the techniques they use is the corruption of correctional employees as a means of neutralizing or improving their conditions of confinement (for example, through the smuggling of drugs, food, radios, or money, or the purchase of privileges).

In her journalistic study of an inmate incarcerated in a maximum-security prison, Sheehan made the following comment regarding the motivation of inmates in prison:

> Most men in the prison are in prison precisely because they were not willing to go without on the street. They are no more willing to go without in prison, so they hustle to afford what they cannot afford to buy (1978:9).

Hustling usually brings the inmates and/or confederates into situations in which they need the cooperation of a staff member, either to overlook an infraction, perform a favor, or smuggle in some item. As such, the incentives or pressures for inmates to influence the reward and punishment structure through corruption are enormous. Gardiner and Lyman underscore this point when they state: "Corruption can only occur when officials have an opportunity to exercise their authority in ways which would lead others to want to pay for favorable treatment" (1978:141). When it comes to the prison, nowhere in society are deprivations found that exceed the harsh conditions of confinement found in the deep end of confinement facilities.

INCENTIVES FOR CORRUPTION

There are many incentives for employees to take advantage of the power associated with their position in an institutional setting. They range from structural and organizational characteristics of prison management to individual factors (e.g., honesty of staff, the financial needs of employees, etc.).

A major incentive for corrupt practices results from defects in the prison organization's control structure. The prison, which is essentially a coercive organization, formally bases its control on the use of coercive power (Etzioni, 1964:59). However, correctional employees, particularly line staff, find that there are limits to the degree of compliance achieved through the use of coercive power (Cloward, 1960; Sykes, 1958). In order to do the job successfully, coercive power must be supplemented with informal exchange relations with inmates. These informal control practices are utilized by staff for control purposes and are responsible for the smooth functioning of the institution and for maintaining an uneasy peace (Cloward, 1960; Irwin, 1980; Sykes, 1958). As Sykes pointed out more than 50 years ago:

> The custodians (guards) . . . are under strong pressure to compromise with their captives for it is a paradox that they can insure their dominance only by allowing it to be corrupted. Only by tolerating violations of minor rules and regulations can the guard secure compliance in the major areas of the custodial regime (1956:158).

According to Sykes, three factors are responsible for undermining the formal control structure of the prison: (1) friendships with inmates, (2) reciprocal relationships, and (3) defaults. Each of these factors develops at the line-staff level as a function of long-term and close working associations between guards and inmates in a close setting. Irwin (1980), in a contemporary update, cited corrupt favoritism as a significant factor in the day-to-day management of the prison.

Corruption through friendship evolves from the close contact that prisoners and guards share in their daily interactions. In many cases, they get to know one another as individuals, and friendships may develop. These friendships may, in turn, affect how staff members use their authority. Corruption through reciprocity occurs as an indirect consequence of the exchange relations that develop between inmates and staff: "You do something for me, I'll do something for you." Corruption through default occurs when staff members (e.g., cellblock officers) begin to rely on inmates to assist them with their duties, such as report writing and cell checks. In time, the employee depends on the inmates for their assistance in satisfactorily performing his or her duties.

Cloward (1960) also pointed out how defects in the prison organization's control apparatus lead staff members to develop informal means of control through the development of various accommodations between the keepers and the kept. Material accommodations occur when staff provide certain inmates with access to forbidden goods and services or contraband in return for their cooperation. Cloward provides an example of this when he quotes an inmate explaining how he makes home brew:

> You go to make arrangements with the mess sergeant. He gets the ingredients and when we're in business . . . it's one of those you do this for me and I'll do this for you sort of thing. . . . The

> sergeant has to feed 1,500 men. It don't look good if he goofs. He
> wants the job done right. Now we're the ones who do the work, the
> cooking and all of that. So the sergeant, he says, okay you can make
> a little drink. But see to it that you get that food on the lines or the
> deal's off (1960:7).

Power accommodations occur when selected inmates are provided with access to restricted information, such as the date and time of an impending shakedown (search of cells) or access to key correctional personnel. Frequently, these take the form of reciprocal relationships in which valuable information is exchanged by both staff and inmates. Inmates inform on one another, and staff in turn may disclose administration plans regarding such activities as the time and place of cell searches.

Status accommodations result when staff provide special deference to certain inmates. According to Cloward:

> The right guy . . . seems to be left alone (by staff) in spite of con-
> spicuous deviance from official values, and this mark of untouch-
> ability results in high status among his peers (1960:40).

The cumulative effect of these accommodations may predispose certain correctional employees to take advantage of their situation and attempt to materially benefit from their working relationships with inmates, staff, and contractors.

Another factor that complicates matters is the type and quality of persons recruited and hired to work in correctional facilities. Frequently the quality of the work force is uneven and sometimes substandard because of low pay and poor working conditions. These individuals are placed in situations in which they are given considerable discretionary authority (without much training in its use) in a setting in which the visibility of their actions is quite low. When this occurs, the probability of corrupt practices increases. Another factor that provides an incentive for corruption is the impact of politics. If the selection and promotion of employees are influenced by politics, employee decisions may benefit the political party in power.

CONTROLLING CORRUPTION

First of all, it must be recognized that corruption is a regular feature of government processes. The problem of corruption will always be hovering in the background and can probably never be eradicated; however, certain steps may be taken to reduce and control the problem (Gardiner, 1970:93). In this section, we will examine several strategies that a correctional administrator may adopt to address the problem of corruption within a correctional agency.

A first step in dealing with the problem of corruption is to develop and enforce a strict, zero-tolerance policy on corruption, and implement and communicate a strong and forceful anticorruption policy. This policy should define specifically what the agency means by corruption as well as specify the penalties associated with such practices. (See Ward and McCormack, 1978, for an example of developing an anti-corruption policy for police departments). Once this policy has been formulated, it needs to be disseminated to all workers. Training should also be provided to employees regarding the nature, causes, impact, and consequences of corrupt practices. This training should be integrated into both pre-service and in-service training modules. Without enforcement, these policies will have no impact. For deterrence to work, these policies must be enforced. Employees charged with corruption should be investigated and prosecuted if warranted—not merely asked to resign.

Second, the correctional agency should develop a proactive mechanism to detect and investigate corrupt practices. This includes the establishment of an internal affairs unit and processes that encourage employees, inmates, and civilians to report allegations of staff misconduct. A whistleblower hotline is used by many states to deal with governmental misconduct, and this can be extended to prison systems. In addition, the use of routine and special audit procedures on a random basis will ensure the proper expenditure of funds. In one state, state-level investigators randomly target prisons and conduct interdiction investigations to search for contraband. Inmates, staff, and civilians are subject to searches and drug testing, including a drug-detection system known as Ionscan. In one year these searches resulted in the seizure of a large quantity of drugs (powder cocaine, crack cocaine, and marijuana) and weapons, including 13 firearms and 280 rounds of ammunition in one state system (Florida Department of Corrections, 1997). Drug testing of employees and the screening of correctional employees as they enter and leave institutions should also be considered.

Third, correctional administrators should attempt to improve management of material practices in the prison. This internal reform is directed at improving the control of the organization. In prior studies of corruption, where it was shown that leadership and control of persons were weak, the potential for corruption increased (Gardiner, 1970). Management must take affirmative steps toward reducing the opportunities for corruption. One step in this direction is to structure the use of discretion and make the visibility of low-level decisionmakers more public and subject to review. Guidelines for the use of discretionary rewards and punishments should be public. For example, specific criteria and a review process should be established to review cell changes, job assignments, and transfers or temporary releases. In addition, the disciplinary process should be opened up to review. These decisions should be periodically reviewed by supervisors to ensure the accountability of decisionmakers. An example of the misuse and abuse of the disciplinary process occurred a few years ago in the state of Massa-

Figure 15.1
Zero-Tolerance Memo

State of California   Youth and Adult Correctional Agency

Memorandum

Date   :   February 17, 2004

To   :   All California Department of Corrections Employees

Subject: **ZERO TOLERANCE REGARDING THE "CODE OF SILENCE"**

The California Department of Corrections (CDC) is only as strong as the values held by each of its employees, sworn and non-sworn. How we conduct ourselves inside our institutions and in the Central Office is a reflection of those values.

The "Code of Silence" operates to conceal wrongdoing. One employee, operating alone, can foster a Code of Silence. The Code of Silence also arises because of a conspiracy among staff to fail to report violations of policy, or to retaliate against those employees who report wrongdoing. Fostering the Code of Silence includes the failure to act when there is an ethical and professional obligation to do so.

Every time a correctional employee decides not to report wrongdoing, he or she harms our Department and each one of us by violating the public's trust. As members of law enforcement, all Correctional Officers must remain beyond reproach. The public's trust in this Department is also violated by retaliating against, ostracizing, or in anyway undermining those employees who report wrongdoing and/or cooperate during investigations. There is no excuse for fostering a Code of Silence.

Your hard fought efforts to protect the public deserve recognition. Recently, however, the public's trust has been undermined by the operation of a Code of Silence within the CDC. To correct this problem we are taking steps to ensure the Department exemplifies integrity and instills pride. Part of this effort is the immediate implementation of a zero tolerance policy concerning the Code of Silence. We will not tolerate any form of silence as it pertains to misconduct, unethical, or illegal behavior. We also will not tolerate any form of reprisal against employees who report misconduct or unethical behavior, including their stigmatization or isolation.

Each employee is responsible for reporting conduct that violates Department policy. Each supervisor and manager is responsible for creating an environment conducive to these goals. Supervisors are responsible for acquiring information and immediately conveying it to managers. Managers are responsible for taking all appropriate steps upon receipt of such information, including initiating investigations and promptly disciplining all employees who violate departmental policy.

Any employee, regardless of rank, sworn or non-sworn, who fails to report violations of policy or who acts in a manner that fosters the Code of Silence, shall be subject to discipline up to and including termination.

RICHARD RIMMER   RODERICK Q. HICKMAN
Director (A)   Agency Secretary
California Department of Corrections   Youth and Adult Correctional Agency

Source: http://www.corr.ca.gov/CDC/PDFs/CodeofSilenceMemo.pdf

chusetts, where John Geoghan, a defrocked priest convicted of molesting dozens of children, was falsely accused on disciplinary infractions by guards so that he would be transferred to a more punitive and restrictive setting. Geoghan was later killed by an inmate in a supposedly more secure but more punitive correctional facility. Internal reform should also include screening of employees in order to improve their overall quality.

Another management enhancement practice would be to upgrade employee selection procedures to include psychological testing and formal pre-service training designed to screen out questionable employees. In addition, simple police checks of an individual's background should be expanded to include in-depth background investigations of prospective employees. Some states are finding that members of street gangs are applying for jobs as correctional officers to assist in the expansion of the gang's power inside prisons. Routine investigations have also found that individuals with felony convictions and even escapees have been hired as correctional employees. Another step would entail improving the working conditions of employees so that the quality of correctional worker is raised. Employees making just barely above the minimum wage might be attracted to supplement their incomes through illicit behavior. Improving wage scales, enlarging job responsibilities, and broadening employee participation in decisionmaking, as well as increasing efforts toward professionalism, all will help address the issue of staff commitment to the mission of the agency.

A fourth and final recommendation addresses the political environment of prisons. Prisons are located in the executive branch of government, and top administrators serve at the pleasure of the state governor or President. Correctional administrators have little control over political and community attitudes toward prisons and prisoners, but they should take steps to insulate their employees from external pressure placed on them to act in a way that benefits some constituent or campaign donor who seeks to intervene on behalf of an inmate. By requiring merit selection and promotion of employees, a correctional administrator reduces the impact of political interference in the operation of the agency.

In sum, controlling corruption requires a commitment by correctional administrators to provide leadership in setting high standards of ethical conduct, communicating and upholding standards of ethical behavior, and holding people accountable for their actions. This includes improving and upgrading the general correctional environment (particularly the working conditions for staff) to protect employees from political pressures and to replace a tendency toward complacency with a concern for accountability. Opportunities for corruption must be identified and addressed, and the risks taken by persons predisposed to misconduct must be increased. It is doubtful that corrupt practices can be eliminated, but they can be reduced and controlled. It is important to keep in mind the words of Supreme Court Justice Kennedy when he addressed the American Bar Association:

> We have a greater responsibility, as a profession, and as a people, we should know what happens after the prisoner is taken away. To be sure the prisoner has violated the social contract; to be sure he must be punished to vindicate the law, to acknowledge the suffering of the victim, and to deter future crimes. Still, the prisoner is a person; he or she is part of the family of humankind. It is no defense if our current prison system is more the product of neglect than of purpose. Out of sight, out of mind is an unacceptable excuse for a prison system that incarcerates over two million human beings in the United States.

To upgrade and improve the prison in a democracy we must make sure that the prison be opened to the public and its workings exposed to citizens. The light of day shined on prison practices will ensure that our expectations for ethical conduct will be met.

REFERENCES

Barker, T. (1977). "Social Definitions of Police Corruption," *Criminal Justice Review*, 1 (Fall):101-110.

Blacks Law Dictionary (1968). St. Paul, MN: West.

Belluck, P. (2004). "Inquiry Lists Prison System Errors in Case of Slain Priest." *New York Times*, February 4, A16.

Braswell, M.C. (2005). Chapter 1, this volume.

Boston Prison Discipline Society (1826-1854) (1972). Reprint of 1st-29th Annual Report: An Introductory Report. Montclair, NJ: Patterson-Smith.

Buell, M., E. Layman, S. McCampbell & B. Smith (2003). "Addressing Sexual Misconduct in Community Corrections." *Perspectives: The Journal of the American Probation and Parole Association*, (27)2: 26-37.

Butterfield, F. (2004). "Inmates Use Smuggled Cellphones To Maintain a Foot on the Outside." *New York Times*, June 21:1, 18.

Clark, J.P & R.C. Hollinger (1981). "Theft by Employees in Work Organizations." Minneapolis: University of Minnesota. Cited in *Criminal Justice Abstracts*, 1(March):19.

Cloward, R. (1960). *Theoretical Studies in Social Organization of the Prison*. New York: Social Science Research Council.

Costikyan, E.N. (1974). "The Locus of Corruption." In J.A. Gardiner & D. J. Olsen (eds.), *Theft of the City: Readings on Conuption in Urban America*. Bloomington: Indiana University Press.

Crouch, B. (ed.) (1980). *The Keepers: Prison Guards and Contemporary Corrections.* Springfield, IL: Charles C Thomas.

Davis, K.C. (1960). *Discretionary Justice: A Preliminary Inquiry.* Baton Rouge: Louisiana State University Press.

Duchaine, N. (1979). *The Literature of Police Corruption,* Vol. II. New York: John Jay Press.

Duffee, D. (1974). "The Correction Officer Subculture and Organizational Change" *Journal of Research in Crime and Delinquency,* 2:155-172.

Etzioni, A. (1964). *Modem Organizations.* Englewood Cliffs, NJ: Prentice Hall.

Florida Department of Corrections (1997). *Office of the Inspector General Annual Report.*

Fogel, D. (1979). *"We Are the Living Proof": The Justice Model for Corrections.* Cincinnati: Anderson.

Gardiner, J.A. (1970). *The Politics of Corruption.* New York: The Russell Sage Foundation.

Gardiner, J.A. & T.R. Lyman (1978). *Decisions for Sale, Corruption and Reform in Land Use and Building Regulations.* New York: Praeger.

Goldstein, H. (1977). *Policing in a Free Society.* Cambridge, MA: Ballinger.

Heidenheimer, A. (1970). *Political Corruption: Readings in Comparative Analysis.* New York: Holt, Rinehart & Winston.

Irwin, I. (1980). *Prisons in Turmoil.* Boston: Little, Brown.

Kennedy, A.M. (2003). "An Address to the American Bar Association Annual Meeting." Associate Justice, Supreme Court of the United States, August 9.

Kleinig, I. (1996). *The Ethics of Policing.* New York: Cambridge University Press.

Knapp, W (1973). *Knapp Commission on Police Corruption.* New York: Brazilier.

Lombardo, L.X. (1989). *Guards Imprisoned: Correctional Officers at Work.* Cincinnati: Anderson.

Lyman, T., Fletcher & J. Gardiner (1978). *Prevention, Detection and Correction of Corruption* ed. *in Local Government.* Washington, DC: U.S. Government Printing Office.

McCarthy, B.J. (1981). "Exploratory Study in Corruption in Corrections." Ph.D. dissertation, The Florida State University.

McKorkle, L. (1970). "Guard-Inmate Relationships." In Johnston et al. (eds.), *The Sociology of Punishment and Control.* New York: John Wiley and Sons.

Meyer, J.D. (1976). "Definitional and Etiological Issues in Police Corruption: An Assessment and Synthesis of Competing Perspectives:" *Journal of Police Science and Police Administration,* 4:46-55.

Mitford, J. (1973). *Kind and Usual Punishment: The Prison Business.* New York: Knopf.

National Institute of Corrections (2000). "Sexual Misconduct in Prisons: Law, Remedies, and Incidence." In *Special Issues in Corrections.* Longmont, CO: U.S. Department of Justice.

Reid, S.T. (1981). *The Correctional System.* New York: Holt, Rinehart & Winston.

Rothman, D. (1971). *The Discovery of the Asylum: Social Order in the New Republic.* Boston: Little, Brown.

Sheehan, S. (1978). *A Prison and a Prisoner.* Boston: Houghton Mifflin.

Sherman, L. (1974). *Police Corruption: A Sociological Perspective.* New York: Anchor Books.

Sherman, L. (1978). *Scandal and Reform, Controlling Police Corruption.* Berkeley: University of California Press.

Sherman, L. (1979). "Obtaining Access to Police Internal Affairs Files." *Criminal Law Bulletin,* 15 (September-October):449-461.

Simpson, A. (1978). *The Literature of Police Corruption.* New York: John Jay Press.

Suro, R. (1997). "Officials Wonder if Bribery Arrests at Federal Prison are Isolated or Trend:" *The Washington Post,* June 1:A08.

Sykes, G. (1956). "The Corruption of Authority and Rehabilitation." *Social Forces,* 34:157-162.

Sykes, G. (1958). *The Society of Captives: A Study of a Maximum Security Prison.* Princeton, NJ: Princeton University Press.

Ward, R. & R. McCormack (1979). *An Anti-Corruption Manual for Administrators in Law Enforcement.* New York: John Jay Press.

Whitman, J.Q. (2003). *Harsh Justice: Criminal Punishment and the Widening Divide Between America and Europe.* Oxford University Press.

DISCUSSION QUESTIONS

1.   What kinds of motivations might a correctional officer have for engaging in corruption? Are some forms of corruption worse than others? Explain.

2.   If you were an inmate serving time in a punitive prison would you attempt to curry favor with staff to obtain extra privileges? Would you pay for those privileges?

3. Is corruption an unavoidable result of discretion? Discuss your response in detail.

4. Working in corrections can be morally challenging for employees. What does this mean? What are some of the temptations that might exist?

5. Should the goals of the prison system include degrading and demeaning prisoners?

6. What implications would this have for staff working in prison?

7. You have been serving as a prison commissioner for several months without any political pressure placed on you. During a friendly conversation with the Governor's Chief of Staff, the Chief mentioned that a former political ally doing time for bribery would like to be transferred to a minimum-custody classification facility close to his family's hometown. The Chief said he would really appreciate your assistance in this matter. As an aside, he mentioned your performance review was coming up. How should you respond?

CHAPTER 16

Ethics and Prison: Selected Issues

John T. Whitehead

INTRODUCTION

Prisons are a source of fascination for many of us. Although prisons are intended to repel us, they seem to be a source of mysterious interest. Moviemakers have capitalized on this interest with countless movies set in real or fictitious prisons, especially traditional "Big House" prisons such as Sing Sing or Walla Walla. Another testimony to the uncanny attractiveness of prisons is the conversion of Alcatraz, the former disciplinary prison of the federal prison system, to a museum where tourists can walk around and even be locked in a cell for a few minutes of imaginary incarceration.

This chapter will examine some of the ethical issues about prison. It will discuss prison composition, discrimination, prison conditions, treatment, victimization, elderly offenders, women in prison, and privatization. Guard corruption will not be considered because McCarthy discussed that issue in Chapter 15.

KEY CONCEPTS:

discrimination

elderly offenders

prison composition

prison conditions

privatization

treatment

victimization

WHO BELONGS IN PRISON?

A basic ethical question about prison is: Who belongs there? What kinds of offenders deserve to be sentenced to prison? A number of critics contend that many of the people sent to prison do not need to be there. According to these critics, these prisoners are neither violent nor career criminals, and most citizens do not really want such people incarcerated. Irwin and Austin (1997:58-59), for example, cite 1992 prison admission statistics that show that only 27 percent of prison admittees that year were admitted to prison for a violent crime conviction. Like other prison critics (see, for example, Tonry, 1995), Irwin and Austin note with alarm the increased use of prison for drug crimes (1997:27-28).

Conservatives, on the other hand, applaud the growth in the prison population. DiIulio, for example, argues that average citizens want prisons to be used and that prison incapacitates and saves money: "'prison pays' for most prisoners: it costs society about twice as much to let a prisoner roam the streets in search of fresh victims as it does to keep him locked up for a year" (DiIulio, 1995: 41). DiIulio (1994) also argues that greater use of incarcerative sentences will reduce crime in our nation's crime-ridden neighborhoods.

A complete analysis of this issue is beyond the scope of this chapter,[1] but some consideration is necessary. First, critics of increased incarceration fail to mention several crucial points about prison/prisoner statistics. For example, critics often fail to note that approximately 15 percent of the offenders admitted to prison each year are admitted for burglary (Maguire & Pastore, 1996:567). Although prison critics conventionally label burglary as a "property" crime, many citizens regard this crime as a much more serious crime than other property crimes, such as shoplifting. Burglary involves trespass into one's personal space (one's "castle" or home), and it also involves a very real potential for violence. Either the burglar or the victim may have a weapon at hand and resort to using it. A qualitative indicator of the seriousness with which some people regard burglary is the criminal law allowance of deadly force against burglary in at least one state (see, e.g., Alabama Code, 13A-3-23). Another connection of burglary to violent crime is that many burglars are looking for guns (Wright & Decker, 1994:144). Clearly, there is some probability that these guns will be fenced or otherwise transferred to other criminals directly engaged in violent crime. Second, many of the "nonviolent" offenders admitted to prison in any year were repeat offenders and/or offenders who had been under community supervision of some sort. In 1991, for example, 45.9 percent of all state prisoners were either probation or parole violators at the time of their admission to prison (Cohen, 1995). In 1992, parole violators represented 29 percent of prison admissions (Maguire & Pastore, 1996:567). Thus, it is misleading to argue that only 27 percent of new admissions to prison are violent, when another 15 percent are burglars and another 29 percent are repeat offenders (parole violators).

In addition, in giving *admission* statistics, critics may overlook *composition* statistics. For example, in both 1992 and 1993, almost one-half (48%) of the prisoners in state prisons were in prison for a violent crime (Beck & Gillard, 1995). Another 11 percent were in prison for burglary. Thus, approximately six out of 10 prisoners were in prison for either burglary or a violent crime.

Moreover, drug offenders may be more threatening than Irwin and Austin consider them to be. One investigation found that many crack cocaine users were involved in both crack dealing and other crime. Inciardi and his colleagues (1993) studied serious delinquents in Miami at the start of the crack epidemic in the mid-1980s. They found that more than one-half of the crack users in their sample were dealers and 18 percent were "dealers plus" (i.e., they also manufactured, smuggled, or wholesaled the drug). More importantly, these dealers were far from innocent, recreational purveyors: "Degree of crack-market participation was also related to earlier and greater general crime involvement, *including violent crime* (emphasis in the original) (Inciardi, Horowitz & Pottieger, 1993:178). Further, a number of studies "have shown that lethal violence is used commonly by drug traffickers in the pursuit of their economic interests" (Brownstein et al., 1995:475).

On the other hand, prison proponents also omit or fail to emphasize some important points about prison composition. For example, the contention that the average citizen wants criminals incarcerated (see, for example, DiIulio, 1995) is only partially correct. There is substantial agreement in the literature that the public is not as punitive as surmised but rather still wants rehabilitation and will opt for nonincarcerative sentences for many offenders. When asked in 1995 whether the government should "make a greater effort these days [to] rehabilitate criminals who commit violent crimes or punish and put away criminals who commit violent crimes," 26 percent of the respondents in one public opinion poll favored rehabilitation and another 12 percent favored *both* rehabilitation and punishment (Maguire & Pastore, 1996:177). When asked whether they thought violent criminals could "be rehabilitated given early intervention with the right program," 14 percent of the sample thought most could be rehabilitated, and 45 percent thought that some could be rehabilitated (Maguire & Pastore, 1996:177). Research in California found that citizens did indeed initially express a preference for prison for 25 hypothetical cases varying from petty theft to rape. After being informed of costs and alternatives to incarceration, however, these same citizens wanted only 27 percent of the hypothetical offenders to be incarcerated (DiMascio, 1995). Recent research in Ohio showed that on a global measure of support 88 percent of the sample favored a "three strikes and you're out" law. On more specific measures, however, only 17 percent of the respondents favored life sentences; most favored sentences of five to 15 years in prison. Thus, it is safe to say that "underneath more punitive global attitudes, in specific situations, the American public tends to be less punitive and to favor a more diversified response to crime than simply locking up offenders . . ." (Applegate et al., 1996:519).

Similarly, the matter of incapacitation is much more complex than many prison proponents portray. Spelman (1994) found that collective incapacitation is at best a "gamble" that "may pay off" (p. 289) and that the effect of selective incapacitation is at best—and under ideal conditions—only 4 to 8 percent (p. 289). This led Spelman to caution that "the crime problem can never be substantially reduced through incapacitation alone" (1994:312). Instead,

> criminal justice policies that deter and rehabilitate individual offenders; broader-based policies aimed at ameliorating continuing social problems such as chronic poverty and unemployment,

teenage pregnancy and child abuse, and the like; and entirely different approaches aimed at reducing the number of criminal
opportunities rather than just the number of criminals, all deserve
continued attention (Spelman, 1994:312).

In summary, the debate about who should go to prison is often clouded
by partisan positions that fail to consider some important pieces of information. Critics of prison tend to overemphasize the use of prison for nonviolent offenders. Proponents oversell the alleged benefits of prison and
ignore polling research that indicates the public's willingness to use nonincarcerative options. Hopefully, a peacemaking approach mindful of as much
clarity as possible will help to resolve the debate.

DISCRIMINATION IN SENTENCING

A more specific concern in the larger question of prison composition has
been the alleged discrimination in sentencing to prisons. In 1992, for example, 54 percent of all prison admissions were African Americans (Maguire
& Pastore, 1996). Further, African Americans make up 12 percent of the general population but 31 percent of federal prisoners and 51 percent of state
prisoners (Mumola & Beck, 1997; Walker, Spohn & DeLone, 1996).

The overrepresentation of African Americans in prisons is nothing new.
This group made up 30 percent of the prison population in 1940, more
than 40 percent in 1980 (Walker, Spohn & DeLone, 1996), 46 percent in
1985, and 49 percent in 1990 (Mumola & Beck, 1997). However, one aspect
of the problem that *is* new is the increased number of African Americans
incarcerated for drug offenses (Mumola & Beck, 1997). Several observers
argue that police "target minority communities—where drug dealing is
more visible and where it is thus easier for the police to make arrests—and
tend to give less attention to drug activities in other neighborhoods" (Walker,
Spohn & DeLone, 1996:209).

A few cautions are in order. Drug offenders may be more threatening than
some of the critics of the incarceration of drug offenders consider them to
be. As noted in the previous section, drug use may also mean involvement
in drug dealing, criminal activity, and violence (including lethal violence)
(Brownstein et al., 1995; Inciardi, Horowitz & Pottieger, 1993).

These observations are not meant to justify discriminatory policing
and/or sentencing of African-American drug offenders. They are simply
offered to show that there is some reason for society to be concerned about
drug offending, no matter which racial or ethnic group is involved.

It would seem that the ethical course of action is to pursue a drug policy that treats all races the same. It would also seem that any drug policy
should not discriminate or give the *appearance* of discrimination. At the very
least, our nation's drug policy has failed on the latter account. A number of

observers have judged the drug war to violate the appearance of impartial handling. Steps need to be taken to correct that appearance. If the famous O.J. Simpson murder trial said anything, it is that how the criminal justice system treats African Americans is clearly under scrutiny, and even the perception of bias can have harmful consequences. Continuing the recent drug policy runs the risk of alienating still further minority members who are already substantially alienated.

PRISON CONDITIONS: CODDLING OR TOUGHNESS?

Another fundamental ethical issue concerning prisons is the question of what kind of prison environment society should provide for prisoners. A number of voices are calling for tough, spartan-like prisons with no "frills" such as television, recreational facilities, or athletic equipment. More traditional voices think that prison intrinsically involves a number of pains or deprivations and that we do not need to make it much tougher than it is. To these people, what looks like a frill may in fact be justified for one or more logical reasons.

Van den Haag (1975) is an example of a critic who argues for spartan prisons. He argues that prisoners should work many hours each day for the purpose of punishment and that such hard labor should be sufficient to tire them out. At night they would be so exhausted that they would just rest before bed. This type of prison would serve retributive, incapacitative, and deterrent objectives. It would be tough punishment for crime, it would keep offenders off the streets and away from opportunities to commit crime, and it would serve to frighten potential offenders from committing crime because persons considering crime would not want to be sentenced to a hard-labor prison.

Bidinotto (1997) has criticized our nation's prisons for coddling prisoners. In an article originally published in *Reader's Digest*, he alleged that hard labor was out of fashion. In style, he said, were electronic exercise equipment, horseshoe pits, bocce, conjugal visits (even at such supposedly spartan prisons as Attica Prison in New York), and opera appreciation classes.

More extreme critics argue for even tougher prisons. In addition to removing any frills or amenities from traditional prisons, these individuals contend that prison should be made as tough as possible. Possible changes would be very limited diets and the introduction of chain gangs. Chain gangs would add humiliation to prison labor. Prisoners would be chained to each other and forced to work outside prison walls so that the public could see them at work. In this scenario, scorn would return to the criminal justice system. (See the separate section below on chain gangs.)

More traditional voices note that prison already contains numerous painful features that are sufficient punishment for offenders. These inherent pains of prison are harsh enough to make prison punitive and also serve as a deterrent to potential offenders. Sykes (1958), for example, noted almost 50 years ago that prison involves a number of pains or deprivations. These are deprivation of freedom, autonomy, possessions, security, and heterosexual contact. Deprivation of freedom or liberty is self-explanatory; inmates lose their freedom to come and go as they please. Deprivation of autonomy refers to the removal of choices; inmates are told what to do and when to do it by virtue of a schedule that governs every minute of the day. Unlike free citizens, inmates have no choices about when to get up in the morning, when to go to meals, what to eat, what to wear, when to watch television, and when the lights go out. The prison dictates the decisions that those of us in the community take for granted each day and treats the inmate like a child who is incapable of making autonomous decisions. Likewise, with possessions, the administration allows only minimal possessions such as a picture or poster or two and no distinguishing clothing. In a society that exalts material possessions as signs of status, accomplishment, and individuality, the prison restricts possessions to the minimum and thereby depersonalizes each inmate. Security is far from a given in prison. Inmate assaults are a real possibility, especially for the weak. Even the strong have to fear attacks from groups of inmates who can overpower any one individual (more on this below). Finally, deprivation of heterosexual contact is the norm in most prisons. Very few prisons allow conjugal visitation, and a prisoner must be married to participate.

Guenther (1978) has noted some additional deprivations or pains. The subjective experience of time in prison can be very painful. For example, weekends are periods of "hard time" because the inmate does not have to go to a job that helps him or her pass the time during the week. Through the holiday season, inmates see holiday shows and advertisements that remind them that they are missing contact with loved ones at a special time of the year. Even letters from home can be painful because sometimes the letter writer expresses anger or hurt at the offender for the things the offender did to the writer. Children, for example, may express anger at their father for abandoning them and not being with them to do simple things like take them fishing. Visits can be occasions for other inmates to offer taunts. Other inmates may tease the inmate who receives a visit from his or her spouse, reminding the offender that the spouse is free and might be seeing other people behind the offender's back. Or a visit from a spouse may cause the inmate "to question how 'the government' can deny him sexual access to his spouse" (Guenther, 1978:602). At the very least, visitors have to be searched, and they see the offender in prison clothing that reminds both the visitor and the offender that he or she is a lawbreaker who has been arrested and convicted.

Traditionalists argue that these inherent pains of prison are sufficient suffering. Additional torments such as removing exercise equipment or televisions and radios are unwarranted. Traditionalists also argue that amenities can serve to keep inmates occupied and thereby help prevent restlessness, attacks on other inmates, attacks on guards, and, ultimately, prison riots.

Conrad (1982:313) frames the question aptly: "What do the undeserving deserve?" His answer is worthy of consideration. He argues that they deserve "safety, lawfulness, industriousness, and hope" (Conrad, 1982:328). Safety and lawfulness are self-explanatory; unfortunately, they are often lacking in our prisons. Inmates often fear that they will be victimized in some way while behind bars. By industriousness Conrad does not mean mere busywork but that "everyone puts in a full day of work at jobs that are worth doing and paid accordingly" (p. 328). Hope is the most important consideration: ". . . where everyone has some reason to hope for better things to come— or could have such a reason if he or she were willing to look for it—the prison will not only be safer, but it will also be a place in which its staff can take some pride" (Conrad, 1982:328).

Sometimes the debate over prison conditions can make it sound like prisoners are living in expensive luxury resorts in which every whim is satisfied, but "[i]f our prisons are such resorts, simply open the gates and see how many run out . . . and how many walk in" (Taylor, 1997:92).[2]

TREATMENT/REHABILITATION/PROGRAMMING

Related to the issue of the appropriate conditions for prisoners is the issue of whether treatment opportunities should be provided for prisoners. Although rehabilitation was once routinely provided, many voices question providing anything other than punishment to inmates.

There is no question that most prisoners are in need of various types of assistance. Many prisoners are high-school dropouts, do not have employable skills, had alcohol or other drug problems prior to entering prison, and may suffer from psychological difficulties such as lack of self-esteem.

An argument for providing services to offenders is that such services may help reduce recidivism when the inmate is released. Employment, for example, has been shown to be a clear correlate of success on parole (Pritchard, 1979). Similarly, recent studies of intensive supervision have demonstrated that offenders who received treatment for various problems recidivated less (were less likely to reoffend) than offenders who did not receive appropriate treatment (Petersilia & Turner, 1993). Such empirical evidence for the efficacy of treatment (see also, Gendreau, 1996) suggests that the ethically correct course of action is to provide treatment opportunities.

In spite of its effectiveness, some still argue that treatment is not appropriate for prisoners. One argument is the principle of least eligibility, which maintains that prisoners do not deserve anything better than what is given to the least eligible in our society. Because many people cannot afford college or vocational training or psychological counseling, a strict adherent of this principle might argue that prisoners should not benefit from any such treatments. To do so would give them something better than that had by a significant minority of the free population.

One response to this is that the deprived status of the neediest in American society is not sufficient justification for depriving inmates. The answer is to address both problems. Law-abiding citizens deserve the opportunity to attend college or learn a vocational trade. Prisoners too should have such opportunities, which will hopefully help prevent any return to crime. Years ago, the Vienna Correctional Center in Illinois attempted to solve the problem by opening up a number of prison programs to any interested citizens from the community. That way, the area residents did not feel that the inmates were benefiting from programs that were not available to them (Silberman, 1978).

Another argument against services for inmates is that the prison environment is highly likely to sabotage such efforts. Drawing on the prison research of Sykes (1958), the mental hospital research of Goffman (1961), and other research, some argue that so much suspicion, distrust, and animosity arises between inmates and prison staff that it is impossible to offer meaningful treatment options in the prison environment. In Goffman's terms, inmates are so involved in seeking secondary adjustments that mitigate the intended punishments of prison that they would not benefit from treatment programs. In Sykes's terms, inmates are so busy trying to soften the pains of prison by such strategies as making home-brewed alcoholic beverages, achieving status by boisterousness or physical prowess, or prowling for sexual conquests that any treatment efforts would fall on deaf ears. The counter argument is that prison officials have often failed to implement rehabilitation programs as needed. Instead, wardens and guards put custody concerns over treatment concerns in terms of both dollars and emphasis. Thus, prison staff get what they want: custody rather than rehabilitation.

An important reminder in any debate over providing treatment is that most offenders will be released back into society. If society makes no effort to educate or train offenders for gainful employment after release, the offenders will not have a legal means of support and may well resort to crime. Releasing offenders without any improvement of their condition seems highly unlikely to improve their chances for success.

CHAIN GANGS

Chain gangs were reintroduced in Alabama in 1995, but the move was followed by court challenges. Governor Fob James justified their use as a way to save money and to make incarceration tougher. He argued that a prison guard can supervise only 20 unchained men on a road crew but the number doubles to 40 prisoners if the men are shackled. Concerning toughness, he argued that some men were declining parole because they thought incarceration was easier (Morris, 1997). An argument can also be made that chain gangs are constitutional because the Thirteenth Amendment to the United States Constitution prohibits involuntary servitude "except as punishment for crime."

A major argument against chain gangs is that they are discriminatory or, at best, give the appearance of discrimination. Observers have noted that 70 to 90 percent of the Alabama chain gang prisoners were black (Corsentino, 1997). For African Americans, chain gangs are a reminder of the Reconstruction Era in the South when racism was still rampant. After the Civil War, the South needed to rebuild railroads and roads, and prison labor was leased out to contractors to engage in such direly needed projects. Many of the prisoners were blacks, as the South used its criminal justice systems as a way to get around the legal abolition of slavery. As in slavery, the offenders were classified as "full hands" or "half hands," tacit recognition that slavery had simply taken another form (McKelvey, 1997). A constitutional question is whether the use of chain gangs violates the cruel and unusual punishment prohibition of the Eighth Amendment.

Another argument against reintroducing chain gangs is von Hirsch's (1990) principle of acceptable penal content. What he means is that sanctions are only acceptable if the offender can endure them and still maintain his or her human dignity. Von Hirsch, who argues that punishments such as bumper stickers on the cars of drunk drivers proclaiming their DUI (driving under the influence of alcohol) status are too demeaning, would oppose chain gangs because they are intrinsically humiliating and do not allow the offender the necessary minimum condition of human dignity.

Finally, it is important to consider what emotions might be generated in offenders by the use of measures like chain gangs, especially after release. Do we want offenders living next to us who have been humiliated and scorned? Or do we want offenders who feel that prison was a painful but appropriate punishment for the wrongs they committed?

SAFETY/SECURITY IN PRISON

As noted, Sykes (1958) listed deprivation of security as one of the pains that prisoners suffer. There is some controversy about how much lack of security prisoners should undergo. A number of studies have detailed the victimization that many prisoners have had to face. Lockwood (1980), for example, found that approximately 25 percent of the male inmates he studied had been a target of sexual assault. Nacci and Kane (1983) did a similar study of federal prisoners and found that 9 percent of them had been targets of sexual aggression in any prison and that 2 percent had been targeted in a federal institution. Marquart (1986), conducting participant observation research, personally witnessed 50 guard beatings of inmates. Wachtler (1997), former Chief Judge of the New York Court of Appeals, reported being stabbed in a federal facility. Therefore, it appears that although federal facilities are supposed to be relatively safe and secure, even a prominent white-collar criminal has a considerable risk of being attacked in prison.

More generally, Bowker (1980) provides a thorough (but now-dated) catalogue of the various types of victimization that prisoners suffer. Irwin and Austin have argued that prison produces harmful effects on offenders: "The disturbing truth is that growing numbers of prisoners are leaving our prisons socially crippled and profoundly alienated" (1997:82). They are also concerned that the increasing use of maximum-security confinement compounds the harmful effects of prison so that contemporary prison systems are "spewing out such damaged human material" (Irwin & Austin, 1997:106). Indeed, a survey of prisoners revealed disciplinary practices, including beatings that were characterized as capricious and brutal (Hamm et al., 1994).

Several studies, however, have painted a less negative picture. A study of coping in New York prisons concluded that "most prisoners serve fairly trouble-free terms" and that their overall experience in prison is "no more overwhelming to them than other constraining situations they have encountered in their lives" (Toch & Adams, 1989:254). A longitudinal study of the incarceration experience in Canada led Zamble and Porporino to compare a prison sentence to a "deep freeze" after which the offenders are unchanged: "As they had done on the outside, most of the inmates in this study followed a path of least resistance, and they focused on the fine line of present time passing" (1988:150). A 1990 review of prison studies failed "to show any sort of profound detrimental effects" (Bonta & Gendreau, 1994:57).

In summary, a number of studies have shown that victimization is problematic in at least some prisons or for some prisoners in many prisons. Other studies have shown that a number of prisons are relatively secure and safe and that a considerable number of offenders come out unscathed. The ethical mandate is to make all prisons safe and lawful. Even the undeserving deserve this minimal guarantee (Conrad, 1982).

ELDERLY PRISONERS

With longer sentences, mandatory sentences, and "three strikes and you're out" laws, state prison systems and the federal prison system can expect an increase in the number of elderly offenders. This increase raises some ethical issues.

A basic question concerns the release of elderly prisoners once they are no longer a danger to others. In other words, given some of the changes in sentencing in the last 10 years, it is reasonable to expect that prison officials will see increasing numbers of prisoners in their sixties, seventies, or eighties. As prisoners become elderly in prison, it is clear that many of them will be little or no danger to society. A prisoner who has Alzheimer's disease or arthritis or heart disease is hardly at risk of engaging in burglary, armed robbery, or murder. At some point, age reduces the risk of further criminal behavior to zero or close to zero.

If there is little incapacitative or rehabilitative value in keeping such prisoners locked up, should we release them? Or does the goal of retribution dictate that they stay in prison for as long as their original sentence dictated? If a prisoner gets to the point at which he or she does not even understand where he or she is (for example, due to a disease like Alzheimer's), does it make any retributive sense to keep the prisoner confined? Doesn't the concept of punishment require that the prisoner understand what is being done to him or her?

Conversely, society may want to release elderly offenders to save money. As prisoners age, it is logical to expect that their health care expenses will rise. They generally will need increasing medical care. Should society keep these offenders in prison so that they can receive the medical attention they need, or should society release them to save money? Parenthetically, a system of national health care could eliminate this dilemma by removing any incentive to release them.

WOMEN IN PRISON

Women make up a small but significant proportion of the United States prison population. At year-end 2003, there were 101,179 female prisoners in state and federal institutions, constituting 6.9 percent of the total prison population (Harrison & Beck, 2004).

Although prison conditions are not as violent for women as for men, there are some problems that are unique to women's prisons. Because women constitute a much smaller proportion of any state's prison population, there are usually fewer prisons for women and also fewer opportunities for education and training. Part of this is related to stereotyped conceptions of the appropriate role for women in society. Traditional notions of appropriate roles have played a part in providing programs to train women to become cosmetologists or cooks instead of auto mechanics or television repair workers. Traditional notions of appropriate female behavior have also led to prison disciplinary practices that can be more dictatorial than those found in men's prisons. Beliefs that women should be "prim and proper" have influenced many officials to enforce rules against arguing and talking back to guards more stringently in women's prisons than in men's prisons. Thus, while women's prisons may look more pleasant than men's prisons, the appearance of a softer regime may in fact belie an institution that oppresses by intruding into more dimensions of behavior than occurs in the typical male prison.

Perhaps the fundamental ethical question is that suggested by Durham (1994): Would it be right to treat women exactly like men when such a shift in orientation might very well take away some of the benefits—such as single rooms rather than cells—that have benefited many women prisoners? Equal treatment would mean some positive changes, such as increased opportunities for vocational training, but would the overall results be beneficial for women, or would equal treatment actually mean generally worse conditions for women?

PRIVATIZATION

Another ethical issue is whether states should privatize prisons or continue to keep them public. As noted in Chapter 13 on ethical issues in probation and parole, proponents of privatization argue that there are several benefits for turning over prisons to private corporations. One alleged benefit is budgetary savings. Proponents claim that private enterprise can do things more efficiently and less expensively than the government. Government operation is equated with waste and inefficiency. Some of this is attributed to the civil service system that guarantees job tenure except in extreme circumstances when jobs are abolished. Civil service workers are not under the same pressures as workers in private industry who must constantly show a profit. Competition forces private industry to be effective, efficient, and accountable (Logan, 1990).

Opponents of privatization argue that government agencies *can* be efficient and effective. Government offices can adopt strategies that enhance efficiency and effectiveness just as can privately run agencies.

A number of states have turned over some of their prisons to private corporations. Several evaluations of private prisons, jails, and juvenile facilities have been conducted. In most of these studies, a private prison and a public prison from the same state are compared in terms of costs and inmate and/or staff satisfaction. One reviewer of a number of such studies concluded that they "seem to show a somewhat lower cost and higher quality of services in private facilities" (Shichor, 1995:231). The reviewer went on to note, however, that one particular private prison has been the subject of several of the studies and that some of the researchers finding such positive results were "active supporters" of privatization rather than neutral observers (Shichor, 1995:231). Shichor thus agrees with the conclusion of the General Accounting Office study that private prisons have not yet been proven superior.

Perhaps the main argument against privatization is whether it is appropriate for the government to turn over functions as basic as correctional supervision of offenders to private businesses. Many question whether the symbolic task of punishing offenders can be handed over to workers who wear uniforms that say "Acme Corrections Company" rather than the "State Department of Corrections" (American Bar Association, 1986). The most dramatic example of this would be for "Brand X Corrections" to carry out capital punishment. Should the state surrender the symbolism of the state executing an offender? Less dramatically, is it right for the state to allow private companies to impose deprivation of liberty and serious disciplinary measures such as solitary confinement? Or does incarceration involve a basic right that ought not to be relinquished by the government? Going further, is it right to bring the profit motive into this area? One answer is that it is wrong to do so; "it can be found morally troubling that corporations will try to make a profit on the punishment of people (which is a deliberate cause of suffering by representatives of society)" (Shichor, 1995:258).

Another concern regarding privatization is whether the profit motive can debase corrections. For example, would private prisons be under pressure to keep clients incarcerated beyond an appropriate release time so as to keep prison populations and reimbursements high? Would these companies begin to lobby for lengthier sentences and fewer release opportunities? Would private prisons try to pay guards fair salaries or would profit pressures work to minimize salaries and benefits for officers? Would private agencies try to cut services for inmates (counseling, drug treatment) to a minimum?

In the nineteenth century, the profit motive did operate to cause significant problems in many state prison systems. In one juvenile system, for example, boys were leased out to private contractors for their labor. Hardworking boys would be kept under supervision longer than necessary because the contractor did not want to lose their productivity (Pisciotta, 1982).

A response to such problems is spelling out a private agency's responsibilities to offenders in a carefully devised contract and then monitoring the implementation of the contract. If state inspectors enforce the contract conditions, then problems can be prevented or quickly resolved. If a private agency does not resolve any problems, it is in violation of the contract and the agency can be dropped. Opponents of privatization contend that there is a problem with this argument. If the state wants to end a contract, there may not be another service provider willing and able to step in and take over the contracted service. At the very least, it would take some time for another company to be ready to do so.

Still another problem with privatization is that private agencies can be overly selective of the clients (offenders) they want to manage. Private agencies in corrections and in areas such as welfare have been criticized for picking the most capable clients (Rosin, 1997). The criticism is that these individuals may have been able to succeed on probation or in getting off of public assistance with little or no help. Statistics showing them to be success stories are thereby misleading. The private agency selected the individuals most likely to succeed and ignored the individuals most in need of intervention. The state is left to deal with these more difficult cases.

Proponents of privatization argue that contracting of services can make spending on correctional services more visible. When the government operates its own prisons, the prisons "have been ignored by the public and given . . . 'hands-off' treatment by the courts" (Logan, 1990:256). Because there has been some criticism of contracting, there would be a number of eyes scrutinizing the privately run prisons.

In summary, proponents of prison privatization argue that private agencies can provide needed services more effectively and more efficiently than the government has done in the past. Opponents argue that government agencies can become more effective and efficient. Opponents also contend that there can be serious problems with privatization and question whether it is right to allow the state to give away the highly symbolic function of depriving citizens of their freedom and supervising that deprivation of liberty.

SUMMARY

This chapter has examined a number of ethical issues pertaining to prisons. Probably the most basic question is Conrad's: What do the undeserving deserve? One's choice of answer to this question permeates most of the other issues raised in this chapter. At this moment in our nation's history, it appears that many answer that prisoners deserve little or nothing. Because they treated their victims with no compassion, they deserve no compassion in return.

The three theories that form the framework for this book, however, suggest that the current answer to Conrad's question may not be the ethical answer. Kant's categorical imperative urges us to treat others as subjects. Utilitarianism urges us to consider the consequences of our actions, including the consequences of treating inmates very harshly for years and then simply releasing them back onto the streets. The peacemaking perspective reminds us that we are all connected, including offender, victim, and public, and that caring is a basic ethical principle. It seems that all three ethical theories suggest that while punishment is appropriate, we cannot lose sight of the humanity of offenders even when they have appeared to lose sight of their own humanity and the humanity of others.

The challenge for the next century is to try to punish offenders in ways that are fitting and to remain mindful of the need to treat offenders with dignity. The Quakers and others tried to do this 200 years ago. It is not an easy task.

NOTES

1. For a more thorough analysis of the issue of prison composition, see Irwin & Austin (1997) and Braswell & Whitehead (1997). This section of the chapter relies heavily on the latter source.

2. Ironically, one conservative critic of soft prisons, former Governor J. Fife Symington III of Arizona, who removed many frills from his state's prisons, recently pleaded guilty to fraud. He may be forced to experience firsthand the tougher prison environment that he orchestrated.

REFERENCES

Alabama Code, 13A-3-23.

American Bar Association (1986). *Section of Criminal Justice, Report to the House of Delegates*. Chicago: American Bar Association.

Applegate, B.K., F.T. Cullen, M.G. Turner & J.L. Sundt (1996). "Assessing Public Support for Three-Strikes-and-You're Out Laws: Global versus Specific Attitudes." *Crime & Delinquency*, 42:517-534.

Beck, A.J. & D.K. Gillard (1995). *Prisoners in 1994*. Washington, DC: U.S. Department of Justice.

Beck, A.J. & P.M. Harrison (2001). *Prisoners in 2001*. Washington, DC: U.S. Department of Justice.

Bidinotto, R.J. (1997). "Prisons Should Not Coddle Inmates." In Cozic, C.P. (ed.), *America's Prisons: Opposing Viewpoints* (pp. 85-92). San Diego: Greenhaven Press.

Bonta, J. & P. Gendreau (1994). "Reexamining the Cruel and Unusual Punishment of Prison Life." In M.C. Braswell, R.H. Montgomery & L.X. Lombardo (eds.), *Prison Violence in America,* 2nd ed. (pp. 39-68). Cincinnati: Anderson.

Bowker, L.H. (1980). *Prison Victimization*. New York: Elsevier.

Braswell, M. & J. Whitehead (1997). "The Middle Way: The Debate about Prisons." Paper presented at the 1997 Annual Meeting of the Southern Criminal Justice Association, Richmond, VA.

Brownstein, H.H., B.J. Spunt, S.M. Crimmins & S.C. Langley (1995). "Women Who Kill in Drug Market Situations." *Justice Quarterly*, 12:473-498.

Cohen, R.L. (1995). *Probation and Parole Violators in State Prison, 1991*. Washington, DC: U.S. Department of Justice.

Conrad, J.P. (1982). "What Do the Undeserving Deserve?" In R. Johnson & H. Toch (eds.), *The Pains of Imprisonment* (pp. 313-330). Beverly Hills, CA: Sage.

Corsentino, M. (1997). "Inmate Chain Gangs are an Improper Form of Punishment." In Cozic, C.P. (ed.), *America's Prisons: Opposing Viewpoints* (pp. 120-127). San Diego: Greenhaven Press.

DiIulio, J.J., Jr. (1994). "The Question of Black Crime." *The Public Interest*, 117:3-32.

DiIulio, J.J., Jr. (1995). "White Lies about Black Crime." *The Public Interest,* 118:30-44.

DiMascio, W.M. (1995). *Seeking Justice: Crime and Punishment in America*. New York: Edna McConnell Clark Foundation.

Durham, A.M. (1994). *Crisis and Reform: Current Issues in American Punishment*. Boston: Little, Brown.

Gendreau, P. (1996). "The Principles of Effective Intervention with Offenders." In A.T. Harland (ed.), *Choosing Correctional Options that Work: Defining the Demand and Evaluating the Supply* (pp. 117-130). Thousand Oaks, CA: Sage.

Goffman, E. (1961). *Asylums: Essays on the Social Situation of Mental Patients and Other Inmates*. Garden City, NY: Anchor Books.

Guenther, A. (1978). "The Impact of Confinement." In N. Johnston & L.D. Savitz (eds.), *Justice and Corrections* (pp. 596-603). New York: John Wiley & Sons.

Hamm, M.S., T. Coupez, F.E. Hoze. & C. Weinstein (1994). "The Myth of Humane Imprisonment: A Critical Analysis of Severe Discipline in U.S. Maximum Security Prisons, 1945-1990." In M.C. Braswell, R.H. Montgomery & L.X. Lombardo (eds.), *Prison Violence in America,* 2nd ed. (pp. 167-200). Cincinnati: Anderson.

Harrison, P.M. & A.J. Beck (2004). *Prisoners in 2003*. Washington, DC: U.S. Department of Justice.

Inciardi, J.A., R. Horowitz & A.E. Pottieger (1993). *Street Kids, Street Drugs, Street Crime: An Examination of Drug Use and Serious Delinquency in Miami*. Belmont, CA: Wadsworth.

Irwin, J. & J. Austin (1997). *It's About Time: America's Imprisonment Binge,* 2nd ed. Belmont, CA: Wadsworth.

Lockwood, D. (1980). *Prison Sexual Violence*. New York: Elsevier.

Logan, C.H. (1990). *Private Prisons: Cons and Pros*. New York: Oxford.

Maguire, K. & A.L. Pastore (eds.) (1996). *Sourcebook of Criminal Justice Statistics 1995*. Washington, DC: U.S. Department of Justice.

Marquart, J.W. (1986). "Doing Research in Prison: The Strengths and Weaknesses of Full Participation as a Guard." *Justice Quarterly*, 3:15-32.

McKelvey, B. (1997). "American Prisons: A Study in American Social History Prior to 1915." In J.W. Marquart & J.R. Sorenson (eds.), *Correctional Contexts: Contemporary and Classical Readings* (pp. 84-94). Los Angeles: Roxbury.

Morris, R.L. (1997). "Inmate Chain Gangs are a Proper Form of Punishment." In C.P. Cozic (ed.), *America's Prisons: Opposing Viewpoints* (pp. 111-119). San Diego: Greenhaven Press.

Mumola, C.J. & A.J. Beck (1997). "Prisoners in 1996." *Bureau of Justice Statistics Bulletin*. Washington, DC: U.S. Department of Justice.

Nacci, P.L. & T.R. Kane (1983). "The Incidence of Sex and Sexual Aggression in Federal Prisons." *Federal Probation*, 7(4:)31-36.

Petersilia, J. & S. Turner (1993). "Intensive Probation and Parole." In M. Tonry (ed.), *Crime and Justice: A Review of Research* (Vol. 17). Chicago: University of Chicago Press.

Pisciotta, A.W. (1982). "Saving the Children: The Promise and Practice of *Parens Patriae,* 1838-98." *Crime & Delinquency*, 28:410-425.

Pritchard, D.A. (1979). "Stable Predictors of Recidivism: A Summary." *Criminology*, 17:15-21.

Rosin, H. (1997). "About Face: The Appearance of Welfare Success." *New Republic*, 217 (August, 4): 16-19.

Shichor, D. (1995). *Punishment for Profit: Private Prisons/Public Concerns*. Thousand Oaks, CA: Sage.

Silberman, C.E (1978). *Criminal Violence, Criminal Justice*. New York: Random House.

Spelman, W. (1994). *Criminal Incapacitation*. New York: Plenum Press.

Sykes, G.M. (1958). *The Society of Captives: A Study of a Maximum Security Prison*. Princeton, NJ: Princeton University Press.

Taylor, J.M. (1997). "Prisons Do Not Coddle Inmates." In C.P. Cozic (ed.), *America's Prisons: Opposing Viewpoints* (pp. 85-92). San Diego: Greenhaven Press.

Toch, H. & K. Adams, with J.D. Grant (1989). *Coping: Maladaptation in Prisons*. New Brunswick, NJ: Transaction.

Tonry, M. (1995). *Malign Neglect—Race, Crime, and Punishment in America*. New York: Oxford.

van den Haag, E. (1975). *Punishing Criminals: Concerning a Very Old and Painful Question*. New York: Basic Books.

von Hirsch, A. (1990). "The Ethics of Community-Based Sanctions." *Crime & Delinquency*, 36:162-173.

Wachtler, S. (1997). *After the Madness: A Judge's Own Prison Memoir*. New York: Random House.

Walker, S., C. Spohn & M. DeLone (1996). *The Color of Justice: Race, Ethnicity, and Crime in America*. Belmont, CA: Wadsworth.

Wright, R.T. & S. Decker (1994). *Burglars on the Job*. Boston: Northeastern University Press.

Zamble, E. & F.J. Porporino (1988). *Coping, Behavior, and Adaptation in Prison Inmates*. New York: Springer-Verlag.

Zimring, F.E. & G. Hawkins (1995). *Incapacitation: Penal Confinement and the Restraint of Crime*. New York: Oxford University Press.

Discussion Questions

1. What do you think the "undeserving deserve"? Describe an ethical prison. What would it look like? How would prisoners live? What would be their daily regimen? If you were a state commissioner of corrections and could design your own prison system, what would it be like? Could you sell your ideal system to the governor and to the public?

2. Is there any place for chain gangs or other harsh measures in an ethical prison? Why or why not?

3. Is there a point at which elderly offenders should be released even if they have five, 10, or more years to serve on their sentences? Discuss.

4. Should women prisoners be treated exactly like male prisoners? Would equal treatment be advantageous for female prisoners? Discuss.

5. Is it desirable for a state to contract out its prison operations to a private correctional company? What are the ethical considerations in doing so?

Section V: Ethical Issues in Crime Control Policy and Research

> Justice and power must be brought together, so that whatever is just may be powerful, and whatever is powerful may be just.
>
> —Blaise Pascal

How should we approach problems related to crime control? We are spending increasing sums of money in areas of law enforcement and corrections, and we have continued to pass new legislation with an eye toward developing more effective crime control policies. Still, crime continues to increase. In addition, we have to contend with public perceptions regarding crime and the justice system's response that are largely shaped by the media. Newspaper headlines, television programs, and films each try to attract readers or viewers. How much is fact and how much is fiction? Whether founded entirely on fact or not, our citizens' fear of crime is certainly real to them.

An increasing awareness of the scope and nature of corporate crime challenges the abilities and resources of our justice system on additional fronts. Our traditional approach to controlling crime seems more comfortable when addressing familiar criminal behavior in such areas as burglary, robbery, and assault. The "bad guys" are typically more clearly defined. This is not always the case with much of corporate crime. Problems involving consumer safety, pollution, and other related issues often involve business executives who are considered upstanding members of their communities, and with the rapid development of the computer, such crimes are increasingly difficult to track down. In some ways it seems that our traditional approach to administering justice is simply not adequate to resolve the more sophisticated problems of much of the corporate world. Still, the demands of culture can encourage and stimulate us to develop new ways of thinking about crime and, as a result, more innovative responses to crime-related problems.

There are also a variety of ethical concerns surrounding criminal justice research. The scientific life provides no barrier to unethical conduct. The problem of employing unethical means to an otherwise desirable end is ever present in the research setting, where scientists are sometimes tempted to sacrifice the well-being of their subjects for the sake of scientific knowledge. Subjects can easily come to be viewed as the means to an end when the products of scientific research are equated with the utilitarian's "greater good."

In the name of scientific research, subjects may experience invasions of privacy, unknowing participation in simulated research experiments, and physical and emotional stress. In experimental research designs, which systematically withhold an intervention from one group while exposing another, research subjects may be denied participation in programs offering medical, educational, or psychological treatment.

Although the nature of the research task poses many ethical dilemmas, additional problems involve the political context of the research. No one wants to hear bad news about a popular new law enforcement or correctional program, least of all the people who administer the program. Researchers can find themselves in very difficult circumstances when results indicate that the program is not achieving its goals. Is the correct response to redo the results until a more palatable outcome is achieved, or to report findings honestly? How is this decision affected when the people administering the program are the same ones paying the researcher's salary?

Researchers should police themselves, using standards of professional ethics and censure to provide appropriate guidance. It must be recognized, however, that there are significant pressures against the objective exercise of such standards. Competition for research funds is considerable—few universities or research centers are interested in forfeiting research funds on ethical grounds, and few scholars are interested in creating any more obstacles for their research efforts than necessary. It is therefore very important to establish a climate of high ethical standards in the graduate schools that produce researchers and in the organizations ultimately responsible for conducting research.

CHAPTER 17

Crime, Criminals, and Crime Control Policy Myths

Robert M. Bohm

INTRODUCTION

Despite recognition that the reality of crime is socially constructed, the task of debunking myths about crime, criminals and crime control policy has received only limited attention (Quinney, 1970; 1979; 1979b; Pearce, 1976; Milakovich & Weis, 1977; Reiman, 1979; Simon, 1981; Pepinsky & Jesilow, 1984; Walker, 1985). Myths continue to be perpetuated.[1] Moreover, some of them have become part of an ideology that informs, and is informed by, public interests in the area of social control in general and of crime and crime control in particular.[2] This has resulted in at least two undesirable consequences for the vast majority of Americans. First is a myopic focus on short-term interests of dubious value and a near total obliviousness to long-range interests which promise greater

> **KEY CONCEPTS:**
>
> **crime control myths**
>
> **crime myths**
>
> **criminal myths**
>
> **undesirable consequences**

relief from criminal victimization. Obliviousness to future interests makes exploitation easier.[3] A second undesirable consequence for most Americans is the contradictions that occur when actions are based on myth-laden ideology. Though not inevitable, contradictions, when they arise, sometimes adversely affect both short- and long-term interests. For many people, control policies based on myth-laden ideology result in an exacerbation of harm and suffering.

The focus of this essay, however, is not crime control ideology per se, but rather the myths that inform that ideology. Specifically, the purpose is threefold: first, to identify some of the myths that inform the currently dominant crime control ideology in the United States; second, to examine

Reprinted with permission of the Academy of Criminal Justice Sciences. Robert M. Bohm, "Crime, Criminals and Crime Control Policy Myths" (1986). *Justice Quarterly*, (3)2:193-214.

some of the sources of and reasons for the perpetuation of the myths; and third, to consider some of the contradictions and consequences of beliefs and policies based on myths.

CRIME, CRIMINALS, AND CRIME CONTROL POLICY MYTHS

Due to space limitations, the following discussion considers only some of the myths that inform the prevailing "politically conservative," "law and order" ideology in the United States. Most of the myths examined are not new—testimony to both their enduring quality and their ability to be adapted to different, often opposing purposes.

Crime Myths

The foundation of the entire crime mythology edifice is the definition of crime. The problem is a lack of clarity as to what the concept of crime refers. Historically, crime has been used to label an extraordinarily large and a seemingly unrelated number of actions and inactions. A legal definition of crime, moreover, does not solve the problem. The law is rather arbitrary about what kinds of phenomena are regarded as crime and has generally expanded and contracted depending on the interests of the dominant groups in the social struggle. All definitions of crime, legal or otherwise, include actions or inactions that arguably should be excluded and exclude actions or inactions that arguably should be included. This is inevitable, given the political nature of crime. Consequently, a critical issue is whether there is a socially unacceptable and generally unknown bias in including or excluding certain actions or inactions as crime. Considerable evidence indicates that there is (Pepinsky & Jesilow, 1984; Simon & Eitzen, 1982; Reiman & Headlee, 1981:43; Reiman, 1979; Quinney, 1979:62; Lieberman, 1973; Mintz & Cohen, 1971:25-26; American Friends Service Committee, 1971). For example, consider the crime of murder. According to the 1982 *Crime in the United States,* there were 21,012 murders and nonnegligent manslaughters. These murders represent only a fraction of those killed intentionally or negligently. Conservative estimates indicate that each year at least 10,000 lives are lost to unnecessary surgeries, 20,000 to errors in prescribing drugs, 20,000 to doctors spreading diseases in hospitals, 100,000 to industrial disease, 14,000 to industrial accidents, 200,000 to environmentally caused cancer, and an unknown number from lethal industrial products (Reiman, 1979; Simon & Eitzen, 1982; Pepinsky & Jesilow, 1984). Yet, few of the latter actions or inactions are defined legally as murder or manslaughter. One reason is the myth that "white-collar crime" is nonviolent.

Another problem with criminal definitions that contributes to myths is the presumption that all laws are enforced and/or enforced fairly. Just as there is a socially unacceptable and generally unknown bias in the definition of crime, there is a similar bias in the enforcement of law. One reason so few white-collar crimes are brought to light, for example, is the inadequate enforcement mechanism. A myth that effectively obscures this inadequacy is that regulatory agencies can prevent white-collar crime. While there is little doubt that there would be more white-collar crime if regulatory agencies did not exist, it is not at all clear how much white-collar crime is prevented by their existence. In any event, the myth can be sustained only by ignoring the history of efforts at federal regulation of corporate crime. Humphries and Greenberg (1981:236) argue that "regulatory agencies were the Progressive Era's solution to the problem of controlling business in a manner that did not delegitimize capitalism by tarnishing capitalists with the stigma of criminality." Similarly, Pearce (1976:88) maintains that the state intentionally created agencies responsive to the interests of big business (also see Pepinsky & Jesilow, 1984:66-79). Furthermore, while the prosecution of corporate crime has increased dramatically in recent years, it may well be, as Pearce (1976:90) suggests, merely a symbolic effort to vindicate the myth that the state is neutral and to reinforce the myth that the law is applied uniformly to all persons. In the wake of lost legitimacy following Watergate and other scandals of the 1970s, an increase in the prosecution of elite criminality is not surprising. In any event, two problems lie at the heart of the myth of crime: the definitional problem and the enforcement problem.

Another myth is that crime in the United States is primarily violent. This myth is derived partly from the Uniform Crime Reports. These reports give the impression that the crime problem in the United States consists primarily of the eight "index offenses": murder and nonnegligent manslaughter, forcible rape, robbery, aggravated assault, burglary, larceny-theft, motor vehicle theft, and, beginning in 1979, arson. Three or possibly four of the eight "index crimes" are clearly "violent" (murder and nonnegligent manslaughter, forcible rape, aggravated assault and, possibly, robbery). Yet, according to recent Uniform Crime Reports, only about 10 percent of all the crime known to the police is violent. In addition, if the new arson category is excluded, no more than ten percent of all persons arrested are charged with *any* of the index crimes (Milakovich & Weis, 1977:339). It is hard to justify the crime problem, as conceptualized in the Uniform Crime Reports, as a problem of violence.

Another common myth is that crime is increasing. This myth is also sustained primarily by the data reported in the Uniform Crime Reports. However, if data in the Uniform Crime Reports are compared with the findings of the Census Bureau's National Crime Surveys from 1973 to 1980, one finds a major discrepancy. The Uniform Crime Reports show a substantial increase in the crime rate during the period, while the Census Bureau statistics indicate no increase in the proportion of victims reporting the same crimes. In some cases, the Census Bureau reports slight decreases (Paez & Dodge, 1982). Indeed, a careful examination of the historical record provides no basis for the belief that street crime, the type of crime most people fear, is rising: "People today are in no greater danger of being robbed or physically hurt than 150 years ago" (Pepinsky & Jesilow, 1984:22; also Ferdinand, 1977:353).

A final myth is that crime is an inevitable concomitant of complex, populous and industrialized societies. This myth has been advanced by Shelley in *Crime and Modernization: The Impact of Industrialization and Urbanization* (1981). Besides the serious problems with comparing crime statistics cross-culturally (cf. Sutherland & Cressey, 1974:25), there are at least four other problems with Shelley's proposition. First, it fails to account for the great variation in crime rates of different complex, populous and industrialized societies. For example, the crime rates of Japan and West Germany are much lower than those of the United States (Reiman, 1979:20; Martin & Conger, 1980; also see Clinard, 1978; Stack, 1984, especially Appendix 1). Second, the proposition fails to account for the great variation in crime rates within modern, complex, populous, and urbanized nations. For example, according to the 1984 Uniform Crime Report, the homicide rate in the United States varied from a low of one in New Hampshire to a high of 13.1 in Texas (per 100,000 persons). Similar variation is found for other crimes (cf. Lyerly & Skipper, 1981). Third, the proposition fails to account for the lack of correlation between a city's crime rate and its population and population density. According to the 1984 Uniform Crime Report, for example, the city with the highest homicide rate was Gary, Indiana. The three most populated cities in the United States—New York, Los Angeles, and Chicago—are not found among the top ten cities with the highest homicide rate (also see Reiman, 1979:21-23, especially Table 1). A fourth problem with the proposition is that the claim of inevitability in the social sciences is always tenuous and suspect.

Criminal Myths

Several myths inform popular conceptions of criminals. For example, one myth holds that some groups are more law abiding than others (Pepinsky & Jesilow, 1984:47). Evidence indicates however, that over 90 percent of all Americans have committed some crime for which they could be incarcerated (Silver, 1968; Wallerstein & Wyle, 1947). The observation does not deny that crime may be more concentrated in some groups, but only that it is unlikely to be absent in others. The myth seems credible because the crimes of some (e.g., physicians or corporate executives) are not easily detected, or there is not as much effort exerted detecting them. These two problems sustain another myth: that most crime is committed by poor, young males between the ages of 15 and 24 (Pepinsky & Jesilow, 1984; Reiman, 1979). As noted, if law enforcement were able or willing to detect all crimes, it would be more evenly distributed among rich and poor and all age groups, though it may remain more highly concentrated in some groups. With regard to age discrimination, an additional problem with the myth is that "the crime rate is growing much faster than either the absolute number of young people or their percentage of the population" (Reiman, 1979:24).

Crime Control Policy Myths

Myths about crime and criminals often form the basis of crime control policy. Historically, the use of myth in effecting crime legislation is perhaps the most transparent in the "educational campaign" mounted by the Federal Bureau of Narcotics to outlaw the consumption of marijuana (Grinspoon, 1977; Becker, 1973; Smith, 1970). Under the leadership of Commissioner H.J. Anslinger, the myth of the eleventh-century Persian Assassins was employed in the 1930s to substantiate a link between marijuana, violence, and crime. To obtain stiffer penalties in the 1950s, the attack on marijuana by Anslinger and the Federal Bureau of Narcotics shifted to the myth that marijuana use led to heroin use. Although there is speculation on the motives behind the campaign (cf. Helmer, 1975; Becker, 1973; Musto, 1973), suffice it to say that it was successful in achieving its ends. A result has been that somewhere between twelve and thirty-four million otherwise generally law-abiding citizens have been made criminals.

A number of myths inform public conceptions of law enforcement and law enforcement policy. One of the more pervasive myths is that the police are primarily crime-fighters. Nothing could be further from the truth. Only a small fraction of police time (perhaps less than 10%) is devoted to crime fighting. The vast majority of police time entails public service and traffic activities (Pepinsky, 1980:107; Manning, 1978; 1977:16; Bittner, 1975:42; 1967:700; Wilson, 1975:81; 1968:6; Garmire et al., 1972:25; Reiss, 1971:100).

Related to the myth of police as crime-fighters is one that holds that the police solve crimes. Evidence suggests otherwise (see sources cited in the paragraph above). According to recent editions of the Uniform Crime Report, the official overall clearance rate of the police in the United States is around 25 percent. The true rate, however, is probably closer to 13 percent (Walker, 1985:26).

A final myth of crime control policy to be considered is that eliminating injustices from the criminal justice system will reduce the level of serious crime. Eliminating injustices from the criminal justice system is certainly a worthwhile pursuit. However, it is unlikely to have an appreciable effect on serious crime. The causes of most crime are to be found in general social arrangements and not in the operation of the criminal justice system (Walker, 1985:206; Bohm, 1982).

The preceding list of myths is by no means exhaustive and is only intended as an indication of some of the myths that inform the now dominant "politically conservative," "law and order" ideology in the United States. Based largely on this ideology, crime prevention and enforcement resources have been expended recently on some of the following priorities: mandatory sentencing, habitual-criminal statutes, increased numbers of police officers, more effective police officers, changes in Miranda warnings, preventive detention, changes in plea bargaining, changes in the exclusionary rule, changes in the insanity defense, career criminal programs, prison industries and capital punishment. While each of these policies is intended to accomplish one or more bureaucratic goals (e.g., crime reduction, cost-effectiveness, or greater efficiency), none is likely to have a significant effect on the harm and suffering experienced by the vast majority of the American public. They do not adequately address the fundamental social structural elements of the crime problem (cf. Pepinsky & Jesilow, 1984; Walker, 1985; Bohm, 1982). The task now is to examine some of the sources of and reasons for the perpetuation of myths that do not contribute to pervasive harm and suffering.

SOURCES OF AND REASONS FOR THE MYTHS: CONTRADICTIONS AND CONSEQUENCES

Myths about crime, criminals and crime control policy are perpetuated because they serve a variety of interests. Among the interests served are those of the general public, the media, politicians, academic criminologists, criminal justice officials and social elites. One of the problems with previous discussions of crime-related mythology is the emphasis on the way elite interests are served (cf. Reiman, 1979; Quinney, 1979; 1979b). This emphasis is probably derived from the seminal observations of Marx and Engels, who wrote that "the ideas of the ruling class are in every epoch the ruling ideas . . ." (1970:64). They noted that in order for the ruling class to carry out its ideas, it is necessary for the ruling class "to represent its interest as the common interest of all the members of society, that is, expressed in ideal form: it has to give its ideas the form of universatility and represent them as the only rational, universally valid ones" (Marx & Engels, 1970:65-6). This, of course, includes ideas about crime.

A problem with Marx's and Engels' observations is that they failed to distinguish between short- and long-term interests. While in the long-run elite interests are served by myths about crime, criminals and crime control policy, and the general public is duped into believing that their long-run interests are also served, it is unlikely that the myths could find such universal appeal if they did not also serve real short-term interests of the general public. It is maintained here that myths about crime, criminals and crime control policy are perpetuated because they actually do serve the general short-term interest, as well as long-term elite interests.

This section examines some of the ways that myths serve both general and elite interests. It also considers some of the contradictions and consequences of beliefs and policies based on myths. While there is obvious overlap in groups served by myths (e.g., members of the media, politicians, academic criminologists, criminal justice officials and elites are also part of the general public), the ways that each group contributes to and is served by myths are a little different. For this reason, each group is considered separately.

The General Public

The general public contributes to their own myth-laden conception of crime in at least four ways. The first is by overgeneralizing from personal experience. If people have been crime victims, they may consider their own experience typical or representative of crime in general. A problem is that it is unlikely that there is such a thing as "typical" crime, and the crime most people know and experience is not representative of crime in general. A second way the public contributes to myths is by relying on inaccurate communication. Some people embellish crime experiences and thus distort their own conceptions or the conception of those to whom they communicate. A third way the public contributes to myths is by relying on atypical information. For those who are not aware that they have experienced crime, part of their conceptions of crime may come from atypical and unrepresentative experiences, embellished or otherwise, of family or friends, who may or may not have been victims themselves. Finally, the public contributes to myths through a lack of consciousness. There are many cases where the general public has no knowledge of victimization. For example, in cases of consumer fraud or medical negligence, people may never know that a crime has been perpetrated against them. In such cases, it would be difficult to conceptualize such actions as criminal.

The public perpetuates myths about crime, criminals and crime control policy because they serve at least three short-term interests: (1) they offer identities, (2) they aid comprehension by creating order, and (3) they help forge common bonds and create and reinforce a sense of community. Implicit in each of these interests, however, are important contradictions. Myths about "criminals" and "law-abiding citizens" offer identities. For many people, it is comforting to conceive of themselves as law-abiding citizens. Given the daily temptations to violate the law, those who do not, even in the face of great material deprivation, demonstrate a moral courage and a self-control that often forms the basis of their self-identities. Additionally, abiding by the law is considered by many an aspect of patriotism. This does not mean that law-violators necessarily consider themselves unpatriotic, but only that to be law-abiding and patriotic is an important part of many people's identities. This facet of patriotism is an emotion that politicians find it advantageous to exploit. For these reasons, many people find it in their interests to believe in and perpetuate the myth of the criminal and law-abiding citizen.

In reality, however, many self-conceived law-abiding citizens are engaging in self-delusion. No doubt there are a few paragons of virtue, but not many. Most people manifest common human frailties. For example, evidence suggests that over 90 percent of all Americans have committed some crime for which they could be incarcerated (Silver, 1968; Wallerstein & Wyle, 1947). This is not to imply that most Americans are murderers or robbers, for they are not. Criminality is a relative (and political) phenomenon. In his discussion of delinquency, Matza (1964) captures this relativity when he writes that juveniles drift between law-abiding and law-violating behavior. Whether a juvenile actually engages in a delinquent act depends on a host of factors, not the least of which is available opportunity. There are few delinquents or criminals whose entire life orientation is centered around delinquent or criminal activities. Consequently, it makes little sense to label an individual a "delinquent" or a "criminal" who occasionally gets into a fight, steals from a store, exceeds the speed limit, or cheats on income taxes. While these are "criminal" acts, the people who perpetrate them are not "criminals."

A contradiction is that the criminal role offers a different kind of identity to another segment of the population. For some, the criminal label is actively sought. The literature on juvenile delinquency is replete with examples of juveniles whose identity is based on their "rep" (reputation) for toughness, sexual prowess, institutional experience, etc. Many of those who assassinate or attempt to assassinate famous people are likely seeking a public identity that could not be achieved legitimately. This applies as well to many "notorious" criminals. A problem with labeling theory, in this regard, is an overemphasis on the negative consequences of the label or stigma— that individuals actively seek to avoid it. In many cases, as noted above, individuals actively seek the label as a goal. Myths do offer identities, criminal or otherwise, real or imagined; and people find it in their interest to believe in and perpetuate the myth of the criminal and law-abiding citizen.

Another way in which myths about crime and criminals contribute to identity is through the reinforcement and perpetuation of the myth of the individual. The concept of "individual," as used here, does not deny "individualism" but only refers in a limited sense to the idea of the "free-willed" being who acts on society without being acted on by society. Although the myth of the individual has informed philosophical and criminological thought at least since the Enlightenment, it became a part of popular consciousness and identity through existentialism and the human potential and other movements of the 1960s. It began influencing crime control policy again significantly by the mid-1970s.

However, as Foucault (1977:194) explains, "The individual is no doubt the fictitious atom of the 'ideological' representation of society. . . ." The idea of the individual, as used here and portrayed in existentialism, for example, is an illusion precisely because human beings are necessarily social. Not only are human beings social by virtue of the social nature of self-identity and of relations with others, but also because of the social component (e.g., language) in the ability of human beings to conceive of anything at all (Ollman, 1976; Mead, 1972).

The idea of the "free-willed individual" finds characteristic expression in the current politically conservative interpretation of the "criminal" and his or her behavior. In this view, the criminal is considered an isolated being whose social environment is generally inconsequential or, at least, legally irrelevant to his or her criminal actions. Kennedy (1976:39) maintains that the notion of the criminal as individual was the product of an historical transformation from "the ethic of shared responsibility for individual conduct (the cooperative ethic) to the ethic of individual responsibility." He adds that this transformation "was fundamental to the birth of crime and penal sanction" and "to political, economic, religious, and familistic transformation generally. . . ." Thus, states Kennedy (1976:38), "individualism as an attitude of self is basic to guilt, and as a premise of both civil and criminal law it is elemental to the whole legal practice of incrimination." A consequence is that the belief that the individual alone is responsible for his or her conduct diverts attention away from the structural elements in society that inevitably contribute to criminal behavior. (This last point will be discussed further in another context later.)

Another reason that myths find popular support is that they aid comprehension by creating order. Myths aid comprehension in two ways. They reduce contradictions and simplify complex phenomena.

As previously noted, myths about crime and criminals create a simple dichotomy that separates the "good guys" from the "bad guys." Quinney (1977:14) maintains that the myth of crime "provides the metaphor for our human nature; crime represents human nature in its 'less attractive form.'" Consequently, for many people, the "criminal" is conceived as abnormal, irrational, evil or untrustworthy, while the "law-abiding citizen" is normal, rational, good and trustworthy. While dichotomies such as these can be useful heuristic devices, they necessarily abstract and distort reality.

Myths also aid comprehension by reducing contradictions, which is especially important when it comes to public conceptions about crime and crime control. One of the major contradictions that confronts American society is that one of the wealthiest and technologically advanced countries in the world contains widespread poverty, unemployment and crime. Historically, a myth that has been perpetrated to resolve this contradiction is that crime is an individual problem, the result of personal defect—especially of poor, young males between the ages of 15 and 24. Conceived of in this way, it follows that there is no social or structural solution to the problem of crime.

Another contradiction that perplexes many Americans is that at a time when more effort was expended and more money spent on crime control, the worse the problem got. Myths help people cope with the knowledge that crime control efforts have not lived up to expectations. For example, during the heyday of LEAA, when billions of dollars were presumably spent on crime control, crime became, in the minds of many, epidemic. However, when

LEAA was disbanded and the monies expended on crime control were greatly reduced, the crime problem, according to official statistics, decreased. No doubt other factors were operating, but the impression given to many people must have been that the more we do, the worse we fail, which for many is a very disconcerting observation. It is likely that the current punitive attitude of a large segment of the public and the call for a result to the punishment model in crime control can be attributed at least in part to the simple solution that the punishment model offers to a seemingly intractable problem. A result is that the United States currently holds the distinction of incarcerating more of its citizens than any other country in the world with the exception of the Soviet Union and South Africa, and it is among one of the last countries outside of Africa and Asia to impose the death penalty.

Finally, crime myths contribute to public fear which helps forge common bonds and creates and reinforces a sense of community. Fear of crime makes people feel that they share the same boat. Crime crosses social barriers. In reality, however, the chance of actual victimization from the crimes most people fear is very unevenly divided among social groupings. Nevertheless, that matters little, since it is the abstract fear that helps unite people. Fear of crime also creates and reinforces a sense of community. Recent enthusiasm over neighborhood watch programs and the recent increase in vigilantism are two examples of the way that fear of crime brings people together.

A contradiction is that fear of crime also inhibits community. Because of fear, people are afraid to leave their homes and are suspicious of strangers. It is fear of crime, moreover, that politicians play upon in their "law and order" campaigns. Weighted together, it is likely that factors that inhibit community are more influential than those that create community.

In sum, the public perpetuates myths about crime, criminals or crime control policy because they serve at least three short-term interests:

1) they offer identities;

2) they aid comprehension by creating order; and

3) they help forge common bonds and create and reinforce a sense of community.

THE MEDIA

Perhaps the most important source of common conceptions and myths of crime, criminals and crime control policy is the media. As Vold observed, "crime waves are now and probably always have been products of newspaper headlines" (1935:803; also see Fishman, 1978). One thing is certain: the media presents a distorted crime picture to the public. According to one study, the factors that influence crime news selection are the seriousness of the offense, whimsical or unusual elements, sentimental or dramatic aspects and the involvement of famous or high-status persons (Roshier, 1973:34-35; also see Graber, 1980; Sheley & Ashkins, 1981).

The entertainment media has a particularly distorting effect on public conceptions of crime, criminals and crime control policies. Crime-related television programs have been estimated to account for about one-third of all television entertainment shows (Dominick, 1978). Information that the public receives from these shows is anything but accurate. Studies have indicated that

1) the least committed crimes, such as murder and assault, appear more frequently than those crimes committed more often, such as burglary and larceny;

2) violent crimes are portrayed as caused by greed or attempts to avoid detection rather than by passion accompanying arguments as is more typical;

3) the necessary use of violence in police work is exaggerated;

4) the use of illegal police tactics is seemingly sanctioned;

5) police officers are unfettered by procedural law; and

6) the police nearly always capture the "bad guys," usually in violent confrontations (Dominick, 1973; Pandiani, 1978; Gitlin, 1979).

Perhaps the principal reason why the entertainment media perpetuates such myths is that they attract a large viewing audience which, in turn, sells advertising. Whether more accurate presentations would be less appealing, however, is an empirical question yet to be answered. In any event, whether intentional or not, crime myths perpetuated by the media often do serve elite interests by, among other things, portraying crime in a particular manner. (Other ways in which crime myths serve elite interests are examined in a later section.) The fact that most of the mass media in the United States are either owned by large corporations or are dependent on corporate advertising has been taken as evidence of a conspiracy among the elite to control public consciousness (Miliband, 1969; Halberstam, 1979; Dreier, 1982; Evans and Lundman, 1983). While such a view has a certain intuitive appeal and some empirical evidence to support it, the fact remains that the mass media, particularly of late, has been at the vanguard at exposing elite malfeasance. Whether the effort is sincere or merely an attempt to legitimate the media as an institution that serves the interests of the general public, as was the case with the federal regulation of corporate crime, is not clear. Intentions aside, there is no question that the mass media perpetuates a false conception of crime to the general public.

Another, though subtle, way the media affects common conceptions about crime, criminals and crime control policy is through public opinion polls. Erskine (1974) argues that the public's conception of crime may be the result of categories selected by pollsters. Erskine reports that 1965 was the first year (since 1935 when Gallup polled his first respondent) that crime appeared as a response to the question: "What do you think is the most important problem facing this country today?" The crime response, however, did not appear alone as a single category but was grouped in a category that included "immorality, crime and juvenile delinquency." Crime did not appear again as a response when the same question was asked until 1968 when it was grouped in a category of "crime and lawlessness, including riots, looting, and juvenile delinquency." The importance of the category in which crime is grouped in generating a response is underscored by Erskine who notes, "When categories such as unrest, polarization, student protest, moral decay, drugs, and youth problems began to be itemized separately, crime 'per se' began to rank relatively lower than it had previously" (1974:131). Furthermore, in response to the Harris Survey question—"In the past year, do you feel the crime rate in your neighborhood has been increasing, decreasing, or has it remained about the same as it was before?"—the conception of crime appears to be tied to a variety of events such as racial violence, assassination, war protest and campus unrest, as well as criminal activity (Erskine, 1974:131-2). In short, it is conceivable that people who were polled in both Gallup and Harris Surveys were responding either to non-criminal problems (e.g., unrest, polarization, student protest, moral decay, etc.) arbitrarily grouped together in a category that also included crime or to dramatic social events that artificially raised people's conceptions of the crime rate.

POLITICIANS

A third source of crime-related myths is politicians. As members of the public, politicians derive much of their knowledge in the same way as does the rest of the public. However, unlike much of the public, politicians also get knowledge about crime, criminals and crime control policy from academic criminologists and especially criminal justice officials. Since "law and order" rhetoric is often politically advantageous (for reasons already discussed), many politicians find it difficult not to disseminate popular myths.

ACADEMIC CRIMINOLOGISTS AND CRIMINAL JUSTICE OFFICIALS

A fourth source of crime-related myths is academic criminologists and criminal justice officials. Like politicians, they are members of the public and thus derive part of their conception of these subjects from their own experiences. However, if blame is to be leveled at any one group for perpetuating myths, then it should fall here, because academic criminologists and criminal justice officials should and often do know better. They are in the best position to dispel the myths. There are several reasons why they do not.

Many academic criminologists find it in both their short- and long-term interests to perpetuate myths. These interests, moreover, may be either cognitive or structural. Regarding the former, many academic criminologists, like other members of the general public, have internalized the myths as part of their social "reality." To challenge the myths would be, for many, to undermine long-established and fundamental conceptions of society. For many academic criminologists, what has been considered here as myth simply makes sense or attunes with preconceived ideas. To question the myths might create cognitive dissonance.

Other academic criminologists perpetuate myths because it is in their structural interests to do so. Platt (1975:106-7) suggests that this is because of academic repression and cooptation. My impression is that prestigious university appointments and promotions in general typically go to those academics whose work does not fundamentally challenge myths supportive of the status quo. It appears that prestigious journals rarely publish articles that radically deviate from an accepted, often myth-laden perspective (though this may reflect considerations other than ideology). Similarly, major research grants generally seem to be awarded to academics whose proposals do not fundamentally undermine privileged positions or deviate from preconceived, often myth-laden wisdom. Whether or not myths are perpetuated because of academic repression and cooptation, academic life is generally more pleasant for those who do not make waves.

Criminal justice officials perpetuate myths for at least four reasons. First, employment and advancement often depend on a responsiveness to the interests of political and economic elites. Administrators, in particular, are generally either elected to their positions or appointed to them by political electees. Since political election or appointment often depends on the support of political and economic elites, those who would dispel myths that serve interests of political and economic elites are not likely to find support forthcoming.

Second, in case of the police, the myth of increasing crime is used to justify larger budgets for more police officers and higher pay (Pepinsky & Jesilow, 1984:16-17 and 30). Third, as was the case with the general public, myths also provide order to the potentially chaotic role of the police officer. They allow police officers to believe that they can do the job (i.e., prevent or control crime). Finally, as was also the case with the general public, myths provide police officers with a basis of solidarity, common purpose and collective unity in the face of a hostile and potentially threatening environment.

SOCIAL ELITES

As part of the general public, social elites contribute to the perpetuation of myths in much the same way as do other members of the general public. It is doubtful, moreover, that political and economic elites conspire to perpetuate myths primarily because it is unnecessary for them to do so. Because myths serve at least the short-term interests of virtually all members of society, myths of crime, criminals and crime control policy probably would be perpetuated whether they served the interests of social elites or not. Nevertheless, social elites receive more significant and long-lasting advantages from the myths than any other social grouping. Social elites are also affected by the adverse consequences of the myths.

The principal way that myths about crime, criminals and crime control policy serve elite interests is by helping to secure and legitimate the social status quo with its gross disparities of wealth, privilege and opportunity. Two interrelated means by which myths help to accomplish this are by providing a scapegoat and by redirecting the defusing dissent.

In the first place, the "crime problem" in general has been used as a scapegoat for increasing political and economic distress (Quinney, 1977:6). Secondly, by focusing public attention on particular forms of crime (e.g., crimes of the poor), the belief that such crime is the basic cause of social problems obscures "the conditions of inequality, powerlessness, institutional violence, and so on, which lie at the bases of our tortured society" (Liazos, 1977:155).

In effect, almost every type of "reported crime" has served as a "scapegoat" for political and economic contradictions. Examples include: organized crime (Galliher & McCartney, 1977:376; Pearce, 1976; Simon, 1981), street crime (Center for Research on Criminal Justice, 1977:14), rape (Griffin, 1976:237), and juvenile delinquency (Platt, 1977:192; Foucault, 1977). Even the occasional prosecution of corporate crime has its advantages for social elites. It serves as a symbolic gesture that reinforces the belief that the law is applied uniformly to all persons (Pearce, 1976:90).

A major result of scapegoating is the polarization of the population into a "confident and supportive majority" and an "alienated and repressible minority" (Clements, 1974). By creating a readily identifiable criminal group through scapegoating, willing obedience and popular support of the "noncriminal" majority are made less problematic, thus reducing the need for compulsion. If polarization were not accomplished, or if people (e.g., the poor) were not divided through a fear of being criminally victimized, for example, then they might unite to the detriment of social elites to press for the realization of their common interests (Wright, 1973:21; Chambliss, 1976:7; Pearce, 1976:90; Quinney, 1979).

Another result of scapegoating and another way that myths serve the interest of social elites is by redirecting or defusing dissent. One means by which dissent is redirected is the perpetuation of the myth that crime is primarily the work of the poor. Belief in this myth diverts the attention to the poor from the social and economic exploitation they experience to the criminality of their own class (Chambliss, 1976:8). Furthermore, the myth "deflects the discontent and potential hostility of middle America away from the classes above them and toward the classes below them" (Reiman, 1979:5; also see Pepinsky and Jesilow, 1984:42). In both cases, myth has the effect of directing attention away from the sources of crime that have the most detrimental consequences for society.

A primary way that dissent is defused is by supervising or institution-alizing potential dissidents. As Gordon (1976:208) relates, "If the system did not effect this neutralization, if so many of the poor were not trapped in the debilitating system of crime and punishment, then they might otherwise gather the strength to oppose the system which reinforces their misery." Thus, the criminalization of the poor negates their potential "for developing an ide-ologically sophisticated understanding of their situation . . . and by incar-cerating them it is made difficult for them to organize and realize their ideas" (Pearce, 1976:81).

Ultimately, the success or failure of redirecting or defusing dissent depends on the degree to which the public accepts myths of crime, criminals and crime control policy as accurate descriptions of reality. Fortunately for social elites, myths are likely to be critically accepted by the public for the following reasons (besides those already noted): First, the ethic of indi-vidual responsibility, a "legal fiction" which is both socially and psycho-logically insupportable, obscures the state's causal role in crime (Kennedy, 1976:48). Second, most individuals have been socialized, to varying extents, to behave in conformity with the law (Schumann, 1976:292). Third, most criminal behavior represents impulsive reactions to unspecific social con-flicts which rarely victimize the opponent in the underlying conflict, thus obscuring the "real" sources of social conflict (Schumann, 1976:292). Iron-ically, for the exploited, "much, if not most, crime continues to victimize those who are already oppressed . . . and does little more than reproduce the existing order" (Quinney, 1977:103). Fourth, most individuals who commit crimes attempt to conceal their illegal behavior from others, and, thus, remain isolated instead of attempting to develop solidarity with others (Schumann, 1976:292). Finally, most individuals are insulated from any abridgment of justice so that interpretations of justice made by the state are credible. For example, "systematic elimination or incarceration of a certain 'criminal element' must always be the objective and professional pursuit of the role of law. . . ." (Clements, 1974:176).

CONCLUSION

As the preceding discussion shows, common conceptions of crime, crim-inals and crime control policy are to a rather large degree informed by myths. The myths are perpetuated not only because they serve elite interests, but also because they serve short-term interests of much of the general public.

Because myths serve elite interests by helping to secure and to legitimate the social status quo, and because social elites are less affected by the crimes most people fear, social elites have little incentive to dispel myths or to reduce crime. Ironically, social elites are the one group that could have a profound effect on changing the system that creates these problems (cf. Reiman, 1979).

The real irony is that the rest of the public helps perpetuate myths that inhibit the reduction of those actions or inactions that cause them harm and suffering. While myths do serve, in a perverted way, short-term interests of the general public, in the long-run, they inhibit comprehension of the fundamental changes necessary to bring about a reduction in harm and suffering. The poor, as a result, bear the bulk of the blame while continuing to be the most victimized; and the middle class, also victimized, must bear the bulk of the costs of policies that would not provide them the protection and the security they are seeking.

There are people who would like to perpetuate the myth that nothing can be done to significantly reduce crime in the United States. If the ameliorative reforms of the past are the sole indication, they may be right. However, there remains the possibility that a significant reduction can be achieved through, as yet tried, fundamental social change. Although the details of such a program are beyond the scope of this essay,[4] a first step is demystifying the myths that inform the ideology that inhibits fundamental social change. A promising means by which to achieve this goal is the development and the employment of a self-reflexive critical theory grounded in justifiable human interests (cf. Gouldner, 1976:292).

According to Ollman (1976), "reflexivity" may be distinguished by three characteristics. First is an awareness of oneself as an individual active in pursuing his own ends (Ollman, 1976:82). Evidence of this endowment includes: (1) the ability to choose whether or not to act in any given situation (this includes the ability to forego gratification of short-term interests for achievement of long-term interests); (2) a purposefulness or an ability to plan actions before engaging in them; and (3) a mental and physical flexibility in regard to one's tasks (Ollman, 1976:110-112). Second is an awareness that actions of others have aims similar to, and even connected to, one's own (Ollman, 1976:82). For this reason, human activity is always social: "Even when it is not done with or for other men, production is social because it is based on the assumptions and language of a particular society" (Ollman, 1976:112). The last characteristic is an awareness of a past, which is the record of one's successes and failures in attaining one's aims and of the possibilities which constitute one's failure (Ollman, 1976:82). In sum, "reflexivity" is the "conscious, willed, purposive, flexible, concentrated and social facets which enable man to pursue the unique demands of his species" (Ollman, 1976:112).

Critical theory involves the critique of contemporary society, especially "the system of information publicly available through the concretely organized mass media" (Gouldner, 1976:159). Critical theory makes problematic generally unquestioned traditional belief. In this sense, critical theory is similar to traditional sociology, except in two important respects: (1) in the emancipatory values it explicitly seeks and (2) in the reflexive relation it has toward its own value commitments (Gouldner, 1976:292).

A self-reflexive critical theory, then, does not transcend ideology because of the assumption that nearly all human actions, and ideologies that inform them, are necessarily grounded in partisan interests. Since ideology cannot be transcended, it can only be reconstituted around other interests. Consequently, self-reflexive critical theory grounds its ideology in justifiable human interests and makes these interests problematic or subject to examination in their own right. Ultimately, self-reflexive critical theory seeks to demonstrate connections between knowledge, belief and human interests. It is hoped that this essay has contributed to that effort.

NOTES

1. According to Nimmo and Combs (1980:6), "at best, myths are simplistic and distorted beliefs based upon emotion rather than rigorous analysis; at worst, myths are dangerous falsifications." Specifically, a "myth" is:

   . . . a credible, dramatic, socially constructed re-presentation of perceived realities that people accept as permanent, fixed knowledge of reality while forgetting (if they were ever aware of it) its tentative, imaginative, created, and perhaps fictional qualities (Nimmo and Combs, 1980:16).

   For examples of myths of crime, criminals, and crime control policy, see especially Reiman, 1979; Pepinsky and Jesilow, 1984; Walker, 1985.

2. For Gouldner (1976:30), "ideology" is "a call to action—a 'command' grounded in social theory," ideology "presents a map of 'what is' in society; a 'report' of how it is working, how it is failing, and also how it could be changed" (Gouldner, 1976:30). "Interests," on the other hand, refer to "what it makes sense for people to want and do, given their overall situation" (Ollman, 1976:122). Although ideologies are partly legitimated by their claim to represent the "public interest," in practice, they nearly always represent private interests. This does not necessarily forebode undesirable social consequences however, because there is often hidden public value in vested private interests (Gouldner, 1976:282).

3. "Exploitation," in this context, refers to the activity of one group preventing another group from "getting what they may as yet have no idea of, and therefore do not desire, but would prefer to their present condition if only they knew about it" (Plamenatz, 1963:322).

4. For some interesting "new" ideas, see Pepinsky and Jesilow, 1984.

REFERENCES

American Friends Service Committee Working Party (1971). *Struggle for Justice*. New York: Hill and Wang.

Becker, H.S. (1973). *Outsiders: Studies in the Sociology of Deviance.* New York: Free Press.

Bittner, E. (1967). "The Police on Skid Row: A Study of Peace-Keeping." *American Sociological Review*, 32:699-715.

Bittner, E. (1975). *The Functions of the Police in Modern Society.* New York: Jason Aronson.

Bohm, R.M. (1982). "Radical Criminology: An Explication." *Criminology*, 19:565-589.

Center for Research on Criminal Justice (1977). *The Iron Fist and the Velvet Glove.* Berkeley: Center for Research on Criminal Justice.

Chambliss, W.J. (1976). "Functional and Conflict Theories of Crime: the Heritage of Emile Durkheim and Karl Marx." In W.J. Chambliss & M. Mankoff (eds.), *Whose Law? What Order? A Conflict Approach to Criminology.* New York: Wiley.

Clements, J.M. (1974). "Repression: Beyond the Rhetoric." In C.E. Reasons (ed.), *The Criminologist: Crime and the Criminal.* Pacific Palisades, CA: Goodyear.

Clinard, M.B. (1978). *Cities with Little Crime: The Case of Switzerland.* Cambridge, England: Cambridge University Press.

Dominick, J.R. (1973). "Crime and Law Enforcement on Prime-time Television." *Public Opinion Quarterly*, 37:241-250.

Dreier, P. (1982). "The Position of the Press in the U.S. Power Structure." *Social Problems*, 29:298-310.

Erskine, H. (1974). "The Polls: Fear of Violence and Crime." *Public Opinion Quarterly,* (Spring) 131-145.

Evans, S.S. & R.J. Lundman (1983). "Newspaper Coverage of Corporate Price-Fixing: A Replication." *Criminology*, 21:529-541.

Ferdinand, T.N. (1977). "The Criminal Patterns of Boston Since 1849." In J.F. Galliher & J.L. McCartney (eds.), *Criminology: Power, Crime and Criminal Law.* Homewood, IL: Dorsey.

Fishman, M. (1978). "Crime Waves as Ideology." *Social Problems*, 25:531-543.

Foucault, M. (1977). *Discipline and Punish.* New York: Pantheon.

Galliher, J.F. & J.L. McCartney (1977). *Criminology: Power, Crime and Criminal Law.* Homewood, IL: Dorsey.

Garmire, F., J. Rubin & J.Q. Wilson (1972). *The Police and the Community.* Baltimore: Johns Hopkins University Press.

Gitlin, T. (1979). "Prime Time Ideology: The Hegemonic Process in Television Entertainment." *Social Problems*, 26:251-266.

Gordon, D.M. (1976). "Class and the Economics of Crime." In W.J. Chambliss & M. Mankoff (eds.), *Whose Law? What Order? A Conflict Approach to Criminology.* New York: Wiley.

Gouldner, A.W. (1976). *The Dialectic of Ideology and Technology: The Origins, Grammar, and Future of Ideology.* New York: Seabury.

Graber, D.A. (1980). *Crime News and the Public.* New York: Praeger.

Griffin, S. (1976). "Rape: the All-American Crime." In W.J. Chambliss and M. Mankoff (eds.), *Whose Law? What Order? A Conflict Approach to Criminology*. New York: Wiley.

Grinspoon, L. (1977). *Marijuana Reconsidered,* 2nd ed. Cambridge, MA: Harvard University Press.

Halberstam, D. (1979). *The Powers That Be*. New York: Knopf.

Helmer, J. (1975). *Drugs and Minority Oppression*. New York: Seabury.

Humphries, D. & D.F. Greenberg (1981). "The Dialectics of Crime Control." In D. Greenberg (ed.), *Crime and Capitalism*. Palo Alto, CA: Mayfield.

Kennedy, M.C. (1976). "Beyond Incrimination." In W.J. Chambliss & M. Mankoff (eds.), *Whose Law? What Order? A Conflict Approach to Criminology*. New York: Wiley.

Liazos, A. (1977). "The Poverty of the Sociology of Deviance: Nuts, Sluts, and Perverts." In J.F. Galliher & J.L. McCartney (eds.), *Criminology: Power, Crime and Criminal Law*. Homewood, IL: Dorsey.

Lieberman, J.K. (1973). *How the Government Breaks the Law*. Baltimore: Penguin.

Lyerly, R.R. & J.K. Skipper, Jr. (1981). "Differential Rates of Rural-Urban Delinquency: A Social Control Approach." *Criminology*, 19:385-399.

Manning, P. (1977). *Police Work*. Cambridge, MA: MIT Press.

Manning, P. (1978). "Dramatic Aspects of Policing." In P. Wickman & P. Whitten (eds.), *Readings in Criminology*. Lexington, MA: D.C. Heath.

Martin, R.G. & R.D. Conger (1980). "A Comparison of Delinquency Trends: Japan and the United States." *Criminology*, 18:53-61.

Marx, K. & F. Engels (1970). *The German Ideology*. New York: International Publishers.

Matza, D. (1964). *Delinquency and Drift*. New York: Wiley.

Mead, G.H. (1972). *On Social Psychology*. Chicago: The University of Chicago Press.

Milakovich, M.D. & K. Weis (1977). "Politics and Measures of Success in the War on Crime." In J.F. Galliher & J.M. McCartney (eds.), *Criminology: Power, Crime and Criminal Law*. Homewood, IL: Dorsey.

Miliband, R. (1969). *The State in Capitalist Society*. New York: Basic Books.

Mintz, M. & J.S. Cohen (1971). *American Inc.: Who Owns and Operates the United States?* New York: Dial.

Musto, D.F. (1973). *The American Disease: Origins of Narcotic Control*. New Haven: Yale University Press.

Nimmo, D. & J.E. Combs (1980). *Subliminal Politics: Myths and Mythmakers in America*. Englewood Cliffs, NJ: Prentice Hall.

Ollman, B. (1976). *Alienation,* Second Edition. Cambridge: Cambridge University Press.

Paez, A.L. & R.W. Dodge (1982). "Criminal Victimization in the United States." Washington, DC: U.S. Department of Justice.

Pandiani, J.A. (1978). "Crime Time TV: If All We Know is What We Saw . . ." *Contemporary Crises*, 2:237-258.

Pearce, F. (1976). *Crimes of the Powerful.* London: Pluto Press.

Pepinsky, H.E. (1980). *Crime Control Strategies: An Introduction to the Study of Crime.* New York: Oxford University Press.

Pepinsky, H.E. & P. Jesilow (1984). *Myths that Cause Crime.* Cabin John, MD: Seven Locks.

Plamenatz, J. (1963). *Man and Society,* Vol. 2. New York: McGraw-Hill.

Platt, T. (1975). "Prospects for a Radical Criminology in the USA." In I. Taylor, P. Walton and J. Young (eds.), *Critical Criminology.* Boston: Routledge and Kegan Paul.

Platt, T. (1977). *The Child Savers.* Chicago: The University of Chicago Press.

Quinney, R. (1970). *The Social Reality of Crime.* Boston: Little, Brown.

Quinney, R. (1977). *Class, State and Crime.* New York: David McKay.

Quinney, R. (1979). *Criminology,* 2nd ed. Boston: Little, Brown.

Quinney, R. (1979b). "The Production of Criminology," *Criminology*, 16:445-457.

Reiman, J.H. (1979). *The Rich Get Richer and the Poor Get Prison: Ideology, Class and Criminal Justice.* New York: Wiley.

Reiman, J.H. & S. Headlee (1981). "Marxism and Criminal Justice Policy." *Crime & Delinquency*, 27:24-47.

Reiss, A. (1971). *The Police and the Public.* New Haven: Yale University Press.

Roshier, B. (1973). "The Selection of Crime News by the Press." In S. Cohen and J. Young (eds.), *The Manufacture of News.* Beverly Hills, CA: Sage.

Schumann, K.F. (1976). "Theoretical Presuppositions for Criminology as a Critical Enterprise." *International Journal of Criminology and Penology*, 4:285-294.

Sheley, J.F. & C.D. Ashkins (1981). "Crime, Crime News, and Crime Views." *Public Opinion Quarterly*, 45:492-506.

Shelley, L.I. (1981). *Crime and Modernization: The Impact of Industrialization and Urbanization on Crime.* Carbondale, IL: Southern Illinois University Press.

Silver, I. (1968). *Introduction to The Challenge of Crime in a Free Society.* New York: Avon.

Simon, D.R. (1981). "The Political Economy of Crime." In S.G. McNall (eds.), *Political Economy: A Critique of American Society.* Glenview, IL: Scott, Foresman.

Simon, D.R. & D.S. Eitzen (1982). *Elite Deviance.* Boston: Allyn & Bacon.

Smith, R.C. (1970). "U.S. Marijuana Legislation and the Creation of a Social Problem." In D.E. Smith (ed.), *The New Social Drug: Cultural, Medical, and Legal Perspectives on Marijuana.* Englewood Cliffs, NJ: Prentice Hall.

Stack, S. (1984). "Income Inequality and Property Crime: A Cross-National Analysis of Relative Deprivation Theory." *Criminology*, 22:229-257.

Sutherland, E.H. & D.R. Cressey (1974). *Criminology,* Ninth Edition. Philadelphia: J.B. Lippincott.

Vold, G.B. (1935). "The Amount and Nature of Crime." *American Journal of Sociology*, 40:496-803.

Walker, S. (1985). *Sense and Nonsense About Crime: A Police Guide.* Monterey, CA: Brooks/Cole.

Wallerstein, J.S. & C.J. Wyle (1947). "Our Law-Abiding Lawbreakers." *Probation,* 25:107-112.

Wilson, J.Q. (1968). *Varieties of Police Behavior.* Cambridge, MA: Harvard University Press.

Wilson, J.Q. (1975). *Thinking About Crime.* New York: Vintage.

Wright, E.O. (1973). *The Politics of Punishment: A Critical Analysis of Prisons in America.* New York: Harper & Row.

DISCUSSION QUESTIONS

1. The author discusses a "self-reflexive critical theory grounded in justifiable human interests." What does he mean by this and how could it have a positive effect on myths and their consequences?

2. What role does the media play in perpetuating the current myths about crime and crime control policy? How do they exacerbate the problem and how could they be used to diminish the problem effectively?

3. Identify the myths as explained by the author. Discuss each one in detail, and explain why you think they are relevant to the criminal justice system. Which one do you think is most relevant?

CHAPTER 18

The Ford Pinto Case and Beyond: Assessing Blame

Francis T. Cullen, William J. Maakestad & Gray Cavender

In 1968, the President's Commission on Law Enforcement and Administration of Justice concluded that "the public tends to be indifferent to business crime or even to sympathize with the offenders who have been caught" (1968:84). Now some might question the accuracy of the commission's assessment; indeed, it appears that the public has never been quite so sanguine about white-collar crime as governmental officials and academicians have led us to believe (see Braithwaite, 1982a:732-733). Nevertheless, it would be too much to assert that the commission's evaluation of the views of the American citizenry was fully without empirical referent. For if the commission underestimated the willingness of the public to punish criminals of any sort, it was perhaps more correct in sensing that citizens had yet to define white-collar and corporate criminality as anything approaching a social problem.

> **KEY CONCEPTS:**
>
> **corporate misconduct**
>
> **political ethics**
>
> **white-collar crime**

By contrast, few social commentators today would seek to sustain the notion that the public considers upperworld illegality as "morally neutral conduct" (Kadish, 1963). To be sure, there are now and undoubtedly will continue to be calls for citizens both to sharpen their awareness of the dangers posed by the lawlessness of the rich and to demand that the state take steps to shield them from this victimization. Nonetheless, public awareness of white-collar and corporate crime has reached the point where the concept has become part of the common vernacular. Further, survey data indicate that the public judges such criminality to be more serious than ever before, is quite prepared to sanction white-collar offenders, and is far more cognizant of the costs of upperworld crime than had been previously imagined (Cullen, Clark, et al., 1982; Cullen et al., 1982, 1983).

Adapted from Frances T. Cullen, William J. Maakestad, and Gray Cavender, *Corporate Crime Under Attack: The Ford Pinto Case and Beyond* (Cincinnati: Anderson), 1989.

In light of the events of the past decade and a half, the finding that upper-world crime has emerged as an increasingly salient social issue is not surprising. Indeed, during this time we have witnessed what Katz (1980) has termed "the social movement against white collar crime" (Clinard & Yeager, 1978:258-262; 1980:12-15). Thus, with Watergate and Abscam representing the more celebrated examples, prosecutions for political corruption have climbed markedly (Katz, 1980:161-164). Similarly, consumer groups have scrutinized corporate activities and asked what officials planned to do to put a halt to "crime in the suites" (Nader & Green, 1972). Meanwhile, investigative news reporters and news shows such as "60 Minutes" have told us much about improprieties ranging from kickbacks to the illegal dumping of chemical wastes that endanger lives (Brown, 1980). Mistrust has run so deep that physicians are now suspected of fraudulent Medicaid schemes, and hence states have moved to establish enforcement agencies to combat this possibility (Cullen & Heiner, 1979; Pontell et al., 1982). In 1977, the notion that white-collar crime is a serious problem received further reification when U.S. Attorney General Griffin Bell remarked that he would make such illegality his "number one priority."

It is clear, then, that consciousness about upperworld lawlessness rose, perhaps substantially, since the President's Commission on Law Enforcement and Administration of Justice [President's Commission] (1968) characterized public opinion about such matters as essentially disinterested. However, it is equally important to be sensitive to the particular content that this consciousness came to assume. On the one hand, the social movement Katz speaks of alerted people to the enormous costs incurred by white-collar crime (Conklin, 1977; Schrager and Short, 1978); yet it did much more than this: it provided the additional message that the rich and powerful could exact these harms with impunity. Consequently, questions of justice and moral right were immediately suggested. The matter was thus not merely one of preventing victimization but of confronting why crime allows "the rich to get richer and the poor to get prison" (Reiman, 1979). As Katz (1980:178-179) has observed:

> The demand supporting the movement to date has been much more than a utilitarian concern for the efficient deterrence of antisocial conduct. . . . In order to understand the expansion of "white collar crime," we must understand the demand that unjust enrichment and unjustly acquired power be made criminal; not just that it be made unprofitable but that it be defined officially as abominable, that it be treated as qualitatively alien to the basic moral character of society.

In short, a core element of the movement against white-collar crime was to assert that the harms committed by the more and less advantaged be subject to the same moral mandates, particularly within our courts. Of course, the very attempt to reshape moral boundaries is itself a manifestation of broader changes in the social context of any historical era (Erikson, 1966;

Farrell & Swigert, 1982:27-51; Gusfield, 1967). While a complicated matter, two circumstances would appear to have done much to encourage and structure the nature of the attack on upperworld criminality that has emerged in recent times.

First, the unfolding of the civil rights movement focused attention on the intimate link between social and criminal justice. Pernicious patterns of racism and class discrimination were thus seen to be reproduced within the legal system. In turn, it became incumbent upon political elites to explain why such inequities were allowed to prevail in our courts. Significantly, a second circumstance made answering this charge of perpetuating injustice an essential task for those in government: the "legitimacy crisis" facing the state (Friedrichs, 1979). Indeed, such poignant happenings as Attica, Kent State, Vietnam, and Watergate, as well as the failure of the "Great Society" programs to fulfill promises of greater distributive justice, all combined to shake people's trust in the benevolence of the government (Rothman, 1978). In response, elected officials (like Jimmy Carter) felt compelled to campaign on their integrity and to claim that they would not show favor to criminals of any class. That is, political elites, under the press of the call for "equal justice," were placed in the position of having to publicly support the notion that the harms of the rich be brought within the reach of the criminal law. And as Piven and Cloward (1971, 1977) have demonstrated, when necessity moves political elites to define existing arrangements as unfair, the possibility of a social movement to refashion the social order is greatly enhanced. It would thus appear that, at least in part, elite definitions lent legitimacy and helped give life to the movement against white-collar crime.

Now, in this social climate, the behavior of corporations took on new meaning. The world of big business was seen to suffer, in Durkheim's (1951) terms, from "chronic anomie," a breakdown of any sense of ethical regulation. It was thus common to encounter articles which first asked, "How lawless are big companies?" and then answered that "a surprising number of them have been involved in blatant illegalities" (Ross, 1980). What is more, these infringements of existing legal and administrative standards not only involved enormous and ostensibly intentional harm, but also were seen to be greeted only rarely with the full force of the criminal law. Corporate actors were thus depicted as readily sacrificing human well-being for unjustly acquired profits with little worry over paying any real price; meanwhile, those who had the misfortune of stealing lesser amounts through more customary means could anticipate no immunity from state sanction.

Notably, such imagery helped to precipitate not only public discussion and popular accounts about corporate malfeasance (e.g., Caudill, 1977; Dowie, 1979; Rodgers, 1974; Stern, 1976; Vandivier, 1972; Wright, 1979), but a proliferation of scholarship on the topic as well (e.g., Braithwaite, 1979, 1982b; Braithwaite & Geis, 1982; Coleman, 1975; Duchnick & Imhoff, 1978; Elkins, 1976; Fisse, 1971, 1973, 1981; Geis, 1972; Geis & Edelhertz, 1973; Kramer, 1979; Kriesberg, 1976; Yoder, 1979;). Typically, these

academic writings followed a pattern of initially identifying the large costs
of corporate illegality and lamenting the failure of existing enforcement
strategies to diminish this pressing problem. The commentary would then turn
to a consideration of whether such activity should be brought under the
umbrella of the criminal law. In particular, two issues were debated:
(1) Should corporations and their executives be held responsible for unlawful acts just as street criminals are? (2) Will efforts to use criminal sanctions
really result in a reduction of corporate illegality?

These latter concerns as well as those discussed previously furnish a context for understanding both the very occurrence and importance of Ford Motor
Company's prosecution for reckless homicide by the State of Indiana. It
appears that the Ford Pinto case was very much a child of the times; succinctly
stated, it is doubtful that Ford would have been brought to trial during a previous era. Yet, as the case is best seen as a manifestation of the broad movement
against white-collar crime—and, in particular, against corporate crime—it is
also unique in the legal precedent it set, the publicity it received, and in the
opportunity it provides to examine how more theoretical insights on corporate
responsibility and control are shaped by the realities of the courtroom.

With these issues in mind the current endeavor attempts to present a case
study of Ford's prosecution.[1] To be more exact, four matters are discussed
below: Why was an indictment brought against Ford in Indiana? Why did the
courts permit a corporation itself to be tried for a criminal offense? What transpired at the trial? And what will be the meaning of the case in the time ahead?

ASSESSING BLAME

On August 10, 1978, Judy and Lyn Ulrich and their cousin visiting
from Illinois, Donna Ulrich, set out to play volleyball at a church some twenty
miles away. While on U.S. Highway 33 in northern Indiana, the yellow
1973 Pinto they were driving was struck in the rear by a van. Within seconds
their car was engulfed in flames. Two of the teenagers, trapped inside the vehicle, died quickly; the driver, Judy was thrown clear of the blazing Pinto with
third-degree burns on more than 95 percent of her body. Though conscious
following the accident, she died at a hospital eight hours later (Strobel, 1980).

As might be anticipated, the accident stunned those who witnessed the
aftermath of the crash and soon sent shock waves throughout the local
community of Elkhart. Yet, like many other fatal collisions, this might have
been defined exclusively as a tragedy. Or, if wrongdoing was involved, law
enforcement officials might have prosecuted the driver of the van. Indeed,
as a 21-year-old who had just recently reacquired a suspended license and
who was driving a van that was labeled "Peace Train" and contained half-
empty beer bottles as well as the remains of marijuana cigarettes scattered
on the floor, he would have made a likely candidate to take the rap.

However, both the particulars of the accident and the tenor of the times led the blame to be placed elsewhere. In particular the observations of State Trooper Neil Graves were crucial in determining that this was not a "normal crime" (Sudnow, 1965). After arriving at the scene of the crash, Graves discovered that gasoline had somehow soaked the front floorboard of the car. He found as well that the van had sustained only minor damage, and its driver, Richard Duggar, was only mildly injured. By contrast, the Ulrichs' Pinto was viciously crushed in the rear and, of course, badly charred. This oddity was made even more poignant when eyewitnesses reported that the van was not speeding and that it looked initially like the accident was going to be nothing more than a fender-bender (Strobel, 1980).

These inconsistencies might have been set aside had it not been that Trooper Graves recalled reading an exposé about the Pinto some months before. This piece, written by Mark Dowie (1977) and entitled "Pinto Madness," alleged that the placement of the gas tank on the Pinto constituted a lethal hazard. Specifically, Dowie noted that the location of the tank adjacent to the rear bumper made it highly susceptible to puncture by the fender's bolts during a rear-end collision. In turn, this meant that the Pinto would experience considerable fuel leakage and hence fires when hit even at low speeds.

Yet this is not all that Dowie claimed. Far more controversial was his assertion that Ford was fully aware of this problem in the initial stages of production but chose not to fix the Pinto's defect because it was not cost efficient. To bolster this conclusion, he presented secret Ford memoranda that revealed that the financial loss of a recall exceeded the loss incurred as the result of injuries and fatalities "associated with crash-induced fuel leakage and fires." In the name of profit, Dowie believed, "for seven years the Ford Motor Company sold cars in which it knew hundreds of people would needlessly burn to death."[2]

Sensitized to the potential dangers of the Pinto, Graves was thus aware that the blame for the accident might rest with Ford. This sentiment was reinforced when he began to receive calls from news reporters around the country inquiring about the crash and the possibility that the fuel tank defect may have been responsible for the deaths of the three teenagers. Meanwhile, Michael A. Cosentino, Elkhart County's State's Attorney, was apprised of the accident. When he had an opportunity to review photographs of the crash, he too was troubled by the discrepancy between the minimal damage to the van and the wreckage of the Ulrich girls' Pinto. And then there was the emotional, human side to the accident: the pictures of the charred remains of the victims and the reality that three teenagers had suffered a terrible death (Cosentino interview; Strobel, 1980).

As a 41-year-old conservative Republican county prosecutor, Cosentino was an unlikely candidate to try to bring Ford Motor Company within the reach of the criminal law. Like many people at this time, he had heard about the problems associated with the Pinto and about the recall of the car that Ford had begun earlier in the summer. However, he had not read Dowie's article, and he was not inclined to attack corporations because of an ideological persuasion that they constituted a menace to society. Indeed, even now, Cosentino is convinced that the civil law should be used to deal with "99 percent" of all cases involving alleged corporate misbehavior (Cosentino interview).

Yet in light of the facts surrounding the accident and of conversations with Neil Graves (who by this time had called and talked with Mark Dowie), Cosentino could not easily put the matter aside. He was aware as well that Indiana's revised criminal code, which had become effective on October 1, 1977, less than a year before the accident, contained a provision for the offense of "reckless homicide." Section 35-42-1-5 of the Indiana Code thus read: "A person who recklessly kills another human being commits reckless homicide." Taken together, these considerations led Cosentino to wonder whether the Ford Motor Company could or should be criminally prosecuted. Because of the novelty of the case, the power of Ford, and the difficulty of piercing the corporate veil, Cosentino did not seriously consider prosecuting individual Ford executives (Cosentino interview).

Cosentino, however, set out to explore whether Ford could in fact be prosecuted under Indiana law. Since Section 35-41-1-2 of the penal code included "corporation" under its definition of "person," his staff reported that a prosecution was legally permissible. This conclusion was corroborated by William Conour of the Indiana Prosecuting Attorney's Office, who had been involved in drafting the reckless homicide statute (Strobel, 1980).

But even though the potential for prosecution seemed to exist, the question remained whether Ford really should be charged with a criminal offense. Research conducted by Cosentino and his staff suggested that it should be. Particularly influential were the conversations with and documents supplied by those involved in civil judgments against Ford. The prosecutor was in contact, for example, with automobile experts who had testified against Ford in civil hearings and with Mark Robinson, who was the lawyer in the Alan Grimshaw case.[3] As the evidence from these varied sources who had been close to the Pinto scene accumulated, it became clear that Ford knew that its Pinto was defective and chose to risk human life by not moving quickly to fix it. Thoughts of criminal culpability did not seem out of place in this context.

It is important to note here that, without the mounting attention concerning Ford's handling of the Pinto, it would have been unlikely that Cosentino would have come to blame Ford for the deaths of the three teenagers. Had the accident occurred several years before, he might have been forced, perhaps reluctantly, to put aside the peculiarities of the crash and move on to other cases. Yet now the social climate worked against this option and, alternatively, made a criminal prosecution seem plausible, if not obligatory. By August of 1978, the attack against Ford and its Pinto had emerged as a "symbolic crusade" (Gusfield, 1967), a movement aimed at showing that Ford, like other powerful corporations, felt comfortable in operating outside accepted moral boundaries in its irresponsible pursuit of profit. Ford's handling of the Pinto thus came to symbolize what was wrong with corporate America.

In general terms, Dowie's (1977) "Pinto Madness" article, its release trumpeted at a press conference sponsored by Ralph Nader, signaled the beginning of the "crusade" against Ford. With concern over corporate crime running high, Dowie's article earned national exposure. In February of 1978 the movement intensified still further with the announcement of the exorbitant financial damages awarded in the Grimshaw civil case. At the same time the National Highway Traffic Safety Administration (NHTSA), a federal regulatory body, had undertaken tests on the Pinto. In May of 1978, NHTSA notified Ford that there had been "an initial determination of the existence of a safety-related defect" (quoted in Strobel, 1980:23). Denying any wrongdoing but faced with pressure on all sides, Ford subsequently issued a recall of all Pintos manufactured from 1971-1976 and all 1975-1976 Bobcats, a total of 1.5 million cars (Strobel, 1980). As might be expected, this series of events sparked a marked escalation in the focus placed by the media on Pinto issues (Swigert & Farrell, 1980-1981). Indeed, it was clear that reporters had come to view the Ford Pinto matter as a fascinating and eminently newsworthy upperworld scandal.

Thus, it is significant that Mike Cosentino confronted the Ulrichs' tragic accident in the midst of a general crusade against Ford, for in several ways this necessarily shaped what the case could and did come to mean to him. First, unlike the traffic fatalities he had processed in the past, the numerous calls that his office and Neil Graves received from reporters across the nation alerted him, if only vaguely at the start, to the fact that any Pinto crash was potentially of national concern. Second, the movement against Ford, while certainly informal and unorganized, nevertheless created invaluable informational networks. This meant that in a matter of days Cosentino acquired revealing documents and expert feedback from parties who harbored strong sentiments against Ford. Under normal circumstances, such material would have either been unavailable or taken months to uncover, a task beyond the resources of a county prosecutor. Third, the ideological framework of the Pinto crusade provided the conservative state's attorney with a vocabulary about the case that encouraged a response by the criminal law. As Swigert and Farrell (1980-1981) have demonstrated, accounts of the Pinto appearing at this time increasingly characterized Ford as willfully and without repentance inflicting harm on innocent citizens. In a sense, then, Ford was being designated as a sociopath that knew no social responsibility.

In short, Cosentino quickly learned that the death of the Ulrich girls was not a local or isolated occurrence and that Ford, like the worst of criminals, endangered its victims not inadvertently but intentionally. He was aware as well that evidence existed that made a prosecution feasible. Taken together, these considerations personally convinced Cosentino that Ford had acted recklessly and should be prosecuted. Again, he did not wish to initiate a campaign calling for the use of criminal sanctions to deal with all corporate wrongdoing. However, it was manifest to him that Ford had been largely unaffected by traditional forms of control; after all, Ford's conduct surrounding the Pinto had already triggered nearly every legal response possible other than criminal prosecution: civil cases involving compensatory damages, civil cases involving both compensatory and punitive damages, and federal administrative agency actions. In absence of effective regulation and where corporate behavior is so outrageous as to affront moral sensibilities, Cosentino could see the application of the criminal law as appropriate. And from what he knew of the Pinto case, it seemed that this was just such an instance, where justice demanded that a corporation be held criminally responsible for its behavior (Cosentino interview; Maakestad, 1981). However, the very novelty of this idea caused Cosentino to exercise caution. While he believed that Ford should be indicted and that he possessed the authority to do so, he was not certain that the community would support such a prosecution. Consequently, he convened a grand jury to consider an indictment under the reckless homicide statute. From the beginning of the hearing, Cosentino consciously made every effort not to sway the grand jury one way or the other (Cosentino interview). Nevertheless, after entertaining testimony from both Ford officials and safety experts who had previously served as witnesses in civil cases against Ford, the grand jury unanimously returned indictments against Ford Motor Company for three counts of reckless homicide. In essence, the six-member panel agreed with Cosentino that there was sufficient evidence to believe that Ford had acted with moral irresponsibility. Swigert and Farrell (1980-1981:180) captured this point when they wrote:

> The indictment against Ford may be viewed as an attempt on the part of the state to assert moral integrity in the face of enemy deviation. In its decision to contest civil suits, the corporation refused to recognize that moral boundaries had been transgressed. This opened the way to a definition of the manufacturer as a force against whom the power of the law must be directed.[4]

GETTING TO TRIAL

Word of Ford's indictment immediately received front-page attention in newspapers across the nation. It now appeared that Ford Motor Company, at that moment the fourth largest corporation in the world (Clinard & Yeager, 1980:3), would go to trial for reckless homicide. While a guilty verdict would bring only a $30,000 fine ($10,000 on each count), company officials viewed the prospect of a trial with considerable consternation. With Pinto sales already down 40 percent, due to the recent recall, a lengthy, highly publicized criminal case could only serve to erode still further consumer confidence in the car and, more generally, in the corporation. Equally troubling was that a prosecution could encourage state's attorneys elsewhere to bring criminal charges against the company and alert other Pinto victims (or surviving families) to the fact that Ford should be held civilly liable for burn injuries occurring in rear-end collisions (Strobel, 1980). Moreover, executives realized that a criminal conviction would be powerful evidence of Ford's culpability in any subsequent civil suits. With the potential costs of a prosecution running high, Ford thus quickly mobilized to see that the case would never come before a jury.

The task of preventing a trial was given to the prestigious Chicago law firm of Mayer, Brown, and Platt. With a ten-member team assigned to the case, the result of the firm's efforts was a 55-page motion that argued that the criminal indictment should be dismissed on both conceptual and constitutional grounds. In fashioning a response to this attack, Cosentino and his small staff realized that they could well benefit from additional assistance. However, all such help would have to come from volunteers. Cosentino had asked Elkhart County for a special fund of $20,000 to try the case, and he had promised not to request any additional moneys. This figure would have to be stretched far in the fight against Ford; in fact, Cosentino would eventually spend money of his own to defray expenses (Strobel, 1980). Yet, given the prevailing social context, finding law professors to join the prosecution's team did not prove overly difficult. After all, corporate liability and the criminal law was a "hot topic," and the Pinto case obviously possessed both important national and legal ramifications. Again, whether a local prosecutor could have so readily acquired such expert assistance in a previous decade or on a different case is questionable. Bruce Berner, one of the two law professors who worked full time on the case,[5] wrote that "originally, of course, I got involved because of the novel legal questions presented by the indictment." However, it should also be realized that, after agreeing to become part of the prosecution's staff, the appeal of legal novelties was not all that sustained the commitment of volunteers to the case. There was also and always the reality of the horrible deaths of the Ulrich girls. In Berner's words (letter to author, February 21, 1982):

> It was only after I became involved that I saw the photographs [of the girls following the crash] and met the families of the girls. It is nevertheless hard for me to separate the motivating force of the legal issues from that of the personal aspect of the tragedy. . . . Part of what we were saying is that a corporation like all other persons must be forced at all times to look at the very personal tragedies it causes. It seems to me that Ford's whole effort in keeping the pictures of the girls out of evidence, including the pictures of them while they were alive, was in part a way to disconnect themselves from what they had wrought to some very nice people. All I can say about the "Car Wars" photos was that they made me ill and that I cannot, to this day, get them out of my head.[6]

While numerous arguments were voiced in the debate over whether Ford could be brought to trial, the continued vitality of the indictment hinged on two central issues (Maakestad, 1980, 1981). To begin with, Ford's legal brief contended that conceptually the reckless homicide statute could not be applied to corporate entities. For one thing the statute defines the offense as "a person who recklessly kills another human being." Ford claimed in turn that the meaning of "another" was "one of the same kind." Consequently, since the victim is referred to as "another human being," it followed that the perpetrator of the crime must also be human (Clark, 1979). For another thing, the brief asserted that the use of the word "person" in other places in the criminal code clearly is not meant to apply to corporations. Conceptual consistency thus would preclude corporations from being charged with violently oriented offenses like reckless homicide. Quoting Ford's memorandum:

> There are numerous examples in the Criminal Code where the legislature has used the word "person" to refer exclusively to human beings. See, e.g., the section prohibiting rape. . . . ("A person who knowingly or intentionally has sexual intercourse with a member of the opposite sex . . .") Thus, although corporations may generally be covered by the definition of "persons," there are clearly crimes—essentially crimes of violence against other human beings—where it is irrational to read the statutes as applying to corporations.

In response to this line of reasoning, the prosecution initially turned to the penal code itself. First, it observed that the code distinguishes between a "person" ("a human being, corporation, partnership, unincorporated association, or governmental entity") and a "human being" ("an individual who is born and alive"). Because the statute defines reckless homicide as a "person who recklessly kills another human being," rather than as a "human being who recklessly kills another human being," it is evident that the legislative intent here is to encompass corporate behavior. Second, the prosecution noted that the Indiana criminal code explicitly reads that a corporation "may be prosecuted for any offense . . . if it is proved that the offense was committed by its agent within the scope of his authority." Finally, the state's brief dismissed the idea that "corporations" cannot physically commit violent crimes like rape and homicide by emphasizing the realities of the corporation as a legal fiction:

> The major premise that "person" cannot include corporation in the rape statute is simply incorrect. This argument patently exploits the corporate fiction. It attempts to show corporate inability to commit rape. . . . Of course, a corporation cannot itself engage in sexual intercourse; a corporation cannot itself do anything. As it is a fictional person, it can act only through its natural-person agents. A corporation has no genitals, to be sure, but neither does it have a trigger finger, a hand to forge a check, an arm to extend a bribe nor a mind to form an intent or to "consciously disregard" the safety of others. Nevertheless, a corporation is liable for all crimes of its agents acting within their authority. The unlikelihood of corporate rape liability is because sexual intercourse by its agents will almost always be outside the scope of their authority—not because the crime is definitionally ridiculous.

Apart from conceptual considerations Ford maintained that there were two constitutional barriers to its being brought to trial. First, there was the matter that the National Traffic and Motor Vehicle Safety Act had already created a federal apparatus to supervise the automobile industry. Consequently, Ford argued, Congress intended that this system would preempt any state, including Indiana, from regulating the same field. In rebuttal, the prosecution argued that the federal measure was not invoked to deprive states of their police power, and they observed that Ford was unable to cite "a single case where a traditional, general criminal statute was found to have been preempted by a federal regulatory scheme."

Yet there was a second, more serious constitutional matter raised by Ford's lawyers: the ex post facto provision of both the Indiana and U.S. Constitutions. As may be recalled, the revised Indiana code which contained the new reckless homicide crime category became law only on October 1, 1977. Moreover, it was not until July 1, 1978—41 days prior to the Ulrichs' crash—that the reckless homicide offense was amended to include acts of omission as well as commission. Significantly, it is the amended version of the statute that was employed to indict Ford. In light of these two dates, Ford reminded the court that it was being charged with recklessly designing and manufacturing a car that was a 1973 model. It was thus being prosecuted for an act that had transpired several years before enactment of the very law under which it was being charged. Even if its acts were reckless, such ex post facto application of the law constitutionally barred prosecution.

The prosecution assaulted Ford's logic on two fronts. First, issue was taken with Ford's interpretation of when its offense occurred. Contrary to Ford's assertions, the prosecution argued that it is the date the offense is completed, not the date of the first element of the crime, that determines whether ex post facto provisions have been violated. Thus, since the accident postdated the reckless homicide law, the company was potentially subject to criminal sanction. Second, the prosecution maintained that the defendant's omissions in regard to its obligation to either repair the Ulrichs' 1973 Pinto or warn them of the car's hazards were important elements of the offense. That is, Ford was being charged with reckless homicide not only for an act of commission (building a dangerous vehicle), but for an act of omission (ignoring its duty to protect owners from the Pinto's known dangers). The prosecution then went on to propose that once either proscribed acts or omissions are shown to have taken place after a criminal statute is enacted, all of the defendant's prior acts and omissions can properly and constitutionally be considered by the court.

On February 2, 1979, Judge Donald W. Jones succinctly rendered his decision: "There are substantial factors in this case for which there are no precedents. The indictment is sufficient. I therefore deny the motion to dismiss" (quoted in Strobel, 1980:55). In large part, Judge Jones embraced the prosecution's reasoning, agreeing that Indiana law does permit a corporation to be charged for reckless homicide and that federal regulatory statutes did not in this instance preempt the state's rights to seek retributive and deterrent goals unique to the criminal sanction. However, he was only partially persuaded by the prosecution's thoughts on the ex post facto aspects of the case, and thus he attempted to clarify exactly what Ford could and could not be tried under.

In essence Jones's ruling declared that since the vehicle was marketed in 1973, Ford could not be charged for recklessly designing and manufacturing the Pinto. Instead, its actions with regard to the actual production of the Pinto were relevant only to the extent that they constituted antecedents for Ford's alleged recklessness in repairing the vehicle. Alternatively, Ford could be charged with failure to fulfill its obligation to repair, because such recklessness could potentially have occurred in the 41 days between the enactment of the omission amendment to the reckless homicide statute on July 1 and the Ulrich girls' deaths on August 10.

The problems surrounding the ex post facto issue clearly complicated the prosecution's case. At least in theory it would no longer be sufficient to convince the jury that Ford had recklessly assembled the Pinto. To be sure, this much would have to be proven in order to show that Ford knew its product was unsafe and thus had a duty to warn its customers, including the Ulrichs, of this fact. However, Ford could now only be convicted if it could also be revealed that the company had recklessly ignored its duty to inform the Ulrichs of the Pinto's dangers in the period following July 1.

In sum, with the help of law professors and other volunteers, Cosentino had succeeded in getting Ford to trial. However, the legal constraints on his case, the realities of the courtroom, and the resources at his opponent's disposal would make getting a conviction another matter.

TRYING FORD

Ford's failure to quash the indictment taught the company that their foes were perhaps more formidable than initially imagined. It was now manifest that nothing could be spared in order to avert the shame of a criminal stigmatization. In particular, Ford's lawyers would be given a blank check; they would be free to craft the best defense money could buy.

For Ford, two orders of business were immediately at hand. First, there was the crucial matter of whom to select to head the defense team. The choice proved to be a wise, if expensive, one; James J. Neal, a former special prosecutor during Watergate.[7] The second pressing concern was to move Cosentino off his home turf by securing a change of venue. Based on evidence gathered from a survey of Elkhart residents about the case (commissioned by Ford) and the testimony of $1,000-a-day consultant Hans Zeisel (co-author with Harry Kalven of *The American Jury*), Ford argued that it could not receive a fair trial in Elkhart.[8] Judge Jones agreed, and the case was moved to Winamac, a town of 2,450 located in Pulaski County some 55 miles southwest. Sixty-year-old Judge Harold Staffeldt would preside over the trial (Strobel, 1980).

The move to Winamac and the additional living expenses this entailed further strained the prosecution's budget; Cosentino himself would shoulder much of this new burden. However, as would become evident throughout the trial, there appeared to be no limit to the resources that Ford was able and willing to devote to its defense. The cost of the survey employed to justify the change of venue itself approximated the entire Cosentino budget. Other facts are equally revealing. For instance, after the place of the trial became known, Ford quickly made an attractive offer to and succeeded in retaining a local Winamac lawyer who was a close friend of Judge Staffeldt and who had practiced with the judge for 22 years. Similarly, the bill for housing the Ford defense team, which at times reached 40, ran to $27,000 a month. Later they would undertake additional crash tests on Pintos at a cost of around $80,000. Importantly, they were also able to purchase daily transcripts of the trial at $9 a page, with the total expenditure for the trial transcripts being $50,000 (Strobel, 1980). Since the complexity and length of the trial meant that a private firm supplied the court stenographers and thus that the transcripts were not available free to the prosecution, budgetary constraints precluded Cosentino from having access to this material. In his opinion, the inability to review previous testimony (e.g., to prepare for cross-examination) was one of the largest disadvantages plaguing the prosecution (Cosentino interview). In the end, it is estimated that Ford may have spent anywhere from $1.5 million to $2 million on its defense.

In launching its case, the prosecution wanted to impress upon the members of the jury that they were not merely dealing with statistical casualties; like other homicide cases, they were being asked to assess whether Ford should be held responsible for the horrible burn deaths of three vibrant teenagers. James Neal, however, fully realized that it would be important to neutralize this emotional factor. In a skillful maneuver he thus submitted a document that first admitted that the Ulrich girls had died as a result of burns and then declared that there was no need for the jury to see the grotesque pictures of or hear testimony about the girls' charred bodies. The prosecution countered that Neal was endeavoring to "sanitize" the girls' deaths and that it is common practice to present evidence on cause of death in a homicide trial. Somewhat amazingly, Judge Staffeldt agreed with Neal and prevented the jury from seeing or hearing about what the reality of the crash entailed. Stymied on this front, the emotional advantage of the prosecution was largely confined to the remarks of the victims' mother, Mrs. Mattie Ulrich, who told the court that she would have gotten rid of the Pinto had she known of its dangers. She then remarked that she had in fact received notice of the Pinto recall; however, it came to her house in February of 1979, several months after the crash in which her two daughters and niece had perished (Strobel, 1980).

Despite this setback, the prosecution remained optimistic. After all, the foundation of its case was not erected upon the angle of playing on the jurors' sympathies. Instead, Cosentino felt that the Pinto had a defective fuel tank placement. This material included internal Ford memos and documents commenting on the Pinto's safety as well as the results of crash tests on 1971 and 1972 models, conducted by Ford and the government, showing that the vehicle exploded in flames at low impact speeds. These tests would be crucial, Cosentino reasoned, because they revealed that in planning the production of the 1973 Pinto, Ford had concrete evidence of the car's defects yet chose not to rectify them. Moreover, Cosentino did not have crash tests at low speeds for the 1973 model, and his tight budget precluded his conducting them at this stage.

Recognizing the damaging nature of this evidence, Neal moved quickly to challenge the admission of any testimony or tests that were not directly related to the 1973 Pinto, the model year of the Ulrichs' car. In a series of rulings over the course of the trial, Judge Staffeldt concurred with Neal and barred nearly all materials that predated 1973. Needless to say, this had the result of seriously undermining the state's case. In the end, only a small percentage, perhaps as low as 5 percent, of the documents the prosecution had compiled were admitted as evidence (Anderson, 1981:370, n.20).

The judge's reluctance to permit the jury to consider the totality of the prosecution's case points up the difficulty of transporting what has traditionally been a product liability case from civil into criminal court. To a large extent, it appears that the rural judge was never fully comfortable in knowing how this was to be done. Indeed, his grabbing onto 1973 as his evidentiary standard reveals that he either did not fully comprehend the logic of the prosecution's case or did not embrace the legal theory on which it was based. It seems that he wished to treat the 1973 Pinto as he would any other weapon in a homicide case: Since it was this weapon that caused the crime, evidence on other weapons was irrelevant. Of course, at the heart of the prosecution's case was the understanding that Ford's recklessness with regard to the 1973 Pinto was intimately contingent on what the corporation had done in its product development of the car line in the previous years. Whether rightly or wrongly, Judge Staffeldt failed to appreciate this distinction between the recklessness of corporate decisionmaking and that involved in more traditional forms of criminality.

Now with much of its case set aside, the prosecution presented two major lines of argument to the jury. First, it called in auto safety experts, including a former Ford executive who testified that the fuel tank on the Pinto was placed in a potentially lethal position. Second, Cosentino relied upon eyewitnesses to prove that Duggar's van was traveling at 50 miles per hour or less and that the Ulrichs' Pinto was still moving when hit from behind. Taken together, these facts indicated that the speed differential at the moment of impact was around 30. In turn, establishing this low differential was crucial to the prosecution's case because it explained both why so little damage was done to the van and why the girls died from their burns but not from injuries sustained in the crash, as would be expected in a high-velocity collision. Most importantly, however, it showed that the Pinto the girls were driving exploded despite being hit at a relatively low speed. The implication was thus clear: Because of Ford's reckless construction of the Pinto, three girls died in an accident that should have been little more than a fender-bender.

Having done much to diminish the force of the prosecution's case, James Neal began Ford's defense by vigorously rejecting the claim that the Pinto was an unsafe vehicle. For instance, Neal brought his own automotive experts before the jury to testify that the 1973 Pinto met prevailing federal automotive standards and was just as safe as comparable subcompacts manufactured at that time. He also produced Ford executives who testified that they had such faith in the car that they had purchased Pintos for members of their own families. Neal then challenged the prosecution's version of the speed differential between the van and the Ulrichs' Pinto. Crucial in this regard were the dramatic accounts of two surprise witnesses; both claimed that prior to her death in the hospital Judy Ulrich had said that her car was stopped on the highway. If so, the speed at impact would have been 50 miles per hour, a collision that no small car could have withstood. This reasoning was given added credence when Ford presented newly conducted crash tests which showed that at 50 miles per hour a van would sustain only minimal damage despite the large crushing effect it exerted on the rear of the Pinto. Neal thus concluded from this that the small front-end wreckage of Duggar's van was not evidence of a low-impact accident but was normal, even at speeds exceeding 50 (Strobel, 1980).

The defense also took pains to remind the jurors that Ford itself had voluntarily agreed to recall the Pinto two months before the Ulrich accident and thus during all 41 days following the enactment of the omission amendment to the reckless homicide statute. Ford employees testified that during this period the company had pressured them to contact Pinto owners about the recall as quickly as possible. To accomplish this task, workers were given overtime pay, and airplanes were used to hurry recall kits across the nation. With 1.5 million customers it was not surprising, though of course terribly regrettable, that the Ulrichs' notification did not arrive until February 1979. Indeed, Ford had done everything feasible to warn Pinto owners; it certainly had not been reckless in this duty (Strobel, 1980).

After four days of exhausting deliberations, the jurors returned their verdict: not guilty. The initial vote was 8–4 to acquit. Twenty-five ballots later, the final holdout changed his mind and joined the majority. Some on the jury felt that the hazards of the Pinto were basically inherent in all small cars and that owners took certain risks when they chose a vehicle that was less costly and consequently less sturdy. A number of other jurors, however, were convinced that Ford had marketed a defective automobile, but that the prosecution simply had not proven that the corporation was reckless in its recall efforts during the 41 days in which it was criminally liable (Strobel, 1980).

Regardless, the 10-week Ford Pinto trial was now over. As might be anticipated, there was much jubilation and relief at Ford headquarters in Dearborn, Michigan (*Time,* 1980). Meanwhile, Cosentino and his staff were left to contemplate the bitterness of an unsuccessful crusade and to wonder what might have occurred had a different judge presided over the case and the prosecution not been burdened by a tight budget and ex post facto considerations.

CONCLUSION: THE FORD PINTO CASE

The Ford Pinto trial was regularly hailed in the media as "one of the most significant criminal court trials in American corporate history" (*Newsweek,* 1980). This notoriety clearly signifies the uniqueness of the case. While Ford's prosecution was not totally devoid of legal precedents (Maakestad, 1981), it was certainly the most poignant example of a corporation being brought within the reach of the criminal law for allegedly visiting violence upon innocent citizens (Anderson, 1981). In this light, it thus provided a rare and concrete glimpse of the power that corporations can bring to bear in order to avoid conviction. Similarly, it revealed that prosecution of corporations for offenses of a product liability type will necessarily involve legal theories with which participants in the criminal justice system are only vaguely familiar and perhaps find inappropriate for their arena. Indeed, from an ideological standpoint, the potential for irony here is pronounced: We can expect conservative jurists now to be inclined to look favorably on the rights of the defendant (the corporation) and their more liberal brethren to furnish a more generous interpretation of the prerogatives enjoyed by the state. Finally, the very fact of prosecution is notable not merely for its role in bolstering formal legal precedent but in breaking psychological barriers. The legal community is now sensitized to the possibility that companies that recklessly endanger the physical well-being of the public may, even by a local state's attorney, be held criminally responsible for their conduct.

Yet the special character of the Pinto case should not mask the realization that Ford's prosecution was very much a social product. As argued earlier, the more general crusade against the Pinto, itself a manifestation of a broader movement attacking corporate crime that sought to question the appropriate moral boundaries of corporate behavior, was integral in creating the opportunity for Cosentino to prosecute Ford. In turn, this perspective suggests that the ultimate, long-range meaning of the Pinto trial may depend less on the legal precedent that has been set and more on the nature of the social context that comes to prevail. That is, will the time ahead sustain the movement against corporate crime and thus encourage attempts to build upon the Pinto prosecution, or will concern with upperworld illegality diminish any interest in criminally sanctioning corporations commensurately decline?

The answer to the question is by no means certain. To be sure, the Reagan Administration moved to reinterpret the moral character of corporate America and to officially clarify what "real" crime is (Reiman, 1979). Thus, Reagan's loosening of regulatory controls on business was accompanied by a renewed concern over violent street crimes and the trafficking of drugs; meanwhile, white-collar and corporate criminality were placed on the back burner (Cullen & Wozniak, 1982; Gordon, 1980). Notably, like many of his other social policies, Reagan's crime control agenda was informed by his implicit view of human nature: the productive respond to incentives (opportunities for profit), while the unproductive respond to punishments, thus the need for harsh sanctions for the crimes of the poor (Piven & Cloward, 1982:39).

However, these policies and the sentiments that underlie them may very well have the unanticipated consequence of fueling the public's concern over upperworld lawlessness. The ostensible failure of Reagan's domestic programs to effect promised benefits for working people made his administration susceptible to charges of injustice, an image that Democrats across the nation constantly tried to make more salient. In this climate, sensitivity to collusion between government and big business, as in the EPA incident involving the dumping of chemical wastes, should run high (*Time,* 1983). Corporate conduct should thus remain a matter of continuing public concern, and in turn it will be difficult for the state to retain legitimacy if it chooses to ignore flagrant affronts to existing moral boundaries. If this analysis is correct, we should see additional, if only intermittent, criminal prosecutions within the immediate future of corporations who persist in recklessly endangering the public's well-being.

NOTES

1. The account of the Pinto case presented here was drawn from four sources: (1) several telephone interviews by the authors with prosecutor Michael Cosentino; these were conducted in late February 1983; (2) the personal observations of one of the authors, William J. Maakestad, who served as Special Deputy Prosecuting Attorney during the case; (3) the detailed information compiled by newsman Lee Strobel (1980) in his fascinating chronicle of the case; and (4) news reports and scholarly commentary written about the trial. Please note that data taken from the talks with Cosentino is cited in the text as "Cosentino interview."

2. The estimated cost of fixing the fuel tank defect has generally been placed at $11, though the price has at times been set as low as $6. Also, it should be noted that the memo printed by Dowie in which Ford calculated the costs of fixing the Pinto versus the financial loss due to death and injury pertained to problems in the fuel tank during rollover tests conducted by Ford and not during rear-end crash tests. Nevertheless, the mode of thinking suggested by the memo vividly reinforces Dowie's point that, with regard to the Pinto, profit was more important to Ford than consumer safety.

3.   In this latter instance, Grimshaw, who had undergone over 50 operations to correct burn injuries suffered during a Pinto crash-turned-inferno, was awarded $2.8 million in compensatory damages and $125 million in punitive damages (reduced to a total of $6.6 million two weeks after the trial).

4.   Interestingly, Swigert and Farrell reached this conclusion without talking with Cosentino. Thus, while their observations were drawn from a broad understanding of the social meaning of the case, their comments captured much of what was going on inside prosecutor Consentino's mind.

5.   Berner was on the law faculty at Valparaiso. The second professor working full time on the case was Terry Kiely of DePaul University. A few other lawyers, including author William Maakestad, also volunteered substantial amounts of time at points in the case. Finally, Berner and Kiely recruited up to 15 law students to conduct research and otherwise assist the prosecution.

6.   During the course of the trial, tired members of the prosecution's team, especially the law students helping with research, would look at the post-crash photographs of the girls in order to remember what the case was really about and hence bolster their resolve to continue working.

7.   As Strobel (1980:60) noted, Neal's salary in other cases is reputed to have been as much as $800,000.

8.   The survey showed that 56 percent of the residents sampled felt that Ford was either guilty or probably guilty (Strobel, 1980:66). Interestingly, Cosentino believed that about half his community initially supported the idea of prosecuting Ford, while the other half thought he was "crazy." However, by the time of the trial, it was his perception that the vast majority of his constituents were in his camp (Cosentino interview).

REFERENCES

Anderson, D. (1981). "Corporate Homicide: The Stark Realities of Artificial Beings and Legal Fictions." *Pepperdine Law Review*, 8:367-417.

Braithwaite, J. (1979). "Transnational Corporations and Corruption: Towards Some International Solutions," *International Journal of Sociology of Law*, 7:125-142.

Braithwaite, J. (1980). "Inegalitarian Consequences of Egalitarian Reforms to Control Corporate Crime." *Temple Law Quarterly*, 53:1127-1146.

Braithwaite, J. (1982a). "Challenging Just Deserts: Punishing White Collar Criminals." *Journal of Criminal Law and Criminology*, 73 (Summer):723-763.

Braithwaite, J. (1982b). "Enforced Self-Regulation: A New Strategy for Corporate Crime Control." *Michigan Law Review*, 80 (June):1466-1507.

Braithwaite, J. & G. Geis (1982). "On Theory and Action for Corporate Crime Control." *Crime & Delinquency*, 28 (April):292-314.

Brown, M. (1980). *Laying Waste: The Poisoning of America by Toxic Chemicals*. New York: Pantheon.

Caudill, H. (1977). "Manslaughter in a Coal Mine." *Nation*, 224 (April 23):492-497.

Clark, G. (1979). "Corporate Homicide: A New Assault on Corporate Decision-Making." *Notre Dame Lawyer*, 54 (June): 911-924.

Clinard, M. & P. Yeager (1978). "Corporate Crime: Issues in Research." *Criminology,* 16 (August): 255-272.

Clinard, M. & P. Yeager (1980). *Corporate Crime.* New York: Free Press.

Clinard, M., P. Yeager, J. Brissette, D. Petrashek & E. Harries (1979). *Illegal Corporate Behavior.* Washington, DC: U.S. Government Printing Office.

Coleman, B. (1975). "Is Corporate Criminal Liability Really Necessary?" *Southwestern Law Journal*, 29:908-927.

Conklin, J. (1977). *Illegal but Not Criminal: Business Crime in America.* Englewood Cliffs, NJ: Prentice Hall.

Cullen, F. & K. Heiner (1979). "Provider Medicaid Fraud: A Note on White-Coat Crime." Presented at the annual meeting of the American Society of Criminology.

Cullen, F. & J. Wozniak (1982). "Fighting the Appeal of Repression." *Crime and Social Justice*, IX (Winter):23-33.

Cullen, F., B. Link & C. Polanzi (1982). "The Seriousness of Crime Revisited; Have Attitudes Toward White Collar Crime Changed?" *Criminology*, 20 (May): 82-102.

Cullen, F., R. Mathers, G. Clark & J. Cullen (1983). "Public Support for Punishing White Collar Crime: Blaming the Victim Revisited." *Journal of Criminal Justice,* 11(6):481-493.

Cullen, F., G. Clark, B. Link, R. Mathers, J. Lee & M. Sheahan (1982). "Dissecting White Collar Crime: Offense-Type and Punitiveness." Presented at the annual meeting of the Academy of Criminal Justice Sciences.

Dowie, M. (1977). "Pinto Madness." *Mother Jones*, (September-October):18-32.

Dowie, M. (1979). "The Corporate Crime of the Century." *Mother Jones*, (November):23-38, 49.

Duchnick, J. & M. Imhoff (1978). "A New Outlook on the White Collar Criminal as it Relates to Deterring White Collar Crime." *Criminal Justice Journal*, 2 (Winter): 57-76.

Durkheim, E. (1951). *Suicide.* New York: Free Press.

Elkins, J. (1976). "Corporations and the Criminal Law: An Uneasy Alliance," *Kentucky Law Journal*, 65: 73-129.

Erikson, K. (1966). *Wayward Puritans.* New York: John Wiley.

Farrell, R. & V. Swigert (1982). *Deviance and Social Control.* Glenview, IL: Scott, Foresman.

Fisse, B. (1971). "The Use of Publicity as a Criminal Sanction Against Business Corporations." *Melbourne University Law Review*, 8 (June):107-150.

Fisse, B. (1973). "Responsibility, Prevention, and Corporate Crime." *New Zealand University Law Review*, 5 (April):250-279.

Fisse, B. (1981). "Community Service as a Sanction Against Corporations." *Wisconsin Law Review*, (September):970-1017.

Friedrichs, D. (1979). "The Law and the Legitimacy Crisis: A Critical Issue for Criminal Justice." In R. Iacovetta & D. Chang (eds.), *Critical Issues in Criminal Justice,* pp. 290-311. Durham, NC: Carolina Academic Press.

Geis, G. (1972). "Criminal Penalties for Corporate Criminals." *Criminal Law Bulletin*, 8 (June): 377-392.

Geis, G. & H. Edelhertz (1973). "Criminal Law and Consumer Fraud: A Sociological View," *American Criminal Law Review*, 11 (Summer):989-1010.

Gordon, D. (1980). *Doing Violence to the Crime Problem: A Response to the Attorney General's Task Force.* Hackensack, NJ: NCCD.

Gusfield, J. (1967). "Moral Passage: The Symbolic Process in Public Designations of Deviance." *Social Problems*, 15 (Fall):175-188.

Kadish, S. (1963). "Some Observations on the Use of Criminal Sanctions in Enforcing Economic Regulations." *University of Chicago Law Review*, 30 (Spring):423-449.

Katz, J. (1980). "The Social Movement Against White Collar Crime." In E. Bittner & S. Messinger (eds.), *Criminology Review Yearbook,* Vol. 2, pp. 161-184. Beverly Hills: Sage.

Kramer, R. (1979). "The Ford Pinto Homicide Prosecution: Criminological Questions and Issues Concerning the Control of Corporate Crime." Presented at the annual meeting of the American Society of Criminology.

Kriesberg, S. (1976). "Decisionmaking Models and the Control of Corporate Crime." *Yale Law Journal*, 85 (July):1091-1129.

Maakestad, W. (1980). "The Pinto Case: Conceptual and Constitutional Problems in the Criminal Indictment of an American Corporation." Presented at the annual meeting of the American Business Law Association.

Maakestad, W. (1981). "A Historical Survey of Corporate Homicide in the United States: Could it be Prosecuted in Illinois?" *Illinois Bar Journal*, 69 (August):2-7.

Nader, R. & M. Green (1972). "Crime in the Suites: Coddling the Corporations." *New Republic*, 166 (April 20):18.

Newsweek (1980). "Ford's Pinto: Not Guilty." March 24:74.

Piven, F. & R. Cloward (1971). *Regulating the Poor: The Functions of Public Welfare.* New York: Pantheon.

Piven, F. & R. Cloward (1977). *Poor People's Movements: Why They Succeed, How They Fail.* New York: Pantheon.

Piven, F. & R. Cloward (1982). *The New Class War: Reagan's Attack of the Welfare State and Its Consequences.* New York: Pantheon.

Pontell, H., P. Jesilow & G. Geis (1982). "Policing Physicians: Practitioner Fraud and Abuse in a Government Medicaid Program." *Social Problems,* 30 (October):117-125.

President's Commission on Law Enforcement and Administration of Justice (1968). *Challenge of Crime in a Free Society.* New York: Avon.

Reiman, J. (1979). *The Rich Get Richer and the Poor Get Prison.* New York: John Wiley.

Rodgers, W. (1974). "IBM on Trial." *Harper's Magazine,* 248 (May):79-84.

Ross, I. (1980). "How Lawless are Big Companies?" *Fortune,* 102 (December 1):56-64.

Rothman, D. (1978). "The State as Parent: Social Policy in the Progressive Era." In W. Gaylin et al., *Doing Good: The Limits of Benevolence,* pp. 67-96. New York: Pantheon.

Schrager, L. & J. Short (1978). "Toward a Sociology of Organizational Crime." *Social Problems,* 25 (April):407-419.

Stern, G. (1976). *The Buffalo Creek Disaster.* New York: Vintage.

Strobel, L. (1980). *Reckless Homicide? Ford's Pinto Trial.* South Bend, IN: And Books.

Sudnow, D. (1965). "Normal Crimes: Sociological Features of the Penal Code in a Public Defender's Office." *Social Problems,* 12 (Winter):255-276.

Swigert, V. & R. Farrell (1980-1981). "Corporate Homicide: Definitional Processes in the Creation of Deviance," *Law & Society Review,* 15(1):171-182.

Time (1980). "Three Cheers in Dearborn." March 24:24.

Time (1983). "Superfund, Supermess." February 21:14-16.

Vandivier, K. (1972). "The Aircraft Brake Scandal." *Harper's Magazine,* 244 (April):45-52.

Wright, J. (1979). *On a Clear Day You Can See General Motors: John A. DeLorean's Look Inside the Automotive Giant.* New York: Avon.

Yoder, S. (1979). "Criminal Sanctions for Corporate Illegality." *Journal of Criminal Law and Criminology,* 69 (Spring):40-58.

DISCUSSION QUESTIONS

1. What role did the 21-year-old driver of the "peace train" van play in the events as evidenced in the Ford case? Should he have been implicated? Why or why not? Explain.

2. List some additional "corporate crimes" that are committed today that you feel should be dealt with on the criminal level?

3. Should corporations be held equally responsible for unlawful acts as compared to street criminals? If so, would the same penalties and sanctions work on white-collar criminals?

4. What features are shared by organized and white-collar criminals? How does the ideology of criminal justice policy work to obscure these similarities?

CHAPTER 19

The Corrections Corporation of America: aka The Prison Realty Trust, Inc.

Alan Mobley & Gilbert Geis

The Corrections Corporation of America (CCA) is the largest private prison entrepreneur in the United States and, undoubtedly, in the world as well. Based in Nashville, Tennessee, CCA has existed since 1983, time enough to discern a sense of its mission and its ethos and to examine its experiences. This chapter primarily considers some of the more distressing episodes in the corporate life of CCA. Part of the reason for such a focus on failure is that success stories, though they may get some passing attention, rarely capture headlines. Much more importantly, CCA is a far-flung enterprise and difficulties that have arisen in its prison operations need to be gathered together for analysis in regard to judgments concerned with the privatization of prisons.

KEY CONCEPTS:

"cherry picking"

conflict of interest

excessive force

inadequate training

inmate abuse

privatization

The record of CCA must be scrutinized with an awareness of the performance of state-run penal facilities. If government-operated correctional facilities had an even halfway decent record they would not have been as vulnerable to encroachment by groups such as CCA. State-run prisons are marked by overcrowding, inmate suicides, escapes, brutality, and explosive riots. These circumstances have given them a deservedly unsavory reputation and made them easier targets for takeover. Other considerations as well, particularly speculative cost-benefit analyses and the astounding escalation of recourse to imprisonment in the United States, have played into the emergence and growth of privatized corrections. There are, for instance, now about 1.8 million persons confined in penal facilities in the United States, a figure double the total of a decade ago.

Reprinted with permission from David Shichor and Michael J. Gilbert (eds.), *Privatization in Criminal Justice: Past, Present and Future* (Cincinnati: Anderson), 2001.

We cannot as yet provide more than faint indicia of the "success" and the "failure" of privatization on the basis of our brief case history of a particular corporate entity. For one thing, elements of such judgments hinge upon very intricate and, almost invariably, rather inconclusive comparisons, in large part because of the difficulty of locating satisfactorily equivalent representations of the two approaches to corrections. The episodes we detail below offer lessons only about possible shortcomings in the privatization approach. Whether these shortcomings are remediable and will be remedied remain open questions.

Financial issues are often at the center of the privatization debate. Complicated calculations of savings or losses to taxpayers underlie much of the discussion. Claims have been made backing both sides of the fiscal debate concerning the costs of privatization (Logan, 1992; General Accounting Office, 1996; McDonald, Fournier, Russell-Einhorn & Crawford, 1998). Although these matters can be of great concern to both citizens and shareholders, they are not considerations to which most of the following pages will be devoted. While the evidence on taxpayer savings from privatization remains mixed, the prevailing opinion continues to be that most private prisons save the state some money, at least in terms of direct outlays. Yet Douglas McDonald (1990:91), after considerable study, concluded that "the claims of the private sector's superior cost-effectiveness . . . are less robust than they might first appear." Beyond that, it can be said that the financial rewards for CCA itself have been extraordinary, indeed spectacular.

Finally, this introduction would be inadequate without our personal testimony that on ideological grounds we are opposed to private prisons and, more generally, that we are dismayed by this country's increasing reliance on imprisonment to solve what we see as pressing social problems. We would add that although we are by no means enamored with the way that state-run correctional facilities are operated, we would prefer, perhaps naively, to seek as a first recourse to reform that system rather than to turn it over to private profit-generating enterprises. Our bias may very well bear upon those things that we report and the manner in which they are reported. We shall try assiduously to keep our personal beliefs under control, but it seems essential to place them on record.

The Evolution of CCA and The Prison Realty Trust

The renaissance of private prison management has its roots in the variety of circumstances addressed in other contributions to this volume. The particular story of Corrections Corporation of America exemplifies many elements of the economic and ideological debate that has coalesced around prison privatization during the past 15 years.

Thomas W. Beasley and Doctor R. Crants, two Nashville businessmen, lawyers, and members of the 1966 West Point graduating class, founded CCA in 1983. Beasley and Crants were attracted to the field of corrections by the fact that American prisons were beleaguered by court orders mandating lower facility populations while at the same time public and political opinion was pressing toward the incarceration of a larger percentage of the American population. The ballooning ranks of prisoners was the result primarily of the increasing incarceration of nonviolent offenders, most particularly drug users who in previous times would have been enrolled in treatment programs or other alternative approaches to imprisonment. CCA entered the fray, promoting privatization as a solution: "You just sell it like you were selling cars, or real estate, or hamburgers," Beasley has said (Schlosser, 1998:70). The firm sometimes has used arguable campaign tactics to gain marketshare, stating that its main competitor, the government, "can't do anything very well" (Bates, 1999:593).

Persuaded that the era of "big government" was over, CCA's founders sensed that the approximately $35 billion spent each year in the United States on corrections represented an attractive opportunity for private business. By the end of 1989 CCA had a contracted caseload of 3,448 beds. Expansion in the 1990s was remarkably vigorous: CCA now has 71,851 beds in 81 facilities, making it the sixth largest prison system in the country. It owns and operates 44 prisons and jails and manages 35 others (PR Newswire, 1999a), employing more than 14,000 persons (Wilson, 1998).

CCA's success in acquiring contracts did not go unnoticed on Wall Street. From 1992 through 1997, CCA shares showed a compound annual growth rate of 70 percent, making the company one of the five top performers on the New York Stock Exchange (Johnston, 1998). The value of its shares rose from $50 million when it first went public in 1986 to more than $3.5 billion at its peak, which was toward the end of 1997. Crants owned 1.6 million CCA shares, while Beasley controlled well over two million (Vickers, 1999). CCA's largest stockholder—with 16 percent of the common stock—is Sodexho Alliance, a facilities management and food services conglomerate headquartered in France. Sodexho is also CCA's partner in UK Detention Services, a private prison company based in Europe. The French company also holds a majority stake in Sodexho Marriott of North America, whose board of directors includes Crants.

CCA's stock recently has moved downward. Perhaps in anticipation of this turn, just weeks before the decline in stock price Crants and Beasley sold 200,000 and 122,000 shares, respectively, saving themselves millions in losses (Corrections Corporation of America, 1998d; Schlosser, 1998). Further declines have followed since CCA shareholders approved a complicated plan that allowed the company to be merged into CCA Prison Realty Trust (PRT), a real estate investment trust, or REIT, that had been spun off by CCA into a separate company in mid-1997. REITs are corporate entities that pay no federal taxes—estimated for CCA to be about $50 million in 1998—but they are required to distribute to shareholders at least 95 percent of what would have been their taxable income (Johnston, 1998). PRT's founding president was Robert Crants III. The 28-year-old Crants is Princeton-educated, a former Goldman Sachs REIT specialist, and son of CCA Chairman Doctor Crants.

The merger was accomplished over the objections of several of the nation's largest pension funds whose managers claimed that the deal was not in the best interest of shareholders but rather that it favored company executives (Hartmann, 1998). The Prison Realty Corporation, the newly formed REIT, is publicly traded under the symbol PZN, with PrisonR its newspaper listing. One wonders if the recent acquisition by CCA of one of its competitors, U.S. Corrections Corporation, will result in the company's market listing evolving further into PRISONS-R-US.

The stock price for Prison Realty at the time of the new arrangement was in the low 30s. The company received some "buy" endorsements after analysts were told that PZN would pay CCA $400 for each bed in facilities that PZN acquired and farmed out to CCA to run. Later it was announced that the original $400 figure had been renegotiated to $4,000. PZN's stock price then cascaded downward into the low teens (Associated Press, 1999).

Company officials have also admitted that the costs to operate and develop prisons are much higher than those represented to shareholders in connection with the merger. Some people expressed puzzlement:"How the company could not have known about an $80 million shortfall is beyond me" (PR Newswire, 1999b:1). A person associated with Legg Mason Securities, said: "The way they disclosed the problem is very disappointing. It raises serious questions about the credibility of the management team. People are debating whether these guys are incompetent or thieves" (PR Newswire, 1999b:1).

Nevertheless, CCA plans to move forward and take advantage of its REIT affiliation by buying additional government-managed prisons, a strategy believed to provide a more stable, if slower growing business than the current focus on negotiating contracts to manage such facilities (Skerrert, 1998). Management chores will fall to now-private CCA, whose officers and directors are nearly indistinguishable from the REIT's. A CCA board member has declared that there is nothing for clients to fear from the corporate restructuring: "It's the same company. It's just a different way of doing business" (Thompson, 1998:B4).[1]

Lobbying for Lucrative Leverage

Soon after its formation, CCA had "achieved a certain notoriety because of its political and financial ancestry" (Ryan & Ward, 1989:13). Beasley was the former chairman of the Tennessee State Republican Party, and his new company was backed by capital supplied by the Massey Burch Investment Group, which funded the Kentucky Fried Chicken operation. Massey Burch, more relevantly, had founded the Hospital Corporation of America (HCA), which, like most HMOs, is now under almost constant consumer siege.

The blueprint for the operation of CCA generally followed much the same lines as the HMOs. Service is not to be driven by need but by cost. As one critic puts it: "Private prisons companies are more concerned with doing well than with doing good" (Robbins, 1986:25). In a 1997 prospectus, CCA was quite forthright about its overarching aims: "The Company's primary business objectives are to maximize current returns to shareholders through increases in cash flow available for distribution and to increase long-term total returns to shareholders through appreciation of the value of the Common Shares" (Prison Realty Trust, 1997:24). Costs are to be kept under control by bulk purchasing and, most importantly, by control of wages and benefits. About 60 to 80 percent of the operating costs in correctional facilities are represented by wages, and CCA routinely pays about 15 percent less than state-run facilities, though its administrators usually earn a great deal more than their state counterparts (Schlosser, 1998).

Tennessee Tactics

In 1984, a Tennessee court threatened to order the immediate release of 300 inmates from the state prison system if some arrangement to reduce violence was not put into place. The predicament worsened a year later when a policy calling for new prison uniforms with stripes along the pants legs led to disturbances throughout the system, causing $11 million in damages (Associated Press, 1985).

Seeing an opportunity where others saw disaster, CCA offered to buy the entire Tennessee prison system for $50 million down and $50 million over the next 20 years, along with another $150 million it would spend on improvements and new construction. For its operation of the prisons, CCA was to be paid from the state treasury a sum not to exceed the $175 million annual operating budget of the corrections department (Cody & Bennett, 1987). While the proposal was being considered, it was discovered that the wife of Lamar Alexander, Tennessee's governor, and Ned McWherter, the speaker of the state Assembly and later Alexander's successor as governor, had invested money in CCA and together owned 1.5 percent of the company's stock (United Press International, 1985). The list of original stockholders also included current and former Alexander cabinet officials. Conflict of interest charges led Ms. Alexander to exchange her shares for an equivalent amount of another Massey Burch-financed company. She eventually sold these for a six-figure profit (Marcus, 1995:A19). Ultimately, CCA's purchase offer was rejected by the state legislature (see further discussion in Hallett & Lee, this volume).

Today, CCA's lobbying tactics in Tennessee continue apace. The wife of the speaker of the legislature is the company's chief lobbyist in the state (Aucher, 1997), while a son of the county employee responsible for monitoring a CCA work farm near Chattanooga was put on the CCA payroll. In addition, five state officials, including the governor, the House speaker, and the sponsor of the privatization bill, are partners with Beasley in several barbecue restaurants (Bates, 1999).

Elsewhere, CCA is equally aggressive. Crants and other CCA employees have made substantial campaign contributions to Governor Tommy Thompson of Wisconsin, whose state leads the nation in prisoners outsourced to other states (Jones, 1998b:1), and to Governor Frank Keating of Oklahoma, a state where the majority of medium-security beds are in private hands (Swope, 1998). CCA broadened the scope of its political reach in 1997 when it added Joseph Johnson to its board of directors. Johnson had been a long-time Washington DC Council member and former mayoral candidate John Ray's top political strategist. Before that, he was National Campaign Manager for the presidential campaign of Governor Douglas Wilder of Virginia; and in the 1980s he served as Secretary of Health for the state of New Mexico, and Executive Director of Jesse Jackson's Rainbow Coalition. Along with his appointment to the board, Johnson was given options on 140,000 shares of company stock, at least 80,000 of which was priced at $18.25. The closing price of CCA stock the day the options were granted was $32.50, providing Johnson with an immediate windfall of more than $1 million (Corrections Corporation of America, 1998d:30). The rationale for the stock award reads as follows:

> The company granted Mr. Johnson the Option in consideration for his extensive efforts in building and facilitating the Company's business relationship with certain governmental departments, agencies, and entities. (Corrections Corporation of America, 1998d:30)

THE YOUNGSTOWN DEBACLE

Events that took place in 1997 and 1998 at CCA's Northeast Ohio Correctional Center (NOCC) in Youngstown expose a dark side of private prison management. Problems that led to violence at the facility have been detailed in a post-mortem review conducted by a committee headed by a federal government official. Among a variety of matters, the committee pinpointed the curious manner in which CCA entered into a full-service detention contract with the District of Columbia, virtually bypassing the competitive process said to be an especially advantageous aspect of prison privatization:

> The immediate need for prison bed-space by [District of Columbia Department of Corrections] officials, coupled with the desire by CCA to fill its new vacant prison facility in Ohio, led to a request for bids that . . . virtually eliminated competition (Clark, 1998, chap. 2:1).

What followed in Youngstown may be no more than a private-prison analog of the considerably more awful events that in earlier years marked the life stories of state-run prisons such as that in Attica, New York (Wicker, 1975) and Jackson, Michigan (Martin, 1954) and, more recently, at the Corcoran facility in California (Gladstone & Arax, 1999). Alternatively, Youngstown may be the result of something else, the drive by private managers to maximize profits. The escapes, murders, and assaults that plagued the Youngstown prison were blamed on inadequate numbers of staff and inexperience on the part of those staff present. It is reasonable to attribute the penny-pinching on personnel to attempts by managers to lower costs by downsizing their operation. But the brutality that followed, where guards were instructed by management to engage in violent, degrading treatment of inmates (Clark, 1998) is typical of any prison, public or private, that is out of control.

Court and financial pressures bearing upon the District of Columbia led to the decision to dismantle parts of its Lorton, Virginia correctional complex and transfer 1,700 medium-security inmates to the CCA-operated prison in Youngstown, a site said by CCA officials to be "within a reasonable distance for families to visit District inmates" (Ray, 1998:A20). We should perhaps note that 300 miles may be a reasonable distance for families with corporate-provided chauffeurs and paid-for airline trips. But for the poor families of the predominantly African-American prisoners the cost of the trip often was prohibitive. The prisoners' considerable distance from home likely was an important contributor to the trouble that exploded at NOCC.

The prison had been built for $57 million by CCA on an abandoned industrial site sold to the company by the city of Youngstown for $1. The city gave CCA a 100 percent tax abatement for three years as an additional incentive to place the prison in their economically troubled area (Clark, 1998, chap.1:2). As a sign of the prosperity to come the spanking new prison featured a sign in front displaying CCA's daily stock price.

Within 14 months of the Youngstown facility's opening there were two fatal stabbings and 47 assaults, 20 of them involving knives. Assault victims were about evenly divided among inmates and guards. The violence went unreported to local authorities but became known after some of the injured prisoners were taken to a hospital. The lack of communication between the prison and local officials occurred despite a contract provision that called for the police to investigate all serious felonies within the facility (Tatge, 1998b). One prisoner was stabbed to death by inmates who were supposed to be shackled but who had obtained keys to remove their restraints. The other murdered man, Bryson Chisely, was a medium-security prisoner housed in a segregated protective custody unit. Chisely's wife had complained to CCA officials both in Youngstown and Nashville that he was in danger. She had also written to members of the D.C. Council, telling them three weeks before her husband was slain that "he fears for his life" (Jaffe & Brooks, 1998:A8).

Shortly after CCA spokespeople declared they had things under control at Youngstown, six men escaped (all were eventually recaptured); five were convicted murderers. They had cut through two 12-foot fences and evaded surveillance cameras and a defective motion detector. An employee was believed to have helped the inmates flee (Tatge, 1998b).

The investigative report prepared for the federal Department of Justice by a team headed by D.C. Corrections Trustee John Clark faulted both the District government and CCA. The $182 million, five-year contract between D.C. and CCA was negotiated, the report indicates, at a "somewhat inflated price" and marked by "weak requirements on the contractor and minimal provisions for enforcement." District of Columbia prisoners had been transferred to Youngstown at a pace that created chaos. A total of 904 inmates had been moved in 17 days, before any policies were established and before the security system had been set up. The CCA staff was inexperienced and poorly trained, and there were few educational and work opportunities for inmates. In the words of the Clark Report: "The District's rush combined with CCA's awareness of lack of competition proved to be advantageous to the company and cost D.C. more than $27 million over the life of the contract" (Clark, 1998, chap.2:3). CCA's successful lead lobbyists on the project were John Ray, late of the D.C. Council, and Joseph Johnson.

For its part, CCA responded, as it routinely does to problems, with a practiced calmness and reassurance that glitches were to be expected, and that they would remedy them in the future. "The idea was to move folks to a much safer environment [than Lorton]," said a CCA board member. "That was all we had to achieve. We had some problems, early on problems that we have addressed and will continue to address. But we'll never be a problem-free facility" (Thompson, 1998). The former mayor of Youngstown who had helped bring CCA to the city to create job opportunities was not placated. He termed CCA the "most deceitful, dishonest corporation I have ever dealt with" (Jaffe & Brooks, 1998:A8).

CCA's public declaration failed to address the allegation that the company conspired with D.C. officials to ship numerous violent, maximum-security prisoners to Youngstown, a move at odds with the contract that permitted the transfer of only medium-security prisoners. Neither D.C. nor CCA officials at Lorton had furnished the records necessary to show that many of the men were dangerous and that some were to be separated from one another. D.C. and CCA had created a classification system for Lorton inmates that lowered some prisoners' custody level from "high" or "maximum" to "medium" and "high-medium" (Clark, 1998), a security designation heretofore unknown, but one which the colluding officials thought would legitimate transfer to NOCC. Youngstown's mayor commented: "Under this company's classification system, Jack the Ripper would be classified as medium-security" (Tatge, 1998b). The attorney representing the inmates put it another way: "Instead of removing a lot of maximum-security inmates, they have just called them something else" (Tatge, 1998a:5B). An independent consultant appointed by the courts found that 319 of the 1,700 inmates were incorrectly classified. For their part, CCA had willingly accepted all comers to NOCC, well aware that the more beds it filled the greater would be its profit.

Unsound correctional practices as detailed in the Clark Report were surely at the root of the NOCC fiasco, but how such a situation was allowed to develop remains a point of contention between CCA leaders and Youngstown city officials. NOCC is a state-of-the-art facility planned as a showpiece for the CCA way of corrections. An accreditation team of the American Correctional Association had given the facility a near perfect rating, even with the mayhem of the first 15 months. Company officials hoped that the 1,700 D.C. inmates sent to NOCC would be but a first installment, since the entire Lorton complex of prisons had to be closed by December 31, 2001. A creditable showing at NOCC would have put CCA in the driver's seat to essentially assume control of D.C. corrections and to prove that it could do what it proposed all along—operate a jurisdiction's complete correctional system.

JOLTS IN OTHER JURISDICTIONS

Youngstown was not the only CCA trouble spot, though it was the most egregious. The need for CCA to keep up its image in order to retain and obtain business can on occasion lead to controversial and seemingly self-serving (rather than socially desirable) tactics.

Tennessee

CCA has been sued for inmate abuse, including the misuse of electric stun guns at its Whiteville, Tennessee facility. Allegations of excessive force against Wisconsin prisoners housed at Whiteville were repeatedly and vehemently denied by CCA until a Wisconsin state delegation investigating the matter uncovered convincing evidence. In response, CCA admitted wrongdoing and dismissed eight employees, including the prison's director of security. Wisconsin officials have asked the FBI to investigate a cover-up (Jones, 1998a:1).

CCA's reticence to own up to problems or to allow oversight at Whiteville would come as no surprise to Ohio authorities. When two legislators in that state tried to go into the NOCC to make a spot inspection, prison employees refused them entry because a pair of Ohio corrections officers were accompanying them. The incident led one lawmaker to observe sarcastically: "Turns out it's a lot easier for prisoners to get out than for the lawmakers to get in" (Turnbull, 1998:2A).

In another incident, in mid-1998 CCA abruptly transferred inmate Alex Friedmann from its lockup in Clifton, Tennessee. Friedmann said that he had been accused of "efforts to degrade CCA with negative articles" published in "outside sources" (Bates, 1998a:5). The CCA warden thought he had his finger on the problem: "Alex is intelligent," the warden said, "but once he gets in his mind that something's wrong, he's going to hit it with a vengeance, forever and ever, amen." Friedmann's sin was that he had been quoted in a cover story published in *The Nation* (Bates, 1999) that criticized CCA's operation of the facility. He lost an appeal seeking administrative remedy on the grounds that he had made "a deliberate effort to disseminate material which is negatively oriented to the prison operating company," apparently something not to be tolerated by CCA, despite First Amendment guarantees (Bates, 1998a).

The Friedmann incident is especially interesting as it mirrors a much-publicized event marring the otherwise exemplary career of the current CEO of CCA, J. Michael Quinlan. Quinlan was director of the Federal Bureau of Prisons from 1987 to 1992 under presidents Reagan and Bush. Shortly before the 1988 presidential election, an inmate at the federal prison in El Reno, Oklahoma contacted media sources alleging that he once sold marijuana to Bush's vice-presidential running mate, Dan Quayle. Nina Totenberg, a correspondent for National Public Radio, got in touch with members of Quayle's staff regarding the inmate's charge. They maintained that there was no truth in the report. A senior Quayle advisor then called Quinlan to discuss the matter. Soon after, the inmate, Brett Kimberlain, was placed in administrative segregation and held incommunicado until after the election. Quinlan insisted that political motives played no part in his decision to order Kimberlain segregated. He said that he was told Kimberlain feared for his safety and that the transfer to protective custody had been at his own request. Both Kimberlain and Totenberg refute Quinlan's account. An investigation of the matter by the inspector general of the Justice Department concluded that the extraordinary intervention of the bureau's chief in disciplining an inmate was inappropriate (Isikoff, 1991:A3). Quinlan resigned his post as director before the inspector general's report was made public, citing health reasons (Ostrow, 1992:A39).

North Carolina

The high business tide upon which CCA has been riding can be illustrated by its experiences in North Carolina. The company contracted to build a facility in rural Pimlico County, near the Atlantic Ocean coast, and another in the mountains on the Mitchell-Avery county line. The rationale for going private offered by a Republican state representative is the usual one: "The private sector can provide services and facilities at much less cost to the taxpayer and provide the same level of service" (Gray, 1998:1). The legislator also noted that the innovations wrought by CCA can impel improved state procedures; thus, the state, following CCA's lead, had begun to use preset concrete and steel cells, making construction cheaper than when done with more traditional methods.

The peculiar aspect of the North Carolina CCA involvement is that the state does not have run-down hellholes for prisons nor is there a public employee union whose wage levels can be undercut. The Department of Corrections runs a most unusual operation, one that not only pays for itself, but contributes about $1 million a year to the general fund and $500,000 to the program to compensate crime victims. But as often has been the case, CCA negotiated a notably sweet deal, stipulating that the state will assign to its facilities only able-bodied inmates who are willing to work. "They're not obliged to take mad or mean convicts or sick ones," complained one state prison superintendent. "If I can go through and pick the best prisoners, I can run a cheap prison too" (Gray, 1998:1).

Others have seconded concerns with "cherry picking," and accuse CCA of taking in only the healthiest and most docile inmates. "When a prisoner falls ill or proves troublesome, CCA simply ships him back into a state-run prison, where the bill is picked up by taxpayers instead of company share-holders" (Bates, 1999:598). Not only can this selection process make the operation of CCA prisons less costly, but facilities can be rendered less hazardous places in which to work and to "do time." This practice would surely produce a noticeable disparity between the quality of CCA and public institutions, with public facilities finding themselves in an ever more precarious predicament because of the congregation inside their walls of the most needy and aggressive inmates.

CCA apparently plans on plucking not just the "best" prisoners from public penal systems, but the best prisons as well. As mentioned earlier, the new Prison Realty REIT has as its goal the acquisition of penal facilities, primarily those now publicly owned. By purchasing the best prisons and stocking them with the least costly prisoners, CCA stands poised to outperform public facilities in terms of cost and safety. As older, more hazardous government-operated prisons become ever more expensive to run, CCA will be able to portray itself as an efficiency-oriented, cost-cutting corporate savior, instead of, as some view it, as a politically savvy and highly skilled poacher of prisons, extracting the pick of state correctional systems.

CCA facilities might then be used as rewards for cooperative prisoners, even as the company verges on becoming the gilded revolving door through which state-trained prison workers pass. Kathleen Hawk, the present director of the Federal Bureau of Prisons, recently voiced to Congress her concerns over the potential departure of a large percentage of the bureau's executive staff (Hawk, 1995). The latest case of a senior civil officer leaving for the private-prison sector is the early retirement of Percy Pitzer, a 48-year-old warden. Pitzer became the new head of CCA's troubled Whitcville, Tennessee facility (Jones, 1998a:1). Michael Quinlan, Hawk's predecessor, traded his $123,100 annual salary for a CCA compensation package that included $3 million in stock (Hallihan, 1997:A26).

Healthcare: Florida, Tennessee, and Ohio

The attempt by CCA to avoid paying medical costs is indicated by a 1994 arrangement under which prisoners in the Hernando County Jail in Florida had to bear the expense for their own healthcare. The money was taken from a prisoner's account; if the inmate had no funds he left prison with a debt that the county could seek to collect by seizing property or other assets. This procedure was said by the resident prison doctor to encourage inmates "to find the most appropriate way to treat their problems. They learn to treat minor medical conditions [themselves] and to seek professional care when necessary" (Stern, 1998:41-42).

A Tennessee contract with CCA bars prisoners with AIDS from being sent to a CCA facility and places a $4,000 per inmate cap on medical services; if the cost is greater the excess has to be paid by the state (Aucher, 1997). In regard to the CCA facility at Clifton, Tennessee, the mother of a deceased 28-year-old inmate claims CCA reduced its average daily medical care costs from $3.07 per inmate per day in 1994 to $1.68 per inmate per day in 1997. The facility's medical expenses stayed the same during that period—around $1 million—even though the inmate population grew from 1,000 to 1,500 (Associated Press, 1998c).

In addition, 250 of the first 900 prisoners to enter NOCC at Youngstown in its first 17 days required chronic health care treatment for ailments such as asthma, HIV, diabetes, high blood pressure, and heart disease. Not a single prisoner was turned away by CCA even though the medical department was overwhelmed by the pace of new arrivals and incapable of meeting their healthcare needs (Clark, 1998:21).

South Carolina

State officials refused to renew a contract with CCA to run a juvenile detention facility when child welfare advocates claimed that the company's employees were mistreating some boys and had confined as many as 18 in a one-person cell where they had only cups for toilets. One boy was said to have been hog-tied on at least 30 occasions. CCA has filed a suit in court seeking to recover $12 million it spent to renovate the facility and build wilderness camps. Said a CCA spokesperson, "We did the best that could be done under the circumstances. We're proud that we prevented South Carolina from paying substantial fines" (*Corrections Professional*, 1997:2).

Texas Tribulations

CCA's Houston Processing Center for suspected illegal immigrants, with a design capacity for 411 beds, also brings into question the quality of the facilities that the corporation creates and runs. The Houston Center was built in April 1984 and represents CCA's first design, construction, and management contract. The following sketch, though perhaps telling, has to be read with some caution, since it is the product of a site visit by members of the British Prison Officers' Association, hardly a neutral source:

> The inmates were . . . in large dormitories each containing between 540 and 600 beds with no privacy whatsoever, no lockers, no screening around toilets or showers which were open to view by both male and female staff. . . . The few officers we saw were scruffy and thug-like in appearance. . . . [W]e have never witnessed such shocking conditions, which considering the state of some of our prisons, is a terrible condemnation. . . . We have never seen so many prisoners obviously confused and despairing. (Ryan & Ward, 1989:49-50)

The British report might be seen as a warning sign regarding what was to occur later, when two sex offenders escaped from the facility. One of the two escapees was serving time for sexual abuse, the other for beating and rape of an 88-year-old woman. They climbed a fence topped with razor-wire and, once outside, assaulted a guard and stole his car.

CCA had sought to increase the Houston's facility's population (and profitability) when it found itself receiving fewer immigrant detainees. On its own initiative, CCA brought in 244 sex offenders from Oregon—"some of the worst Oregon had," according to one Texas legislator (Turner, 1996:33). State and local officials were unaware of the transfers, since the facility previously housed only federal offenders. "Who the hell would have thought that someone would do something like this?" a Texas state legislator said, referring to the Oregon transportees (Bardwell, 1996:1).

Meanwhile, in 1996, at the 1,000 bed CCA-run facility in Eden, Texas, a disturbance led to the injury of 17 persons. The inmates said that they were protesting against poor food, inadequate recreation, and what they regarded as other subpar institutional conditions (Turner, 1996). Pressure to provide decent arrangements and still come in under budget has apparently been too much for CCA at some of its Texas facilities. The company recently announced that it is in the process of closing three of them (Hallihan, 1998).

ISSUES OF EVALUATION

Social science and economic evaluations of the consequences of prison privatization presents a formidable challenge. As Adrian James and his colleagues aptly observe: "[T]here are no simple and yet truthful answers which encompass the myriad of complex practical, moral and theoretical questions raised by an initiative such as contracting-out . . . not least because the data are open to various interpretations" (James, Bottomley, Liebling & Clare, 1997:169). John Donahue adds a point particularly relevant to our scrutiny of the activities of CCA:

> Ideologically fervent commentators of every political stripe too often
> neglect . . . [the fact] that no set of studies can prove any universal
> assertion about either public or private institutions. . . . The best that
> any empirical survey can hope for is to find some suggestive ten-
> dency in the way the evidence falls (Donahue, 1989:57).

In an early attempt to quantify the relative advantages of private and public prisons, Charles Logan measured 333 indicators of quality of confinement. He derived his numerical evidence from institutional records and
surveys of inmates and staff at two New Mexico facilities, one run by CCA,
and the federal institution at Alderson, West Virginia. All three prisons
held female inmates and were deemed to be "of high quality." The private
CCA-operated facility was said to have "outperformed its governmental counterparts on nearly every dimension" (Logan, 1992:577).

Logan's findings have been called into question by critics (Ryan, 1997).
Furthermore, the New Mexico Department of Corrections later accused
CCA of overcharging the state nearly $2 million for its running of the facil-
ity. It did so, the New Mexico officials said, by including in its $95 fee for
each inmate each day $22 that represented debt service. It was also charged
that the women inmates in CCA's New Mexico facility lost good time credits at a rate nearly eight times higher than men in the state-run facility
(Bates, 1999). As Jerome Miller says, "The problem is all the incentive in
privately run prisons is to keep them full and to get as many people in
there for as long as possible" (Hammack, 1995:G1).

Although Logan himself lists shortcomings of his study that might render the findings suspect, he is unwilling to touch the issue of recidivism, that
is, the success experienced by inmates in the different facilities upon their
release. He offers this defense of his decision to bypass outcome measures:

> The criteria proposed here for comparative evaluation of prisons
> are normative, rather than consequentialist or utilitarian. They
> are based on a belief that individual prisons ought to be judged pri-
> marily according to the propriety and quality of what goes on inside
> their walls—factors over which prison officials may have con-
> siderable control (Logan, 1992:579).

He adds: "It is neither fair nor methodologically feasible to compare
Prison A with Prison B in terms of external outcome—that is, in terms of each
one's relative contribution to crime control" (Logan, 1992:579). It is this
methodological complexity that leads us to regard skeptically the purported
first-ever recidivism study comparing private and state-facilities. This study
found both a lower re-offending rate and less serious offenses after one year
for inmates released from private compared to public facilities (Lanza-
Kaduce, Parker & Thomas, 1999). Aside from the overly short time span of
the study, it takes for granted the problematic equivalence of the facilities.
In addition, the Florida Ethics Commission ruled that one of the authors,

Charles Thomas, had a conflict of interest in his work on private prisons. He has or will receive more than $3 million in cash, stock options, and fees for serving on the Prison Realty Trust Board of Trustees (for further details see Geis, Mobley & Shichor, 1999).

The matter of recidivism measurement is not, however, unfeasible methodologically. It can be carried out rather elegantly by recourse to random assignment, the most powerful experimental tool science possesses. A pool of eligibles can be created on a random basis: Prisoner A can be placed in a private prison and Prisoner B in the state-run facility to which it is being compared. There inevitably will be glitches in the purity of the design (knowledge that their assignment was randomly determined, for instance, may disproportionately affect the members of one or the other group). Also, of course, such work takes time for the outcome to become known. We suspect that recidivism may not differ greatly between private and state run institutions, but we are not certain. There are hypotheses that cut both ways. Some say, for instance, that juvenile recidivism is encouraged when locked-up delinquents discover that they can manage quite well in an affable institution; the obverse is that less indulgent facilities create a stronger sense of not desiring to repeat the experience.

STAFFING PRIVATE PRISONS

CCA officials and spokespersons often insist that staffing difficulties, common enough in any pioneering endeavor, lay at the root of difficulties that the company has experienced at various sites. They maintain that such things as staff inexperience are no more than a temporary difficulty that in time will be resolved.

It is arguable, however, whether CCA staff difficulties represent only a short-term problem. Staffing issues are crucial to CCA and all private prison companies since personnel costs are at the core of the industry's profitability. Private prisons aim to operate more cheaply than public prisons by lowering costs, especially labor costs which, as noted earlier, account for approximately 60 to 80 percent of total expenses (Schlosser, 1998). This can be done in three ways: (a) by employing fewer workers than state prisons; (b) by paying the same or a similar number of workers less; or (c) by doing both simultaneously. Any of these approaches can exacerbate long-standing problems of prison management.

Employing fewer workers per shift is standard procedure for CCA operations. Technology allows a very small number of guards to oversee large prison populations, but only if prisoner movement is tightly constrained. In CCA's Youngstown facility, for example, a typical day found inmates contained in their two-man cells, within the dayrooms of 36-man pods, or within recreation areas along with the 216 men from their adjacent housing units (Clark, 1998). Using such tactics, even a prison of 2,000 or more inmates theoretically can be managed with no more difficulty than a jail with a 200-person population. Such a high level of containment over a prolonged term, however, breeds apathy, despair, and violence (Johnson & Toch, 1982).

The alternative, employing a higher number of less well-paid staff, permits a more fluid prison operation, as larger numbers of prisoners can be set in motion simultaneously while appropriate levels of staff supervision are maintained. This approach both permits and demands activities to fill idle hands and minds, and it makes the orderly running of the institution more dependent on staff personnel, particularly on line staff, and less reliant on architecture and technology.

More of a human touch increases the options available for programming, work assignments, and other activities, but it also looms as a potential liability. Employees often are responsible for the illegalities that transpire behind prison walls. Staff members import drugs, weapons, escape tools, and other contraband into prison facilities, and staff allow prisoners to engage in officially proscribed activities, such as the sanctioned killings recently reported at a California state facility (Gladstone & Arax, 1999:A3). Persons from all social classes and of all caliber working in prisons have proven vulnerable to being corrupted by the near absolute power of their positions (Haney & Zimbardo, 1998). Poorly trained and poorly paid employees of CCA prisons must surely be prone to such potentially deadly mischief.

Systems such as the Federal Bureau of Prisons have tried to lessen the allure of employee opportunism by paying staff relatively well, offering benefits representative of the middle-class, and by promoting an inclusive "bureau family" atmosphere. Staff members who see the bureau as a career and not transient employment probably stand a much better chance of resisting temptations. Nonetheless, even prisons and prison systems offering the highest wages have great difficulty retaining employees. No doubt it is the nature of the work (not just the stigma of it) that drives people away. What then can the likes of CCA expect from line staff? Paltry wages, few benefits, and no retirement plan do not command much loyalty in today's economy, particularly when the work is so difficult and potentially dangerous.

CCA no doubt expects very high rates of staff turnover, meaning that CCA prisons may be perpetually manned by inexperienced crews. Since acute prison problems such as assaults, riots, brutality, and homicides are often the result of poor decisions made by inexperienced staff unfamiliar with procedures, institution staff may emerge as CCA's greatest liability. It is a curious situation where prison managers are compelled by their corporate responsibilities to see prisoners as capital assets and employees as costly threats to corporate profitability.

Conclusion

An examination of prisons operated by CCA involves, at its heart, consideration of the real and possible virtues and deficits of the two major economic and ideological positions of our times, capitalism and state socialism. Scrutiny of the achievements and setbacks of CCA obviously cannot resolve that larger and formidable debate, which at its core is both a moral and an empirical issue. But it can provide information bearing upon it, and can offer facts and judgments that might be relevant to legislative enactments, court decisions, and public attitudes concerning private prison operation.

On one side of the ideological battlefield stands the extraordinarily powerful critical analysis of the dynamics of capitalism propounded by Karl Marx and Friedrich Engels. Put into the context of responsibility for prison management, it insists that the press of private enterprise inevitably and inexorably will be toward exploiting those it employs and supervises. In prisons, profit-driven corporate employers will tend to look to their own benefit when negotiating staff size, experience, salaries, and benefits, and the maintenance expense of prisoners. Every cent saved is a cent that reflects favorably on the managers and contributes to an escalation of corporate profits and the enhanced wealth of stockholders.

Shareholders likely will know little and care less about how the private prisons are operated. Profits are regarded as their rightful reward for having risked their money in the hope that the organization they bought into will pay off. Such profits, going into the pockets of private citizens, are not seen as subtracting from either prison or public funds but rather are regarded as a consequence of savings achieved by operational skill and intelligence. Private prison corporations have been able to ignore the need for voter approval for bond issues to build new prisons. If the public were directly confronted with the fact that punitive penal policies were being paid for by increasingly heavy burdens on their personal incomes, they might well re-examine their support of such policies. As it is, CCA and other companies allow legislatures to have prisons built, still at public expense, but without public consideration and formal approval.

There are, of course, limits beyond which profit-making cannot reach. Wages and benefits, for instance, must be enough to attract reasonably competent workers. Prisoners may not have the status of medical patients at health maintenance organizations who can stir up a mountain of agitation if they believe they are being ill treated. But, though unable to vote and carrying a social stigma, prisoners nonetheless must be kept sufficiently satisfied so that they do not riot or otherwise call attention to what they may see as inadequacies of the private regime (Sykes, 1957).

If a profit is made from the operation of government-operated prisons (and that is unlikely), that sum would be returned to the state to be used to upgrade prisons, or, more likely, to be incorporated into the government's general operating budget. There is no notable incentive in public prisons to be particularly careful, much less adventuresome, in regard to the reduction of expenses and the burden of work. Prison staff typically unionize and press for the best working arrangements that negotiations can secure. Prisoners, under this arrangement, remain relatively powerless unless they adopt attention-gathering (and dangerous) tactics to seek to call attention to and gain sympathy for what they regard as unacceptable conditions.

Free-market economic theories suggest that CCA will continue to improve its operations and remedy failures out of its own corporate self-interest. But CCA appears to have a marked predilection to repeat the mistakes of its past. Although it operates one of the largest prison systems in the country, it discourages the circulation among its institutions of written reports detailing problem areas. Lapses in security, escapes, management blunders, and even circumstances leading to injury and death are later repeated in other institutions because of this lack of communication.

An incident involving Washington DC inmates transferred from Ohio to another CCA facility provides a chilling example. In August 1998, five months after the Chisely killing, two inmates who were supposed to be separated from one another were housed on the same tier and removed from their cells at the same time. Both produced weapons and one, Corey Smith, was killed. The survivor had removed his handcuffs, presumably through the use of a tool, and attacked the other. How could a homicide so remarkably similar to one at Youngstown occur? The answer lies in the fact that CCA took no steps to warn receiving prisons about the strategies peculiar to the most violent D.C. prisoners. Not only does the company prohibit the dissemination of reports following mishaps, corporate policy forbids the very writing of such reports out of a concern that written documents could be used in litigation (Clark, 1998, chap. 7:3).

This bottom-line-oriented policy almost surely permitted what the Clark Report (1998, chap. 2:16) called "a carbon copy . . . of the Chisely case." Other maximum-security inmates shipped from Youngstown attacked and beat five guards at the CCA Estancia, New Mexico prison. That institution, like Youngstown, was said to be intended only for minimum- and medium-security inmates (Beyerlein, 1998). But perhaps the most distressing incident occurred at the Clifton, Tennessee CCA site, where four inmates convicted of crimes such as rape and murder escaped into the surrounding community. They fled through holes cut in both perimeter fences while on the recreation yard in a re-enactment of the mass escape at Youngstown. Once again a staff member, this time a supervisor, is suspected of facilitating the escape (Warren, 1998).

The following quote epitomizes the way in which CCA presents itself in a press release: "A safe and secure correctional environment for staff, inmates and the community is paramount at ALL CCA facilities, all of which have numerous features designed to provide that secure environment" (Tatge, 1998c:4B).

The evidence that we have accumulated in this chapter indicates that in many respects the company has seriously failed to realize the goals that it claims to have set for itself. The Clark Report tells how it views CCA's work to date: "[CCA] has not demonstrated the capability to identify and correct its own problems. Numerous major changes have been spurred primarily in reaction to intervening negative events or external forces" (Clark, 1999, chap. 7:4).

Prisons may be a "necessary evil" to hold captive persons who truly represent a serious threat to other human beings, people who deserve better. In the United States, we seem to have concluded, senselessly, that the only cure for the maladies that are characteristic of prisons are more prisons. We have failed to attend to the horrors of imprisonment and to the fact that there are more effective and more decent alternatives. Private companies see prisons as a source of financial profit, with their income dependent on a flourishing trade in more prisons and more prisoners. If the early history of CCA is a fair indication, the movement to privatize prisons will only worsen rather than relieve a problem desperately in need of correction, and not a euphemistic parody of the term.

ENDNOTE

[1]   See Chapter 3 in [Shichor, D. & M.J. Gilbert (2001). *Privatization in Criminal Justice: Past, Present and Future*. Cincinnati: Anderson] for later developments.

REFERENCES

Associated Press (1985). "Prison Damage Set at $11 Million." *New York Times*, (July 4):A9.

Associated Press (1998, September 6). "Mother of Dead Inmate Among CCA's Growing List of Critics." *Regional News, AM Cycle*. [Online: LEXIS-NEXIS Academic Universe, *http://web.lexis-nexis.com* as of September 29, 1999].

Associated Press (1999, May 18). "Prison Realty Stock Plummets Amid Increased Jail Costs." *Regional News, AM Cycle*. [Online: LEXIS-NEXIS Academic Universe, *http://web.lexis-nexis.com* as of September 29, 1999].

Aucher, R. (1997). "Activists Cow to Defeat Prison Privatization." *Executive Intelligence Review*, 29 (December 12):61-64.

Bardwell, S.K. (1996). "Local Private Jail Begins Moving Oregon Inmates." *Houston Chronicle*, (August 10):A-1.

Bates, E. (1998). "Prisons for Profit." *The Nation*, 266:5.

Bates, E. (1999). "Prisons for Profit." In K. Haas & G.P. Alpert (eds.), *The Dilemmas of Corrections: Contemporary Readings*, 4th ed. Prospect Heights, IL: Waveland.

Beyerlein, T. (1998). "Senator: Prison Company Lied." *Dayton Daily News*, (August 13):1B.

Clark, J.L. (1998). *Report to the Attorney General: Inspection and Review of the Northeast Ohio Correctional Center.* Washington, DC: Office of the Corrections Trustee (November 25).

Cody, W.J.M. & A.D. Bennett. (1987). "The Privatization of Correctional Institutions: The Tennessee Experience." *Vanderbilt Law Journal,* 40:829-849.

Corrections Corporation of America (1998). *Proxy Statement.* Washington, DC: Securities and Exchange Commission.

Corrections Professional (1997). "South Carolina Ends CCA Contract, Learns Slow Approach Needed." *LRP Publications,* (May 23):*2.*

Donahue, J. (1989). *The Privatization Decision: Public Ends, Private Means.* New York, NY: Basic Books.

Geis, G., Mobley, A. & D. Shichor (1999). "Private Prisons, Criminological Research, and Conflict of Interest: A Case Study." *Crime & Delinquency,* 45(3):372-388.

General Accounting Office (1986, August). *Private and Public Prisons—Studies Comparing Operational Cost and the Quality of Services.* Washington, DC: GAO.

Gladstone, M. & M. Arax (1999). "State to Form Special Unit to Probe Prison Guards." *Los Angeles Times,* (February 2):A1, A3.

Gray, T. (1998). "What Happens When State Loses Its Locks on Prisons: Transfer of Prison Control to Private Corporations." *Raleigh News and Observer,* (November 10):1, 12.

Hallihan, J.T. (1997). "Private Prisons Go Public with Bang." *New Orleans Times Picayune,* (August 17):A26.

Hallihan, J.T. (1998). "Private Prisons Not Saving: Strapped Company Closing Three in Texas." *New Orleans Times Picayune,* (December 31):A10.

Hammack, L. (1995). "Profit Behind Bars." *Roanoke Times and World News,* (February 26):G1.

Haney, C. & P. Zimbardo (1998). "The Past and Future of United States Prison Policy." *American Psychologist,* 73:709-725.

Hawk, K. (1995, June 8). *Testimony Before the House Subcommittee on Crime, Committee on the Judiciary.* Washington, DC: Federal Document Clearing House.

Isikoff, M. (1991). "Inmate Who Claimed to Be Quayle's Drug Dealer Presses Rights Case." *Washington Post,* (November 19):A3.

Jaffe, G. & R. Brooks (1998). "Violence at Prison Run by Corrections Corp. Irks Youngstown, Ohio." *Wall Street Journal,* (August 5):A1, A8.

James, A., A.K. Bottomley, A. Liebling & E. Clare (1997). *Privatizing Prisons: Rhetoric and Reality.* London: Sage.

Johnson, R. & H. Toch (eds.) (1982). *The Pains of Imprisonment.* Beverly Hills, CA: Sage.

Jones, R.P. (1998a). "State Now Admits Private Prison Abuse." *Milwaukee Journal Sentinel,* (November 11):1.

Jones, R.P. (1998b). "Legislators to Visit Private Prison." *Milwaukee Journal Sentinel*, (November 12):1.

Lanza-Kaduce, L., K.F. Parker & C.W. Thomas (1999). "A Comparative Recidivism Analysis of Releases from Private and Public Prisons." *Crime & Delinquency*, 45:28-47.

Logan, C.H. (1992). "Well Kept: Comparing Quality of Confinement in Private and Public Prisons." *Journal of Criminal Law and Criminology*, 83(3):577-613.

Marcus, R. (1995). "Ventures During Public Service Multiplied Net Worth by 10." *Washington Post*, (February 26):A19.

Martin, J.B. (1954). *Break Down the Walls*. New York: Ballantine.

McDonald, D.C. (1990). "The Cost of Operating Public and Private Correctional Facilities." In D.C. McDonald (ed.), *Private Prisons and Public Interests*. New Brunswick, NJ: Rutgers University Press.

McDonald, D.C., E. Fournier, M. Russell-Einhorn & S. Crawford (1998). *Private Prisons in the United States: An Assessment of Current Practices*. Cambridge, MA: Abt Associates.

Ostrow, R. (1992). "Federal Prison Chief Expected to Resign Soon Due to Illness." *Los Angeles Times*, (December 4):A39.

PR Newswire (1999a). "PZN Finalizes Merger with CCA." *PR Newswire Association*, (January 4):1.

PR Newswire (1999b). "Wolf Popper LLP Accuses Prison Realty Trust Inc. of Securities Violations." *PR Newswire Association*, (June 3):1-2.

Prison Realty Trust (1997, July 15). *Prospectus: 18,500,000 Shares*. Nashville: Author.

Ray, J. (1998). "Contracting out Corrections (Letter to the Editor)." *Washington Post*, (April 3):A-20.

Robbins, I.P. (1986). "Privatization of Corrections: Defining the Issues." *Federal Probation*, 50 (September):24-30.

Ryan, M. (1997). "Review: The State of Our Prisons." *British Journal of Criminology*, 37:300.

Ryan, M. & T. Ward (1989). *Privatization and the Penal System: The American Experience and the Debate in Britain*. Milton Keynes, UK: Open University Press.

Schlosser, E. (1998). "The Prison Industrial Complex." *The Atlantic Monthly*, 282 (6):51-77.

Skerrett, J. (1998). "Corrections Corp. Firm Joins with Affiliate in REIT Bid." *Chicago Tribune*, (April 21):2A.

Stern, V. (1998). *A Sin Against the Future: Imprisonment in the World*. Boston: Northeastern University Press.

Swope, C. (1998). "The Inmate Bazaar." *Congressional Quarterly DBA Governing Magazine*, (October):18.

Sykes, G. (1957). *The Society of Captives*. Princeton, NJ: Princeton University Press.

Tatge, M. (1998a). "Judge to Rule on Youngstown Prison Security Issue." *Cleveland Plain Dealer*, (July 17):5B.

Tatge, M. (1998b). "More CCA Prison Assaults Revealed." *Cleveland Plain Dealer*, (August 18):5B.

Tatge, M. (1998). "Transferred Inmates Attack New Mexico Guards." *Cleveland Plain Dealer*, (September 2):4B.

Thompson, C. (1998). "D.C. Prisoner Transfer Faulted." *Washington Post*, (December 5):B1.

Turnbull, L. (1998). "Breakout Spurs Talk of Prison Closing." *Columbus Dispatch*, (July 27):1A, 2A.

Turner, A. (1996). "Feds to Review Handling or Riot at Texas Prison." *Houston Chronicle*, (August 23):A33.

United Press International (1985). "McWherter Sells Stock in CCA, Honey Alexander Undecided." *Regional News, AM Cycle,* April 12.

Vickers, T. (1999). *Insider Trading.* Available at: http://www.vickers-stock.com

Warren, B. (1998). "Prison Official Fired as Escape Probe Continues." *The Tennessean*, (October 22):A1.

Wicker, T. (1975). *A Time to Die*. New York: Quadrangle/New York Times Book Co.

Wilson, J. (1998). "CCA Firm Celebrates Growth at Silverdale Anniversary Event." *Chattanooga News Free-Press*, (October 16):A-4.

DISCUSSION QUESTIONS

1. How have politics played a role in the emergence and growth of private corrections?

2. Define "cherry picking." How can this selection process affect evaluation outcomes of private versus public corrections?

3. List three potential problems concerning staff at private correctional facilities.

4. What are the major differences between private and public corrections?

5. Based upon your understanding of private corrections, what do you think the future holds for privatization in corrections?

CHAPTER 20

Ethics and Criminal Justice Research

Belinda R. McCarthy & Robin J. King

No area of life or work is free of ethical dilemmas, and the field of research is no exception. In recent years a number of scandals surrounding the professional behavior of academic researchers have made newspaper headlines and stirred government inquiries. Academic researchers have been charged with falsifying data to obtain additional research funding and to falsify publication of results.

Of a different nature, a conflict within a sociology department at Texas A&M University has left faculty choosing sides in a nasty dispute (*Chronicle of Higher Education*, 1999). Three professors have accused each other of plagiarism and theft of data. While no amicable resolutions have been made, the department has suffered a major public relations blow. The incident escalated to a degree requiring investigation by the university, the National Science Foundation, and the American Sociological Association (*Chronicle of Higher Education*, 1999).

> **KEY CONCEPTS:**
>
> **codes of ethics**
>
> **coercing participation**
>
> **confidentiality**
>
> **privacy**
>
> **randomization**
>
> **self-determination**
>
> **willingness to participate**

A noted criminologist was investigated by the Florida Commission on Ethics when it was disclosed that he had been paid millions of dollars by private corrections firms while simultaneously being paid via a contract as an academic consultant (*Miami Herald*, 1999). The professor admitted that his involvement in both research projects was a conflict of interest (*Miami Herald*, 1999).

The issue of plagiarism in academic publication is an area that deserves much attention in the literature. Published research has the potential to influence the conduct of practitioners and policy within criminal justice and other social professions (Jones, 1999). Thus, it is imperative that criminal justice researchers are conscious of these potential pressures when disseminating results from research projects.

One might think that scientific endeavors, with their objective and unbiased approach to the world, would create fewer dilemmas than other occupational activities. Although most researchers are not faced with the same kind of corrupting influences confronting street-level criminal justice officials, the pressures of "grantsmanship" and publication provide significant motivations. The dilemmas of working with human subjects in a political environment are equally challenging. Moreover, the goal of scientific purity, of unbiased objectivity, may be corrupting as well, as researchers are tempted to put scientific objectives before their concern for the welfare of others.

In this chapter we will examine the nature of ethical dilemmas confronting the criminal justice researcher. To a large degree these problems are comparable to those difficulties faced by other social scientists. Additional problems arise as a result of the particular focus of research on deviance and law-breaking.

PROBLEMS INVOLVING WORK WITH HUMAN SUBJECTS

Stuart Cook (1976) lists the following ethical considerations surrounding research with human subjects:

1. Involving people in research without their knowledge or consent.

2. Coercing people to participate.

3. Withholding from the participant the true nature of the research.

4. Deceiving the research participant.

5. Leading the research participants to commit acts which diminish their self-respect.

6. Violating the right to self-determination: research on behavior control and character change.

7. Exposing the research participant to physical or mental stress.

8. Invading the privacy of the research participant.

9. Withholding benefits from participants in control groups.

10. Failing to treat research participants fairly and to show them consideration and respect (p. 202).

INVOLVING PEOPLE IN RESEARCH WITHOUT THEIR KNOWLEDGE OR CONSENT

Often the best way to study human behavior is to observe people in a natural setting without their knowledge. Self-reported descriptions of behavior may be unreliable because people forget or are uncertain about their actions. Although most people might tell you that they would attempt to return a lost wallet, a hidden camera focused on a wallet lying on the sidewalk might reveal very different behaviors. People who know they are being watched often act differently, especially when unethical, deviant, or criminal behaviors are involved. For these reasons, studies of deviance often involve direct observation, which involves listening as well as visual observation.

At times, the observer participates to some degree in the activities being studied. Whyte's (1955) study of street-corner society involved just this form of participant observation. Humphreys's (1970) examination of homosexual behavior in public restrooms, Short and Strodtbeck's (1965) study of delinquency in Chicago, and Cohen's (1980) observations of female prostitutes in New York all involved the observation of persons who never consented to become research subjects.

Studies of persons on the other side of the criminal justice process have also been undertaken without the consent of those participating in the research. Meltzer (1953), for example, studied jury deliberations through the use of hidden microphones. The importance of discretion in the criminal justice process and the hidden nature of most decisionmaking support the greater use of such techniques in efforts to understand how police, prosecutors, and correctional personnel carry out their duties.

The ethical dilemma, however, is a complicated one: Is the value of the research such that persons should be turned into study "subjects" without their permission? The conditions of the research are extremely important to this deliberation. If the behaviors being studied would have occurred without the researcher's intervention, the lack of consent seems less troubling. Such studies involve little personal cost to unknowing subjects. Unobtrusive research that involves only behaviors that occur in public view is also less questionable, because the invasion of personal privacy is not at issue.

But what about experiments that create situations to which subjects must react, such as those involving a "lost" wallet? Or a study of witness response to crime that involves an actor or actress screaming and running from an apparent assailant down a crowded street? Observation might be the only method of determining how citizens would really respond, but the personal cost of being studied might be considerable.

> "Human subjects have the right to full disclosure of the purposes of the research as early as it is appropriate to the research process, and they have the right to an opportunity to have their questions answered about the purpose and usage of the research" (Academy of Criminal Justice Sciences Code of Ethics, 2000:5).

Not only may such research be troubling for the persons involved, but when sensitive activities that are normally considered private or confidential are the subject of study, additional problems may arise. Cook (1976) reports that Meltzer encountered such difficulties in his study of jury deliberations:

> Members of Congress reacted to the jury recording as a threat to fundamental institutions. When the news of the study came out, a congressional investigation resulted. Following the investigation legislation was passed establishing a fine of a thousand dollars and imprisonment for a year for whoever might attempt to record the proceedings of any jury in the United States while the jury is deliberating or voting (p. 205).

Although the response might be less severe, one can anticipate similar objections to the taping of discussions involving police, attorneys, judges, correctional officials, and probation and parole authorities.

COERCING PEOPLE TO PARTICIPATE

You have probably received a questionnaire in the mail at some time that offered you some small incentive for completing the form—perhaps a free pen or a dollar bill. This practice is a common one, reflecting the assumption that people who are compensated for their efforts may be more likely to participate in a research endeavor than those who receive nothing. Similarly, college students are often provided a grade incentive for participation in their instructor's research. When, though, does compensation become coercion? When is the researcher justified to compel participation? The issues here involve the freedom not to participate, and the nature and quantity of the incentives that can be ethically provided without creating an undue influence.

The person receiving the questionnaire in the mail is free to keep the compensation and toss away the form. Students may be similarly free not to participate in their instructor's research, but the instructor's power over the grading process may make students feel quite ill at ease doing so. Thus, the relationship between students and researcher as teacher can be particularly coercive. One example of the coercive nature of this relationship can be seen when researchers, acting as teachers, *require* student participation in a research project as part of their course grade (Moreno, 1998). Again, there is a discernable differential in power that would eliminate the students' ability to refuse to participate in the research project.

It might seem that the easiest way out of this dilemma is to simply rely on volunteers for research subjects. But volunteers are different from others simply by virtue of their willingness to participate. At a minimum they are more highly motivated than nonvolunteers. It is important to obtain a more representative sample of participants, a group that mirrors the actual characteristics of those persons to whom study results will be applied.

This problem becomes especially critical when research subjects are vulnerable to coercion. Although students might be considered a captive population, jail and prison inmates are clearly the most vulnerable of research subjects.

> "Criminologists must not coerce or deceive students into serving as research subjects" (American Society of Criminology Code of Ethics, 1999:6).

The history of inmate involvement in research is not a very proud one. Prisoners have been used as "guinea pigs" by pharmaceutical companies that set up laboratories at correctional institutions. For minimal compensation, or the possibility that participation might assist in gaining parole, inmates have participated in a variety of medical research projects.

In the United States, the first use of correctional subjects for medical experiments took place at the Mississippi state prison in 1914, when researchers attempted to discover the relationship between diet and the disease pellagra. The Governor of Mississippi promised pardons to persons volunteering for the experiment. The situation may be contrasted to a more recent experiment in New York in which eight prisoners were inoculated with a venereal infection in order

> Criminologists "should inform research participants about aspects of the research that might affect their willingness to participate, such as physical risks, discomfort, and/or unpleasant emotional experiences" (Academy of Criminal Justice Sciences Code of Ethics, 2000:5).

to test possible cures. In exchange for their voluntary participation, the subjects, in their own words, "got syphilis and a carton of cigarettes" (Geis, 1980:226). Today, prisoners are forbidden to engage in such research efforts, but inmates are frequently required to participate in efforts to evaluate the impact of correctional treatment, work, or education programs.

In the early 1990s, research on prisoners was allowed under federal regulations. In order to pass federal guidelines, research on prisoners had to take one of four forms: (1) studies of treatment or therapies that were implemented with the goal of helping prisoners, (2) low-risk research examining inmate behavior and inmate criminality, (3) studies of correctional institutions, and (4) research that examines inmates as a class or group (Moreno, 1998). Currently, the standards by which prisoner or prison research is determined to be ethical depends on the degree to which the research will ultimately benefit individual prisoners or prisoners as a class or group (Moreno, 1998).

The reason for requiring participation is the same as that stated above. Volunteers are sufficiently different from others that relying on their participation would probably produce more positive outcomes than the intervention alone would warrant. Freedom of choice is highly valued in this society, but how much freedom of choice should prisoners have? Before denying a subject the opportunity to refuse participation, it should be clear that the overall value of the research outweighs the harm of coercion. In this consideration, the nature of the participation must be carefully evaluated—coercion to participate in weekly group therapy is quite different from coercion to participate in eight weeks of paramilitary training. One must also assess whether coercion is the only or best means available to obtain research results. Confronting this dilemma requires a balancing of such matters with a concern for individual rights.

WITHHOLDING FROM THE PARTICIPANT THE TRUE NATURE OF THE RESEARCH

Informed consent requires that subjects know fully the nature of the research, its possible effects, and the uses to be made of the data collected. However, even in the most benign circumstances, written notification may deter further action. Full and complete notification has the added potential of prejudicing responses. Often more accurate assessments are achieved when the subject believes that one aspect of his or her behavior is the focus when research interest is really on something else.

Researchers are understandably reluctant to provide too much information in this regard, especially in the early stages of a project, when the need to develop rapport and a willingness to cooperate are especially important. From a research perspective, fully disclosing the purpose of the research could severely limit findings of the study. For example, a participant's mindfulness of being observed can seriously alter his or her behaviors. Specifically, research participants are typically less willing and likely to admit to undesirable attitudes or behaviors if they know they are being studied (Singleton & Straits, 1988). This *social desirability effect* can produce error in the data collected from the research. Ethically speaking, informed consent should precede involvement in the study, so that individuals are given a meaningful opportunity to decline further participation.

"Criminologists should not mislead respondents involved in a research project as to the purpose for which that research is being conducted" (American Society of Criminology Code of Ethics, 1999:3).

Balancing research interests and respect for human dignity requires that subjects be informed about all aspects of the research that might reasonably influence their willingness to participate. Any risks that the subjects may expect to face should be fully discussed. Geis (1980) recommends that researchers remember the example of Walter Reed, who participated as a subject in his own experiments on yellow fever because he could ask no one to undergo anything that he himself was not willing to suffer.

DECEIVING THE RESEARCH PARTICIPANT

Perhaps the most flagrant example of deception in criminological research is provided by Humphreys's (1970) study, *Tearoom Trade*. Humphreys assumed the role of lookout in public restrooms so that strangers unaware of his research objective could engage uninterrupted in homosexual activity. He copied down the automobile license tags of the subjects and obtained their addresses. Later, he went to their homes, explaining that he was conducting a health survey. He asked the respondents many personal questions that became part of his research on public homosexual conduct.

"Members of the Academy should take culturally appropriate steps to secure informed consent and to avoid invasions of privacy" (Academy of Criminal Justice Sciences Code of Ethics, 1999:3).

The rationale for such deception emphasizes the importance of the research and the difficulties of obtaining accurate information through other means. All deceptive acts are not equal. There are differences between active lying and a conscious failure to provide all available information. Deception may be considered an affront to individual autonomy and self-respect or an occasionally legitimate means to be used in service of a higher value (Cook, 1976).

One alternative to deception is to provide only general information about the research project prior to the experiment and offer full disclosure after the research has been completed. Another technique relies on subjects to role-play their behavior after the nature of the research project has been explained. There is mixed evidence, however, on the effectiveness of this technique (Cook, 1976).

In regard to deception, the researcher must evaluate the nature of the research and weigh its value against the impact of the deception on the integrity of participants. The degree to which privacy is invaded and the sensitivity of the behaviors involved are important considerations. Finally, the possibility of harming the research participant should be considered before attempting to deceive the participant. If the nature of the research is potentially harmful, the research participant should be able to fully assess whethe he or she wishes to risk participating in the study.

LEADING THE RESEARCH PARTICIPANTS TO COMMIT ACTS THAT DIMINISH THEIR SELF-RESPECT

Research subjects have been experimentally induced into states of extreme passivity and extreme aggression. Efforts to provoke subjects to lie, cheat, steal, and harm have proven very effective. Cook (1976) describes a study in which students were recruited to participate in a theft of records from a business firm. The inducements described included an opportunity to perform a patriotic service for a department of federal government. A substantial number of students were significantly encouraged to take part in the theft, although ultimately the burglary was not carried out.

Research by Haney, Banks, and Zimbardo (1973) involved the simulation of prison conditions, with 21 subjects assuming the roles of prisoners and guards. After a very short time, the guards began behaving in an aggressive and physically threatening manner. Their use of power became self-aggrandizing and self-perpetuating. The prisoners quickly experienced a loss of personal identity, exhibiting flattened affect and dependency; eventually they were emotionally emasculated by the encounters.

Because of the extreme nature of the subjects' responses, the project was terminated after only six days. The debriefing sessions that followed the research yielded the following comments:

Guards:

"They (the prisoners) seemed to lose touch with the reality of the experiment—they took me so seriously."

". . . I didn't interfere with any of the guards' actions. Usually if what they were doing bothered me, I would walk out and take another duty."

". . . looking back, I am impressed by how little I felt for them . . ."

"They (the prisoners) didn't see it as an experiment. It was real, and they were fighting to keep their identity. But we were always there to show them just who was boss."

"I was tired of seeing the prisoners in their rags and smelling the strong odors of their bodies that filled the cells. I watched them tear at each other, on orders given by us."

". . . Acting authoritatively can be fun. Power can be a great pleasure."

". . . During the inspection, I went to cell 2 to mess up a bed which the prisoner had made and he grabbed me, screaming that he had just made it, and he wasn't going to let me mess it up. He grabbed my throat, and although he was laughing, I was pretty scared. I lashed out with my stick and hit him in the chin (although not very hard), and when I freed myself I became angry."

Prisoners:

". . . The way we were made to degrade ourselves really brought us down, and that's why we all sat docile towards the end of the experiment."

". . . I realize now (after it's over) that no matter how together I thought I was inside my head, my prison behavior was often less under my control than I realized. No matter how open, friendly and helpful I was with other prisoners I was still operating as an isolated, self-centered person, being rational rather than compassionate."

> "... I began to feel I was losing my identity, that the person I call
> _____, the person who volunteered to get me into this prison
> (because it was a prison to me, it still is a prison to me, I don't
> regard it as an experiment or a simulation . . .) was distant from me,
> was remote until finally I wasn't that person; I was 416. I was really
> my number, and 416 was really going to have to decide what to do."

> "I learned that people can easily forget that others are human."

In Milgram's (1974) research, participants showed "blind obedience" to a white-coated "researcher" who ordered them to provide what appeared to be electric shocks of increasing severity to subjects who failed to respond correctly to a series of questions. Although they were emotionally upset, the subjects continued to follow their instructions as the "shocked" subjects screamed in agony.

Follow-up research revealed that Milgram's subjects experienced only minor and temporary disturbances (Ring, Wallston & Corey, 1970). One might argue that the subjects even benefited from the project as a result of their greater self-awareness, but the fact that the educational experience occurred without their initial understanding or consent raises ethical concerns.

To what degree should subjects be asked to unknowingly engage in activities that may damage their self-esteem? Again, the researcher is required to engage in a balancing act, reconciling research objectives and the availability of alternative methods with a concern for the integrity of subjects. At a minimum, such research efforts should provide means to address any possible harm to subjects, including debriefings at the conclusion of the research and follow-up counseling as needed.

VIOLATING THE RIGHT TO SELF-DETERMINATION: RESEARCH ON BEHAVIOR CONTROL AND CHARACTER CHANGE

The film *A Clockwork Orange* provides an excellent illustration of the dilemmas of behavior-modifying research. In the film, a thoroughly violent and irredeemable individual named Alex is subjected to therapy that requires him to observe violent acts on film at the same time that the chemicals he has ingested make him physically ill. After a while, the acts that he has observed make him sick as well, and he is changed from a violent individual to one who avoids violence at all cost, including that required for his own self-defense. At the end of the film, the "powers that be" decide to reverse his treatment for political reasons.

Although there is little possibility of behavior modification being used to exact such effect in the near future, the question remains: To what extent should experimental efforts be made to alter human behavior against the will of the participant? Remembering the vulnerability of the inmate to coercion (in the film, Alex only participated in the violence control project because he thought it would help him gain early release), it becomes clear that the greatest desire to use behavior control strategies will be evident in areas involving those persons most vulnerable to coercion—criminals and persons with problems of substance abuse. Although research on crime prevention and control generally has only the most laudable aims, it should be remembered that it is often well-intentioned actions that pose the greatest threat to individual freedoms.

Exposing the Research Participant to Physical or Mental Stress

How would you evaluate the ethics of the following research project: an evaluation of a treatment program in which persons convicted of drunk driving are required to watch and listen to hours of films depicting gory automobile accidents, followed by horrifying emergency room visits and interviews with grieving relatives? Would it matter whether the actions of the drunk drivers had contributed to similar accidents? If your answer is yes, you are probably considering whether the viewers deserve the "punishment" of what they are forced to observe on film.

This not-so-hypothetical scenario raises a difficult issue. Is it acceptable for a research project to engage in activities that punish and perhaps harm the subject? To test various outcomes, subjects in different settings have been exposed to events provoking feelings of horror, shock, threatened sexual identity, personal failure, fear, and emotional shock (Cook, 1976). The subjects in Haney, Banks, and Zimbardo's research and Milgram's research were clearly stressed by their research experiences. To what extent is it acceptable to engage in these practices for the objective of scientific inquiry?

In most situations, it is impossible to observe human reactions such as those described above in their natural settings, so researchers feel justified in creating experiments that produce these reactions. The extent of possible harm raises ethical dilemmas, however, because theoretically there is no limit to what might be contrived to create a "researchable" reaction. The balancing of research objectives with a respect for human subjects is a delicate undertaking, requiring researchers to scrutinize their objectives and the value of their proposed studies dispassionately.

Invading the Privacy of the Research Participant

The issues of privacy and confidentiality are related concerns. Ethical questions are raised by research that invades an individual's privacy without his or her consent. When information on subjects has been obtained for reasons other than research (e.g., the development of a criminal history file), there are questions about the extent to which data should be released to researchers. Some records are more sensitive than others in this regard, depending on how easily the offender's identity can be obtained, as well as the quantity and nature of the information recorded. Even when consent has been given and the information has been gathered expressly for research purposes, maintaining the confidentiality of responses may be a difficult matter when the responses contain information of a sensitive and/or illegal nature.

CONFIDENTIALITY

The issue of confidentiality is especially important in the study of crime and deviance. Subjects will generally not agree to provide information in this area unless their responses are to remain confidential. This may be a more difficult task than it appears. Generally, it is important to be able to identify a subject so that his or her responses can be linked to other sources of data on the individual. Institutionalized delinquents might be asked in confidence about their involvement in drug use and other forms of misconduct during confinement. An important part of the research would involve gathering background information from the offender's institutional files to determine what types of offenders are most likely to be involved in institutional misconduct. To do this, the individual's confidential responses need to be identifiable; therefore, complete anonymity is unfeasible.

> "Subjects of research are entitled to rights of personal confidentiality unless they are waived" (Academy of Criminal Justice Sciences Code of Ethics, 2000:5).

As long as only dispassionate researchers have access to this information, there may be no problem. Difficulties arise when third parties, especially criminal justice authorities, become interested in the research responses. Then the issue becomes one of protecting the data (and the offender) from officials who have the power to invoke the criminal justice process.

One response to this dilemma is to store identifying information in a remote place; some researchers have even recommended sending sensitive information out of the country. Because the relationship between the researcher and his or her informants is not privileged, researchers can be called upon to provide information to the courts.

Lewis Yablonsky, a criminologist/practitioner, while testifying in defense of Gridley White, one of Yablonsky's main informants in his hippie study, was asked by the judge nine times if he had witnessed Gridley smoking marijuana. Yablonsky refused to answer because of the rights guaranteed him in the Fifth Amendment of the U.S. Constitution. Although he was not legally sanctioned, he said the incident was humiliating and suggested that researchers should have guarantees of immunity (Wolfgang, 1982:396).

It is also important that researchers prepare their presentation of research findings in a manner that ensures that the particular responses of an individual cannot be discerned. Presentation of only aggregate findings was especially important for Marvin Wolfgang (1982) when he reinterviewed persons included in his earlier study of delinquency in a birth cohort. His follow-up consisted of hour-long interviews with about 600 youths. The subjects were asked many personal questions, including many about their involvement in delinquency and crime. Four of his respondents admitted committing criminal homicide, and 75 admitted to forcible rape. Many other serious crimes were also described, for which none of the participants had been arrested.

At the time of the research, all of the respondents were orally assured that the results of the research would remain confidential, but Wolfgang raises a number of ethical questions surrounding this practice. Should written consent forms have been provided to the subjects, detailing the nature of the research? Wolfgang concludes that such forms would have raised more questions than they answered. Could a court order impound the records? Could persons attempting to protect the data be prosecuted for their actions? Could the data be successfully concealed?

The general willingness to protect subjects who admit to serious crimes also requires close ethical scrutiny. Wolfgang (1982) takes the traditional scientific stance on this issue, proposing that such information belongs to science. Because the information would have not been discovered without the research effort, its protection neither helps nor hinders police. The ethical judgment here requires a weighing of interests—the importance of scientific research balanced against society's interest in capturing a particular individual.

It should be noted that if researchers began to inform on their subjects routinely, all future research relying on self-reports would be jeopardized. Thus, the issue at hand is not simply that of the value of a particular study, but the value of all research utilizing subject disclosures. Researchers are generally advised not to undertake such research unless they feel comfortable about protecting their sources. This requires that all research involving the use of confidential information provide for controlled access to sensitive data and protect the information from unauthorized searches, inadvertent access, and the compulsory legal process (Cook, 1976).

WITHHOLDING BENEFITS TO PARTICIPANTS IN CONTROL GROUPS

The necessity of excluding some potential beneficiaries from initial program participation arises whenever a classical experimental design is to be used to evaluate the program. This research design requires the random assignment of subjects to experimental and control groups. Subjects in the control group are excluded from the program and/or receive "standard" rather than "experimental" treatment.

In a program evaluation, it is important that some subjects receive the benefits of the program while others do not, to ensure that the outcomes observed are the direct result of the experimental intervention and not something else (subject enthusiasm or background characteristics, for example). It is imperative that those who receive the intervention (the experimental group) and those who do not (the control group) be as identical in the aggregate as possible, so that a clear assessment of program impact, untainted by variation in the nature of subjects, can be obtained. Though randomization is important from a methodological point of view, the participants who, by chance, end up in the control group are often denied treatment, or possibly services, that could be of the utmost importance to their lives. The Minneapolis Domestic Violence Experiment is a classic example of how those persons involved the control group were denied potential law enforcement interventions that could have benefited them. Figure 20.1 is a description of Sherman and Berk's (1984) study that looked at various responses to domestic violence.

The best way to ensure that experimental and control subjects are identical is randomization. Randomization is to be distinguished from arbitrariness. Randomization requires that every subject have an equal chance to be assigned to either the experimental or control group; arbitrariness involves no such equality of opportunity.

In many ways, randomization may be more fair than standard practice based on good intentions. Geis (1980) reports:

> For most of us, it would be unthinkable that a sample of armed robbers be divided into two groups on the basis of random assignment—one group to spend 10 years in prison, the second to receive a sentence of 2 years on probation. Nonetheless, at a federal judicial conference, after examining an elaborate presentence report concerning a bank robber, 17 judges said they would have imprisoned the man, while 10 indicated they favored probation. Those voting for imprisonment set sentences ranging from 6 months to 15 years (p. 221).

Randomization is also acceptable under law, because its use is reasonably related to a governmental objective, that is, testing the effectiveness of a program intervention (Erez, 1986).

Although randomization is inherently fair, it often appears less so to the subjects involved. Surveys of prisoners have indicated that need, merit, and "first come, first served" are more acceptable criteria than a method that the offenders equated with gambler's luck (Erez, 1986). Consider Morris's (1966) description of "the burglar's nightmare":

> If eighty burglars alike in all relevant particulars were assigned randomly to experimental and control groups, forty each, with the

experimentals to be released six months or a year earlier than they ordinarily would be and the control released at their regularly appointed time, how would the burglar assigned to the control group respond? It is unfair, unjust, unethical, he could say, for me to be put into the control group. If people like me, he might complain, are being released early, I too deserve the same treatment (cited in Erez, 1986:394).

Program staff are also frequently unhappy with randomization because it fails to utilize their clinical skills in the selection of appropriate candidates for intervention. Extending this line of thought, consider the likely response of judges requested to sentence burglary offenders randomly to prison or probation. While this might be the best method of determining the effectiveness of these sanctions, the judicial response (and perhaps community response as well) would probably be less than enthusiastic. This is because it is assumed, often without any evidence, that standard practice is achieving some reasonable objective, such as individualizing justice or preventing crime.

Figure 20.1
The Minneapolis Domestic Violence Experiment

Domestic violence was beginning to be recognized as a major public affairs and criminal justice problem. Victim advocates were demanding the automatic arrest for domestic violence offenders. However, there was no empirical research that showed that arresting domestic violence offenders deterred future acts of domestic violence. Thus, Sherman and Berk, sponsored by funding from the National Institute of Justice, designed a randomized experiment that looked at the effects of arrest on domestic violence.

Sherman and Berk enlisted the help of the Minneapolis Police Department. When on misdemeanor domestic violence calls, the police were to respond to the call depending on the random call response they were assigned. There were three responses with which the police could respond to the misdemeanor domestic violence call: arrest, removal of batterer from the premises without an arrest, or counsel the batterer and leave the premises. While the initial findings of this research indicated that arresting domestic violence offenders reduced the incidence of future incidents, the methodology and ethics of this experiment have been heavily scrutinized. The victims of the misdemeanor domestic violence certainly did not consent to the randomized assignment of response to the situation. Thus, not only were potential benefits withheld from the certain women, some victims could have been placed at greater risk as a result of the random treatment. While the benevolent intentions behind this research agenda were admirable, the implementation of the experiment and the variable being randomized (i.e., type of response to domestic violence) should have been further considered before implementation of the research.

Based on Sherman L.W. & R.A. Berk (1984). "The Specific Deterrent Effects of Arrest for Domestic Assault." *American Sociological Review*, 49(2):261-272.

Randomization does produce winners and losers. Of critical importance in weighing the consequences of randomization are the differences in
treatment experienced by the experimental and control groups. Six factors
are relevant here:

1. *Significance of the interest affected.* Early release is of much
   greater consequence than a change of institutional diet.

2. *Extent of difference.* Six months early release is of greater significance than one week's early release.

3. *Comparison of the disparity with standard treatment.* If both
   experimental and control group treatment is an improvement
   over standard treatment, then the discrepancy between the
   experimental and control group is of less concern.

4. *Whether disparity reflects differences in qualifications of
   subjects.* If the disparity is reasonably related to some characteristic of the subjects, the denial of benefits to the control
   group is less significant.

5. *Whether the experimental treatment is harmful or beneficial to
   subjects compared with the treatment they would otherwise
   receive.* A program that assigns members of the experimental
   group to six weeks of "boot camp" may be more demanding of
   inmates than the standard treatment of six months' incarceration.

6. *Whether participation is mandatory or voluntary.* Voluntary
   participation mitigates the concern of denial of benefit, while
   coercion exacerbates the dilemma (Federal Judicial Center,
   1981:31-40).

Similar to the management of other ethical dilemmas, an effort is
required to balance values of human decency and justice with the need for
accurate information on intervention effectiveness. Problems arise not in the
extreme cases of disparity but in more routine circumstances. Consider the
following example: How do we judge a situation in which a foundation grant
permits attorneys to be supplied for all cases being heard by a juvenile court
in which attorneys have previously appeared only in rare instances? A
fundamental study hypothesis may be that the presence of an attorney
tends to result in a more favorable disposition for the client. This idea may
be tested by comparing dispositions prior to the beginning of the experiment
with those ensuing subsequently, though it would be more satisfactory to
supply attorneys to a sample of the cases and withhold them from the
remainder, in order to calculate in a more experimentally uncontaminated
manner the differences between the outcomes in the two situations.

The matter takes on additional complexity if the researchers desire to
determine what particular attorney role is the most efficacious in the juvenile court. They may suspect that an attorney who acts as a friend of the court,
knowingly taking its viewpoint as *parens patriae,* and attempting to inter-

pret the court's interest to his or her client, will produce more desirable results than one who doggedly challenges the courtroom procedure and the judge's interpretation of fact, picks at the probation report, raises constant objections, and fights for his or her client as he would in a criminal court. But what results are "more desirable" (Geis, 1980:222-223)?

It could be contended that little is really known about how attorney roles influence dispositions and that, without the project, no one would have any kind of representation. Over the long term, all juveniles stand to benefit. On the other hand, it could be argued that it is wrong to deprive anyone of the best judgment of his or her attorney by requiring a particular legal approach. What if there are only enough funds to supply one-half of the juveniles with attorneys anyway? Is randomization more or less fair than trying to decide which cases "need" representation the most?

Randomization imposes a special ethical burden because it purposefully counters efforts to determine the best course of action with the element of chance. The practice is justifiable because the pursuit of knowledge is a desirable objective—as long as the overall benefits outweigh the risks. The balancing of risks and benefits is complicated by the fact that judgments must often be made in a context of ambiguity, attempting to predict the benefits of an intervention that is being tested precisely because its impact is unknown.

The Federal Judicial Center (1981) recommends that program evaluations should only be considered when certain threshold conditions are met:

> First, the status quo warrants substantial improvements or is of doubtful effectiveness.
>
> Second, there must be significant uncertainty about the value or effectiveness of the innovation.
>
> Third, information needed to clarify the uncertainty must be feasibly obtainable by the program experimentation but not readily obtainable by other means.
>
> And fourth, the information sought must pertain directly to the decision whether or not to adopt the proposed innovation on a general, non-experimental basis (p. 7).

Several conditions lessen the ethical burdens of evaluative research. Random assignment is especially acceptable when resources are scarce and demand for the benefit is high. Denying benefits to the control group is quite acceptable when members of the control group can participate at a later date. Finally, discrepancies between the treatment of experimental and control groups are decreased when the groups are geographically separated (Federal Judicial Center, 1981).

FAILING TO TREAT RESEARCH PARTICIPANTS FAIRLY AND TO SHOW THEM CONSIDERATION AND RESPECT

The basic tenets of professionalism require that researchers treat subjects with courtesy and fulfill the variety of commitments they make to subjects. In an effort to obtain cooperation, subjects are often promised a follow-up report on the findings of the research; such reports may be forgotten once the study has been completed. Subjects are often led to believe that they will achieve some personal benefit from the research. This may be one of the more difficult obligations to fulfill.

Researchers need to treat their human subjects with constant recognition of their integrity and their contribution to the research endeavor. This is especially important when subjects are powerless and vulnerable. Although such treatment may be a time-consuming chore, it is the only ethical way to practice scientific research.

BALANCING SCIENTIFIC AND ETHICAL CONCERNS

This discussion has emphasized the importance of balancing a concern for subjects against the potential benefits of the research. Cook (1976) identifies the following potential benefits of a research project:

1. Advances in scientific theory that contribute to a general understanding of human behavior.

2. Advances in knowledge of practical value to society.

3. Gains for the research participant, such as increased understanding, satisfaction in making a contribution to science or to the solution of social problems, needed money or special privileges, knowledge of social science or of research methods, and so on (p. 235).

The potential costs to subjects are considerable, however, and it is often difficult for the researcher to be objective in assessing the issues. For this reason, many professional associations have established guidelines and procedures for ethical research conduct. Generally, because little active monitoring occurs, the professional is honor-bound to follow these guidelines.

INSTITUTIONAL REVIEW BOARDS AND SETTING ETHICAL STANDARDS

To ensure that their faculty follow acceptable procedures (and to protect themselves from liability), universities have established institutional review boards to scrutinize each research project that involves the use of human subjects. These review boards serve a valuable function in that they review the specifications of each research project prior to implementation. They are generally incapable of providing direct monitoring of projects so, again, the responsibility for ethical conduct falls on the researcher.

How are the ethical standards being set within the criminal justice community, and how and to what degree are ethics being taught in criminology and criminal justice academic settings? McSkimming, Sever, and King (2000) analyzed 11 research methods textbooks that are frequently used in criminal justice and criminology courses. The authors looked at the extent to which ethical issues were addressed within the criminal justice texts and the type of ethical issues that were covered within the texts. The authors found that there was no collective format being utilized in the major criminal justice texts regarding ethics in criminal justice. Furthermore, the significance and positive functions of institutional review boards were rarely mentioned.

Of further concern was the noticeable absence of some important ethical topics in these criminal justice research methods texts. These topic areas concerned ethics related to the dissemination of information into the criminal justice audience. These areas concerned "plagiarism, fabrication of data, Institutional Review Boards, authorship rank, and ethical considerations in journal editing and grant-writing" (p. 58).

Institutional review boards are often the only source for ethical guidance and standards for the criminal justice academic researcher (McSkimming, Sever & King, 2000). It is imperative that graduate students, publishing professors, and other disseminators of information within the criminal justice discipline have some guideline or gauge with which to measure ethical standards.

Ethical Codes

In order to address some of these (and other) ethical considerations, associations of academic researchers develop and make known standards or codes of ethics. The Academy of Criminal Justice Sciences (ACJS) has advanced a standard for those persons researching and writing within the discipline of criminal justice. It addresses the ethical standards of conducting social science research as well as the dissemination of information within the criminal justice discipline. The ACJS code provides criminologists with ethical standards concerning fair treatment; the use of students in research; objectivity and integrity in the conduct of research; confidentiality, disclosure, and respect for research populations; publication and authorship standards; and employment practices (ACJS Code of Ethics, 2000).

Ethical/Political Considerations

Applied social research, that is, research that examines the effectiveness of social policies and programs, carries with it additional ethical responsibilities. Such research influences the course of human events in a direct fashion—often work, education, future opportunities, and deeply held values and beliefs are affected by the outcomes. Researchers must be prepared to deal with a variety of pressures and demands as they undertake the practice and dissemination of research.

It is generally acknowledged that organizations asked to measure their own effectiveness often produce biased results. Crime statistics provide a notorious example of data that tend to be used to show either an effective police department (falling crime figures) or a need for more resources (rising crime figures). Criminal justice researchers are often asked to study matters that are equally sensitive. A correctional treatment program found to be ineffective may lose its funding. A study that reveals extensive use of plea bargaining may cost a prosecutor his or her election.

Often the truth is complicated. A survey that reveals that drug use is declining in the general population may prove troublesome for those trying to lobby for the establishment of more drug treatment facilities. The survey results may lead the public to believe that there is no problem at the same time that the need for treatment facilities for the indigent is substantial.

Such research has been known to produce unintended consequences. The publication of selected results of a study on the effectiveness of correctional treatment programs (Martinson, 1974) was used by many persons to justify limiting funds for education and treatment programs in correctional institutions. The research revealed that there was little evidence that correctional treatment programs were effective means of reducing recidivism (a finding that has been widely challenged). Rather than stimulating the development of more theoretically sound programs and rigorous evaluations of these efforts, the apparent product of the research was a decrease in the humaneness of conditions of confinement.

Sometimes research results conflict with cherished beliefs. Studies of preventive police patrol (Kelling et al., 1974) and detective investigations (Chaiken, Greenwood & Petersilia, 1977) both revealed that these practices, long assumed to be essential elements of effective law enforcement, were of little value. Researchers can expect findings such as these to meet with considerable resistance.

Researchers may be asked to utilize their skills and their aura of objectivity to provide an organization or agency with what it wants. When the group that pays the bills has a direct interest in the nature of the outcome, the pressures can be considerable. Marvin Wolfgang (1982) reports:

> I was once invited to do research by an organization whose views are almost completely antithetical to mine on the issue of gun control. Complete freedom and a considerable amount of money to

explore the relationship between gun control legislation and robbery were promised. I would not perform the research under those auspices. But the real clincher in the decision was that if the research produced conclusions opposite from that the organization wanted, the agency would not publish the results nor allow me to publish them. Perhaps their behavior, within their ideological framework, was not unethical. But within my framework, as a scientist who values freedom of publication as well as of scientific inquiry, I would have engaged in an unethical act of prostituting my integrity had I accepted those conditions. (p. 395)

In-house researchers, who are employed by the organization for which the research is being conducted, face special problems in this regard, because they lack the freedom to pick and choose their research topic. These problems must balance their concern for rigorous scientific inquiry with their need for continued employment.

Generally, the issues confronted are subtle and complex. Although researchers may be directly told to conceal or falsify results, more often they are subtly encouraged to design their research with an eye toward the desired results. The greatest barrier to such pressures is the development of a truly independent professional research unit within the organization. Such independence protects the researcher from political pressures and at the same time promotes the credibility of the research being conducted. Without this protection, the individual is left to his or her own devices and standards of ethical conduct.

THE PURITY OF SCIENTIFIC RESEARCH

The ideal of scientific inquiry is the pure, objective examination of the empirical world, untainted by personal prejudice. However, research is carried out by human beings, not automatons, and they have a variety of motivations for undertaking the research that they do. Topics may be selected because of curiosity or a perceived need to address a specific social problem, but the availability of grants in a particular field may also encourage researchers to direct their attention to these areas. This is critical if one is working for a research organization dependent upon "soft" money. The need for university faculty to publish and establish a name for themselves in a particular area may encourage them to seek "hot" topics for their research, or to identify an extremely narrow research focus in which they can become identified as an expert.

There is some evidence that the nature of one's research findings influences the likelihood of publication (*Chronicle of Higher Education*, 1989d). A curious author submitted almost identical articles to a number of journals. The manuscripts differed only in one respect—the nature of the conclusions. One version of the article showed that the experiment had no effect; the other described a positive result. His experiment produced some interesting find-ings—the article with positive outcomes was more likely to be accepted for publication than the other manuscript.

If research that concludes that "the experiment didn't work" or that "differences between Groups A and B were insignificant" are indeed less likely to see the light of day, then pressures to revise one's research focus or rewrite one's hypotheses to match the results produced can be anticipated.

None of the practices described above involve scandalous violations of ethical conduct. Their presentation should function, however, to remind us that actions justified in the name of scientific inquiry may be motivated by factors far less "pure" than the objective they serve.

PUBLIC POLICY PRONOUNCEMENTS AND TEACHING CRIMINAL JUSTICE

When is a researcher speaking from the facts and when is he or she pro-moting personal ideology? If there were any fully conclusive and definitive studies in the social sciences, this question would not arise. However, research findings are always tentative, and statements describing them invari-ably require conditional language. On the other hand, researchers have val-ues and beliefs like everyone else, and few of us want to employ the same conditional language required to discuss research when we state our views on matters of public policy and morality. Researchers thus have a special oblig-ation to carefully evaluate their remarks and clearly distinguish between opinion and apparent empirical fact. This is not always an easy task, but it is the only way to safeguard the objectivity that is critically important to sci-entific inquiry. Furthermore, criminal justice researchers acting as teachers and mentors have a responsibility to their students, due to the influence their position has over the lives of the students (ACJS, 2000). Specifically, a researcher's influence and authority used inappropriately has the potential to mislead and distort the perspectives of their students by disseminating infor-mation that was merely personal ideology as opposed to scientific findings.

CONCLUSION

Conducting scientific research in criminal justice and criminology in an ethical fashion is a difficult task. It requires a constant weighing and balancing of objectives and motivations. It would be nice to conclude that the best research is that which is undertaken in an ethical fashion, but such a state-ment would skirt the dilemma. This is the exact nature of the problem: those actions required to meet the demands of scientific rigor sometimes run counter to ethical behavior.

Evaluating rather than avoiding ethical dilemmas does provide a learning experience, though, the benefits of which can be expected to spill over into all aspects of human endeavor. Thinking and doing in an ethical fashion requires practice, and conducting research provides considerable opportunity for the development of experience.

REFERENCES

ACJS (2000). "Academy of Criminal Justice Sciences: Code of Ethics."

Chaiken, J., P. Greenwood & J. Petersilia (1977). "The Criminal Investigation Process: A Summary Report." *Policy Analysis* 3:187-217.

Chronicle of Higher Education (1989a), January 25:A44.

Chronicle of Higher Education (1989b), June 14:A44.

Chronicle of Higher Education (1989c), July 19:A4.

Chronicle of Higher Education (1989d), August 2:A5.

Chronicle of Higher Education (1999), November 46:A18.

Cohen, B. (1980). *Deviant Street Networks: Prostitution in New York City.* Cambridge, MA: Lexington Books.

Cook, S.W. (1976). "Ethical Issues in the Conduct of Research in Social Relations." In *Research Methods in Social Relations*, 3rd ed., Claire Sellitz, Lawrence Rightsman & Stuart Cook (eds.). New York: Holt, Rinehart and Winston.

Driscoll, A. (1999). "UF Prof Who Touted Privatized Prisons Admits Firm Paid Him." *Miami Herald*, April 21:A1.

Erez, E. (1986). "Randomized Experiments in Correctional Context: Legal, Ethical and Practical Concerns." *Journal of Criminal Justice*, 14: 389-400.

Federal Judicial Center (1981). *Experimentation in the Law. Report of the Federal Judicial Center Advisory Committee on Experimentation in the Law.* Washington, DC: Federal Judicial Center.

Geis, G. (1980). "Ethical and Legal Issues in Experiments with Offender Populations." In *Criminal Justice Research: Approaches, Problems & Policy*, S. Talarico (ed.). Cincinnati: Anderson.

Haney, C., C. Banks & P. Zimbardo (1973). "Interpersonal Dynamics in a Simulated Prison." *International Journal of Criminology and Penology*, 1:69-97.

Humphreys, L. (1970). *Tearoom Trade: Impersonal Sex in Public Places.* Chicago: Aldine.

Jones, K.D. (1999). "Ethics in Publication." *Counseling and Values*, 43:99-106.

Kelling, G.L., T. Page, D. Dieckman & C.E. Browne (1974). *The Kansas City Preventive Patrol Experiment*. Washington, DC: The Police Foundation.

Martinson, R. (1974). "What Works?—Questions and Answers About Prison Reform." *Public Interest*, 35:25-54.

McSkimming, M.J., B. Sever & R.S. King (2000). "The Coverage of Ethics in Research Methods Textbooks." *Journal of Criminal Justice Education*, 11:51-63.

Meltzer, B.A. (1953). "A Projected Study of the Jury as a Working Institution." *The Annals of the American Academy of Political and Social Sciences*, 287:97-102.

Milgram, S. (1974). *Obedience to Authority: An Experimental View*. New York: Harper and Row.

Moreno, J.D. (1998). "Convenient and Captive Populations." In J.P. Kahn, A.C. Mastroianni & J. Sugarman (eds.), *Beyond Consent: Seeking Justice in Research*. New York: Oxford University Press, pp. 111-130.

Morris, N. (1966). "Impediments to Penal Reform." *Chicago Law Review*, 33:646-653.

New York Times (1983). February 26:7.

Ring, K., K. Wallston & M. Corey (1970). "Mode of Debriefing as a Factor Affecting Subjective Reaction to a Milgram Type Obedience Experience: An Ethical Inquiry." *Representative Research in Social Psychology*, 1:67-88.

Sherman, L.W. & R.A. Berk (1984). "The Specific Deterrent Effects of Arrest for Domestic Assault." *American Sociological Review*, 49:261-272.

Short, J.F., Jr. & F. Strodtbeck (1965). *Group Processes and Gang Delinquency*. Chicago: University of Chicago Press.

Singleton, Jr., R.A. & B.C. Straits (1988). *Approaches to Social Research*, 3rd ed. New York: Oxford University Press.

Whyte, W.F. (1955). *Streetcorner Society*. Chicago: University of Chicago Press.

Wolfgang, M. (1982). "Ethics and Research." In *Ethics, Public Policy and Criminal Justice*, F. Elliston & N. Bowie (eds.). Cambridge, MA: Oelgeschlager, Gunn and Hain.

DISCUSSION QUESTIONS

1. Are there any circumstances in which it is acceptable for a research project to involve activities that punish and perhaps harm the subject? Where should the researcher draw the line? Can you think of any situation in which the ends justify the means? Support your answer.

2. What are some of the benefits to be gained by doing a research project? Do the benefits outweigh the costs to the subjects and participants? Explain. What are some of the pressures that may be placed on researchers that could compromise the integrity of their research results?

CHAPTER 21

Research Ethics and Research Funding: A Case Study of Easy Virtue

Gary W. Potter & Victor E. Kappeler

INTRODUCTION

The single most important fact in criminal justice and criminological research is that what we do, how we do it, and what we say all have consequences. Sometimes those consequences are not as great as we would like, and we find our work ignored or confined to esoteric discussions within the discipline. Sometimes, however, and more often when we have official state partners in our research, our work becomes the basis of policies that impact thousands or even millions of people—or becomes the justification for programs and policies we never intended to justify. Often small pieces and tidbits of our research are used in support of policies and crime control initiatives that the body of scientific knowledge has clearly shown to be deficient

KEY CONCEPTS:

causal analysis vs. policy analysis

conflict of interest

false dichotomies

federal funding trends

pure research vs. applied research

social construction of crime

theory vs. practice

or even counterproductive, such as capital punishment and mandatory sentencing schemes. In the late 1980s, published research, based on a deficient methodology, led to widespread public, media, and governmental attention being focused on the problem of "crack babies." The early research had involved "nonblind" studies in which babies with crack-using mothers were identified to researchers, who then identified a plethora of medical, social, and psychological dysfunctions in those infants. Follow-up research, which utilized a correct methodology by not identifying the "crack babies," consistently failed to identify (1) any pattern of dysfunction in those infants, and (2) was unable to identify infants whose mothers had been crack users. Nonetheless, by the time the faulty research had been corrected, immense damage had been done. States passed laws that required physicians and nurses to identify crack-using mothers to child welfare authorities, which allowed state bureaucracies to remove those babies from maternal care and, in some cases, allowed the mother to be prosecuted as a "drug trafficker." This legislation had the impact of deterring expectant mothers from seeking prenatal care and scaring them away from postnatal care for their infants. This took place despite the fact that the follow-up research had clearly indicated that the dysfunctions identified in newborns emanated from a lack of proper nutrition, a lack of prenatal and postnatal care, and fetal alcohol syndrome, rather than the consumption of crack cocaine (Coffin, 1996). Children, both those with crack-using mothers and others, were placed at even greater risk because of draconian and uncalled for state policies emanating from careless research. The further irony of this case is that those unfortunate crack babies who had been removed from maternal care were almost impossible to place with foster parents because they had already been labeled as behavioral problems by the state.

In a similar case, the misuse of laboratory studies by the Meese Commission on the effects of pornography, despite the pleas of the researchers who had conducted the studies to be careful in interpreting their data, virtually sabotaged any legitimate discussion of the role of pornography in contributing to violent crime (Donnerstein & Lintz, 1986). The Meese Commission, appointed by President Reagan, was "stacked" with pornography opponents. The callous political misuse of potentially useful data, and the refusal of the Commission to address pornography as a symptom rather than a cause in a patriarchal, sexist society, made it virtually impossible to pursue constructive research or policy formulation. Instead of linking sexism and patriarchy to rape and violent crime, the Commission insisted on a direct causal link to pornography, despite a series of studies disputing that link (Kimmel, 1993; McCormack, 1985; Schwartz & DeKeseredy, 1997).

Often, when our work contradicts state policies and programs, it is ignored and confined to the dust-laden journals on library shelves. The dozens of studies finding no utility—and, in fact, considerable damage—caused by three-strikes laws and mandatory sentencing are universally ignored by policymakers. The hundreds of studies finding direct links between violence and economic inequality, employment opportunities for youth, patterns of mortgage investment, and the extraction of profit are similarly anathema to policymakers. Compelling research looking at successful alternatives to the "drug war" that are being implemented by the European democracies are confined to classroom discourse.

By the very nature of our work as researchers and professors of scientific truth, we carry a heavy social responsibility to be meticulously ethical in how we state that truth and how we conduct that research. The potential consequences of what we say, how we say it, and in what manner we conduct inquiries are awesome. The possibility that a passage from our work may result in support for the death penalty, one person being confined to the horrors of prison, or a child becoming the ward of the state should humble us, frighten us, and make us extremely circumspect.

Even the purest and most basic science can have horrifying and unintended impacts. Einstein and Teller went to their deathbeds lamenting the creation of the atom bomb. Nobel's guilt over the creation of gunpowder led him to redistribute much of his wealth in a search for world peace. In criminal justice, though, no case of lamentable science is more compelling than the case of Bob Martinson. In the Winter of 1980, with his teenage son looking on, Bob Martinson, who had become through his research the most celebrated critic of rehabilitation in corrections, threw himself out the window of his Manhattan apartment, killing himself. Martinson had surveyed 231 evaluation research studies on offender rehabilitation. That study would become political dynamite. While Martinson's co-authors tempered their findings in their writings, he took a more public and flamboyant approach, writing a series of newspaper opinion columns, magazine stories, and journal articles, most containing in their titles the phrase "nothing works." While the more cautious statements of his colleagues were generally ignored, the media and politicians enthusiastically repeated Martinson's catch phrase. Lost in the simplistic reporting and political interpretation of Martinson's work were his many cautions. For example, he warned that rehabilitation had never been properly supported or funded by the state nor implemented by correctional institutions. He cautioned that while overall the research could not say rehabilitation worked, some studies showed that some programs had promise but had simply not been given a chance. Lost in the feeding frenzy over "nothing works" was the whole point of Martinson's research. Martinson was not suggesting that prisons should be transformed into cruel, harsh warehouses for the underclass; he was, in fact, suggesting that the prisons be abolished. He wrote, "the long history of 'prison reform' is over. On the whole, the prisons have played out their allotted role. They cannot be reformed and must be gradually torn down." But Martinson did not know or understand the danger of research running headlong into politics. Bob Martinson died for what he did not understand (Miller, 1989). He committed suicide in no small part because of the misuse, primarily by state agencies and the media, of his critique of rehabilitation programs. Those dangers are compounded exponentially when the issue of state sponsorship is added to the mix. State sponsorship not only can lead to policy initiatives never even conceived of by social scientists but can also fundamentally alter the nature of the scientific enterprise itself.

The Martinson case is emblematic of the misuse of research by the state. The state also often tries to prevent research and discourse altogether. In fact, research by Geis and Goff (1992) demonstrates clearly that the FBI tried to control, through intimidation, the whole field of criminology as it was developing in the United States. The research shows that J. Edgar Hoover used the FBI's intelligence-gathering resources against Harry Barnes, author of *New Horizons in Criminology* and one of the founders of criminology as a discipline, as early as 1936. Barnes had given two lectures in which he had criticized the FBI's unwillingness to address the issues of organized crime. He also criticized the FBI for its vigorous, public-relations-inspired obsession with what Barnes called "second-rate" criminals like the bank robber John Dillinger. As a result of these lectures, Hoover put Barnes's name on the "custodial index file," a list of allegedly dangerous and disloyal persons who were to be seized by force and interned in the event of a serious threat to the internal security of the United States. Hoover also singled out Edwin Sutherland, arguably the most prominent American criminologist, because Sutherland favored parole and had written critically of Hoover's opposition to it. Sutherland was denied access to basic, public documents, such as the Uniform Crime Reports and other FBI data, and was placed on a "no contact" list of persons who had been critical of the FBI. In yet another case, the power of the FBI was unleashed against Abraham Blumberg, a John Jay College professor and leading critic of the operations of the American court system. Blumberg had been critical of the FBI in some of his lectures at John Jay. Hoover ordered all FBI agents taking courses at John Jay to leave the school if Blumberg was not fired. In addition, FBI agent John Shaw, who was a student at John Jay, had written a letter to one of his professors criticizing and sometimes agreeing with Blumberg's criticisms of the FBI. The FBI secretary who typed the letter for Shaw sent a copy to Hoover, who promptly transferred Shaw to the FBI's Butte, Montana, office.

Two decades ago, Marvin Wolfgang (1982) warned us sternly that the source of research funds constitutes a major moral and ethical dilemma in criminology. Wolfgang suggested that researchers avoid all sponsorship in which the funding agency seeks to control the research through suggested methodologies or suggested types of data. He further warned that a sponsor who politicizes the findings is one that takes the researcher across the moral boundaries of science and one whose sponsorship must be refused.

More recently, Gil Geis and his colleagues made it clear that researchers have an ethical obligation to disclose any financial self-interest in the agency or issue they are evaluating or researching (Geis, Mobley & Shichor, 1999). The case study addressed by Geis and his colleagues involved a researcher who received a summer salary from the institution he was researching and served as a trustee on the board of another institution he was evaluating. The implications of this case study are far-reaching. Clearly, any researcher who, for example, has a consulting relationship with an agency, a salaried training relationship with that agency, or the expectation of continued financial support for research has an ethical obligation to specify those relationships up-front—and may have a moral obligation to decline participation in any form of evaluative research. The importance of avoiding the appearance of a conflict of interest has been repeatedly stressed in the literature (Geis, Mobley & Shichor, 1999; Hagan, 1998; McShane, 1996; Wolfgang, 1982).

THE SOCIAL CONSTRUCTION OF CRIME BY FUNDING AGENCIES

The scientific method assumes that criminologists and other social scientists will select topics of inquiry based on three criteria: (1) their own scholarly interests and expertise, (2) the needs of society, and (3) the availability of accurate, valid, and reliable data, or the existence of methodologies to develop accurate data. Since the inception of the Law Enforcement Assistance Administration in the 1960s, through the current programs for research at the National Institute of Justice (NIJ), the Office of Juvenile Justice and Delinquency Prevention (OJJDP), and other federal agencies both inside and outside of the Department of Justice, a flood of federal funds has altered the direction of scientific inquiry in criminology and criminal justice. Certainly, the availability of copious amounts of federal dollars for research has stimulated scientific inquiry with regard to crime and justice. However, it has also played a significant role in dictating the topics to be studied, in determining how they will be studied, and in pointing to data sources for those studies. It is true that scholars who choose not to study topics regarded as significant by federal funding agencies, or who reject prescribed methodologies and data sets, are free to look elsewhere for funding. But it is equally true that the ready availability of funding attracts many scholars who would otherwise not have tackled a particular area of inquiry. A study by Dennis Longmire (1983), which sampled members of the American Society of Criminology, found that 63 percent of them had experienced ethical dilemmas and had felt pressure to engage in undesired research. This has the effect of artificially stimulating a body of knowledge, which has subsequently proliferated in the scholarly journals, that might not have otherwise been pursued, regarded as important, or have been dictated by the state of criminological science.

Government-sponsored research on the drug war is instructive. From 1994 to 1998, NIJ funded 50 grants to universities for drug research. Eleven of those grants focused on applications for drug testing, such as the Drug Use Forecasting system, that allow state agencies to identify more efficiently those the state feels need enhanced social control. Most of the other grants dealt either with more efficient means to manage those already identified and arrested or with clearly spurious attempts, already discredited by a vast body of criminological literature, to tie drug use to violent crime (see Kappeler, Blumberg & Potter, 2000). Not a single grant explored the efficacy of harm reduction, drug maintenance, or de-escalation of the drug war (Kearns, 2000). NIJ grants in the area of policing were similarly directed toward efficient processing, management, and amelioration of community fears about crime. From 1994 to 1998, NIJ gave universities 82 research grants to study policing. Fifty-five of those grants targeted community policing, the panacea de jour, despite no evidence that community policing has any impact on the prevalence or incidence of crime (Greene & Mastrofski, 1988). At the same time, the federal government has published countless "community policing profiles" asserting that problem-solving policing has reduced crime, never mentioning that victimization rates in the United States began their 30-year decline (Kappeler, Blumberg & Potter, 2000) before the advent of community policing. Twenty-five of those grants addressed efficiency and mass processing of the "dangerous classes" by the police. Only 12 addressed the issue of police "integrity" during a period in which serious issues regarding police brutality, corruption, and police sexual violence against women had resurfaced (Kearns, 2000). By any assessment, even the most benevolent, this means that federal funding agencies are fundamentally altering the content, scope, and definitions of scientific inquiry to fit their political agenda rather than the objective criteria of social science. This means that federal funding agencies are acting as moral or political entrepreneurs in the social construction of a reality of crime which is substantially false. Federal funding often focuses on the poor and the social "junk" of society. We may be compelled to study heroin-addicted female prostitutes rather than liquor- or barbiturate-addicted male corporate executives. We may be compelled to study armed robbers, not environmental polluters. We may ask whether the "moral inferiority" of the poor, disguised as discussions of family breakdown and social control, is correlated with violence but not whether the consumption patterns of the rich are correlated with corruption, graft, exploitation, and white-collar deviance.

Equally important as selecting topics for study, the existence of federal "Requests for Proposals" (RFPs) may cull out and suppress other areas of inquiry. In fact, a survey of American Society of Criminology officers from 1988 to 1993 found widespread concern regarding areas of research that were neglected due to funding restrictions (Vohryzek-Bolden, 1997). In that study, it was also reported by several respondents that the findings of their research had not been released, or had been delayed in their release, because their results were not compliant with agency ideology and goals. Vohryzek-Bolden (1997:131) also reported that the "respondents overwhelmingly agree, and some strongly so, that we have been co-opted and that our research agendas have been set by the federal government." While huge sums of money are being devoted to studying the dubious question of criminal careers in a society in which self-report surveys tell us that virtually everyone appears to be a criminal recidivist, funds for other explorations are hard to come by. For example, NIJ is deficient in sponsoring research on political corruption. In fact, from 1994 to 1998, no such studies were funded by NIJ (Kearns, 2000). Corporate and organized crime scarcely gets a mention in NIJ program documents. From 1994 to 1998, out of 433 research proposals funded to universities, only six dealt with white-collar or organized crime. While the average NIJ research grant to universities was about $197,222, grants dealing with organized and white-collar crime averaged less than one-half that amount at $91,449 (Kearns, 2000). While crime against women and children receives some attention, the research is directed away from consideration of the potentially criminogenic role of the traditional family in a patriarchal society. In fact, all of these funds were directed toward risk assessment, court programs, and victim and witness assistance programs. Not a single one addressed the etiology of violence against women in American society (Kearns, 2000).

Overall, the distribution of NIJ research funds to universities is highly instructive. On their face, the data demonstrate a commitment by NIJ to the preservation and extension of policies and programs scientifically shown to be inefficacious, programs that are "shopworn versions of failed policies of the past: more cops, longer prison sentences, extensions of capital punishment, and a tad of community prevention programs" (Levine, 1995:175). They demonstrate a commitment by NIJ to a social construction of crime that paints the crimes of the poor and disenfranchised as more compelling and dangerous than crimes of the powerful. The 433 NIJ university research grants from 1994 to 1998 break down as in Figure 21.1.

Figure 21.1
NIJ Research Grant Topics, 1994-1998

Topic Area	Number of Grants	Percentage of all Grants
Violence	91	21.0%
Policing	82	18.9%
Technological Development	54	12.5%
Corrections	51	11.8%
Drugs and Crime	50	11.5%
Crime Prevention	52	9.7%
Development, Information Dissemination & Support of the Criminal Justice System	30	6.9%
Courts and Sentencing	19	4.4%
Public Housing	9	2.1%
Family Support Programs	3	0.7%
International Crime	2	0.5%

Source: Kearns, A. (2000).

The deviance of the poor is emphasized, while the deviance of the powerful is typically ignored. This becomes much more than a constructionist controversy. At this level, the direction of scholarly inquiry toward questions that are relevant only to the efficacy of harsh crime control programs, and that fail to meet the basic criteria for study selection enumerated above, is unethical by any definition of science.

Knowledge is defined and limited by what we already know. Only research that has been done can inform research that is to be done. Only the produced body of knowledge can be passed from teacher to student. Existing knowledge defines the issues we raise and the questions we ask. In some respects, this is good in that it provides structure, but structure can be quite limiting by telling us that we can only look for possible answers in the areas that have been predefined by past practice, ideology, and politics. If an agency or funding entity has played a preeminent role in deciding what questions are asked, how they are asked, and what data shall answer them, that funding entity has gained a disproportionate influence in the process of accumulating knowledge. Reliance on secondary data collected, processed, and stored by state agencies rather than the collection of independent data based on researcher's observations ensures that state definitions and ideologies are embedded in our scientific inquires. The definitions of crime become those created by the state, the practices of justice system officials become those documented by agencies, and the reality of crime and justice becomes distorted.

This is not the only way that such agencies restrict and restrain the growth of knowledge and the expanse of science. Methodology also plays a key role. Overwhelmingly, funding agencies produce RFPs that call for quantitative analyses, frequently of data sets produced by that agency or by another criminal justice system agency. This creates two dilemmas of science. The first is that quantitative analysis, even the most elegant, can achieve only highly limited objectives. Such analyses can answer only small, precisely defined questions. Usually those answers can be stated only as correlations, which as any freshman research student knows is a far distance from causation. Such analyses cannot address unexpected questions or questions that exceed the range of the agency-collected data being analyzed. If data that might be critical of the agency are not collected, and there is good reason to believe an agency will not collect such data, then the data cannot be analyzed. The probability of police departments collecting accurate data on police corruption or violence is minuscule. Therefore, any police-agency-produced data sets will by default lead researchers away from these questions. Of course, the solution to this problem is to temper quantitative analyses with qualitative research, which, while difficult to generalize from, can ask and answer a wide range of questions, including those related to meanings and intentions. The discipline was founded on rigorous qualitative research, but such research lost favor among our most generous sponsors. And why has this happened? As indicated, it is difficult to generalize in sweeping panoramas from qualitative data. Qualitative research also takes time. The real reason, though, is that qualitative research is unbounded; it leads the researcher where it leads the researcher. That is highly problematic to funding agencies. Searching for facts and understandings outside of the constraints of extant data sets or limited methodologies is dangerous stuff. It has the potential to point out inconsistencies, contrary ideas, and imponderables in social life. Those questions are anathema to social control agencies; therefore, methodologies that raise them are best left unused.

When qualitative research studies are funded by federal agencies, the methods researchers are allowed to use ensure predetermined and favorable outcomes. The techniques used to achieve desired outcomes include studying the "best practices" of criminal justice agencies and programs, limiting research to highly selective and innovative agencies, requiring letters of support for the project from agency officials, and having practitioners review and approve the funding of research projects. The "best practices" technique requires researchers to do case studies of only the most innovative agencies, programs, and practices. By using this technique, the average or even worst programs, practices, and agencies are never examined. Requiring sponsorship and letters of support from officials ensures that the agency is conformable with the researcher and is relatively sure that the outcome of the research will be palatable to the agency. By allowing practitioners to pass judgment on the viability, quality, and funding of the research, sensitive questions are not addressed or at least the questions posed are those that are viewed as "practical." Perhaps the most damaging aspect of governmental funding of a few qualitative research studies is that it gives the appearance of balance, rigor, and objectivity. While clearly the preferred mode of inquiry, balanced forms of research utilizing mixed methodologies or following quantitative analyses with qualitative research to address inconsistencies and contradictions are not favored by federal funding agencies.

The emphasis on quantitative and highly suspect qualitative research also has a debilitating impact on the creation of a body of knowledge and, therefore, on the integrity of the academic process. Criminology and criminal justice departments eager to attract research funds train graduate students in the methods most useful to the principle investigators on those grants. The emphasis on quantitative techniques and those highly suspect techniques means we are producing future teachers who are able only to pass on these techniques. As new faculty, these former students will use the limited methodological skills with which they have been invested to secure more federal grants, which will produce more graduate students with limited qualitative skills, and the cycle will be continued into infinity.

STATE FUNDING AND CONFLICTS OF INTEREST

The vital importance of objectivity to science is clear (Weber, 1949). Objectivity is a basic canon of the scientific method. Unfortunately, when an institution offering research funding is itself a primary focus of the research, objectivity can be hard to come by. When the Department of Justice, through NIJ, offers research funds, it is not likely to offer funds for research that would negatively impact its own reputation or operations. Rare indeed is the RFP that solicits research on corruption of federal law enforcement agents, or the violence of federal SWAT teams, or perjury in affidavits for search warrants proffered to federal judges by DEA agents, or the misuse of informants, and so on. Moreover, what about the impact of funding on those research topics that are solicited by the federal government? If a researcher is too critical, or too troublesome, or insufficiently solicitous of bureaucratic needs and desires, he or she may find getting funds to be a particularly difficult matter. If he or she produces research that is too troubling, raises too many issues, or does so in a manner that is too pointed for bureaucratic niceties, that researcher may find future funding imperiled.

Researchers in crime and criminal justice play many roles. They are often researchers, practitioners, professors, citizens living in their community, and political actors. As such, they face role conflicts that are vital to the research enterprise and that may create additional conflicts of interest. Conflicts of interest are particularly compounded by the set and setting of most research. Universities typically employ scholars and researchers. Those scholars are under considerable pressure to accumulate external funding, upon which universities have become increasingly dependent. With universities typically extracting a 40 to 60 percent overhead charge on research monies and a 20 to 30 percent surcharge to pay for faculty salaries and benefits, research grants readily translate into buildings, equipment, and personnel lines. In many universities, the decision to hire a new faculty member is made by determining whether the applicant can fund her own position by demonstrating a track record of securing governmental grants—not necessarily the ability to conduct scientific research or perform quality teaching. When we add to this mix the university's control of the tenure and promotion process, the potential for conflicts of interest become compelling.

Our academic brethren, however, find cover for these conflicts in three false dichotomies that are often advanced by those who wish to accept funding or who promote without worrying about conflicts of interest. Those three false dichotomies, which seek to hide fundamental ethical questions under the guise of scholarly debate, are: (1) theory vs. practice, (2) causal analysis vs. policy analysis, and (3) pure research vs. applied research.

THEORY VS. PRACTICE

The subject matter of research on crime and justice is fundamentally different than that of the natural sciences. Because we focus on crime, criminals, victims, behaviors, and the criminal justice system, we must be concerned with attitudes, groups, organizations, human societies, politics, economics, and social psychology. The perception that this subject matter is more imprecise and less subject to the laws of the universe than the natural sciences leads to a controversy about theory and practice.

One of the fundamental false dichotomies in the research debate is that of theory versus practice. Theory is simply an attempt to structure, summarize, and develop reasonable explanations of reality based upon the available scientific evidence. Theories seek to inform inquiry, to provide fundamental insights into how things work, and to illuminate areas of confusion and controversy. Without theory, criminology and criminal justice research is conceptually bankrupt, merely a collection of apocryphal war stories selected for an ideological purpose. Without theory, there is no practice, there is no research, and there is no scholarship. As Hagan (1998:22) perceptively points out, "studying a field devoid of theory would be akin to a mystery novel in which the author never told us 'whodunit' and how and why they did it." Research without theory and practice uninformed by theory are vacuous enterprises.

Drug enforcement provides a classical example of atheoretical practice. Drug crackdowns and street sweeps are predicated on the assumption that an overwhelming show of police force and a large number of arrests of drug sellers and buyers will disrupt drug markets, causing them to close down. These very expensive police operations do stop drug selling at the point of impact temporarily. However, they have several deleterious impacts (Sherman, 1990). First, they inevitably displace open-air drug markets, moving them a few blocks in another direction or forcing them indoors. This leads to the creation of SWAT teams, drug raids, and other more dangerous invasions into personal space, as well as the growth of the police institution rather than the reduction of drug trafficking. Second, they perform a vital service for organized crime. By removing disorganized and not particularly adept pushers from the streets, they allow syndicates to gain total control of the illicit drug market. In essence, the police act as a kind of personnel department for the syndicate, "firing" through arrest the slothful, unimaginative, slow, lazy, and careless among them. Inevitably, organized crime syndicates do two things. They reduce the price of drugs and increase the supply in the community as a means of acquiring all of the customers formerly served by less organized or independent entrepreneurs. Enterprise theory, which explains organized crime as a simple extension of legitimate business activities into illegal product markets, would have told police that aggressive crackdowns were not only useless but counterproductive and would have suggested other, less expensive and more effective means of reducing public sales of drugs. A drug policy uninformed by theory not only makes the situation worse but also costs much more in the expenditure of public resources. Evaluation research, which emphases the number of arrests (once again, uninformed by theory), would suggest the possibility of success or progress in such crackdowns. Studies emphasizing the drug market would show no impact and an overall worsening of the situation.

Another example of practice uninformed by theory is the widely held belief by media representatives, politicians, and the public that increasing the number of police officers can impact on the prevalence and incidence of violent crime. Such an approach is expensive, illogical, and thoroughly nonproductive for several reasons. First of all, most violent crime occurs between people who know each other and are indoors. How can more police patrolling the streets prevent what they cannot see? Even for crimes that do occur on the street, such as armed robbery, the chances that a patrolling police officer will be passing by the precise location at the precise time that such a robbery is occurring would still be minuscule even if we tripled or quadrupled the number of police. If police are observed by a potential criminal, the criminal will usually wait until they are gone to commit whatever predation was being contemplated. "Common sense," uninformed by theory, is usually not very sensible. Yet, much of the research being conducted today is aimed at the resurrection of theoretically bankrupt notion of crime and crime control—the deterrence of police patrol and the death penalty, the power of punishment and rehabilitation, and the ability to discern between law-abiding and not-so-law-abiding citizens.

Think about the potential absurdity of formulating policy on violent crime devoid of theory. For example, 86 percent of all arrests for violent crime are of males. Practice, devoid of theory, might suggest that simply imprisoning all males at birth would reduce the violent crime rate. Practice, informed by theory, would indicate that it is not the sex of the offender but his gender within the society that is the problem. Such theory directs our attention to the way we raise boys—to their socialization into competitiveness, violence, and aggression. Theory directs our research toward schools, parenting, sports, sexism, and the media, not toward prediction and detention focused on genitalia.

CAUSAL ANALYSIS VS. POLICY ANALYSIS

Theory and research should provide us with facts and valid explanations regarding crime and criminal justice. Ideology, on the other hand, is a belief system about what should happen that frames viewpoints about political directions of social policy. James Q. Wilson draws a clear distinction between what he calls causal analysis and policy analysis. Wilson's dichotomy parallels the theory–practice debate in that he argues that causal analysis (theory) is an impractical intellectual pursuit because causation is not readily subject to change. Wilson (1975: 51) says that the assumption that "no problem is adequately addressed unless its causes are eliminated" is causal fallacy. This atheoretical assertion about causation misses the fact that causation exists on a number of conceptual levels; Wilson misstates the dilemma. The issue is not whether "causes are eliminated"; the issue is that no problem is adequately addressed unless its causes and the level of causal abstraction are acknowledged, recognized, and considered. No problem is adequately addressed unless theory, which offers explanations of problems, is the grounding for policy.

Take the case of heroin. Evidence clearly indicates that heroin addicts commit proportionately more crime, and more serious crime, than other people in American society. Policy, devoid of theory, would tell us that heroin, therefore, causes crime, and those heroin addicts should be rounded up and imprisoned willy-nilly. That, however, would be wrong. At the highest level of causal abstraction, laws cause crime—both the crimes of substance abuse and the property crime the government wants to associate with it. Furthermore, heroin in fact sedates addicts. A heroin addict who has a ready supply of heroin has no desire to rob a liquor store and even less motivation than a non-heroin-using citizen. At this level of causal abstraction, the absence of heroin causes crime. It is the absence of heroin that provides the impetus for an act the addict does not wish to commit, save the need for money to buy more heroin. Switzerland, Great Britain, the Netherlands, and Germany have adopted practices consistent with this reality by supplying heroin and clean needles to addicts. In the United States, we continue with uninformed policies that can only antagonize an already bad situation.

Take the heroin example one step further. At the turn of twentieth century, heroin was a legal, over-the-counter drug in the United States. It was sold in a variety of flavored elixirs (cherry-flavored heroin, licorice-flavored heroin, distilled liquor and heroin). Comparatively, we had far more addicts per capita then than now. However, addicts at the turn of the century were predominantly white, middle-class, middle-aged, rural women. There was no concern that they would run out and rob a liquor store or that heroin abuse was leading them to crimes of predation against society. By today's atheoretical policy standards, police should have arrested half a million or so grandmothers and slammed them in prison for long mandatory sentences. The absurdity of such a policy in 1898 is obvious. The absurdity of the same policy today should be equally obvious.

PURE RESEARCH VS. APPLIED RESEARCH

One of the most rancorous, and in many ways one of the most contrived, arguments in criminology and criminal justice is found in the disagreements between those who pursue "pure research" and those who find value in "applied research." In essence, pure research is centered on the discovery of knowledge for the sake of knowledge. Such research may have no current utility; it simply exists to contribute to the continuing development of science. Applied research has many definitions. In essence, it is centered on addressing questions with direct relevance to present policy or practice. The distinction is contrived because the best research of both types has overlapping characteristics (Rabow, 1964). In addition, the proper conduct of all research creates a context that should make "applied" research contingent upon and secondary to "pure" research. It is hard to realistically imagine any form of pure social science research that does not have either an application or an implication for application.

How can this be so? First, while pure research is often dismissed as the ivory tower musings of detached intellectuals, it is in fact the basis of all critical breakthroughs in science, both social and natural. Einstein, Galileo, Copernicus, and Pasteur were not applied researchers. They are representative of what Thomas Kuhn (1970) terms "scientific revolutions." According to Kuhn, scientific revolutions are those quantum leaps of knowledge in science that were heretofore unimagined and often heretical. There would have been no discovery of America if we still believed the world was flat. There would be no space program if we still believed that the earth was the center of the universe. There would be no modern medicine if we had not learned about infection and were still exorcising evil spirits. Scientific revolutions result in paradigm shifts in which all of science is changed in terms of conceptualization, instrumentation, and observation. They challenge the old truths and the old methods. As acts of scientific heresy, they prevent researcher ideology from becoming scientific religion. The primacy of pure research and the accumulation of knowledge in the development of science is both practically and ethically obvious. It also defines an area of overlap because applied research that is not informed by and within the context of pure research is simply bad science.

On the other hand, applied research need not be the domain of charlatans, quacks, and bureaucrats, as is often alleged. In fact, it should be the domain in which pure knowledge finds it practical application. To fill this role, it must be both scientifically rigorous and ethical—and there's the rub. Is there anything wrong, scientifically or ethically, with seeking policy applications or evaluating current programs? Of course not, as long as it is done as science—not ideology and not religion. In order to be science, applied research must be conducted within the confines of the scientific method, and that means the following things must be true:

1. *It must be objective.* For pure research, objectivity revolves around the method and practitioner. With applied research, additional considerations come to the fore. A significant amount of applied research in criminology and criminal justice is funded by governmental agencies at the federal level, some at the state and local level, and some by private foundations. This creates a number of difficult problems, which were discussed previously. How do we assure objectivity when we are subjects of institutional funding that requires us to evaluate that institution or its practices? The answer is that social scientists must insist upon adherence to the scientific method. The scientific method ensures "honesty" by insisting that researchers be autonomous and totally free of external restrictions and constraints (Kaplan, 1963). The integrity of science is protected by (1) peer review, a process in which our fellow scientists review our findings to assure the absence of bias and error; and, perhaps more importantly, by (2) replication, which assures that our work can be repeated in other settings, thereby providing the basis of intersubjective agreement or controversy depending on the findings. What may not constrain scientific inquiry is political pressure.

The scientific method requires that we be forthright in addressing issues of methodology and data. If a methodology is inadequate, even if prescribed by a funding agency, it must be denounced as such by the researcher.

If the data set is polluted with regard to validity or reliability, the researcher must expose it. No ideological consideration, political reality, funding decision, or act of university governance may interfere. To do less is unethical and is academic malpractice of the worst kind.

At one point early in his career, one of the authors of this chapter was asked to accept a grant to analyze drug arrest data. The data were very limited. Being arrest data, they told us much about what the police were doing and nothing about patterns of drug use or consumption or the seriousness of the drug problem. The data were analyzed, careful comment was included on the limitations of the data, and an analysis of what could be said from the data was prepared. The federal funding agency was not happy. It suggested that police chiefs, the media, and other officials were put off by "too many words" in this kind of research report. It would be better, they thought, to include a lot of graphs, tables, and charts, but much less explanation. Much of the text was excised, new illustrations were included, and because data does not speak for itself, a relatively benign (but nonetheless fraudulent) report was issued by the funding agency, after removing one of the authors names at his insistence. The university still got the money, the agency got its pretty picture of "drug abuse," and only one person's sensibilities were offended.

2. *The research must be in context.* It is very easy for a social scientist to escape the constraints of science by using data that deal with a very limited issue or a very limited aspect of an issue. Because much research, particularly that funded by the state, deals with specific issues, data sets, or applications, it often seems easy for a researcher to avoid the larger issues and maintain adherence to the rigors of science by avoiding those more encompassing controversies. A classic example is the federal government's Drug Use Forecasting programs, which make assessments on the prevalence of drug use and the connections between drugs and crime by drug testing arrested and incarcerated samples. That data, while politically useful in suggesting, for example, that some number of armed robbers may have one point or another used cocaine, is scientific fraud if it does not similarly test the population as a whole and tell us how many people using cocaine are not armed robbers. Would we not reach the same conclusions if we tested physicians performing surgeries, college professors lecturing, or police officers on patrol? This is data and research without context, without a means of evaluating its actual meaning. It is here that the crux of much of the causal versus policy, pure versus applied debates is found.

Several decades ago, a leading researcher in the area of organized crime told one of the authors about a report he was preparing for a state agency. Being something of a computer expert in a time when such expertise was limited, he was asked to construct a database of organized crime activity. He had carefully accumulated and listed all of the individuals listed in intelligence reports or arrested for organized-crime-type offenses (i.e., gambling, fencing stolen goods, prostitution, drug trafficking, etc.). As he was preparing to analyze that data, he was told to remove non-Italian individuals from his data set. The state had a vested interest in producing an image of organized crime as a small, easily containable "Mafia," against which law enforcement successes could be duly noted. The state had no interested in a report that would show that two-thirds of the organized crime associated individuals were non-Italian, some with strong political connections, and most unmolested by federal or state enforcement operations. About 10 years after this incident, one of the authors of this chapter received a frantic call from a student interning with an organized crime intelligence collection agency. She had been collecting newspaper accounts of organized crime activities and creating a database of individuals and incidents. When the time came to analyze the data for the agency's annual report, she was told to find and isolate only the Italian-Americans in her database. She thought this was unethical and fraudulent. She was right. It seems that social reality is often much more important to criminal justice agencies than truth. It is the obligation of the researcher to hold in check these tendencies to obfuscate the truth as a means of enhancing agency goals.

In recent years, violence in schools and school safety is a heavily invested federal and state topic of concern. Is it possible to demonstrate the degree of dangerous criminality in schools by merely recording and analyzing lists of students disciplined or admonished by teachers and administrators? No, it is not. Violent crime and in-school disorder are two entirely separate issues. Nonetheless, violations of administrative rules have consistently been used to supplement the rather small number of violent crimes in schools as a way of exaggerating both the danger and changing the context of the question. It is imperative that researchers conducting such studies "just say no." Is it possible to address the issue of school safety by evaluating the usefulness of locking school doors to outsiders without addressing the context of the school safety issue? No, it is not. It is scientific fraud to ask that question without considering why those doors might be locked in the first place. If the data were to indicate that school violence was exceptionally rare and declining; if the data were to indicate that juvenile violence is exceptionally rare, confined to specific locales, and declining; if the data were to suggest that most juvenile victimization occurs at the hands of adults, not other children—then the question of why the doors should be locked to begin with must be discussed to place the research in context. In other words, why are individuals who are not the source of the problem being singled out for state action?

Is it ethical to ask if community members feel safer in their neighborhood as a result of community policing initiatives, without addressing the reality of victimization in that community or the utility of community policing as a crime control strategy? No, it is not. If there is little victimization to begin with, the question is moot. If the community has not been impacted by rates of victimization, the question is moot. The question of public fear of crime may be addressed, but the answer must be contextualized.

All social scientists and researchers have an incumbent obligation to present the whole truth as we presently know it and understand it. We may not need to show that the cause of a problem has been removed, but we do need to show the impact of not addressing those causes on the present program or question being researched or evaluated. For example, if we focus research efforts on the abduction of children by strangers, we must acknowledge that (1) stranger abductions are rare (about 300 a year in the United States); (2) we are ignoring 90 percent of actual abductions of children (abductions by parents in custody disputes); and (3) we are ignoring the vast majority of cases of missing children, who either ran away and did not return (possibly as many as 50,000 a year) or ran away and returned within 48 hours (possibly as many as 1,500,000) (Kappeler, Blumberg & Potter, 2000). We must acknowledge that policy and research directed at stranger abduction will have virtually no impact on the issue of missing children and that such research ignores the principle issue of dysfunctions in the traditional family that make running away a preferable alternative to staying home. The fact that a specific crime control program does not address those issues is a debilitating criticism of that program. To fail to state it clearly (even if it is not the question we were paid to address) is inherently deceptive. We may not need to address the breath of an entire issue in a single piece of research, but we must show where the present question or evaluation is located within that issue. Science does not limit truth to meet the exigencies of cleverly limited questions. In fact, science has an obligation to ask why that question is being pursued.

PROTECTING ACADEMIC FREEDOM

So, where does the obligation to protect science rest? The answer is with the individual researcher. We as social scientists must be strong enough and ethical enough to say no to projects and their attendant funds that compromise the requirements of science. We are the last line of defense against the politicization of crime by state agencies and against the denigration of research to a discount store shopping spree by universities. If there is no grounding in theory to study community policing as crime reduction strategy, or if the wrong questions are being asked, or if the issue is simply implementation rather than efficacy, then we should not ask them. The simple existence of 50 NIJ grants to universities, averaging $225,067.50 each, between 1994 and 1998, dealing with community policing is not a sufficient justification to take on the research. In fact, it may be a reason *not* to accept such funding. The rapacious appetite of universities for research grants, combined with a government's need to find any data supportive of its policies, prostitutes science and challenges academic credibility (Kappeler, 1999:486). As faculty, we also sit on promotion and tenure committees. We can decide what to reward and what to vilify. Constructive critiques of colleagues' work that are designed to assist them in avoiding undue pressure and assist them in the production of ethical scientific products are among our responsibilities. We should not shrink from them.

Some obligations also are inherent in the discipline. Most of us are referees for journals, reviewers for publishers, and even peer-reviewers for NIJ and other funding agencies. In every case, we must ask if the scientific method was followed, if the results were polluted by the requirements of funding agencies or pre-selected methodologies or data sets, and if the question being asked is worthy of explication. We should be applying the highest standards when asking these questions, and we should not be afraid to say a resounding no when science is being subverted to state policy agendas.

What about our friends at NIJ, BJS, NIDA, OJJDP, and other agencies that offer to fund our inquiries, or rather solicit us to conduct theirs? The truth is, they do rather well. They are state agencies, representing state interests and dedicated to achieving state-defined goals. They offer the veneer of peer-review on proposals while keeping most of their reviewers very close to their bosoms. Can we expect them to fund an all-out assault on the crime control ideology that created them? Probably not. We can only expect them to be as honest and rigorous as possible in pursing their goals, which are not always congruent with the goals of science.

In the end, it is universities that will resolve the issue. Universities must protect pure research and reward it to a greater degree than applied or policy research. Universities must stop measuring productivity in dollars and start measuring it in effort. Universities must protect and promote the kind of discourse that may not be politically ameliorative but that raises fundamental dilemmas of science and fact. Universities must guard against becoming the research arm of the state. Failure to do so will do more violence to the quality of education than would the withdrawal of all the research monies from all the disciplines.

REFERENCES

Coffin, P. (1996). *Cocaine and Pregnancy: The Truth About Crack Babies*. New York: The Lindesmith Center.

Donnerstein, E. & D. Lintz (1986). "The Question of Pornography." *Psychology Today*, (December):56-59.

Geis, G. & C. Goff (1992). "Lifting the Cover from Undercover Operations: J. Edgar Hoover and Some of the Other Criminologists." *Crime, Law and Social Change*, 18(1-2):91-104.

Geis, G., A. Mobley & D. Shichor (1999). "Private Prisons, Criminological Research, and Conflict of Interest: A Case Study." *Crime & Delinquency*, 45(3):372-388.

Greene, J. & S. Mastrofski (1988). *Community Policing: Rhetoric or Reality?* New York: Praeger

Hagan, F. (1998). *Introduction to Criminology*. Chicago: Nelson-Hall.

Kaplan, A. (1970). *The Conduct of Inquiry*. Scranton, PA: Chandler.

Kappeler, V. (1999). *The Police and Society: Touchstone Readings*, 2nd ed. Prospect Heights, IL: Waveland.

Kappeler, V., M. Blumberg & G. Potter (2000). *The Mythology of Crime and Criminal Justice*, 3rd ed. Prospect Heights, IL: Waveland.

Kearns, A. (2000). "NIJ and the Social Construction of Crime, 1994-1998." Paper presented at the annual meeting of the Academy of Criminal Justice Sciences, New Orleans, LA (March 23).

Kimmel, M. (1993). "Does Pornography Cause Rape?" *Violence Update*, 3(10):18.

Kuhn, T. (1970.) *The Structure of Scientific Revolutions*, 2nd ed. Chicago: University of Chicago Press.

Levine, J. (1995). "Federal Crime Legislation Through the Eyes of Alexis de Tocquiville." *Crime, Law and Social Change*, 31:347-362.

McCormack, T. (1985). "Making Sense of Research on Pornography." In *Women Against Censorship*, edited by V. Burstyn, pp. 181-205. Toronto: Douglas and McIntyre.

McShane, M. (1996). "Producing a Successful Grant Proposal." *Corrections Today*, 58(4):144-147.

Miller, J. (1989). "The Debate on Rehabilitating Criminals: Is it True that Nothing Works?" *Washington Post*, (March).

Rabow, J. (1964). "Research and Rehabilitation: The Conflict of Scientific and Treatment Roles in Corrections." *Journal of Research in Crime and Delinquency*, 1 (January):67-79.

Schwartz, M. & W. DeKeseredy (1997). *Sexual Assault on the College Campus: The Role of Male Peer Support*. Thousand Oaks, CA: Sage.

Sherman, L. (1990). "Police Crackdowns: Institutional and Residual Deterrence." In *Crime and Justice: A Review of Research*, Vol. 8, M. Tonry & N. Morris (eds.). Chicago: University of Chicago Press, pp. 1-48.

Vohryzek-Bolden, M. (1997). "Ethical Dilemmas Confronting Criminological Researchers." *Journal of Crime and Justice*, 20(2):121-138.

Weber, M. (1949). *The Methodology of Social Sciences*. E.A. Shils & H.A. Finch (trans.). New York: The Free Press.

Wilson, J. (1975). *Thinking About Crime*. New York: Basic Books.

Wolfgang, M. (1982). "Ethics and Research." In *Ethics, Public Policy, and Criminal Justice*, F. Elliston & N. Bowie (eds.), pp. 391-418. Boston: Oelgeschlager, Gunn and Hain.

Discussion Questions

1. Is it possible for a researcher, who has an ongoing relationship working with an agency implementing a new program, training employees for that program, and helping to write policy, to evaluate that program ethically?

2. Can a researcher who is asked to evaluate a police department–generated set of data on drug arrests perform that task without (1) pointing out the limitations of the data, (2) insisting that additional types of data be collected to clarify and put in the context the departmental data, and/or (3) insisting that the Request for Proposal be modified to be more scientifically valid?

3. Is it possible for a federal research agency such as NIJ (which is housed in the Department of Justice) to be objective in soliciting and evaluating research? How might objectivity be enhanced? Could a peer-review system that explicitly excluded any NIJ grant recipients be more objective and more ethical than a peer-review system of past grant recipients?

4. Suppose you were employed by a state agency with responsibility for analyzing statistical crime-related data. In analyzing drug arrests, you were told to drop from your data set arrests for possession of cocaine-hydrochloride (a crime most commonly committed by the middle and upper classes) but to include arrests for possession of crack cocaine (a crime most commonly committed by the poor). What would you do? Would you protest? Would you resign? Would you tell the media what you had been asked to do? Or would you simply perform the assigned task with your eye firmly fixed on your retirement?

5. If a researcher knows that the preponderance of the scholarly literature rejects the question he or she is asked to research, should the research move forward? How should it move forward? What must the researcher do to protect objectivity?

6. Should universities give more weight in promotion and tenure considerations to pure research rather than applied or evaluation research? Which is more potentially important for society? Which is more protective of academic integrity? Should funding be eliminated altogether from promotion and tenure considerations?

CHAPTER 22

The Canary's Song:
Guantanamo and the War on Terrorism

John P. Crank & Patricia Gregor

If I were to stand in a crowd and yell the word "Guantanamo," I would likely get more attention (and more controversy) than if I yelled "Fire." The U.S. prison camp at Guantanamo Bay in Cuba is characteristic of the war on terrorism in a profound way: It is at the nexus of all the controversies that are associated with the war on terrorism. Legally, it is at the fore of a broad-ranging reassessment of the relationship between crime control and due process. Ethically, it is a watershed event: Advocates of legal fair play contend that Guantanamo is in violation of all U.S. and international notions of justice, while supporters of Guantanamo detainment argue that the war on terrorism is so important that the way it is carried out should be outside the bounds of the law.

KEY CONCEPTS:

contested concept

freedom fighter

Guantanamo Bay prison camp

habeas corpus

mens rea

terrorism

terrorist

Many people have correctly pointed out that the war on terror lacks clear focus and specificity. Guantanamo, however, is a thing, clear and specific—a geographic space located off American soil where prisoners picked up in the war on terrorism are held. Beyond that, all else is controversial. Guantanamo is ethically restless, providing little moral satisfaction for those who are embroiled in its controversies. In discussions of Guantanamo, there is no neutral ground. Why is this?

Adapted from John Crank and Patricia Gregor (2004). *Counter-Terrorism After 9/11: Justice, Security, and Ethics Reconsidered*. Cincinnati: Anderson/Lexis-Nexis.

The Problems with Defining Terrorism

Guantanamo and its associated post-911 controversies stem from the way we think about the war on terrorism. The moral battleground on which Guantanamo is discussed and dissected, advocated and damned, is a direct consequence of the war on terrorism. So this paper begins with a discussion of the war, discussing why the terminology of the phrase "war on terrorism" is inherently controversial.

To comprehend a war on terrorism, we have to be able to answer the question, "What are we fighting against?" Because we are fighting a war on terrorism, the question becomes, "What is terrorism?" It is important to note that this is a war on a concept—"terrorism"—not on a category of people "terrorists." The United States has selected to go to war against an idea rather than an articulable enemy, and that has many implications for the war, especially when the idea is so diffuse and contestable. Guantanamo, we argue throughout this paper, is controversial precisely because terrorism is a contested concept. Consequently, we begin our discussion of Guantanamo with a brief review of definitions of terrorism.

There are many definitions of terrorism. For example, Rush (1994:333) has a four-part definition that is quite useful:

1. The calculated use of violence to obtain political goals through instilling fear, intimidation, or coercion.

2. A climate of fear or intimidation created by means of threats or violent actions, causing sustained fear for personal safety, in order to achieve social or political goals.

3. An organized pattern of violent behavior designed to influence government policy or intimidate the population.

4. Violent criminal behavior designed primarily to generate fear in the community . . . for political purposes.

This definition provides a set of criteria that are focused on motive rather than behavior. One can imagine a wide variety of behaviors that might constitute the crime, from the serious felony of murder to the relatively minor crime of assault. It is in the criminal intent, the *mens rea*, that we determine whether the event is terrorist. Moreover, Rush has provided us with a four-pronged test to assess the intent.

Rush's definition is fine for analytical or theoretical purposes, such as those used by social scientists who wish to catalogue behaviors or determine the meanings and intents associated with particular acts. However, it has little to do with how the government defines terrorism. And the terms of the conflict in which we have been engaged since 9/11 are determined by the government—particularly the executive branch of government—not the social scientists. So how does government define terrorism? According to U.S. Code

Title 18 (Crimes and Criminal Procedure), Section 2331, international terrorism refers to activities that

(A)   involve violent acts or acts dangerous to human life that are a violation of the criminal laws of the United States or of any State, or that would be a criminal violation if committed within the jurisdiction of the United States or of any State;

(B)   appear to be intended (i) to intimidate or coerce a civilian population; (ii) to influence the policy of a government by intimidation or coercion; or (iii) to affect the conduct of a government by mass destruction, assassination, or kidnaping; and

(C)   occur primarily outside the territorial jurisdiction of the United States, or transcend national boundaries in terms of the means by which they are accomplished, the persons they appear intended to intimidate or coerce, or the locale in which their perpetrators operate or seek asylum;

According to the same reference, domestic terrorism refers to activities that

(A)   involve acts dangerous to human life that are a violation of the criminal laws of the United States or of any State; (B) appear to be intended as used in this chapter.

The USA PATRIOT Act expanded the definition of domestic terrorism in Section 802 as follows:

(B)   (see Title 18 above, last line) appear to be intended—

  (i)   to intimidate or coerce a civilian population;

  (ii) to influence the policy of a government by intimidation or coercion; or

  (iii) to affect the conduct of a government by mass destruction, assassination, or kidnapping; and

(C)   occur primarily within the territorial jurisdiction of the United States.

The legal definition distinguishes between intent and act, and between domestic and international terrorism. The body of the crime of terrorism is assessed as to whether it is in violation of the U.S. criminal law or the criminal laws of any state. There are two other definitions of terrorism in Title 18. Acts of terrorism transcending national boundaries involve incidents in which someone from one country enters the United States to commit acts of terrorism. In addition, the federal crime of terrorism is any act whose intent is "calculated to influence or affect the conduct or government by intimidation or coercion, or to retaliate against governmental conduct." The acts that constitute the crime (the body of the crime) are described in detail in the statute, but, as in the definition, involve the violation of a currently exist-ing criminal statute.

These definitions of terrorism are not useful for extralegal responses to terrorism, including the use of military power. They provide no insight into the way in which the United States responded to the terrorist attacks of 9/11. When the United States declared war on terrorism and invaded Afghanistan, the administration did not base its behavior on the legalistic definitions of terrorism described above. Nor when we undertook the war on terrorism did we assess, in a legal setting, whether U.S. laws were broken by individuals fighting for al Qaeda or the Taliban. So why, if we have such clear federal laws regarding the conduct of the United States in regard to terrorism, do we have a war against it?

There is an easy answer to this question. The easy answer is the dan-gerousness of the threat argument, which states that we step up the level of response according to the level of the threat facing the country. Law enforce-ment is adequate if the source of the threat can be isolated to particular indi-viduals. However, once state-supported players become involved, a more robust response involving the U.S. military is required.

There is also a historical reason. The historical reason is that President Bush elected to declare a "war on terrorism." The U.S. Congress has agreed that it was the President's prerogative to do so. If this history were to be replayed, he might well have named it something different. Perhaps on deeper reflection he would have declared war on al Qaeda. But he did not.

The controversy hidden in both these seemingly straightforward reasons for using extralegal force is that they relocate the working definition of ter-rorism to the executive branch of government, hereafter referred to as the Executive. When a threat is responded to with military action, it means that the Executive has made a decision to treat terrorism under the rules of war. In the current instance, the war on terror that provides the setting for Guan-tanamo and the controversies surrounding the war on terrorism stem from the fact that they were an Executive decision. Put differently, the two sim-ple theories for the war on terrorism actually complicate things considerably. We have to trust the way the Executive defines the threat, identifies the actors responsible for the threat, and determines their intent in order to believe that the war is legitimate. We shift the working definition of terrorism from a body of articulable U.S. law, as determined by the legislature and carried out by the judiciary, to the Executive.

What, then, is the Executive's working definition of terrorism? The 1996 Antiterrorism and Effective Death Penalty Act gave the Secretary of State the discretion to decide who was on the government's terrorism list. As of October 2003, this list had 36 organizations on it. The following conse-quences apply to members of these groups:

1. Contributing money to these groups, even if for humanitarian rea-sons, is a crime.

2. Members of these groups are barred from entering the U.S. and can be deported if they are already in the U.S.

3. Banks can freeze the funds of these organizations and their agents (Cole & Dempsey, 2002).

U.S. security agents also have a master list of five million people worldwide thought to be potential terrorists or criminals. According to a senior Canadian immigration official, "The U.S. lookout index contains some five million names of known terrorists and other persons representing a potential problem." Names are compared against those flying internationally or entering the United States on visa. Anyone whose name matches the list is stopped and questioned (Godfrey, 2004).

Citizens of individual "terrorist" nation-states are also on the watch list. These states are Cuba, Iran, Iraq, Lybia, Syria, Sudan, and the Democratic People's Republic of Korea. Citizens from these states also were required to register under The National Security Entry-Exit Registration System (NSEERS). This program, which was replaced by US-VISIT in 2004, was implemented by the Department of Justice to track individuals in the United States from these countries.

What we see in the "working definition of terrorism" is that it is categorical; that is, it is based on lists of known individuals, terrorist organizations, and nation-states. All of these elements tend to focus on identifiable terrorist groups; for example, the labeling of nation states as terrorist is associated with states that are friendly to terrorist groups, and the identification of individuals who are dangerous is largely determined by their membership or association with terrorist groups.

TERRORISM AS A CONTESTED CONCEPT

Terrorist or freedom fighter? Once we move from a theoretical or legal definition carried by the criminal law to a practicing definition, we encounter problems of arbitrariness. In brief, "One man's terrorist is another man's freedom fighter." This has two elements.

The first element is that the way in which the label "terrorism" is applied changes over time. Perhaps no individual fits this notion better than Osama bin Laden, the accused mastermind of the 9/11 terrorist attacks. In the Afghanistan–Soviet Union conflict, bin Laden was a member of the Afghani resistance, characterized by President Reagan as freedom fighters and supported militarily by the United States. Certainly, that description is inappropriate today. This shows us how the working definition, and how individuals conform to it, depends on time and place. Ariel Sharon, head of state of Israel, was once on the U.S. terrorist list, yet today is viewed as a strong ally of the United States. Muammar Khadaffi, head of state of Libya, was viewed for many years as one of the world's leading terrorists. However, in December 2003, after extensive secret diplomacy sought by Khadaffi for many years and carried out principally by Great Britain, Libya agreed to full nuclear inspections, and today Libya is seen as a developing ally of the United States in its war on terrorism.

The second element is that individuals who are seen as heroes or freedom fighters by one group are seen as terrorists by others. This means that the definition of terrorism is largely one of political utility. A widely cited example is that of American citizens who fought in the revolutionary war in the United States. For U.S. citizens, these individuals are freedom fighters and highly regarded "founding fathers." For the British, they were terrorists attacking a legitimate state authority. In other words, who is a terrorist and who is a freedom fighter depends not only time and place but also on which side of a conflict someone is on.

Once we move from legal or theoretical to the working definition of terrorism, terrorism becomes an "essentially contested concept" (National Research Council, 2001). We can see this in the uncomfortable juxtaposition of terrorist and freedom fighter. With contested concepts there are no agreed-on definitions of the meaning of the concept—in fact, in the real world, there is significant disagreement as to the core meaning of the term. The meaning shifts and changes with different contexts, and can change dramatically and suddenly. Witness the political and moral rehabilitation of Muammar Khadaffi, whom the United States has attempted to kill, and who today is treated as the leader of a state in a Mideast transition toward democracy.

The central problem with a contested definition of terrorism is that its working definition is created and acted out in a political environment, influenced by emotional, ideological, and religious predispositions of those in power. Consequently, a contested definition will tend to favor a simple categorization of "us" and "them." This steers us away from the capacity to form more strategic responses to terrorism, focusing instead on what appear to be immediate tactical threats. We noted elsewhere (Crank & Gregor, 2004) that

> The notion of contestation complicates efforts to develop (independent) definitions of terrorism and freedom fighting. By creating definitions that distinguish between the two, we make an artificial distinction that removes us from the real world where conflict . . . is acted out. Our definitions are not objective. They tend to reflect and reinforce our international alliances, organizational missions, or political or cultural preferences (Crank & Gregor, 2004:12).

"War versus crime" as a contested arena. The contested definition of terrorism is particularly evident in the debate over whether terrorism should be considered an act of war or a crime. Currently, counterterrorism is car-

ried out as a war, and the Executive has resisted having aspects of the "war" reviewed by any currently operative judicial entity except the FISA court, which provides only a procedural overview and does so in secret.

The "war or crime" issue asks whether individuals should be treated as criminals, which would mean that they have access to the U.S. court system. However, it also involves a broader question: Should some standard of fair play apply to individuals accused of being terrorists? This might involve applications to U.S. law, or it might entail treaty obligations under international law, such as Geneva Convention rights. Or are detainees outside all legal protections altogether? Should we be more focused on interrogation and the acquisition of information about future terrorist attacks, and treat accused terrorists as so dangerous that they can be held indefinitely without out legal recourse? Arguments are quite strong on both sides.

Soros (2003), for example, argues that 9/11 should have been treated as a crime against humanity. Protection against terrorism, he notes, requires precautionary measures, awareness, and intelligence gathering. All these protective measures depend on the support of the populations in which terrorists operate. Treating it as a war, on the other hand, antagonizes the population and expands terrorist support. The state of war produces victims among the local population, which produces more terrorists, which produces more war, in a never-ending cycle. If the war on terrorism had been treated as a crime, only al Qaeda would have been attacked, and we would not be involved in military actions such as Iraq, in which we have become deeply embedded.

Turk (2003), on the other hand, argues that there are fundamental limitations to individualized justice as provided by the U.S. justice system. Democracies, he argues, construct justice around the notion that each individual life has meaning. The law ensures that individual worth is protected. For the state to strip an individual of worth—conceived as life, liberty, and the pursuit of happiness—the state must establish the criminality of the individual's behavior according to some legal standard, usually "beyond a reasonable doubt."

Individualized justice, however, is ineffective under some conditions. The enemy faced in the war on terror is "dedicated to our cultural extermination and willing to kill all of us" (Turk, 2003:281). The substantial dangerousness of terrorism must be addressed in any efforts to develop counter-terrorist measures. He argues in favor of war, stating that we need to recognize the enemy as a special case requiring exceptional non-legal and extralegal measures.

Guantanamo

What is Guantanamo? Guantanamo stands at the nexus of the war/crime controversy. We have been at war in a very real way—we have used military troops to defeat regimes in Afghanistan and Iraq and are using military forces to try to stabilize and rebuild the political and economic infrastructures of those countries. As a result of the Afghanistan war, we have acquired prisoners. Detention authority was provided to Secretary of Defense Donald Rumsfeld under the military order "Detention, Treatment, and Trial of Certain Non-Citizens in the War against Terrorism." That order permitted Secretary Rumsfeld to direct anyone subject to the order to: (1) be detained at an appropriate location, selected by the Secretary, (2) be provided humane treatment, (3) be provided adequate food, drinking water, shelter, clothing, and medical treatment, (4) be permitted the free exercise of religion, and (5) be detained in accordance with any other provisions determined by the Secretary (Office of Press Secretary, 2001).

Secretary Rumsfeld subsequently undertook the establishment of a high-security detention facility at the U.S. Naval Base in Guantanamo. Designed to take about 100 prisoners initially and hold up to 2,000, it was staffed by Joint Task Force 160, comprised of about 1,000 soldiers from various bases in the United States. Prisoners arrived at what came to be called Camp X-Ray, where they were fingerprinted, photographed, and underwent initial interrogation. They were housed in cells that measured 1.8 meters by 2.4 meters, or about six feet wide by about eight feet long and eight feet high. The cells had corrugated metal roofs, wire mesh walls, and concrete bases.

In April 2002, Camp X-ray was closed, and prisoners were relocated to Camp Delta. Camp Delta has blocks of 48 cages, with two rows of mesh cages separated by a narrow corridor. Each cell had a through-the-floor toilet, a sink, and a bed. The cells had electric ventilators in the ceilings to help compensate for the scorching temperatures of Cuban summers. Specialized blocks were also set up. Those in Camp 4 were for prisoners who cooperated and were rewarded with dormitory-style life. A block was set aside for juvenile prisoners. India Block was used for punishment isolation cells, which were windowless metal cages. Delta Block was used for prisoners with mental problems.

What does it mean to hold detainees in Guantanamo? The principal reason for holding detainees at Guantanamo is that it is not on U.S. soil. Under *Johnson v. Eisentrager* (1950), enemy aliens not on U.S. soil are not permitted access to U.S. courts. Hence, their only appeal is through the Executive. They are given only that procedural recourse permitted by the executive branch of the government. So far, there has been none. The Executive has not permitted due process or *habeas corpus*, and has held prisoners without charges under terms of indefinite detention.

Critics have argued that some legal standard of fair play should be provided for detainees. One standard widely discussed is the international standard of the Geneva Convention. However, any international status conferred on the detainees has been steadfastly refused by the administration. Indeed, Secretary Rumsfeld has refused to call the detainees "prisoners," arguing that such a designation would confer legal status on them (Serrano & Hendren, 2002). One has to have some sort of international status in order to have rights. No international or national legal status equals no rights. The

Inter-American Commission on Human rights, a committee of the Organization of American States (OAS), has asked the United States to provide some sort of legal status for all detainees. OAS members, they reminded the United States, are subject to international legal obligations, and so, while it is making up its mind on what legal status they should have, the United States should provide them temporarily with prisoner-of-war (POW) status. The United States responded by saying that this was not an OAS jurisdictional matter (Weissbrodt, Fitzpatrick & Newman, 2002). Amnesty International (AI) has expressed concerns about the treatment of detainees. AI has expressed concern that, though detainees were seized during armed conflict, the Executive has refused to grant them POW status. AI expressed particular concern about their being held without charges, access to the courts, or access to relatives (Amnesty International, 2003a). In her annual address, the Secretary General of AI noted that the war on terrorism contributed to a "roll-back of human rights gains of the past five decades . . ." and that the collective system of security provided by international law was increasingly ignored or undermined" (Amnesty International, 2003b [1]).

According to the Geneva Convention, to be considered POWs, irregular militias must satisfy certain criteria. The U.S. government has justified its refusal to provide Geneva Convention protections to detainees for two reasons, based on those criteria: (1) Al Qaeda tried to blend into civilian populations, did not carry fixed insignia recognizable from a distance, and did not conduct their operations in accordance with the customs of war. Moreover, al Qaeda is a nonstate entity and not a signatory to the Geneva Convention. (2) The Taliban represented Afghanistan, which was a signatory and did conduct themselves as military units. However, they did not wear fixed insignia, nor did some of them bear arms openly (Dorf, 2002).

The government consequently achieved three objectives by refusing to allow international standards of human rights under the Geneva Convention: (1) Prisoners can be interrogated. Under the Geneva convention, prisoners cannot be interrogated. (2) Under Article 118 of the Geneva convention, prisoners of war must be repatriated at the end of hostilities. However, there is no intent to repatriate prisoners. Indeed, a permanent prison is currently being built that is anticipated to house detainees indefinitely, and the state department continues to plan for trials of prisoners. (3) If prisoners were granted POW status, the government could not carry out military tribunals. If they were recognized as POWs, they would be provided internationally recognized procedural rights.

Why hold detainees in Guantanamo? From where does this profound intent to refuse any sort of procedural recourse for detainees come? It cannot be simply a matter of interrogation: The value of information gained during interrogation for anti-terrorism purposes is likely to deteriorate fairly quickly in time. There is certainly little that can be gained by interrogating someone after a year's passage and multiple previous interrogations. Nor is it simply a rational calculus of the technical fit of a detainee to POW status.

If the Executive Branch of government were morally committed to international conventions on prisoners of war or some other international or national standard of fair play, it would find a way to make some legal recourse available to detainees. Certainly, a chorus of international actors have made it clear that they would provide their support for such an endeavor.

Detainees are held for another reason: Fear of overlooking a very dangerous terrorist who might commit or has committed grave acts against the United States. Simply stated, it is the fear of missing a potential terrorist who might carry out a mission against the United States. Consider the words of a military commander who was asked why the United States continued to hold at Guantanamo detainees it knew to be innocent: "No one wanted to be the guy who released the 21st hijacker" (Miller, 2002).

This fear is driven by the magnitude of 9/11. The central feature of 9/11 was not that a terrorist attack had occurred in the United States—there have been many such—but that it had been so catastrophically successful. The magnitude of threat from terrorism post-9/11 is so substantial that, for many, traditional ideas of citizens' rights must be reconsidered.

This response to fear reveals a reversal of a moral way of thinking about justice. That moral way of thinking was stated by Supreme Court Justice Benjamin Cardoza, who said it was better that 10 guilty men go free than one innocent man be imprisoned. In the war on terror, and in our treatment of detainees at Guantanamo, we see a negation of Cardoza's maxim. The comment of the soldier at Guantanamo implies that a guilty person might be mistakenly released if we decided to release those we thought were truly innocent. How much of a chance are we willing to take that we would release a guilty person by mistake? As Ricks and Slevin (2003) noted, Secretary of State Rumsfeld argued that the greater the threat facing the United States, the less evidence we would need for attacking someone: "Focusing on the danger of nuclear and biological weapons falling into the hands of groups that want to attack the United States," Rumsfeld said, "I would submit that the hurdle, the bar that one must go over, changes depending on the potential lethality of the act." In other words, if our fear is great enough that someone potentially will do something truly horrendous, then we are willing to take no chance.

What does this way of thinking mean for justice as we know it? Fear of terrorism has changed, in a fundamental way, the way in which we think about fair play for terror suspects—and increasingly, for criminal suspects as well. The practice of justice is increasingly one in which the relationship between crime control and due process is not adversarial, but in which crime control issues—retexted as security issues and treated administratively through the Executive—receive priority over due process. Due process and access to court remedy is permitted only after the Executive is satisfied that security issues are resolved.

Military tribunals for Guantanamo detainees. Guantanamo is controversial not only because detainees are held there deliberately to evade U.S. court relief, but also because the Executive has proposed holding military tribunals for selected detainees.

President Bush authorized the creation of military tribunals on November 13, 2001, to try noncitizens on charges of terrorism. Secretary of State Rumsfeld was given authority to carry out tribunals, and issued an order on March 21 titled "Procedures for Trials by Military Commission of Certain Non-United States Citizens in the War on Terrorism." The authority included approval of charges, sending detainees to trial, selecting military officers to sit on commissions, and making decisions on procedures, motions, and facts (Migration Policy Institute, 2003). Elements critical and supportive of tribunals are briefly reviewed below.

Lawrence Tribe (2001) argued that access to the courts was a part of the cultural fabric of the United States. Our unique cultural identity was framed by the Constitution and worked out in court processes. That cultural identity is possible because the constitution creates a legal definition of U.S. persons to whom the government must grant certain rights. The use of military tribunals violated the core notion of what it means to be a U.S. person to such an extent that it challenged the notion of freedom itself. Tribunals are an immediate threat to 20 million resident aliens in the United States. Moreover, the decision about who should be subject to tribunal is wholly Executive and is unreviewable. This means that the traditional separation of authority into three branches of government is abrogated, with the Executive acting as judge, jury, and executioner. Moreover, the definition of who is a terrorist is vague. That the United States holds prisoners in indefinite detention, without *habeas corpus*, and holds secret trials, is inherently offensive to American notions of justice.

Others have asked: If we fail to provide protections to aliens, how will U.S. prisoners be treated in international conflicts—in which the U.S. seems increasingly involved (see Glaberson, 2001). The United States has specifically criticized other countries for the use of precisely the kind of tribunals that are being arranged in Guantanamo. The text of the order violates the International Covenant on Civil and Political Rights, which was ratified by the United States in 1992 and obligates signers to provide due process to all persons subject to criminal proceedings.

Tribunal supporters have responded that military tribunals have a long history of use in the United States. For example, Dean (2001a, 2001b) argued that both Lincoln and Roosevelt used military tribunals during wartime. We are, Dean reminds us, under conditions of a declared war. Moreover, criminal trials for terrorists are long and expensive, exposing participants to terrorist revenge. Addicot (2001) argues that tribunals are legitimated by Articles I and II of the Constitution, that congress has the power to define and punish offenses against nations, and that the executive is the Commander in Chief. Further, Article 21 of the Uniform Code of Military Justice provides for the use of military commissions.

Since first establishing them, the Executive has modified the rules under which a tribunal would be conducted. In 2002, the rules were revised as follows: Conviction and sentencing would require a two-thirds majority. There would be three to seven panelists who would be military officers. Evidence would have probative value to a reasonable person, including secondhand and hearsay evidence. Defendants would be provided with military attorneys and could acquire civilian attorneys. However, defendants cannot appeal to the federal courts. They could appeal to a panel of review, which would include military officers and civilians.

The guidelines were revised again in February 2004 to give lawyers more information about whether the government will eavesdrop on conversations between lawyers and detainees, although the government continues to retain the right to eavesdrop. Lawyers can get help from their offices and other lawyers even if they are not part of a pre-approved Pentagon pool.

Yet, the actual carrying out of military tribunals poses a dilemma for the Executive. If individuals are found guilty in the tribunals, the Executive will be accused internationally and by many groups in the United States of kangaroo justice against 9/11 detainees. If detainees are found innocent, the Executive will be accused of overreaching, and its justification for Guantanamo will be undercut. Finally, if the Executive selects only certain individuals for trial, many will ask that if cases are not strong enough for those who are not brought to trial, why are they being held? Why is the government cherry-picking cases? The tribunals thus pose a perilous dilemma for the Executive, in which all outcomes carry enormous potential to delegitimize the government's case. This may be why the government has slowed down its rush to tribunals. Yet this slowdown is itself controversial, because an increasing chorus of voices is asking why detainees are being held indefinitely without the opportunity to have their cases heard.

In the military order establishing tribunals, we again see the Executive attempting to establish a procedure that works outside existing justice processes. It has made concessions to due process, perhaps to dampen the volume of criticism about them. However, we can see in the organization of the tribunals—in the low quality of allowable evidence, in the overall secrecy of the trials, and in the somewhat arbitrary and truncated nature of the highly limited appeals process—the assertion of security issues over due process. Due process seems to be included only begrudgingly, and then only after enormous international and internal pressure.

REDEFINING JUSTICE IN THE WAR ON TERRORISM

The war on terror has permitted the redefinition of the relationship between crime control and due process. Traditionally, this relationship has been conceived of as adversarial, though the widespread practice of plea bargaining and the disproportionate state funding for prosecutors over defense counsel overall has placed crime control in a dominant position. The veneer of due process, though thin, was nevertheless present. Although overall, criminal justice system behavior is weighted toward crime control, a fundamental belief in due process remained. However, the war on terror has changed this relationship.

In the new model, crime control issues are prioritized over due process. Crime control issues are reframed as security issues. Only after security issues are resolved are due process concerns considered. The decision as to whether security issues have been adequately addressed is at the discretion of the Executive. At Guantanamo, the use of that discretion is to permit no opportunity for due process.

One might argue that issues of security are advanced over due process for a relatively narrow population of detainees. Yet, the same principles have been applied to those holding visas as well. Historically, visa holders, and indeed anyone on U.S. soil, are protected by a core body of rights. If they have been suspected of illegal behavior, they have been permitted *habeas corpus*, the right to appeal the assertion of the holding authority to some court to have their case reviewed.

In the war on terror, the use of the courts has been interceded by administrative decisionmaking in the Justice Department. There is no appeal for the decisions made by the Justice Department, and detention and evidence may be kept secret. Review is permitted only by the Foreign Intelligence Surveillance Act (FISA) court, and then it is only a review of the conformance of the conduct of the court with that required by law. As we noted elsewhere (Crank & Gregor, 2004),

> The determination about whether they (detainees) have that right (access to American courts) is a Justice Department decision. Once security concerns are resolved, the person may be released to return to their families, if they are in fact in the country legally and have been uncontroversial. Or they may be turned over to the justice department for prosecution if an investigation into their activities has produced evidence of criminal wrongdoing. Or they may be deported to their country of origin. Or, for an unfortunate few, they may be held indefinitely, without charges. But first, the security is resolved to the satisfaction of the Justice Department (p. 22).

What recourse does a person have under these circumstances? Without access to the courts, the only opportunity a person has may be to plead guilty during interrogation and hope for leniency from the Justice Department. And in the war on terrorism, there has been scarce leniency.

One might respond that the preemption of crime control through administrative decisionmaking over due process or fair play concerns is justified for the treatment of war prisoners (though recall that there is resistance to calling them prisoners, because this confers status). However, the preemption of security issues can also be seen in the roundup of immigrants after 9/11.

Inspector General of the Justice Department, Glenn Fine, issued a report in 2003 on the treatment of immigrants held after September 11 attacks (*September 11 Detainees*, 2003). Many immigrants were placed in highly restrictive 23-hour lockdown confinement. Relatives were not told that their family members were arrested. The bringing of charges was delayed indefinitely because of the extraordinary circumstances clause in the USA PATRIOT Act. Moreover, the authority to make release decisions was shifted from the Immigration and Naturalization Service to the FBI. Anyone picked up was held, regardless of the strength of the evidence, and was presumed to be a terrorist until cleared by the FBI. In particular, the use of the material witness statute permitted the government to hold individuals for long periods without bringing charges.

Fine further noted that the FBI issued a no-bond policy that resulted in long-term detention of individuals with no connection to terrorism. Some were held for clearance investigation, even though they had received orders for voluntary departure. Ultimately, none of the 762 immigrants picked up for questioning were charged as terrorists. In this example, we again see that crime control issues are revamped as security issues, and their relationship to crime control is one of preemption.

The elevation of crime control over due process can also be seen in the attitudes of members of the Justice Department toward U.S. citizens. Three senior justice officials in 2003 said that U.S. citizens classified as enemy combatants "should gain access to attorneys only after they have disclosed everything they know about terrorist operations." The goal, they said, was not to deny counsel, "only to delay it until interrogations are finished" (*Port St. Lucie News*, 2003). Similarly, many aspects of the USA PATRIOT Act are being used against American citizens involved in street crime. Laws intended primarily for counter-terrorism are being used in crime fighting. The deputy chief for legal policy in the Justice Department's asset forfeiture and money laundering section, Stefan Castella, said that the PATRIOT Act contained many elements that were on prosecutors' wish lists for years. A spokesman for the National Association of Attorneys complained that the Justice Department was conducting seminars on how to stretch the wiretapping laws beyond terrorism cases (CNN.com, 2003).

The Song of the Canary

"If you want a definition of this place, you don't have a right to have rights." This comment, from a detainee in Guantanamo, was one of the few political comments that slipped past the censors (Meek, 2003, Part 1:2). The comment shows the frustration of individuals held in terms of indefinite detention, without legal recourse, without the opportunity to request that the government in fact find out if they should be there.

Guantanamo is in many ways the canary in the coal mine. What happens in Guantanamo harkens to wider justice trends toward a reframed notion of crime control as security and prioritized over due process. The opening quote in this section is the song of the canary. It is the frustration and hopelessness of those caught in a system of justice determined by administrative prerogatives rather than by adversariness. The problem we encounter when we think about the song of the canary is this. We do not have in place a legal mechanism to determine if they are who the government claims they are. Maybe they are truly and unrepentantly dangerous. Maybe they are innocents caught up in red tape. We don't know. We don't have a way to tell. As long as administrative process trumps judicial review or *habeas corpus*, we will never know. The truth of their individual cases is inaccessible through democratic processes of justice.

Should the detainees be there? Are they all, as Richard Meyers, Chair of the Joint Chiefs of Staff described the first 20 detainees to arrive, "people who would gnaw through the hydraulic lines in the back of a C-17 to bring it down" (Cnn.com, 2002). The *Los Angeles Times* said that at least 59 of them were of no intelligence value after being interrogated in Afghanistan. Many seemed to have been caught up in bureaucratic processes from which they could not escape. According to Miller (2002), once a name was on an interrogation list, it remained on the list regardless of the outcome of the interrogation. Many of the names gradually filtered to the top, primarily because they could be removed only if senior intelligence officers worked through a thicket of red tape. In 2004, five detainees who were British citizens were allowed to be returned to the United Kingdom. They were arrested by the British on arrival and then freed the following day. The Department of Defense also noted in March 2004 that 88 detainees had been released and 12 had been transferred to other countries, but provided no additional information.

Do American citizens want the government to have the authority to treat people this way? Ah, there's the rub. Some of us do. Some of us don't. And there are very few in the middle. The issue of detainee treatment as Executive prerogative in Guantanamo as well as elsewhere—in the New York jails following 9/11, in the proposed military tribunals, in INS special registrations of Middle-Easterners that converted into sweeps in some places, in other offshore prisons that the United States uses, or under conditions of extraordinary rendition in which other countries are provided the opportunity to interrogate detainees—is highly polarizing.

The canary's song is a paradox. One might counter that the grief and suffering associated with the terrorist strike against the Wolrd Trade Center twin towers and the Pentagon that launched the war on terror was the canary's song. Indeed, this is the position of many advocates of the war on terrorism. Viet Dinh (2003), whom many consider the architect of the USA PATRIOT Act, quoted a spokesperson for the Irish Republican Army on a failed assassination attempt on Margaret Thatcher in the 2003 annual American Bar Association conference: "Today we were unlucky. But remember: We only have to be lucky once. You have to be lucky always." In the terrorist attacks, the United States was unlucky once. Like the canary's song, 9/11 was a warning that someone is at war with the United States, and failure to respond at the war-like level of the attacks would only increase our vulnerability.

The canary's song, for both sides in the contested war on terrorism and as acted out at Guantanamo, is filled with suffering and injustice. This is the paradox: In the way we conduct the war on terrorism today, the more one side seeks to reestablish its sense of justice, the greater the injustice is to the other side. The more the United States seeks to protect itself against terrorist threats associated with Muslim fundamentalism—and it is only in terrorism tied in some way to Muslim identity, and in no other area of terrorism, that we are treating terrorism as a war and not a crime—that we see perceptions of injustice on both sides. In the paradox, we understand better the opening oft-cited quote: "One person's terrorist is another person's freedom fighter." Both sides feel vulnerability, grief, and loss. In a war on a contested term, the outcomes of the war will themselves be contested, and wars have a long history of ending badly, sowing the seeds for future conflicts.

CONCLUSIONS

Terrorism, liberty, and security. We return to the central problem with a war on terrorism. It is a war on a contested concept. The central contestation is between security and liberty, which can be framed in terms of the importance of utilitarian good ends versus the rightness of fair play. It is the conflict between security and liberty that is contested in Guantanamo, and increasingly in other areas where the Executive is asserting control over traditional areas of jurisprudence.

There is a long history to the growth and dominance of crime control. The prioritization of crime control over due process as acted out in Guantanamo and in other areas of the war on terrorism did not emerge whole-cloth post-9/11. Prioritization is the cumulative outcome of trends in the United States over an extended period. Diane Gordon (1991) described the dramatic expansion of the war on crime and the growth of the criminal justice system as a justice juggernaut. She expressed concerns that its growth, particularly in terms of surveillance and intrusion into civilian affairs through surveillance, was likely to continue into the future. Expansion of government authority can be seen most recently in the war on drugs and in the political utility of harsh penalties for crimes generally. Among Republicans, crime and drug control is a "stalking horse" for attacks on the welfare state and cultural permissiveness (Gordon, 1991). Among Democrats, the expansion of the criminal law has followed support for the protection of vulnerable populations, especially battered women, victims, and minorities under hate crime legislation. In other words, bipartisan support for the expansion of the crime control system was fully in place before 9/11.

Moreover, the reach of Executive authority in the USA PATRIOT Act was probably less than the 1996 anti-terrorism act signed into law by President Clinton. The authority of the Executive to intervene in the affairs of immigrants should be more properly traced to President Clinton and the 1996 Immigration Act than the PATRIOT Act. The anti-terrorism court permitting the secret review of evidence, commonly called the FISA court, was signed into law in 1978. That post-9/11 security and traditional notions of crime control are closely associated can be seen in a speech given by Attorney General John Ashcroft near the second anniversary of 9/11. He noted that, "We have proven that the right ideas—tough laws, tough sentences, and constant cooperation—are stronger than the criminal or the terrorist cell" (Meek, 2003, Part 2:2). The particular changes brought about by 9/11 were: (1) the retexting of crime control in terms of the language of international security, whether security were international or internal to the United States, and (2) the broadening of administrative control of suspects by the Executive in the name of security, in lieu of due process or *habeas corpus*.

Currently, we can roughly map the contenders in the debate between security and liberty. The side of security is carried out by the Executive branch of government, with a great deal of public support. The Executive has taken a utilitarian view of the war: It has had an unremitting focus on good ends, and has sought to avoid any use of the courts that would disrupt its effort to bring about those good ends. Utilitarianism argues for a forceful response to terrorism. If legal rules of conventional society have to be set aside for the duration of the war, then we need to consider whether a greater good will come from aggressively attacking terrorism than the inevitable harm of imprisoning some who are factually innocent. It also means that we can use the same dirty means that terrorists use if that's what we need to do to defeat them. Smith (2003:117) cites an old Texas saying to describe this view: "When you wrestle with a hog, you both get dirty, but the hog likes it." Terrorism, according to this view, is a dirty business, and to deal with it one must get dirty, too.

This view is opposed by those who believe in the importance of fair play, or ethical formalism, in the treatment of aliens, be they detainees at Guantanamo or immigrants and visa holders. This view is also held by many citizens and by groups such as the American Library Association, and is widely expressed internationally, for example, in Europe and in the work of international organizations such as Amnesty International. According to this view, to act at the level of the terrorists is to be no morally different from terrorists. For democracy to work, respect for the practice of law and due process in all its activities is required. Within the United States, we respect the Constitution and Bill of Rights, and internationally, we work within a framework of international law, be it the Geneva Convention or a code of the Organization of American States. Chomsky expresses the view that the United States has the moral obligation to treat aliens as it treats its own citizens. One must be willing to apply the standards to oneself that one applies to others. Once we do this, he observes, we realize that our treatment of aliens does not rise to even a minimal moral level (*Brothers and Others*, 2002).

The tension between these views is unresolved and the voices on each side strident. If, as some say, the elements that make up the foundings of great enterprises are carried with them through the length of their histories, then the contestedness between freedom and liberty is likely to be enjoined for a quite long period. We are in a war without end. As Soros (2003) noted, the war on terrorism may bring about a permanent state of war. Terrorists will never disappear. A war on a contested term may consequently institutionalize the current highly polarizing conflicts between liberty and security.

The war on terrorism is carried out in ongoing conflict in Iraq in the current era, and the American people have tended to display a fundamental non-reality about Iraq and terrorism. A year after the war was started, a poll of Americans carried out by the Knowledge Networks between March 16 and March 22, 2004, showed that 57 percent of Americans believed that Saddam Hussein gave material support to al Qaeda terrorists. In addition, 45 percent believed that clear evidence was found that Iraq worked closely with al Qaeda, and 38 percent believed that Iraq had weapons of mass destruction just before the war (Davies, 2004). Yet the evidence is compelling that all of these statements are false. This suggests that most people continue to look at security issues through the lens of terrorism, whether or not that is a correct way to consider them.

A CNN/Gallup poll in February 2004 asked respondents if they thought the USA PATRIOT Act went too far, was about right, or did not go far enough in restricting people's civil liberties in order to fight terrorism. Twenty-six thought it went too far, 43 percent thought it was about right, 21 percent thought it did not go far enough, and 10 percent had no opinion. When queried about individual statutes of the PATRIOT Act, respondents tended to split as well. Only when respondents were asked whether federal agents should be allowed to secretly search a U.S. citizen's home without informing the person of that search for an unspecified period of time did respondents take a clear side: Only 26 percent approved, while 71 percent disapproved. In all other areas, responses were evenly divided.

Summing these polls, Brookings scholar Thomas Mann said, "We are so polarized right now that people are seeing what they want to see through a very partisan lens" (Davies, 2004). We might add to his comment that partisanship, at least at this juncture, is somewhat nonmaleable to the presence of fact. In other words, the political and moral contestedness of the war on terrorism is likely to be among its enduring characteristics.

REFERENCES

Addicot, J. (2002). "Military Tribunals are Constitutional." *Jurist*. Available at: http://jurist. law.pitt.edu/forum/forumnew51.php

Amnesty International (2003). "U.S.: 'Operation Liberty Shield': An Attack on Asylum-Seekers' Rights." Available at: http://www.web.amnesty.org/web/web.nsf/print/ usa-270303-action-eng

Amnesty International (2003b). "USA." In Report 2003, 'Counter-Terrorism' and Human Rights." Available at: http://web.amnesty.org/web/web.nsf/prit/usa-summary-eng

Brothers and Others (2002). Worldlink Special. Baraka Productions.

CNN.com (2003). "Anti-Terror Laws Increasingly Used Against Common Criminals." September 15. Available at: http://www.cnn.com/2003/LAW/09/14/anti.terror.laws.ap/ index.html

CNN.com (2002). "Shackled Prisoners Arrive at Guantanamo." Available at: http://edition. cnn.com/2002/WORLD/asiapcf/central/01/11/ret.detainee.transfer

Cole, D. & J. Dempsey (2002). *Terrorism and the Constitution*. New York: The Free Press.

Crank, J. & P. Gregor (2004). *Counter-Terrorism After 9/11: Justice, Security, and Ethics Reconsidered*. Newark, NJ: Anderson/Lexis-Nexis.

Davies, Frank (2004). "Many Believe Hussein Backed Terror." *Miami Herald*, April 23. Available at: http://www.miami.com

Dean, J. (2001a). "Military Tribunals: A Long and Mostly Honorable History." Findlaw. December 7. Available at: http://writ.findlaw.com/dean/20011207.html

Dean, J. (2001b). "Appropriate Justice for Terrorists: Using Military Tribunals Rather than Criminal Courts." Findlaw. September 28. Available at: http://writ.findlaw.com/ dean/20010928.html

Dinh, V. (2003). "Security and Privacy in the United States.' Invited panel presentation at the annual meeting of the American Bar Association.

Dorf, M. (2002). "What is an 'Unlawful Combatant,' and Why it Matters: The Status of Detained al Qaeda and Taliban Fighters." Findlaw's Legal Commentary. Available at: http://writ.findlaw.com/dorf/20020123.html

Glaberson, W. (2001). "Critic's Attack on Tribunals Turns to Law Among Nations." *The New York Times*, December 26. Available at: http:/www.nytimes.com/2001/12/26/national/ 26LAW.html

Godfrey, T. (2004). "5 Million on Terrorism List." *Toronto Sun*, January 20. Available at: http:// www.canoe.ca/NewsStand/TorontoSun/News/2004/01/20/318488.html

Gordon, D. (1991). *The Justice Juggernaught: Fighting Street Crime, Controlling Citizens*. New Brunswick and London: Rutgers University Press.

Meek, J. (2003a). "People that Law Forgot." Parts 1 and 2. December 3. Available at: http:// www.guardian.cc.uk

Migration Policy Institute (2003). "Chronology of Events Since September 11, 2001 Related to Immigration and National Security." Available at: http://www.migrationinformation. org/USfocus/display.cfm?ID=116

Miller, G. (2002). "Many Held at Guatanamo not Likely Terrorists." *Los Angeles Times*, December 22. Available at: http://www.latimes.com/news/nationworld/world/ la-na-gitmo22dec22.story?null

National Research Council (2001). "Terrorism: Perspectives from the Behavioral and Social Sciences." Washington, DC: The National Academies Press.

Port St. Lucie News (2003). "Enemy Combatants Should Give Info First." December 17:A13.

Ricks, T. & P. Slevin (2003). "General Acknowledges Some U.S. Personnel Already are Inside Iraq." *Idaho Statesman*, January 30:3.

Rush, G. (1994). *The Dictionary of Criminal Justice*, 4th ed. Guilford, CT: Dushkin.

September 11 Detainees (2003). "A Review of the Treatment of Aliens Held on Immigration Charges in Connection with the Investigation of the September 11 Attacks." Inspector General, Department of Justice. Washington, DC: Department of Justice.

Serrano, R. & J. Hendren (2002). "Rumsfeld Strongly Denies Mistreatment of Prisoners." *Los Angeles Times*. Available at: http://www.latimes.com/news/nationworld/nation/la-012302gitmo.story

Smith, L. (2003). "Expanded Police Powers are Needed to Ensure U.S. Security." In M. Williams (ed.), *The Terrorist Attack on America*, pp. 115-119. Current Controversies Series. New York: Greenhaven Press.

Soros, G. (2003). "The Bubble of American Supremacy." *The Atlantic*, December. Available at: http://www.theatlantic.com

Tribe, L. (2001). "Military Tribunals Undermine the Constitution." Testimony Given Before a Senate Subcommittee, December 6. Available at: http://www.counterpunch.org/ltribe1.html

Turk, A. (2002). "Policing International Terrorism: Options." *Police Practice and Research: An International Journal*, 3(4):279-286.

U.S. Department of Defense, (2004). "Transfer of British Detainees Complete." March 9. Available at: http://www.defenselink.mil/releases/2004/nr20040309-0443.html

Weissbrodt, D., J. Fitzpatrick & F. Newman (2001). *International Human Rights: Law, Policy and Process*, 3rd ed. Cincinnati: Anderson.

DISCUSSION QUESTIONS

1. Explain what domestic terrorism is.

2. How does the government define terrorism?

3. Explain what the phrase, "One man's terrorist is another man's freedom fighter," means.

4. Discuss the current situation in Guantanamo Bay. What are your personal opinions on this issue?

5. How does terrorism impact one's personal and professional ethics?

Section VI: Ethics and the Future

> **Where there is life there is hope.**
>
> **—Latin proverb**

When thinking about the future of our institutions of justice and other processes that are related to them, a number of questions come to mind. What philosophical model or models will guide us personally and professionally? How will we attempt to balance the rights of the individual with the needs of the larger community? How will these same models help to define and redefine the roles of the courts, policing, and corrections? The heart and mind of our system of justice from which our policies and programs spring forth is composed of our personal and professional philosophical models. Will our collective heart and mind of justice use its long arms of the law to simply keep the peace, or will it begin to try to encourage and contribute to the peace? And how will all the interrelated aspects of this process be evaluated? How will we define success in the future?

It seems evident that as we come to the last section of this book, there are many more questions than answers. Perhaps that is as it should be. As we look to our future, we may find the beginnings of the answers we seek through the asking of clear, accurate, meaningful questions about our personal sense of justice and how it is expressed through our formal justice process.

CHAPTER 23

Criminal Justice:
An Ethic for the Future

Michael C. Braswell

Now that we have come to the end of this volume, we would like to finish by once again considering its beginning. The first three chapters were concerned with developing a philosophical framework through which we could consider the ethical implications of a variety of criminal justice issues from personal, social, and criminal justice perspectives. Now that we have attempted to examine contemporary issues within this framework, we are challenged to look toward the future of criminal justice, a future that is found hidden in its present. How are we to find the eyes to see such a future—a vision that can empower us to contribute to its promise? Will our contributions as individuals and institutions be expressed in the context of a community of hope or a community of fear and cynicism? Will we protect and serve the status quo (focus on the criminal), or will we move ahead, riding the crest of a long shot—that the larger sense of justice is what will be accentuated and that the possibility of social peace can increasingly become a reality? Are we only to be engaged in colorful, crisis-minded rhetoric, or can we translate contemporary justice dilemmas into opportunities for encouraging more substantial policies and practical applications toward restitution and reconciliation?

If we choose to commit to seeking justice and peace in a community of hope, we will need to begin acting on an enlarged vision that includes an ethic for the future. Of course, to some, this sort of thinking may seem to be too romantic a notion when considered against the hard realities of today's justice problems. Still, it would appear that an attitude of hope that empowers us on a personal as well as systemic level, and is anchored in something more than another blue-ribbon task force or budget increase, is worth pursuing. Whether in reference to offenders, victims, citizens, or criminal justice professionals, it seems to be in our best interests to recognize and encourage an attitude of personal empowerment, that perhaps we need to restore

> **KEY CONCEPTS:**
>
> **mindfulness**
>
> **order-keeping**
>
> **peacemaking**

the balance of our interaction with our environment, that problems and solutions come from the inside-out as well as from the outside in. Thich Nhat Hanh writes:

> The problem is to see reality as it is. A pessimistic attitude can never create the calm. But, in fact, when we are angry, *we ourselves* are anger. When we are happy, we ourselves are happiness. When we have certain thoughts, *we are those thoughts*. . . . In a family, if there is one person who practices mindfulness, the entire family will be mindful. . . . And in one class, if one student lives in mindfulness, the entire class is influenced" (emphasis added) (pp. 40, 52, 64).

THE NEED FOR MINDFULNESS

If we are to develop an ethic for the future of criminal justice, we need to become more mindful and conscious of ethical truths concerning justice that are found in the present. For example, the utilitarian's priority for community good and the individual integrity of the deontologist become conscious of one another in the context of connectedness and, more importantly, reconciled in an ongoing response of active care. At some point in our lives, we are inclined to become aware that no matter how strong our personal needs and interests are, no one is an island. We need to be with other people in the community in order to survive and grow.

Whether we live in suburbia, the inner city, or rural America, we begin to realize that we are connected: parents to children, teachers to students, guards to prisoners, and offenders to victims. We like the ideas of "one for all and all for one" and "one nation under God with liberty and justice for all," and we are also connected to our environment. Drought, acid rain, forest fires, and oil spills all raise our consciousness of our interdependence with our physical environment as well.

The dynamic interaction between the community and the individual along a continuum of connectedness and care can be demonstrated in a specifically criminal justice context. We may still find it necessary to remove an offender from society. We may decide to place this person in prison "for the good of the community," yet, even in prison, we need to realize that offenders are entitled to certain rights of basic care and safety. In other words, we need to see that they are treated humanely on ethical and moral grounds, even if in some cases we may feel they are not deserving because of the crimes they have committed or that our correctional treatment efforts have little effect on their behavior.

Although the offender may be inside prison and we may be outside in the community, we are still connected in a number of ways. We are bound together from the past by the fear and suffering of the victim and the vicarious feelings and perceptions of our citizens. There is also the fear and suffering of the offender and the offender's family, who may also be victims. We are brought together in the present through the quality of life of the prison staff, who are also members of the community and are tied to the offenders they supervise and with whom they interact. The promise of the future connects us in the knowledge that, especially with current overcrowding problems, most offenders will eventually return to our communities. We might even consider the notion that how we as a community allow prisoners to be treated in prison and in correctional programs may say much about how we see ourselves and expect to be treated. Becoming more mindful can allow us, as individuals and communities, to take greater care in seeing and responding more meaningfully to the connections that bind us together in relationships.

ORDER-KEEPING AND PEACEMAKING

Hans Mattick (in Conrad, 1981) once said, "If I could sum up my entire education experience and reflection in a single sentence, it would be: 'Things are not what they seem'" (p. 14). Yet, often in our haste to find and keep order, we try to do just the opposite of what Mattick suggests: we try to eliminate the ambiguity and paradox from human behavior—we try to make things "be as they seem." If we limit our search for justice to crime and criminals, we are likely to miss the larger truth of Mattick's point. Our search for justice can instead become subverted to a search for order. It is even possible that the ambiguity that is an inevitable part of democracy's birthright can, over time, be replaced by the certainty and predictability of a totalitarian society.

Too much emphasis on order-keeping encourages us to review problems or failures in the justice process as technological difficulties that can be corrected through sound engineering rather than fundamental problems of design. We imagine that if we can just do things more efficiently, crime and justice problems can eventually be solved or at least reduced to an insignificant level. Unfortunately, an order-keeping focus may inhibit us from expanding our area of concern to include the impact of the interaction within the larger social arena, which addresses more specific crime and justice issues. It is worth remembering that if we have not asked the right questions, which include a variety of diverse perspectives, our solutions—no matter how efficiently implemented—are no solutions at all; rather, they simply add another layer to the confusion and difficulty that already exists, and end up creating additional problems and suffering.

The importance of viewing criminal justice and related issues from a variety of perspectives is well illustrated by a Sufi writer: "What is fate?," Nasrudin was asked by a scholar. "An endless succession of intertwined events influencing each other," Nasrudin replied. "That is hardly a satisfactory answer. I believe in cause and effect." "Very well," said the Mulla, "look at that." He pointed to a procession passing in the street. "That man is being taken to be hanged. Is that because someone gave him a silver piece to buy the knife with which he committed murder, or because someone saw him do it, or because nobody stopped him?" (Meredith, 1984:48).

While keeping the order is important, keeping the peace is more than that. Peacekeeping represents a larger vision with potentially profound implications for the individual and the community. Peacekeeping can in fact emerge into a practice of peacemaking. Such a practice requires that we encourage a greater sense of mindfulness that allows us to remain conscious that human behavior is not an either/or proposition but a continuum that includes and connects offenders, victims, and nonoffenders. Order-keeping focuses on the "guilty few," while the mindfulness of peacekeeping and peacemaking remind us that "few may be guilty, but all are responsible" (Quinney, 1980).

Isaiah (32:17) states, "Justice will bring about peace, right will produce calm and security." Is that what is happening in our crime and justice–conscious culture? Are our citizens experiencing a greater sense of peace, calm, and security? How can we in a meaningful and balanced way maintain that order yet keep and even contribute to the peacefulness, calm, and security in our communities? Such existential questions seem challenging at best and overwhelming at worst. It is easy enough to think and talk about peacemaking, but quite another thing to put it into mindful action. Hubert Van Zeller (in Castle, 1988) adds yet another twist when he writes, "Thinking about interior peace destroys interior peace. The patient who constantly feels his pulse is not getting better" (p. 180). Van Zeller would lead us to believe that if we are able to contribute to the peacefulness, calm, and security of our community, we must learn to be more peaceful, calm, and secure within ourselves. Can we offer calm if we are angry, security if we are fearful, or hope if we are cynical? It seems that if we are to contribute to a more just society, we must not simply think, talk, or write about peacekeeping and peacemaking but personally struggle to increasingly *be* peace. Quinney (1987) writes, "Rather than attempting to create a good society first, and then trying to make ourselves better human beings, we have to work on the two simultaneously. . . . Without peace within us and in our actions, there can be no peace in our results" (pp. 19, 23). Critics of peacemaking as a viable way to improve our justice process would point to its impracticality. Such an approach seems to have little in common with popular notions such as "getting tough" on crime. Unfortunately, while such popular notions may get people elected to political office and make many of us feel better emotionally, their practical applications have done little to reduce crime or increase the calm and security of citizens. Although perhaps requiring an alternative mind set, peacemaking may not be as impractical as many critics would suggest. Dass and Gorman (1985) offer an account by a police officer who struggled to see himself primarily as a peacekeeper and peacemaker:

Now there are two theories about crime and how to deal with it. Anticrime guys say, "You have to think like a criminal." And some police learn that so well they get a kind of criminal mentality themselves.

How I'm working with it is really pretty different. I see that man is essentially pure and innocent and of one good nature. That's who he is by birthright. And that's what I'm affirming in the course of a day on the job. In fact, that is my job. The "cop" part of it . . . well, they call us "cops," to me, my job is *I'm a peace officer.*

So I work not only to prevent the crime but to eliminate its causes—its causes in fear and greed, not just the social causes everyone talks about.

Even when it gets to conflict. I had arrested a very angry black man who singled me out for real animosity. When I had to take him to a paddy wagon, he spit in my face—that was something—and he went after me with a chair. We handcuffed him and put him in the truck. Well, on the way I just had to get past this picture of things, and again I affirmed to myself, "This guy and I are brothers." . . . When I got to the station, I was moved spontaneously to say, "Look, if I've done anything to offend you, I apologize." The paddy wagon driver looked at me as if I was totally nuts.

The next day I had to take him from where he'd been housed overnight to criminal court. When I picked him up, I thought, "Well, if you trust this vision, you're not going to have to handcuff him." And I didn't. We got to a spot in the middle of the corridor, which was the place where he'd have jumped me if he had that intention, and he stopped suddenly. So did I. Then he said, "You know, I thought about what you said yesterday, and I want to apologize." I just feel deep appreciation.

Turned out on his rap sheet he'd done a lot of time in Michigan and had trouble with guards in jail. I symbolized something. And I saw that turnaround, saw a kind of healing, I believe.

So what really happens if you're going to explore whether or not this vision of nature really has power? Maybe people will say you're taking chances. But you're taking chances without any vision; your vision is your protection. Maybe they'll say you're sentimentalizing people. But it's not about people. It's about principle and truth. It's about how the universe is. Maybe they'll think it's idealistic; things could never be this way. Well, for me, things are this way already; it's just up to us to know that more clearly.

I see that my work is to hold to an image of who we all truly are and to be guided by that. And I have been guided by that, to greater strength and security . . . within myself and on the street.

SOME SUGGESTIONS FOR CRIMINAL JUSTICE

If we are to look to the future of criminal justice with some measure of hope rather than a growing sense of cynicism, we must seek out fresh possibilities rather than defend traditional certainties. We need not be naive to remain open to creative alternatives concerning justice philosophy, policy, and programming. As Geis (1984) suggests, we need to "stand apart from the parade" to see old problems with a new perspective. Nettler (1982) exhorts us to spend more time and energy in asking the right questions *before* seeking answers. We need reflection before action. Lozoff puts our dilemma in perspective when he writes, "We all want to know the way, but very few of us are willing to study the maps" (1989:3).

It seems more important than ever for us to look past our individual and agency interests into the larger community of which we are a part. The corporate body of this larger community includes both the best and the worst that we have to offer. The sinner and saint, offender and victim all share the consequences of our formal and informal responses to matters of crime and justice. The choice between prevention, intervention, or no response at all holds meaning for each part of our community as well as the whole. We have to keep trying to look at the problems of crime and justice with fresh eyes, through the eyes of overworked bureaucrats, prison guards, caseworkers, victims, and offenders. We need to look beyond the next career opportunity and try to see through the eyes of our children, and even their children, for we are responsible to them as well. The following suggestions are offered as observations to consider, as food for thought.

Law and Justice

Can legal statutes or the justice system make up for our lack of community, for our feelings and experiences of fragmentation? Can morality or a responsible and caring community be legislated? The answer to both questions is, of course, no. However, the way we define laws and the way our justice system enforces them can enhance or diminish our opportunities for more peaceful and orderly communities. While conflict and ambiguity are an inevitable part of how social ills are connected to problems of crime and justice, intervention (in the form of prevention efforts) must occur before as well as after crimes are committed. Adequate health care and opportunities for meaningful work are at least as important than simply improving the efficiency of the criminal justice process. As we consider how laws must be changed and our justice system needs to be improved, an expanded vision can allow us to create a space in which we can more honestly address differences between how we view the justice process ideally and how it often functions in reality. Myths—such as (1) white-collar crime is nonviolent, (2) the rich and poor are equal before the law, (3) the punishment can fit the crime, and (4) law makes people behave—can be examined and responded to in a more enlightened context of community.

There are also issues of law and justice that must be struggled with on a personal basis, both in terms of our being criminal justice professionals and as members of families and social communities. For example, it seems that many persons have come to believe that a legal act and a moral act are essentially the same thing. Politicians or corporate executives charged with crimes typically declare to the press and the public that they have done nothing illegal and, indeed, they may often be correct. But does that make it right? Can legal behavior be immoral and illegal behavior moral? Were Martin Luther King Jr. and Mahatma Gandhi criminals or heroes? In a society in which success is measured primarily in terms of money and prestige, are we encouraged to do whatever is necessary within (and sometimes outside) the law to be successful (Braswell & LaFollette, 1988)? We are appalled when public figures are convicted of large-scale fraud, yet we may consider cheating on our income taxes or college exams acceptable. It seems as if we are saying, "It's all right to do something wrong as long as we don't get caught at it." Of course, in life or in criminal court, when we do get caught, our plea is for mercy. From minor greed to major fraud, when we are the victim, we are inclined to want retribution, yet when we are the offender, we want mercy. This contrasting desire seems true in personal relationships as well as in a professional or criminal justice context. Can we truly have it both ways: mercy when we are the offender and retribution or revenge when we are the victim? Or do we need to accept responsibility and make a stand for one way or the other?

Policing

With more minorities and women entering police work, the opportunity exists for a greater openness in defining and redefining police roles and function. In addition, as issues surrounding the family such as domestic violence and child abuse are translated into law and criminal justice policies, the need for police officers to possess meaningful communication and interpersonal skills should become more apparent. It seems ironic that police officers are expected to intervene with families who are in crisis, while few, if any, helping services are available to many of them when they experience family crisis situations. Shift work and a closed professional system are just several of the factors that can contribute to difficulties regarding family life. To make matters worse, in some instances, a stigma perceived as weakness is identified with those officers who do seek professional help for family-related problems (Miller & Braswell, 1997).

Police agencies are also responsible for detaining offenders in jails until courts dispense with them. Current problems associated with prison overcrowding have also spilled over into jails, turning many of them into little more than institutions for extended incarceration. Most jails are operated by law enforcement agencies more inclined toward enforcement and order maintenance strategies than correctional intervention with offenders. And the offenders who end up in jail are typically from the underclass and represent the least affluent in the community because they often cannot afford bail. Suggestions for more creative options such as pretrial release, diversion programs, and speedier trials have long been a possibility, but they are often not utilized. Such an attitude of neglect has additional implications for one of the criminal justice system's most missed opportunities: its potential impact on first-time offenders who have their initial contact with the system at the jail. It seems ironic that the point in the justice process at which the first-time offender is usually the most open to intervention is also the place where the least resources are allocated.

Are police officers tough, unyielding crime fighters, or are they much more than that? Many police officers consider social services calls as "garbage calls," not worthy of their time and effort, yet the majority of their typical work day is spent dealing with human service situations. Paradoxically, the more mindful they are of the ethic of care, as translated through effective communication and interpersonal skills, the less likely they are to have to get tough with the people with whom they come in contact. Still, the image persists: "Dirty Harry" crime fighter or peacemaker? It is interesting to note that an informal survey given each semester to introductory criminal justice students consistently reveals that the overwhelming majority of them would prefer, all things being equal (i.e., job responsibilities, pay, etc.), to be identified as a police officer or deputy sheriff rather than as a public safety officer. How can we enlarge our vision of police work to include a primary emphasis on peacemaking as well as law enforcement? It is not just a matter of knowing how to shoot well but also knowing when to shoot—as well as being open to possible nonviolent alternatives. Given the litigious nature of today's world, such an orientation has pragmatic as well as peacemaking advantages. It is unfortunate that the nature and tradition of contemporary police work would make the previous example of the police officer who saw himself as primarily a peace officer seem so unusual (Dass & Gorman, 1985). With so much research focused on police corruption and deviance, we might find it worthwhile to follow A.H. Maslow's (1954) example and turn our attention to what motivates well-adjusted, creative, and psychologically healthy police officers. Given the discretion and immediacy of response necessary for police officers in the community setting, there is perhaps no other criminal justice professional who is as connected to the community and who has as great an opportunity to contribute to the community's sense of care and well-being. There are a number of positive developments in policing, particularly in the area of community policing (Trojanowicz et al., 1998).

Corrections

Corrections directly addresses the "least of the community"—the two-time losers, the nuisance factor, the disenfranchised, and the violent. Along the continuum of connectedness, offenders appear to be the least useful to the community. They have demonstrated their disdain or inability to do their duty as citizens, to adequately contribute to the common good, or to provide meaningful care. As a result, the larger community often retributively feels that such persons themselves are deserving of the least care. Ironically, while we want them to pay for crimes and be corrected, we are not particularly supportive of their feeling good about themselves. The paradox "be good, but don't feel good about it" can often put our correctional process at odds with itself. Is our priority to provide corrections or punishment? Is our emphasis to repair the connection and restore both offender and victim to our community, or to disconnect and distance one or the other or both from community? Are we to be more interested in restitution and reconciliation whenever possible, or in retribution? Thomas Merton writes, "You cannot save the world with merely a system. You cannot have peace without charity" (in Quinney, 1988:71).

While the effectiveness of correctional treatment is a worthy and important topic for debate between the pro- and anti-rehabilitation factions in criminal justice (Cullen & Gilbert, 1982; Whitehead & Lab, 1989), is it the only (or even the most important) basis for funding and providing correctional treatment services for offenders? Are the moral and ethical grounds for treating offenders at least as important, if not more so, than the utilitarian demands for effectiveness? Perhaps we need to develop and articulate a treatment ethic that is restorative in nature and that more honestly addresses the community's (including its lowest-status members) sense of duty to itself. Such a turn of focus also allows us to pay closer attention to the art of correctional treatment rather than strictly to its scientific aspect—to the creation as well as the operation of correctional process. The restorative justice and peacemaking movements, through such nonprofit organizations as The Prison Fellowship (Van Ness & Strong, 1997) and Human Kindness Foundation (Bazemore & Schiff, 2001; Braswell, Fuller & Lozoff, 2001; Fuller, 1998), offer a correctional alternative that encourages offenders to take responsibility for their actions and be restored to a sense of community in which personal and spiritual transformation can take place.

It is interesting that when we think of correctional treatment interventions we are inclined to think of them more as treatment systems or clinical approaches to be evaluated and less as existential processes to be experienced. While this tendency may also be true of our psychotherapeutic colleagues, there are more among them that are sensitive to and grounded in a vital sense of the existential that makes the philosophy and science of theory come alive in the art and process of relationship (Rogers, 1980; Satir, 1973). It is worth noting the substantial and continually evolving research of Robert

Carkhuff and his associates (1969, 1987), which indicates that the further graduate students progress in clinical help professions, the more proficient they become in diagnostic, assessment, and evaluation skills, but the less effective they seem to become in demonstrating meaningful and effective communication skills.

To put the "art of treatment" perspective into a more specifically correctional context, we can turn to the groundbreaking work of John Augustus and Alexander Maconochie. We can become so enamored of their innovative approaches that we can easily forget, or at least take for granted, the inner aspect of who they were that made their approaches come alive in experience. David Dressler (1959) writes of John Augustus's interaction with offenders in a police court: "It is probable that some of them know him, for as he walks to the box two or three turn their blood-shot eyes toward him with eager glances. . . . In a moment he is with them, gently reproving the hardened ones, and cheering . . . those in whom are visible signs of penitence" (p. 25). Dressler continues in commenting on Maconochie's restorative impact on an incorrigible and disturbed inmate: "He was out of touch with reality most of the time, unaware of what was going on about him, but when Maconochie, his wife, or their children, visited him, he returned to reality, recognized his callers. He showed affection for them to the day he died" (p. 67). It is true that evaluating treatment effectiveness is important, as is educating and training competent clinical professionals in diagnostic, assessment, and evaluation skills. However, the art of helping requires more than cognitive or affective sensitivity; it requires a synthesis of both these dimensions and more—emerging from within and lived out in experience with others. "A staff person who's calm and strong and happy is worth his or her weight in gold. People who are living examples of truthfulness, good humor, patience, and courage are going to change more lives—even if they're employed as janitors—than the counselors who can't get their own lives in order" (Lozoff & Braswell, 1989:52).

Perhaps we can begin to rethink our attitude regarding corrections. Do we really want it to work or not? Is corrections to be little more than an opportunity for an incomplete community to express its feelings of retribution, or can it be more than that? Can we realize the possibility that corrections, even with its need for punishment, can also include restitution, rehabilitation, and restoration as a means for the community to experience reconciliation? After speaking to a local Kiwanis group about juvenile crime and corrections in their community, one speaker was asked by one of the group members what they could do to help. His response: "Create recreation opportunities for the least of your community and for yourselves—join the local PTA."

JUSTICE AS A WAY RATHER THAN A DESTINATION

It is in our best interests to begin to see justice as an evolutionary way of service rather than as an efficiently engineered technological destination. We need an ethic for our future that will empower us to act on an enlarged vision of what justice is about—a vision that will include the community of which we are all a part, the best of us and the worst of us (and the best in each of us and the worst in each of us). We need a prophetic vision to energize the empowerment of such an ethic. The passion of prophetic vision resounds in the words of Amos (5:24) in the Bible and is repeated by Martin Luther King Jr. in a striking address: "Let justice roll down like waters. And righteousness like a mighty stream." Quinney (1980) adds, "For the prophets, justice is like a mighty stream, not merely a category or mechanical process. In contrast, the moralists discuss, suggest, counsel; the prophets proclaim, demand, insist" (p. 25).

Justice as a way of service requires more than just the passionate zeal of the visionary, it also requires the mindfulness of quiet compassion. Creative and humane policies and plans are one thing, but making them work is something else. It is the compassionate professionals in public schools, courts, law enforcement, corrections, and other human service agencies that make the ethic of care come alive in the community. Such persons are mindful of the suffering that crime and social injustice creates for victims and offenders. Their mindfulness is born of their own suffering as well. Dietrich Bonhoeffer, himself incarcerated and finally executed in a Nazi prison camp, wrote (in Castle, 1988), "We must learn to respond to people less in the light of what they do or omit to do, and more in the light of what they suffer." Seeing a Ted Bundy or Charles Manson through the eyes of compassion keeps us from closing ourselves off from the terrible suffering they have given and received. Their acts are not excused, nor is our irresponsibility in choosing not to commit our collective resources and energies toward preventing the creation of future Bundys or Mansons. Compassionate professionals realize it is not how much they do, but rather how mindfully they do whatever they do. To put it another way, as Mother Teresa suggested, "It is not how much you do, but how much you do with love." From a compassionate way of service comes a sense of peace and well-being.

Success, happiness, and even justice are all preludes at best, and second-rate substitutes at worst, to what we really seek—peace. Only peace has the potential to remain calm and resolute even in the midst of suffering that connects each of us to the other in community. Peace comes from the inside out. It cannot be implemented organizationally from the top down. People at peace with themselves create peaceful organizations that can then become instruments for peacemaking in the larger community. To reiterate Dass and Gorman's (1985) cogent observation: "If we ourselves cannot know peace, be peaceful, how will our acts disarm hatred and violence?" (p. 165). And to borrow once again from Isaiah (2:17): "How else will our justice system bring about peace, produce calm and security for our people?"

REFERENCES

Amos 5:24.

Bazemore, G. & M. Schiff (2001). *Restorative Community Justice: Repairing Harm and Transforming Communities*. Cincinnati: Anderson.

Braswell, M.C. (1989). "Correctional Treatment and the Human Spirit: A Focus on Relationship," *Federal Probation*, (June):49-60.

Braswell, M.C., J. Fuller & B. Lozoff (2001). *Corrections, Peacemaking and Restorative Justice*. Cincinnati: Anderson.

Braswell, M.C. & H. LaFollette (1988). "Seeking Justice: The Advantages and Disadvantages of Being Educated." *American Journal of Criminal Justice*, (Spring):135-147.

Carkhuff, R. (1987). *The Art of Helping III*. Amherst, MA: Human Resource Development Press.

Carkhuff, R. (1969). *Helping Human Relations, Vol. II*. New York: Holt, Rinehart, and Winston.

Castle, T. (1988). *The New Book of Christian Quotations*. New York: Crossroad.

Conrad, J. (1981). *Justice and Consequences*. Lexington, MA: Lexington Books.

Cullen, F. & K. Gilbert (1982). *Reaffirming Rehabilitation*. Cincinnati: Anderson.

Dass, R. & P. Gorman (1985). *How Can I Help?* New York: Alfred A. Knopf.

Dressler, D. (1959). *Practice and Theory of Probation and Parole*. New York: Columbia University Press.

Fuller, J.R. (1998). *Criminal Justice: A Peacemaking Perspective*. Boston: Allyn & Bacon.

Geis, G. (1984). "Foreword." In H. Pepinsky & P. Jesilow, *Myths that Cause Crime*. Cabin John, MD: Seven Locks Press.

Gendreau, P. & R. Ron (1987). "Revivification of Rehabilitation: Evidence from the 1980's." *Justice Quarterly*, 4:349-409.

Hanh, T.N. (1987). *Being Peace*. Berkeley, CA: Parallax Press.

Isaiah 32:17.

Lozoff, B. (1989). "Editorial," *Human Kindness Foundation Newsletter*, 3.

Lozoff, B. (1987). *We're All Doing Time*. Chapel Hill, NC: Human Kindness Foundation.

Lozoff, B. & M. Braswell (1989). *Inner Corrections: Finding Peace and Peace Making*. Cincinnati: Anderson.

Maslow, A. (1954). *Motivation and Personality*. New York: Harper.

Meredith, N. (1984). "The Murder Epidemic." *Science*, (December):48.

Miller, L. & M. Braswell (1997). *Human Relations and Police Work,* 4th ed. Prospect Heights, IL: Waveland.

Nettler, G. (1982). *Explaining Criminals*. Cincinnati: Anderson.

Pepinsky, H. & P. Jesilow (1984). *Myths That Cause Crime*. Cabin John, MD: Seven Locks Press.

Quinney, R. (1988). "Crime, Suffering, and Service: Toward a Criminology of Peacemaking." *The Quest*, (Winter):71.

Quinney, R. (1987). "The Way of Peace: On Crime, Suffering, and Service." Unpublished paper, (November):19, 23.

Quinney, R. (1980). *Providence: The Reconstruction of Social and Moral Order*. New York: Longman.

Rogers, C. (1980). *A Way of Being*. Boston: Houghton Mifflin.

Satir, V. (1973). *Peoplemaking*. Palo Alto, CA: Science and Behavior Books.

Trojanowicz, R., V.E. Kappeler, L.K. Gaines & B. Bucqueroux (1998). *Community Policing: A Contemporary Perspective*, 2nd ed. Cincinnati: Anderson.

Van Ness, D. & K.H. Strong (1997). *Restoring Justice*. Cincinnati: Anderson.

Whitehead, J. & . Lab (1989). A Response to "Does Correctional Treatment Work?" Unpublished paper.

DISCUSSION QUESTIONS

1. Can legal behavior be immoral and illegal behavior moral? Give your opinion on this statement, and defend your answer with examples.

2. Braswell thinks an ethic for the future can improve the criminal justice system. Do you agree or disagree with his viewpoint? Why or why not?

3. Why is mindfulness important to one's personal and professional life? Can you think of any personal example?

Index